LE JUGEMENT DU ROY DE BEHAIGNE

AND

REMEDE DE FORTUNE

Comment lamant fait une complainte de fortune et de sa roe.

Car elle nest
ferme ne estable.
Juste loyal
ne veritable.
Quant on la cuide
charitable.
Elle est avere.
Dure. diverse. espouvantable.

Traistre poignant decevable.
Et quant on la cuide amiab[…]
Lors est amere.
Car la soit ce quamie ap[…]
Douce com miel vraie commere.
La pointure dune vipere.
Quest mortable.
En riens a li ne se compere.

GUILLAUME DE MACHAUT

Le Jugement du roy de Behaigne

AND

Remede de Fortune

EDITED BY

JAMES I. WIMSATT

AND

WILLIAM W. KIBLER

MUSIC EDITED BY

REBECCA A. BALTZER

THE CHAUCER LIBRARY

THE UNIVERSITY OF GEORGIA PRESS

ATHENS AND LONDON

Set in Mergenthaler Bembo
The paper in this book meets the guidelines for permanence and durability of the Committee on Production Guidelines for Book Longevity of the Council on Library Resources.

92 91 90 89 88 5 4 3 2 1

Library of Congress Cataloging in Publication Data

Guillaume, de Machaut, ca. 1300–1377.
Le jugement du roy de Behaigne; and, Remede de fortune.

(The Chaucer library)
1. Guillaume, de Machaut, ca. 1300–1377—Translations, English. 2. Love poetry, French. 3. Love poetry, French—Translations into English. 4. Love poetry, English—Translations from French. 5. Chaucer, Geoffrey, d. 1400—Sources. 6. Love poetry, French—Manuscripts. 7. Manuscripts, French. I. Wimsatt, James I. II. Kibler, William W., 1942– . III. Guillaume, de Machaut, ca. 1300–1377. Remede de fortune. English. 1987. IV. Title. V. Series.
PQ1483.G5A2 1988 841′.1 86-11241

Printed Digitally

Paperback ISBN-13: 978-0-8203-5353-1

2017 hardcover reissue ISBN-13: 978-0-8032-5354-8

CONTENTS

FOREWORD

The purpose of the Chaucer Library is to present the classical and medieval works that the English poet Geoffrey Chaucer (ca. 1343–1400) knew, translated, or made use of in his writings in versions that are as close as possible to those that were in existence, circulating, and being read by him and his contemporaries. These versions were, of course, not critical editions—they were filled with readings that the original authors did not write, with additions and omissions, and sometimes with glosses and commentaries—and the Chaucer Library was created in 1946 in the belief that only by reproducing such non-original material could one have a true understanding of the ways in which classical and medieval texts were read and understood by medieval readers. The Chaucer Library has followed this traditional policy, as in the first volume published by the University of Georgia Press, Pope Innocent III's *De Miseria Condicionis Humane*, and will continue to do so, while at the same time striving to present readable texts, with punctuation and capitalization modernized, abbreviations expanded, some letters regularized, and accompanied by English translations.

It is clear, however, that some works known to and used by Chaucer do not warrant this kind of presentation, and the Chaucer Library has widened its range of editorial possibilities to include critical editions. Nicholas of Lynn's *Kalendarium* and the *Summa virtutum de remediis anime*, the last two volumes, were critical editions, and the present volume of two of Guillaume de Machaut's long *dits amoureux* is one as well. As Professors Wimsatt and Kibler show in their introduction, there are "significant parallels in plot, characterization, and technique, as well as in verbal expression," between *Le Jugement du roy de Behaigne* and Chaucer's works and broader and more widespread parallels between the *Remede de Fortune* and his works, but the verbal evidence of the French manuscripts is too evenly balanced to permit them to choose a single manuscript to be printed in its entirety for either *dit*. In both cases, however, the evidence points to Chaucer's use of a manuscript or manuscripts of the "early tradition," and Wimsatt and Kibler present a critical edition of the manuscripts of this tradition, which brings us very close both to the manuscript Chaucer had before him and to Machaut's original. In addition, for the first *dit* all readings closer to Chaucer's borrowings have been marked with an asterisk in the critical apparatus so that one can see at a glance where Chaucer's manuscript would have differed from the edited text; and for the second there is a good possibility that Chaucer may have known the base manuscript. It is therefore with great pleasure that the Chaucer Library Committee now adds these two *dits amoureux* by Machaut to the list of books in Chaucer's library.

Robert E. Lewis, General Editor

For the Chaucer Library Committee:
John H. Fisher
William W. Kibler
Traugott Lawler
A. G. Rigg
Siegfried Wenzel
Edward Wilson
James I. Wimsatt

PREFACE

The two poems of Guillaume de Machaut which this edition presents are very appropriate texts for the Chaucer Library, whose fundamental purpose is to make available to modern audiences the literature that Chaucer knew. On the one hand, it is demonstrable that the English poet knew the whole of these poems well, and on the other, it is a fact that today's readers have not commonly known or appreciated them, in large part because access to the poems has been difficult. Though Ernest Hoepffner's edition of them has served well, its now-dated text has inevitable shortcomings; and Hoepffner provides no annotations of the individual lines, much less commentary on the uses to which Chaucer put the works. As with all editions of the Chaucer Library the chief aim of this one is to supply insofar as possible what a student of Chaucer needs or wants to know of the works and the poet's use of them. It also serves the purposes of the scholar who is mainly interested in Machaut. Our text, apparatus, translation, and notes present much that can be found nowhere else.

Working with Machaut's *dits* over a number of years has helped us to understand the poetic virtues that led Chaucer to the French poet, and we hope that our edition will in turn lead others to appreciate his work. In the course of our efforts we have profited from the expertise of a number of people. By far the most important have been the general editor of the Chaucer Library, Robert E. Lewis, and the former chairman of the Chaucer Library Committee, Robert A. Pratt, who have given guidance and encouragement from the inception. Others who have provided assistance for which we are most grateful are Professor James Atkinson, M. François Avril, Professor Lawrence Earp, Professor John Fisher, Dr. Karen Gould, and Dr. Nigel Wilkins. And we especially thank Professor Robert A. Taylor who read the manuscript for the Chaucer Library. We are indebted to the American Council of Learned Societies for a grant to James I. Wimsatt in 1974–75, and to the University of Texas Research Institute for a grant to William W. Kibler in 1983, which freed the respective editors for essential full-time work on the project. We would also like to thank the University of Texas Research Institute for generously supporting the edition with computer time and supplies, and especially for the generous grant that made possible the color frontispiece, which helps to convey the splendor of the original manuscript.

The beginning of every edition such as ours is in the collections which house the originals of the text, and we are very grateful for the principle of accessibility and assistance which prevails at all the libraries that hold manuscripts of *Le Jugement du roy de Behaigne* and *Remede de Fortune*. The librarians readily gave us access to them, had them reproduced on microfilm, and have allowed us to use them for this edition. Of the libraries our primary debt is to the Bibliothèque Nationale in Paris, which holds twelve of the twenty extant manuscripts that contain the works, including both of those that we use as bases for the texts. We also are indebted to the Bibliothèque Municipale of Arras, the Burgerbibliothek in Bern, the Pepys Library of Magdalene College in Cambridge, the Pierpont Morgan Library in New York City, the Bibliothèque de l'Arsenal in Paris, the Royal Library in Stockholm, and Wildenstein and Company and H. P. Kraus in New York City.

Each of the main editors has participated importantly in all parts of the work so that it represents a genuine collaborative effort throughout. Nevertheless, each has naturally concentrated more on the parts to which his expertise applies. James Wimsatt has been especially concerned with Chaucerian aspects of the text, and William Kibler with French language aspects. As the title page indicates, Rebecca Baltzer has edited and annotated the music of *Remede de Fortune*.

INTRODUCTION

GUILLAUME DE MACHAUT: LIFE AND CAREER

Guillaume de Machaut is the most important French poet and musical composer of the fourteenth century. With his poetry he firmly established, though he did not originate, the fashions which dominated Middle French poetry. His many short poems are mainly composed in the demanding *formes fixes* (so-called) of ballade, rondeau, lai, and virelai. His long poems stand in the line of development from the *Roman de la Rose* and provide the models for most subsequent Middle French *dits amoureux*. Moreover, the influence of his poetry and music extended quite beyond France, to Czechoslovakia, Italy, Spain, England, and the Low Countries. His influence on the work of Geoffrey Chaucer provides the ultimate impetus for this edition.

As with most medieval writers, little precise information exists about Machaut's life, but details of his poems and a few public records remain to provide a rough idea of his biography.[1] One gathers that he was born to middle class parents in about 1300 (no later than 1302) near Reims in Champagne, the city and province with which he is always identified. As the common reference to him as "maître" suggests, he probably received his master of arts degree at a university; his self-designation as "clerc," moreover, indicates that he went on to study theology, but he did not become a priest.

After his studies, Machaut served from about 1323 to the end of the 1330s as personal secretary and clerk to Jean l'Aveugle of Luxembourg, king of Bohemia. For most of these years he followed the peripatetic Jean in his travels through central and western Europe. In the late 1330s Jean became blind; nevertheless, in 1346 at the battle of Crécy, heroically or foolishly, he insisted on throwing himself into the melée and was cut down. At the time of the king's death, Machaut was no longer associated with him on a day-to-day basis. In 1333 Jean had gotten the poet a canonry at Reims, and in 1337 the chapter formally received him. After 1340 Machaut's name appears regularly in the records of Reims and of the chapter of canons.

Almost till his death King Jean had actively sponsored both Machaut and his brother, also a canon at Reims, and the poet enthusiastically eulogized him. But Machaut did not lack for patrons after 1346; Jean's daughter Bonne was one patron. In 1332 Bonne had married the heir to the throne of France, the future Jean le Bon, though she died in 1349, the year before he became king. Machaut wrote his *Remede de Fortune* for Bonne (see Introduction to *Remede* below), and in *La Prise d'Alexandrie* he gratefully memorialized her as a fine lady for whom he had performed important services. In addition, she was the mother of two men who became major patrons of his, Jean, duke of Berry, and Charles, duke of Normandy, later Charles V. As early as 1349 Machaut also established an important association with Charles le Mauvais, king of Navarre, whose family had hereditary associations with Champagne and who had married a daughter of Bonne and Jean le Bon. The poet was still profiting from Charles' patronage in 1361 despite that king's grave problems with the king of France.[2]

In any event, by 1360 Machaut's attentions were mainly turned to the French royal family. In that year, or shortly afterward, he wrote a long poem for the duke of Berry, the *Dit de la fonteinne amoureuse*. Also testifying to his close relationship with that powerful patron is a rich manuscript of Machaut's works, Bibliothèque Nationale fonds français 9221, which carries the duke's personal signature. Equally good evidence exists of Machaut's familiar relationship with Charles V. A record from 1361 shows that Charles, then duke of Normandy, stayed in Machaut's home on a visit at Reims. And in Machaut's *Voir dit* (c. 1364) the poet speaks proudly of his own extended sojourn with the most important man in the kingdom "save for one," i.e., except for King Jean. At the time that Charles was crowned at Reims in 1364, Machaut evidently established a friendship with another royal personage, Pierre de Lusignan, king of Cyprus. For a number of years Pierre was the leading crusader of Europe. An accomplished courtier and a jouster of prowess, he captured the imagination of pope and king, courtier and clerk. Machaut was among his greatest admirers and wrote his last major poem, *La Prise d'Alexandrie*, about Pierre's career.

After he finished the *Prise* in about 1370, Machaut's activities obviously diminished. One record does indicate that he continued to cultivate powerful patrons. In 1371 Amadée, the Green Count of Savoy, gave the poet three hundred gold francs for a "romanzo," probably a manuscript collection of his works. Machaut perhaps wrote his important *Prologue* in 1372; otherwise, no major work of his dates from after the *Prise*, and public records do not speak further of him till his death in April 1377. He was buried beside his brother in the cathedral at Reims. Two celebrated ballades of Eustache Deschamps commemorate "la mort Machaut, le noble rhetorique."[3]

MACHAUT'S *OEUVRE*

While he was following Jean of Luxembourg around Europe, no doubt somewhat breathlessly, Machaut's artistic output was not large. One motet and its accompanying music can be assigned with some certainty to the year 1324,[4] and doubtless he wrote a number of other lyrics in the

1320s and 1330s, but the bulk of his short poems and music, and all but one or two of the long poems, date from after he settled down at Reims when middle age was upon him. Despite the late start, Machaut was blessed with long life, and the body of his eventual production is impressive in both extent and quality. All in all his poetry totals some sixty thousand lines (cf. Chaucer's thirty-eight thousand), including a substantial number of both lyrics and long poems.

Machaut wrote some 420 lyric poems, most of them in the *formes fixes* of chant royal (eight extant), ballade (239), rondeau (seventy-seven), virelai (forty), and lai (twenty-three). He also composed twenty-three motets and nine complaintes. He set about 140 of these lyrics to music, providing polyphonic notation for the ballades, rondeaux, and motets, and monodic for the lais, virelais, one complainte, and one chant royal. The manuscripts also include music for a famous Messe de Nostre Dame, and a double hocket.

Machaut's other poetic works include eight long *dits amoureux* and four shorter *dits*. Two of the long *dits* are edited here, *Le Jugement du roy de Behaigne* and *Remede de Fortune*. These are second and third in order of composition. The *Dit du vergier* precedes. The subsequent five long *dits*, in approximate chronological order, are the *Dit du lyon* (sometimes thought to be the original of Chaucer's lost *Book of the Lion*), *Le Jugement du roy de Navarre* (which is a response to *Le Jugement du roy de Behaigne*), a bird allegory called the *Dit de l'alerion*, the *Dit de la fonteinne amoureuse*, and the pseudo-autobiographical *Voir dit*. The shorter *dits amoureux* include two Marguerite poems and the *Dit de la rose* and *Dit de la harpe*. The remaining extant works of Machaut are an extensive poem of comfort and counsel, entitled *Confort d'ami*, written for Charles of Navarre when Jean le Bon had imprisoned him (1356–57); the long verse chronicle, *La Prise d'Alexandrie*; and the *Prologue*, in which he sets forth in succinct allegory some of his ideas about poetry.

Scholars commonly treat Machaut's music and poetry separately, with the musicologists having done a more thorough job with the music than the literary scholars have with the poetry. The sharp division of scholarly labor, and the comparative neglect of the poetry, of course, are not sanctioned by the spirit in which the works were created. Machaut's *Prologue* shows that he considered himself a composer of poems in which understanding, rhetoric, and music were integral components of more or less equal status. By no means did he feel that the words were secondary, nor *a fortiori* did he have a sense that he was better at composing the music than at finding the words. Like his contemporaries his usual procedure was to write the words, then add the music, if indeed there was to be music. The fact is that most of his poetry lacked accompanying notation. His collection of lyrics without music, the *Louange des dames*, includes about two-thirds of his total production in the shorter forms; and except for some intercalated lyrics in *Remede* and *Voir dit* his long poems are without music. In the manuscripts, moreover, the musical pieces are not given a position of precedence; the *Louange des dames* and the long poems are always placed ahead of the music. This is not to minimize the importance of his music, whose place of honor in history is assured, but rather to suggest the importance of the poetry from a Machauvian perspective.

THE MACHAUT TRADITION IN FRENCH LITERATURE

Though there were writers after Machaut who combined the skills of poet and musical composer, the technical requirements of the new modes of music made it particularly difficult for most poets to provide notation for their lyrics. As a consequence, the outstanding French poets who followed Machaut were not composers, and his influence on them mainly involves the words rather than the music he wrote. Notwithstanding, his successors were conscious of music as a component of poetry. Since the lyric forms they used originally accommodated music, they sometimes refer to musical performance of their poems, and they sometimes had their works set to music by others.[5] Moreover, at least one prominent treatise of the time sees the words themselves as constituting music. In his *Art de dictier* Eustache Deschamps speaks of the verse as being of itself "natural music"; the notation makes "artificial music."[6]

In finding music in the words, Deschamps perhaps was trying to reinforce the ties of his own verse and that of his peers, which lacked notation, with Machaut's pieces set to music. Himself a Champenois and perhaps a nephew of the older man, he acknowledged that Machaut had educated him. But whatever the precise implication of his characterization of verse as "natural music," it is especially apt for the literary tradition which Machaut in part fathered, and in greater part fixed, and which Daniel Poirion accurately labels the "Machaut tradition."[7] Its mode is thoroughly lyric, emphasizing metrical skill and representation of emotion and thought through conventional expression and imagery. Even in the long works, characterization and narrative are highly conventional, reinforcing the lyric content rather than competing with it.

Into the sixteenth century in France, poetry largely adhered to the Machaut tradition. In the latter part of the fourteenth century, Jean Froissart imaginatively built his poetic *oeuvre*, form by form and work by work, on the Machaut model; Deschamps found inspiration for his large production mainly in the lyrics of the master, though he developed his own emphasis on political and moral commentary; and Oton de Granson with less originality followed Machaut's lead closely as far as he was able. The same close imitation holds true of most of the minor poets who contributed to the *Cent Ballades* and its "Responses," or who are represented in the later large anthology, the *Jardin de Plaisance*. The major fifteenth century writers are more distinctive in their work, but at the same time they are central participants in the tradition: Christine de Pizan, Alain Chartier, Charles d'Orléans, Jean de Garancières, and even François Villon.

Since the Machaut tradition comprises mainly a court poetry dependent on a select audience initiated into its modes, it is not surprising that it died out in the late fifteenth century and fell into oblivion until scholars with antiquarian interests began studying and selectively editing the manuscripts from about 1750. Given the specialized, highly lyric nature of the tradition, it is also not surprising that the modern reception of the poetry has been very cool. Those critics who have read the work have generally seen it as the detritus of a noble literature which had played itself out in the thirteenth century. Alfred Jeanroy's assessment of Machaut's lyrics is representative. Though Jeanroy recognized the poet as a major innovator, he saw the innovations as particularly baneful, with their emphasis on music and versification stifling to the essential aspects of poetry. Among Machaut's many lyrics, he claimed to be unable to find twenty verses worth citing.[8]

Despite the failure of scholars, with notable exceptions, to appreciate Middle French poetry, Machaut's works did find good editors in the late nineteenth and early twentieth centuries. It was natural for those editors, with their bias toward modern fiction, to seize first on the works which seem to have most topical content. In 1875 Paulin Paris edited the *Voir dit*, which parades as a record of the aging poet's love life;[9] and in 1877 L. de Mas-Latrie published the long biographical commemoration of Pierre of Cyprus, the *Prise d'Alexandrie*.[10] Thirty years later the bulk of the remaining work appeared in two monumental editions: the other eight long poems were edited by Ernest Hoepffner in three volumes (1908–21), and the lyrics by V.-F. Chichmaref in two volumes (1909). After editing the poems, however, literary scholars largely abandoned Machaut's work to the musicologists, who among numerous valuable publications have produced two fine editions of the complete music, those by Friedrich Ludwig (1926–43)[11] and Leo Schrade (1956).[12]

Present trends in literary study now seem to be producing a Machaut renaissance. Since about 1965, the year in which Poirion's *Le Poète et le prince* appeared, literary scholars have increasingly come to devote attention to Middle French poetry. A part of their activity, like the present edition, has had its impetus in Chaucer's large debt to Machaut, which is by no means confined to his hypothetical "French period." His very use of Machaut, of course, is witness to the worth of the poetry: if such a writer as Chaucer found continuing inspiration in the French poet's work, surely the values are not all ephemeral and illusory. But present-day scholars are not depending on such second-hand testimony, however impressive. Placing the works in their proper milieux and defining their proper values, they are demonstrating the poetry's great independent value. At last, then, late in the twentieth century, the efforts of French scholars are converging with those of musicologists and Chaucerians in showing the importance and merit of Guillaume de Machaut's large *oeuvre* and of the tradition he fathered. The belated recognition is witnessed notably by two recent Machaut conferences and their published proceedings.[13]

Of all fourteenth-century French love poems, the two edited here are probably the most important; they certainly were the most influential on Chaucer. Together they rival even the *Roman de la Rose* as seminal texts for him. Their narratives represent the canonical versions of the love stories that were current; the concepts and emotions expressed in them extend across the range of the standard literary philosophy and psychology; and their language codifies verbal expression for subsequent love poems. As Chaucer's direct borrowings in the *Book of the Duchess* and *Troilus and Criseyde* especially demonstrate, and as others of his love poems reveal in various ways, *Jugement* and *Remede* provided primary prototypes for his writing about love and lovers.

LE JUGEMENT DU ROY DE BEHAIGNE

Contents, Sources, and Influence

If number of manuscripts and frequency of imitation are reliable indicators, *Jugement* was the most popular French *dit* of the fourteenth century. The substance of its 2,079 lines is a debate centering on a *demande d'amour* and its resolution by Jean l'Aveugle of Luxembourg, king of Bohemia. The participation in the narrative of a historical king in an actual castle helps to impart to it an air of realism new to the *dit amoureux*. The work evidently was composed before the death of Jean l'Aveugle in 1346, and in all likelihood before 1342, the date of Machaut's *Dit du lyon*, which comes after *Jugement* in the manuscripts. The question which is debated is who suffers more, the lover whose mate proves unfaithful, or the one whose beloved has died. *Jugement* figures forth the question with two stricken lovers. A lady and a knight, encountering one another by chance in a wood, in turn reveal their sorrows and then contest which of them has been more grievously wounded: her faithful lover has died; his faithless lady has taken a new *ami.* Eventually they decide to submit the question to a judge, but where can they find one? The narrator, who has been eavesdropping, reveals himself in order to recommend as arbiter the king of Bohemia, who is to be found at the Castle of Durbuy nearby. The debaters are willing, so all proceed to the castle where the king, aided by counselors who are his virtues personified, decides in favor of the knight. Afterwards he entertains the disputants for several days before sending them off with magnificent gifts.

The question of love presented in *Jugement* was familiar in French literature; it is dealt with in several extant *jeux partis,* or lyric debates.[14] The main antecedents of Machaut's plot, however, are found in longer poems which treat of another *demande d'amour.* These are the *Altercatio Phyllidis et Florae* and its French and Latin analogues which center about the question of who is the better lover, a clerk or a knight.[15] In the *Altercatio* the problem is debated by two girls who eventually have recourse to the God of Love. As with *Jugement,* after an extended discussion the disputants travel to a royal court where they ask the monarch to render a judgment. *Jugement* is especially close to the *Altercatio* in its serial narration of the girls' meeting in a *locus amoenus,* of their journey to the court, and of Love's seeking advice from personified counselors, here Usus and Natura, before rendering a decision in favor of the clerk. The *Altercatio* also provides an antecedent to the four-line stanzas of *Jugement,* though the monorhyme quatrains of two French debates are closer.[16] A second Latin poem, the *Concile de Remiremont,* is much less like *Jugement* than the *Altercatio* except in the fact that its debate is given a historical site and some of the participants are identified by full name.[17] The several French poems likewise are less like *Jugement* in most respects, and particularly in that the counselors of the king are birds who ultimately settle the debate by judicial duels. Nevertheless, in the fact that in these vernacular poems Love has numerous counselors (as against two in the *Altercatio*), and that the debate is quite extended, they provide a closer model to Machaut's *dit.* Furthermore, one of the French poems[18] resembles *Jugement* in having the opening of a *roman d'aventure*; the debate of the girls is overheard by a narrator who one fair morning enters a garden spot. It is possible that Machaut had an examplar that didn't survive which incorporated the motifs found separately in various antecedent poems, but it is more likely that he simply derived inspiration from various works in the tradition.

In the treatment of its materials, furthermore, *Jugement* has marked differences from its antecedents. There are numerous elements of verisimilitude in Machaut's poem which the earlier works do not possess: the little bird which leads the narrator into the *destour,* the lady's dog which runs up to him and bites his cloak when he comes out of hiding, and the king holding court, a historical person in a well-known castle. And the lyric effects of the rhetorical elaboration are more pervasive than in the Phyllis and Flora debates. Lyricism is especially marked in the ceremonial diction and behavior of the participants, in the elaborate description of the lady, and in the presentations of the castle high upon its rock foundation and of the peerless king with his allegorical companions. Particularly in the lyric excursuses Machaut may have been influenced by rhetorical treatises. The knight's description of his lady, lines 302–95, is an obvious example; parallels in it to Geoffrey of Vinsauf's *Poetria Nova* are documented in the Notes to the Texts.

The semi-stanzaic form of the poem also adds to its lyric nature. The metrical units are markedly different even from the four-line stanzas of prior works referred to above; they are interlocking quatrains, rhyming *aaab bbbc cccd*, etc., with the first three lines of each quatrain decasyllabic and the fourth tetrasyllabic. Machaut subsequently made use of a closely related stanza in several poems, notably in the complainte in *Remede*, and in the complainte and the "comfort" of the *Fonteinne amoureuse*. The same lyric stanza was later taken up by Froissart, Granson, and others in poetic complaintes. Chaucer uses the lyric rhyme scheme, though he varies the line length, in two stanzas of *Anelida and Arcite* (ll. 256–71, 308–24).

Jugement is found in nineteen manuscripts: eleven collections of Machaut's works, and eight manuscripts that do not contain other Machaut *dits*. Of his other long poems only the *Dit du vergier* appears in so many Machaut collections; moreover, no other one appears independent of other Machaut *dits* in more than three manuscripts. *Jugement*'s popularity is shown also in its substantial influence on later poems. Froissart uses the same versification and several of the narrative motifs in the *Dit du Bleu Chevalier*, and he employs something of the plot in the *Plaidorie de la rose et de la violette*; Christine de Pizan uses both versification and plot in three debate poems, the *Débat de deux amans*, the *Livre des trois jugements*, and the *Dit de Poissy*; and Alain Chartier likewise employs the metrics and debate format in the *Débat des deux fortunés d'amours* and the *Livre des quatre dames*. Also in the early fifteenth century Martin le Franc refers to *Jugement* in declaring his disagreement with the king's decision in the poem. Machaut himself presented a contrary decision in *Le Jugement du roy de Navarre*, which is a palinode to *Jugement* very much as Chaucer's *Legend of Good Women* is a palinode to *Troilus and Criseyde*. The influence of the pairing of the *Jugements* on Chaucer's sequence is patent.

The Manuscript Tradition of *Jugement*

Jugement is preserved in the following nineteen manuscripts, identified either by the one-letter sigla assigned them by Ernest Hoepffner,[19] or, lacking traditional notation, by two-letter sigla we have assigned:

A	Paris, Bibliothèque Nationale, fonds français 1584
B	Paris, Bibliothèque Nationale, fonds français 1585
C	Paris, Bibliothèque Nationale, fonds français 1586
D	Paris, Bibliothèque Nationale, fonds français 1587
E	Paris, Bibliothèque Nationale, fonds français 9221
F	Paris, Bibliothèque Nationale, fonds français 22545
J	Paris, Bibliothèque de l'Arsenal 5203
K	Bern, Burgerbibliothek 218
M	Paris, Bibliothèque Nationale, fonds français 843
P	Paris, Bibliothèque Nationale, fonds français 2166
R	Paris, Bibliothèque Nationale, fonds français 2230
Ar	Arras, Bibliothèque Municipale 897
Kr	New York, H. P. Kraus
Pc	Paris, Bibliothèque Nationale, fonds français 1149
Pm	New York, Pierpont Morgan Library 396
Ra	Paris, Bibliothèque Nationale, fonds français 20026
St	Stockholm, Kungliga Biblioteket Vu 22
Vg	New York, Wildenstein Gallery
Ys	Paris, Bibliothèque Nationale, fonds français 1595

Of the above, the following manuscripts contain more or less complete collections of Machaut's works: A, B, C, E, F, J, K, M, Pm, and Vg. Manuscript D is a partial collection. In each of the remaining manuscripts, P, R, Ar, Kr, Pc, Ra, St, and Ys, *Jugement* is the only long poem by Machaut. Eighteen of the nineteen manuscripts have most or all of *Jugement*; Ys has only the first sixty-six lines. The present discussion is based on inspection and complete collation of the original manuscripts, except for Kr, from which we could obtain only representative readings; Vg, which we collated from a microfilm in Columbia University Library; and St, also collated from microfilm.

Previous to our edition, only Ernest Hoepffner has made a full critical edition of *Jugement* from the manuscripts;[20] he founded his text on the eleven manuscripts which he knew and had available, using A as his base manuscript. Another edition, together with a translation in English, has been made by J. Barton Palmer, his text being based mainly on Hoepffner's.[21] Barry Windeatt also has translated *Jugement* into English.[22]

The stemma which Hoepffner set up for the complete manuscripts[23] does not hold for *Jugement*, nor does it seem possible to establish a reliable stemma, though groupings that Hoepffner suggested can be maintained with modifications. In place of his three-part division of the manuscripts, a binary separation seems indicated in which his middle (beta) group is split between his original first and third branches. The first branch then is composed of C, the earliest of the collections; E, J, and K, "secondary" collections with inferior texts; and the eight independent texts of the poem listed above. The other branch is formed by the seven closely related collections which have been presumed to represent Machaut's text as it developed after 1360 under his supervision: A, B, D, F, M, Pm, and Vg. Because of the relationship of all of the texts in the first branch to C, and despite the lateness of some of its manuscripts, we identify that branch as the "early text tradition." The other group, then, makes up the "late text tradition."

The standard view of the Machaut manuscripts, which was pioneered by Hoepffner[24], is that the "primary collections"—those of the late tradition plus C—were derived rather directly from an exemplar that the author kept in his possession and presumably perfected over the years, and that at least A and Vg were probably overseen personally by Machaut. On this assumption, Hoepffner chose for his base A, relying next on the closely related F-G. However, the changes that the text of *Jugement* underwent from C and its related manuscripts to the late-tradition manuscripts do not support the established view of authorial supervision which other considerations have seemed to invite. Indeed, the best texts of the poem seem to be found in C and in the still-better independent versions in P and Pc.

Especially since study of the *Jugement* manuscripts suggests that the received view of the development of Machaut's texts is in error, it will be useful to substantiate rather fully the binary division of the manuscripts that we propose, and then to consider what the changes in the text from early to late indicate about the presumed authorial supervision. Two matters seem particularly relevant to this demonstration: included and omitted passages, and substantive differences in the individual readings among the texts.

The manuscripts of the early tradition most obviously are distinguished from the late by having four passages which are omitted consistently from the others: lines 980–83, 1000–1047, 1816–19, and 1861–84 (the last also missing in C and P). Hoepffner's edition, though based on late manuscripts that do not have these passages, includes them without comment. In each of the four cases the omission seems unplanned and deleterious. The omission of 980–83 leaves line 984 ("De ceste amour") dangling and does not introduce the situation that requires the subjunctives of 985 and 987; the deletion of lines 1000–1047 destroys the logic of the lover's response to the lady, wherein he had promised to reply to her charges point by point (line 974), by omitting the section on Souvenir, which in turn is needed to explain the introduction of Pensee in 1048; without 1816–19, Raison's reply to Amours is colorless and undeveloped; and the loss of 1861–84 leaves the sentence begun by Youth in 1857–60 incomplete and meaningless, and also deletes the antecedent for the relative *qui* in 1885. (Moreover, this last omission is much better explained as a scribal slip *du même au même*, from *Qu'amours* of 1860 to *Qu'Amour* of 1884.) Thus these omissions bring strongly into question hypotheses of continuing authorial supervision, as well as the existence of a dependable exemplar of *Jugement* which Machaut maintained for the purpose of having copies made from it.

The evidence of the individual readings points to the same conclusions that the omitted passages do, though the presentation of the evidence is more complicated. For our purposes, the best and clearest contrast between the two sets of manuscripts is found in the instances in which there are two competing and distinctly different readings, each of which has substantial support in the manuscripts. Idiosyncratic readings of one, two, or three manuscripts may of course have authority, but there are not many of these which are not clear blunders, and in any event they tend to blur the larger picture. We look, then, for competing readings supported by more than three manuscripts. Our survey of the corpus of variants for all of the nineteen manuscripts reveals ninety-one instances of two distinct readings with such support. Following are the variants for these from all nineteen manuscripts. The entries here differ from the critical apparatus presented with the text of the poem in that they include the seven late-tradition manuscripts and focus on the word or words in question rather than the whole lines. To point up the early-late division, the sigla of the early-tradition manuscripts are italicized. The lemmas are the same, sometimes truncated, as those used in the critical apparatus (generally from P). As with the critical apparatus, those manuscripts which accord with the lemma are not itemized in the individual entry.

9 **En** a ABDF*ArPc*PmVg; Ad M. 13 **Atemprez** atrempres *C*; attrempre *E*; atremprez *J*; attrempe *RPcRaYs*. 113 **que** qua ABD*E*FM*Ar*PmVg. 147 **Et en tous** En trestous ABDFM*RPc*Pm*Ra*Vg. 151 **et** *om* ADFM*Pc*Vg. 193 **n'avendra** ne vendra ABD*E*F-*J*M*Pc*Pm; nen vendra Vg. 246 **N'est merveille** nest pas merveille *P*BCD*EJKRArRa*. 262 **ne comprendre** et comprendre A*CE*F*RArPc*Pm*RaSt*. 286 **une** lune ABDFM*Pc*Vg. 317 **trop** moult AB*CE*FM*ArPc*PmVg; pou D. 330 **nestoient** nestoit AFMPmVg. 341 **et** *om* ABF*J*KM*Kr*PmVg. 342 **et** *om* AB*EFJK*MPmVg. 359 **quant on** ains quon AB-D*E*FM*Pc*PmVg. 367 **Et si** Car elle ABDPmVg; aussi *R*. 384 **ce** du *EJKArSt*; de D. 393 **com** de ABCDFMPmVg; comme *ERRa*. 493 **dueil** voeul *PCJKMSt*.

532 **Bon** Son ABD*EF*S*t*Vg. 541 **Pour ce** Si que ABD*EFJK*MPmVg. 545 **Ne** Et ABDFMPmVg; Qui *E*. 547 **Rien** Plus ABD*EFJK*MPmVg. 567 **fust** soit ABD*E*FMPmVg. 651 **nostre** vostre *CDEKRArSt*. 678 **renvoisiez** envoisies ABDFM*ArPc*PmVg. 701 **Car** Que ABD*E*FMPmVg. 712 **M'ont** Moult *CEJKPc*. 715 **le** je ABDFMPmVg. 722 **partir** palir *CJKRRa*. 733 **fait** voit A*E*FMPmVg. 734 **le bas en haut** en haut les bas *CJK*; hault en bas *Ar*; de hault embas *St*. 759 **chierir** encherir BC*Ar*Vg; enrichir *ERPcRaSt*. 790 **Qu'el** Qui ABCDM*ArPc*Pm*St*Vg; Quelle *RRa*. 806 **maint** tant ABD*E*FMPmVg. 809 **firent grant** si firent *C*Pm; furent en D; feirent ABFM*Pc*Vg. 821 **n'a Fortune** a fortune CD*JKRPcRa*. 849 **me prenray** men prenray *CEArSt*; men plaindray *JK*; men penray ABDFMPmVg. 857 **prendray** penray ABFMPmVg. 864 **qui** quil *JRAr*Pm*RaSt*. 888 **n'a** nait ABCFM*Ar*PmVg. 933 **pooie** savoie *CFJKRAr*Pm*RaSt*. 961 **au** a D*EJKRArRa*.

1051 **lasse mourne** morne lasse ABD*EFJK*MPmVg. 1055 **en change** au change CF*JK*M*RRa*. 1067 **mouvoir** doloir ABD*EFJK*MPmVg. 1127 **jour heure** heure jour D*JKRRaSt*. 1145 **repentoie** departoie ABCDFM*ArPc*Pm*St*Vg. 1197 **puiz** pris ADFM*ArPc*Vg; prins B. 1214 **me** men ABCFM*Ar*Vg. 1218 **son poil toudis** toudis son poil ABDFMPmVg; son poil tous jours *Ar*. 1257 **demanda** apparla ABDFM*RPc*Pm*Ra*Vg; emparla *C*; appella *St*. 1286 **Et ma** Et de ma *P*CD*RRa*; Et du ma *EJK*. 1301 **tout le bien** tout bien *P*BCD*Pc*Vg; tous biens *RArRaSt*. 1325 **les estours** et les tours *PCEJKRArRa*; et tours D; et estours *St*. 1334 **soit** fust ABD*EFJK*MPmVg. 1342 **raison** bien drois ABDFMPmVg. 1343 **de mere et de pere** de pere et de mere *CEJKRArRaSt*. 1350 **vous** nous *P*ABDFMPmVg. 1371 **dame prie** dame en prie ABDFMPmVg; daler prie *E*. 1403 **oïr** en nul ABDFMPmVg; estre en *C*; avoir *Ar*. 1421 **longue large** largue longe P; large longue AFM*R*Pm*Ra*. 1435 **iere** estre ABDFM*RArPcRaSt*Vg. 1443 **que** com ABD*EFJK*M*Pc*PmVg. 1497 **le prisa** les prisa A*E*FM*R*Pm*Ra*.

1510 **flory** foillu *EJKRArRa*. 1514 **poy se peüst** peu si peust ADF*Pc*Pm*St*; penser peut *RRa*. 1538 **durement** doucement BD*EJKRRa*Vg. 1546 **assouvi** assevi ABDFMPmVg; affeni *C*; ay promi *E*. 1553 **Le pris le senz** Le sens le pris ABDFMPm*St*Vg. 1570 **Avec s'amour** Amant samour *P*; Son cuer samour ABDFMPmVg; Avec son cuer *C*. 1577 **a li** ailleurs AFMPm; lui *JK*. 1581 **noz** mes ABCDFMPmVg; ces *EJK*. 1671 **Et** Ne *EJKRRa*. 1702 **tres** trop *JKRArRa*. 1704 **dame** femme *JK*; ame ABDFMPmVg. 1721 **moult** tant ABDFM*PAr*Vg. 1729 **sont** font *JKRArRa*. 1753 **assez mieux** mieus assez ABCD*E*FM*RRa*Vg. 1775 **tant** trop *ERArPcRaSt*. 1789 **moustree** moustre BCD*EJKRRa*Vg. 1801 **faire fait** fait faire *EJKRRaSt*. 1830 **acquiert** acuet ABDFMPmVg; acqueut *C*; acquier *E*. 1831 **fausse** haute ACD*EJK*M*Ar*. 1834 **a** en *CJKRRa*. 1846 **elle a fait** elle fait ACFM*P*Pm. 1915 **ferai** ferons *P*; faire ABFMVg; feres D; fera *CArSt*. 1973 **conforte** deporte *CRArPcRaSt*. 1986 **se deffont** se meffont AB*C*FMPmVg. 1987 **seront** se font ABFMPmVg; feront *E*. 2031 **moult vous font** vous font moult ACDFM*R*Pm*Ra*. 2053 **plus ne** plus nen ABCD*E*FM*Pc*Vg.

A cursory review of the above readings will show that there is no watertight division between early and late; each of the manuscripts shares frequently in the variant readings. Thus, though our text, represented by the lemmas, is based on the early tradition, most of the variant readings listed are to be found in the early as well as the late tradition. Notwithstanding, there remains sound support for the binary division that we have posited. To demonstrate, we may analyze the sixty-three cases in which A agrees with the variant reading (the reading that differs from the lemma). In these cases other manuscripts concur with A quite in accord with the early-late division: F joins A in sixty (of the sixty-three) cases; M in fifty-six, B and Vg in fifty-two, Pm in forty-nine, and D in forty-four. These six late-tradition texts are therefore from 70 to 95 percent in agreement with A in these readings. By contrast no early-tradition manuscript embodies the variants of A as much as a third of the time: *E* joins A in twenty cases, *Pc* in nineteen, *C* in seventeen, *Ar* in thirteen, *J*, *K*, and *St* in ten, *Ra* in nine, *R* in eight, and *P* in six.

The divergent readings provide further significant information of a different sort. The variety of the early-tradition texts, for one thing, is indicated by the fact that thirty of the ninety-one variant readings listed find stronger support in the early tradition than in the late, even though our text is based on early-tradition manuscripts. *C*, for example, presents the alternate in thirty-three cases. In agreeing with the reading of the text in the sixty-one other cases, *C* demonstrates its early-tradition alliances, but in its divergences from that tradition it finds no manuscript or set of manuscripts with which it is consistently allied, and none from which it is cut off. It is joined by F in eighteen variant readings; A, D, *R*, and *Ra* in seventeen; M and *Ar* in sixteen; D, B, and Vg in fifteen; *Pc* and Pm in thirteen; *E*, *J*, *K*, and *St* in twelve; and *P* in seven. Since *P* normally provides our readings, it would be expected to present few of the variants. The numbers other than for *P* are quite uniform, ranging narrowly from twelve to eighteen. A *C* variant is just a little more likely to appear in a late text than in an early version. There is no evidence here for either systematic adoption or purging of new readings.

More compelling proof that there was no special authorial oversight or revision of the successive *Jugement* texts is provided by a comparison of the quality of these variant readings. As previously stated, the set of variants listed above presents the cases we have found in which each of two competing readings has substantial manuscript support. In all cases both readings make sense, but this does not mean that they are always equally good. Our careful evaluation finds that forty-three of the ninety-one show a distinct difference in quality between the early and late readings. Of the forty-three, fourteen of the late-tradition readings are to be preferred, and twenty-nine of the early, a two-to-one advantage for the early. A simple example is presented in line 532, where the adjective "Bon" of the early tradition is preferable to the colorless "Son." More complex is a case like line 147, in which the early tradition presents an "et" between "amoureux" and "discrez," while the late readings omit it. The difference in syllable count is made up in most manuscripts by the use of "trestous" rather than "tous" early in the line. The sense, grammar, and metrics of the variant line are satisfactory, but the "et" between the adjectives makes the better line, both because a conjunction is normal between such compound predicate adjectives and because it balances well with the previous line's "loyaulz et secrez." There is no doubt a subjective element in such judgments, but certain objective criteria are also usually present. In any event, the independent evaluations of the two editors proved to be extremely close. We find the early readings better for the following lines (italics indicate readings strongly preferred): 147, 193, 317, 341, 342, 367, 393, *532*, *541*, 547, 678, 701, *790*, 809, 849, 888, *1145*, *1257*, 1350, *1403*, 1497, *1570*, 1577, 1581, 1704, 1831, 1846, 1986, and 1987; the late are better for 151, 246, 330, *493*, 626, 715, 821, 1067, 1197, 1286, 1301, *1325*, *1343*, and 1514.

Further striking evidence of a lack of continuing authorial oversight can be drawn from another feature of these variants. Not only do the early-text manuscripts have the better readings more than twice as many times as the late, but of those fourteen instances in which the late seem better, only three readings (330, 1067, 1301) are not represented in one of the better early manuscripts, i.e., *C*, *P*, and *Pc*. Conversely, of the twenty-nine readings in which the early seem better, only three (367, 532, 1831) are represented in the late manuscripts that Hoepffner favored, A and F. From this one would infer that almost none of the better readings originate in the later texts, while once the good readings were lost, they remained lost. All the evidence of the manuscript texts of *Jugement* thus paints a different picture of the development of the Machaut text from that which a broader, but less complete and detailed, study of the complete manuscripts has presented. It is clear that at least with *Jugement* Machaut did not carefully supervise the text of the later manuscripts. The situation with *Remede* is somewhat different, but we can assert with confidence that previous editions of *Jugement* have not been based on the best manuscripts of the poem.

The best texts, which belong to the early tradition, are those which our study of Chaucer's use of Machaut have led us to edit. Since all of the independent texts of *Jugement* (*Pr, Ar, Kr, Pc, Ra, St,* and *Ys*) represent the early tradition, it obviously had a much wider dissemination than did the late tradition. Thus it is not surprising that all indications are that Chaucer read and used a text or texts of the early tradition, as we show below. The evidence points to no one manuscript in the early group. J and K have several unique readings which must have been Chaucer's, but they also have as many which could not have been his. Therefore, we have chosen to make a critical edition of the set, *C, E, J, K, P, R, Ar, Kr, Pc, Ra, St,* and *Ys*, the last six of which Hoepffner did not include in his edition. The present edition, we believe, produces a version as near as possible to Machaut's original, the version he composed and sanctioned, which in almost all cases is also as near as possible to that which Chaucer used.

Description of Manuscripts Used for This Edition

C Paris, Bibliothèque Nationale, fonds français 1586. Vellum, 225 folios measuring 30 × 22 cm., 1350–56. C is the base manuscript for the present edition of *Remede*. It was assigned a fifteenth-century date in Bibliothèque Impériale, Département des Manuscrits, *Catalogue des manuscrits français*, tome I, Ancien fonds (Paris: Firmin Didot, 1868), p. 259; and by Schrade.[25] However, François Avril has demonstrated the dating 1350–56 on art-historical grounds.[26]

Contents: The manuscript has most of the *oeuvre* of Guillaume de Machaut before *Le Jugement du roy de Navarre* (1349): *Jugement*, ff. 1–22; *Remede*, ff. 23–58; *Dit de l'alerion*, ff. 59–92; *Dit du vergier*, ff. 93–102; *Dit du lyon*, ff. 103–120; *Louange des dames*, ff. 121–148v; lyrics set to music, ff. 148v-225.

This deluxe manuscript was probably prepared for Jean le Bon.[27] With *Jugement*, as with the rest of the manuscript, the text is written in a handsome *littera textualis formata* in two columns, generally of thirty-eight lines, measuring 21.5 × 14 cm. Of the 107 miniatures of the manuscript, *Jugement* has nine and *Remede* has thirty-four.[28] The manuscript has extensive musical notation, including the seven musical compositions of *Remede*.

E Paris, Bibliothèque Nationale, fonds français 9221.[29] Parchment, five flyleaves and 238 folios, 40.6 × 30 cm., about 1390. Though this manuscript traditionally has been seen as having been written in Machaut's lifetime (d. 1377), Avril has argued convincingly for the later date.[30]

Contents: The works of Machaut. Shorter *Prologue*, f. 1; *Louange des dames*, ff. 1v-17; *Dit du vergier*, 18–21v; *Remede*, ff. 22–36v; *Jugement*, ff. 37–42v; *Jugement du roy de Navarre*, ff. 45–56v; *Lai de plour*, ff. 57–58; *Dit du lyon*, ff. 61–67; *Dit de l'alerion*, ff. 69–82v; *Dit de la fonteinne amoureuse*, ff. 83–91; *Confort d'ami*, ff. 93–104; *Dit de la harpe*, ff. 105–106 (displaced to the beginning of the manuscript); lyrics set to music, ff. 107–164; Mass, ff. 164v-170; *Voir dit*, ff. 171–211; *Prise d'Alexandrie*, ff. 213–238.

This very large and elaborate codex was prepared for Jean, duke of Berry, who signed it. The texts of *Jugement* and *Remede*, written in a very fine *littera textualis formata*, are presented in three columns of sixty lines which cover 29.3 × 21 cm. Of the thirty-nine miniatures of E, one (on folio 37) belongs to *Jugement*; it depicts the knight speaking to the lady, whose train is being held by her serving girl, and the narrator behind some trees. There are two miniatures for *Remede*. The full musical notation of the manuscript includes the seven compositions in *Remede*.

J Paris, Bibliothèque de l'Arsenal 5203.[31] Parchment, 164 folios (numbered 161 with three numbers duplicated), 29 × 21 cm., double columns of thirty-six lines, fourteenth century.

Contents: Much of Machaut's *oeuvre* with some apocryphal pieces. *Louange des dames*, ff. 1–20v; *Dit du vergier*, ff. 21–30; *Jugement*, ff. 30v-44v; *Lai de plour*, ff. 45–46; *Chanson desesperee*, f. 46v; *Remede*, ff. 47–76; *Dit du lyon*, ff. 77–90v; *Confort d'ami*, ff. 91–117v; *Dit de la fonteinne amoureuse*, ff. 118–137v; *Dit de la harpe*, ff. 138–139v; lais, f. 139v-146; anonymous works and short pieces of Machaut, ff. 146v-161v.

J, composed in a very even and regular *littera textualis formata*, is very closely related to K. Hoepffner thinks it a copy "pure et simple" of K. Nevertheless, there are some differences between the two manuscripts in the texts of *Jugement* and *Remede*, and the original contents of the two codices probably differed somewhat in the later parts. It is possible that J was made for Robert d'Alençon (d.1377).[32] At the head of *Jugement* is a large illumination depicting the king with the knight and the lady, accompanied by her serving-girl and her dog; in the background the narrator rather comically looks out from behind some bushes. There are five miniatures for *Remede*.

K Bern, Burgerbibliothek 218.[33] Parchment; originally 140 folios (numbered 138 with two numbers duplicated), but only 106 folios remain; 29.5 × 20.2 cm.; dated 11 April 1371, written in *littera textualis formata* in two columns of forty-two lines.

Contents (using original folio numbers): *Louange des dames*, ff. 1–20v; *Dit du vergier*, ff. 21–29v; *Jugement*, ff. 30–41; *Lai de plour*, f. 42 r-v; *Chanson desesperee*, f. 42v; *Remede*, ff. 43–68v; *Dit du lyon*, ff. 69–83v; *Confort d'ami*, ff. 84–107v; *Dit de la fonteinne amoureuse*, ff. 108–124v; *Dit de la harpe*, ff. 125–126v; lais, ff. 127–132; anonymous works and short pieces by Machaut, ff. 132–138.

For the relationship of J and K, see the description of J above. Many of the numerous folios removed from K may have been decorated with miniatures. The first folio of *Jugement* with the first 160 lines of the poem is missing, and the next two folios are reversed; two later folios of the poem also are reversed. No miniatures for *Jugement* survive, but there are three for *Remede*. Poirion suggests that K is the "roman" for which Amadée of Savoy gave Machaut three hundred gold francs in 1371, but Earp considers this unlikely because of the apocryphal contents included in K.[34] The manuscript includes the music of the two ballades of *Remede*.

P Paris, Bibliothèque Nationale, fonds français 2166.[35] Vellum, ninety-six folios, single columns of thirty-two lines, 22.8 × 17.2 cm., mid to late fourteenth century. P is the base manuscript for the present edition of *Jugement*. The *Catalogue des manuscrits français*, p. 366, identifies it as fifteenth century, but this catalog is unreliable (as the misdating of C demonstrates). Its script seems earlier. Karen Gould makes the following comment, based on inspection of a microfilm of P: "The most outstanding characteristics are the pronounced ascenders and descenders: *f* and *s* rise far above the line looping to the right and descend well below the line tapering to a point. The ascending portion of *b* and *d* forms a loop that is often an exaggerated curve . . . Scripts with similar characteristics which could be classified as *littera cursiva textualis* appear in French manuscripts of the second half of the fourteenth century." The contents also suggest a fourteenth-century dating.

Contents: P is a continuation of Bibliothèque Nationale, fonds français 2165, and is like it in format and execution. The 104 folios of 2165 contain over three-fourths of the *Voeux du Paon* of Jacques de Longuyon (1312). The last part of the *Voeux* is found in 2166 (P), ff. 1–32v. The continuation of Jacques' poem, *Le Restor du Paon*, written by Brisebarre de Douai (d. 1340), occupies folios 32v-63v, but with no distinguishing incipit. *Jugement*, lines 1–2058, takes up folios 64r-95v (actually folios 65r-96v, since two successive folios bear number 45).

Manuscripts 2165 and 2166 together are made up of twenty-five quires of eight folios, two hundred folios total. The scribe arrived at the end of the last folio with only eighteen lines remaining of *Jugement*. It would seem natural for this conscientious scribe to have made an attempt to complete the poem in some fashion; nevertheless, all evidence of the manuscript indicates that, having arrived at the end of the quire, he was content to leave the poem hanging. (However, the final eighteen lines have been added on the inside flyleaf of the back cover in what is probably a nineteenth-century hand.) There are three miniatures each in 2165 and 2166, with one on folio 64r at the beginning of *Jugement*. The king is shown with four counselors behind him, and a man and woman pleading before him.

R Paris, Bibliothèque Nationale, fonds français 2230.[36] Vellum, two flyleaves and 248 folios, 21 × 15.5 cm., mid-fifteenth century (after 1445).

Contents: Works of Alain Chartier. *Jugement*, identified in the explicit as "Le Jugement d'Amours" with no mention of Machaut, is found on folios 27v-61.

A coat of arms identifies the manuscript as made for Marguerite de Rohan, wife of Jean d'Angoulême. It has one miniature; none for *Jugement*. Ra, described below, is written by the same scribe and very closely related to R. The text of *Jugement*, in *littera cursiva textualis*, is in single columns of thirty lines measuring 14 × 7.5 cm.

Ar Arras, Bibliothèque Municipale 897.[37] Parchment, 182 folios, 30 × 20 cm., double column of thirty-eight lines, 1370.

Contents: *Roman de la Rose*, ff. 1–120v; *Testament Jean de Meun*. ff. 121–134; *Vision of St. Fulbert*, in quatrains, ff. 134–136v; poem "Fils de Dieu," f. 136v; two untitled serventois, ff. 136v-137v; *Purgatory of St. Patrick*, ff. 137v-141; *Prise amoureuse* by Jehan Acart de Hesdin (1332), ff.

141v-152; *Jugement* ff. 152v-166v; poem on care of birds, f. 166v; *Thobie*, in prose, ff. 167–171v; prose life of St. John the Baptist, ff. 172–177v; verse life of St. John Chrysostum, ff. 177v-182v. The only miniature for *Jugement* occurs at the beginning of the poem on folio 152v; it depicts the knight meeting the lady accompanied by her dog, with the poet hidden behind some trees. The text of *Jugement* is in a clear and regular *littera textualis*.

Kr New York, H. P. Kraus (formerly Phillipps 6740). Vellum, forty-one folios (numbered 49; folios 33–40 missing) measuring 18.5 × 13.5 cm. Advertised as third quarter of fourteenth century, but probably later.

Contents: Untitled poem, "Ou mois qui est peres de joie," ff. 1–17; *Jugement*, ff. 18–41. Because of the missing gathering, *Jugement* lacks lines 1038–1542.

We were unable to do more than sample the readings in this manuscript, but our inspection indicates that it is of secondary importance for establishing the text. The other poem in the manuscript seems an imitation of the narrative of *Jugement* in octosyllabic couplets. The manuscript could have been made for the unidentified poet of the imitation.

Pc Paris, Bibliothèque Nationale, fonds français 1149.[38] Vellum, 183 folios, double columns of thirty-four lines, last quarter of fourteenth or early fifteenth century (estimate of Karen Gould). The contents suggest the fourteenth century. A space was left on folio 167r for a miniature that was never executed. Approximately a third of folio 179 was cut out, causing the loss of forty lines of *Jugement*. The manuscript is written in *littera cursiva textualis*.

Contents: *Vision de Jean Dupin* (1340), ff. 1–123v; *Anticlaudianus*, French translation, ff. 124–166; *Jugement*, ff. 167–182.

Ra Paris, Bibliothèque Nationale, fonds français 20026.[39] Vellum, 3 flyleaves and 179 folios, 22 × 15 cm., mid-fifteenth century (after 1440).

Contents: Works of Alain Chartier.[40] *Jugement* called "Jugement d'Amours," is found on folios 81v-115r.

This manuscript bears the arms of Marie de Clèves, wife of Charles d'Orléans and sister-in-law of Marguerite de Rohan, for whom the closely-related R was made. *Jugement* is in single-column format, thirty lines per column, measuring 13.5 × 7 cm. It was written by the same scribe as R in *littera cursiva textualis* and, like R, is decorated with elaborate floral borders in the outside and bottom margins of folios on which major items begin.

St Stockholm, Kungliga Biblioteket Vu 22.[41] Paper, 272 folios measuring 20.5 × 14.5 cm., fifteenth century.

Of the 114 French texts of various kinds in this manuscript, Machaut is represented by two motets, ff. 138v-140; a rondel, f. 141v; and *Juge-*

ment, ff. 160–182v (missing the first 152 lines). The text is written in single columns of forty lines measuring 16.5 × 9 cm. *Jugement* is in an irregular *littera cursiva currens* with very thick descenders on *p*, *q*, *s*, *f*, *j* and broad strokes in *d*, *h*, *b*, and *l*.

Ys Paris, Bibliothèque Nationale, fonds français 1595.[42] Vellum, thirty-eight folios, single columns of thirty lines, last quarter of fourteenth century (though previously identified as fifteenth by L. Hervieux, *Les Fabulistes latins* [Paris: Firmin-Didot, 1893], and in the catalog of the Bibliothèque Impériale). The text is in *littera textualis currens*.

Contents: *Ysopet*, ff. 1–36; *Jugement*, ff. 36v–37v, with the text broken off near the middle of the page after the first half of line 66.

Choice of the Base Manuscript

The texts of the manuscripts we edit vary greatly in quality and, as we have suggested, have interesting and surprising convergences and divergences. As a consequence, it is not possible to construct a stemma that will explain satisfactorily the contamination among the many manuscripts involved. Nonetheless, it is possible to see certain groupings, of which the most evident are EJK–RRa–ArSt–CPPc.

Both J and K are missing a number of lines that the other manuscripts consistently include (175, 205, 307, 410, 844–47, 990, 1039, 1252–54, 1386, 1414, 1417), and the two texts share almost all significant variants (e.g., 486, 570–71, 718–19, 757–58, 906–7, 991, 1041–43, 1525, 1770–71, 1858–59, 1994–95). For *Jugement*, in contrast to *Remede* as we shall see, E is often allied with J and K against the individual manuscripts (P, R, Ar, Kr, Pc, Ra, St, and Ys) and against C. E, J, and K reverse lines 1122 and 1123, and share important variants at 37, 95, 247, 333, 507, 541, 547, 743, 746, 941, 997, 1006, 1008, 1036, 1051, 1067, 1082, 1131, 1155, 1169, 1170, 1171, 1215, 1285–87, 1323, 1329, 1334, 1355, 1391, 1395, 1407, 1409, 1437, 1455, 1472–73, 1511, 1514, 1520, 1521, 1531, 1539, 1563, 1581, 1615, 1627, 1630, 1657, 1694, 1698, 1749, 1759, 1778, 1782, 1791, 1817, 1843, 1937, 1941, 1953, 1974, 1985, 2069, 2079. Since E does not omit the many lines missing in J and K, nor repeat numerous errors contained in those manuscripts alone, E, J, and K must have been copied independently from an earlier manuscript containing these (and other) errors. The relatively few variants in the sixty-six lines contained in Ys suggest that it was copied from a fairly early source, and is possibly allied with the EJK group.

Like J and K, R and Ra share almost all of the significant variants that they present, including omitted lines at 199, 438, 505–40, 590, 639, 1176–79, 1495, 1498, 1715, 1767, 1820–23, 1862, 1886, 1910–11, 1955, 2061. Significant substantive errors and the omission of additional lines at 243,

551, and 626 in R suggest that R was a copy of Ra. R and Ra are associated with J (and usually K) by the omission of lines 1176–79 and variants at 14, 18, 20, 57, 58, 73, 74, 194, 218, 235, 607, 808, 821, 823, 927, 1063, 1127, 1180, 1387, 1638, 1646, 1718, 1729, 1789, 1801; with E at 15, 50, 82, 94, 111, 185, 281, 378, 393, 465, 490, 661, 787, 833, 845, 926, 989, 1103, 1104, 1159, 1194, 1497, 1501, 1574, 1667, 1889, 1919, 1996, 2050, and 2059; and with the EJK tradition by a number of important variants (1293, 1365, 1510, 1759, 1858) and by many minor ones. On the whole, however, R and Ra are quite independent and quite eccentric, and of almost no value in the establishment of the text. Forty-five variants ally Pc with R and Ra: 13, 14, 41, 55, 74, 85, 102, 107, 147, 150, 180, 218, 486, 562, 586, 610, 759, 778, 821, 903, 969, 1035, 1039, 1131, 1155 (twice), 1171, 1175, 1249, 1257, 1322, 1390, 1462, 1533, 1582, 1586, 1625, 1639, 1775, 1858, 1873, 1882, 1950, 1973, 2043. Of these forty-five, twenty-one further link R and Ra with Ar (74, 85, 102, 107, 486, 562, 586, 610, 778, 1035, 1155, 1171, 1249, 1462, 1533, 1586, 1775, 1858, 1873, 1950, 1973), and many of these same variants also show a link with St (759, 778, 1035, 1171, 1175, 1249, 1322, 1462, 1533, 1582, 1639, 1775, 1858, 1873, 1973).

Ar and St share a number of variants in common with other manuscripts of the early tradition, but both are independent and not easily assimilable to the tradition as a whole. Ar was transcribed in Picardy with a strongly dialectal orthography; it omits lines 1079, 1595, and 1910–13, and transposes lines 394–95 and 625–26. St has lost lines 1–152, due to loss of its initial folio, and is also missing lines 740–43, 847, 853, 1528–31, and 2019. The additional transposition of some twenty lines and the numerous infractions of the meter offer ample evidence of a hastily copied text. Ar (and less frequently St) can be associated with E, J, and K or with E alone (35, 109, 113, 179, 303, 365, 379, 384, 386, 402, 409, 421–22, 526, 542, 678, 706, 841, 867, 870, 993, 1053, 1095, 1106, 1137, 1147, 1197, 1410, 1450, 1569, 1795, 1819, 1858, 1861, 1948, 1981). The few variant readings that we were able to take from Kr, which is privately held, do not suffice to demonstrate its affiliations beyond showing that it belongs to the early group and is not one of the best texts.

Occasional variants ally C with E (occasionally in conjunction with J and K) and with R and Ra, but C is more closely linked to P. Both offer relatively faithful and non-eccentric versions of the poem; both are early in date; and both omit a lengthy passage (1861–84) also missing in manuscripts of the late tradition. P and C, together with Pc, offer the best versions of *Jugement*, as even the most superficial comparison of the texts proves.

Most of the early-text manuscripts have features that make them unsuited to providing a base for this edition:

E (prepared in the last decade of the fourteenth century for the Duke of Berry) is notoriously inaccurate in its text: in the first five hundred lines of *Jugement* it has unsupported readings in 105 instances; throughout the poem it omits six lines and inverts another six. Manuscripts J and K (K commences at line 152) have ninety-seven variant readings not shared with other manuscripts in these same five hundred lines; they omit seventeen lines, invert fourteen, and repeat eight. R and Ra are even more eccentric, having over 120 unsubstantiated readings in the initial five hundred lines, and omitting some fifty-six lines and inverting fifteen through the course of the poem. Ar, with its markedly Picard dialectal traits, and St, with its numerous omissions, transpositions, and generally sloppy text, are both quite unsuitable as base manuscripts.

C, P, and Pc are all considerably more accurate than E, J, K, R, Ar, Kr, Ra, and St: C has only fifty-two individual unsupported readings in the initial five-hundred-line sample, while P and Pc have seventeen and eighteen respectively. Pc, as we have seen above, is linked by a number of variants to the RRa group, as well as to the ArSt tradition. The majority of these variants, however, are inconsequential: change of word order, choice of a synonym, plural/singular, etc., and were probably found in a lost early model. The numerous errors of R and Ra were introduced at a later stage and do not affect Pc. Pc omits only lines 602–5, but lines 1673–92 and 1707–26 have been cut out of the manuscript; Pc alone provides the correct reading at line 1325, and joins only with P in having the correct reading for line 1343. Pc does introduce a number of errors in the initial five hundred lines which affect either the meter or the rhyme (21, 77, 114, 131, 151, 346, 367, 421), and Pc also neglects the case system almost entirely except where it affects meter or rhyme, but this does not alter the fact that Pc is an exceptionally good text. P and C clearly go back to a common model, which was quite accurate, but which, lacking 1861–84, could not have been Machaut's original. In copying his model, scribe C was less meticulous than scribe P, often introducing readings that are at variance with the meter. C has fifty-six metrically irregular lines, at 10, 14, 146, 233, 271, 345, 353, 354, 369, 399, 457, 535, 601, 693, 717, 822, 881, 918, 935, 971, 1013, 1025, 1102, 1183, 1205, 1286, 1287, 1298, 1301, 1305, 1382, 1389, 1393, 1414, 1446, 1499, 1505, 1523, 1585, 1594, 1609, 1669, 1693, 1747, 1750, 1763, 1822, 1831, 1858, 1941, 1955, 1967, 1971, 1979, 1994, 2011. The scribe of P, on the other hand, was more attentive to the meter and meaning of his text, to the point of occasionally supplying lines of his own confection, either because he encountered an error in his model or was not happy with it for some reason (see the variants at 870, 917, 1306, and 1886–87). In addition to the common error with C at 1861–84, P omits four lines at 1708–

11, and is missing 2061–79, which would constitute the final folio of the manuscript. C omits only one additional line (214), but transposes several: 138–39, 869 and 871, and 1586–87.

Because of its unusual accuracy, and in spite of the lacuna at the end, we have chosen P as our base manuscript for *Jugement*. C, nevertheless, has unusual importance which we elaborate on in our discussion of the manuscripts of *Remede* (for whose text C is our base manuscript). P's lacunae at 1708–11 and 2061–79 have been supplied from C. Lines 1861–84, missing in both C and P, are transcribed from Pc. Pc rivals P in accuracy, and it does include 1861–84 (not in C or P), but P is more in the mainstream of the early-text tradition, and its readings, much more than those of Pc, ally it with E, J, and K, those manuscripts which generally show Chaucer's reading, as the discussion of Chaucer's Machaut manuscript below shows.

In presenting our text, we have followed the orthography of P, which is unremarkable save for the preference of *-z* for final *-s* (*puiz*, 7; *nez*, 14; *douz*, 24) and a very slight tendency to include etymological letters (*soubz*, 4; *conjoinctement*, 172; *maulx*, 467; *serfi*, 703).

Whenever there are competing readings of comparable quality, we have sought to present the text that most nearly approaches that which Machaut might have originally written. The emendations have been arrived at by an evaluation of all variant readings of the manuscripts representing the early tradition, and all emendations have the authority of at least one manuscript. Whenever a reading of P has been rejected for metrical reasons, this is indicated by (+1) or (−1) in the corpus of variants. Whenever we have selected a reading from a witness or witnesses other than P, our choice has been guided by the recension of the respective variants and the nature of the probable error. The relative weight assigned the witnesses generally follows the manuscript groupings PPcC–EJK–ArSt–RRa.

We have made the standard editorial interventions expected in editions of medieval French texts: we have expanded all abbreviations (except numerals) in conformity with forms found in full elsewhere in the manuscript; we have distinguished *i* from *j* and *u* from *v* according to accepted usage; we have added capitals and punctuation where required, respecting the manuscript's capitalization at the beginning of each line of verse; we have followed the recommendations in Foulet and Speer[43] on the use of the diaresis. Elision of feminine *e* of most monosyllables is noted by the use of the apostrophe (*s'y*, *l'amoit*, *qu'elle*, *n'a*, etc.), where in the manuscript the words are regularly conjoined. In some thirty cases in P this feminine *e* is written by the scribe and we have included it (lines 23, 82, 83, 90, 150, 267, 531, 627, 842, 851, 883, 899, 933, 943, 992, 1039, 1059, 1088, 1092, 1095, 1269, 1403, 1441, 1530, 1685, 1772, 1803, 1984, and

2073). However, when Machaut intended a feminine *e* to count to fill out his line, whether on monosyllables or polysyllables, we have so indicated by the use of the diaresis (lines 217, 238, 414, 525, 538, 899, 943, 1013, 1050, 1182, 1198, 1407, 1528, 1557, 1615, 1695, 1705, 1810, 1850, 1914, 2063, and 2079). We have indicated folio numbers of the base manuscript in the right margin and have maintained the divisions of the text as indicated by the blanks left in it for the rubricator to supply large capitals.

The critical apparatus lists the lemma, followed by any rejected reading from P, then all variant readings in the order C, E, J, K, R, Ar, Kr, Pc, Ra, St, Ys. Thus, the variant readings should be understood as follows:

13 **attemprez** atrempres C; attrempre E; attrempe RPcRaYs.

The reading **attemprez** of the text is found in P, J, K, Ar, Kr, and St; C reads *atrempres*; E has *attrempre*; and R, Pc, Ra, and Ys all have *attrempe*.

15 **La** Et la PERRaYs (+1); Que la Ar.

The reading of the base text P, attested also in E, R, Ra, and Ys, has been rejected as unmetrical in favor of that found in C, J, K, Kr, Pc, and St; Ar also has an unmetrical reading that has been rejected.

In the apparatus the only abbreviation used is *om* to indicate omissions of words or lines.

The critical apparatus is intended to indicate all differences in word choice or meaning, no matter how subtle. Only minor spelling differences that do not affect meaning or meter have not been included among the variant readings. Thus, *seur/sur/sus* have all been considered spelling variations of *sur* ("upon") and are not noted. The spellings *li/lui/luy* are not noted when they are clearly variant spellings of the masculine pronoun, but are indicated whenever *li* is or could be understood as a feminine form. Similarly, *fu/fui* are not listed when they are variant spellings of the first person singular preterit, but are listed when the use of *fu* could indicate the choice of a third person subject rather than first person. Doublets such as *avec/avecques*, *ains/ainçois*, are noted only when the use of one for the other affects the syllable count of the line in question. In cases of doubt, we have preferred to list variants. Thus, although *ce* and *se* frequently are no more than spelling variants, they could also represent the choice of a demonstrative versus a reflexive pronoun, so we have indicated them. In like manner, we have preferred to distinguish *qui/qu'il*, *ne/ni/n'y*, *me/m'en*, *se/sa*, *c'est/ceste/s'est*, etc. However, we have not picked up the frequent differences in case usage or in agreements of past participles, unless they affect the meter.

When giving variants, the spelling shown is that of the first witness that follows the variant. Thus:

35 **Souz** Dessoubz EArYs; Entre RRa.

The spelling **souz** is that of the base manuscript P; other manuscripts attesting that reading (C, J, K, Kr, Pc, and St) do not necessarily record the same exact spelling. *Dessoubz* is recorded in E, but Ar and Ys could spell *dessous/desous/dessoubs*, etc. *Entre* is the spelling of R, but not necessarily of Ra.

Chaucer's Manuscript of *Jugement*

That Chaucer knew *Jugement* well is clear; his extensive use of the poem's language, ideas, and literary features shows his thorough familiarity with it. The Notes to the Texts quote the passages from Chaucer's poetry that present significant parallels to *Jugement*; these are itemized in the table below. We qualify with "Cf." some of the citations of Chaucer's works in the notes, indicating that direct indebtedness to the French poem is less than certain. For the sake of pointing up word-for-word similarities, we have chosen to compare the texts in mainly one- and two-line segments. The brevity of these passages sometimes obscures the broader context of the borrowings which is often essential for understanding the relationships. The reader may compensate for this limitation by referring to the full passages and to the borrowings before and after the line(s) in question. Nevertheless, it is finally impossible to pinpoint and schematize adequately the matter of influence. The best test is a careful reading of the French poem in the light of Chaucer's works, with reference to what has been written about Chaucer's use of *Jugement*.

Such study shows significant parallels in plot, characterization, and technique, as well as in verbal expression; it leaves no doubt that the poem exercised a major formative influence on the English writer's work and provided continuing inspiration to him. *Jugement*'s relationship to the *Book of the Duchess* and *Troilus and Criseyde* is especially important. It is basic in the *Book of the Duchess*, where most of the borrowings are found in the elegy proper; they recur continually from the point when the Black Knight recites his sad song (lines 475–86) until he rides away to the rich hill (1311–20). The contribution of *Jugement* to the *Book of the Duchess* is notably strong in the conversational exchange between the dreamer and the Knight, the Knight's fainting and resuscitation, his account of his first sight of White, the physical details of his description of her, and his ultimate confession to her. In *Troilus and Criseyde*, while the influence of *Jugement* is often ancillary to that of *Remede*, it comes to the fore in particular when Troilus faints beside Criseyde's bed in Book III and composes a prayer to Love shortly thereafter.

The chart below, which does not pretend to be exhaustive, lists 198 passages of *Jugement* which have parallels in Chaucer. Of these, counterparts to 157 are found in the *Book of the Duchess*, thirty-one in *Troilus and*

Criseyde, nine in the *Canterbury Tales*, five in *Complaint of Mars*, and one in the *Legend of Good Women*. Three-fourths of the parallels listed occur in the first third of Machaut's poem, but some are found in all parts of the work.

Jugement Line Nos.	**Chaucer's Work**	**Chaucer Line Nos.**
13	Book of the Duchess	341
14	Book of the Duchess	340, 342
17	Book of the Duchess	340
19	Book of the Duchess	346
26–27	Book of the Duchess	397
30	Book of the Duchess	400
43–44	Book of the Duchess	398–99
50	Book of the Duchess	452
59	Book of the Duchess	533–34
60–62	Book of the Duchess	503–4
70	Book of the Duchess	520–21
71	Book of the Duchess	509–10
73–74	Book of the Duchess	525
74	Book of the Duchess	519
75–76	Book of the Duchess	529
77	Book of the Duchess	526–27
78	Book of the Duchess	528
79–80	Book of the Duchess	555
79, 86	Book of the Duchess	538
88	Book of the Duchess	547
89	Book of the Duchess	553
90	Book of the Duchess	548–49
91	Book of the Duchess	554
92	Book of the Duchess	551
93	Book of the Duchess	560
94–96	Book of the Duchess	563
97	Book of the Duchess	564
123–24	Book of the Duchess	749–50
125	Book of the Duchess	37, 759
126	Book of the Duchess	764–65
127	Book of the Duchess	766
128–29	Book of the Duchess	759–60
130–33	Book of the Duchess	767–70
149–50	Book of the Duchess	1036
151–59	Book of the Duchess	1038–40
166	Book of the Duchess	1289
167	Book of the Duchess	1290–91
169–72	Book of the Duchess	1292–94
173	Book of the Duchess	1295
184–85	Book of the Duchess	609–10
186	Book of the Duchess	608
191	Book of the Duchess	608

Jugement Line Nos.	**Chaucer's Work**	**Chaucer Line Nos.**
194	Book of the Duchess	476
195–96	Book of the Duchess	481–82
199–200	Book of the Duchess	483
201	Book of the Duchess	478
204	Book of the Duchess	475
213	Book of the Duchess	507
215	Book of the Duchess	488–89
215	Troilus and Criseyde	III 1088–89
217	Book of the Duchess	510
220	Book of the Duchess	488
220	Troilus and Criseyde	III 1092
221–23	Troilus and Criseyde	III 1114–15
227–28	Troilus and Criseyde	III 1119–20
232–33	Book of the Duchess	714–15
234	Book of the Duchess	725
253–56	Book of the Duchess	749–52
254	Book of the Duchess	555–56
261	Book of the Duchess	759–60
262	Book of the Duchess	761–62
263	Book of the Duchess	763–64
265	Book of the Duchess	775
266	Book of the Duchess	776
268	Book of the Duchess	766
269	Book of the Duchess	771
270–71	Book of the Duchess	772, 774
272–73	Book of the Duchess	773
281–82	Book of the Duchess	805, 807–8
284	Book of the Duchess	811
285	Book of the Duchess	812
285	cf. Troilus and Criseyde	IV 5
286	Book of the Duchess	817–18
287	Book of the Duchess	821, 824
288	Book of the Duchess	822
289–90	Book of the Duchess	826–27
292–96	cf. Book of the Duchess	895–903
297	Book of the Duchess	848
298	Book of the Duchess	849
299	Book of the Duchess	850
300	Book of the Duchess	853
301	Book of the Duchess	854
302	Book of the Duchess	855, 858
303	Book of the Duchess	857
312	Book of the Duchess	859
314–15	Book of the Duchess	866–67, 883
316–18	Book of the Duchess	860–61
321	Book of the Duchess	872
322	Book of the Duchess	861
323	Book of the Duchess	864–65

Jugement Line Nos.	Chaucer's Work	Chaucer Line Nos.
326	Book of the Duchess	883
329	Book of the Duchess	866–67
330	Book of the Duchess	874
331–35	cf. Book of the Duchess	883–87
331	cf. Troilus and Criseyde	I 325
337–38	cf. Canterbury Tales	A 150
341	cf. Canterbury Tales	A 153
342	cf. Canterbury Tales	A 3261
346	cf. Canterbury Tales	A 3735
357–58	Book of the Duchess	904–5
361	Book of the Duchess	942, 947
362–63	Book of the Duchess	939–41, 943, 945
365–66	Book of the Duchess	952–54
367	Book of the Duchess	955
369–70	Book of the Duchess	956
373	Book of the Duchess	952
374–75	Book of the Duchess	954
376–77	Book of the Duchess	956–57
382	Book of the Duchess	959
382–83	Troilus and Criseyde	I 282–83
390	Book of the Duchess	950
394	cf. Troilus and Criseyde	I 289–91
398–99	Book of the Duchess	908–9
402–3	Book of the Duchess	910–11
411–14	Book of the Duchess	913
411–14	Troilus and Criseyde	I 297–98
412	cf. Troilus and Criseyde	I 366
421	Book of the Duchess	1056, 1060; cf. 368
422	Book of the Duchess	1072
437–39	Troilus and Criseyde	I 289–91
440–41	Troilus and Criseyde	I 301
442	Book of the Duchess	1218
442–44	Troilus and Criseyde	I 306–7
451–52	Troilus and Criseyde	I 361–62
453–56	Book of the Duchess	1186–91
461–62	Book of the Duchess	1196–98
461–62	Troilus and Criseyde	I 898–99
466	Book of the Duchess	1191–92
468–70	Book of the Duchess	1212–14
471	Book of the Duchess	1211
473	Book of the Duchess	1218
474	cf. Troilus and Criseyde	III 79
499	Book of the Duchess	1214–15
504	Book of the Duchess	1224
505	Book of the Duchess	1219
505–6	cf. Canterbury Tales	F 978
509	Book of the Duchess	1236
521	cf. Canterbury Tales	A 119

Jugement Line Nos.	Chaucer's Work	Chaucer Line Nos.
541–48	cf. Book of the Duchess	1239–44
580–81	Book of the Duchess	917–18
582	Book of the Duchess	910–11
596–97	Book of the Duchess	1261–63
598	Book of the Duchess	1264
610	Book of the Duchess	1271
622	Book of the Duchess	1277–78
622	cf. Troilus and Criseyde	III 1243
623	Book of the Duchess	1280
635	Book of the Duchess	1216
641	Book of the Duchess	1270
656	Book of the Duchess	1227–28
658	Book of the Duchess	1230
659–60	Book of the Duchess	1234–35
663	Book of the Duchess	1040
663	Legend of Good Women	F Prologue 95
665–67	Troilus and Criseyde	III 1294–95
670	Book of the Duchess	1270
675–77	Book of the Duchess	1296–97
684–85	cf. Troilus and Criseyde	IV 2–3
686	cf. Troilus and Criseyde	III 1271
688	Troilus and Criseyde	IV 7
689	Troilus and Criseyde	IV 8–9
690–91	Troilus and Criseyde	IV 6, 11
710	cf. Book of the Duchess	905
722	cf. Book of the Duchess	488
723–24	Complaint of Mars	191–92
740	Book of the Duchess	631
747	Complaint of Mars	193
808–9	Complaint d'Amour	57–58
811	Complaint of Mars	268
826	cf. Book of the Duchess	608
834–36	cf. Book of the Duchess	1049–53
849–50	Complaint of Mars	191
854–55	Complaint of Mars	267–68
861–63	cf. Canterbury Tales	A 715–16
861–62	cf. Book of the Duchess	1129–30
1039	cf. Book of the Duchess	616
1072	Book of the Duchess	645
1074	Book of the Duchess	646
1078	Book of the Duchess	648
1097–99	cf. Troilus and Criseyde	II 925–30
1143	Book of the Duchess	1115–17
1145	cf. Book of the Duchess	1114–16
1204	cf. Book of the Duchess	389
1212	cf. Book of the Duchess	395
1224–25	Book of the Duchess	529, 533–34
1226	Book of the Duchess	454

Jugement Line Nos.	Chaucer's Work	Chaucer Line Nos.
1273	Book of the Duchess	398–99
1297	cf. Book of the Duchess	1059–65
1423	cf. Book of the Duchess	43
1466–67	cf. Troilus and Criseyde	II 80–82
1474–75	Troilus and Criseyde	II 83–84
1513	cf. Book of the Duchess	301–2
1525–26	cf. Book of the Duchess	502–3
1540–41	cf. Book of the Duchess	537–38
1595–96	cf. Canterbury Tales	B 2154
1642	cf. Book of the Duchess	1049–50
1676–78, 1687	cf. Troilus and Criseyde	IV 423–24, 427
1709–11	cf. Troilus and Criseyde	IV 418–20
1753	cf. Book of the Duchess	843–45
1796–99	cf. Troilus and Criseyde	I 818–19
1803–4	Troilus and Criseyde	I 813, 816
1805–7	cf. Troilus and Criseyde	I 810, 812
1823	cf. Canterbury Tales	D 484, 487
1918–20	cf. Book of the Duchess	723–25
1918–20	cf. Troilus and Criseyde	IV 623, 327–29
1986–88	Troilus and Criseyde	I 823–24
2012–43	cf. Troilus and Criseyde	V 435–48, 477–504

We have then substantial materials that may provide indications of what Chaucer's *Jugement* manuscript was like: a good number of manuscripts of the poem and a large corpus of borrowings. However, the manuscript texts of *Jugement* are relatively uniform, and no major variants appear to reveal Chaucer's personal text, nor do omissions of substantial passages provide clues. There do show up twenty-six more limited cases in which Chaucer's specific reading is indicated by contrasting variants which make sense. For these twenty-six cases we have provided in the Notes to the Texts complete variants from all *Jugement* manuscripts together with commentary explaining the relationships to Chaucer's text; each case is signalled in the Notes with the heading, *Chaucer's manuscript reading*. Of the twenty-six variants, nine (lines 173, 194, 201, 289, 321, 473, 722, 747, and 1986), while of interest, provide less strong or equivocal indications of Chaucer's reading. The remaining seventeen (lines 17, 129, 204, 263, 269, 286, 288, 301, 314, 366, 382, 438, 597, 667, 723 and 849, 1074, and 1145) have substantial value as evidence. In these instances the indicated Chaucer reading appears almost exclusively in the early-tradition manuscripts; there are only three instances in which late-tradition manuscripts are even represented, once by F and M (line 288), and twice by Pm (lines 286 and 301). All early-tradition texts (except for the fragment Ys) have two or more of the Chaucer variants, but there is a wide variation in the number: J has thirteen; K, eleven; E, seven; P, six; Kr and St, five; R and Ra, four; C and Ar, three; and Pc, two. All details for each of these readings may be found in the Notes to the Texts.

Since a Chaucer Library edition should be based on the manuscript nearest to Chaucer's original, the foregoing figures would suggest that our base text should be the closely related J and K, which have clearly the largest number of Chaucer readings. However, these manuscripts have quite defective texts, and they contain inferior or unintelligible readings for a number of lines for which Chaucer obviously had a better model: 170, 201, 290, 302, 412, 505, 580, 582, 597, 623, 747, 1039, and 1753. The nature of these readings may be seen in the critical apparatus. The next candidate, E, has a notoriously poor text, as a cursory review of the critical apparatus will show. The result is that scribal error has cancelled out the usefulness of E, J, and K as base texts for an edition, though their exemplars may well have been closer than any surviving manuscript to Chaucer's text.

Happily, there is a way to preserve the Chaucer readings while presenting a good text of the poem; that is, through a critical edition of the early-tradition manuscripts. Even if Chaucer had access to several *Jugement* manuscripts, as is quite possible, it seems almost certain that they all would have been from the early tradition. The critical edition thus preserves all of the relevant readings, in some rare cases in the critical apparatus rather than in the text. Where the Chaucer variants differ from the text, the Chaucer reading is marked by an asterisk (*) in the critical apparatus. It is also fortunate that there is available a very good text to use as base, P, which shows the largest number of Chaucer readings after E, J, and K. Making this critical edition of *Jugement* has had advantages which we did not originally anticipate. As the discussion of the manuscripts shows, in addition to indicating what the English poet's text was like, the variants provide new insights into the development—actually the deterioration—of the Machaut text. As a consequence of these insights, our critical edition of the early version produces a text substantially superior to that of previous editions.

REMEDE DE FORTUNE

Occasion, Contents, Sources, and Influence

Remede de Fortune is probably the most important French love poem of the fourteenth century, and it may also be the best. Consisting of 4,300 lines, primarily octosyllabic couplets, it is the progenitor of several major

Middle French poems constructed on the simple narrative pattern of lover's complaint answered by some deeds and many words which provide comfort.[44] The date of composition of *Remede* has been a matter of disagreement. Since in the manuscript collections of Machaut's work it always comes after *Jugement*, which was probably composed in the late 1330s, and precedes the *Dit du lyon*, which is firmly attached to the date April 3, 1342, Hoepffner would place it c. 1340.[45] Dating Machaut's works by manuscript order, however, presents problems, particularly because the order differs in some manuscripts.

Another suggestion of a date for *Remede*, put forward by Daniel Poirion, is c. 1350. Though Poirion barely indicates his argument,[46] it seems to run as follows. In some major manuscripts *Le Jugement du roy de Navarre* and *Lai de plour* directly precede *Remede*, so the three works were probably composed in that order. As its prologue on the Black Plague indicates, *Navarre* was written in 1349 or shortly thereafter, having been conceived—so Poirion believes—as a poem for Bonne of Luxembourg, represented in the poem by Lady Bonneurté.[47] When Bonne died in 1349 Machaut recast the work to honor her son-in-law Charles of Navarre. The *Lai de plour* which follows evidently represents the poet's penance assigned in *Navarre* (just as in Chaucer's *Legend of Good Women* the legends which follow the prologue represent the poet's penance). Furthermore, since the *Lai* presents a lament by a lady for her dead lover, it comprises an appropriate veiled reference to Bonne and her death. As for *Remede*, its line 4258 (4256 in Hoepffner) repeats the identifying first line of the *Lai*, "Qui bien aimme a tart oublie,"[48] thereby making a further reference to Bonne and confirming its chronological posteriority.

The argument, however, is not finally convincing. Hoepffner has satisfactorily explained why *Navarre* is found out of place chronologically in the manuscripts: being a palinode for *Jugement*, the maker of the manuscript moved it up to follow that poem directly. Moreover, the recurring line in *Remede* provides a slender reed on which to base a dating, especially since the line is proverbial.[49] The more probable time of composition for *Remede*, then, is Hoepffner's c. 1340. At the same time, the special treatment which *Remede* receives in manuscript C, discussed below, evokes the possibility that the poem underwent revision at the time the manuscript was made, between 1350 and 1356, and lends some color to aspects of Poirion's thesis.

For determining the poem's occasion, a further suggestion by Poirion probably points more in the right direction. He sees the poet's address to Bonne Amours at the end of *Remede* (4277–4300) as directed to Bonne. Other factors substantiate this suggestion. Bonne Amours is in fact the title which Machaut gives to love throughout *Jugement* and *Remede*; thus, even though Amours could take either gender in medieval French and was clearly masculine in the *Roman de la Rose*, in both Machaut works it is treated as feminine. One therefore might see the very conception of Love in the two works as put under the aegis of Bonne in her powerful position as daughter of King Jean of Bohemia and wife of Jean le Bon, heir to the French throne. But one can find evidence which is much less speculative to associate *Remede* with Bonne; such evidence does not identify her directly with Amours but with the beloved lady of the poem.

The lady is presented as mistress of a grand château and as she whom all follow.[50] The factual description of the castle and the activities in and around it, and the fact that an actual place name is assigned to the park nearby, the park of Hesdin, indicate that an actual lady and a real place are referred to. That this lady represents Bonne, the poet tells us unequivocally near the beginning of the work:

> . . . ma dame, qui est clamee
> De tous seur toutes belle et bonne.
> Chascun par droit ce non li donne. (54–56)

She is called "beautiful and *Bonne*, everyone properly gives her this name." The pun on the name is substantiated both by Machaut's poetic practice and by historical circumstance. Machaut was fond of hiding names in his poems, as numerous acrostics and anagrams show, including the anagram of line 4297 in this work. Bonne, moreover, is the lady of prominence most closely associated with Machaut, particularly in the 1330s and 1340s. She was daughter, mother, and mother-in-law of the poet's most important patrons, and was herself a valued patroness.[51] If doubt remains, the pun is repeated in lines 268–69, where the lover says the lady was to him "mestresse bonne" who taught him in a "bonne escole," and comparably in lines 3816–17. It is finally confirmed by Chaucer in his elegy for Blanche of Lancaster, the *Book of the Duchess*. Modelling his words directly on *Remede* 54–56, quoted above, Chaucer identifies the object of his elegy by means of the same kind of *double entendre*:

> And good faire White she het;
> That was my lady name ryght.
> She was bothe fair and bryght;
> She hadde not hir name wrong. (948–51)

Chaucer's play on White/Blanche is conclusive evidence that he recognized and imitated Machaut's word play.

Writing in 1368 when he could connect *Remede* with a well-known lady who had died young, Chaucer could have viewed Machaut's poem as a commemoration like his own of an important duchess. For Machaut at the time of composition, on the other hand, *Remede* would have been a celebration of a young lady whom he had known from infancy. One need not be concerned that the poem appears to treat of a secret love affair between the poet and the lady. If Machaut at the end identifies himself by name as first-person poet, he carefully distances his own person from that of the lover. At the time of composition Machaut was a bookish canon of Reims of about forty, while the lover of *Remede* is a young courtier anxious to learn the skills of jousting and tourneying (lines 4115–34); there is nothing in the presentation of him to identify him closely with Machaut. It is true that Amant is a writer of love poems, but all good courtiers should be. And though he is humble and self-deprecatory, this is only appropriate for a proper lover of whatever station. Moreover, there is little individualizing humor attached to the person of the narrator such as we find with the narrators of *Navarre* and *Fonteinne amoureuse*. Corroborating this distinction between the first-person narrators in *Remede* and a poem like *Navarre* is the fact that the manuscripts which provide rubrics for the lover's speeches in *Remede* consistently identify him as "Amant," while comparable rubrics in *Navarre* present the narrator as "Guillaume." On the one hand is the generalized lover, Amant; on the other is the very specific poet, Guillaume. In *Remede* the love affair is between this generic lover and a literary stand-in for Bonne; in the idealized court world of the poem, the lady's kind word and sweet look suffice to any but the most treacherous lovers. The poem then would provide no basis for suspicion or jealousy on the part of Jean le Bon.[52] Indeed, if manuscript C was made for him in the early 1350s, as seems probable, then we find him particularly honoring the work after her death.

That the poem was composed for Bonne as mistress of Jean's household also accords with the one undisguised—and very suggestive—proper name in the work. When the lover suddenly leaves the lady's château in confusion, he goes off to complain in the park of Hesdin. Hesdin, which lies in the plain of northwest France on the river Canche, was the site of one of the great castles and parks of the Middle Ages, now disappeared and almost forgotten.[53] The town reached initial prominence after the construction of a "château magnifique" in 1068 by Baudouin de Mons on an ancient fortified site along the north bank of the river. Baudouin also established a park north of the castle proper, in which he placed a large number of wild animals for hunting. Hesdin assumed greater importance after it came into the possession of the French royal family in the thirteenth century. In 1244, Robert I of Artois, having been given the property by his brother King Louis IX, established his residence in a new château built to replace the earlier Romanesque structure.

However, the real glory days of Hesdin were under Robert's son, Robert II of Artois, and the latter's daughter, the countess Mahaut. Very complete financial records maintained in the so-called Treasure of Artois Charters in the archives of the Pas-de-Calais show that between 1295 and his death in 1302 Robert II undertook an extensive renovation of both the castle and the park. [54] To the latter he added an extensive walled enclosure and numerous hydraulically operated automata. By 1300 the park was a major attraction in northern France that one modern historian has termed "the Versailles of the Middle Ages." [55] Work on the park was continued by Robert II's daughter, Mahaut of Artois, who was a prominent patron of the arts, having her chambers decorated with portraits of the kings and queens, and writing romances and translating literary works. In 1311, to develop the new gardens, Mahaut hired a Parisian gardener, one Guillaume Rosce, named perhaps after his flowers.[56] During Mahaut's occupancy "Li Manage" was built along the Canche and the château was a frequent object of royal visits. Documents from the fourteenth century show that the park was maintained on an annual basis. It was obviously a continuing attraction for royal and other prominent visitors, and the depiction of the park in *Remede* is clearly based upon personal knowledge. Machaut's patron, Jean l'Aveugle of Luxembourg, whose daughter Bonne was married to the heir of the French throne, spent the 1330s moving from castle to castle in northern France. It is quite likely that both Jean l'Aveugle accompanied by his secretary Machaut, and Jean le Bon, accompanied by his wife Bonne, would have joined the royal visit to Hesdin of Philippe VI recorded in 1335.[57]

Two further records suggest that Hesdin was a favorite resort for Philippe and his son, Jean le Bon. The *Chronicle of St. Denis* states that in 1347 Philippe of Valois and his son (no doubt Jean) stayed several weeks at Hesdin while waiting for reinforcements to relieve Calais;[58] and Froissart notes that Edward III on his way to Calais had passed by the fortifications of Hesdin without assaulting them, "car il est trop fort."[59] Froissart relates further, perhaps relying on Jean le Bon's personal testimony, that three days before Christmas in 1364, when Jean was returning to England from Paris, he arrived in Hesdin, where he was joined by Louis de Mâle of Flanders. The two celebrated Christmas there, staying till December 28. Hesdin obviously offered special amenities. That Bonne had acted as mistress of the château—or at least its leading lady—on regular stays there in the 1340s is very likely. Evidently Machaut too had been a visitor there and envisioned it as the site of *Remede*.

As already suggested, the story of *Remede* is hardly complex. The Amant begins by describing his early service to Amour. He long loved his chosen lady in silence. Her noble deportment and behavior served as valuable instruction to him, but he dared not confess his love for fear of rejection. To pass his time he writes poems about his love and circulates them anonymously. Then one day a lai of his comes into his lady's hands when he is present. Not only does she have him recite it, but then she demands to know who wrote it. Unable to speak, he departs in despondency without taking leave, retreating to the Park of Hesdin where he delivers a lengthy complainte against Love and Fortune.

The complainte prompts the appearance of Lady Esperance who proceeds to act as moral physician to him; she demonstrates that Fortune has served him as Fortune must and not always against his interests, and that Amour has actually caused him to behave to his advantage. When Esperance finishes her consolation and advice and has promised always to aid the lover, she disappears, only to return when he loses his courage on the way back to the château. After giving him first a good scolding and then encouragement, Esperance leaves again and the lover goes at once in search of his lady. When he confesses his love to her and tells of his experience with Esperance, she receives him as her *ami*, and they exchange rings. They then hear Mass, dine, assist at a musical entertainment, and play parlor games; he finally goes off to participate in chivalric sports. When he returns to the château, however, the lady ignores him. Her later explanation is that she was motivated by Bien-Celer (Hide-Well). The Amant, a naive and trusting person, feels compelled to accept the explanation, and the poem ends on this ambiguous note.

The salient characteristic of *Remede* is its didacticism. It is a manual for courtiers—for lover-poets—represented in the poem by the Amant. Love is the teacher, acting within the work through her deputies, Esperance and the lady. Their lessons are drawn primarily from two spectacularly successful didactic works of the Middle Ages, the *Consolation of Philosophy* by Boethius and the *Roman de la Rose*, mainly the section by Guillaume de Lorris. Proverbial lore also plays an important part in their teaching.

Many features of Machaut's plot use either the *Roman de la Rose* or Boethius as a model. The lover's retreat to the Park of Hesdin and his ensuing complainte are based on the *Roman de la Rose*, while the main inspiration for the coming of Lady Esperance and for her alternately sweet and sharp consolation is Boethius. Apparently original with Machaut are the initial situation in which the Amant recites his lai, then hurries away, and the concluding events involving the lovers getting together, the realistic portrayal of the feast and entertainment, and the lady's subsequent neglect of the Amant. The characterizations also have identifiable sources which are substantially modified. In his naiveté and emotionalism the lover is like the Amant of the *Roman de la Rose*, but in his modest desire for just a sweet look from the lady he reveals a more particular kinship with the lover of the court lyrics as that figure had developed in the fourteenth century. The lady also reflects contemporary court poetry. Instead of being a complex of abstractions like the lady in the *Roman de la Rose*, she is rather the superior and wise paragon found in the court lyrics. The third major figure, Esperance, who personifies the main recourse of unfulfilled lovers, owes her origin as personification to the God of Love's lecture in the *Roman de la Rose*, where Hope is promised; but in her character as garrulous consoler she is modelled on Lady Philosophy in Boethius and to a lesser extent on Reason in the *Roman de la Rose*. At the same time, as a result of echoes of the Bible and conventional Christian phraseology, she goes beyond the abstract signification of her name to take on the character of priestess who unites the lovers.

Since Machaut's purpose differs from the aims of the theodicy of Boethius and the art of love of the *Roman de la Rose*, in *Remede* he often adapts the lessons of those works to rather different ends. In the *Roman de la Rose* the God of Love lectures Amant on the procedures and conduct which will conduce to his purpose of gaining the Rose; there is a strong practical element in his advice. The end in *Remede* is to make Amant worthy to be a lover; it is the exemplar of the lady which instructs him. Thus, while Machaut uses parts of the God of Love's presentation, he selects and modifies it. His art of love aims at refinement of emotion rather than conquest. The philosophy of love also differs from the *Roman de la Rose*'s presentation in which the God of Love and Reason are rival and conflicting figures, with Reason basing her opposition to Love mainly on arguments drawn from Boethius. By contrast, in *Remede* it is for the purpose of defending Amour that Esperance, Amant's main docent and bulwark, draws many of her lessons word-for-word from Lady Philosophy. Obviously, Machaut had to modify Boethius' vindication of a monotheistic God in order to make it serve Esperance's theodicy of love. As is appropriate for the character of Hope, to be sure, the main aims of Esperance are psychological rather than philosophical. Thus she draws mainly from the earlier parts of Boethius, where there is an emphasis on assuaging the narrator's anguish. The greater part of the borrowings from Boethius are from Book II, the book in which Fortune is treated as an actual entity for Philosophy's therapeutic purposes. Esperance also makes reference to Book I, in which the nature of the complainer's problem is determined, and to Book III, largely devoted to distinguishing between illusory and transcendent good.

In the Notes to the Texts we have identified fifty-seven proverbs, and had we fully annotated the discussions of Fortune, we might have adduced several in addition. Many of the proverbs are identified in the manuscripts by "nota" in the margins, but in classifying the expressions as proverbs we have relied mainly on three proverb dictionaries, documented in the notes: Hassell's of Middle French, Morawski's of Old

French, and Whiting's of medieval English. As mentioned, the numerous proverbs and proverbial expressions bolster the general didacticism of the work; they also serve purposes of characterization. Of the fifty-seven proverbs, twenty-three occur in the speeches of Esperance, already filled by the wisdom of Boethius and the *Roman de la Rose*. A series of five proverbs which she enunciates in a space of fifteen lines, 2979–93, is particularly effective in pointing up her tendency to pedantry. Even more striking are the nine identified aphorisms with which the lady instructs and warns the lover in the brief space of twenty-two lines (3777–98); she is responding to a single maxim of his (3771–72), evidently showing him that if either of them is to be the teacher, it will be she. Pandarus and Criseyde show a related aphoristic bent.

The didactic nature of *Remede* is also manifested importantly in its series of intercalated lyrics, complete with appropriate musical settings. One model for such insertion was Boethius with his thirty-nine lyrics set between the proses. Philosophy sings some of these to Boethius even as Esperance sings two to the Amant in *Remede*. There were also numerous antecedent French love poems which provided Machaut with models for inserting lyrics in his story; he clearly knew Jean de le Mote's *Regret Guillaume Conte de Hainault* (1339) and Nicole de Margival's *Dit de la panthère d'amours* (c. 1300).[60] The latter in particular is relevant to *Remede* since in its final five hundred lines, a sort of epilogue, Nicole inserts an abbreviated tableau of the *formes fixes*. In similarly providing a set of the forms, though a more complete one, Machaut evidently follows the *Panthère*; he includes one each of lai, chanson royal, ballade, virelai, and rondeau, plus two other types that did not become standard, complainte and baladelle. Not only does Machaut present the forms, but he also discusses their nature and provides in the narrative appropriate occasions for their presentation; for instance, as was traditional, the virelai is sung without instrumental accompaniment while the company dances (3451–96). Taken together, the lyrics form the most obvious part of the implicit art of poetry which *Remede* provides.

Remede was the culmination of a poetic type, and at the same time made a new beginning. It was the last and best of the line of French love poems which integrate lyrics with music into a narrative. As is set forward more fully in the introduction to the music of *Remede*, the musical composition is highly sophisticated and of remarkable quality. *Remede* was also very influential on the nonmusical works of later poets. Among the fourteenth-century works for which it provided a model are Machaut's own *Dit de la fonteinne amoureuse*, Froissart's *Paradys d'Amours* and *Joli buisson de jonece*, the anonymous *Songe vert*, and Granson's *Complainte de l'an nouvel*. Most significantly, it was a major seminal work for Chaucer: for the wording of the *Book of the Duchess*, for the structure of

Anelida and Arcite, and—to a degree that has been hardly suspected—for many aspects of *Troilus and Criseyde*. Chaucer's debt to *Remede* is treated further in the discussion of his manuscript below, and his verbal uses are documented in the Notes to the Texts insofar as these have been set forth in the scholarship.[61]

The Manuscript Tradition of *Remede*

Remede is preserved in eleven manuscripts, ten Machaut collections and one manuscript in which it and an anonymous prose work comprise the contents. The ten collections all contain *Jugement*, and are identified above with the manuscripts of that poem according to their mainly traditional sigla A, B, C, E, F, J, K, M, Pm, and Vg. The other manuscript, which is described below, is Pe, Cambridge, Magdalene College, Bibliotheca Pepysiana 1594. All manuscripts except J and K have virtually complete texts; J and K have substantial lacunae, and K additionally is missing some leaves.

As with *Jugement*, Hoepffner's three-part stemma is not satisfactory for the text of *Remede*. In place of a stemma we suggest a three-part grouping (different from Hoepffner's) that is very similar to the two-part division we proposed for *Jugement*. Again there is an early-text group, composed of manuscripts related to C, the earliest Machaut collection; but this time only three belong to this group: C; E, a "secondary" collection; and Pe, the only independent text of the poem. With *Jugement* the early-text tradition similarly included C, E, and all independent texts of the work. There is likewise a later-text group, composed of six quite full Machaut collections, A, B, F, M, Pm, and Vg, all included in the similar grouping of seven *Jugement* manuscripts. (Manuscript D does not contain *Remede*.) The main difference from *Jugement* in the *Remede* categories is that J and K are no longer closely allied to the early manuscripts and form a third, intermediate group. As with the earlier poem, their texts for *Remede* have numerous distinctive and almost always inferior readings. At the same time, when their readings agree with other manuscripts, J and K have mixed affiliations. Up to line 1100, their versions mainly agree with the early tradition, and from line 1100 to the end they agree with the late tradition more often. On the whole, in contrast to all other manuscripts, J and K do not show substantial allegiance to either early or late tradition. Nevertheless, because of the many readings they share with the early texts, and their numerous distinctive readings that may represent the early tradition, we include them with the early texts for editorial purposes.

The development of the *Remede* text from early to late is by no means as consistent as that of *Jugement*. With *Jugement* the later text shows considerable deterioration, both in the deletion of needed passages and in numerous inferior readings. With *Remede* only two lines are wholly missing from either group: C, E, and Pe lack 2111–12 (though J and K have them). On the other hand only C and E have 3225, necessary for the form of the prayer, though M makes another substitution. A and Pm additionally lack 3724–25, which Hoepffner omits from his edition because of his reliance on A. A complete list of omissions is found in the description of the manuscripts below.

Even as the testimony of the missing lines is negligible, so also the competing readings, which are so telling in the case of *Jugement*, do not reveal clear superiority for either group. In the first place there are proportionately fewer distinct, competing readings for *Remede*, only seventy-four as compared with ninety-one for *Jugement*, a poem only half as long as *Remede*. Clearly, there is not as much total variation between the early and late text traditions. Furthermore, where differences do exist between them, the late reading is as often superior to the early as it is inferior, but no more often. Following is the list of competing and distinctly different readings, each with substantial manuscript support, which our collation of all the manuscripts has turned up. As with the list in the introduction to *Jugement*, the lemmas used here are the same as those used in the critical apparatus, but here, in contrast to the entries in the critical apparatus, the six late-tradition manuscripts are included. In making the entries here again, the sigla of the early-tradition manuscripts, as well as those of J and K, are italicized to point up the early-late division. As with the critical apparatus, those manuscripts which accord with the lemma are not itemized in the individual entry.

30 **ou** et AB*E*FM*Pe*PmVg. 134 **autre amour n'aray** autre nameray ABFMPmVg (*no JK*). 220 **affremee** affermee *EPe*; affervee *J*; afirvee *K*; affrenee ABFMPmVg. 400 **Et loyaux** Amoureux ABF*JK*MPmVg. 426 **C'est** Sest ABFMPm*Pe*; Est *E*. 448 **En** Et *CEJK*. 508 **Joie en croy** A lottroy ABFM*Pe*PmVg. 509 **Pour ce mon** Et de mon ABFM*Pe*PmVg. 510 **Remaint** Demeure *JK*; Qui maint ABFMPmVg. 537 **que moy** quautrui ABFMPmVg. 611 **Met** Mest ABFMPmVg (*no JK*). 669 **Servir, celer** Servir, doubter ABFMPmVg; Celeement et tendrement E. 733 **despondre** espondre *JK*; respondre ABFMPmVg. 740 **quil** qui *Pe*; com ABF*JK*MPmVg. 1007 **sa** la ABFMPmVg. 1169 *om* ABF*J*MPmVg. 1170 *After this line* ABF*J*MPmVg *add* En desconforte se reconforte. 1295 **Si** Et ABF*JK*MVg. 1304 **Quoy** Que ABF*JK*MVg. 1390 **Et** Se ABFM*Pe*Pm. 1489 **noiez** baigniez *CPe*; baillies *E*. 1581 **pensoit** savoit ABFMPmVg (*no JK*). 1784 **noires rouges** rouges noires BFMPmVg; rouges jaunes A. 1836 **soutil parabole** soutive parole *CJK*; soubtille parole *E*. 1872 **qui** quil ABFMVG. 1921 **se cueve** se couve ABVg; se queuve M; ce quouve *E*; se lienne F*JK*Pm.

2102 **pou** plus *CEPe*. 2184 **desordonees** desortenees *C*; desmesurez *JK*; desmesurees BFMVg. 2240 **Joye pl.** Joie et pl. ABFM*Pe*PmVg. 2246 **nouvel et g.** noel et g. *E*; noiel et *Pe*; et nouvel g. ABFMPmVg. 2277 **en ma** a ta ABPmVg; en ta FM. 2340 **les** le *CEMPe*.

2401 **estordre** destordre ABF*J**K*MPmVg. 2477 **Qu'en** Que ABF*J**K*MPmVg. 2478 **ne** en *CEPe*. 2576 **fera tant** sera temps *E*; face tant ABF*J**K*MPmVg. 2719 **en meschiet** mal en chiet *CEPe*. 2801 **en compte** sans conte *CEPe*. 2812 **en siege de g.** en haut de g. *C*; en siecle de g. *JK*; ou ciel de g. *Pe*. 2984 **baées** *CJ* bees; *K* beez. 2993 **ce a mal ne me doit t.** ce a mal me devoit t. *C*; ce mal ne me doit t. *E*; ce a mal me doit t. *Pe*.

3019 **fait** font ABFMPmVg. 3060 **ne** nen ABFPmVg. 3074 **Il** y AB*C*FMVg. 3196 **ja** la ABF*J*MPmVg. 3215 **Quant** Que ABF*J*MPmVg. 3225 *om* ABF*J*MPmVg. 3240 **Par** Pour ABF*J*MPmVg. 3246 **ce** *om* ABF*J*PmVg. 3267 **raport** ressort AFMPm. 3345 **m'enrichir** moy enrichir *CEPe* (+1). 3382 **ne ame** ne jame ABFMPmVg. 3391 **Qu'Esperance m'ot dit de cuer** Que javoie escript en mon cuer ABF*J*MPmVg. 3400 **Me** Le ABF*J*MPmVg. 3423 **Il** Y AB*C*FMPmVg. 3441 **estoie** estoit ABF*J*MPmVg. 3542 **un moult parfont** un plaint et un ABF*J*MPmVg. 3601 **destraint** estaint *C*; estraint AB*E*FMPmVg. 3643 **force de** force et de ABF*J*MPmVg. 3671 **La demonstrance de l'escu** Les armes qui sont en lescu ABF*J*MPmVg. 3762 **puet** vuet ABF*J*MPmVg. 3772 **donner nest de** loenge de ABF*J*MPmVg. 3808 **et** *om* B*E*FMVg. 3861 **l'amour** lonneur ABFMPmVg (*no J*). 3871 **les** *om C*; le *EPe*. 3884 **sentoie** pensoie ABFMPmVg (*no J*). 3903 **vigour** honnour *CEPe*.

4040 **vous** nous ABFM*Pe*PmVg. 4089 **avant** avec AB*E*F*J*MPmVg. 4111 **Par** De ABF*J*MPmVg. 4136 **Que** Car ABF*J*MPmVg. 4150 **Je** Jen ABF*J*MPmVg. 4162 **doulour** doubte ABF*J*MPmVg. 4200 **Vostre** Nostre ABF*J*MPmVg.

When treating the similar significant variants in the text of *Jugement*, we noted that there was no "watertight division" between the early and late traditions; every manuscript joined each of the others in the variant readings a substantial number of times. With the text of *Remede* this is no longer true; the division is much sharper, and the manuscripts within each group are impressively uniform. The early-text group, C, E, and Pe, on the one hand, and the later-text group, A, B, F, M, Pm, and Vg, on the other, have nearly identical texts. To illustrate, we may use the test we employed for *Jugement*, i.e., we may compare the number of times each manuscript joins A in showing the same variant reading. With *Jugement* the late-tradition manuscripts agree with the A variant 70 to 95 percent of the time, with the average being 85 percent; the early tradition manuscripts agree with the A variant from 10 to 32 percent of the time, with the average being 18 percent. The case of *Remede* presents a clear contrast. There are fifty-eight instances in which manuscript A presents the variant reading for the seventy-four lemmas listed above. It is joined by B, F, and Vg in fifty-seven of these fifty-eight, by M in fifty-six, and by Pm in fifty-three; but by *C* and *E* in only two and *Pe* in seven. Thus the late tradition agrees with the A variant from 90 to 98 percent of the time, with the average being 97 percent, while the early agrees with the A variant 3 to 12 percent of the time, with the average being 5 percent. Manuscript J (and K), showing no consistent affiliation with either early or late, shares the A variant in twenty-seven cases, about 47 percent of the time. As we have said, J and K belong in a separate, third category.

Putting them aside, one sees clearly that there is much less contamination between the early and late text tradition of *Remede* than there is for *Jugement*.

The texts of the poems in the Machaut collections obviously need to be studied separately. With the text of *Remede* the relationship of C to E, of C and E to J and K, and of all of these to A, B, F, M, Pm, and Vg, is different from the same relationships for *Jugement*. However, despite the differences, the text of *Remede* offers little more reason than *Jugement* does to suppose that Machaut actively revised the poem, or even oversaw the copying of the text in the successive manuscripts. Just as the lacunae are of minor importance, so the significant variants are equally divided in the matter of quality. We find that forty-two of the seventy-four variants show a difference in quality between early and late, twenty-one of them being better in the early tradition and twenty-one in the late. Similarly, inspection of the individual readings does not suggest at all the hand of a revising poet. We find the early readings better for the following lines: 220, 537, 611, 733, 740, 1169, 1170, 1295, 2277, 2477, 2576, 3019, 3074, 3225, 3246, 3267, 3382, 3423, 3762, 4089, and 4111. The late seem better for lines 426, 448, 669, 1489, 1836, 2102, 2240, 2340, 2478, 2719, 2801, 2812, 2984, 2993, 3345, 3391, 3861, 3871, 3903, 4040, and 4200. We discuss a number of the different readings in the Notes to the Texts, but we might speak of the two here which embody the most substantive apparent revisions in the text between early and late.

The first of these occurs in lines 507–10, where our text of the lai, based on C, reads, "Car en moy / Joie en croy, / Pour ce mon cuer vray / Remaint en soy" ("For joy grows within me, since my true heart lives in her"). The later text has it, "Car de moy / A l'ottroy / Et de mon cuer vray / Qui maint en soy" ("For she has the gift of me and my true heart, which lives in her"). One might find the early text just a shade better because of the parallel and contrast between "en moy" and "en soy." At the least it does not seem possible to claim a significant improvement in the late tradition. With the second case, there is a decline. Manuscript C presents the following for lines 1169–71 (description of Fortune): "Sa foy est qu'a nul foy ne porte, / Sa force est qu'en chëant est forte, / En riant meschëance aporte" ("Her faith is that she's faithful to no one, / Her strength is that she's strong in falling, / Laughing, she brings misfortune"). The late text reads, "Sa force est qu'en chëant est forte; / En desconfort se reconforte; / En riant meschëance aporte" ("Her strength is that she's strong in falling; / In discomforting, she comforts herself, / Laughing, she brings misfortune"). The later passage here seems clearly inferior, particularly in the broad context. The smooth syntax and nice rhetorical parallelism of the first two lines from the earlier manuscripts contrast with the rather dull parallel set up in the second and third lines from the later, which is driven into the ground in the quatrain that follows. Scribes rather than the poet were at work.

One probable explanation for the fact that between the early and late versions the *Jugement* text deteriorated, while that of *Remede* remained qualitatively comparable, is that *Jugement* was written earlier than *Remede* and was copied more times over a longer period. There were as a consequence many more opportunities for error to be introduced into the text before the group A, F, M, Pm, and Vg began to be composed in the early 1360s. The explanation perhaps does not account wholly for the difference in development. Notwithstanding, it is clear that the text tradition of neither poem indicates that Machaut revised the texts or oversaw directly the copying of the manuscripts.

Our study of Chaucer's use of Machaut has led us to edit the manuscripts of the early-text tradition of *Remede*. There are only a few readings, discussed below and in the Notes to the Texts, which indicate a Chaucer manuscript or manuscripts, and these almost exclusively point to C, E, Pe, J, and K. Again, we believe that our edition produces a version as near as possible to Machaut's original, and also to the text(s) which Chaucer read and used.

Description of Manuscripts Used for This Edition

C, E, J, and K These manuscripts are described in the introduction to *Jugement*.

Pe Cambridge, Magdalene College, Bibliotheca Pepysiana 1594.[62] Parchment, forty-four folios measuring 21 × 152 cm., fifteenth century. *Remede* is written in double columns of thirty-two lines in a careful *littera cursiva formata* with prominent loops on *b*, *h*, and *l*.

Contents: *Remede*, entitled *Remede d'Amour*, ff. 1–36v; prose treatise on love, beginning "Hugues de Saint Victor dit ou livre que len appelle Arraste," ff. 37–43. There is one small miniature on folio 12b in which Esperance appears to a robed and apparently tonsured Amant.

It is not known where Samuel Pepys acquired this manuscript, though it appears to be of French origin. Professor Robert Latham, formerly librarian for the Pepys collection, stated to one of the editors that Pepys obtained most of his manuscripts from London, and that indications are he did not own this one for long.

Choice of the Base Manuscript

The manuscripts of *Remede* are less numerous than those of *Jugement* and their texts are more uniform. J and K are by far the least reliable, largely because of the omission of substantial portions of the text. Due to the loss of several folios, K is missing lines 948–1263 and 3029–4300. J has omitted lines 1169, 1764, 1848, 3134, 3198, 3225, 3295, 3305, 3397, 3434, 3451–70, 3544, 3622, 3653, 3688, 3849–90, 4104, and 4219–56. In addition, J and K have common lacunae at 412, 497–98, 559–680, 727, 734, 860, 914, 932–33, 1486, 1577–1606, 1894, 1988–93, 2439, 2591, 2642, 2688, 2845, 2891, and 2896. K is thus missing 1763 lines, or more than 40 percent of the text; J is missing 252 lines, or approximately 6 percent of the poem. Moreover, the JK tradition rewrites seven lines (46, 352, 1175, 2632, 2642, 3391, and 3671), has inversions involving sixteen (65–66, 538–44, 1089, 1293–94, 1645–46, 2817–18), and repeats three (1225, 1378, 1561).

E offers a better text of *Remede* than it does of *Jugement*. It has lacunae at 2033–38 and 3485–87; reversed lines at 2153–54, 2845–46, 3569–70, 3975–76, and 4223–24; a repetition at 4293; and reformulated lines at 1873, 2641, 2657, and 3128. It joins with C and Pe in omitting lines 2111–12. E is allied with J (and K) in presenting common errors against C and Pe at 293, 541, 803, 1166, 1529, 1717, 1978, 2193, 2234, 2961, 3027, 3168, 3384, 3499, 3518, 3625, 3638, 3705, 3829, 4089, and 4290. However, E allies itself more frequently with C and Pe against J and K (errors at 109, 748, 1489, 2102, 2224, 2340, 2478, 2634, 2759, 2801, 3345, 3545, etc.); occasionally with C alone (7, 299, 315, 1517, 1618, 1727, 1941, 1957, 2012, 2095, 2239, 2265, 2415, 2757, 2909, etc.); or more rarely with Pe (38, 41, 421, 426, 1049, 2454, 3940, etc.).

Easily the most reliable version of *Remede*, however, is that preserved in C and Pe. These manuscripts have common lacunae at 2578 and 3709–10, and join with E in omitting lines 2111–12. C and Pe have most readings in common, including errors at 279, 1097, 1489, 1529, 1590, 1837, 2028, 2215, 2563, 2644, 2712, 2732, 2765, 3531, 3764, and 4236. There is relatively little to choose between C and Pe. They are closely related as the common lacunae and numerous variants show. They present about the same percentage of individual readings, with both scribes being exceptionally conscientious. However, Pe omits line 1727, displaces 3634, and presents a unique rondelet at 4109–16. C has no individual omissions or inversions, and rewrites only line 2722. Furthermore, as François Avril has shown,[63] C was prepared between 1350 and 1356, probably for Jean le Bon, perhaps under the direct supervision of Machaut, and is an unusually significant manuscript for its text, music, and illuminations (with potential Chaucerian implications, as stated below).

In editing *Remede*, we have followed the text of C except where the comparison with the other manuscripts of the early tradition demonstrates that it is clearly inferior, as well as in some few instances where it incorporates graphies that might mislead the reader. Whenever there are competing readings of comparable quality, we have sought to present the text that most nearly approaches that which Machaut might have originally composed. The emendations have been arrived at by an evaluation of all variant readings of the manuscripts of the early tradition (including J and K), and all have the authority of at least one manuscript. Whenever a reading of C has been rejected for reasons of meter, this has been indicated by (+1) or (−1) in the critical apparatus. Most errors in C were due to scribal inattention, and rarely are of major consequence. Typical errors include *comme* for *com* (109, 1164, 2035, 2196), *jusques a* for *jusqu'a* (1958), *perdue* for *perdu* (2125), *raies* for *rais* (2197), *porroiee* for *porroie* (3020), etc., all giving an extra syllable in the meter; the addition or omission of a conjunction or a pronoun rendering a line unmetrical (683, 794, 902, 1039, 1490, 1734, 2012, 2239, 2358, 2379, 2454, 2569, 2634, 2644, 2736, 2759, 2909, etc.); substitution of one pronoun for another (695, 1529, 2150, 2340, 2765, etc.); inversion of proper word order (247, 315, 1832, 1910); and inadvertent addition or omission of a minim (984, 1946, 3260, 3695, 3789, 3933, and 4247).

Although C is a more carefully prepared and transcribed manuscript than any other of *Remede*, it does contain occasional phonological and orthographical peculiarities that merit comment. Chief among these are the effacement of final *l* in words ending with *il*, typical of Middle French[64], affecting especially *qu'il* and *il* (e.g., at 1051, 2701, 2751, 3074, 3423, 3978); the confusion of *c* and *s*,[65] as at 299, 426, 974, 1085, 2263, 2450, 2473, 2541, 2542, 2600, 3161, 3691, etc.; intrusive *i* after close *e* in several words (at 1305, 1861, and 3897); and the use of *que* for *car* or *com*, at 121, 748, and 2742 and elsewhere. All such occurrences could be defended as dialectal variations, but since they occur only rarely in the language of our scribe and are potentially misleading to the reader, we have preferred to correct them.

Among scribal peculiarities of note in C are the occasional confusion of final *z* and final *s* (e.g., 1627, 1647–48, 1703–4, 1706, 1723–24, 1791), and a small number of Picardisms.

We have made the same editorial interventions in *Remede* as we made in preparing the text of *Jugement*, and the critical apparatus has been prepared using the same criteria.[66]

Chaucer's Manuscript of *Remede*

As with *Jugement*, it is certain that Chaucer knew *Remede* well, though the relationship of *Remede* to his work differs somewhat from that of *Jugement*. His familiarity with *Jugement* shows up primarily in his manifold word-for-word adoption of lines and passages for the *Book of the Duchess*, and secondarily in his use of it for other works: about thirty passages for *Troilus and Criseyde* and a few for the *Canterbury Tales* and the rest. With *Remede* the uses are often less exactly word-for-word and the parallels tend to be broader; at the same time, while there are fewer identified parallels of the poem with the *Book of the Duchess*, there are more than twice as many with *Troilus and Criseyde* and Chaucer's other works.

Following our procedure for *Jugement*, in the Notes to the Texts we usually quote the significant parallels to Chaucer's works, summarizing his uses in the table below. The caution expressed previously about the quotations by Chaucer is applicable here. The quotations tend to be brief. However, the broad context of the passages cited, as well as of the Machaut passages, needs to be taken into account to understand the full implications, and sometimes to recognize that the relationships involve more than conventional uses of poetic expression. The most important affiliations of *Remede*, in particular, with Chaucer's poetry are revealed in an appreciative reading of the full work, which is in large measure the main fourteenth-century embodiment of the prototypical love story.

The presence of *Remede* as a prototype for Chaucer's work is felt most strongly in the *Book of the Duchess* and *Troilus and Criseyde*, and numerous direct parallels in phraseology between *Remede* and the two Chaucer works substantiate the broad relationship. The important correspondences of the *Book of the Duchess* to *Remede* are concentrated in the elegy portion. Here *Remede* is generally secondary to *Jugement* as a direct source, but its influence comes to the fore in the Black Knight's complaint against Fortune, and in his relating his early experiences with Love and the lady. The impact of *Remede* on *Troilus and Criseyde* is of great significance. It is imperfectly reflected in the enumeration of parallel passages, many of which we qualify with "cf.," indicating a less than certain connection. Notwithstanding, the parallels listed indicate numerous places where the influence is particularly palpable. Among these are Troilus' early experiences with love, including his initial sight of Criseyde and its immediate consequences, his agonizing in his chamber, and Pandarus' advice to him toward the end of Book I; the passages on Fortune in Book I and the opening of Book IV; and Troilus' encounters with Criseyde in Book III, at the beginning of the book and when he comes to her bed. The influence is much reduced in the body of Book IV and in Book V. A substantial number of parallels to other works appear in the chart; important examples are the counterparts which *Jugement* provides to the passage on "mastery" in the Franklin's Tale, and to the nature description in the *Legend of Good Women*. Many of the parallels have to do with the conventional practices of lovers.

The chart enumerates 186 passages of *Remede*. Of these, the *Book of the Duchess* shows significant similarities to 103, *Troilus and Criseyde* to sixty-three, the *Canterbury Tales* to fifteen, the *Legend of Good Women* to seven, the *House of Fame* to two, and the *Parliament of Fowls, Anelida and Arcite*, and *Fortune* to one apiece. As was the case with *Jugement*, the parallels are more numerous in the first part of the poem; about a third are found in the first five hundred lines (11 percent) of the work. But they are of sufficient frequency throughout Machaut's poem to assure Chaucer's close familiarity with all of it.

Remede Line Nos.	Chaucer's Work	Chaucer Line Nos.
23	Book of the Duchess	793
24–25	Book of the Duchess	794–96
26	cf. Book of the Duchess	797
26–30	Book of the Duchess	779–83
31–34	cf. Canterbury Tales	E 1429–30, 2117
37–40	Book of the Duchess	786–88
45–48	Book of the Duchess	797–99
49–51	Book of the Duchess	801–4
54–56	Book of the Duchess	948–51; 1049–53
55–60	Canterbury Tales	C 7–11
61	cf. Book of the Duchess	1092
64	Book of the Duchess	1095
65	Book of the Duchess	1101
89	Book of the Duchess	1089
92–95	Book of the Duchess	1090–93
96–98	Book of the Duchess	839–42
109	Book of the Duchess	1072
110–11	Book of the Duchess	1059–61
112–13	Book of the Duchess	1064–65
116	Book of the Duchess	1056–57
118–22	cf. Book of the Duchess	717–19
123–24	Book of the Duchess	986–87
123–24	cf. Legend of Good Women	F 250
123–24	cf. Canterbury Tales	E 1744–45
130	cf. Book of the Duchess	1129
131	cf. Book of the Duchess	1146
132–33	Book of the Duchess	1226–28
134	Book of the Duchess	1229
137–40	Book of the Duchess	1285–86
143–44	Book of the Duchess	1098
146	cf. Book of the Duchess	1040
147–49	Book of the Duchess	1262–63
147–49	cf. Troilus and Criseyde	III 165–66
164	cf. Book of the Duchess	1286
170	cf. Canterbury Tales	E 1754
171	Book of the Duchess	911–12
197	Book of the Duchess	833
197	Troilus and Criseyde	I 182
198	cf. Book of the Duchess	1052–53

Remede Line Nos.	Chaucer's Work	Chaucer Line Nos.
198	cf. Troilus and Criseyde	I 173, 176
199	Book of the Duchess	834
200	cf. Troilus and Criseyde	I 174
209	cf. Book of the Duchess	834
217	Book of the Duchess	919
219–22	Book of the Duchess	921–22
226–27	Book of the Duchess	930–31
232–37	cf. Book of the Duchess	927
238	Book of the Duchess	937
299–302	Book of the Duchess	1102–5
330	cf. Book of the Duchess	834
359–61	Book of the Duchess	1146–47
363–64	Book of the Duchess	1149–50
371–78	cf. Troilus and Criseyde	III 78–98
375	Book of the Duchess	1215
396	Book of the Duchess	1216
402–3	Book of the Duchess	1156–57
402–3	cf. Book of the Duchess	471
403–4	cf. Canterbury Tales	F 947–48
405	Book of the Duchess	1171–72
405	cf. Canterbury Tales	F 944–45
423–24	cf. Book of the Duchess	1172
430	Book of the Duchess	471, 1171
436–39	cf. Troilus and Criseyde	I 526, 969
497	cf. Canterbury Tales	A 119
662–64	cf. Book of the Duchess	1211–15
693–98	cf. Book of the Duchess	1212–17
703–7	cf. Troilus and Criseyde	III 78–81
705	cf. Book of the Duchess	310
708	cf. Book of the Duchess	1218
733–34	Book of the Duchess	1250
737–38	cf. Troilus and Criseyde	III 1319–20
751–52	cf. Book of the Duchess	1250–51
757	Troilus and Criseyde	I 543
830–32	cf. Book of the Duchess	398–401
891	Book of the Duchess	645
905	cf. Book of the Duchess	599–600
912–14	Troilus and Criseyde	I 848–50
916–18	Troilus and Criseyde	IV 10–11
918	Book of the Duchess	635
926	cf. Book of the Duchess	620,813
982–84	cf. Book of the Duchess	718–19
988–90	cf. Canterbury Tales	E 2059
988–90	cf. Book of the Duchess	636–41
1052–56	cf. Troilus and Criseyde	IV 5
1052–53	cf. Book of the Duchess	647
1054	Book of the Duchess	621
1057	Troilus and Criseyde	IV 11
1059–60	Canterbury Tales	D 792

Remede Line Nos.	Chaucer's Work	Chaucer Line Nos.
1061–62	Troilus and Criseyde	IV 6–7
1078	cf. Book of the Duchess	637, 639
1113–14	Book of the Duchess	673–74
1129–53	cf. Book of the Duchess	598–615
1133	cf. Book of the Duchess	607
1138	Book of the Duchess	642
1153–57	cf. Book of the Duchess	630–31
1162	Book of the Duchess	633–34
1167	Book of the Duchess	622
1169	Book of the Duchess	632
1177	cf. Book of the Duchess	632
1191	cf. Book of the Duchess	659–60
1246–48	Book of the Duchess	1190
1265–67	cf. Book of the Duchess	1217–19
1270	cf. Troilus and Criseyde	I 274
1271	Book of the Duchess	1211–12
1271	cf. Troilus and Criseyde	I 278–79
1278–80	cf. Troilus and Criseyde	I 305–7; III 129, 306–7
1289–90	cf. Troilus and Criseyde	I 422–23
1304	cf. Troilus and Criseyde	I 427
1319–20	Troilus and Criseyde	I 538; III 129–30
1323–24	cf. Troilus and Criseyde	III 129–30
1351–52	cf. Book of the Duchess	764–66
1362	cf. Canterbury Tales	A 1238
1374–75	cf. Book of the Duchess	659–60
1445–59	cf. Troilus and Criseyde	I 544–46
1461–64	cf. Troilus and Criseyde	I 533–36
1465–66	Troilus and Criseyde	I 440
1470–72	Troilus and Criseyde	I 436, 490; cf. I 445, 448
1481–82	Book of the Duchess	504–5
1481–82	Troilus and Criseyde	IV 1083–84
1483	cf. Book of the Duchess	487
1488	cf. Troilus and Criseyde	I 484–85
1489	cf. Troilus and Criseyde	I 543
1490–93	Troilus and Criseyde	III 1088–91
1491–93	Book of the Duchess	488–89
1499–1500	cf. Book of the Duchess	184–85
1572–73	cf. Book of the Duchess	450, 502
1577–84	cf. Book of the Duchess	490–92
1629–30	Book of the Duchess	906
1636	cf. Troilus and Criseyde	I 813
1639–40	Troilus and Criseyde	I 817–19
1643–48	Troilus and Criseyde	I 817–19
1662–63	Troilus and Criseyde	I 813
1671–82	Troilus and Criseyde	I 897–900
1684	Troilus and Criseyde	I 901
1686	Troilus and Criseyde	III 1282; cf. III 1267
1686	Legend of Good Women	F 161–62
1686	Canterbury Tales	A 3089

Remede Line Nos.	Chaucer's Work	Chaucer Line Nos.
1721–22	cf. Troilus and Criseyde	I 807–8
1733–84	cf. Troilus and Criseyde	III, V
1737–38	cf. Canterbury Tales	F 510–11
1751–75	cf. Troilus and Criseyde	III 82–98
1790–92	cf. Troilus and Criseyde	I 818–19
1794–96	cf. Troilus and Criseyde	I 879–89
1865–69	cf. Troilus and Criseyde	III 1370–71
1887–88	cf. Troilus and Criseyde	IV 1584
1984	cf. Book of the Duchess	310
2039–49	cf. House of Fame	853–57
2079	cf. Canterbury Tales	B 4633
2089	cf. Troilus and Criseyde	II 1276
2094–96	cf. Book of the Duchess	1273
2133–28	cf. Book of the Duchess	1277–78
2193–94	Book of the Duchess	752–55
2199–2222	cf. Book of the Duchess	410–15
2199–2222	cf. Legend of Good Women	F 125–29
2205–8	Legend of Good Women	F 128–29
2209	cf. Legend of Good Women	F 131
2253–57	cf. Book of the Duchess	410–15
2253–57	cf. Legend of Good Women	F 125–29
2283–86	cf. Legend of Good Women	F 510–19
2296–97	cf. Troilus and Criseyde	II 835–36
2305	cf. Troilus and Criseyde	II 842
2310–11	cf. Troilus and Criseyde	II 844–45
2317–26	cf. Book of the Duchess	435–42
2336	cf. Troilus and Criseyde	I 969
2364–65	cf. Anelida and Arcite	131
2370	cf. Book of the Duchess	1003–5
2461–63	Troilus and Criseyde	III 813–14, 817
2485–90	Troilus and Criseyde	IV 1583–88
2510	cf. Book of the Duchess	620, 813
2531–40	Troilus and Criseyde	I 848–51
2541	Book of the Duchess	631
2692	cf. Book of the Duchess	623
2706	cf. Fortune	10
2709	cf. Troilus and Criseyde	III 1271
3093–94	cf. Troilus and Criseyde	III 737
3313–14	cf. Canterbury Tales	E 1332
3168	cf. Troilus and Criseyde	I 448–49
3190–92	cf. Troilus and Criseyde	II 1201
3201–2	cf. Legend of Good Women	2268–69
3201–2	cf. Canterbury Tales	E 141
3241–48	cf. Troilus and Criseyde	I 932–38
3379	cf. Book of the Duchess	805–6
3381	cf. Book of the Duchess	832
3395	Troilus and Criseyde	III 50
3419–20	Troilus and Criseyde	II 1257–58
3420–22	Book of the Duchess	1215

Remede Line Nos.	Chaucer's Work	Chaucer Line Nos.
3420–22	Troilus and Criseyde	III 94–95
3424–26	Troilus and Criseyde	III 85
3533–36	cf. Book of the Duchess	746–48
3537–38	Troilus and Criseyde	III 148–49
3578	cf. Book of the Duchess	1129
3692	cf. Troilus and Criseyde	IV 623
3959–88	cf. House of Fame	1201–59
4001–8	cf. Book of the Duchess	1160–70
4049–54	Canterbury Tales	F 745–47, 764–66, 794–95
4075–78	cf. Troilus and Criseyde	III 1368
4075–78	cf. Book of the Duchess	1273
4085–88	cf. Troilus and Criseyde	III 136–38
4199–4200	cf. Troilus and Criseyde	V 1606, 1610
4258	cf. Parliament of Fowls	rondeau heading, l.679
4291	cf. Book of the Duchess	1331
4292	cf. Canterbury Tales	B 47–48

Again with *Remede*, as with *Jugement*, though we can document a large number of parallels between it and Chaucer's works, there are no major variants to indicate which of the eleven extant manuscripts is closest to Chaucer's. Again too, there are some minor variants that point to some manuscripts rather than others, though there are substantially fewer of these than was the case with *Jugement*. Nevertheless, such as one finds once more point consistently to the early-text tradition. In the Notes to the Texts appear complete variants for thirteen readings relevant to Chaucer's text (23, 24, 30, 50, 134, 220, 403, 733, 1169, 1198, 1319–20, 1489, and 1492), together with commentary on their relationships to Chaucer. These are signalled in each case by the rubric *Chaucer's manuscript reading*. Five of the variants concern readings of J and K which are suggestive for Chaucer, but equivocal or negative in import (23, 50, 403, 1198, 1492). One is a variant of Pm involving a missing minim that may well have also been omitted from Chaucer's manuscript by convergent error.

The remaining seven variants involve manuscript C. One of these appears in C only (1319) and bears uncertain significance. Four appear in C, E, and Pe (134, 220, 1169, 1489), with the last being a reading that was not Chaucer's, but with the other three providing positive associations of C to Chaucer's manuscript. Of the remaining two, both also positive, one appears in C, J, and Pm and one in C, E, J, K, and Pe. Five, then, provide clear-cut positive indications that C is like Chaucer's manuscript. Because C has all of these readings there is no case in *Remede* in which an asterisk is needed in the variants to indicate a Chaucer reading which is not that of our edition. There is only one line (1489), representing a probable rather than certain use, in which the later tradition (joined here by J and K) shows the indicated Chaucer reading. Otherwise, aside from two cases involving only Pm, the late tradition is completely unrepresented. It is therefore again logical to base an edition such as this, which aims to recover insofar as possible Chaucer's manuscript of Machaut's poem, on the early-text tradition, using C as the base. As explained above, C presents a very good text of the poem. Moreover, there is the further reason for choosing C that Chaucer may have known this specific manuscript.

The possibility that Chaucer knew the manuscript may be inferred from the recent study made by François Avril of the illuminations of the splendid Machaut manuscripts in the Bibliothèque Nationale. Avril accords great attention and praise to the thirty-four illuminations of *Remede* in C, denominating the "remarquable" artist the "maître du *Remède de Fortune*," and identifying him with an illuminator who worked on several manuscripts which were executed for Jean le Bon between 1350 and 1356.[67] Though it is not recorded that C was made for Jean, the identification of the lady of the poem with his wife Bonne, and the location of the action at Hesdin, particularly encourage its association with him. Bonne had died in 1349, so the special attention given to *Remede* by the chief artist of the manuscript could have resulted from Jean's desire to make the codex a memorial to her. Furthermore, since the manuscript would have been completed in the years just before the Battle of Poitiers, the chances that Jean took this major artifact combining literature, art, and music with him to England after he was captured in the battle seem excellent.

Jean travelled to England with a large company, including poets and musicians. Such a portable masterpiece would have had use for reading and musical performance, and would have supplied aesthetic pleasure and a means of impressing Jean's lenient jailer-hosts with the superior art of France. And if Jean did carry this treasure with him, the further probability that young Chaucer saw it appears strong. It is quite conceivable that it provided his first acquaintance with the poem, and even was the exemplar for a copy made in England that Chaucer had continuing access to. Its illuminations and decorations, moreover, could have supplied a model for manuscripts made of Chaucer's poems; in particular, for a decorated manuscript of the *Book of the Duchess*, which celebrated another patroness who had died. C suggests, perhaps as well as any manuscript extant, how early elaborate court manuscripts of Chaucer's works might have been arranged and illuminated. For this reason, we have thought it of particular importance to present the contents of the C version of *Remede* as fully as possible. Both the music and the reproductions of the illuminations are therefore included in the appendices of this edition. The illuminations provide visual testimony to the development of the long love poem from the abstractions of the *Roman de la Rose* to the augmented realism of Machaut. It was at this point in history that Chaucer entered the evolutionary process to which Machaut had supplied the main impetus.

NOTES TO INTRODUCTION

1. The most satisfactory biographies of Machaut available are Armand Machabey, *Guillaume de Machaut, 130?-1377: la vie et l'oeuvre musical*, Bibliothèque d'Etudes Musicales, vol. 1 (Paris: Masse, 1955), pp. 1–83; and *Oeuvres de Guillaume de Machaut*, ed. Ernest Hoepffner, Société des Anciens Textes Français, 3 vols. (Paris: Firmin-Didot, 1908–21), 1:ii–xliii.

2. That Machaut's relationship to Charles of Navarre continued as late as 1361 is documented in Jacques Chailley, "Du cheval de Guillaume de Machaut à Charles de Navarre," *Romania* 94 (1973): 251–58.

3. *Oeuvres complètes de Eustache Deschamps*, ed. le marquis de Queux de Saint-Hilaire and Gaston Raynaud, Société des Anciens Textes Français, 11 vols. (Paris: Firmin-Didot, 1878–1903), vol. 1, nos. 123, 124.

4. Motet XVIII in Guillaume de Machaut, *Poésies lyriques*, ed. V.-F. Chichmaref, vol. 1. (Paris: Champion, 1909), pp. 518–20.

5. Deschamps's twin ballades on the death of Machaut, set to music by Andrieu, offer one example of notation provided for a nonmusician poet's work. See Nigel Wilkins, ed., *One Hundred Ballades, Rondeaux and Virelais from the Late Middle Ages* (Cambridge: Cambridge University Press, 1969), pp. 67–68, 132.

6. *Oeuvres complètes de Deschamps*, vol. 7, no. 272.

7. Daniel Poirion, *Le Poète et le prince: l'évolution du lyrisme courtois de Guillaume de Machaut à Charles d'Orléans*, Université de Grenoble, Publications de la Faculté des Lettres et Sciences Humaines, no. 35 (Paris: Presses Universitaires de France, 1965). For Machaut's place at the head of the tradition, see esp. pp. 192–93, 203–5.

8. Alfred Jeanroy, *Histoire des lettres*, vol. 12 of *Histoire de la nation française*, ed. Gabriel Hanotaux (Paris: Plon-Nourrit, 1921), p. 465.

9. Guillaume de Machaut, *Le Voir-dit*, ed. Paulin Paris (Paris: Société des Bibliophiles Français, 1875).

10. Guillaume de Machaut, *La Prise d'Alexandrie*, ed. L. de Mas-Latrie, Société Historique de l'Orient Latin, série historique, no. 1 (Geneva: Fick, 1877).

11. Guillaume de Machaut, *Musikalische Werke*, vols. 1–3 edited by Friedrich Ludwig; vol. 4 edited by Heinrich Besseler (1926–43; reprint, Leipzig: Breitkopf and Härtel, 1954).

12. *Polyphonic Music of the Fourteenth Century*, ed. Leo Schrade, vols. 2 and 3, *The Works of Guillaume de Machaut* (Monaco: Editions de l'Oiseau-Lyre, 1956).

13. Madeleine Pelner Cosman and Bruce Chandler, eds., *Machaut's World: Science and Art in the Fourteenth Century*, Annals of the New York Academy of Sci-

ences, 1978; *Guillaume de Machaut,* Colloque–Table Ronde Organisé par l'Université de Reims, Actes et Colloques, no. 23 (Paris: Klincksieck, 1982).

14. For the *jeux partis* see William Calin, *A Poet at the Fountain: Essays on the Narrative Verse of Guillaume de Machaut* (Lexington: University of Kentucky Press, 1974), pp. 39–40.

15. The *Altercatio Phyllidis et Florae* is found in Alfons Hilka and Otto Schumann, eds., *Carmina Burana,* vol. 2 (Heidelberg: Winter, 1941), pp. 94–119. For other such debates in Latin and French, see Charles Oulmont, ed., *Les Débats du clerc et du chevalier* (Paris: Champion, 1911), and Paul Meyer, "Notice du ms. 25970 de la Bibliothèque Phillipps (Cheltenham)," *Romania* 37 (1908): 209–35.

16. Oulmont, *Les Débats,* pp. 197–222.

17. Ibid., pp. 93–100.

18. Ibid., pp. 167–83.

19. *Oeuvres de Machaut,* 1:xliv–xlv.

20. *Oeuvres de Machaut,* 1:57–135.

21. *The Judgment of the King of Bohemia,* ed. and trans. J. Barton Palmer, Garland Library of Medieval Literature, ser. A, vol. 9 (New York: Garland, 1984).

22. Barry A. Windeatt, *Chaucer's Dream Poetry: Sources and Analogues,* Chaucer Studies, no. 7 (Cambridge: Brewer, 1982), pp. 3–25.

23. *Oeuvres de Machaut,* 1:xliv–li.

24. *Oeuvres de Machaut,* 1:xliv.

25. *Polyphonic Music,* ed. Schrade, Commentary to vols. 2 and 3, pp. 27–28.

26. François Avril, "Les Manuscrits enluminés de Guillaume de Machaut," in *Guillaume de Machaut,* Colloque–Table Ronde, pp. 118–24.

27. See Avril, "Les Manuscrits enluminés," p. 120; and introduction to *Remede.*

28. Descriptions of the handwriting of the manuscripts are based on the categories proposed by G. I. Lieftinck in B. Bischoff, G. I. Lieftinck, and G. Battelli, *Nomenclature des écritures livresques du IXe au XVIe siècle* (Paris: CNRS, 1954).

The miniatures for *Remede* are reproduced at the end of this volume. For a concordance of all the miniatures of C and other manuscripts, see Lawrence M. Earp, "Scribal Practice, Manuscript Production and the Transmission of Music in Late Medieval France" (Ph.D. diss., Princeton University, 1983), pp. 390–423. Color reproductions of three miniatures from *Remede* are in François Avril, *Manuscript Painting at the Court of France: The Fourteenth Century* (New York: Braziller, 1978), plates 23–25.

29. Standard descriptions in Henri Omont, *Catalogue générale des manuscrits français,* Bibliothèque Nationale, Ancien supplément français, vol. 1, nos. 6171–9560. (Paris: Leroux, 1895), p. 326; and in *Polyphonic Music,* ed. Schrade, Commentary to vols. 2 and 3, pp. 33–34.

30. Avril, "Les Manuscrits enluminés," p. 128.

31. Standard descriptions in Henry Martin, *Catalogue des manuscrits de la Bibliothèque de l'Arsenal,* vol. 5 (Paris: Plon, 1889), pp. 143–49; and in *Polyphonic Music,* ed. Schrade, Commentary to vols. 2 and 3, pp. 33–34.

32. See Earp, "Scribal Practice," p. 38.

33. Standard description in *Polyphonic Music,* ed. Schrade, Commentary to vols. 2 and 3, pp. 32–33.

34. Poirion, *Le Poète et le prince*, p. 195; Earp, "Scribal Practice," p. 34, n. 75.

35. Standard description in Bibliothèque Impériale, Département des Manuscrits, *Catalogue des manuscrits français*, tome 1, Ancien fonds (Paris: Firmin-Didot, 1868), p. 366.

36. Standard description in *Catalogue des manuscrits français*, p. 388. A more accurate and more detailed description is now available in J. C. Laidlaw, ed., *The Poetical Works of Alain Chartier* (Cambridge: Cambridge University Press, 1974), pp. 108–9.

37. Standard description in Ernest Langlois, *Les Manuscrits du Roman de la Rose, description et classement*, Travaux et Mémoires de l'Université de Lille, new series, 7 (Paris: H. Champion, 1910), pp. 110–16.

38. Standard descriptions in *Catalogue des manuscrits français*, pp. 193–94; and in *Polyphonic Music*, ed. Schrade, Commentary to vols. 2 and 3, p. 38.

39. Standard description in Omont, *Catalogue générale*, pp. 463–464. See also Laidlaw, *Poetical Works*, pp. 111–12, and P. Champion, "Un *Liber amicorum* du XVe siècle," *Revue des bibliothèques* 20 (1910):320–36.

40. These works of Chartier are enumerated in Laidlaw, *Poetical Works*, pp. 111–12.

41. Standard description in *Polyphonic Music*, ed. Schrade, Commentary to vols. 2 and 3, p. 38.

42. Standard description in *Catalogue des manuscrits français*, p. 270.

43. Alfred Foulet and Mary B. Speer, *On Editing Old French Texts* (Lawrence: Regents Press of Kansas, 1979), pp. 69–73.

44. See James I. Wimsatt, *Chaucer and the French Love Poets*, University of North Carolina Studies in Comparative Literature, no. 43 (Chapel Hill: University of North Carolina Press, 1968), pp. 103–50.

45. *Oeuvres de Machaut*, 1:lxiv–lxv; 2:i–iii.

46. Poirion, *Le Poète et le prince*, pp. 194, 201 and n.

47. Ibid., p. 194. Bonneurté has an exalted position in the work appropriate to her representing Bonne.

48. For the *Lai de plour*, see *Oeuvres de Machaut*, 1:283–91; Machaut, *Poésies lyriques*, 2:459–73.

49. See note to *Remede*, line 4258.

50. For her leading position, see, e.g., lines 3508–9.

51. For Machaut's salute to Bonne, see the *Prise d'Alexandrie*, lines 768–69.

52. The report by the chronicler Jean le Bel that Bonne was unfaithful to Jean le Bon, repeated by Poirion (*Le Poète et le prince*, p. 194n.), is highly suspect. Froissart excises it from his *Chroniques* in a passage where he is following Jean le Bel closely, and it doesn't agree with other indications her actions provide. See Raymond Cazelles, "Jean II le Bon: Quel homme? Quel roi?" *Revue historique* 98 (1974): 16.

53. The most authoritative study on the park of Hesdin is now that by Anne Hagopian van Buren, "Reality and Literary Romance in the Park of Hesdin," in *Medieval Gardens*, ed. Elizabeth McDougall (New York: Dumbarton Oaks Research Library and Collection, 1986), pp. 117–34. Footnote 16 to this article announces a forthcoming book-length study by van Buren of the castle of Hesdin. Other important sources are Marguerite Charageat, "Le Parc d'Hesdin. Création

monumentale du XIIIe siècle," *Bulletin de la Société de l'histoire de l'art français* (1950): 94–106; C. Dehaisnes, *Documents et extraits divers concernant l'histoire de l'art dans la Flandre, l'Artois, et le Hainaut avant le XVe siècle* (Lille, 1886); and Bruno Danvin, *Vicissitudes, heur et malheur du Vieil-Hesdin* (Saint-Pol: Bécart-Renard, 1866).

54. See van Buren, "Reality," pp. 118–29; Charageat, "Le Parc," pp. 94–98.

55. Charageat, "Le Parc," p. 102.

56. van Buren, "Reality," p. 122.

57. Ibid., p. 123. That Machaut knew the park of Hesdin personally has also been suggested by Derek Pearsall and Elizabeth Salter, *Landscapes and Seasons of the Medieval World* (Toronto: University of Toronto Press, 1973), p. 173.

58. Danvin, *Vicissitudes*, p. 89.

59. Jean Froissart, *Oeuvres de Froissart . . . Chroniques*, ed. Kervyn de Lettenhove, 25 vols. in 26 (Brussels: Devaux, 1867–77), 5:81.

60. For the lyrics in these poems, see the articles of Ernest Hoepffner, "Die Balladen des Dichters Jehan de le Mote," *Zeitschrift für romanische Philologie* 35 (1911): 162–66; and "Les Poésies lyriques du *Dit de la Panthère* de Nicole de Margival," *Romania* 46 (1920): 204–30.

61. The publications which detail Chaucer's debt to *Remede* are George L. Kittredge, "Chaucer's *Troilus* and Guillaume de Machaut," *MLN* 30 (1915): 69; and "Guillaume de Machaut and *The Book of the Duchess*," *PMLA* 30 (1915): 1–24; and Wimsatt, *Chaucer and the French Love Poets*; and "Guillaume de Machaut and Chaucer's *Troilus and Criseyde*," *Medium Aevum* 45 (1976): 277–93.

62. Standard description in *A Descriptive Catalogue of the Library of Samuel Pepys*, part 3, *Medieval Manuscripts*, by M. R. James (London: Sidgwick, 1923), pp. 24–26.

63. Avril, "Les Manuscrits enluminés," pp. 118–24.

64. Mildred K. Pope, *From Latin to Middle French with Especial Consideration of Anglo-Norman* (Manchester: The University Press, 1934), section 392.

65. Ibid., section 722.

66. See introduction to *Jugement*, pp. 24–26.

67. Avril, "Les Manuscrits enluminés," pp. 119–24.

LE JUGEMENT DU ROY DE BEHAIGNE

At Easter time when everything rejoices, when the earth adorns itself with many happy colors, and Good Love enters without a wound beneath the breast of many a fair lady, many a lover, and many a maiden, which afterwards causes them many new joys and many cares; in this sweet season, in the month of May, one morning I arrayed myself like one who loved most perfectly with constant love. The air was temperate, beautiful, clear, luminous, bright and limpid, with no chill. The dew sparkled so brightly on the grass, because of the sun which shone upon it, that it dazzled me when I looked that way. And the birds, for the sweetness of the delightful new season, were all singing so gaily and festively that I followed the call of their sweet song. I caught sight of one in flight which outsang all the others, crying: "Oci, oci!"

I followed it until it came to rest in a secluded place above a stream, near a beautiful tower, where there were many trees and sweet-smelling flowers of various hues. Then I dropped gently to the ground and hid myself as best I could beneath the trees, so it could not see me there, to listen to the very sweet melody of its delightful song. And I took more pleasure in listening to its sweet singing than ever I could tell.

Title Le jugement du roy de behaine J; *lacking in all others.*

1–152 *om* St. 1–160 *om* K. 1 **Au** Ou ERa; *om* Kr. **rien** gent RRa. 2 **Que** Et que EYs. 3 **Se** Yl se E. **dont** de Ra. 4 **Soubz** Sus RRa. 7 **puiz** prins RRa. **lie** joie J; liee Ys. 9 **En** A ArPc. **may** moi J. 10 **m'acesmay** macheminai C; massenay RRa. 11 **Com cilz** Comme celui RRa. 13 **attemprez** atrempres C; attrempre E; attrempe RPcRaYs. 14 **clers . . . froidure** nes luisans sans f. C; net pur sans ordure E; net et pur sans f. JRPcRa; pur et net sans ordure Ys. 15 **La** Et la PERRaYs (+1); Que la Ar. 17 **Si** Tant RRa. 18 **mes . . . part** celle part mes regars Ys. **guenchissoit** regardoit JRRa. 19 **Pour** Par RRa. 20 **cil** si C; li JRRaYs. 21 **Pour** Par RRa; **joli** *om* Pc; **temps** chant J. 22 **Si** Tant RRa. **liement** doucement P. **et de** et par RArRaYs. 23 **je alai** je vins RRa. 25 **en . . . voletant** un en my lair volant E. 26 *after this line* J *adds*: A haulte vois en son doulx chant disant *in a different hand.* **s'en** en PPc. 27 **et . . . sievi** et le sui J. **tant** *om* Ra. 30 **mainte** *om* Ys. 32 **S'ala** Ala RRa. 33 **lessay** laisse Ra. **tout** tant Ar. 34 **me coiti** moy couvry E; me quati J; me boute RRa; me moussay Ys. **si bien** si tres bien Ys. 35 **Souz** Dessoubz EArYs; Entre RRa. **qu'il** con C; qui RArRa. 37 **son de** chant de EJ. 38 **plot . . . deliter** pris lors si fort a deliter E; a loyr RRa. 39 **Son dous chanter** En son doulz chant E; son tres douch chant Ar. **racompter** recorder E.

Au temps pascour que toute rien s'esgaie, f. 64
Que la terre de mainte coulour gaie
Se cointoie, dont pointure sanz plaie
Soubz la mamelle
Fait Bonne Amour a mainte dame belle,
A maint amant, et a mainte pucelle,
Dont il ont puiz mainte lie nouvelle
Et maint esmay;
En ce doux temps, contre le mois de may,
Par .i. matin cointement m'acesmay,
Com cilz qui tres parfaitement amay
D'amour sceüre.
Et li jours fu attemprez par mesure,
Beaus, clers, luisans, purs et nez, sanz froidure.
La rousee par dessus la verdure
Resplendissoit
Si clerement que tout m'esbleuissoit, f. 64v
Quant mes regars celle part guenchissoit,
Pour le soleil qui dessus reluisoit.
Et cil oisel,
Pour la douceur du joli temps nouvel,
Si lïement et de si grant revel
Chantoient tuit que je alai a l'appel
De leur douz chant.
Si en choisi en l'air .i. voletant
Qui dessus tous s'en aloit glatissant:
"Ocy! ocy!" Et je le sievi tant
Qu'en .i. destour,
Sur .i. ruissel, prez d'une belle tour,
Ou il avoit maint arbre et mainte flour
Souëf flairant, de diverse coulour,
S'ala seoir.
Lors me lessay tout bellement cheoir
Et me coiti si bien a mon pooir
Souz les arbres, qu'il ne me pot veoir,
Pour escouter
Le tres dous son de son joli chanter.
Si me plot tant en oïr deliter
Son dous chanter, que jamez racompter
Ne le pourroie.

But just as I was delighting in listening to its sweet song, I saw a lady approaching along a narrow pathway, thick with grass; she was pensive and all alone except for a small dog and a young girl. Yet in her restrained way she seemed overwhelmed with grief.

And from the other side, a short distance from me, a finely attired knight was approaching her unaccompanied; it seemed to me they might be lover and beloved. I ducked beneath the leafy branches, so hidden that they could see nothing of me.

When the lover, whom Nature had fashioned well, came near the noble lady, he greeted her like a gracious, wise, and cultivated person. Yet the lady, beset by thought, passed him by without reply. He turned back at once and, taking her by the skirt, said sweetly to her: "Fair lady, do you hold my greeting in contempt?"

And when she saw him, she replied at once with a sigh: "Indeed, sir, I did not hear you, because my heavy thoughts prevented it; but if I've done anything offensive or wrong, please pardon me."

The knight, without more ado, said softly: "My lady, there is no call for pardon, for there has been no wrong, nor am I angry; but I beg you please to tell me what so preoccupies you."

41 **com je me** que je me RPcRa; si comme Ar. 43 **vi** vus Ra. 45 **pensant** pensent J. 46 **chiennet** chien RRa. 47 **Mais** Et RArRa; **sa maniere** a sa chiere E; **simplete** seulete C. 49 **moy** soy RRa. 50 **noble** bel ERRa. 51 **le** ung Ra. 53 **Si m'apensay** Si me pensay CJPc; Lors mavisay RRa; Lors me pensay Ys. **qu'amis** quamans Ar. **ert** est R. 54 **Lors** Si R; Or Ra; Et Ys. **dedens** dessouz JYs. 55 **embuschiez** embrunchiez ERYs; embuschie J; embuschez R; embuissiez Ar. **qu'il** qui RPcRa; que Ar. 56 **Mais** Et RRa. 57 **assez . . . mis** hut assez de bien mis JRArRaYs; ot mis E. 58 **la** sa R. **de pris** gentilz JRRa. 59 **Com gracïeux** Comme courtois E. 60 **la** le PAr. 61 **que** qui CE; cui Ar. 63 **Et cilz** Maiz cil E; Et celui RRa. **tantost . . . repassa** arrieres tantost si rapassa J. 64 **si** puis Ys. **la** le PAr. 66 Ys *ends in the middle of this line after* tresdoulce *near the top of a folio.* **Tres douce** Ma douce E; Douce J. **avez vous en** avez en R. 67 **le vit** loyt J. 70 **Certes sire** Certainement Ar. 71 **Pour** Par RRa. **mon** le E. 73 **Riens** Chose JRRa. 74 **s'il** si JRArPcRa. 77 **nul** *om* Pc. 78 **meffait** courous P. 79 **que** quen E.

Mais tout ainsi com je me delitoie
En son tres dous chanter que j'escoutoie,
Je vi venir par une estroite voie,
Plaine d'erbete,
Une dame pensant, toute seulete
Fors d'un chiennet et d'une pucelete;
Mais bien sembloit sa maniere simplete
Plaine d'ennoy.
Et d'autre part, .i. petit loing de moy, f. 65
.i. chevalier de moult tres noble arroy
Tout le chemin venoit encontre soy
Sanz compaignie;
Si m'apensay qu'amis ert et amie.
Lors me boutay par dedens la fueillie,
Si embuschiez qu'il ne me virent mie.
Mais quant amis,
En qui Nature assez de bien a mis,
Fu approuchiez de la dame de pris,
Com gracïeux, sages, et bien apris
La salua.
Et la dame que pensee argua,
Sanz rien respondre a li, le trespassa.
Et cilz tantost arrieres repassa,
Et si la prist
Par le giron, et doucement li dist:
"Tres douce dame, avez vous en despit
Le mien salut?" Et quant elle le vit,
Si respondi
En souspirant, que plus n'y attendi:
"Certes, sire, pas ne vous entendi
Pour mon penser qui le me deffendi;
Mais se j'ay fait
Riens ou il ait vilonnie ou meffait,
Veulliez le moy pardonner, s'il vous plaist."
Li chevaliers, sanz faire plus de plait,
Dist doucement:
"Dame, il n'affiert ci nul pardonnement,
Car il n'y a meffait ne maltalent;
Mais je vous pri que vostre pensement
Me veulliez dire."

The lady sighed deeply and said: "In God's name, fair sir, let me be: I have no need for you to cause me more grief and distress than I already feel."

And he came closer to her, to draw out her thoughts, and said to her: "Most sweet and noble lady, I see you in sorrow. But I swear to you and give you my word, that if you'll tell me your trouble I'll do all in my power to set it right."

The lady started to dismiss him, saying: "Sir, no one can help me, and no one except God can lighten the great sorrow which makes my color grow pale and fade, which grips my heart with sadness and tears, and which causes me such heavy languor that, to tell the truth, no heart could ever bear more."

"My lady, what misfortune causes you to grieve so? Tell me, for I believe that I am subject to such grievous, dire, harsh, heavy, and bitter pain, that you can be certain that there is no lady, no human being, nor ever was, who ever endured such pain."

"Indeed sir, I am sure that you do not bear so much sorrow in your heart as I in mine. Therefore you shall know what you seek to learn about my thoughts. But first you will promise to tell me truthfully the nature of your grief."

"Agreed, my lady. I promise you on my soul and solemn word that I shall avow to you fully and without falsehood the anxiety which enkindles and enflames me and which pierces and gnaws at my heart."

82 **me en pais** moy en pais C; men paix ERRa; mestre J. 83 **Car . . . que** Que (Car) nay mestier que JAr. **me faciez plus** plus me faciez E. 84 **de** du C. 85 **Que** Car E. **je** jen RArPcRa. **se** ce E. 86 **Plus . . . pour** Pres delle pour R; Plus pres delle pour Pc; Pres de lui pour Ra. **sa pensee** son pense E. 87 **Et li a** Et si lui RRa. 88 **Triste** Tritte Pc. 89 **jur et promet** promet et jure RRa. 90 **Se a moy** Se me RRa. 91 **je ferai tout** jen feray trestout Ar. 92 **l'adrecier** ladresses Ra. 93 **l'en prist** le prent RRa. 94 **nulz** riens E. **m'en** me ERRa. **aidier** aider RRa. 95 **ne porroit** me puet E; men puet J. 96 **grief** grant J. 101 **cuers** corps RRa. 102 **Dame . . . mal** Dame quelz maulx RArPcRa. **fait** font CRRa. **si fort** ensi Ar. 105 **dure si grevaine** dure et si grevaine EJAr. 106 **Si amere** Et si amere PAr (+1); Si tresamere E. **soiez bien** bien soyes EJ. 107 **Qu'il** Qui RArPcRa. **dame** ame J. 108 **n'iert** nait RRa. 109 **Qui** Que EAr. 110 **croy** say J. **que** quan Ar. 111 **a . . . com** en vo cuer com ERRa; en cuer comme J. 113 **que** qua EAr. 114 **avant . . . prometterez** avant vous me prometres CR; avant ce vous me prometres J; avant me promettrez Pc. 115 **me** moy E. 119 **souvent . . . mort** mon cuer souvent mort CArPc; souvent mort mon cuer J. 120 **Vous gehiray** Je vous diray RRa. 121 **chief en chief** mot en mot P. **ne ja n'en mentirai** que ja nen me tiray E.

Et la dame parfondement souspire f. 65v
Et dit: "Pour Dieu, lessiez me en pais, beau sire,
Car mestier n'ay que me faciez plus de ire
  Ne de contraire
Que je reçoif." Et cilz se prinst a traire
Plus prez de li, pour sa pensee attraire,
Et li a dit: "Tres douce debonnaire,
  Triste vous voy.
Mais je vous jur et promet par ma foy,
Se a moy volez descouvrir vostre ennoy,
Que je ferai tout le pooir de moy
  De l'adrecier."
Et la dame l'en prist a mercïer,
Et dist: "Sire, nulz ne m'en puet aidier,
Ne nulz fors Dieu ne porroit alegier
  La grief dolour
Qui fait palir et taindre ma coulour,
Qui tient mon cuer en tristrece et en plour,
Et qui me met en si dure langour
  Qu'a dire voir
Nulz cuers qui soit n'en porroit plus avoir."
"Dame, et quel mal vous fait si fort doloir?
Dites le moy; car je cuit recevoir
  Si tres grief paine,
Si dolereuse, si dure, si grevaine,
Si amere, que soiez bien certaine,
Qu'il n'est dame, ne creature humaine,
  Ne n'iert jamais,
Qui telle paine endurast onques mais."
"Certes, sire, je croy bien que tel fais
Ne portez pas a vo cuer com je fais.
  Pour ce sarez
Ma pensee que savoir desirez. f. 66
Mais tout avant, vous me prometterez
Que sanz mentir la vostre me direz."
  "Tenez, ma dame:
Je vous promet par ma foy et par m'ame
Que le penser qui m'esprent et enflame
Et qui souvent mon cuer mort et entame
  Vous gehiray
De chief en chief, ne ja n'en mentirai."

"So be it, sir, and I shall tell you mine."

"Tell me then; I'll listen to you most eagerly."

"Sir, for fully seven or eight years now, my heart has been in the service and pay of Good Love, whose paths I've followed since youth. For since first I knew her, I happily set heart, body, power, life, possessions, strength, and all that was mine, to serving her. She accepted my homage and gave me with loyal heart to a fair and good, gentle, gracious, and wise lord, who was the flower of courtliness, perfect honor, and pleasing deportment. He was the best of the best; and he possessed a lithe, handsome, vigorous, and fair body, and he was young, noble, graceful in manner, endowed with all a lover should possess. And he was held worthy to be loved above all others, for he was true, loyal, and circumspect, loving and discreet in all things; and I loved him so sincerely that I devoted all my heart to loving him, and had no other thought. In him were my hope and my joy, my pleasure, my heart, my love, my thoughts and my desires. My heart could enjoy every good simply by seeing and hearing him. He was my every consolation; he was my every pleasure, my every solace, my joy, my treasure; he was

123 **je vous escouterai** et je lescouteray P. 125 **Sire . . . .viii.** Sire loyal bien a sept ans RRa. 126 **rentiers** entiers Ar. 127 **si qu'apris** si qua CJE. **ses sentiers** se sentier Pc. 128 **tres** des Pc. **m'enfance** mon enfance Ra. 129 **des . . . que** depuis ce que E; des lors que RRa. **j'euch sa cognoissance** *je oy cognoissance J. 130 **Cuer . . . vie** Mon cuer mon corps P; Que corps vie povoir RRa; Cuer corps avoir vie J. **avoir et poissance** avoir vie puissance E; vie avoir et poissance J; et puissance CJ; amour et puissance RRa. 131 **canqu'il fu** quanque fu J; quanques jay fust RRa; quanquay fu Ar; quanques il fu Pc. **moy mis** mi mais C. 133 **retint** recut J. **homage** servage *corrected above line to* hommage J. 134 **me** moy E. 135 **bel et bon** bon et bel E. **doux gracïeux** gracieux doulz J; et gracieux RRa. 138 *om* J. 138–39 *inverted in* C. 139 **Et . . . meillour** Entre les bons estoit tousdis m. RRa. 140–43 *om* J. 140 **s'ot** sont RRa. 141 **faitiz . . . joli** cointe appert et joly RRa; faitich lonc apert et joli Ar. 142 **gentil** joyeux E. **de . . . garni** et de mamour garny RRa. 143 **Plein de** Et de P. **qui** que E; quil Ar. 146 **vrais loyaulz** vrais et loyaux C. 147 **Et en tous** En trestous RPcRa. **fais** cas P. **discrez** secrez Ar. 150 ne *om* RPcRa. 151 **Qu'en li** En lui J. **m'esperance et** ma plaisance Pc. 153 **mon desir** mi desir J. 154 **tous les** trestous EArSt. **pooit** se peut RRa. 155 **Par** Pour St. 157–58 *inverted in* RRa. 157 **en li** trestous E. **c'estoit tous** et trestous Ar. **depors** ressors RRa. 158 **Tous mes soulas** Touz mes deduis J; Mes solaz mes deduiz RRa. **mes . . . tresors** cestoit touz mes tresors J; mes deduis mes accorz St; mes deduis mes depors Ra. 159 **mes chasteaux** ma tour et C. **mes ressors** mon effors RRa; mes tresors St.

"Certes, sire, et je le vous dirai."
"Or dites donc; je vous escouterai
Moult volentiers."

"[S]ire, il a bien .vii. ans ou .viii. entiers,
Que mes cuers a esté serfs et rentiers
A Bonne Amour, si qu'apris ses sentiers
Ai tres m'enfance.
Car des premier que j'euch sa cognoissance,
Cuer, corps, pouoir, vie, avoir, et poissance
Et canqu'il fu de moy, mis par plaisance
En son servage.
Et elle me retint en son homage
Et me donna de tres loial courage
A bel et bon, doux, gracïeux, et sage,
Qui de valour,
De courtoisie, et de parfaite honnour
Et de plaisant maintieng avoit la flour,
Et des tres bons estoit tout le meillour.
Et s'ot en li
Gent corps faitiz, cointe, appert, et joli,
Joine, gentil, de maniere garni,
Plein de tout ce qui faut a vray ami;
Et d'estre amez
Par dessus tous estoit dignes clamez, f. 66v
Car il estoit vrais, loyaulz, et secrez,
Et en tous fais amoureux et discrez;
Et je l'amoie
Si loyaument que tout mon cuer mettoie
En li amer, ne autre entente n'avoie:
Qu'en li estoit m'esperance et ma joie
Et mon plaisir,
Mon cuer, m'amour, mon penser, mon desir.
De tous les biens pooit mon cuer joïr.
Par li veoir seulement et oïr.
Tous mes confors
Estoit en li; c'estoit tous mes depors,
Tous mes soulas, mes deduis, mes tresors;
C'estoit mes murs, mes chasteaux, mes ressors.

my wall, my fortress, my refuge. He loved me, and he served and respected me above all others. He called me his heart, his love, his lady. He was mine entirely, my heart well knew it; nothing could displease him that would please me. Our two hearts were so well paired that never did one oppose the other; instead, they were of one accord, of one mind; they were alike in will and in desire; they felt as one each good, each trial, each joy; nor was it ever otherwise between them, rather they were always so faithful that there was never a base thought in our love.

"Alas! Unhappy me! Now all's reversed, for my pleasures have become grief-filled toils and my joys are bitter grief; my thoughts, which once brought consolation to my heart and comforted it sweetly in its sorrows, are and will always be painful, sad, and bitter. My days will be dark, full of woe; my hopes will remain unfulfilled; and my grief will be hard and unremitting, for I must ceaselessly grow pale, tremble, blush and quake, grieve, weep, sigh and moan, and shudder in the dread of despair. Nor will any good ever come to my weary heart, nor will it expect any comfort or joy until Death takes me, who does me great wrong when she does not begin to devour me with her doleful

161–325 *In* K *these lines, which compose f. 31 (new numbering 16), follow lines 326–494, which compose f. 30 (new numbering 15).* 161 **tous** toutes PRArRa (+1). **cremoit** pasoit R; prisoit Ra. 162 **Son** Mon RRa. 163 **miens** siens PJArSt. **mes cuers** mon cuer JSt; son cueur RRa. 165 **moy deüst** moy si deust RRa. 166 **si juste** tout une E. 167 **ne fu** ne furent RArRa. 170 **de desir** de dit JK. **se sembloient** sassembloient P; ce ressembloient JK; ressembloient ArSt. 173 **fu entr'eulz .ii.** fu entreulz deulz CJK; furent eux deux E; fust entre eulx doux RRa. 174 **Ainz** Mais CERArPcRaSt. **a** sa CRArRaSt. **toudiz esté** este toudis JKRRa; este toujours Ar. 175 *om* K. *added by later hand in* J. **n'ot** ny eust RRa; ni ot ArSt. **.i.** nul Ar. 177 **a rebours** au rebours EJ. 179 **Et mes joyes** Et mes grans joyes EAr. **ameres** agues JK. 180 **mi** mon RPcRa. 181 **En qui** Encor St. **mes cuers** mon cuer CJK. **se souloit** souloit soy St. 182 **de tous** en tous RRa; de ses JK. 183 **Sont et seront** Souvent seront C; Or sont et seront St. **dolent** dolour E. 185 **mi jour** un jour C; mes jours ERRa. 186 **mi espoir** mon espoir CRRa; mes espoirs E. 187 **douceur** dolour JK. **dure durté** dure adurte JK. 188 **Car** Et C. 189 **Taindre** Craindre E. **muer** muet E. 191 **de desespoir** de sespoir E. **fremir** fenir RRaSt. 192 **Me** Moy E. 193 **N'a . . . n'avendra** Ne jamaiz bien en mon cuer ne v. E; Ne mes las cuer j. b. n. St. **n'avendra** ne vendra EJPc; navera St. 194–95 *inverted in* St. 194 **Ne** Na CRArPcSt. **ne joie** de joie JKRRa; na joie CArPcSt. **n'attendra** nateindra CAr; ne tendra St. 195 **la** *om* J.

Et il m'amoit;
Par dessus tous me servoit et cremoit.
Son cuer, s'amour, sa dame me clamoit.
Tous estoit miens; mes cuers bien le savoit;
Ne riens desplaire
Ne li peüst qui a moy deüst plaire.
De noz .ii. cuers estoit si juste paire
C'onques ne fu l'un a l'autre contraire;
Ainçoiz estoient
Tout d'un accort; une pensee avoient;
De volenté, de desir se sembloient;
.i. bien, .i. mal, une joie sentoient
Conjoinctement;
N'onques ne fu entr'eulz .ii. autrement,
Ainz a toudiz esté si loyaument
Qu'il n'ot onques .i. vilain pensement
En noz amours.
Lasse, dolente! Or est bien a rebours, f. 67
Car mes douceurs sont dolereux labours
Et mes joyes sont ameres dolours;
Et mi penser,
En qui mes cuers se souloit deliter
Et doucement de tous mals conforter,
Sont et seront dolent, tristre, et amer.
En obscurté
Seront mi jour, plain de maleürté;
Et mi espoir sanz nulle sceürté,
Et ma douceur sera dure durté;
Car sanz faillir
Taindre, trembler, muer, et tressaillir,
Plaindre, plorer, souspirer, et gemir,
Et en paour de desespoir fremir
Me couvendra.
N'a mon las cuer jamez bien n'avendra,
Ne nul confort ne joie n'attendra,
Jusques atant que la Mors me prendra,
Qui a grant tort
Par devers moy, quant elle ne s'amort
A moy mordre de son dolereux mort,

bite, now that she has swallowed up and taken from me entirely my sweet friend whom I loved faithfully, and he me. After him—alas! woe! ah me!—I do not desire to live a day, or even half a day, in such bitter grief; rather, I want to die of the hurt of which I complain."

And I who was hidden within the bushes, saw that at this word the sweet lady fell as if dead. But he who had a fine and noble character constantly begged and pleaded with her very sweetly to take comfort; but it was to no avail, for the lady who was assailed by deep sorrow for her beloved felt such a harsh onset that her strength and breath failed her. When he understood that the lady heard nothing he said, he was as sad as he could possibly be; he came to realize that the lady had fainted. Then in his hands he gathered dew from the green grass; he moistened the eyes of her tearful face so gently that the lady who had for a long while lost her strength, feeling, and understanding, opened her eyes and began to sigh deeply, mourning him who made her desire Death out of loyal love.

He whose heart was open and without bitterness said: "Dear lady, as God is merciful, try to regain your composure. Such conduct is killing you, for I see that you are paying too dearly for your love for him. Don't show such weakness of heart, for it is not noble, good, or honorable."

199 *om* RRa. 201 **de fin cuer** loyaument JK; de cuer fin RRa. **il** lui RRa. 202 **li lasse** le laisse Ra. 203 **jamez vivre** vivre jamaiz ESt. **jour ne** ne jour ne R. 204 **grief** *grant EJKRRa. 205 *om* JK. **Ainz voel** Mais veult RRa. 206 **boutez** repous PSt; mussie RRa. **dedens** dessouz JK. **le** cest St. 207 **ce** cest CSt. **dous** bel St. JK *add after this line*: De desconfort de doleur et de dueil. 208 **com** comme RRa. 209 **noble . . . sorte** noble gentil sorte C; noble et gente force JK. 212 **ne** ny EJKRaSt. 213 **Car** Mais RRa. **que** qui CSt; cui Ar. **grief** fine RRa. 214 *om* C. **sent .i.** font un E; sentoit Ar. 215 **Qu'en li** Qui la C; Quen lui JKERSt. **deffaut** si faut E. 217 **l'entent në oyt** lentent ne ooit E; lentent ne voit RRa; nentent ne ne oit St. 218 **pooit** porroit JKRPcRa. 219 **Et** Mais CPcSt. **que bien perçoit** et appercoit J; appercoit K; que bien persait R. 222 **si l'en a** dont il la Ar. 223 **Par** En CEArPcRa. **les lieux** les yex JK. 227 **les** ses RRa. 229 **desirer** souspirer JK. 230 **par** pour CRRaSt. **loyaument** lardanment JK. 231 **Mais** Et Ar. **sanz** et Ar. 232 **Dist** Dist a la RRa. 233 **Dieu merci** dieu a mercy C. **reprenez** refrenez P. 234 **de** a St. 235 **Car** Maiz E. **moult** trop JKRRa; vous EPc. 237 **le cuer ainsi** ainsi le cuer RPcSt. 238 **Car . . . preu** Car ce n'est preux JKRArRa. **në . . . aussi** bien ni honneur aussi JK; ne point honneur aussy RRa; ne honneurs autressi Ar.

Quant elle m'a du tout tolu et mort
Mon douz ami
Que j'amoie de fin cuer et il mi.
Mais aprez li, lasse! dolente! hemy!
Ne quier jamez vivre jour ne demi
En si grief duel,
Ainz voel morir du mal dont je me duel."
Et je qui fui boutez dedens le bruel
Vi qu'a ce mot la dame au dous accueil
Cheï com morte.
Mais cilz qui fu de noble et gentil sorte f. 67v
Souventesfois li deprie et ennorte
Moult doucement qu'elle se reconforte;
Mais rien ne vault,
Car la dame que grief dolour assaut
Pour son ami sent .i. si dur assaut
Qu'en li vigour et alaine deffaut.
Et quant il voit
Que la dame pas ne l'entent në oyt,
Tant fu dolens qu'estre plus ne pooit;
Et nonpourquant tant fait que bien perçoit
Qu'elle est pasmee.
Lors en sa main cueilli de la rousee
Sur l'erbe vert; si l'en a arrousee
Par tous les lieux de sa face esplouree
Si doucement,
Que la dame qui avoit longuement
Perdu vigour, senz, et entendement
Ouvri les yeux et prist parfondement
A souspirer,
En regretant celi qui desirer
Li fait la Mort par loyaument amer.
Mais cilz qui ot le cuer franc sanz amer
Dist: "Dame chiere,
Pour Dieu merci, reprenez vo maniere;
Vous vous tuez de faire telle chiere,
Car je voy bien que moult comparez chiere
L'amour de li.
Si n'aiez pas le cuer ainsi failli,
Car ce n'est pas preu, në honnour aussi."

"You speak the truth, sir, but most unhappy was the hour and day I first loved with such perfect love, for by no device can I escape; instead, I perceive my death inevitable."

"My lady, listen to what I shall say and don't take it amiss: it's no wonder you are distraught, and quite right that you're upset. But truly one could find relief sooner for your troubles than for mine."

"Sir, how could that be? Tell me, and keep your promise."

"Most willingly; but you must listen to me, my lady, and dismiss sorrow from your heart so that you can give all your attention to what I say."

"Indeed, sir, I can't be very happy. But I'll do my best, in truth."

"Then without more delay I'll tell you of the sorrows I have to suffer. My lady, ever since I attained understanding and my heart could feel and comprehend what love was, I constantly sought to be loved. Thus, in order to earn the name of lover, for a long time before my heart was assigned or given, granted or allotted to any lady, I pleaded often and devoutedly with Good Love that she place my heart so as to honor her in whom it would rest, that the lady might receive renown and glory through it, and that if ever my heart were able to do anything which might merit her notice or might deserve any reward for service

239 **mar vi** matui C; mal vi EJKArPc; mauldy RRa. 242 **je** jour Ar. 243 *om* R. **Ainz y** Ainsi St. **y cognois** icy voy Ra. **nul** *om* E. 245 **l'aiez** soiez JK. 246 **N'est merveille** Nest pas merveille PCEJKRArRa (+1). 247 **Car bien est** Ains est bien EJK. **soiez** en soyez St. 249 **On** En JK. 250 **En** A RRa. **et** *om* JKRArSt. 251 **vo serement** vostre serement E; vostre serment RRa. 254 **Et que** Dame et JK. **getez** ostez JK. 255 **Par quoy** Affin que JK; Pourquoy St. **toute** du tout Ar. 256 **En** A EJKRRaSt. 257–60 *om* St. 257 **me** men C. 258 **j'en** je C. 259 **quiex mals** je que maux E. **j'ai a sentir** jay assentir CJ. 261 **Dame . . . que** Dame des lors que P; Voir est dame tresdont que St; Dame depuis que E. **je me sceuz** me peuch Ar; seux St. 262 **Et** Ne JK. **pot** sot C. **sentir ne comprendre** savoir ne comprendre P; sentir et comprendre CERArPcRaSt. 263 **Qu'estoit amer** Que cest amour C; Que cest damer EPcSt; Que ciert damer JKKr; Quest vraye amour RRa. **je ne finay** mes mon cueur RRa. **de tendre** datendre JK; sans reprendre RRa; dentendre KrSt. 265 **amis** *om* RRa. 266 **fust** soit Ar. 267 **Ne a** A JK. **dame nulle** nulle dame CRRa. **n'assenez** nagraiez JK; nassure RRa; ne donnez St. 268 **A** Na C. 269 **Par . . . fiz** *Fis maintes foiz E. **devote** devottement E; parfaitte St. 270 **Qu'elle** Quamours RRa. **a l'onnour** a honnour RRaKr. 271 **son** *om* C. 272 **ce** *om* Ar. 273 **et gloire** et grace E. 274 **que** *om* RRa. **se . . . cuer** se james cuers CSt; mon cuer se ja JK; jamais mon cueur RRa. **faire peüst** faire sceust JK; faire si peust RRa. 275 **de . . . deüst** a son vueil qui plaire li deust JK; de quoy souvenir si lui deust RRa. 276 **Ou** En E; Ne JK. 277 **Nul** Ou St. **par** pour RRa.

"Vous dites voir, sire; mes trop mar vi
L'eure et le jour
C'onques amay de si parfaite amour, f. 68
Car je n'en puiz eschaper par nul tour;
Ainz y cognois ma mort sanz nul retor."
"Dame, or oyez
Ce que dirai et a mal ne l'aiez:
N'est merveille se vous vous esmaiez,
Car bien est drois que dolente soiez.
Mais vraiement
On trouveroit plus tost alegement
En vostre mal qu'ou mien." "Sire, et comment?
Dites le moy, et de vo serement
Vous acquittez."
"Moult volentiers, mes que vous m'escoutez,
Et que vo cuer de tristrece getez,
Par quoy toute vostre entente mettez
En moy oïr."
"Certes, sire, poy me puiz resjoïr,
Mais j'en ferai mon pooir, sanz mentir."
"Donc vous dirai quiex mals j'ai a sentir,
Sanz plus attendre.

[D]ame, tres dont que je me sceuz entendre,
Et que mon cuer pot sentir ne comprendre
Qu'estoit amer, je ne finay de tendre
A estre amez;
Si que lonc temps, pour estre amis clamez,
Ainz que mon cuer fust assis ne donnez
Ne a dame nulle ottroiez n'assenez,
A Bonne Amour
Par maintes fois fiz devote clamour
Qu'elle mon cuer asseïst a l'onnour
De celle en qui il feroit son sejour,
Et que ce fust
Si que loenge et gloire en receüst f. 68v
Et que se ja mon cuer faire peüst
Chose de quoy souvenir li deüst
Ou desservir
Nul guerredon de dame par servir,

to a lady, that at such time she should remember me who wish to be hers, inseparable, for all my life. Then it happened that Fortune, who lies too much to everyone, brought me to a company of many beautiful ladies, all young, noble, joyful, and gay. I caught sight of one among them who, just as the sun outshines the moon in brightness, outshone the others in worth, honor, grace, and beauty. She was so simple and unassuming that truly one could not select her equal in all the world, nor could the whole world suffice to describe her beauty perfectly. For I saw her dance so gracefully and then sing so very prettily, laugh and play so delightfully, that never before was a more blissful treasure seen.

"Her hair was like strands of gold, neither too blond nor too brown; her forehead was white and smooth, unwrinkled, perfectly formed without fault, so that it was neither too broad nor too narrow; and her eyebrows, which were perfectly shaped, seemed a black thread above the white, for which they were prized over a hundred thousand others. And her two eyes, which sought to cross over the threshold of my heart by their power and their fair welcome to give me the sorrow which grieves me, were laughing, yet not too bright, so as to be more

278 **Qu'en** En P. **daignast** deust JK. 279 **partir** mentir RRa. 280 **toute** tante Pc. 281 **qu'en** en ERRa. 282 **jolie** ilie Ar. 283 **gentil** gente RRa. **joyeuse et envoisie** de maniere garnie JK; joieuse et engaye RRa. 284 **Vins** Vint Ra. **par** et Ar. 285 **est a tous** a tous est CJKArPcSt. 286 **une** lune Pc. 287 **aussi** ainsi EJKRArKrPcSt. **com** que Pc. 288 **Vaint de** Veu que de RRa; Donne Ar; Passe de Kr. 289 **Avoit elle** Par avoit elle E; Avoit celle K. 290 **d'onneur de grace** de grace donneur RRa; donnour de senz E. **et** *om* JKArSt. 291 **Et tant estoit** Tant fu E. **humble et simple** humble simple ArPc; simple et humble St. 292 **Quë a** Quau PE (−1); Car a CPcSt; Que au JK; Car au Ar. 293 **On** En JK 294 **Sa** La C. **ne tous** trestout E. 295 **a sa** pour sa PJKSt; sa grant Ar. 298 **tres** *om* E. 299 **et** *om* St. 301 **fu** fust RRa. **plus** *si EKrSt. **gracïeux** amoureux Kr. 302 **Car si chevel** Si cheveulz JK. **resembloient** souloyent Ar. **fil d'or** filz dor JK; a fin or E; de fin or Ar. 303 **Et n'estoient** Et si nestoient EArPc; Ne si nestoient RRa; Ne ilz nestoient St. 305 **poli** joliz RRa. 307 *om* JK. **Que trop** Que point trop E; Trop nestoit Ar. **large** les Ar. **ne trop estroit** ne trop nestoit estroit Ar; ne trop petit nestoit St. 309 **Qui** Aussi E. **tres** si C; trop RRa; tant Ar. 310 **sembloient .i. noir** sembloient bien voir C; sembloient dun noir RRaSt; ressambloient noir Ar. 311 **il feussent** il bien fuissent Ar. **entre** contre St. 312 **Mais** Et J. **doy** doulz RArRa. 314 **rigeur** *regart JK; vigueur RRaSt. 315 **Pour . . . dont** Me donnerent le mal ceur Ar. 317 **trop** moult CEArPc. **pour estre plus** pour plus estre E.

Qu'en aucun temps li daignast souvenir
De moy qui voeil estre siens, sanz partir,
Toute ma vie.
Tant qu'il avint qu'en une compaignie
Ou il avoit mainte dame jolie,
Joine, gentil, joyeuse, et envoisie,
Vins par Fortune,
Qui de mentir est a tous trop commune.
Si en choisi entre les autres une
Qui, tout aussi com li solaus la lune
Vaint de clarté,
Avoit elle les autres surmonté
De pris, d'onneur, de grace, et de beauté.
Et tant estoit humble et simple, a mon gré,
Quë, a voir dire,
On ne porroit en tout le monde eslire
Sa pareille, ne tous li mons soffire
Ne porroit pas, a sa beauté descripre
Parfaitement.
Car je la vi danser si cointement
Et puiz chanter si tres joliement,
Rire et joer si gracïeusement,
Qu'onques encor
Ne fu veü plus gracïeux tresor.
Car si chevel resembloient fil d'or
Et n'estoient ne trop blont ne trop sor;
Son front estoit
Blanc et poli, ne fronce n'y avoit, f. 69
Sanz vice nul compassé si a droit
Que trop large n'estoit, ne trop estroit;
Et si sourcil
Qui estoient de taille tres gentil
Dessus le blanc sembloient .i. noir fil,
Dont il feussent prisiez entre .c. mil.
Mais si doy oeil,
Qui de mon cuer volrent passer le suel
Par leur rigeur et par leur bel acueil,
Pour moy donner le mal dont je me duel,
Furent riant,
Non pas trop vair, pour estre plus poignant

piercing and sharp, more sweet, modest, and attractive, full of snares to entrap a lover into pure love. And they were modestly lowered, with lids almost touching, attracting all with their sweet darts. And when they flashed, no man alive could keep from being struck right through his heart, if they wished, and kept for their own. But their gaze, bringing mercy with their glances, was not scattered idly among fools; for when she wished to launch one of her arrows, she did it so astutely and subtly that no one except he for whom it was intended would rightly know it.

"Without blemish, sensitive, long, and straight, her nose was perfectly proportioned to her face; for it was neither too small nor too large. But her red, rounded, properly small, constantly laughing, delicious, and sweet little mouth makes me languish as my heart recalls her. For whoever heard her mouth speak becomingly, and saw it laughing, and gathered its sweetnesses, would esteem it above all others and acknowledge it so. When she smiled her cheeks, which were pink and white and slightly plump, made two dimples, which increased her beauty. And what is more, she had small, white, evenly-spaced teeth, and her chin was slightly cleft, gently curved below and round above. Her complexion was wondrous, unlike any other's, for it was lively,

318 **attraiant** ataignant St. 319 **lïer** lacier P. 321 **s'estoient** si estoient EKRa; se estoyent Ar. **clingnetans** clinet JK; clingniet ArKr; cloant St. **par mesure** et par mesure JK; tout par mesure St. 323 **Tout** Tant C. **leur** *om* Ar. 324 **N'a** A Ar. 325 **Ne se peüst** Ne saparceust JK; Ne peut RRa; Ne se pourroit St. **soit** fort RRa. 327 **S'il** Si EJRRa. **eulz** les RRa. 329 **donnans** donnent CJK; donnoient RRa; crier Kr. **aux** au JK; a RKrRa. 330 **pas** mie PCERArPcRaSt (+1). **foletement** trop folement Kr. 331 **Car** Et St. **lancier vouloit** larchier volet RRa; vouloit lancer St. 333 **savoit** voloit JK. **si soutivement** tressoutilement E; si tres subtilment JK. 334 **nel** ne le PcSt. 335 **cilz** cellui RRa; cheulz Ar. **cheoit** venoit JK; seoit St. 336 **Nez** Et JK; Mais RRa. 337 **traitiz** traittible RRa. **seant** faisant JK. 338 **Avoit le** Et si estoit St. **viaire afferant** viaire aufferrant C; visaige bien gent RRa. 341 **et** *om* JKKr. 342–43 *inverted in* E. 342 **savoureuse** samoureuse E. **et** *om* EJK. 343 **Me** Moy ESt. 345 **et rire la** et si ne C; et puis rire le RRa. 346–47 *inverted in* St, *but noted in margin by the scribe.* 346 **les douceurs** la douceur P. **saveur** savoir JK. **recueillist** recueillir Pc. 349 **sousriant** son riant E. **ses** les St. 350 **Qui estoient** Qui moult estoient E. **vermeillettes** vermeilles Ra. 351 **Pour** Et pour E. **et** *om*. PAr. **petit grossettes** petitet grossettes PAr; petit crassetes E; petit grassetez RRaSt. 352 **Et encor plus** Encore plus JK. 353 **avoit blans** ot blanches C; avoit blanches RRa. **serrez et menus** serreez et menues C; et serres et menuz E; serrees et menuz RRa. 354 **Et son menton** Son mentonnet E. **poy fendus** petit fendus C; pou fourchuz RRa. 355 **rondez** rondel RRa. 357 **nonpareille** despareille PArPcSt; se pareille C. 358 **fu** estoit St. **vive fresche** frece vive Ar.

Et plus agu, doux, humble, et attraiant,
Tout plain de las pour lïer .i. amant
En amour pure;
Et s'estoient clingnetans par mesure,
Fendus a point, sanz trop grant ouverture,
Tout acquerans par leur douce pointure;
N'a l'entrouvrir
Ne se peüst nulz homs qui soit couvrir
Qu'en mi le cuer ne l'alassent ferir,
S'il leur pleüst, et pour eulz retenir.
Mais leur regars
Merci donnans par semblant, aux musars
N'estoient pas foletement espars;
Car quant lancier vouloit .i. de ses dars,
Si sagement
Le savoit faire et si soutivement
Que nulz savoir nel peüst bonnement,
Fors cilz sur qui il cheoit proprement.
Nez, odorant,
Lonc et traitiz, de taille bien seant f. 69v
Avoit le nez au viaire afferant;
Car il n'estoit trop petit ne trop grant.
Mais sa bouchete,
Petite a droit, vermeillette et grossette,
Toudis riant, savoureuse et doucete,
Me fait languir, quant mon cuer la regrete.
Car qui l'oïst
Parler a point, et rire la veïst,
Et les douceurs par saveur recueillist,
Il la prisast sur toutes et deïst;
Que .ii. fossettes
En sousriant faisoient ses jöettes
Qui estoient blanches et vermeillettes
Pour embelir, et .i. petit grossettes.
Et encor plus:
Les denz avoit blans, serrez, et menus,
Et son menton estoit .i. poy fendus,
Voltis dessouz et rondez par dessus.
Mais a merveille
Fu sa coulour, des autres nonpareille,
Car elle fu vive, fresche, et vermeille,

fresh, and pinker than any new-picked rose in May. To speak briefly, her throat was white as snow, smooth, of pleasing shape, without prominent bone or wrinkle, and she had a lovely neck for which I prized and esteemed her.

"It's also proper that I speak of her long, straight arms, which were shapely in every part; and she had white hands with slender fingers.

"Her breasts were just to my liking: white, firm, and high set, pointed, rounded, and small, in perfect accord with her body, graceful and proportioned.

"Her body was fashioned without a flaw: fair, graceful, pretty, young, gentle, supple, long, straight, proportioned, comely, pert, and slender. She had well-shaped hips, thighs, and legs, and her feet were arched, rounded, beautiful, shapely, and shod with the most elegant taste.

"Of the rest, which I did not see, I can assure you, my lady, that it was in perfect accord with Nature, pleasing in shape and contour. This remaining part, which I wish to speak no more of here, must be held without comparison to be sweeter and more beautiful than any other.

"She had white, soft, and delicate skin, outshining everything, so that one marvelled at it. She had no faults or blemishes. Her flesh was sweet and firm, tender as the dew; she was graced with a modest and confident manner, and with excellent bearing.

359 **la** *om* RRa. **may** moy JK. **quant on** ains quon EPc. **la** *om* ArKr. 361 **com** que Ar. **polie** et polie RRa. 362 **Fu sa gorge** Fu sa gorgete PAr (+1); Ot la gorgete JK; Fust sa gorge RRa; Et en la gorge Kr. **n'y ot** navait Kr. 363 **Et s'ot Et ot CSt; Et si eust RRa. col** corps CSt. **la** le CArRaSt. 364 **Aussi** Ainsi P. 365 **je parle** je parole EAr; de joye RRa; je die St. **de ses bras** des bras ses St. 366 **Qui . . . bien** Qui bien estoient E; *Quelle avoit bien JK. **tous** trestous E. **endrois** droiz J. 367 **Et si** Aussi R. **avoit** avoient Pc. 368 **devis** avis ArRa. 369 **dur** *om* C; droit JK. 371 **le** son RRa. 372 **mestrait** mal trait CJKRRaSt. 374 **jeune . . . grasset** rondelet et crasset JK; jeune et tresbien fait St. 375 **appert** *om* E. **grellet** parfait St. 377 **Hanches cuisses** Blanches cuissez C; Avoit les jambes E; Blanches cuissettes RRa; Hanste les cuisses Ar; Hanstes cuisses St. **ot et les** et autressi les E; ot et lonc St. 378 **grossez** grasses ESt. **bel et bien** bien et bel CESt; bien et beau RRa. **entailliez** enjointies ERRaSt; esjointies ArPc. 379 **Par maistrise** Et par maistrie EAr; Par mestrie CPc; Par mesure JK. **chauciez** chausses Ra. 380 **Du** Au RRa. 381 **vous di je** vous diray E; vous dire JK; je vous en dy RRa. 382 **Qu'a** Que PArSt. **tout . . . respondant** tout estoit fait respondant P (+1); toute estoit respondant C; *estoit tant respondant JKSt. 383 **Bien façonné** De sa facon JK. **excellent** plaisant JK. 384 **ce** du EJKArSt. 385 **Dont** Dame E; Pour St. **je ne voeil maintenant** ne veul maintenant E; maintenant jou ne vuel Ar; maintenant ne vueil je St. 386 **Devoit estre** Devoit bien estre E; Bien devoit estre Ar. 387 **douz** bel St. **et . . . nulz** et a plus bel tenuz C; que veoir peust nus JK; et a plus doulz que nus St. 391 **Vice tache** Vice ne tache PRAr (+1); Vilte chaste E; Ne nulle tache St. 392 **serree** sucree E. 393 **tendrete com** tendrete de C; tendre comme ERRa; tendre com JK. 394–95 *inverted in* Ar. 394 **humble et asseüree** simple et acesmee C; douche et aseuree Ar; si humble et asseuree St. 397 **Tant fu** Tant par fu E; Tant estoit Ar.

Plus que la rose en may, quant on la cueille;
Et a briefs mos,
Blanche com noif, polie, de beau gros
Fu sa gorge, n'y ot fronce në os;
Et s'ot beau col dont je la prise et los.
Aussi est drois
Que je parle de ses bras loncz et drois
Qui estoient bien fais en tous endrois,
Et si avoit blanches mains et longs dois.
A mon devis
Avoit le saim blanc, dur, et haut assis, f. 70
Poignant, rondet, et si estoit petiz,
Selon le corps, gracïeux et faitiz.
Sanz nul mestrait
Avoit le corps par mesure pourtrait:
Gent, joint, joli, jeune, gentil, grasset,
Long, drois, faitiz, cointe, appert, et grellet.
Tres bien tailliez
Hanches, cuisses, jambes ot, et les piez
Voltis, grossez, bel et bien entailliez,
Par maistrise mignotement chauciez.
Du remanant
Que pas ne vi, dame, vous di je tant
Qu'a Nature tout estoit respondant,
Bien façonné et de taille excellent.
Et ce surplus
Dont je ne voeil maintenant dire plus
Devoit estre sanz comparer tenuz
A plus tres douz et a plus bel que nulz.
Delié cuirien
Blanc et souëf avoit, sur toute rien
Resplendissant, si c'on s'y mirast bien;
Vice, tache n'y avoit fors que bien.
Douce et serree
Avoit la char, tendrete com rousee;
Mais de maniere humble et asseüree
Et de tres beau maintieng estoit paree.
Et vraiement
Tant fu belle, que je croy fermement,

"And truly she was so beautiful that I firmly believe that if Nature who fashions all things skillfully wished to make another equal to her, she'd fail and could never aspire to succeed, had she not for model this lady who surpasses all others in beauty. And thus I tell you that never in my life have I seen a woman's body more beautifully formed.

"She was fourteen and a half, or thereabouts. Thus, my lady, when I saw her appearance which was so beautiful and unblemished, the sweet image of her face was so imprinted within my heart that it remains there ever, and has never left, for which reason I undergo many sorrows and much doleful duress. And without a doubt, before I left her presence, Plaisance so fixed herself within my heart as I gazed at her sweet countenance that you can be sure that if I had Octavian's wealth combined with Galen's wisdom, and if moreover all the world's treasures were mine, I would abandon them all if only I could see her to my heart's content or do anything which might prove pleasing to her.

"But Love, who saw that I was taken captive through Plaisance's trick, who had put me in her tower as I gazed upon my lady's gracious person, caused her to cast a sweet laughing glance into my heart, and so ensnare me that Love without a threat forced me to submit to her sweet

398 **Se Nature** Que se nature JAr; Que nature K. **tout** tant RRaSt. **subtilment** soustevement RRa. 399 **faire une** une faire C. 401 *follows* 403 *in* St. **Et que** Ne que JK. **assener** assenez K. **saroit** pourroit E. 402 **l'exemple** lexemplaire EAr. **ceste** celle R. **ci n'avoit** ne prenoit St. 403 **Qui** Et E. 405 **encor . . . vie** encores en ma vie E; en ma vie encore RRa. 406 **Corps de dame** Si gentilz corps E; Corps nul de dame Ar. **si tres bien** ne si bien E. **assouvi** asservy E. 407 **Mais elle avoit** Et si avoit St. 409 **Si que dame** Si que ma dame EAr. 410 *om* JK. 411 **la** *om* RRa. **impression** emprise on RRa; mesproison Ar. 412 **De sa figure** De sa douce figure JK; Que sa figure RRa. 413 **qu'elle y dure** que el dure C; quelle dure E. 414 **puiz** *om* E; jour C. 415 **durté** paine JK. 416 **Et** Car RSt. 418 **se . . . si** si ficha si Pc; se ficha sa R; sembati sa St. 421 **Se j'eüsse** Si je eusse EAr; Que se tant eusse R; Que se tout eusse Ra; Que se jeusse Pc; Se tout eusse St. 422 **Et sceüsse** Et si sceusse PSt (+1); Et se (si) eusse EArPc; Et avec ce sceusse J; Aussi que je eusse RRa. **le . . . Galïen** tout le sens Galien CJK. 423 **Et . . . bien** Et tuit li bien du monde J. **fuissent mien** si fust mien RRa. 424 **Je tout** Et que tout RRa; Que tout St. 425 **si que** ce que E. **la** le PRRa. 426 **ou** et St. 427 **a** *om* Ar. **son** mon C. **dont** que JK. **plaire li** plaise lui RRa. **deüsse** peusse Ra. 429 **le tour** lestour St. 430 **De . . . qui** Et plaisance si E. **m'ot** meust RRa. 431 **regardant** remirant E. **gracïeux** precieux JK. 433 **me fist** me si fist Ar. 435 **Qu'il** Qui JKPc. 437 **ploit** pleust RRa. **cilz** li C; ce ERPcSt; son JK. **a santir** assentir C.

Se Nature qui tout fait subtilment
En vouloit faire une aussi proprement,
Qu'elle y faurroit
Et que jamez assener n'y saroit, f. 70v
Se l'exemple de ceste ci n'avoit
Qui de beauté toutes autres passoit.
Et si vous di
C'onques encor en ma vie ne vi
Corps de dame si tres bien assouvi.
Mais elle avoit .xiiii. ans et demi
Ou environ.
Si que, dame, quant je vi sa façon
Qui tant estoit belle sanz meffaçon,
Dedens mon cuer la douce impression
De sa figure
Fu tellement empraínte qu'elle y dure
Në onques puiz n'en parti, dont j'endure
Mainte dolour et mainte durté dure.
Et sanz doubtance,
Ainz que partis fuisse de sa presence,
Dedens mon cuer se ficha si Plaisance,
En remirant sa douce contenance,
Que sachiez bien,
Se j'eüsse l'avoir Othevïen,
Et sceüsse le senz de Galïen,
Et avec ce tout li bien fuissent mien,
Je tout eüsse
Guerpi par si que veoir la peüsse
A mon voloir ou que faire sceüsse
Chose a son voeil, dont plaire li deüsse.
Mais Fine Amour
Qui vit que pris estoie par le tour
De Plaisance qui m'ot mis en sa tour,
En regardant son gracïeux atour,
Sanz mennacier
.i. dous regart riant me fist lancier f. 71
Par mi le cuer, et moy si enlacier,
Qu'il me sousmist en son tres doux dangier
Sanz repentir.
Si me ploit tant cilz dangiers a santir,

dominion. It so pleased me to feel her dominion, when she deigned to let her glance fall upon me that, to tell the truth, I didn't know what was happening to me nor where I was; for I felt myself so enamoured by her eyes that I lost sense, strength, and composure.

"Then the desire to be loved by her burned so hot in my heart that afterwards, sighing, I proclaimed myself 'poor captive' a hundred times; for in my desire I felt such pain that my strength was drained, and in contemplating her sweet face I became downcast. Gladly would I have gone to tell her how I loved her in my heart, forever; but fear of rejection kept me from this. On the other hand, Fair Welcome summoned me, her smiling Sweet Glance enticed me, and Sweet Hope gently whispered in loyalty to me and assured me that never could there be such great beauty without pity. These three so encouraged me that at length I resolved to speak to her of my love. Alas! when I was alone I came to this decision, but when I was about to tell her of my troubles, my heart was so fearful, so feeble, so weary, so anguished, so beaten, so trembling, so embarrassed, and so overcome by lovesickness, that in it there was no sense, direction, or wit; instead, it was overwhelmed and vanquished when I was able to see her unblemished

438 *om* RRa. **Quant** Que Pc. **ses** cilz CArPcSt; son E. **se** si C. 439 **que** car E. 441 **Qu'il** Qui CJRRaSt. **m'avenoit** me menoit C; mamenoit RRa. **quelle part** quel part CRArRa; quelque part E. 443 **Si durement** Tant durement JK; Si doucement St. 445 **desir d'estre** cuidai estre C; je desiray estre RRa. 446 **En** Et C; A St. **mon** *om* RRa. **fu** fui E. **tres fort** forment St. 447 **puiz m'en sui** men sui puiz P. **.c. foiz chetis** chetif cent foiz RRa. 449 **dolour** doucour E. 450 **en aloit** sen aloit Ar; en aloie EJ. 451 **remirant** desirant E. 452 **Son douz** Du douch Ar. 454–55 *inverted in* St. 454 **Comment de** Comment du PJK; Comme de RRa. 457 **part bel** part le bel C. **bel acueil** bellacueil P. **m'appelloit** macueilloit E. 458 **Son** Ses Ar; Et St. **m'asseüroit** masavouroit JK; me rasseuroit St. 459 **dous** *om* St. **me** moy E. 462 **Ne pot estre** Si ne pourroit estre E; **qu'il** qui ERPcRa. 463 **m'ont cil** moult cil C; mont les E; mont cy JKPc; mont ces RSt. 465 **Je** Que St. **diroie** donroie PERRaSt. 466 **tous . . . ainsi** ainssi tout seul CEKR; ensi tous Ar. 467 **mes maulx** mon mal Pc. **cuidoie** vouloie E. 469 **vains** vils P. **si . . . las** si mas si mors E; si las si mas Ar. **si angoisseux** si dolereux P. 473 **Qu'en li** Quen moy JK. **maniere** mesure PC. 474 **estoit** estoie K. 475 **Quant** Que JK. **veoir . . . vis** povoit veoir son viz a viz St. 477 **estoit** yere C.

Quant ses regars se daignoit assentir
A descendre sur moy, que, sanz mentir,
Je ne savoie
Qu'il m'avenoit ne quelle part j'estoie;
Car senz, vigour, et maniere perdoie,
Si durement par ses yeux me sentoie
Enamourez.
Adonc desir d'estre de li amez
En mon cuer fu si tres fort enflamez,
Que puiz m'en sui .c. foiz chetis clamez
En souspirant;
Car tel dolour sentoie en desirant
Que ma vigour en aloit empirant
Et maint penser avoie, en remirant
Son douz viaire.
Car volentiers li alasse retraire
Comment de cuer l'amoie, sanz retraire.
Mais la paour d'escondire ce faire
Me deffendoit.
Et d'autre part Bel Acueil m'appelloit,
Son Dous Regart riant m'asseüroit,
Et Dous Espoir doucement me disoit
En loyauté
Et m'affermoit c'onques si grant beauté
Ne pot estre, qu'il n'y eüst pité.
Si m'ont cil troy tant dit et ennorté
Que toutevoye
Je m'accorday que m'amour li diroie. f. 71v
Helas! tous seulz ainsi me debatoie.
Mais quant mes maulx retraire li cuidoie,
Si paoureux,
Si vains, si mas, si las, si angoisseux,
Si desconfis, si tremblans, si honteux
Estoit mon cuer et du mal amoureux
Si fort espris,
Qu'en li n'avoit senz, maniere, n'avis;
Ainçoiz estoit com transis et ravis,
Quant bien veoir pooie vis a vis
Sa beauté pure.
Lors estoit mors d'amoureuse morsure

beauty face to face. Then my heart was bitten by Love's bite, stung by a joyful sting, and nourished with sweet food by Sweet Thought, who caused my sorrows to cease completely and gave me hope of healing. Thus from love I often had both joy and suffering.

"I remained in this state for a long while, one hour happy and the next in pain, never knowing where to seek relief for my sufferings. Nonetheless, love's distress, burning desire, and cruel languor, which I'd endured for many a day, and her Fair Welcome, hope of ending my grief, her great beauty, her sweet laughing gray eyes, and the fact that there was not a drop of pride in her, all gave me the audacity to seek mercy meekly. So, overwhelmed, I said to her humbly and fearfully: 'My dear lady, your beauty enflames and consumes my heart, such that I love you above all others, blamelessly, with heart, body, soul, and true desire. Therefore I beg you, sweet lady, to have pity on me, for truly I shall die of this love if I receive no relief from your heart, which has made mine black.'

"And when thus I'd told her my suffering, it seemed to me I saw her sweet countenance change a little, and I was afraid of being rebuffed; but her look, her gentleness, and her gracious smile kept reassuring me, so that by them I was emboldened to say: 'Alas,

478 **cuers et poins** coeurs est poins Ar; cuers com poins St. **de joyeuse** damoureuse ESt. 481 **Qui** Que J. 483 **Ainsi** Ains E. 485 **Si** La JK. **demouray** demourra C. 486 **et . . . dolent** et une autre dolent ESt; et une autre en tourment JK; et l'aultre heure doulent RArPcRa. 487 **n'ozay** ne soy CJK. 489 **grant** la JK. **destrece** destrainte St. 490 **Ardant** Dardant E. **et** la CERArPcRaSt. 491 **Ou j'avoie** Ou avoie C; Ou je avoie EAr. 493 **de terminer** daterminer RRa. **dueil** voeul PCJKSt. 494 **son** si Pc. **vair** bel RRa. *After this line* K *inserts lines* 161–325. 499 **tresmuez** redoubtant St. **paoureusement** tres paourement R; tres paoureusement Ra. 501 **mon cuer art** art mon cuer JK. **enflame** entame P. **ma** barred through before **cuer** P. 502 **sur . . . aim** servir vous vueil E; sur toutes vous ayme RArRa. 505–40 *om* RRa. 505 **Douce** Gentilz JK. **qu'aiez** aiez JK. 506 **d'amer** damour E. 507 **nerci** nouri EJK. 508 **n'ai** na Ar. 511 **vis** *om* JK. **fui** sui EPc. 514 **ris** vis CJK. 515 **encor fui** encor sui E; fu encor JKSt; fui encor Ar. **enhardis** si hardiz St.

Mes cuers et poins de joyeuse pointure
Et repeüz de douce nourreture
Par Douz Penser,
Qui ma dolour faisoit toute cesser
Et garison me faisoit esperer.
Ainsi souvent avoie pour amer
Joye et tourment.
Si demouray en ce point longuement,
Une heure lie et autre heure dolent,
C'onques n'ozay requerre alegement
De ma dolour.
Mais nonpourquant grant destrece d'amour,
Ardant desir, et crueuse langour,
Ou j'avoie demouré par maint jour,
Son Bel Acueil,
Esperance de terminer mon dueil,
Sa grant beauté, son dous riant vair oeil,
Et ce qu'en li n'avoit goute d'orgueil,
Le hardement
De requerre mercy couardement f. 72
Me donnerent; si li diz humblement,
Moult tresmuez, et paoureusement:
'Ma chiere dame,
Vostre beauté mon cuer art et enflame,
Si que sur tous vous aim, sanz penser blame,
De cuer, de corps, de vray desir, et d'ame.
Si vous depri,
Douce dame, qu'aiez de moy merci;
Car vraiement, je mourray d'amer ci,
Se de vo cuer, qui a le mien nerci,
N'ai alejance.'

[E]t quant ainsi li oy dit ma grevance,
.i. poy muer vi sa douce semblance,
Ce me fu vis; dont je fui en doubtance
D'estre escondiz;
Mais ses regars m'asseüroit toudis,
Et sa douceur, et son gracïeux ris,
Si que par eulz encor fui enhardis
De dire: 'Helas!

sweet lady, for God's sake don't slay your loyal lover, who is so entrapped in your snares that he is losing all solace and joy.'

"Then the unassuming and modest lady, on whose account Love overpowered and ruled me, said: 'My friend, indeed I'd never wish to do anything which might cause anyone suffering or grief, nor should one do anything to another that he'd not wish done to himself; and, fair friend, there is no good deed that goes unrewarded, nor any evil that remains unpunished; so thus, if Love has enkindled you to love, she will offer you a proper reward in time and season, if you love without thought of deceit. And if she finds you to be other than good, do not doubt that she will be your mortal enemy, and that healing and succor for your sorrows will never be given or granted you by her. Therefore, fair friend, go before Love and make your laments and your clamor to her, for your death and salvation lie in her, not in me; and I don't believe that I'm the cause of your grief, nor should I suffer because of it. In faith, I know nothing more to tell you: I bid you farewell.'

"Thereupon the beautiful one left me, she who had brought me so much pain that my heart nearly deserted me when she left. But the sweetness of her pleasing glance caught my attention by its gentle art;

517 **Gentil** Gentille Ar. 521 **Lors se traïst** Lorez se traist P; Et lors se traist CAr; Adont se traist JK; Lors se tray E; Lors se tourna St. **et** *om* PEAr. 522 **Pour** Par PAr. **qui** quoy Ar. **maistroie** destroye St. 525 **ne** ny J. 526 **Ne l'en** Ne on EJKArSt. **faire chose** riens faire C. 527 **Qu'on ne vousist** Quon ne vausist PSt; Quon vouldroit E. 529 **qui** quil ArSt. 530 **aussi mals qui** aussi nul mal JK; aussi mauls quil Ar; nulz maulx qui St. **soit** soient St. 531 **damer** damour Pc. 532 **Bon** Son ESt. 533 **Vous en rendra** Vous en rendre E; Vous rendera St. 534 **Se vous l'amez** Se le servez P; Se vous lamer JK. 535 **Et s'elle** Et elle J; Et celle KPcSt. **trouvoit** trueve C. 538 **Ne que** Et que PSt; Si que E. **garison** garnison E. 539 **par li** jamaiz St. **donnee** donne CESt. 541 **Pour ce** Si que EJK. 542 **Si lui faites** Et si li faites EAr; Et li faites JK. **plains . . . clamours** plaintes et clamours P; clains et voz clamours St. 543 **mort . . . secours** mors ou vo secours C; maux et vo dolours J; maux et vo secours K; corps et voz secours St. 544 **en** a E. 545 **Ne . . . sui** Qui pas ne sui E; Ne pas suis RRa. 546 **si que** pour ce E; ne que Ar. **m'en** me RRa; en Ar. 547 **Rien . . . plus** Plus ne vous sce que EJK. 549 **Adonc . . . parti** Ainsi la belle de moy se departy RRa; Ainsi de moy la belle se parti St. 550 **de si grant** si tresgrant E. **departi** reparti EJKAr; party RRa. 551 *om* R. **par** pour RaSt. **que mon cuer** le mien cuer E; li cuers ne JK; mon cuer Ra. **ne parti** ne se parti Ra. 552–59 *om* Ar. 554 **son douz art** sa doulceur RRa; son doulx chant St. **j'en os** vostre C; je vos Pc. 555 **Qu'au departir** Au partir E; Quant departi JK.

Gentil dame, pour Dieu, n'ocïez pas
Vostre loyal ami, qui en voz las
Est si laciez qu'il en pert tous soulas
Et toute joie.'
Lor se traïst vers moy la simple et coye,
Pour qui Amours me destraint et maistroie,
Et dist: 'Amis, certes rien ne vaurroie
Faire a nulluy,
Dont il eüst grevance në ennuy;
Ne l'en ne doit faire chose a autrui
Qu'on ne vousist quë on feïst a lui;
Et, beaux amis,
Il n'est nulz biens qui ne soit remeris, f. 72v
N'il n'est aussi mals qui ne soit pugnis;
Si que, se Amours vous a d'amer espris,
Bon guerredon
Vous en rendra en temps et en saison,
Se vous l'amez sanz penser traïson.
Et s'elle vous trouvoit autre que bon,
Ne doubtez mie
Qu'elle ne fust vo mortel ennemie,
Ne que jamez garison në aÿe
Vous fust par li donnee n'ottroïe
De voz dolours.
Pour ce, beau sire, alez devers Amours,
Si lui faites vos plains et vos clamours;
Car en li gist vo mort et vo secours,
Non pas en moy;
Ne pas ne sui cause de vostre ennoy,
Ce m'est aviz, si que soffrir m'en doy.
Rien ne vous sçai plus dire, en bonne foy:
Adieu vous di.'

[A]donc de moy la belle se parti,
Qui de si grant dolour me departi
Que par .i. poy que mon cuer ne parti
De son depart.
Mais la douceur de son plesant regart
Par son douz art fist que j'en os regart;
Qu'au departir de moy, se Dieus me gart,

when she left me, so help me God, she looked at me so sweetly that I really thought her expression was telling me truly: 'Friend, I love you very deeply.' I was completely comforted by the noble power of this look, which afterwards was so valuable to me that it always nourished me and sustained me in good hope. Had there been no parting glance, I believe I'd surely have tumbled into despair, but there was nothing that could make me sad when her eyes smiled upon me. So that, my lady, her glance comforted and aided me in every way in my grief.

"I remained alone and greatly troubled there, until in my thoughts I began to consider her demeanor, her great sweetness, her complexion, her worth, her fine manner, her way of coming and her going, her noble body, her gracious words, her proper bearing, her pleasing look, and her face, which was so sweet, unassuming, and refined, that it was the model of all beauty. And after I had rehearsed her perfections, indeed I was overjoyed and perfectly happy, and considered myself most fortunate, simply because I loved her truly.

"Afterwards I was so diligent and intent upon serving her that her service became my only pleasure, and I could perform no other task. I served, loved, feared, protected, and obeyed her for a long while, all without any recompense. But at last, I so loved and cherished her that

556 **Si** Car si E. 557 **qu'il** qui JKRPcRa. **m'iert vis** mest vis CSt; mert vis E; met vis J; mest advis RRa. 559 **je . . . tres** je tayme si tres R. 562 **m'a puiz tant** tant ma puis C; puis ma trop JK; puis ma tant RArPcRa; puis tant ma St. 563 **Qu'il** Que E; Qui JKPc. **m'a toudiz** ma tous jours PAr; toudis ma E. 565 **Et s'il** Car cil JK; si RRa. 566 **Que . . . cheüz** Que fuisse ore cheus Ar. 567 **Mais** Ne RRa. **fust** soit E. **ne me feïst** ne me fist tant P; si ne me fist RRa. 568 **Quant** Que P. **esgars** espars PCPc; regars ArRaSt. 569 **Estoit sur moy** Quant sur moy ert P; Estoient sur moy JK. **en . . . espars** et souvent et espars JK. 570–71 *inverted in* JK. **ainsi** aussi JK. 571 **aidoit** ardoit CJK; estoit ArSt. 573 **La demourai** Demoure la RRa. **freour** errour J. 574 **Si . . . pensant** Si que penser E; Siques passant RRa. **son atour** a son tour C. 575 **douçour** valour JK. **coulour** douceur JK. **valour** colour JK. 577–78 *inverted in* Ra. 581 **douz . . . et** humble et ESt; doulz humble JAr; humble doulx et RRa. 582 **Que de toute** Et de toute E; Que toute RRa. **beauté** bonte JK. **fust l'exemplaire** fu examplaire JKArSt. 583 **remiré** retraitie E. 585 **et moult** et tres P. 586 **Et pour tres** Et a tres JK. **boneüré** bien eureux JKRArPcRa. **b. me** b. je me St. 587 **sanz** sam C. **loyalment amoie** loyaument l'amoie CE. 589 **li servir** lui amer JK; la servir RRa. **fui** sui CEArPcSt; fu JK. **fui . . . duiz** me tournay et me mis RRa. 590 *om* RRa. **s'est mis** estoit P; ay mis E; fu mis JK; cest mis St. 592 **Si la servi** Si le servi PSt; Si servi suis RRa. 593 **Amay** Ayme RRa. **doubtay celay** celay doubtay EJKSt; selle doubte RRa. 594–95. *inverted in* P *but scribe noted the error and corrected himself by marking "b" in the margin before 594 and "a" before 595.* 594 **me** men JK. 595 **l'amay** lenmay C; layme R.

Si doucement
Me regarda qu'il m'iert vis proprement
Que ses regars me disoit vraiement:
'Amis, je t'aim tres amoureusement.'
Si que je fu
Tous confortez par la noble vertu f. 73
De ce regart qui m'a puiz tant valu
Qu'il m'a toudiz nourri et soustenu
En bon espoir.
Et s'il ne fust, certainement j'espoir
Que je fuisse cheüz en desespoir;
Mais riens qui fust ne me feïst doloir
Quant ses esgars
Estoit sur moy en sousriant espars.
Si que, ma dame, ainsi de toutes pars
Me confortoit et aidoit ses regars
De ma dolour.
La demourai tous seulz en grant freour,
Si qu'en pensant commençay son atour,
Sa grant douçour, sa coulour, sa valour
A remirer,
Son beau maintieng, son venir, son aler,
Son gentil corps, son gracïeux parler,
Son noble port, son plaisant regarder,
Et son viaire
Qui tant estoit douz, humble, et debonnaire
Que de toute beauté fust l'exemplaire.
Et quant j'euch tout remiré son affaire,
Certes j'avoie
Moult grant deduit et moult parfaite joie,
Et pour tres boneüré me tenoie,
Pour ce, sanz plus, que loyalment amoie.
Si que depuiz
A li servir fui si tournez et duiz,
Qu'en li servir s'est mis tous mes deduiz,
N'autre labour ailleurs faire ne puiz.
Si la servi,
Amay, doubtay, celay, et obeÿ f. 73v
Moult longuement, que rien ne me meri.
Mais en la fin, tant l'amay et chiery

she realized I wanted only what was honorable and good for her, and that my heart loved her above all else. I was so attentive that she took me as her own in such a way that with a good cheerful heart and a smile on her face she said to me, 'Beloved, behold your dear love who no longer desires to be haughty toward you; Love wishes this, who moves me to love you with a good heart. And truly, it cannot be otherwise, for a very great thing compels this. Therefore I give you my love and my heart, with no going back; I beg you to preserve my honor, for I love and honor you above all others.'

"And when I saw that my lady called me her beloved so sweetly, and that she had granted me her love without condition, you need not wonder, sweet lady, whether I was happy. For beforehand I was disconsolate, poor, lost, disdained, in exile without hope of relief, when I lacked her sweet comforting. But I was restored, brought back from the dead, powerful above all, full of great consolation, and without tribulation when she said to me, 'Beloved, I give myself to you with my whole heart.' And this sweet gift made me a hundred thousand times greater than any king; no one could recount my joy, for I was so happy that I couldn't find the words to thank her. Yet finally, like a loyal lover with a true heart enflamed by love and without any thought of deceit, I said to her most humbly and calmly, with head bowed and

597 **je . . . a** *ne tendoye qua St. **s'onneur** samour RRa. **et son** a son CEJKAr. 599 **Si** Et E. 601 **de . . . riant** de bon cuer loyal P; de moi riant C; du bon cuer riant J. **lie** bonne E. 602–5 *om* Pc. 603 **envers . . . fiere** cuida vous estre chiere St. 604 **Qu'Amours** Car amours RRa; Camours Ar. 605 **m'esmuet** me sueust JK. 606 **Et vraiement** Et pour ce que E; Car vraiement RRaSt. 607 **Car . . . chose** Et que ainsi faire E; Car moult de chose RRa. **a en faire** a ce faire JKRRa. **l'estuet** le mestuet E; lesqueult RRa. 608 **Pour ce** Du tout E. 609 **nul** *om* RRa. 610 **Si vous depri** Et si vous pri RRaSt; Et vous prie Pc. **m'onnour** mamour RArPcRa. 611 **et** a RRa. 613 **ma** la P. 614 **que** quant Ar. 616 **Se . . . liez** Si fu moult liez C; Je fu lyez RRa. 617 **en merveilliez** esmerveilliez RArSt. 618 **Car j'estoie** Car estoie J. 619 **exilliez** desvoiez St. 621 **tres** *om* St. 622 **Mais recouvrez** Me recouvray R; Me recouvre Ra. 623 **Riche au dessus** Au dessus riche St. **reconfort** desconfort J. 624 **Et** Car St. 625–26 *inverted in* Ar. 625 **toy** ce C; ti Pc. 626 *om* R. **ce . . . ottroy** de tres dous ottroy PCESt; de tres bon arroy JK; de che douch ottroy Ar. 627 **fois** tamps Ar. **plus . . . .i.** greigneur quains JK; plus de joye quau RRa; plus grant dun Ar. 629 **Ne . . . nulz** Nul ne pourroit RRa. 630 **fui liez** je fu liez R. **ne l'en** ne le Ra. **pouoie** savoie P; pourroye RRa. 631 **ne** neis Pc. **savoie** pooie P; sauroie RRa. 633 **Com fin** Com fu JK; Comme fins RRa. 634–35 *inverted in* E. 635 **humblement** doucement P. **le chief** de chief RRa; de coeur Ar.

Qu'elle vit bien
Que je tendoie a s'onneur et son bien,
Et que mon cuer l'amoit sur toute rien;
Si que tant fiz qu'elle me tint pour sien
En tel maniere
Que de bon cuer riant, a lie chiere,
Me dist: 'Amis, vesci t'amie chiere
Qui plus ne voelt envers toy estre fiere;
Qu'Amours le voelt,
Qui de bon cuer a ce faire m'esmuet.
Et vraiement, estre autrement ne puet,
Car moult grant chose a en faire l'estuet.
Pour ce m'amour
Avec mon cuer vous doing, sanz nul retour;
Si vous depri que vous gardez m'onnour,
Car je vous aim dessus tous et honnour.'
Et quant je vi
Que ma dame m'appelloit son ami
Si doucement, et que le dous ottri
M'avoit donné de s'amour sanz nul si,
Se je fui liez,
Douce dame, ne vous en merveilliez.
Car j'estoie devant desconseilliez,
Povres, perduz, despris, et exilliez,
Sanz nul ressort,
Quant je failloye a son tres dous confort.
Mais recouvrez, resuscitez de mort,
Riche au dessus, plain de grant reconfort,
Et sanz ennoy
Fui quant me dist: 'Amis, a toy m'ottroy f. 74
De tres bon cuer.' Et ce tres dous ottroy
.c.m. fois me fist plus grant que .i. roy,
Si que la joye
Ne porroit nulz racompter que j'avoie,
Car tant fui liez que je ne l'en pouoie
Remercïer ne parler ne savoie.
Mais en la fin,
Com fin loyaux amoureux, de cuer fin
Espris d'amer, sanz penser mal engin,
Moult humblement li diz, le chief enclin,

calmly, 'My lady, whom I love more than any other, even myself, to whom I devote my mind, time, heart, life, and love, as much as I am able, yet not as much as I ought, I thank you for the noble gift of your sweet mercy. For you have so nobly enriched me, given me such joy, so healed and so rewarded me that in truth, if all there is, was, or will be beneath the heavens were given me without condition to do with as I wished, I would not love it a hundredth part as much as I do your grace. And I beg God that I never do anything against you which might diminish our love, and that I might ever do your will as I want to do it—humbly, without haughtiness or pride; for, if possible, I will love and serve you loyally in my heart even better than I have; and I shall preserve your honor in all things; and I shall not do anything in word, deed, or thought against you or others where it might incite your anger; instead, you'll be my lady and my sweetheart, my earthly goddess, adored above all others. And without doubt, if I do anything contrary to your pleasure, or bring anger or suffering to your heart, you can be sure it is out of negligence.'

"My lady, thus I thanked her as you have heard for the noble gift of her sweet mercy. And she too swore and pledged to me most firmly that henceforth she would love me truly, without leaving or abandon-

636 **effroy** esroy J. 637 **que** qui Ar. **qu'autres** quautrui CArPc. **que** *om* St. 638 **Et** En Ra. **senz temps** son temps RRa. **cuer** *om* J. **vie amour** vie et amour P (+1); bien amour E; vie a mort JK; vie et RRa. 639 *om* RRa. **Tant com** Tant que PcSt. 640 **Vous remercy** Je vous merci JK. 641 **mercy** amour cy E. 642 **poissanment** richement E; noblement J. 643–44 *inverted in* RRa. 643 **si gari** si ame JK; si garny RRa. **tant mery** si gueri JK; si meri ArSt. 645 **Se . . . a** Se canqu'il est P; Que quanques fust RRa. 646 **canqu'il fu** quanque fu JK; quanques qu'il fust RRa. **quittement** quintement JK. 647 **Me fust** Mestoit E. 649 **de** des Pc. **pars** tans P. **com** que C. 650 **que . . . face** que je jamais ne face C; que jamez ne mefface EJKR. 651 *om* J. **qui** que E. **nostre** vostre CEKRArSt. **efface** defface RSt; mefface K. 652 **Et** Si ESt. **vo** vostre RRa; no Ar. 653 **ainsi** aussi C. **je le voeil** com je sueil C; com je vueil RRa; com je le sueil St. 654 **hautece n'orgueil** hautece d'orgueil PSt; hontage n'orgueil RRa. 657 **de cuer et amerai** et de cuer ameray E; de cueur vous aymeray RRa. 659 **penser** pensee RRa. 661 **N'envers autrui** Ne vers autrui CERRa; Nenvers aucun JK. 662 **et** *om* Ar. 663 **Mon** Mais K. **terrien** humains C; en terre JK; terrestre RRaSt; chams (?) Ar. **aouré** honnoures E. **dessus** par dessus JK. 665 **faiz rien** meffais JK; scay rien RRa. **contre vostre** encontre vo JAr. 666 **Ne . . . ait** Dont vos cuers ait ne P. **courous** dolour E; ennuy RArRaSt. 667 **voir** vray ERRa. **c'ert** cest JKRRaSt; siet Pc. **negligence** *ignorance JKAr. 669 **La** Le PSt; Len E; Bien Ar. **com vous avez** comme avez RRa; dont vous avez St. 670 **douce** noble St. 671 **plevi** pluvy J. 672 **durement** doucement CPcSt; humblement JK; liement RRa. 673 **Qu'a** Que Ra. **mes** *om* RRa. 674 **et sanz** sans faire RRa. 675 **regnay** jaymay RRa.

Et sanz effroy:
'Dame que j'aim plus qu'autres, ne que moy,
Et qui senz, temps, cuer, vie, amour employ,
Tant com je puiz, non pas tant com je doy,
Vous remercy
Du noble don de vo douce mercy.
Car tant m'avez poissanment enrichi,
Tant resjoÿ, si gari, tant mery,
Que vraiement,
Se canqu'il a dessous le firmament,
Et canqu'il fu et sera, quittement
Me fust donné pour faire mon talent,
Je ne l'amasse
Tant de .c. pars com je faiz vostre grace.
Si pri a Dieu que jamez je ne face
Chose envers vous qui nostre amour efface,
Et que vo voeil
Puisse acomplir, ainsi com je le voeil
Faire: humblement, sanz hautece n'orgueil;
Car, se je puiz, assez mieux que ne sueil
Vous serviray
Tres loyaument de cuer et amerai; f. 74v
Et vostre honnour en tous cas garderai,
N'en dit, n'en fait, n'en penser ne ferai
Chose envers vous,
N'envers autrui dont vous aiez courous;
Ainçoiz serez ma dame et mon cuer doux,
Mon dieu terrien, aouré dessus tous.
Et sanz doubtance,
Se je faiz rien contre vostre plaisance,
Ne dont voz cuers ait courous ne grevance,
Sachiez de voir que c'ert par negligence.'
Ma dame, ainsi
La merciai com vous avez oÿ
Du noble don de sa douce merci.
Et elle aussi me jura et plevi
Moult durement
Qu'a tous jours mes m'ameroit loyaument,
Sanz moy guerpir et sanz departement.
Ainsi regnay en joie longuement,

ing me. Thus I dwelt a long while in joy and felt nothing which opposed my joy; rather, I was happier and livelier, more radiant and gay than ever I'd been; and it was fitting that I should be as gracious and serviceable as I could, for I believe I was the best-loved of all lovers, and their king.

"But when Fortune the traitor, who behaves differently to each one, had thus raised me on high, like a sullen scoundrel she didn't give a fig for me or my happiness; instead, she made a face at me, renounced me, and turned her cheek from me. After she had placed me atop her wheel, she turned it, and I was cast down into the mud. But the traitor, always eager and swift to betray those she's taken under her wing, did this because God and Fair Nature, when they formed the one I love, took so much pleasure in the beauty they gave her that they forgot to place any loyalty in her. And this is evident, for I know well and see clearly that my lady, whose body is so perfect, and whom my heart fears, loves, obeys, and serves, has newly taken a lover, without reason, other than myself. Therefore, my lady, if I weep and moan deeply and often repeat: 'Ah me!', it is no wonder, since she has taken away her unrivaled beauty and her lively, fresh, rosy complexion, and her sweet glance which causes me to suffer; and has cast me off completely and removed and distanced me from every good. Alas! how could my heart be

677 **Nulle** Quelle C. 678 **renvoisiez** envoisies ArPc; reveleux St. **resveilliez** reveleus EArPc; amoureux JK; resjouis RRa; envoisiez St. 679 **Jolis et gais** Gay et joliz RRa. 681 *follows* 683 *in* RRa. **fuisse** feisse JK; je estoie RRa. **genz et adrois** jeux esbanois JK; gent et drois RRa; gais et adroiz St. 683 **Li . . . amans** De tous aultres mieulx aymez RRa. 685 **desloyal** triste RRa. **qui** que E. 686 **M'ot** Meust RArRa. **com** comme ERRa; *om* Ar. **mauvaise et enfrune** mauvaise enfrune E; mauvaise yvrongne R; mauvaise effroyne Ra. 688 **Ains** Mais RRa. 689 **renoya . . . tourna** rechigna et retourna RRa; renoya et retourna St. **joe** roe Ar. 690 **m'ot . . . roe** ainsi meust mis dessus la roe RRa. 691 **Puiz la tourna** Puiz le tourna PArRa; Plus la tourna K; Puis retourna R. **si** et EAr. 693 **La** Le EAr. **traÿtre** trahitouse Ar; traite RaSt. **tous jours** tousdiz CJKRRa; conduis E. **preste** est preste C; prest E; prant RRa. 694 **De . . . met** Fait cheoir ceulx que met RRa. **dessous s'elle** souz sesselle JK; dessus sa selle RRa; dessoubz elle St. 697 **j'aim** jay RRa. **fort** bien E. **se** si JKRRa. 698 **qu'il** qui RPcRa; que St. 699 **Que** Car E. **a mettre y** y mettre ils RRa. 701 **Car** Que E. 703 **Que** Qui K. **criemt** ayme RRa. **aime** croit RRaSt. 705 **que mi** de my E. 706 **Si que dame** Si que ma dame EAr; Doncques dame RRa. **se** *om* Ar. 707 **et di souvent** et souvent dy E. 708 **N'est pas** Nen est pas RRa. 709 **Quant** car P. **fine** *om* R. 710–11 *inverted in* RRa. 710 **vermeille** nouvelle RRa. 711 **Et** En Pc. **me traveille** mapareille St. 712 **M'ont** Moult CEJKPc. 713 **Et qu'elle** Et elle RRa. 714 **privé** sevre RRa. 715 **Helas comment** Las et comment JK.

Que je n'avoie
Nulle chose qui fust contraire a joie,
Mais renvoisiez et resveilliez estoie,
Jolis et gais, trop plus que ne souloie;
Et c'estoit drois
Qu'a mon pooir fuisse genz et adrois,
Car par cuidier estoie en tous endrois
Li mieux amez des amans et li roys.
Mais quant Fortune,
La desloyal, qui n'est pas a tous une,
M'ot si haut mis, com mauvaise et enfrune,
Moy ne mes biens ne prisa une prune;
Ains fist la moe,
Moy renoya et me tourna la joe; f. 75
Quant elle m'ot assis dessus sa roe,
Puiz la tourna, si cheï en la boe.
Mais ce fist elle,
La traÿtre, tous jours preste et isnelle
De ceulz trahir qu'elle met dessous s'elle,
Pour ce que Dieus et Nature la belle,
Quant il fourmerent
Celle que j'aim, si fort se deliterent
En la tres grant beauté qu'il lui donnerent,
Que loyauté a mettre y oubliërent.
Et bien y pert:
Car je sçay bien et voy tout en appert
Que ma dame, qui tant a corps appert,
Que mon cuer crient, aime, obeïst, et serft,
A fait ami
Nouvellement, sanz cause, autre que mi.
Si que, dame, se je pleur et gemi
Parfondement et di souvent: 'Emi!',
N'est pas merveille,
Quant sa fine beauté qui n'a pareille
Et sa coulour vive, fresche, et vermeille,
Et son tres dous regart qui me traveille,
M'ont eslongié,
Et qu'elle m'a du tout donné congié
Et de tous biens privé et estrangié.
Helas! comment aroie le cuer lié?

happy? Most wrongfully has she taken away my joy and comfort; and she has put me in such great distress that I know that I shall die of it; nothing can prevent it and nothing can comfort me in any way.

"But what makes my heart shatter and break is that I don't know to whom to complain of my distress, for although Fortune in whom I do not trust or depend has cast me down from the high place to which I'd risen, to speak the truth, I believe that I must not hold it against her, for in doing so Fortune only did her duty, and she has no obligation other than to betray those she advances and enriches, and to cause the lowly to rise up; nor can she favor anyone enough to give him assurance by her good will that he'll never be raised up or cast down from his present state, be it bad or good. Such is her nature: her blessings are rightly haphazard; they are but a wind, a deceiving presence, a joy which is worth little and quickly disappears. One's a fool to trust her! She deceives one and all without warning.

"And if I say that I can lay the blame on my pretty lady for the death that wastes me, by what right do I do it? For what cause? She is in Love's power, to whom she has given herself completely, and wishes her to have true regal command over her, as her sovereign, so that she

716 **Et** Car C; En St. 717 **M'a . . . joie** Ma tolu ma joie C; Ma joie ma tolu JK; Ma tout tollu mon deduit RRa. **et mon confort** et mon deport E; mon deport RRa. 718–19 *inverted in* JK. 718 **grant** dur RRa. 721 **neiz .i. seul** non .j. seul P; ne nul bon JK. **confort** conseil JK; soulaz RRa. 722 **Mais ce qui** Maiz ce que E; Mes cest che qui Ar. **fait mon cuer** men coeur fait Ar. **partir et fendre** palir et tendre C; palir et freindre JK; palir et fendre RRa; fait partir mon cuer et fendre Pc. 723 **C'est . . . qui** Cest que ne scay a qui me doye RRa; Chest che que jou ne say mais a cui Ar. **prendre** *plaindre JKAr; complaindre RRa. 725 **m'est vis** mest advis RRa; me dit St. **se** que P. 726 **du degré** du dangier JK; des degrez Ra. **fui** suy R. 727 **je . . . n'apuy** je me fie et apui JKAr; je fier ne me puy RRa. 728 **A** Au JKAr. 729 **ne li en** je ne len St. 732 **Fors** Que JK. 733 **fait** voit E. 734 **le . . . haut** en haut les bas CJK; hault en bas Ar; de hault embas St. 735 **puet** puent K. 736 **Que** Quen RRa. 737 **Li face avoir** Avoir lui face St. 738 **Soit . . . soit** Ou soit de joye ou Ar. 739 **ou jus** au niant JK. **ne . . . tost** nait elle tost RRa; ne lait tantost ArSt. **hurté** gete Ar. 740–43 *om* St. 741 **que** *om* E. 742 **Ce** Si E. **qu'uns vens** que vens E; que un veux JK. **une fausse** que une fausse P; une seule RRa. **estature** estadure JK. 743 **Une . . . qui** Une joie qui EJK; Que une joye qui RRa; Chest une joye qui Ar. 744 **C'est fol s'y** Si est fol qui si RRa. 746 **se je di** se di JK; si di je E. **qui m'aigrie** magrie EJK; me guerrie RRa; ma magrie Ar. 747 **Puiz** Vueil JK. **ma** *om* JK. 748 **Par** Pour E. 749 **je** *om* Ar. **ne** et P. 750 **Elle s'est** Elle est E; Quelle soit JK; Selle cest RRa; Ele fust St. **subjection** submission E. 751 **a qui** a cui Ar; en qui St. 753 **qu'elle** quil JKSt. 754 **Com ses souvrains** Com souveraine P; Com ses souverains CER; Com ses servans J; Com ses ses servans K; Comme ses souverain Ra. 755 **Si . . . puet** Si quelle ne puet CE; Siques ne puis RRa; Siques ne poeut Ar; Si que ne peut St.

Et a grant tort
M'a retolu ma joie et mon confort,
Et si m'a mis en si grant desconfort,
Que je sçai bien que j'en avrai la mort;
Ne rien deffendre
Ne m'en porroit, neiz .i. seul confort rendre; f. 75v
Mais ce qui fait mon cuer partir et fendre,
C'est ce que je ne me sçay a qui prendre
De mon ennuy.
Car il m'est vis, se par Fortune sui
Jus du degré ou jadiz montez fui
Par li en qui je ne me fi n'apuy,
A dire voir,
Que nul mal gré ne li en doy savoir,
Car elle fist du faire son devoir,
N'elle ne doit autre mestier avoir
Fors de trahir
Ceulz qu'elle fait monter et enrichir,
Et de faire le bas en haut venir;
N'elle ne puet personne tant chierir
Que sceürté
Li face avoir de sa beneürté,
Soit de joye, soit de maleürté,
Que sus ou jus ne l'ait moult tost hurté.
C'est sa nature:
Si bien ne sont fors que droite aventure;
Ce n'est qu'uns vens, une fausse estature;
Une joye est qui poy vault et poy dure.
C'est fol s'y fie!
Chascun deçoipt et nului ne deffie.
Et se je di que la mort qui m'aigrie
Puiz demander a ma dame jolie,
Par quel raison
Le ferai je, ne par quelle achoison?
Elle s'est mise en la subjection
D'Amours a qui elle a fait de li don
Entierement,
Et voelt qu'elle ait tres souverainement, f. 76
Com ses souvrains, sur li commandement
Si qu'el ne puet contrester nullement

can in no way contest Love's desire, but must obey her in everything.

"Therefore, if my lady wishes and is pleased to leave me for another's love, this is Love's doing, not my lady's, who is the abode of all worth, for she is only doing her duty and maintaining her honor by obeying her sovereign lord. Therefore I believe that when Love enkindled my love, that Love more than my worthy lady transgressed against me; that is to say, if Love could transgress against me. But I cannot understand this at all, for like a sweet and tender mother Love has nourished me for a long while with her sweet delicacies as best she could; nor have I yet noticed, in any misfortune I've had, that she failed to remain at my side or to serve me every course, first tears and afterwards sighs. Such is my nourishment; my appetite requires and requests nothing more; nor, by my soul, do I seek anything other than that which breaks my heart. Thus Love grows in my heart in proportion to my sorrow, and leaves me neither night nor day, but rather through her kindness accompanies me in my sad moaning. Therefore I say that this was great friendship to be my mother in prosperity and also in adversity. Thus I cannot complain of her, unless I am truly false, for I find her to be always at my side. Nor have I been brought low by

756 **plaisir** desir St. 757–58 *inverted in* JK. 757 **Ainz** Qui JK. **en tous cas** a amours RRa; en tel cas Ar. 758 **et** *om* St. 759 **chierir** encherir CAr; enrichir ERPcRaSt. 761 **en . . . a** en qui toute JK; qui tant a de RRa; en qui a tout Ar. 762 **Car elle** Maint quelle JK; **devoir** desir E. 763 **son** *om* E. **souverain** souvrain ArSt. 764 **Si qu'il m'est vis** Si quil mest avis E; Com mest advis RRa. 765 **estoie** estoit EK. **espris** espis J. 766 **Qu'en** Quay E. 769 **mesprendre** entendre JK; dessendre St. 770 **ce comprendre** recomprendre C. 771 **longuement** bonnement E. **com** que Ar. **et** *om* EArSt. 772 **repeü** receu St. 773 **De . . . qu'elle** Moult doulcement de ce quelle St. 774 **pas** point RRa. 775 **Pour nul** Par nul JK; Que pour Pc. **receü** apperceu E. 776 **tout adez** tost apres RRa. 777 **Elle** Quelle Ar. **com amie esté** este amie et RRa; este amye PcSt. 778 **Et . . . m'ait** Et quelle ne mait CE; Et quel ne met JK; Et que ne mait RArPcRaSt. 779 **devant** avant E. 781 **vuelt** voeil PEJRArPc. 782 **Ne par m'ame** Et par mame P; Ne ma vie C; Ne par mon ame RArRa. **rien n'est** nest riens Ar. **a quoy** a qui E. **je tende** jentende ERSt. 783 **fende** tende JK. 785 **en** *om* E. **au . . . ma** au fier de ma E; moult crueuse JK. 786 **s'en part** se pert RRa. 787 **m'acompaigne** me compaingne CERArPcRaSt. 789 **Si que je** Et pour ce RRa. 790 **Qu'el** Qui CArPcSt; Quelle RRa. **m'a . . . en** mest mere en grant Ar. 791 **Et encor est** Et est encore E; Encores est RRa; Et encor mest ArSt. 793 **se trop** si tres JK. 794 **Car sanz partir** Quamie et pres JK; Puis que sans partir RRa. **de moy toudiz** o moy tousjours RRa. 795 **Ne** Que RRa.

A son plaisir,
Ainz li couvient en tous cas obeïr.
Dont, se ma dame a plaisance et desir
De moy lessier pour .i. autre chierir,
Ce fait Amour,
Non pas ma dame en qui tant a valour,
Car elle fait son devoir et s'onnour
D'obeïr a son souverain seignour.
Si qu'il m'est vis,
Quant par Amour d'amer estoie espris,
Qu'en ce faisant Amours a plus mespris
Par devers moy que ma dame de pris;
C'est a entendre,
S'Amours pooit par devers moy mesprendre.
Mez nullement je ne puiz ce comprendre;
Car longuement, com douce mere et tendre,
M'a repeü
De ses dous biens au mieux qu'elle a peü;
Ne je n'ay pas encor apparceü,
Pour nul meschief que j'aie receü,
Que tout adez
Elle ne m'ait com amie esté prez
Et qu'el ne m'ait servi de tous mes mes,
De plours devant et de souspirs aprez.
C'est ma viande;
Mon appetit plus ne vuelt ne demande,
Ne, par m'ame, rien n'est a quoy je tende
Fors seulement ad ce que mon cuer fende.
Ainsi Amour
Croist en mon cuer au fuer de ma dolour, f. 76v
Ne ne s'en part ne de nuit ne de jour,
Ainz m'acompaigne en mon dolereux plour
Par sa bonté;
Si que je di que c'est grant admisté
Qu'el m'a esté mere en prosperité,
Et encor est en mon adversité.
Si ne me puiz
Plaindre de li, se trop mauvez ne suis,
Car sanz partir de moy toudiz la truiz.
Ne je ne sui mie par li destruiz,

her, for she cannot alter hearts, since God doesn't wish it. For when God created my lady who used to call me her beloved, and for whom my heart now grieves exceedingly, had He and Nature, when they formed her pure and perfect beauty, pleasing above all other creatures, endowed her sweet being with loyalty, I would still be called her beloved, and her heart which had promised me much consolation would never have become my enemy.

"Therefore I say—with all respect to their honor and reverence—that God and Nature made a great blunder when they fashioned such a beautiful semblance without loyalty. For had she a hundred times less beauty, yet remained loyal, that great gift of loyalty would have brought her more honor and been more pleasing than if she'd been a hundred thousand times more beautiful. At any rate, she must have pleased more, for then there would have been nothing with which to reproach her.

"Therefore I believe that I should not hold Good Love, Fortune, or my lady responsible for my sorrows. Yet can I hold myself responsible? Indeed yes! Because I have brought myself from riches to desolation, from security to mortal danger, from joy to grief, by her subtle glance, and from freedom into a servitude where no one loves or values in the least me or my honor, my love or my service, nor thinks my life worth a cherry. Nevertheless, I do not believe I erred in loving her, for it was

797 **les cuers** le cuer CRRa. **puiz que** depuiz que JK. **ne le voelt** le veult JKR. 798 **me suelt** mestuet JK. 800 **S'il** Quil JK; Lui RRa; Soy St. 801 **sa beauté** samblance JK. **fine** clere Ar; nette St. 802 **a . . . toute** sur toutes a toute E; a cous (*sic*) sur toute Ar. 805 **encor** encores E; a tous St. 806 **son cuer** ses doulz coeurs Ar. **qui . . . bien** qui tant des biens E; qui mavoit bien St. **m'avoit promis** mont promis JK; ma promis Ar. 807 **N'eüst . . . esté** Neust este jamais Ar; Et jamaiz neussent este St. 808 **Pour ce di** Si di JKRRa. **qu'en ce** quausse E. 809 **firent . . . ignorance** si firent ignorance C; firent grant oubliance JK; feirent ignorance Pc. 810 **Sauve . . . d'eulz** Sauf l'onneur dieu RRa. 811 **firent** fourmerent P (+1). **belle** douce PAr; noble ESt. 814 **fust . . . bonté** eust bonte et loyaute St. 815 **De** Sa JK. **plus honnouré** plus amonte P; moult plus honnoure R; on plus honnore St. 817 **.c.m.** Mil cent E. **mieux pleüst** mieulx me pleust RRa. 818 **Et . . . trop** En trestouz cas et J; En trestous cas trop K. **plaire** faire E; pleurer RRa. 819 *after this line* JK *insert lines* 848–55; *they are repeated in their proper location.* (*Variants:* 848 **Si ne** Ainsi; 850 **griefs** grans; 851 **a tous je** a trestous; 852 **ce** ça.) 821 **Qu'a** Car E; Que Pc. **n'a fortune** a fortune CJKRPcRa. 822 **Riens . . . dolours** Riens demander ne mes douleurs RRa; De ma dolour riens demander Ar. **ne** *om* C. *After this line, which ends f. 33 (new numbering 18),* K *inserts lines* 995–1161, *which comprise f. 34 (new numbering 19).* 823 **en** *om* JKRRa. **riens . . . moy** riens ne demanderay moy RRa. 825 **en** a C. 826 **en** et Ra. 827 **son regart** un regart C; son engin JK. 828 **franchise** servise JK. 829 **on n'aime** en aimme C; en naime JKRa. 830–31 *inverted in* St. 830 **m'onnour** mon cuer C; ne ma mere Ar; namour St. **m'amour** amour Ar; monnour St. 831 **Ne . . . vaillant** Ne aussi ma vie vaillant Ar; Ne na vaillant St. **une cerise** une seule serise St. 833 **pas ne mespris** jen ay mespris RRa. **quant** tant CERRa. 834 **Je l'enamay** Je ventoye RRa; Je lamay St. **monde** siecle JK. 835 **fust** fu E. **si excellent** plus excellent E; si suffisant JK.

Qu'elle ne puet
Muer les cuers, puiz que Dieus ne le voelt.
Car quant Dieus fist ma dame qui me suelt
Clamer ami, dont li cuers trop me duelt,
S'il et Nature,
Quant il firent sa beauté fine et pure,
Plaisant a tous sur toute creature,
Eüssent lors en sa douce figure
Loyauté mis,
Je fuisse encor appellez ses amis,
Et son cuer qui maint bien m'avoit promis
N'eüst jamez esté mes ennemis.
Pour ce di qu'en ce
Nature et Dieus firent grant ignorance,
Sauve l'onneur d'eulz et leur reverence,
Quant il firent si tres belle semblance
Sanz loyauté.
Car s'elle eüst .c. fois mains de beauté,
Et elle fust loyaulz, la grant bonté
De loyauté l'eüst plus honnouré
Que s'elle fust
.c.m. fois plus belle, et mieux pleüst;
Et en tous cas trop mieux plaire deüst,
Pour ce qu'en li riens a dire n'eüst.
Si que je croy
Qu'a Bonne Amour, n'a Fortune, n'a soy
Riens demander de mes dolours ne doy.
Et en puiz je riens demander a moy?
Certes oïl!
Car je me mis de richece en exil,
De sceürté en .i. mortel peril,
De joie en duel, par son regart subtil,
Et de franchise
En servitude, ou on n'aime ne prise
Moy ne m'onnour, m'amour ne mon service,
Ne ma vie vaillant une cerise.
Et nonpourquant,
Il m'est avis que pas ne mespris quant
Je l'enamay, qu'en ce monde vivant
N'avoit dame qui fust si excellent,

agreed that in this world there is no lady so perfect. So I became hers with good will and expected nothing but good to come of it because of the excellence of her reputation, which has now destroyed me. But all that glitters is not gold, and one should not so love his joy that he is unable to do without it, when it's ended. And were I the most powerful man in the world, I would choose none other than her, and could not choose better, had I found loyalty in her. Thus I don't know whom to blame and complain to for my great sorrows and misfortunes. Should anyone ask me, I'll say to all that God and Nature are responsible; it's a pity and misfortune to have made her body so beautiful, so noble, and so sweet in every aspect, that—were it loyal—it could not have been better. So shall I blame these two for my troubles? I'll not do it, for they are too exalted for me; instead, the best I can do is to suffer from this day forth.

"Now I've told you the way in which Love made me a faithful lover—the condition, the manner, the whole agreement; what became of me, how I was taken prisoner and held, how my lady forgot me, the blessings and tribulations I have had to endure up until this day, how I've had help from no one, and how I cannot find satisfaction for my deep anguish, which has slain and destroyed me. Therefore I say, if you've listened well and heard me, that the sorrow in which I languish,

836 **Ce** Se RSt. 837 **en** par St. 838 **n'y** ne RArSt. 839 **bon** grant JK. 840 **Qui** Or JK. 841 **ce** il Ar. **or . . . reluist** or quanqui reluist C; dor quanquil reluit EAr; or quanquil luist J; or quanquil reluist KSt; or quanques y reluit RRa. 842 **Ne on ne** On ne C. **tant** tout E. 843 **s'en puist** se puist CPc; se puisse RRa. **quant il cuist** quant on cuit CPc; ains quil cuit E; quant est cuit JK; quant on puit St. 844–47 *om* JK. 845 **Tous li mieudres** Com le meillour E; Tout le meilleur RRaSt. **n'esleüsse** ne eusse ERRaSt; nel leusse Ar. 846 **je** *om* RRa. 847 *om* St. 848 **Si . . . sçay** Ainssi nen say JK; Si ne me scay RArRa. 849 **et** ne JKSt. **me prenray** men prenray CEArSt; *men plaindray JK. 850 **griefs** grans JK. **des meschiefs** du meschief E; les meschiefs St. 851 **m'en** me RRa. **a . . . respondrai** a tous en respondrai C; a trestouz respondray JK; a tous responderay ArSt. 852 **ce** ca JKArRaSt. 853 *om* St. 854 **il . . . corps** ilz vivent son corps RRa; son corps firent Ar. 855 **si . . . doulz** si bon si gent P; si doulz si gent E. **c'on ne com ne K. 857 eulz** tous E. 859 **Ainz** Mes JKRRa; Si St. **meilleurs** mieudres Ar. 860 *om* J. **D'ore en avant** Moult douchement Ar. 861 **la** le Ar. 863 **et . . . couvenant** tout le commancement RRa; tout le commence Pc; et li commencement St. 864 **Ce qui** Se qui E; Ce quil JRArRaSt. 865 **fui** fu CEJKRRaSt. 866 **Comment . . . souvint** Comment de moy a ma dame souvint RRa; Et comment moy de ma dame souvint Ar; Comment de moy ma dame lui souvint St. 867 **qu'endurer** que durer EAr. 869–71. 869 *and* 871 *are transposed in* C. 870 *om* P. *After* 871, P *adds*: Et si ny voy ne secours ne refui. **grief** grant EAr. 871 **a par moy** a part moy E; en par moy St. **murdri** mordi Ra. **et destrui** *om* Pc. 874 **la . . . dont** les douleurs ont RRa.

Ce disoit on.
Si devins siens en bonne entencion,
Ne jamez n'y cuidasse se bien non,
Pour la grandeur de son tres bon renom
Qui m'a destruit.
Mais ce n'est pas tout or canque reluist,
Ne on ne doit pas tant amer son deduit
Qu'on ne s'en puist retraire, quant il cuist.
Et se je fuisse
Tous li mieudres du mont, je n'esleüsse
Autre que li, ne mieux je ne peüsse,
Se loyauté en li trouvé eüsse.
Si ne m'en sçay
Que demander et a qui me prenray f. 77v
Des griefs dolours et des meschiefs que j'ay;
Se on m'en demande, a tous je respondrai
Que ce fait Dieus
Et Nature; dont c'est meschiefz et dieuls,
Quant il firent son corps en trestous lieux
Si bel, si gent, si doulz c'on ne puet mieux,
S'il fust loyaulz.
Si me prendray a eulz .ii. de mes malx?
Je non ferai, car il me sont trop haux;
Ainz soufferrai, c'est mes meilleurs consaux,
D'ore en avant.

[O]r vous ai dit la maniere comment
Amours me fist estre loyal amant,
L'estat, la guise, et tout le couvenant,
Ce qui m'avint,
Comment pris fui, comment on me retint,
Comment de moy ma dame ne souvint,
Les biens, les malx qu'endurer me couvint
Jusqu'au jour d'uy,
Comment je n'ay aïde de nullui,
Comment vengier ne puiz mon grief ennui,
Dont a par moy me murdri et destrui.
Si que je di,
Se bien m'avez entendu et oÿ,
Que la dolour dont en mourant languy,

whose rigor has disfigured me and made me pale, is a hundred thousand times greater than yours; for your troubles are like pure joy and perfect sweetness compared to the sorrows that martyr me."

"Indeed, sir, I don't wish to deny that you have great sorrow and tribulation, when you've lost what your heart desires. Yet nonetheless, it is my opinion, and I dare to state it, considering your sorrow and mine, that you have less sorrow and more joy than I. I wish to tell you the reason why: you've told me that you love faithfully this lady who's caused you so much distress, and that you'll love her with a true heart as long as you live. And since you love her in this way, I believe you certainly desire her love. For one rarely sees Love arise without Desire, nor amorous Desire endure without Hope. And sometimes you have Memory of her, such that when your heart is beset by Desire, you recall your golden-haired beauty, of whom you have more than a few memories. So it cannot but be that you have some reminiscence that gives birth to a little joy in your heart, which vanquishes the grief that masters you; so Memory often brings you cheerful thoughts which dissipate and diminish your sorrow.

"But my sorrow intensifies night and day incessantly, and my river

875 **Qui mon viaire** Et mon visaige RRa. **destaint** destruit CRPc; destraint EJAr. 876 **rigour** vigour JK. 877 **Est** Et Ar. **voz mals** mes maux E; vostre mal RRa; vous mains Ar. **.c. mille** centisme RRa. 879 **Sont** Font C; Est RRa. **la** ma ArPcSt. 880 **martire** maistrie Ar. 881 **Certes sire** Certes biau sire C; Beau sire doulz RRa. **vuel desdire** veul dire E. 883 **Se ainsi** Ainssi J. 884 **toutevoie** toutes foiz RRa. 887 **a** *om* Ar. **dolour . . . joie** dennuyz et plus de joye RRa. 888 **n'a** nait CAr. 889 **Si . . . pourquoy** Et vous diray la raison et pourquoy St. 890 **m'avez** avez JK. 891 **Ceste** Cest E; Celle RRa; Ycelie Ar. **tant vous fait** vous fait tant PSt. 893 **comme vifs serez** comme vous vivres JK; com vif vous serez RRa; comme vous serez St. 894 **l'amez** ames Ar. 895 **s'amour** souvent St. 897 **Voy poy** Voit on JK; Voy je St. **qu'amours soit** quamans soit P; que mort soit JK; quamours fait St. 898 **se puist** puisse RRa. 899 **De esperance** Desesperanche Ar. 901 **Dont . . . est** Et dont quant vostre est R; Et dont quant vostre cuer est Ra; Dont voz cuers est St. **desir destrois** desir si destrois St. 902 **la** *om* J. **crins** clins E; crains RRa. 903 **des pensers** pensees PRPcRa; de pensers JK. 904 **puet** peust E. 906–7 *inverted in* JK. 906 **joie . . . fait** joie face en vous P (+1); fois en vous faut JK; joye fault en vous RRa. **qui remestre** remettre E; qua remetre J; que remerte K; que remestre ArSt. 907 **Fait . . . qui** La dolour qui E; Face la douleur qui RRa. **si . . . mestre** si vous tient et metre JK; a vous chiet a maistre St. 908 **Si qu'a** Siques a RRa. 910 **Qui** Ou RRa. **espart** appert RRa. 911 **Mais** Et RRa. **moye** mienne E. **nuit et jour** jour et nuit CAr. 912 **Sanz nul** Et sanz P. 913 **toudiz** tousjours RAr. **li** lui E; le RRa; les St.

Qui mon viaire a destaint et pali
Par sa rigour,
Est de voz mals .c. mille fois grignour;
Car fine joie et parfaite douçour
Sont vostre mal encontre la dolour
Qui me martire."

"[C]ertes, sire, pas ne vous vuel desdire f. 78
Que vous n'aiez moult de dolour et d'ire,
Se ainsi perdez ce que vo cuer desire.
Mais toutevoie,
Il m'est avis, et dire l'ozeroie,
Consideré vo dolour et la moye,
Qu'il a en vous mains dolour et plus joie
Qu'il n'a en moy.
Si vous en voeil dire raison pourquoy:
Vous m'avez dit que vous amez en foy
Ceste dame qui tant vous fait d'ennoy,
Et amerez
De loyal cuer, tant comme vifs serez.
Et puiz qu'il est ainsi que vous l'amez,
Certes, je croy que s'amour dezirez.
Car avenir
Voy poy souvent qu'Amours soit sanz Desir,
Ne que Desir d'amours se puist soffrir
De Esperancë. Et s'avez Souvenir
Aucune fois
Dont, quant vo cuers est par Desir destrois,
Il vous souvient de la belle aux crins bloys,
Dont vous avez des pensers plus de .iii.
Si ne puet estre
Que vous n'aiez aucun penser qui naistre
Aucune joie en vous fait, qui remestre
Fait la dolour qui si vous tient a mestre;
Si qu'a la fie
Par souvenir avez pensee lie
Qui vo dolour espart et entroublie.
Mais la moye nuit et jour multeplie
Sanz nul sejour,
Et toudiz croist li ruisseaux de mon plour, f. 78v

of tears swells constantly; nor is there any way I can have any thought or hope of regaining my love. But by serving, by honoring, by being discreet, by fearing, by happily persisting and suffering, by loving her well, by obeying her quite humbly, you can still win the solace, joy, and love of her to whom your heart inclines. Therefore I say that I am more tormented; and the reason is, I believe, clear and manifest: it is possible for you to regain your lady, but Nature has made it impossible for me to regain my beloved."

"My lady, there is more wisdom, honor, and moderation in you than in any other creature; for by your reasoning I'd quickly be overcome, could I not answer your arguments; yet truly, I'll not be able to do so as well as I should. But I'd like to go over your arguments, if I can.

"You contend that I love faithfully and will love as long as I live without repentance; and since I love, I must have Desire, who cannot flourish or endure without Hope; and I also have Memory, who often moves me and brings me reminiscences of her. Indeed, my lady, all this I grant as true, except that I have no hope. Yet know you very well, my lady—although there is nothing but good will on both sides—that in this matter your opinion and mine do not agree nor accord in any particular, but are opposed, as I intend to demonstrate to you at the

914 **puiz** peut St. 915 **m'amour** amour Ar. 917 *om* P. *After* 919 P *adds*: Et de vo dame faire tout le plaisir. **Par honnourer** Par bien amer JK; Par honneur Pc. **par . . . cremir** par servir par cremir E; et du cuer obeir JK. 918 **lïement et souffrir** liement et par souffrir C; par liement souffrir Ar. 919 **Par . . . obeïr** Et par franchise cuer et corps li offrir JK. 922 **et l'amour** et lonnour C; et amour EArSt. 923 **plus** moult E. 924 **moult** plus RRa; mon St. 925 **Est la** Et la ESt; La K. **et** est ESt. 926 **Car de ravoir** Car ravrir St. **vo dame c'est** vostre dame est ERRaSt. 927 **c'est** est JKRRa. 929 **Dame d'onneur** Loyalle dame RRa; Dame damour St. 930 **en** a E. **autre** nulle PAr. 931 **sens** *om* RRa. 932 **Moult tost** Most tost J; Tantost RRaSt. 933 **pooie** savoie CFJKRArPmRaSt. 934 **Et** Car CER. **le** *om* J. **saroie** pourroie C. 935 **com** comme C; que RArRaSt. **aroie** avoye R. 936 **repeter** repetier C. 937 **Veeil voz raisons** Vous vueil raison St. **g'i puiz** gy scay PJK; je puis E. **assener** assenez K. 939 **com** comme RRa; que ArSt. **porrai** puisse C. 940 **repentir** repartir JK. 941 **Et . . . j'aim** Et puiz quil faut P; Puis que jayme RRa. **il . . . desir** que je aie desir PSt; il faut que je desir EJK; il fault que jaye desir RRa; il fault laye desir Ar. 942 **se** *om* E. **deporter** destourner RRa. 943 **De esperance** Desesperanche Ar. 945 **et maint** a maint EAr. 946–47 *inverted in* St *but noted in margin.* 946 **ce** je PArSt; et R. **ottroy pour** ottroy de RRa; en croy pour St. 947 **Fors** Mes JK. 949 **comment . . . n'ait** comment il na RRa; combien quil nait St. 950 **Qu'en ce vostre** Que vostre ESt; Que se vostre RRa. 951 **accordent en** accordent de P; sacordent de Ar. 952 **Ainz** Mais RRa. 953 **com . . . pense** com je les vous pense P; com je le pense EPc; que le vous pense RRa; com je vous pense Ar. **a** *om* C.

N'avoir ne puiz pensee par nul tour,
Ne esperance de recouvrer m'amour.
Mais par servir,
Par honnourer, par celer, par cremir,
Par endurer lïement et souffrir,
Par bien amer de cuer et obeïr,
Tres humblement,
Povez encor avoir alegement,
Joie, et l'amour de celle ou vo cuer tent.
Si que je di que j'ay plus de tourment;
Et moult visible
Est la raison, ce m'est vis, et sensible:
Car de ravoir vo dame, c'est possible;
Mais mon ami ravoir, c'est impossible
Selon nature."
"[D]ame, d'onneur, de senz, et de mesure
A plus en vous qu'en autre creature;
Car par vo sens mis a desconfiture
Moult tost seroie,
Se a voz raisons respondre ne pooie.
Et vraiement faire ne le saroie
Si sagement com mestier en aroie;
Mais repeter
Veeil voz raisons, se g'i puiz assener.
Vous argüez que j'aime sanz fausser
Et ameray tant com porrai durer
Sanz repentir;
Et puiz que j'aim il faut qu'aie Desir
Qui ne se puet deporter ne souffrir
De Esperancë; et si ai Souvenir
Qui esmouvoir
Me fait souvent et maint penser avoir. f. 79
Certes, dame, ce vous ottroy pour voir,
Fors seulement que je n'ay point d'espoir.
Mais sachiez bien,
Dame, comment qu'il n'ait partout que bien,
Qu'en ce vostre entendement et le mien
Ne se joignent, në accordent en rien,
Ainz sont contraire,
Ainsi com je le vous pense a retraire,

proper time. But I do not wish to pass over in silence what you have said, that I can yet by honoring her, by serving well, persisting, fearing, obeying, loving faithfully, regain my lady in happiness. Nevertheless, it would be very difficult for him who had her to keep her, for her heart will not stay in one place any more than a ball on a sloping roof. And there is no way that you can regain your love, who was so esteemed and worthy, which is why your color is wan and pale. Therefore you say that my sorrows, which are still with me and which I have not deserved, are much less than yours. I shall answer your arguments as best I can, considering each in some detail; and I'll say what I sincerely feel and know about them from my own experiences.

"My lady, it is true that I love faithfully one who hates me—my lady with the fair body, who is my love and my desolation. When I see her love another and have no concern for me, whom she should love faithfully, my love nearly drives me mad, because if she cared for my life or my honor, she would not for the whole world let me languish a single hour in the sorrow in which I live and remain. But first Love and then my lady increase the strength of the wave of grief which over-

954 **point** temps PE. **ce . . . taire** ne me voeil pas taire P; pas ce ne vueil taire C; ce ne veul pas atraire E; che ne voeil pas traire Ar. 955 **dites** dones Pc. **qu'encor puiz je** quen puisse CRRa; quencore puis St. 957 **doubter** celler E. 958 **Par . . . par** Pour obeir et E. 959 **Qu'en joie puiz** Quencores puiz P; Quencore puis je RRa. 961 **maistrise** mestrie C; chose JK; mestier St. **au** a EJKRArRa. 962 **cuer** corps RRa. **n'arresteroit** sesteroit JK. 963 **estuef** estuet P. **toit** doit C. 964 **Et** En St. 965 **tant** *om* Ar. 966 **mes** plus RRa. 967 **vaine et pale** pale et vaine St. 968 **Si** Et Pc. **qu'ainsi** lainsi Ar. 969 **mes** voz RPcRa. **doleurs** doulcours E. 970 **vostres** nostres RRa; moies Pc. 971 **acquis** apris JK. **par** *om* E. **mes** *om* C. 972 **respondrai** respondra J. 973 **ces** ses JK; telz RRa. **au mieux** le miex E. **porrai** saray KRRa. 974 **.i.** et K. 975 **Si** Et JK. **j'en** je PJK. **sens** pens Ar. 977 **voirs** vray E. **j'aim tres loyaument** jaime loyaument JKRRa. 978 **Ce . . . het** Et qui me plaist RRa. 979 **ma mort** mamour KSt. **destruiement** deffinement C. 980 **li** la JRKrRa; le St. 983 **Si qu'a** Si que C; Siques qua RRa. **ne me marvoy** ne morvoy E; mort ne me voy RRa; ne men marvoy St. 985 **Car** Que Ar. **ma . . . m'onnour** et ma vie et monnour P; ma vie et monnour CSt; ma vie et mon honnour RRa. 986 **En** Et Ar. 987 **me** mi Ar. **l'eure d'un** heure de R; heure du Ra. 989 **en vertu** en dolour, *corrected in margin by scribe to* en vertu P; en vertus JK; sa vertu RRa; les vertus Ar; en vray St. **font** fait ERRaSt. 990 *om* JK. *After* 991 JK *add*: Corps joint joli jeune deue faconde. 991 **Amours . . . et** Amour promise a RRa.

Quant point sera. Mais ce ne voeil pas taire
Que vous dites qu'encor puiz je tant faire
Par honnorer,
Par bien servir, par soffrir, par doubter,
Par obeïr, par loyaument amer,
Qu'en joie puiz ma dame recouvrer.
Mes ce seroit
Moult grant maistrise au garder qui l'aroit,
Car en .i. lieu son cuer n'arresteroit
Né que feroit .i. estuef sur .i. toit.
Et vostre amour,
Qui tant avoit de pris et de valour,
Ne poez mes recouvrer par nul tour,
Dont vous avez vaine et pale coulour.
Si qu'ainsi dites
Que mes doleurs sont assez plus petites
Que les vostres, dont je ne sui pas quittes,
Ne que pas n'ay acquis par mes merites.
Si respondrai
A ces raisons au mieux que je porrai,
Et sur chascune .i. poy m'arresterai;
Si en dirai ce que j'en sens et sçay
De sentement.

[D]ame, il est voirs que j'aim tres loyaument f. 79v
Ce qui me het, c'est ma dame au corps gent,
Qui est ma mort et mon destruiement.
Quant je li voy
Autrui amer, et n'a cure de moy
Qu'elle deüst amer en bonne foy,
Si qu'a paine que tout ne me marvoy
De ceste amour;
Car, s'elle amast ma vie, ne m'onnour,
En la dolour ou je vif et demour
Ne me lessast languir l'eure d'un jour
Pour tout le monde.
Mais en vertu font multeplïer l'onde
De la dolour qui en mon cuer habunde
Amours premiers et ma dame seconde.

whelms my heart. Therefore I do have Desire. But for what? To end it all quickly, for I cannot expect healing from anything that might come to me. And if I had her love again better than before, I don't know if I would trust her. Indeed not! Why not? I wouldn't dare. Because they say nature is more powerful than nurture, and the wolf, unless he loses his instinct, always seeks the forest; it's the simple truth. And for this reason there is no hope in my desire; rather, despair is so rooted there that I shall lie vanquished in the blind alley of Memory, whom you say evokes the thought that brings me happiness. Yet indeed, I can never rejoice, nor have I rejoiced, nor seen, nor heard, nor sensed such thought since my lady has taken a new lover; for at that moment it left me. Thus I wish to prove that Memory is what most torments me and what most causes my heart to lose hope. You know, for it's evident—everyone can see it—that if ever I could forget my lady who keeps me in anguish, my sorrow would be forgotten. And if she were forgotten, the forgetting would cause my sorrow to wither away and die; and this could heal all my troubles. But what happens? This Memory, by its subtle artifice, reminds me of the dear face and fair body for whom I suffer in my heart; but it is conceived, born, and perfected, and survives

993 **Mais** Et E. **est il** il est RRa. **morir** fenir EJKArSt. 994 **qui . . . venir** dont il me puist venir JK. 995–1161 *These lines, which comprise f. 34 (new numbering 19) in* K, *follow line* 822. 995 **je peüsse** je puisse J; je me peusse St. **le garir** le guerir JK; desjoir St. 997 **mieux . . . souloie** ainsi com je soloie EJK; mieulx que ne souloie RRa. 998 **pas** mie St. **je** jamaiz RRa. 999 **je n'ozeroie** je ne pourroie JK. 1001 **Si . . . dit** Si com len dit C; Si com dit J; Si comme on dit Ra. 1002 **toudis** tousjours C. **s'il . . . desnature** boinnement par deviaire Ar. 1003 **au** ou JK. **c'est . . . pure** de sa propre nature, *corrected in margin by scribe to* c'est la verité pure P; cest verite pure CSt; sil ne se desnature Ar. 1004 **ce** cil Ar; cel St. 1005 **En** Eus E. 1006 **a li** en lui EJK. **joint** tout C; gist EJK. **desespoir** desespoire Ar. 1007 **j'en** je CERRa. **matez . . . point** mat ou aveugle apoint RRa. 1008 **Du** Dont EJK. 1009 **qui** quil RRa; que Ar. 1010 **me** ma C. 1011 **puiz . . . joïr** puiz je mes joir P; puisse mais jouir C; puis jou plus goir Ar. 1012 **Ne n'en** Je nen P; Ne ne JKRRa. 1013 **Ne ne la** Ne ne le PRa; Ne vere la C; ne ce ne Pc. **senti në oÿ** oy ne senti JK. 1014 **ot** eust RRa. 1015 **adonques** adont JK; droit adonques Ar. **se . . . il** se parti el JK; se departit RArRa. **de mi** de lui RRa. 1017 **puet** fait R. **grever** toucher St. 1019 **savez** le veez RRa. **et . . . cler** et est cler CPPc; et cest tout cler E; que cest cler JKSt; au cler RRa; cest tout cler Ar. 1021 **Que** Ne RRa. 1022 **qui . . . moult** qui me tient si C; qui moult me tient E; qui me tient en St. **destroit** estroit RRa. 1023 **Que ma dolour** Ma grant dolour P; Que ma dame E. 1025 **l'oubliance** loyaute C. **feroit** seroit JKRRaSt. 1026 **mourroit ou cesseroit** moctroit ou se leroit JK. 1027 **Et ce** Et se P; Ainsi RRa; Et bien Ar. **me pourroit** ne pouoit P; me pouoit C; me feroit St. 1029 **Cilz** Se RRa; Ce PcSt. 1030 **ramentoit** ramenteust St. **le viaire** la maniere RRa. 1031 **Et . . . corps** Et le corps gent P; Le gent corps RRa. **pour qui** par qui PJK; pourquoy RRaSt. **mon cuer** mon corps PSt; le mien en RRa.

Pour ce ai Desir.
Mais quelx est il? Il est de tost morir,
Car il n'est riens qui me peüst venir
Dont je peüsse esperer le garir.
Et se j'avoye
L'amour de li mieux que je ne souloie,
Ne sçai je pas se je m'y fieroie.
Certes, nennil! Pour quoy? Je n'ozeroie.
Car nourreture,
Si com on dit, vaint et passe nature;
Et toudis va, s'il ne se desnature,
Li leux au bos; c'est la verité pure.
Et par ce point
En mon desir d'esperance n'a point,
Mais a li joint desespoir si a point
Que j'en serai matez en l'angle point
Du Souvenir,
Que vous dites, qui fait en moy venir f. 80
La pensee qui me fait resjoïr.
Certes, de li ne puiz jamés joïr
Ne n'en joÿ,
Ne ne la vi, ne senti, në oÿ,
Puiz que ma dame ot fait nouvel ami;
Car adonques se parti il de mi.
Si voeil prouver
Que c'est la riens qui plus me puet grever
Et qui plus fait mon cuer desesperer
Que Souvenir. Vous savez, et c'est cler,
Chascuns le voit,
Que se jamez il ne me souvenoit
De ma dame qui me tient moult destroit,
Que ma dolour oubliee seroit.
Et s'elle estoit
Oubliee, l'oubliance feroit
Qu'elle du tout mourroit ou cesseroit;
Et ce garir de tous mals me pourroit.
Mais qu'avient il?
Cilz Souvenirs, par son engin soubtil,
Me ramentoit le viaire gentil
Et le gent corps pour qui mon cuer exil;

all in sorrow. Why? Because I thought that I was well loved when I was affectionately called beloved. Alas! wretched me! Now all is very changed, since my lady has a new love. And can one experience worse, my lady, without hanging himself? Indeed not! For this will bring a lover to ruin; and not one in five hundred thousand could escape such mortal danger.

"And it often happens, when I remember this, that my weary heart becomes so downcast within my body that I must faint. And if Reminiscence is engendered in me by Memory, what is it like? It is disconsolate, sad, mirthless, sorrowful, and dejected. And, I give you my word, every reminiscence I have runs counter to my happiness, and I am the worse off for it. Do you know why? Because I see my lady inconstant. And had the joy I felt, when I was in her good graces, not been greater than I could possibly express, nor than I could conceive or imagine, then the deep sorrow which oppresses me would be much less. But in so much as the joy was greater, by so much my anguish is bitterer. And I can neither imagine nor conceive that I might regain my lady, in whom I have no hope.

"My lady, I'll tell you what makes me grieve: it seems to me that something which divides and gathers in several places, and which

1032 **Mes** Met E; Maist JK; Mest RRa. 1033 **Nez et feniz** Naist et fini RRa. 1034 **dolour** dolours E. **pour quoy** *om* E. 1035 **Cuiday estre** Cuidoie estre CRArPcRaSt; Cuidai bien estre JK. 1036 **doucement** humblement EJK. 1037 **or est bien** or est il P; Et or est C. 1038 **Quant** Que PJK **aime autre** aime (autre *om*) JKAr; a fait amy St. 1039 *om* JK. **Et . . . pis** Peut on or pis St. **dame** nennil Ar. **se on** qui RPcRa; que St. 1041 *om* JK, *which substitute*: Quen mon servise en a encor cent mil (*cf.* 1805). **a** en P. 1042 *om* JK, *which substitute*: Qui aiment tuit pres aussi fort com il (*cf.* 1806). **hors** *om* Ar. **de si** d'un tel P; de ce St. **peril** *om* Pc. 1043 *om* JK, *which substitute*: Et si nen ont la monte dun fuisil (*cf.* 1807). **N'en** Ne PE. **.i. entre** d'un aultre Ar. **.v.** *om* RRa. 1044 **Dont** Et JK. 1046 **devient** sestaint JK. 1047 **me** men Ar. 1051 **lasse mourne** lasse morte C; morne lasse EJK. **et** *om* RRa. 1052 **Et** Ne ArPcSt. 1053 **penser** pensee EAr. 1054 **si** se Ar. 1055 **ma . . . voy** ma dame au change voy CJK; au change ma dame voy RRa. 1056 **Et se** Est ce RRa. 1058 **Ne** Me C. **saroie** scavoye Ar. 1059 **Ne ymaginer** Ymaginer RRa. 1060 **La** Ma E. 1061 **destraint** destruit C; destaint E. **en fust** et fait EJK; et fust RRa. **en . . . menour** et de nuit et de jour Ar. 1062 **que j'euz** com jay E; com la joie JK; joy RRa; que jay Ar. joie iert JK; jolie Ar. 1063 **crueuse** cruelle CRRa. **dolour** langour CJKRRa. 1064 **ravoir** davoir Ar. 1065 **ou . . . nul** je ny ai nul P. 1066 **le** la EJK. 1067 **Si** Ce E. **me** mi CRAr. **mouvoir** douloir EJK. 1069 **part** pert RRa. 1070 **c'elle tremble** elle tremble P; ce el tremble CPc; ce il me semble E; ce se change JK. 1071 **Ne n'arreste** Ne ne sarreste P; Et na test RRa; Ne na arrest Ar. **ne que** neiz que C; que de RRa. **de** qui E.

Mes engenrez,
Nez, et feniz est, et continuez
Tous en dolour. Pour quoy? Pour ce qu'amez
Cuiday estre, quant amis fui clamez
Tres doucement,
Helas! dolens! or est bien autrement,
Quant ma dame aime autre nouvellement.
Et puet on pis, dame, se on ne se pent?
Certes, nennil!
Car c'est pour mettre .i. amant a exil; f. 80v
N'eschaper hors de si mortel peril
N'en devroit pas .i. entre .v.c. mil.
Dont il avient
Par maintes fois, quant de ce me souvient,
Que mon las cuer dedenz mon corps devient
Si dolereux que pasmer me couvient.
Et se Pensee
Par Souvenir est en moy engenree,
Quelle est ellë? Elle est desconfortee,
Tristre, lasse, mourne, et desesperee.
Et, par ma foy,
Je n'ay penser qui ne soit contre moy;
Et si le pren au piz. Savez pour quoy?
Pour ce qu'aler ma dame en change voy.
Et se la joie
Que j'avoie, quant en sa grace estoie,
Ne fust plus grant que dire ne saroie,
Ne ymaginer ne penser ne porroie,
La grief dolour
Qui me destraint en fust assez menour.
Mais de tant plus que j'euz joie grignour,
De tant est plus crueuse ma dolour.
Et que ravoir
Puisse ma dame, ou je n'ai nul espoir,
Ymaginer ne le puiz, ne veoir.
Si vous dirai ce qui me fait mouvoir:
Dame, il me semble
Qu'une chose qui se part et assemble
En pluseurs lieux, et avec c'elle tremble
Ne n'arreste ne que fueille de tremble,

moreover trembles incessantly like an aspen leaf, and is not stable, but instead is constantly fickle and changing—now here, now there, now by the fire, now at table, then elsewhere—is something not to be trusted; for one can in no way be sure of it: it's truly a game of enchantment, for what one believes he holds securely, he does not have at all. In spite of what some may say, my lady, it is thus with my ladylove, who is fickle and changing: she gives and then takes back, she detests and is then a friend, and all her heart is not in one place; and if anyone takes a portion, indeed I think he has a poor share, and that this part will soon be gone from him. To judge properly, no lover can hold a rival so dear that he would be willing to share his love with him, even in thought. Thus it is clear that I cannot fully hold her heart, which makes me lament; because a heart which goes thus from hand to hand, though one should have it tonight, it will be gone tomorrow. Indeed, the true lover is a veritable bird of prey, because the bird wants nothing less than the whole heart of its victim. Wherefore I say that you'll as soon have your lover back as one would change my lady's heart to make it entirely mine forever; but one cannot pull the wolf from its hide without flaying him, nor can one transform an ox into a sparrowhawk, or vice versa.

"And, sweet lady, it is common for both men and women that when the soul has left the body and the body is interred beneath the

1072 **Et** Ne JArSt; Ce Ar. 1073 **Ainz** Mais RRa. **toudiz changant** changant muant P. 1074 **ci** ca CJAr; sa K. **ore . . . a** au feu et a la PCAr; ore au feu ore au E; or au feu a la table Pc; ore a feu ore a St. 1075 **c'est chose** chose est St. 1077 **la** le P. 1079 *om* Ar. **Que** Car EJK. **certainement** seurement EJK. 1081 **Ainsi** Aussi C. **dame** de ma dame RRa. **que nulz die** nuls die K; quon die RRa. 1082 **De ma** Dune EJK; Qui en RRa. **dame qui se** amer ainsi RRa. 1083 **Donne et retolt** Puis rit puis pleure E; Or donne or tault Ar. **or . . . amie** puis het or est amie E; or het or ayme RRa. 1084 **N'en** Non St. 1085 **N'est tous** Cest tout St. **et s'aucuns** et chacun St. 1086 **croy** tieng Ar. **en** y RRa. 1087 **li** celi E. **celle . . . depart** celle part tost depart P; dautre part tost se part C; tantost celle se part JK; celle part tost se pert RArRa; celle part ce depart Pc. 1088 **Ne a** A RRaSt. 1089 **Amant** Au mains PC; Amours RRa; Ja nul amans St. **avoir home** elle home avoir PC (+1); avoir St. **si** tant RRa. 1090 **Qu'il le** Quel ne P; Qui le RRa; On se St. **vousist** vausist PAr; veist St. **a** .i. P. 1091 **En ses** Aincois JK; A ses RRa. **sanz plus neis** et neys E; et vers li JK; nes sans plus Ar; sanz plus ne Ra; semplus neiz Pc. 1092 **Et pour ce** Et pou C; Pour che EJKArPc. 1093 **Ne puiz** Puet on C. **me** men St. 1094 **en** a St. 1095 **ennuit** a nuit EJKAr. **on** len Pc. 1097 **Est vrais amans** Est drois amez P; Est drois amans JK; Amans est le RRa; Est li amant St. **droiz** dous P; vrais E; uns JK; boins Ar. 1098 **joie** proie J. 1099 **tout** que St. 1101 **rariez** ravrez P. 1102 **Comme on aroit** Que on nauroit C; Que on aroit Ar. 1103 **qu'il** qui Pc. **en mi** ami ERRa; a luy St. 1104 **Mis** Maiz ERRaSt. 1105 **Car** Maiz EJK. 1106 **Sanz l'escorchier** Sans escorchier EJRArRaSt. **n'on ne puet** ne con puet P; nen ne puet CPc; ne on peut Ar. **d'un** de C; du EAr. 1107 **Un** Bon C. **et** ne CEArPcRaSt. 1109 **partout** domme C; tous jours Ar. **d'omme et de** humain et de C. 1110 **est** s'est RRa; et Ar. 1111 **Et** Que St. **corps est** corps gist P; *om* Ar. **en terre** enterrez ER. **soubz** desous Ar.

Et n'est estable,
Ainz est toudiz changant et variable— f. 81
Puiz ci, puiz la, ore au feu ore a table,
Et puiz ailleurs—c'est chose moult doubtable;
Car nullement
On ne la puet avoir sceürement:
C'est droitement li gieux d'enchantement,
Que ce c'on cuide avoir certainement
On ne l'a mie.
Ainsi est il, dame, quoy que nulz die,
De ma dame qui se change et varie:
Donne et retolt, or het, or est amie,
N'en une part
N'est tous ses cuers; et s'aucuns y repart,
Certes, je croy qu'il en a povre part,
Et que de li celle part tost depart.
Ne a droit jugier,
Amant ne puet avoir home si chier
Qu'il le vousist avoir a parçonnier
En ses Amours, sanz plus, neis par cuidier.
Et pour ce a plain
Ne puiz avoir son cuer, dont je me plaing;
Car cuer qui va ainsi de main en main,
Se on l'a ennuit, on ne l'a pas demain.
Et toutevoie
Est vrais amans li droiz oyseaux de proie,
Car il ne voelt avoir pour toute joie
Fors tout le cuer de celle ou il s'ottroie.
Si que je di
Que vous rariez aussi tost vostre ami,
Comme on aroit mué le cuer de li
A ce qu'il fust entierement en mi
Mis sanz retraire;
Car on ne puet le leu de sa pel traire, f. 81v
Sanz l'escorchier, n'on ne puet d'un buef faire
Un espervier, et aussi le contraire.
Et, douce dame,
La coustume est partout, d'omme et de femme,
Que, quant du corps est departie l'ame
Et li corps est en terre soubz la lame,

gravestone, it is soon forgotten, although it may be mourned. I've seen no man nor woman weep so long that he'd not found joy again before the year was out, no matter how true his love—and I make no exception for powerful or poor. Truly, I believe that this is reasonable. You'll hold to the pattern; you'll not break it, and you'll not be reproached for this by anyone, though you pray for his soul sincerely. But I cannot put her whom I cannot forget out of my thoughts; for Memory keeps her close to me every day, hour, and minute. I see her very often, which drives me mad, since my eyes accompany her but I have no consolation from her and find no joy; instead, I see another who is joyful. This is what destroys me; for if she had wished to love neither him nor me, then I would have told my troubles to no one, but borne them hidden humbly within my heart, and I would have remained hopeful of joy and dreaded no tribulation or sorrow. Yet I don't wish to take my heart from her, for fear of the separation, since my heart has rested there too long, and truly I could never repent of loving her. I would be a faithless lover were I to repent it, for I gave her my love without condition. So I'll love her, come what may; and I swear I love her so faithfully that I feel ten times more grief for her than

1112 **Qu'en** En Ar. 1113 **Est** Et E. **c'on en pleure** con le pleure RRa; con empleure Ar; que on plour St. 1114 **Car nul** Ne nulz JK. **n'en** ne J. 1115 **son** soit Ar. **qu'a** que EJKRRa. **requeure** sequeure RRa. 1117 **tant soit** comme Ar. 1121 **La Le Ar. la** le ArSt. 1122–23 *inverted in* EJK. 1122 **nul** moy JK; *om* RRa; nulle St. **n'en** ne RRa. 1123 **pour l'ame** Dieu pour lui C. 1125 **pas** point RRa. 1126 **la** le PArSt. **moult** trop Ra; bien St. **de** *om* J. 1127 **departir** repentir P. **jour heure** heure jour JKRRaSt. 1128 **la** le ArSt. 1129 **tout vif** brief RRa. **me** men P. **desvoy** desroy EJK; mervoy RRa. 1130 **Quant** Tant St. **longuement . . . yeux** de mes iex longuement Ar. **la convoy** le convoy PAr; le congnoy RRa. 1131 **Et** *om* Ar. **joie ne bien** bien ne joye EJK. **n'en voy** nen ay CRRa; ny voy E; nen oy RPcRa; si men marvoy Ar. 1132 **Ains** Et P. 1133 **ce dont** ce qui RArRa. 1134 **amer ne vousist** amer ne vausist P; ne vausist amer Ar. 1135 **ne** nen C. 1137 **humblement et celasse** et humblement celasse EAr. 1138 **Et** Si C. **joie** goir Ar. 1139 **meschief ne dolour** dolour ne meschief P. 1141 **N'en** Ne CRRa. **du partir** den partir JK; departir RRaAr. 1142 **Qui** Que EAr. **et** *om* JRa. **mentir** partir JK. 1143 **Je** Ne JK. **a** pour ESt. 1145 **m'en** me PRRa. **repentoie** departoie CArPcSt. 1146 **sanz nul** nul sans Pc. **li donnai** li donne C; se donna Ar. 1147 **Et** Si EJKArPcSt. **m'en** en R. 1149 **j'ay** je E. 1150 **.x.** Cent RRa. **je . . . moy** nay une pour moy E; je naie de moy JK; je nen ay pour moy RRa. 1151 **Quant . . . voy** Quant voy sonnour C; Quar souvent voy E; Quant souvenir voy RRa; Car sonneur voy St. **amenrir car** avenir et E; ensi amenrir Ar; car (amenrir *om*) St.

Qu'en petit d'eure
Est oublié, ja soit ce c'on en pleure.
Car nul n'en voy ne nulle qui demeure
Tant en son plour qu'a joie ne requeure,
Ainz que li ans
Soit acomplis, tant soit loyaulz amans,
Në excepter n'en veeil petis ne grans.
Et vraiement, je croy que ce soit sens.
Si en ferez
La coustume; pas ne la briserez,
Car ja de nul reprise n'en serez,
Et de bon cuer pour l'ame prierez.
Mais en oubli
Ne puiz mettre celle que pas n'oubli;
Car Souvenir la tient moult prez de mi
Sanz departir jour, heure, ne demi,
Et si la voy
Assez souvent, dont tout vif me desvoy,
Quant longuement de mes yeux la convoy
Et je n'en ai joie, ne bien n'en voy,
Ains voy autrui
Qui joie en a. C'est ce dont me destrui;
Car s'elle amer ne vousist moy ne lui,
Les mals que j'ay ne plainsisse a nullui,
Ainz les portasse
Dedenz mon cuer humblement et celasse, f. 82
Et en espoir de joie demourasse,
Si que meschief ne dolour ne doubtasse.
Ne departir
N'en voeil mon cuer, pour doubte du partir,
Qui trop demeure en vie et, sanz mentir,
Je ne saroie amer a repentir.
Et si seroie
Faux amoureux, se je m'en repentoie,
Car sanz nul sy li donnai l'amour moye.
Et l'amerai, quoy qu'avenir m'en doie;
Et, par ma foy,
Si loyaument l'aim que j'ay plus d'ennoy
.x. fois pour li que je n'aye pour moy,
Quant s'onneur voy amenrir; car au doy

for myself, since I see her honor diminished; because all men and women who hear of this affair will point her out, and many will believe every report and consider her faithless from this day forth. For among sins this is such a wicked, ugly vice that he who commits it, no matter how high his stature, will never be wholly absolved and forgiven. Therefore I conclude, my lady, that I have much more sorrow, and that your troubles will be healed much sooner than those by which I am gripped. And I dare expect judgment in my favor, should we find a judge who would make a fair and just decision."

"By my soul, sir, I heartily desire and dare say that my heart likewise seeks quick judgment. Now consider whom we wish to choose, who'd be prepared to judge without delay which of us is wrong; for I believe that the trouble I bear is so painful that one could not suffer more without dying."

"My lady, I would like the judge to be selected according to your wishes."

"Rather according to yours, fair sir; I advise that he be chosen strictly on your advice. You first suggested having a judge, therefore you ought to name him."

"Indeed, my lady, do not wash your hands of this: *you* name him, for you are more knowledgeable than I."

And when I saw that they desired a judgment be given in these sorrowful matters, my heart was completely restored to joy. I didn't know which of two things I should do: go to them, or remain hidden. For

1152 **La** Le Ar. **mousterront** moustront E. 1153 **et** ou Ar. 1154 **la** le ArSt. 1155 **Car** Qua CRArPcRa; Et EJK. **pour** a RPcRaSt. **la** le Ar. 1158 **Car . . . fait** Que quil le fait E; Car qui la RRa; Car sil le Ar. **ja de pooir** ja pour povoir EJK; ja de paour RRa. 1159 **N'iert** Nest ERRa. **effacieé** affaitie RRa. 1161 **Dame que j'ai** Que jai dame P. 1163 **Seroit** Soit E. 1165 **attendre** entendre E. 1166 **nous** vous C; *om* Pc. **aviens** avez C; avons E; voions JK; avions Pc. 1169 **ma part** mon cuer EJK. **je** le ESt. 1170 **de mon cuer** brief mon cuer EJK; de bon cuer RRa. 1171 **Or regardez** Si regardez P; Or regardons CRArPcRaSt. **qui** que E; cui Ar. **nous voulons** vous vouldrez EJK; volons Ar (nous *om*); nous vorrons St. 1174 **Car avis m'est** Or mest il vis E. 1175 **plus** pis RPcRaSt. 1176–79 *om* JKRRa. 1177 **le juge** li jugemens E. **fait . . . voeil** fait a vostre vueil Ar. 1178 **Mais au vostre** Mais tous au vostre Ar. 1179 **que** fors Ar. 1180 **Car** Et JKRRa. 1181 **pour ce** si que C. 1182 **or . . . lavez** mais vous lottroy avez C. 1183 **Mais vous dites** Mais vous le dites PC (+1); Mais vous direz ERa; Mais que vous direz R. **pour . . . savez** que vous plus en savez Ar. 1184 **fais** say Ar. 1185 **qu'il** que JKPc. **voloient** vouloie E. 1186 **leurs** les E; si JK. 1187 **tous** *om* St. 1189 **la** le Ar.

La mousterront
Ceus et celles qui ceste oevre saront,
Et mains assez en tous cas la croiront,
Car tous jours mez pour fausse la tenront.
Car de meffait
C'est .i. vice si vilain et si lait,
Car qui le fait, ja de pooir qu'il ait,
N'iert de tous poins effacié ne deffait.
Pour ce conclus,
Dame, que j'ai de dolour assez plus,
Et que plus tost a garison venus
Seroit voz mals que cilz dont sui tenuz.
Et jugement
En ozeroie attendre vraiement,
Se nous aviens juge qui loyaument
Vausist jugier, et veritablement."
"Par m'ame, sire,
Et de ma part je voeil et oze dire f. 82v
Que de mon cuer le jugement desire.
Or regardez qui nous voulons eslire,
Qui sanz deport
Sache jugier li quielx de nous a tort;
Car avis m'est que le mal que je port
Est si crueuls c'on ne puet plus sanz mort."
"Dame, je voel
Que le juge soit fait tout a vo voeil."
"Mais au vostre, beau sire, et si conseil
Qu'il ne soit fait que par vostre conseil,
Car vous l'avez
Premier requis; pour ce dire devez."
"Certes, damë, or ne vous en lavez;
Mais vous, dites, pour ce que plus savez
Que je ne fais."
[E]t quant je vi qu'il voloient que fais
Fust jugement de leurs dolereus fais,
Mes cuers en fu de joie tous reffais.
Si ne savoie
De .ii. choses la quelle je feroie:
D'aler vers eulz, ou se je m'en tenroie.

willingly would I have directed them to a judge who could offer such a well-considered judgment that there would be nothing to add, and afterwards there would be no cause for quarrel. I thought it over a long while and finally decided I'd go to them. Then without further hesitation I got up and went without being noticed across the thick green grass toward them. When I had come so near them that I could see them quite clearly and openly, the little dog, which didn't know me at all, began to yelp. I noticed that the lady, who well understood proper behavior, was startled and called to it. But the dog paid very little heed to her call; he approached me barking and sunk his teeth into my robe. I grabbed him and, in his fright, he stopped barking. In my heart I was delighted to bring him back to his mistress, for it gave me the opportunity and occasion to go where I wished; therefore I kept stroking his coat. When I came where I desired, I was not shy or abashed; instead, I greeted the whole company with a smile, as it's my habit to do.

The knight, who was wise, courteous, and well-spoken, a tall, slender, and erect man, handsome and courteous and lively, and schooled and practiced in honorable behavior, promptly and courteously advanced to return my greeting. And the lady, upon whom

1191 **mis les eüsse** les eusse mis St. 1193 **qu'a** que E; qui JRRa; en Ar. **entendre** et entendre RRa. 1194 **Si souffissant** Et suffisant C; Si souffisament RRa. **qu'aprendre** que reprendre ERRa; qua reprendre JK; qua prendre Ar. 1195 **Et qu'aprez** Et apres JK. RRa *replace this line with*: Et que le droit du jugement sceust rendre RRa. 1197 **Moult longuement** Longuettement EAr. **puiz** pris ArPc. **mon avis ay** men advisay RRa. 1198 **je** jen St. **lors** *om* R; et Ar. 1199 **Je . . . alay** Dont me levay et vers eulx men alay RRa. 1201 **l'erbe** lerbete Ar; lerbeu Ra. **drue** dure Ar. 1202 **quant** que JK. 1203 **poy** pou C; pos E; peu RRa; pouch Ar; peuz St. 1205 **qui** quil PAr; car RRa. **cognut** conneust C. 1207 **En** Sen RRa. 1209 **prisié son appel a** prisa son appel la EJ; prisa son apel a K; prisoit cest appel la RRa; prisist son apel a Ar. 1210 **Qu'en abaiant** Quant albaiant C; Quant abayant EJK; Car en abaiant RRa; Quen appellant St. **chiennet m'approcha** chiennent mapprocha P; chenet maprocha J; chien si mapprocha RRa. 1211 **que ses dens** qua ma robe RRa; **a** en CSt. **a . . . acrocha** assez il atoucha RRa; ens ma robe ficha Ar. 1213 **de . . . son** de paour tout son RRa. 1214 **me** men CAr. 1215 **Pour** De EJK. **ce** *om* Pc. **qu'a sa** que tost sa Ar. **reportay** portay CRArRa. 1218 **Si** Et C. **toudis** tous jours Ar. **applanioye** applanoye P (−1); aplanissoie R. 1219 **je . . . estre** vinch la ou je Ar. 1221 **Mus n'esbahis** Mus esbahiz C; Mais nesbahis E; Muet ne esbay RRa. 1222 **Ai** Jai JK. **salué** saluee Pc. 1223 **com** comme ArSt. **soz** say JK. 1225 **sages fu** fu sage K. 1226 **Grans . . . drois** Grans bons et drois C; Beaux lons et droiz E; Grans homs et drois JK; Grant long et bel RRa. **beaus et gens** beaus gentilz P; grans et gros E; droit et gent RRa; beaus Pc; beau gent St. 1227 **apris et** apris est et RRa. 1228 **attendre** atetendre Ar. 1230 **volt entendre** voust entendre JK; voult tendre RRa; vaut entendre Ar; vault tendre St.

Car volentiers mis les eüsse en voie
De juge prendre
Tel qu'a jugier leurs fais peüst entendre,
Si souffissant qu'il n'y eüst qu'aprendre,
Et qu'aprez lui n'y eüst que reprendre.
Si m'avisay
Moult longuement, et puiz mon avis ay
Que jë iroie a eulz. Lors sanz delay
Je me levay et devers eulz alay
Tout le couvert
Parmi l'erbe qui estoit drue et vert. f. 83
Et quant je ving si prez d'eulz qu'en appert
Les poy veoir et tout a descouvert,
Le petit chien
Prist a glatir, qui ne me cognut rien,
Dont la dame qui moult savoit de bien
En tressailli—je m'en aperçu bien—
Si l'appella.
Mais moult petit prisié son appel a,
Qu'en abaiant le chiennet m'approcha,
Tant que ses dens a ma robe acrocha.
Si le happay,
Dont il lessa de paour son abay.
Mais en mon cuer forment me deportay,
Pour ce qu'a sa dame le reportay,
Pour avoir voie
Et achoison d'aler ou je vouloie;
Si que son poil toudis applanioye.
Mais quant je ving ou estre desiroie,
Je ne fui mie
Mus n'esbahis; ainçoiz a chiere lie
Ai salué toute la compaignie,
Si com faire le soz de ma partie.
Li chevaliers
Qui sages fu, courtois, et beaux parliers,
Grans, longs, et drois, beaus et gens et legiers,
Et d'onneur faire apris et coustumiers,
Sanz plus attendre,
Courtoisement me vint mon salu rendre.
Et la dame ou Nature volt entendre,

Nature used her greatest art, so that her beauty surpassed all comprehension, moved elegantly, evenly, and gracefully in my direction; her demeanor was very gracious, and her bearing was unassuming, sweet, and perfect; her hair was blond, her eyes laughing, grayer than any falcon's; her body was comely, graceful, fair and slender, more lithe than any sparrowhawk. Her eyes were perfectly spaced, her manner and greeting proper; and her clothing and fair adornments were tasteful and of the very best. She was whiter than snow on the branch, wise, faithful, courteous, and open-hearted, and so perfect in every aspect that she was more beautiful in bearing constancy than beauty itself. In her there was no haughtiness, no cruelty, nor anything contrary to love. And though her bright face was tearful, it was adorned with radiant color and a soft gentleness.

The lady called me to her and then asked and inquired politely whence I came there. And I, who was eager to obey her, told and recounted to her the truth from beginning to end: how I had come there and where I'd been while they told of their misfortunes. Then in a lighthearted way the knight whispered: "I think he heard our whole discussion."

And I told him: "Sir, have no doubt that I attentively and willingly

1231 **Si . . . puet** Si con ne pot PE; Si con quon ne peut St. **sa** si RRa; le Ar. 1233 **a trait** attrait C. 1235 **Et le maintieng** Et si le tiens RRa. **humble doux** dous et humble C; doulx humble RArRaSt. 1236 **Et** Les St. 1237 **Les yeux** Li oeil C; Nes yex Ar. **vairs que nulz** vrais que uns Ar. 1238 **Et son corps** Son corps JK. **joins gentilz** joins (gentilz *om*) E; joint droit gentil JK. 1239 **appers** espers CJK; apres Ar. 1240 **s'ot** eust RRa. 1242 **atour** attrait C; grant attour St. **gent** doulz C. 1243 **Qui** Si RRa. **point de pareil** pas de paroel Ar; point d'orgueil St. 1245 **noif** noiz E; fleur RRa. 1246 **et** *om* C. 1247 **en** de RRa. 1249 **Estoit assez** Assez estoit RArPcRaSt. **que beauté** que clarte EJK; que bonte RRa. 1252–54 *om* JK. 1253 **Fu . . . forment** Fu moult souvent CSt; Estoit forment E. 1255 **Et . . . douçour** De fine doucour E; Mais de fine coulour RRa; Et de douceur cuer St. **estoit paree** estoit elle paree Ar. 1256 **Et** Si Ra. 1257 **m'enquist et demanda** menquist et emparla C; enquist et demanda JK; menquist et apparla RPcRa; menquist et appella St. 1258 **sagement** doucement St. 1259 **Et . . . fui** Et qui fui E. **d'oïr** doirir K; droit RRa. 1262 **la** je E. **j'avoie** avoie C. 1263 **En** Et CJKAr. **meschief** mestier Ar. 1266 **oÿ tous** ouy icy tous RRa. 1267 **n'en** ne EJKRRa. 1268 **Que voirement** Car vraiement C; Que vraiement EJKRArRa. 1269 **Les . . . oïs** Les aie oys EArSt; Ouy les aye RRa. **ententivement** entierement RRa. 1270 **Et volentiers** Suis voulentis RRa.

Si c'on ne puet sa grant beauté comprendre,
Vers moy se trait
Moult belement, doucement, et a trait; f. 83v
Car elle avoit moult gracïeux attrait
Et le maintieng humble, doux, et parfait,
Et cheveus blons,
Les yeux rians, plus vairs que nulz faucons;
Et son corps fu gens, joins, gentilz, et longs,
Et plus appers que nulz esmerillons.
Et s'ot l'entr'oel
Grandet a point, maniere et douz acueil;
Mais son atour et son gent appareil
Qui simples fu n'avoit point de pareil.
Et si fu blanche
Plus que la noif, quant elle est sur la branche,
Sage, loyal, courtoise, et de cuer franche,
Et si parfaite en toute contenance
Qu'en loyauté
Estoit assez plus belle que beauté;
N'en li n'avoit orgueil ne cruauté,
Ne rien qui fust contraire a amisté.
Mais esplouree
Fu moult forment sa face coulouree;
Et nonpourquant de couleur esmeree
Et de fine douçour estoit paree.
Si m'appella
La dame, et puiz m'enquist et demanda
Moult sagement dont je venoie la.
Et je qui fui desirans d'oïr la,
La verité
De chief en chief li ai dit et compté:
Comment la ving et ou j'avoie esté,
En tant qu'il ont leur meschief racompté.
Lors dist en bas
Li chevaliers par maniere de gas: f. 84
"Je croy qu'il ait oÿ tous noz debas."
Et je li diz: "Sire, n'en doubtez pas,
Que voirement
Les ai je oïs moult ententivement
Et volentiers; mez n'aiez pensement

heard it; but don't be concerned that I've found anything but good in all you've said. In truth I'd come along a grassy path above the stream into this orchard, where I was enjoying myself listening to the singing of the birds. Having thus entered here, sir, I noticed you, and I also saw my lady approaching from the other side. Now I'll tell you what I did: I sought out the thickest part of the wood and I hid myself there for fear of disturbing you; from there I listened to your happiness and troubles from start to finish.

"Now I believe that you would like to have judged whose misfortunes are the more painful: yours or my lady's, whose head is bowed. Yet you did not wish to choose the judge, nor did my lady; on that account I came advisedly to suggest the name of a very praiseworthy knight; for neither on this side of the sea nor on the other is there a nobler, more open, and less bitter heart; he surpasses Alexander in generosity and Hector in valor. He is the pillar of all gentility; he is not a slave to his wealth, but seeks only honor from his worldly goods, and is happier when he can say 'It's yours!' than is a miser to receive from his goods. He loves God, the Church, and Loyalty, and is so equitable that he is called 'The Sword of Justice.' To his friends he is unassuming, meek, and full of generosity; to his enemies, proud and fearsome. In

1271 **g'y pense** je pense J; jaie pense RRa; jou y pense Ar. **fors bien car** que bien quant E; que bien et JK. 1273 **Sur .i. ruissel** En ce vergier RRa; Soubz ung ruissel ArSt. 1274 **En ce vergier** Sur ung ruissel RRa. 1275 **Es** Aux RRaSt. **que . . . escoutoie** canter que jescoutoye Ar. 1277 **Y fui** Y sui E; Je suis RRa. 1279 **comment je me** comme je men RRa. 1280 **Je** Et JK. 1281 **Le** Ou RRa. **bruel si m'y** breul si me E; boys je me RRa. 1282 **ennuy moult me** anui me JK; anui je me Ar. 1283 **biens . . . mauls** maulz et vos biens Ar. 1285 **Or** Si EJK; Lors Ar. 1286 **Et ma dame** Et de ma dame PCRRa (+1); Et du ma dame EJK. **tient** tien J; tint Ar. **son** le RRa. 1287 **Du sien** *om* C; Des .ii. EJK; Savez des doulx ArRa. **volentiers** vontiers J. 1289 **Si** Se RRaSt. **voulez** voustes JK. 1290 **Vostre** Voz St. 1291 **venuz sui** venus si J; suis venus St. **aviseement** a advisement E. 1293 **amer** loer EJKRRa. 1294 **deça . . . mer** de ca la mer non pas de la la mer RRa. 1295 **n'a . . . d'amer** ne mainz amer C; ne moins damer E; et sans amer JK; ni avint damer RRa; na mains amer St. 1298 **li estocs** lestoc C; li escoz JK; lestour R. 1299 **n'il ne vit** Il ne vint RRa. **com** comme RRa; que Ar. **a** en CE. 1301 **que** qua C. **tout le bien** tout bien PCPc (−1); tous biens RArRaSt. 1302 **est** sest ArPcSt. 1303 **Qu'uns** Onques RRa. **du** le RRaSt. 1305 **et . . . justice** et bien justise C; quoy que non disce E; bien et justice RRa. 1306 *om* P, *which includes after line* 1307: Nil ne vaurroit mesprendre en nulle guise. **C'on** Car on RRa. 1307 **Humbles . . . plain** Humble doulx et tout plain RRa. 1308 **A** Vers P. 1309 **Fiers** Fel C.

Que g'y pense fors bien. Car vraiement
Venuz estoie
Sur .i. ruissel, par une herbue voie,
En ce vergier ou je me delitoie
Es oyseillons que chanter escoutoie.
Et quant ainsi
Y fui venuz, sire, je vous choisi,
Et d'autre part ma dame venir vi.
Si vous dirai comment je me chevi:
Je regardai
Le plus fueillu du bruel; si m'y boutay,
Car de vous faire ennuy moult me doubtay;
Et la voz biens et voz mauls escoutay
De chief en chief.
Or m'est avis que de vostre meschief,
Et ma dame qui tient enclin son chief
Du sien, sariez volentiers le plus grief
Par jugement.
Si ne voulez prendre premierement
Vostre juge, ne ma dame ensement;
Pour ce venuz sui aviseement
Pour vous nommer
Un chevalier qui moult fait a amer;
Car deça mer n'a pas, ne dela mer,
Plus gentil cuer, plus franc, n'a mains d'amer;
Car de larguece
Passe Alexandre et Hector de proece. f. 84v
C'est li estocs de toute gentillece,
N'il ne vit pas com serfs a sa richece,
Ainz ne veelt rien
Fors que l'onneur de tout le bien terrien,
Et est plus liez quant il puet dire: 'Tien'
Qu'uns couvoiteus n'est de prendre du sien.
Dieu et l'eglise
Et loyauté aime, et si bien justice
C'on le claime l'Espee de justice.
Humbles et doux est et plain de franchise
A ses amis,
Fiers et cruels contre ses ennemis.
Et, a briefs mos, de senz, d'onneur, de pris

short, in the opinion of all he always carries off the prize for wisdom, honor, and glory wherever he goes. And if it happens that he overcome his enemy, Nature and his good heart guide him to be merciful to him. He's a noble companion, for Valor carries his sword everywhere, Bravery guides and encourages him, and Generosity opens to him the door of every heart. Those who are good (I exclude no one), he treats like brothers and sisters, rich, poor, and in between, all alike. And of Love, sir, he knows all the thrusts and devices—the good, the ill, the complaints, and the tears—better than Ovid, who knew all Love's devices. Tell me whether or not you'd like to know his name, which is so fair and illustrious."

"Indeed, my friend, we urge you to reveal it to us, for I believe there has never been, nor ever will be, another as perfect in every respect, both in words and deeds, as he."

"Sir, his battle cry is Lembourc, and he's King of Bohemia, son of Henry the good king of Germany, who by dint of arms, in spite of all opposition, was crowned emperor in Rome, together with his mother. Therefore if he is good, it's only natural: it comes to him from both his father and his mother. Thus, fair sir, it would be well for you to choose such a judge, who'll be able to show and demonstrate which of you suffers more tribulation; I urge you to take him."

The knight replied sagaciously: "I believe God has brought you

1311 **Emporte adez** Emporte apres RRa; Et porte adez St. **au dit** aud Pc. 1312 **Quel** Quelque E. **part** pert Ra. 1314 **A son dessous** Et saudessus RRa. 1315 **Et** En E. **li** lie J. 1317 **s'espee** son espee R. 1318 **Hardiece le conduit** Hardiesse la conduist EJKRRa; Et hardieche le conduit Ar; Et hardiesse lui deprie St. 1320 **De** A RRa. 1321 **fuers** heurs EJK; hors RRa; hoers Ar. 1322 **Avec . . . com** Avec li (lui) sont com CEJK; Avecques eulx est comme R. **sont** *om* RPcRaSt. 1323 **petis moiens** moyens loyaux EJK; moiens Pc. **et** *om* EPc. **a** *om* RRa. 1324 **et** est RRaSt. 1325 **il** *om* Pc. **tous** *om* CRRaSt. **les estours** et les tours PCEJKRArRa; et estours St. 1326 **les . . . plours** et les plaintes et plours RRa; les plaintes les concours St. 1329 **bons** beaux EJK. **et de noble** et noble de St. 1331 **du** de JRRa. **vous** te Ar. 1333 **ne . . . n'iert** ne fust que mourust RRa. 1334 **soit** fust EJK. **en tous** *repeated* C, *but first is lightly crossed through.* 1335 **cilz** cestui RRa; celui St. **par . . . par** en diz et en JK. 1336 **s'enseigne** a son signe RRa. 1337 **et . . . de** et en joye de RRa. **Behaigne** brehengne C. 1338 **Filz de** Folz de RRa; Fieulz fu Ar. 1339 **qui . . . plaigne** qui qui sen plaigne CP; conquist Champaigne RRa. 1340 **Comme emperere** Comme emperiere JKR; Cun empereur St. 1341 **avec** avant JK. 1342 **s'il** cilz E; il J; cil K. **bons** bon chief RRa. **appere** y pere EJKSt; sapere RRa. 1343 **de . . . pere** de pere et de mere CEJKRArRaSt. 1345 **Un tel juge** Tel juge vous JK. 1346 **vous . . . bien** bien saroit vous JK. **moustrer** jugier Ar. 1347 **Li quielx** Siques RRa. **plus de** plus grief Ar. 1349 **respondi** respond RRa. 1350 **dieus** *om* RRaAr. **vous** nous P. **a ci amenez** cy ladivenez RRa.

Emporte adez au dit des bons le pris,
Quel part qu'il viegne.
Et s'il avient que son ennemi tiegne
A son dessous, Nature li enseigne
Et son bon cuer que pitié li en preigne.
C'est noble sorte,
Car Proece partout s'espee porte,
Hardiece le conduit et ennorte,
Et Larguece si li oevre la porte
De tous les cuers.
A ceus qui sont bon (je n'en met nulz fuers),
Avec eulz est com sont freres et suers,
Grans et petis, moiens, et a tous fuers.
Sire, et d'Amours
Cognoist il tous les assaus, les estours,
Les biens, les mals, les plaintes, et les plours
Mieux qu'Ovides, qui en sot tous les tours.
Et se son nom,
Qui tant est bons et de noble renom, f. 85
Voulez savoir, dites le moy, ou non."
"Certes, amis, du savoir vous prion,
Car onques mais,
Si com je croy, ne fu, ne n'iert jamais
Homme qui soit en tous cas si parfais,
Comme cilz est, et par diz et par faiz."
"Sire, s'enseigne
Crie Lembourc, et est roys de Behaigne,
Filz de Henri, le bon roy d'Alemaigne,
Qui par force d'armes, qui que s'en plaigne,
Comme emperere
Fu couronnez a Romme avec sa mere.
Dont s'il est bons, c'est raison qu'il appere:
Car il le doit et de mere et de pere.
Si que, beau sire,
Un tel juge seroit bons a eslire
Qui vous saroit bien moustrer et descripre
Li quielx de vous sueffre plus de martire;
Si le prenez."
Li chevaliers respondi com senez:
"Je croy que Dieus vous a ci amenez."

here." And added: "My lady, if you accept him as judge, I'm in agreement."

And the lady replied without quarrel: "Sir, I've heard so much good said of the king, who is so wise, brave, and well-attended, that I accept him."

"Many thanks, my lady. We are now of one accord. I pray God to comfort the good king, and that he bring us soon to a safe harbor and that we can speak with him wherever we must go."

I replied: "I can easily show you where he is and, if you please, guide you there. I'm sure of the place, because in truth I dined yesterday and drank with his people in Durbuy castle. He's still there and will not leave today; it's not far off, not even a half league, and well within shouting distance."

The knight urged the lady to go there without further delay. She said: "I've no wish to do otherwise, but I don't know which path to take."

I said: "My lady, I'll be glad to show you. Come along, I'll lead and you come after."

I eagerly set off on the path, and when they saw Durbuy nearby, they stopped and marvelled at the sight of it, for they said they'd never in their lives seen such a beautiful and stately castle. Undoubtedly it was most beautiful and very pleasant, fine and fair and easy to defend. For even if the kings of Germany or France laid siege before it, those inside would never be prevented from venturing back and forth into the

1351 **Et . . . s'a** Et dist ma dame sa Ar; Puiz dame se a St. 1354 **tant oy** jay ouy RRa. **dire de bien** dire trestant de bien RRa; de bien dire ArPc; bien dire de ce St. **du** *om* St. 1355 **Tant** Que tant RRa. **preux et** et pleins EJK; et preus et Ar. **bon** bel P. 1357 **a accort** dun accort JK; en acort RRaSt; nous dacort Ar. 1358 **pri** prit St. 1359 **Et . . . maint** Et qui nous maint PPcRa; Puissons trouver St. 1361 **a li** au roy RRa. **ou il** ou si il Ar; ou Pc. 1362 **bien vous sçay** dieu vous sai C; je vous vueil JK; bien scaray RRa. 1363 **est . . . mener** est et si vous plaist m. PPcRa; est sil vous plaist et m. C. 1364 **Certains en** Avecques lui St. 1365 **mengay** meinge JK. **hier** iert Pc. **et buy** o lui EJKRRa; et hui CArSt. 1366 **ses genz** sa gent E. **ou** en PAr; au CSt. **durbuy** dambury R. 1367 **Et il** Et si RRa; Car il St. **ne** et JKSt. 1370 **de . . . quart** le quart de chi Ar. **huchie** haschie E; archie JK. 1371 **d'aler la dame** la dame daler E; daler alors la dame RRa. **prie** emprie Pc. 1372 **Sanz plus** Et sans E; plus *om* R. 1373 **La dame** Et elle EJK. **quier** puis RRa; fier Ar. 1375 **Je** Et je Ar; Ja Pc. **bien le** bien la CEJKR; je le St. 1376 **adez** apres R. 1377 **G'irai** Siray JK. **venrez** yres E. 1378 **Si qu'au** Siques au RRa. **me mis** meuvent JK; menrez St. **engrez** empes J; enpriz K; cuips (?) St. 1379 **Et quant** Et puis quant RRa. **durbuy . . . veü** il ont durbui veü C; ilz ont veu dambury RRa; il ont veu durbui ArSt. **de prez** de bien pres RRa. 1381 *This line follows 1383 in* St. **du** de le RRa. **se merveilloient** sesmerveilloient CEArSt. 1382 **mes** *om* C. **n'avoient** naient J. 1383 **bel** noble RRa. **ce** se RRaAr. 1385 **ert** est CRArRaSt. **fort** beaus PEJK. **tres** moult JKRRa. **plaisance** poissance CAr. 1386 *om* JK. **Beaus** Gays E. **poy de deffense** tres grant plaisanche Ar; tres grant deffence St. 1387 **li roy** les roys ESt. **et** ou JKRRa. 1389 **Cil de dedens** Ycil dedens EJK; Cil dedens PCAr (−1). **ce** riens JK. **ne lairoient** nen brairoient RRa. 1390 **hors et enz** ens et hors St. **s'il vouloient** si vauloient RPcRa.

Et dit: "Dame, s'a juge le tenez,
Je m'y ottroy."
Et la dame respondi sanz desroy:
"Sire, tant oy dire de bien du roy,
Tant est sages, preux, et de bon arroy,
Que je l'acort."
"Grans mercis, dame; or sommes a accort.
Si pri a Dieu que le bon roy confort
Et qu'il nous maint temprement a bon port,
Si que parler
Puissons a li, ou il nous faut aler." f. 85v
Je respondi: "Bien vous sçay assener
La ou il est et, s'il vous plaist, mener.
Certains en sui,
Car vraiement, je mengay hier et buy
Avec ses genz ou chastel de Durbuy.
Et il y est, ne n'en partira huy;
Ne ce n'est mie
Loing, qu'il n'y a ne lieue ne demie,
Non pas de ci le quart d'une huchie."
Li chevaliers d'aler la dame prie
Sanz plus attendre.
La dame dit: "Je ne m'en quier deffendre,
Mais je ne sçay quel part la voye prendre."
Je diz: "Dame, bien le vous voeil aprendre.
Venez adez,
G'irai devant et vous venrez aprez."
Si qu'au chemin me mis d'aler engrez.
Et quant Durbuy orent veü de prez,
Si s'arrestoient
Et du veoir forment se merveilloient,
Car onques mes en leurs vies n'avoient
Veü si bel, ne si gent, ce disoient.
Et, sanz doubtance,
Il ert moult fort et de tres grant plaisance,
Beaus et jolis et de poy de deffense.
Car se li roy d'Alemaigne et de France
Devant estoient,
Cil de dedens ja pour ce ne lairoient
Qu'il n'alassent hors et enz, s'il vouloient,

surrounding countryside, if they wished, as often as required. It is built upon a rock in a valley, surrounded by mighty, rushing, deep, broad, and swift water; and the orchards around it are so beautiful that to judge properly one could not hope for finer. There is such a crowd of birds that day and night the valley resounds with their fuss; the water likewise gently babbles there, so that one cannot hear a more pleasant sound. Next there are great rocks all around, not near the castle, but far enough from it that no lance, battle machine, or arrow can ever reach it. And the building upon the rock is so superb that none more splendid has ever been seen; it has no imperfection. The well is enclosed within the walls; it springs pure, clear, and fresh from the rock, cold as ice and sweeter than the Seine. The pool into which it flows is sculpted from fine variegated marble, and is more beautiful that any since the time of Abel. The meadow along the riverbank is broad, sweeping, and vast, where one finds a variety of plants.

But I must return to my subject: after they had seen the palace, I spoke to them, saying: "It's time to go there. Let's proceed, for we're accomplishing nothing here."

We continued along the way and crossed the bridge, not stopping

1391 **qu'a besoignier** que mestier en EJK. 1393 **enmi une valee** enmi valee C; au mi une valee E. 1394 **tout** *repeated* E. **environnee** avironnee PAr. 1395 **Grande bruiant** Grande et bruiant ArSt. **roide** ronde C; longue EJK. 1396 **li** le CRRa. 1397 **Sont** Est CRRa; Estoyent Ar. **entour** *om* Ar. **si bel** *om* E. **qu'a** a C. 1398 **On** Quon C. **plus** si Ar. 1399 **y a** si a RRa. 1400 **et** ne JK. 1401 **retentist** retantir E. 1402 **seriement** serreement P; souefvement C. **y** si E. 1403 **que on** com Ar. **oïr** estre en C; avoir Ar. 1406 **Ainz** Mais RRa. **sont** *repeated* Ra. **loing** loig J. **du chastel** du noble chastel St. **qu'il n'est** qui nest JK; quil ne E. **fers** feu RRa; sez St. 1407 **Engins** Nengin C. **qui** que St. **gestast** treist E; traist J; truist K. 1409 **Sur . . . est** A sur la roche et E; Est sus la roche RRa; Siet sur la roche St. **c'onques mes hom** conques hom EJK. 1410 **autre . . . belle** autre de si belle E; nulle aultre de si belle Ar; autre de plus noble R. 1411 **Car . . . a** Et si ne veis E; Et si ny a JK; Plaine dartillerie RRa; Car ni a Ar. **nisune meffaçon** une male fasson E; nes une mal facon JK; de carreaulx environ RRa. 1413 **court** tour CJKSt. 1414 *om* JK. **Ainz** Aincoys C; Mais Ra. **vive de roche** muee de roche E; de roche vive RRa; une yaue de roche Ar. 1415 **com glace** comme glacon RRa; que glache Ar. 1417 *om* JK. **chiet** siet E. **taillié a** taillies au Ar; taille a St. 1418 **fin . . . bis** fin blanc et vif C; fin blanc bis E; fu blanc et bis JK; fin blanc (et bis *om*) RRa; bis blanc et fin Ar; bis fin et fort St. 1419 **tels** puis JK. 1421 **Est** Estoit Ar. **longue large** largue longe P; large longue RRa. 1422 **Ou on** Et lon E; Ou on y ArSt. **d'erbe mainte** herbes et de mainte RRa. 1423 **m'estuet** mestoit E; mesqueut RRa. 1425 **veü** veüe PRRa (+1). 1426 **si** *om* Ar. **de . . . est** deulx aler en RRa; il est daler St. 1427 **ci rien** riens ci K.

Toutes les fois qu'a besoignier aroient
  En la contree.
C'est une roche enmi une valee f. 86
Qui tout entour est d'yaue environnee,
Grande, bruiant, parfonde, roide, et lee;
  Et li vergier
Sont tout entour si bel, qu'a droit jugier
On ne porroit nuls plus beaus souhaidier.
Mais d'oiseillons y a si grant frapier
  Que jour et nuit
La valee retentist de leur bruit;
Et l'yaue aussi seriement y bruit,
Si que on ne puet oïr meillour deduit.
  Et puiz aprez
A grans roches tout entour, non pas prez,
Ainz sont si loing du chastel qu'il n'est fers,
Engins, në ars qui y gestast jamez.
  Mais la maison
Sur la roche est si bien c'onques mes hom
Ne vit autre de plus belle façon;
Car il n'y a nisune meffaçon.
  Et la fontaine
Est en la court, qui n'est mie vilaine,
Ainz est vive, de roche clere et saine,
Froide com glace et plus douce que Saine.
  Mais le vaissel
Ou elle chiet est taillié a chisel
D'un marbre fin, blanc et bis, et si bel
Que tels ne fu depuiz le temps Abel.
  Sur la riviere
Est la pree longue, large, et pleniere,
Ou on troeve d'erbe mainte maniere.
Mais revenir m'estuet a ma matiere:
  Quant la maison
Orent veü, je les mis a raison f. 86v
Et si leur diz: "De l'aler est saison.
Alon nous en, car ci rien ne faison."
  Si en alasmes
Tout le chemin et le pont trespassames,
Ne ça ne la nulle part n'arrestasmes

until we'd knocked upon the gate, which the gateman cordially and gladly opened. I, who came first and had knocked, was quite well-known there and spoke thus: "This knight and this lady here wish to speak to the king, if he's here."

The gateman replied at once that he was.

I said: "Friend, see if we can speak with him."

He said he'd go. As soon as he'd left us to go up, a handsome, noble, powerful, attractive, and joyful knight came to us. His name was Honor, and he knew more about it than anyone. Nor did he come to us alone; but keeping him company was a beautiful, gay, light-hearted lady who was named Lady Courtesy. This was evident, for as soon as she saw us she greeted us and welcomed us warmly. Honor did likewise, as was fitting. Then each of them courteously and with a smile, without ado, took one of the pair by the hand. Courtesy, I must tell you, in a gay and friendly manner accompanied the knight; and Honor was pleased to go with the lady. Then they began to converse among themselves; they walked along talking, led along up the marble staircase until they entered the good king's chamber.

And the good king, who was judicious in every respect, faithful,

1431 **qu'a** que J; quan K. **hurtasmes** entrasmes JK. 1432 **Mais** Et E. 1433 **de cuer** de gre E; et bien JK. 1435 **Et . . . yere** De laiens yere JK; Et du chastel estre RRa; Et de laiens estre ArPcSt. 1437 **Cils chevaliers** Chevalier chevalier RRa; Ce chevalier PcSt. **aussi** cy EJKSt. 1438 **Viennent** Veullent JK. 1439 **li portiers** cil portiers JK; adont le portier RRa. **me** si RRa. 1440 **Qu'il y** Qui il C. 1441 **se on** sil Ar. 1442 **li** nous St. 1443 **ainsi** aussi C. **que** com EJKPc. **se partoit** departoit Ar. 1445 **beaus et genz** biaus gens C; bel gent RRa; biaulz et grans Ar. **et corsus** et corporuz RRa. 1446 **Jolis et gaiz** Jolis et gens Ar; Jeune et joly St. **en** si RRa. **a nous** avant JK. 1447 **ot** eust RRa. **s'en sot** cens sot JK; sens eust RRa. 1448 **N'il** Il St. **vint** vient RRa. 1449 **Tous . . . nous** A nous tous seulz JK. **ainz** mais RRa. 1450 **belle gaie** gaie et belle C; belle et gaie EAr. 1451 **Si ot** Si eust RRa; Il ot St. 1453 **aussi** ainssi JK. **qu'elle** que il RRa. **apparçut** apparceust RRa. 1454 **puiz** moult EJK. 1455 **si com** ainsi com EJK; comme RRa; si que Ar. **faire le dubt**faire dut EJK; faire le deust RRa. 1456 **andoy** eulz doi C; au doy (*sic*) EArRa; cil doy St. 1457 **riant** sourriant RRa. 1458 **Prisrent** Print RRa. **l'un des .ii.** lun des deulz C; de nous RRa; ambe deus Ar; lun de nous St. 1459 **ainsi com** aussi com C; ainsi que Ar. *For this line,* RRa *substitute*: Puis apres sans nul aultre deloy. 1461 **Acompaigna** Acompaigne Ar. 1462 **volt** vault ArSt. **compaignier** acompaignier ERArPcRaSt. 1463 **a desraisnier** au desrenier K; a assembler RRa. 1464 **Si** Et RRa. 1465 **il** chil Ar. 1466 **qu'il** qui RRa; ou ilz St. 1467 **qu'en** que Ar. **s'en entrerent** se monterent C; sen alerent St. **au** du Ra. 1468–69 *inverted in* St. 1469 **Qui** Et St. **sages** liberaux St. **en tous endrois** en moult dendroiz RRa; et adroiz St. 1470 **vaillans liberaux** vaillant et liberal RRa; vaillans sages St. **et adrois** a droit RRa; en tous endroiz St.

Jusques a tant qu'a la porte hurtasmes.
Mais li portiers
La porte ouvri de cuer et volentiers.
Je qui hurtay et qui fui li premiers
Et de leans yere assez coustumiers
Parlay ainsi:
"Cils chevaliers et ceste dame aussi
Viennent parler au roy, s'il est ici."
Et li portiers tantost me respondi
Qu'il y estoit.
Je diz: "Amis, pren garde se on porroit
Parler a li." Et il dist qu'il iroit.
Mais tout ainsi que de nous se partoit
Pour aler sus,
Uns chevaliers, beaus, et genz, et corsus,
Jolis, et gais, en est a nous venus;
Honneur ot nom, et s'en sot plus que nulz.
N'il ne vint mie
Tous seulz a nous, ainz li fist compaignie
Une dame belle, gaie, et jolie;
Si ot a nom la dame Courtoisie.
Bien y parut,
Car aussi tost qu'elle nous apparçut,
Nous salua, et puiz bel nous reçupt.
Si fist Honneur, si com faire le dubt.
Adonc andoy
Courtoisement, en riant, sanz effroy, f. 87
Prisrent chascun l'un des .ii. par le doy.
Mais Courtoisie, ainsi com dire doy,
Le chevalier
Acompaigna lïement, sanz dangier,
Et Honneur volt la dame compaignier.
Lors se prinsrent ensemble a desraisnier;
Si s'en alerent,
Tout en parlant, la ou il les menerent,
Par les degrez de marbre qu'il monterent,
Tant qu'en la chambre au bon roy s'en entrerent.
Et li bons roys,
Qui moult estoit sages en tous endrois,
Loyaulz, vaillans, liberaux, et adrois,

brave, generous, and proficient, and gentle, unassuming, and courteous to all, was seated in great joy upon a silken carpet, and a clerk, whom I cannot name, was reading to him from the Battle of Troy. Bravery and her daughter Valor accompanied him, and he lightly held the hand of Generosity, a lady of exceeding gentility. Also present were Wealth, Love, Beauty, Loyalty, and Happiness, Desire, Thought, Will, and Nobility, Sincerity, Honor, Courtesy, and Youth. These sixteen never left the king's company: God and Nature had granted them to him at his birth, and therefore they all served him; it was a special blessing. And should any one do anything in which another might find harm, Reason was there to smooth over the misdeed. Thus reigned the noble king.

When he saw the lady, he arose and took her by the hand, for Courtesy had taught him to do so. Next he took the knight's hand, praising him greatly in his heart, and then he courteously asked them whence they came there, and inquired about their concerns, which greatly interested him.

The knight requested that the lady explain, but she said she wouldn't and that instead it would be more suitable for him to do so. He replied then that he would tell the king everything, just as they'd discussed it, from start to finish.

"Sir," he said, "near here is a green and blooming garden, filled

1471 **doux humbles** liez humbles C; humble doulx RRa. 1472 **En** A EJK; Eust RRa; Et Ar. 1473 **.i.** les EJK. 1474 **S'i ot** Et ot PC; Si eust R. **ne** bien Ar. 1475 **li** *om* R. **la bataille** les batailles Ar. 1477 **Le compaignoit** Lacompaignoit CERSt. 1478 **tint** tien R; tient Ra. **par la** en sa C; par le Ar. 1482 *om* E, *which adds after* 1483: Et puis raison qui de tous fu maistresse. 1483 **courtoisie et joinece** courtoisie jeunesce JKR; courtoisie et jovenche Ar; fut avecques jeunesce St. 1484 **Cil** Ses Pc. 1485 **Avec** Avecques Ra. **n'onques** ne point C. 1487 **qu'il** que C. 1488–91 *om* E. 1488 **grant grace** grace grant grace RRa. 1489 **ne** ou P. 1491 **le . . . efface** le meffait defface RRa; la maison efface St. 1492 **se sist** se fist CRRa; le fist Ar. 1493 **dame vit** dame si vit RRa. 1494 **Il** Si JKRRa. **la main la** le main le Ar. 1495 *om* RRa. 1497 **et** car St. **le prisa** les prisa ERRa. 1498 *om* RRa. **son cuer** sa cambre Ar. **leur** li C. **demanda** demande P. 1499 **venoient** venoit C. 1500 **Et** Si PcRa. 1501 **estre** estat ERRa. **qui** et CAr. **li abelist** li embelist CRRa; leur abelist JKRa. 1503 **Qu'elle li vousist** Que vausist ArPcSt. **et el li dist** et elle li dist PCE (+1); et puis elle lui dist RRa; et elle li a dist Ar; et elle dist PcSt. 1505 **Ainçoiz li dist** Ainçoys dist elle C; Ainçois deist EArPcSt; Ainçois dist JK; Mais si lui dist RRa. **que** quar E. **mieux li afferoit** mieulx il lui seoit RRa. 1506 **qu'il li** que il CSt; qui li JKPc; que tresbien lui RRa. 1507 **estoit** aloit Ar. 1508 **Jusqu'en** Jusques a RRa; Dusqua Ar; Jusqua Pc. 1509 **Sire . . . a** Le roy a icy pres RRa. 1510 **flory** foillu EJKRArRa. **grant tintin** grant tutin CE; grant hutin JKPc; maint hutin RRa.

Et envers tous doux, humbles, et courtois,
En moult grant joye
Estoit assis sur .i. tapis de soye;
S'i ot .i. clerc que nommer ne saroye
Qui li lisoit la bataille de Troye.
Mais Hardiece
Le compaignoit, et sa fille Proece,
Et doucement tint par la main Larguece,
Une dame de moult grant gentillece.
S'y fu Richece,
Amours, Beauté, Loyauté, et Leece,
Desir, Penser, Volenté, et Noblece,
Franchise, Honneur, Courtoisie, et Joinece.
Cil .xvi. estoient
Avec le roy, n'onques ne s'en partoient:
Dieus et Nature ottroié li avoient
Des qu'il fu nez; pour ce tous le servoient;
C'estoit grant grace.
Et s'il y a nulz ne nulle qui face f. 87v
Chose dont nulz puist dire qu'il mefface,
Raison y est qui le meffait efface.
Ainsi se sist
Li gentilz roys. Et quant la dame vit,
Il se leva, et par la main la prist,
Car Courtoisie a faire li aprist.
Aprez pris a
Le chevalier, et forment le prisa
Dedens son cuer, et puiz leur demanda
Moult sagement dont il venoient la,
Et leur enquist
De leur estre qui moult li abelist.
Li chevaliers a la dame requist
Qu'elle li vousist dire; et el li dist
Que non feroit,
Ainçoiz li dist que mieux li afferoit.
Il respondi adonc qu'il li diroit
De chief en chief tout ainsi qu'il estoit,
Jusqu'en la fin.
["S]ire," dit il, "ci prez a .i. jardin
Vert et flory, ou il a grant tintin

with the singing of nightingales; I went there this morning to listen to their beautiful service and their merry singing, although my heart, which nothing can console, could take little pleasure in them. Nonetheless, there I was by chance, filled and overwhelmed by the sufferings which love has sent me, when I saw this lady who's here with me approaching along a grassy, green, and narrow path. She seemed to me disconsolate, so I set off at once across the thick grass in her direction and, when I'd come near, I greeted her; but she answered not a word, which surprised me, nor did she acknowledge me, either by a glance or her manner. Wondering the reason for this, I spoke gently: 'Dear sweet lady, why do you not want to hear what I say?' I caught her by a tuck of her skirt; she was startled, and her beautiful face blushed. She replied at once, and earnestly begged my pardon, for she had been lost in thought. I asked her why her heart was so dispirited. In the end I so spoke and reasoned with her that she told me all I wished to know, on condition that I would pledge and swear on my word of honor to tell her my troubles after she had unburdened herself.

"She told me that she had had a true friend who loved her faithfully,

1511 **ving . . . matin** ving huy matin EJK; y vint huy matin Ra. 1513 **beau** boin Ar. 1514 **Comment** Combien PSt; Comme RRa. **poy se peüst** penser peut RRa; peu si peust PcSt. **deporter** deliter EJK. 1515 **que** qui R. **porroit** pooit J; povoit KRRa. 1516 **Mais** Et E. 1517 **y** *om* K. 1518 **et pensifs** de pensiz R. **maulx** biens JK. **m'envoie** envoie Ar. 1520 **Verde** Vert EJK. 1521 **qu'avec** quavant C; qui est o EJK; qui o RRa. **moy** *om* Ar. 1523 **Si que** Et lors RRa. **pris . . . l'erbe** tout parmi lerbette C; tout parmi lerbe E; tout par tout lerbe JK; parmy lerbete RRa; droit parmi lerbe St. 1524 **Mon . . . ay** Mon adrecay PC; Men adrecay EJKRRaSt. 1525 *This line follows* 1527 *in* JK. **droit vers** envers EJK; droit a St. **li adreçay** elle prins ay RRa. 1526 **fui** sui Ar. **prez je la** prez je le P; pres lors je la RRa; pres moult bien le Ar. 1527 **dist** di E. **dont . . . merveillay** dont je mesmerveillay E; tous men esmervillay Ar. 1528–31 *om* St. 1529 **ne d'oeil** ne doel E; de oeil JK; de diex Ar. 1530 **merveilliez** merveilleux EJRArRa. **pour . . . yere** pour quoy chiere C; de la chiere RRa; pour chiere Ar. 1531 **bellement** humblement EJK. 1533 **entendre** respondre RArPcRaSt. 1534 **tirai** tray JK; tire R. 1535 **S'en tressailli** Dont la dame P; Si tressaillit RRa. **dont sa belle** qui a clere P; sa tres belle JKAr. 1537 **Si respondi** Lors respond RRa; Lors respondit St. 1538–39 *inverted in* RRa. 1538 **durement** doucement EJKRRa. 1539 **De** Pour EJK. **son . . . a** sien penser en RRa. 1541 **ainsi** si fort ArSt. 1542 **fis** fie Pc. 1543 **tout ce que** che pour quoy Ar. **je li quis** li requis P; je lui enquis RSt. 1544 **si** foy RRa. 1545 **Que** Car RRa. **plevi** pluvy J. 1546 *om* E, *which adds after* 1547: Sanz aler contre et je li ay promis. **elle . . . parler** selle avoit son penser St. **assouvi** affeni C; promi E. 1547 **penser** pense Ar. 1548 **Et** Lors P; Si CPc; Se Ar.

De rousignols; s'y ving huy au matin,
Pour escouter
Leur beau service et leur joli chanter,
Comment que poy se peüst deporter
Mon cuer que riens ne porroit conforter.
Mais toutevoie
Ainsi venus d'aventure y estoie,
Plains et pensifs des maulx qu'Amours m'envoie.
Si vi venir par une estroite voie
Verde et herbue
Ceste dame qu'avec moy est venue. f. 88
Si me sembla de maniere esperdue,
Si que tantost pris parmi l'erbe drue
Mon adresse ay
Et mon chemin droit vers li adreçay,
Et quant je fui prez je la saluay;
Mais mot ne dist, dont je me merveillay,
Në onques chiere
Ne fist de moy, ne d'oeil ne de maniere.
Et je qui fui merveilliez pour quoy ce yere,
Diz bellement: 'Tres douce dame chiere,
Pour quel raison
Ne voulez vous entendre a ma raison?'
Et la tirai par le pan du giron;
S'en tressailli, dont sa belle façon
Coulour mua.
Si respondi, que plus n'y arresta,
Et durement envers moy s'excusa
De son penser a quoy elle musa.
Si li enquis
Pour quoy son cuer estoit ainsi pensis.
Finablement tant parlay et tant fis
Qu'elle me dist tout ce que je li quis,
Voire par si
Que par ma foy li juray et plevi,
Quant elle aroit son parler assouvi,
Que le penser li diroie de mi.
Et dist ainsi
Qu'elle souloit avoir loyal ami
Qui loyaument l'amoit, et elle li.

and she him. But Death has taken him from this world. And his valor, worthiness, wisdom, bravery, and honor—in all of which he was the flower, she said—made him the best of the best. For this reason she was deeply depressed and could not recover from it, and in her despondency she wept and lamented, so that her face was bathed in tears. Therefore she maintains that the sorrow she feels because of her beloved is more bitter than that which grips me.

"Yet, sir, I am obliged to maintain the contrary. I love faithfully in my heart and forever the most beautiful girl with the sweetest face that ever Nature could fashion, who once gave and relinquished to me her whole heart with all her love. She called me her beloved and affirmed she loved me above all others. Now it has happened, sir, that she no longer cares for me, but has abandoned me and taken a new lover. And, by my soul, I've not deserved it! Moreover, she gives and shares my rightful reward with him, and I can have no share nor portion: this, sir, is why my heart forsakes me. So I believe, weighing our arguments, that I am worse off than the lady, even though her beloved is dead—may he be with God in Heaven!

"Sir, this clerk who seems to me to be gay, merry, and clever was hidden in the park and ensconced in the thickest part of the green wood. When he had heard our whole discussion he came forward and

1551 *om* JK. 1553 **Le . . . senz** Le sens le pris St. **et** *om* CPc. 1554 **flour** or J; a or K; lour Ra; la flour St. 1555 **tout** *om* RRa. 1558 **le . . . plaignoit** plouroit et se plaignoit JK; se plouroit et plaignoit RRa. 1559 **vis** visaige RRa. 1561 **est plus grief** plus grieve est P; est plus grant RRa. 1562 **tient** vient Ar. 1563 **di . . . couvient** di que faire me couvient EJK; doy faire le mien comment RRa. 1565 **J'aim** Jamay J. **et sanz** sans riens RRa. 1566 **tres** *om* Ar. 1567 **encor** encore EK. **nature peüst** nature si peut RRa; peust nature Ar. 1569 **tout** *om* EAr. **tout et** et tout RRaSt. 1570 **Avec . . . son** Amant samour son P; Avec son cuer et C. **me clama** mappella RRa. 1571 *replaced in* RRa *by*: Et loyaulte me plevy et jura. 1573 **qu'elle que Ra. mez** plus R; jamais Ar. 1574 **Ainz** Maiz ERRaSt. **guerpi** laissie RRa. 1575 **m'ame** mon ame E. **pas** point St. 1577 **Mon** Bon C. **a li donne** donne a li ESt; lui donne JK. 1578 **n'en** ne RRa. **part ne hart** part ne quart RRa; hart ne part St. 1579 **ce** tout Ar. **pour quoy sire** sire pour quoy ER; dire pour quoy JK. 1581 **noz** mes C; ces EJK. **j'ay pis** je pris RRa; jay pris Ar; jay dit St. 1582 **la** ma RPcRaSt. **comment** combien RPcRa. 1583 **l'ait en paradis** li face mercis P; ait lame de lui St. 1584 **cilz** ce RPc; chieus Ar; cest St. 1585 **gais jolis** gais et jolis C; gens jolis JK; jolis gais Ar. **appers** espers J; espars K. 1586–87 *inverted in* C. 1586 **Se . . . jardin** Fu attapis ou jardin CRArPcRa; Fu el jardin tapiz St. 1587 **qui . . . vers** qui est ouvers C; quest tout vert RRa. 1588 **Si** Se Ar. 1589 **il ot** heut Ar. 1590 **Si** Et JK; Se Ar. **loa** compta RRa.

Mais la Mors l'a de ce siecle parti.
Et la valour,
Le pris, le senz, la proece, et l'onnour f. 88v
Qui fu en li, si com elle dist flour,
Le fist des bons estre tout le meillour.
Pour ce pensoit
Parfondement, neë onques ne cessoit,
Et en pensant, le plouroit et plaignoit,
Si que son vis en lermes se baignoit.
Pour ce maintient
Que la dolour est plus grief qui li vient
Pour son ami que celle qui me tient.
Sire, et je di, faire le me couvient,
Tout le contraire.
J'aim loyaument de cuer et sanz retraire
La plus tres belle et le plus douz viaire
C'onques encor Nature peüst faire,
Qui me donna
Jadiz son cuer tout, et habandonna
Avec s'amour. Son ami me clama,
Et par son dit sur tous autres m'ama.
Or est ainsi,
Sire, qu'elle n'a mez cure de mi,
Ainz m'a guerpi, et fait nouvel ami.
Et, par m'ame, pas ne l'ai deservi!
Et d'autre part,
Mon guerredon a li donne et depart,
Ne je n'en puiz avoir ne part ne hart:
C'est ce pour quoy, sire, le cuer me part.
Si m'est avis,
Consideré noz raisons, que j'ay pis
Que la dame, comment que ses amis
Soit trespassez. Dieux l'ait en Paradis!
Sire, et cilz clers
Qui me semble gais, jolis, et appers, f. 89
Se fu tapis ou jardin et couvers
Ou plus espez du brueil qui est tous vers.
Si sailli hors,
Quant il ot bien oÿ tous noz discors.
Si nous loa que li drois et li tors

recommended that you be asked to judge the right and the wrong, and we agreed. Our discussion had lasted a long while and we had advanced many arguments, as is more fully written out above. Now we have come here into your presence so that the right might be determined and made known, and your decision be respected by us both. Thus you can end this quarrel at once, if it please you, for we have selected you to be our judge. Sir, you have now heard our case fully; please pass judgment, for we have long desired to have it, and this lady and I devoutly beg you for it."

When the knight had finished his presentation, like a wise man skilled in such affairs, the noble and enlightened king replied: "As God is my help, you have chosen in me an inexperienced and uninformed judge, for never in my life have I seen or heard of such a case; I have little idea how to render a verdict. Nevertheless I wish to have my courtiers' advice, for I have good and noble people."

Then with a smile he called forth Loyalty who was there, Love, Youth, and Reason who spoke first, and then the noble king asked them: "You who know all the law, what do you say? This noble and upright knight and this golden-haired lady have come here before me to

1591 **mis sur vous** sur vous mis P. **noz** nostre R. 1594 **Et si aviens** Si avons RRa; aviesmes Ar. **arguement** argument C; fort argument RRa; bel argument Ar; autre argument St. 1595 *replaced in* Ar *by*: De tous les biens d'amours et des maulz ensement. **comme il est escript plus** comme yci il est plus E. **est** *om* R. 1598 **Par** Pour ArRaSt. **quoy . . . soit** qui le droit si soit RRa. **sceüs** veus RRa. 1599 **voz** noz JK; vostre RRa. **soit** soient JK. 1600 **ce** cest C. 1601 **s'il** si JKRRa. 1603 **or avez oÿ** pour ce quavez oy RRa. 1607 **devotement** treshumblement St. 1609 **ot** eust RRa. **moustrees ses** moustre les C; moustires ses JK; moustree leur RRa; moustrees les ArPc. 1610 **com . . . homs** et comme gentilz hom RRa. 1612 **Li** Si RRa. 1615 **Në . . . mez** Nonques RRa. **je . . . vi** en ma vie noy EJK. 1617 **Si en** Si nen JK. **petitement** presentement JK. 1618 **Mais** Et EJK. **nonpourquant** non pour ce RRa. 1624 **gentilz** gracieux RRa. 1625 **Que** Quen P. **dites** diriez RPcRa; dires Ar. 1626 **Cilz** Ce RPcRaSt. **est . . . adrois** genz est et adrois PArPc; est gentilz et drois JK; cy est gent et droiz RRa. 1627 **aussi . . . crins** icy a ces crins C; qui porte ses crins (clins E) EJK; belle en tous endroiz St.

Fust mis sur vous. Et ce fu noz accors,
Car longuement
Avoit duré de nous le parlement,
Et si aviens fait maint arguement,
Si comme il est escript plus plenement
Yci dessus.
Or sommes ci par devers vous venus,
Par quoy li drois soit jugiez et sceüs,
Et que vos diz soit de nous .ii. tenus.
Si que ce plait
Povez tantost terminer, s'il vous plaist,
Car nous avons de vous no juge fait.
Sire, or avez oÿ tout nostre fait
Entierement;
Si en veulliez faire le jugement,
Car nous l'avons desiré longuement,
Et ceste dame et moy devotement
Vous en prions."

[Q]uant cilz li ot moustrees ses raisons,
Qui bien le sot faire com sages homs,
Li gentilz roys qui moult estoit preudoms
Li respondi:
"Se Dieus me gart, vous avez pris en mi
Juge ignorent et de sens desgarni,
Në onques mez je n'oÿ ne ne vi
Tel jugement:
Si en saroie juger petitement. f. 89v
Mais nonpourquant le conseil de ma gent
En voeil avoir; car je l'ai bel et gent."
Lors appella
En sousriant Loyauté qui fu la,
Amours, Joinece, et Raison qui parla
Premierement, et puis leur demanda
Li gentilz roys:
"Que dites vous, qui savez tous les drois?
Cilz chevaliers qui est genz et adrois
Et ceste dame aussi a ces crins bloys
Sont venuz ci
Par devers moy, dont je les remerci,

have my judgment, for which I thank them, as to which has more trouble and vexation. The lady had a faithful friend who loved and served her, and she him as much as she was able. Now it has come to pass that all-consuming Death has taken him from her, and her heart is sorrowful and agitated, for in his day he had finer qualities than any other, and no more handsome knight ever lived.

"This knight loves without reservation and with his whole heart the most beautiful lady alive, so he believes. She promised him her unwavering and constant faith, and she retained and loved him truly as her own; he was certain of her love. Yet now the lady has given her heart to another and abandoned this knight totally, and has no concern for him. With his own eyes he sees the fair lady and the man who reaps the sweet recompenses he has earned. Now I've told you why they've come to hear my judgment. There is no doubt that a heart which languishes in this manner consumes itself and lives in great sorrow. Thus you must advise me as best you know how; each of you is my beloved and my confidant, and you know I place great faith in you. So, Reason, I wish to hear your opinion first, for you have given me much good advice."

Reason, who was beautiful and of great renown, replied in this fashion: "Sir, I say that both these lovers are in great distress, since they have lost what they love, and that their hearts are melting, just as wax

1630 **oïr** avoir EJK. 1634 **com elle povoit** que plus ne pouoit C; que pouoit et savoit St. 1635 **reçoipt** dechoit Ar. 1637 **dolent et irascu** tout doulent et vaincu RRa. 1638 **a** en JKRRa. **ot** eust RRa. 1639 **meilleur . . . bel** plus bel ne nul meilleur RPcRaSt. 1643 **foi** aussi P; soy CPc; li E; lui JKSt; et soy RRa. 1644 **Li a promis** Li ay mis JK; Luy ont promis RRa; Lui ot promis St. 1645 **Et . . . fu** Pour ce receu fut RRa. 1647 **autre** aultrui Ar. 1650 **celi** celui CJK. 1651 **les** lor St. **a** avoit RRa. 1653 **venuz . . . dit** orendroit venu chi Ar. 1654 **Et** Car Ra. **doubte** doubter J. 1655 **destruit** destraint RRa. **a** en JK. 1656 **m'en** me PRRa. 1657 **pouez** savez EJK. 1658 **privez** priviez P. 1659 **me** men JK. **vous bien** vous vous Ar. 1660 **Dites raison** Si est raison JK. 1661 **oïr voeil** vueil oir CRArRa. 1666 **quant** qui E. 1667 **aiment** amoient ERRaSt. **que li** qui les P; qui le JK; que leurs RRa. **leur** *om* E. 1668 **Si com** Comme R.

Et jugement voellent oïr de mi,
Li quielx a plus de mal et de souxi.
La dame avoit
Ami loyal qui l'amoit et servoit,
Et elle lui, tant com elle pouoit.
Or est ainsi que Mors qui tout reçoipt
Li a tolu,
S'en a le cuer dolent et irascu,
Car a son temps ot il si grant vertu
Que nul meilleur ne nul plus bel ne fu.
Le chevalier
Sanz repentir aime de cuer entier
La plus belle qui vive, a son cuidier.
Et elle foi sanz muer ne changier
Li a promis,
Et retenuz fu de li com amis
Et bien amez; il en estoit tous fis.
Or a la dame en autre son cuer mis
Et li guerpi
Du tout en tout, et n'a cure de li. f. 90
Et a ses yeux voit la belle et celi
Qui les doux biens a qu'il a desservi.
Or vous ai dit
Pour quoy il sont venuz oïr mon dit.
Et sanz doubte, cuers qui ainsi languist
Se destruit moult et a grant dolour vit.
Si m'en devez
Donner conseil au mieux que vous pouez;
Car chascuns est mes drus et mes privez,
Et moult me fi en vous, bien le savez.
Dites, Raison,
Premier oïr voeil vostre entention;
Car vous m'avez maint conseil donné bon."
Raison, qui fu belle et de bon renom,
Ainsi respont:

["S]ire, je di que cil doy amant sont
Moult angoisseux, quant ainsi perdu ont
Ce qu'il aiment, et que li cuers leur font,
Si com la cyre

wastes away and dissipates before the fire. But I do not wish to say that their martyrdom and misfortunes are completely identical. I want to tell you what sways me, since I must: this lady can never again see her true love, as once she did. Since she will not see him again, it will happen that I shall make her forget him; for the heart will never love anything so much that it won't forget it after separation. Of course, I don't say that it won't suffer and ache for a time; but Youth who is happy and carefree would never permit him to be remembered constantly. For Youth, sir, come what may, soon forgets what she doesn't see. Furthermore, I say that Love is not powerful enough to sustain itself a single hour without a lover or lady. And if one of the three is missing, the other two are incomplete; for Love, lover, and ladylove must be present in love, or the love is worth nothing. And since Love and the lady have lost the lover's company, indeed I wouldn't give a rotten apple for their love—that is to say, for a worldly love. For it's well and good to do one's duty, so that the soul can perceive it, but there's no woman or man alive whose love is so blameless, if he's caught by the amorous flame, who does not love the body much better than the soul. Why is

1669 **feu se degaste** feu degaste C; feu se gaste JK; feu qui se gaste RRa; fu moult degaste Ar. 1670 **tout pareil** en peril RRa. **de** dun JK. 1671 **Et** Ne EJKRRa. **ce . . . pas** je ne vueil pas ce St. 1672 **me muet** men muet E; mesmuet JK. 1673–92 *cut out of* Pc. 1673 **voeil dire** voeul jou dire Ar. **puiz que faire** puis que dire E; pour quoy dire JK; puis quainsi le St. **l'estuet** lesqueut RRa; mesteut St. 1674 **Ceste** Ycheste Ar. **jamez veoir** veoir jamais Ar. 1675 **ainsi** aussi C. **com elle suelt** comme elle sceust K; quelle souloit RRa. 1677 **puiz que plus** puis plus JK. **le** la P. **verra** reverra JK. 1679 **Car . . . tant** Car le cuer tant ja C; Car ja le cueur tant RRaSt. 1680 **Qu'il** Qui RRa. 1681 **Par eslongier** Neslongnier RRa. **je ne di** ne di je PE; ne dire JK. 1682 **Qu'une piece** Que tous les jours RRa; Caucune paine Ar; Que grant peine St. **n'en ait** on ait JK; nait RRa. **paine et haschie** peine et hastie E; et grant hachie ArSt. 1683 **lie** jolie RRa. 1686 **joinece** sioveneche Ar. **comment** comme RRa. **voit** soit P; voist CE. 1687 **moult tost** tantost St. **que** quil EJK; qui RRa. 1689 **pas** point RRa. **en** o E. **li** lui JK. 1690 **se** le St. **ami** ennuy St. 1691 **ne** et Ar. **amie** amy St. 1693 **autres** *om* C. **aront** en auront E; en ont JK. 1694 **Qu'amours ami** Car tout troy estre EJK. **et amie estre** en une amour les EJK; et a dame estre RRa. **faut** fait Pc. 1695 **Tout e.** Tout troi e. Ar. **ou** en St. **l'amour** amours CRArRa. 1697 **la** leur CEJK. 1698 **D'ami** Dame EJK. 1699 **De** En RRa. 1701 **a** *om* RRa. BBqui est mondain qui est mondainne CEArSt; que est ma dame JK; qui est daultre dame RRa. 1702 **Car** Que Ra. **tres** trop JKRArRa. 1703 **l'ame** lamye RRa; li ame Ar. **s'en . . . apparcevoir** puist faire son devoir Pc. 1704 **dame** ame PCE; femme JK. 1705 **Në homs** Domme P; Nomme St. 1706 **S'il** Cil JK. **est tapez** nest frappe RRa. 1707–26 *cut out in* Pc. 1707 **Qu'il** Que Ar. **assez** en ce RRa. 1708–11 *om* P. 1708 **Pour** Par CJK. **quel** quelle E.

Devant le feu se degaste et empire.
Mais qu'il soient tout pareil de martire
Et de meschief, ce ne veeil je pas dire.
Ce qui me muet
Vous voeil dire, puiz que faire l'estuet:
Ceste dame jamez veoir ne puet
Son ami vray, ainsi com elle suelt.
Si avenra
Ainsi que, puiz que plus ne le verra,
Je ferai tant qu'elle l'oublïera;
Car li cuers ja tant chose n'amera
Qu'il ne l'oublie
Par eslongier. Certes, je ne di mie f. 90v
Qu'une piece n'en ait paine et haschie;
Mais Joinece qui tant est gaie et lie
Ne soufferroit
Pour nulle rien que entroublïez ne soit.
Car Joinece, sire, comment qu'il voit,
Met en oubli moult tost ce que ne voit.
Aprez je di
Qu'Amours n'a pas tant de pooir en li
Que soustenir se peüst sanz ami
L'eure d'un jour, ne sanz amie aussi.
Et se l'un faut
Des .iii., les .ii. autres aront deffaut;
Qu'Amours, ami, et amie estre faut
Tout ensemblë, ou l'amour rien ne vault.
Et puiz qu'amie
Et Amours ont perdu la compaignie
D'ami, certes, je ne donroie mie
De leur amour une pome pourrie,
C'est assavoir,
Quant a l'amour, qui est mondain avoir.
Car c'est tres bon de faire son devoir,
Si que l'ame s'en puist apparcevoir;
Mais il n'est dame
Në homs vivant qui aime si sanz blame,
S'il est tapez de l'amoureuse flame,
Qu'il n'aime mieux assez le corps que l'ame.
Pour quel raison?

that? Because Love comes from carnal affection, and its desires and essence all incline to pleasure. No man or woman who wishes to love can avoid all sin and impropriety; it cannot be otherwise; and it is contrary to the soul which sorrows over it. Furthermore, as soon as the soul leaves the body, love withdraws and sets off. As God is my witness, this is what I see everywhere. Therefore the love of this lady of great worth is constantly diminishing from day to day; and in like measure is her sorrow diminishing.

"But this lover, who foolishly fell in love without my advice, and who is so deeply in love, sad knight, that he is totally spent, is tormented by bitter pangs of love within his heart; for Love enflames him night and day, and he would not and cannot forget his enemy. Do you know why? Because Companionship, Love, Beauty, and happy Youth (and Loyalty whom I don't wish to forget) made him languish in great folly, madness, grief, and delirium, in great jealousy, and in danger of losing his soul and life. His sad heart does not quit his lady morning or evening, but accompanies her constantly wherever she goes—and he who is nearest the fire burns the most. His Loyalty prevented his betraying her; but had he heeded my advice when his lady chose a new

1710 **si** son CRRa. **sa** si St. 1711 **a** en E. 1713 **Nulz** A nulz J. **amer** amour E. **voelt** vueil RRa. 1714 **Qu'il** Que Ar. **pechié il l'estuet** pechie il estueut JK; pechier lui esqueil RRa; pechie qui lesteut St. 1715 *om* RRa. **c'est** si est St. **a l'ame** a la dame E. **s'en duelt** se deust JK. 1717 **aussi tost** autressi C; ainssi tost JK; aussi bien RRa. **com** que RRaSt. **se** sen Ar. 1718 **espart** depart JKRRa. 1721 **moult** tant PAr. *After this line* St *includes*: Et quendure souvent maint mal en plour. 1722–23 *inverted in* St. 1722 **toudiz** tous jours JK. 1723 **aussi** ainssi CRRa. **a ce fuer** a cel fuer C; eschauffer RRa. **la** sa RRaAr. 1724 **cilz** cest RRa. 1725 **s'est d'amer** damer sest PR; cest damer CJKRaSt. **entremis** entrepris JKSt. 1726 **et si** et se EArSt; et qui RRa. 1727 R *replaces this line with*: Que douloureux il en est et ravis. 1728 **Les** Des RRa; Li Ar. 1729 **Sont en** A en RRa; Sont a Ar; Sent a Pc. **li sont** li font JKRRa; le font Ar. **trop** tant RRa. **amer** damer JKRRa. 1730 **le** les JKPc; lui St. 1731 **voudroit** vaurroit PAr; verroy St. 1734 **beauté et joinece** joveneche et leeche Ar. 1735 **qu'oublïer** oublier PC. **voeil** voelt PCSt. 1736 **En** Et PCArSt. 1737 **et en** en grant Ar. 1738 **en** a Ra. 1740 **ne** et CRRaArSt. 1742 **Ainz** Maiz EJKRAr. **l'acompaigne** le compaigne EJKAr. 1743 **est plus prez** plus est prez P; plus pres est RRa. **plus s'art** plus art JKRArRaSt. 1744 **Et** En Ar. 1745 **Si** Se Ar. **a** de JKRPcRa. 1746 **s'il eüst** sil en eust St. 1747 **sa dame ot** ot la dame C. **nuef ami recouvré** nouvel amy trouve RRaAr; amy neuf recouvre St.

Amours vient de charnel affection,
Et si desir et sa condiction
Sont tout enclin a delectation.
Si ne se puet
Nulz ne nulle garder qui amer voelt
Qu'il n'y ait vice ou pechié; il l'estuet;
Et c'est contraire a l'ame qui s'en duelt.
Et d'autre part,
Tout aussi tost com l'ame se depart f. 91
Du corps, l'amour s'en esloigne et espart.
Ainsi le voy partout, se Dieus me gart.
Si que l'amour
De ceste dame ou moult a de valour
Apetise toudiz de jour en jour;
Et aussi fait a ce fuer la dolour.
Mais cilz amis
Qui folement s'est d'amer entremis
Sanz mon conseil, et si s'y est si mis,
Li doloreux, qu'il en est tous remis,
Les maulx d'amer
Sont en son cuer qui li sont trop amer;
Qu'Amours le fait nuit et jour enflamer,
N'il ne voudroit, ne porroit oublïer
Son ennemie.
Savez pour quoy? Pour ce que Compaignie,
Amours, Beauté, et Joinece la lie,
Et Loyauté, qu'oublïer ne voeil mie,
En grant folie,
En rage, en duel, et en forsenerie
Le font languir, et en grant jalousie,
Et en peril de l'ame et de la vie.
Car main ne tart
Son dolent cuer de sa dame ne part,
Ainz l'acompaigne en tous lieus sanz depart;
Et cilz qui est plus prez du feu, plus s'art.
Et Loyauté
Si li deffent a faire fausseté;
Mais s'il eüst par mon conseil ouvré,
Quant sa dame ot nuef ami recouvré,

lover he would not have continued loving her. For in such a situation, the lady calls the tune and sets the pace. Afterwards Beauty told him that he did better to languish for love of her than to enjoy another, and so did Love. Youth fed him with folly in this mistake, in this waywardness, for he is losing his strength and mind. Thus this sorrowful creature is languishing in sorrow; for when he sees that in his very presence another enjoys his ladylove, who used to call him her beloved, his heart is so jealous, so distraught, that it's a wonder he doesn't kill himself, or make ready to kill the cause of his distress. Jealousy whispers this into his ear. And if he had her love, as once he did, what would he do with it? Indeed he would do nothing, since he could never trust her. For this reason, I think, he can never find consolation in another, because he cannot forget this lady who causes him such sorrow. Therefore I say that this knight suffers more than this lady, and that his soul is in greater anxiety, because of the reasons which you've heard. And to my mind this knight has spoken well—for I have found it written out above—and has proven his case by reasoning, in my opinion."

When Reason had finished telling her opinion, Love, who was as

1749 **l'amour** amour E. **car** quant EJK. 1750 **Se la** Car se la EJK. **en . . . bas** haut ou bas C; ou haut ou bas JK; ou en hault ou en bas RRa; hault ou em bas St. 1753 **qu'il** qui JKRPcRa. **assez mieux** mieus assez CERRa. **s'il** qui JK; si RRa; sans St. 1754 **li** elle RRa. **se** *om* R. 1755 **fait** faite CEJKAr. **joinece** jovencel JK. **le** la C. 1757 **ce** cest C; cel St. **en** que JK. **celle fole** cel fol St. 1758 **Car** Que RRa. **en pert** emporte E. **le senz** la joie St. 1759 **Ainsi** Et si RRa. **li dolens** cilz dolens EJK; le doulant RRaSt. **dolour** langour EJKRRaSt. 1760 **Car** Et RRa. 1761 **de s'amour** samour lui RRa. **present li** par prent et RRa; prent li Ar; prent St. **autre joit** quautre en jouyt RRa; aultres et goit Ar; lautre et joit St. 1763 **si d.** et si d. C. 1765 **s'occist** se tue RRa. 1766 **D'ocirre ce** De tuer cil RRa; Doccirre cil PcSt. **le traveille** le (la St) pareille ArSt. 1767 *om* RRa. **ce** si EJK. 1768 **Et** Ne RArRaSt. 1769 **ainsi com** aussi com CAr; si comme JK; ainsi comme St. 1770 JK *replace this line with*: Ne sai je pas se (ce K) il si fieroit. **Qu'en** Que RRa. **n'en** ne RRa. 1771 JK *replace this line with*: Certes nenil pourquoy il noseroit. **Car** Ou R. **jour il** en li P; jour en li C. **s'y fieroit** se fieroit P; se firoit C; il noseroit JK. 1772 **Et pour** Pour EJKSt. **espoir** despoir St. 1773 **N'a** Ne ESt. **de . . . autre** jamaiz eure daultre R; a jamais daultre Ar; jamez cure daultre Ra; de autre jamaiz St. **avoir** naroit St. 1774 **Puiz que** Puis quil JKAr. **mettre ne puet** ne puet metre JK. **en nonchaloir** en un chaloir E; a nonchaloir RPcRa. 1775 **qui** que St. **tant** trop ERArPcRaSt. **le** me St. 1778 **plus . . . souxi** greignour soussi EJK. 1781 **Cilz** Cest C; Ce RRaSt. 1782 **l'ai ci** la cy EJK. 1785 **raison ot** jay sceu qua RRa. **tout son aviz** tout son devis C; son devis RRa. 1786 **fu** *om* J. **fu . . . devis** fu beaus et a lis C; biaus fu a devis Ar.

Il n'eüst pas
Continué l'amour; car en tel cas, f. 91v
Se la dame chante en haut ou en bas,
On doit aler ou le trot ou le pas.
Aprez li dit
Beautés qu'il fait assez mieux, s'il languist
Pour li amer, que se d'autre joïst.
Si fait Amour. Joinece le nourrist
Avec folour
En ce meschief, en celle fole errour;
Car il en pert le senz et la vigour.
Ainsi languist li dolens en dolour;
Car quant il voit
Que de s'amour, present li, autre joit,
Qui son ami appeller le souloit,
Il a le cuer si jalous, si destroit,
Que c'est merveille
Qu'il ne s'occist, ou qu'il ne s'appareille
D'ocirre ce qui ainsi le traveille;
Et ce li met Jalousie en l'oreille.
Et s'il avoit
L'amour de li, ainsi com il soloit,
Qu'en feroit il? Certes, rien n'en feroit,
Car jamez jour il ne s'y fieroit.
Et pour ce espoir,
N'a de jamez autre soulas avoir,
Puiz que mettre ne puet en nonchaloir
Ceste dame qui tant le fait doloir.
Si que je di
Qu'il a plus mal que ceste dame ci,
Et que son cuer est en plus grant souxi,
Par les raisons que vous avez oÿ.
Et, a mon gré,
Cilz chevaliers en a moult bien parlé, f. 92
Car en escript l'ai ci dessus trouvé
Et par raison s'entencion prouvé,
Ce m'est aviz."

[Q]uant Raison ot compté tout son aviz,
Amours parla qui fu beaux a devis,

beautiful and gracious in manner and countenance as one could want, spoke up and said: "Reason, you have put forth your case quite well. I agree, except that it would be wrong for him to remove his heart from the prison of that beautiful lady, for whom he feels love's spark. I wish him to love and serve her from whom he's had many a new joy; for could he live a thousand years, and serve her every day, he would never merit by his service the great favors she once did for him. And if Pleasure, who is responsible for many a strange vicissitude, makes him unsure of his lady, should he fall into despair? Indeed not! For there are in my service a hundred thousand more who love as deeply as he without a straw to show for it. It is in my power to heal him or to increase his sufferings; but he no longer has faith and hope in me, and this is what causes him the most suffering."

"What, Love?" said Reason, "is he to love according to your ways, with no reciprocity, she who has given her heart to another? And is he who serves you not to have the remuneration he deserves? Indeed, one's a fool who strives to serve such a master, since he loses his reward."

After this exchange, Loyalty approached Love and said the lover would have done no wrong if he'd made her a sop of the same bread. "It's not right, if he's true, loyal, and good, for him to be one of those

1787 **viz** diz P. 1789 **moustree vo raison** moustre vostré CEJKRRa. 1790 **Si** Et RRa. 1791 **Feroit** Seroit EJK. 1792 **A** Qua E; De St. 1793 **Pour . . . sent** Pour quil aimt JK; Pour quil il sceust RRa; Pour cui il sent Ar; Pourque il sent St. **l'amoureuse estincelle** sceust la voureuse J; sceust lamoureuse K. 1794 **Si** Maiz E. **qu'il l'aimt** quil aimt JK; qui layme RRa. **serve . . . celle** aime come celle E; quil serve ycelle JK; le serve come celle ArPc. 1795 **Dont eü a** Dont eue a C; Dont a eu EJKAr; Dont il a Pc; Dont en a eu Ra; Dont oy a St. **lie** dure St. 1796 **s'il** si K. 1797 **toudiz** tous jours Ar. **la** le PAr. 1798 **par servir** pour servir PER; pour son servir Ra. 1799 **Les** Ses Ar. 1800 **se** sa RRa. 1801 **faire fait** fait faire EJKRRaSt. 1802 **Li** Le EJKRRa; Li a Ar; La PcSt. 1803 **Doit** En doit St. **estre pour ce** pour ce estre P. 1805 **Qu'en** Que E. **service** pouoir RRa. **encor** encore E. **mil** *repeated* E. 1806 **Qui** Quil E. **tuit prez aussi** tuit pres daussi C; tuit aussi JK. **com il** come luy RRa. 1807 **si** sil E. **monte** montance Ra. 1809 **et** ou C. **li desdoloir** li doloir E; lui redouloir JK; lui condouloir RRa; dessus loir St. 1810 **n'a mez** na pas St. 1811 **c'est** ceste J. 1813 **raison** amours JK. **est** sont P. 1814 **secours** recours E; retours JK. 1815 **Celle** Que elle C; De celle RRa. 1817 **Qu'il n'a** Il na EJK; Quil nait RRa. 1819 **Sifait** A sifait Ar; Tel Pc. **meistre** mestier E. **quant . . . pert** quant guerredon y pert C; que son guerredon pert EJKArPcSt. 1820–1823 *om* RRa. 1822 **que riens** que de rien C. 1823 **Se** Ce E; Et Ar. **li eüst souppe** li eust souppes E; leust telle soupe St. 1825 **s'il** cil EJK. **vrais loyaulz** loyaux vrais E. 1826 **Qu'il soit** Qui soit CE; Sil nest St. **de . . . batent** deceu et bate RRa. **buissons** bissons E.

Et gracïeux de maniere et de viz,
Et dit: "Raison,
Moult bien avez moustree vo raison.
Si m'y ottroy, fors tant que mesprison
Feroit d'oster son cuer de la prison
A la tres belle,
Pour qui il sent l'amoureuse estincelle.
Si voeil qu'il l'aimt et serve comme celle
Dont eü a mainte lie nouvelle;
Car s'il povoit
Vivre mil ans, et toudiz la servoit,
Ja par servir il ne desserviroit
Les grans douceurs que faire li soloit.
Et se Plaisance
Qui faire fait mainte estrange muance
Li fait estre de sa dame en doubtance,
Doit il estre pour ce en desesperance?
Certes, nennil!
Qu'en mon service en a encor .c. mil
Qui aiment tuit prez aussi fort com il,
Et si n'en ont la monte d'un fuisil.
Et s'ay pooir
De li garir et de li desdoloir,
Mez il n'a mez fiance në espoir
En moy; c'est ce qui plus le fait doloir."
"Comment, Amours?"
Ce dit Raison, "Est ce donc de voz tours f. 92v
Qu'il amera, sanz avoir nul secours,
Celle qui a donné son cuer aillours?
Et qui vous serft,
Qu'il n'a mie le loyer qu'il desserft?
Certes, folz est qui a servir s'ahert
Sifait meistre, quant son garredon pert."
Aprez ce fait,
Devers Amours Loyauté se retrait
Et dit ainsi, que riens n'eüst meffait
Se d'autel pain li eüst souppe fait.
"N'il n'est raisons
Pour ce, s'il est vrais, loyaulz, et preudoms,
Qu'il soit de ceulz qui batent les buissons

who beats the bushes so others can take the birds. For if the lady, whom I sharply condemn and blame (and it's quite right to do so, for she earns great blame for changing her key in mid-tune), had not first taken her heart from this lover, who was entirely at her command—ah! Love, Love, I would have argued differently. But without a doubt, since he loves with all his might and she has forgotten him without cause, then he must dance as she is dancing; this would not be anything that would put him out of my favor, for if he leaves her and pursues another, I don't claim he is wronging me. Thus I agree fully with Reason's decision (for she has given a good and faithful account) that he is right and that lady, wrong."

And when Youth, who was very cheerful and full of happiness, and who holds to no pledge or promise unless it be in accord with her desires, heard what Reason and Loyalty had said, she thought little of it, for she was filled with her own opinion and said aloud: "To be sure, Reason, your wit fails you, and Loyalty, indeed, is no support to you; for this lover will never be separated from the precious topaz who surpasses all others in beauty, sweetness, and delicate complexion despite any troubles or afflictions Love may cause him. May it never please God that he stop loving the beauty! For if at present she doesn't want

1828 **se** ce E. 1830–31 *inverted in* R. 1830 **c'est** sest Ar; est St. **car . . . grant** car elle acqueut grant C; quar je aquier un grant E; quelle acquiert grant St. 1831 **De muance** De la muance C. **fausse** haute CEJKAr. 1833 **osté** honte RRa. **son** le Ar. 1834 **a** en CJKRRa. 1835 **Amours amours** A mon avis JK. 1837 **Quant il aime** Quant il laime CESt; Puis que lamie RRa. 1839 **aussi** ainsi EJKSt. 1841 **de . . . puist** par quoy y peut E. **ma** sa PC. 1842 **s'il la laist** sil le laist PArSt; cil la lait E; sel le laist JK; sil la laisse RRa. **se** sen RRa. 1843 **Je . . . qu'envers** Je ne di pas quenvers EJK; Il ne tient pas que vers RRa; Je ne tien point quenvers St. 1845 **de** a C. 1846 **elle a fait** elle fait PC. 1847 **Que cilz** Car sil RRa; Et cilz St. **ceste . . . tort** celle dame a tort E; celle dame tort Ar. 1849 **fu** ert Ar. 1850 **n'acompte** ne compte RRa; nen conte St. **don ne** veu ny JK. 1851 **que** qui JK. 1852 **Ot** Et JRRa. 1853 **ot** eust RRa. 1854 **acompté** escoute RRa. 1855 **moult . . . fu** moult fu plaine et P; pleine fu moult E; moult fut plaine RRa; parlans fu Ar; estoit plain St. 1856 **Si** Ci K; Et RArRaSt. 1857 **vostre . . . faut** vo science vous fault RRa. 1858–59 *inverted in* JK. 1858 **sachiez** certes EJKRArPcRaSt. **vous** *om* C. 1859 **cilz** cest CPc; son RRa. 1861–84 *om* PC. 1861 **N'iert** Nest E. **toupasse** compasse EAr. 1862 *om* RRa. **beauté . . . doulceur** doucheur et de biaute ArPcSt. 1863 **Et . . . coleur** De coulour fine et St. **ja dieu** ne dieu EArPc; que ja dieu St. 1864 **Qu'il** Qui JKArPc. 1865 **refraigne** restraingne RRa. 1866 **s'a present** son penser JK; se present Ar. **le veult** lui vault R. **ne n'adaigne** ne ne daingne JK; ne adaigne RArPcSt.

Dont li autre prennent les oyseillons.
Car se la dame,
Que je repren moult durement et blame,
(Et c'est bien droiz, car elle acquiert grant blame
De muance faire en la fausse game,)
Premierement
N'eüst osté son cuer de cest amant
Qui tous estoit a son commandement,
Amours, Amours, je parlasse autrement.
Mais sanz doubtance,
Quant il aime de toute sa poissance,
Et sanz cause le met en oubliance,
Il doit danser aussi comme elle danse,
Non pas qu'il face
Chose de quoy il puist perdre ma grace,
Car s'il la laist, et ailleurs se pourchace,
Je ne tieng pas qu'envers moy se mefface.
Et si m'accort
Du tout en tout de Raison a l'accort f. 93
(Car elle a fait bon et loyal rapport)
Que cilz a droit, et ceste dame a tort."
Et quant Joinece
Qui moult fu gaie et plaine de leece,
Et qui n'acompte a don në a promesse,
Fors seulement que son voloir adrece,
Ot escouté
Ce que Raison ot dit et racompté
Et Loyauté, poy y a acompté,
Quar moult plaine fu de sa volenté,
Si dit en haut:
"Certes, Raison, vostre scïence faut,
Et Loyauté, sachiez, rien ne vous vault;
Car cilz amis, pour mal ne pour assaut
Qu'Amours li face,
N'iert ja partis de la belle toupasse
Qui de beauté et de doulceur tout passe,
Et de fine coleur. Ja Dieu ne place
Qu'il li avieigne
Que ja d'amer la belle se refraigne!
Car s'a present ne le veult ne n'adaigne,

him or esteem him, at least he loves her, and his heart goes with her. Isn't this enough? Must he weary of loving her? Indeed not! For one is not always loved and welcomed and called 'beloved'; no, and that is certain! A lover would be a fool to listen to you, Reason, and follow your teachings and your pathways; I say that whoever does so can't see a lick. And I give you my word that Love, my lady, and myself will do so much that his heart will be so caught and in such bondage that it will not be willing to leave her night or day. And your efforts, I assure you, will never be strong enough to wrest the pure heart of this lover from the beautiful lady in whom it finds little consolation. For Love, my lady, which enkindles his heart, and scorches, burns, and enflames it, and I who am still here with all my passion, will hold him to this love; for, by my soul, it cannot be otherwise. And if more bitter troubles come to him than to this lady who is seated beside him, he's strong enough to bear and endure them well."

Then the noble king reflected and laughed heartily at what Youth had just said; but he did not esteem her any the less for this, because she spoke only as she ought; he placed more value in a pennyworth of her opinion than in ten pounds of profit.

He said: "Fair lady Youth, you and Love are demanding mistresses to hold this lover in such distress, affliction, misery, and sadness. See how this poor man has lost all comfort, and how his heart has no re-

1867 **l'aime il et** la voit et St. **la** le St. 1868 **n'est ce assez** neste asses E; nesce asses Ar. 1871 **conjoïnz** conjois EPcSt; comme roy RRa. **n'amis** mavez RRa; certes namis Ar. 1872 **et sans doubte** est sanz doubte E; est sans doubtance RRa; cest sanz doubte St. 1873 **Raison . . . qui** Raison folz est qui E; Raison raison folz est qui RArPcRaSt. 1874 **ensuit** ainseut Ar; ainsi St. 1875 **qu'il ne** qui ne ERRa; quil ny St. 1877 **tant** *om* RRa. 1878 **Que . . . si** Que son cueur y est si RRa; Ses coeurs sera Ar; Que ses cuers si St. **en** a RRa. 1879 **ne jour** et jour RRaAr. 1881 **Ne** Nen ArPc. **ne . . . fors** ne sera ja fors J; ne seront ja si fors Pc; ja ne sera si fors St. 1882–83 *inverted in* RRa. 1882 **fin** sien RRa. **fors** fort RRa. 1883 **De** A R. 1884 **Qu'amour ma** Quamours confesse ma St. 1885 **son cuer** son cuert P; mon cuer JK; tout son cueur R. **art** *om* PRRa (−1). **taint . . . enflame** taint et bruit et entache P; tant bruist et enflame JKAr; bruit et enflame Ra. 1886 *om* RRa. P *replaces lines* 1886–87 *with*: Ne guerpira sa dame ne sa fache / Et je di bien et voeil que chascun sache. 1886 **Et** En ArSt. **ma** la St. 1887 **ceste** cest C. **tenrons** tenez RRa. **car** que Ra. 1888 **Il** Quil P. 1889 **se des** de ses PERRa. **plus** pis RRa. 1890 **Qu'a** Que PRRaAr; Car E; Par JK. **la dame** de la dame R. 1891 **les** le CRAr. 1895 **l'en prisa** le prisa J; lemprisa Ar. 1897 **ce . . . disoit** ce quelle faisoit JK; quanques elle disoit RRa. 1898 **Et** Car RRa. **voeil** veult JK. **denree avoit** demie amoit C; denree avoir JK. 1899 **Que .x. Que .xv. JK; Que de dix RRa. livres** *om* JK. **de son proffit** sa prouffit RRa. **n'avoit** naroit PSt; revenoit RRa. 1900 **Si** Et C; Ce RRaSt. 1902 **Qui** Que E; Quant JKRArRaSt. **en . . . destrece** en tel destresse EJK; a grant destresse RRa; en grant tristresse Ar. 1903 **tristrece** destresse Ar. 1904 **Vous et** En voz St. 1905 **tout secours** son secours P; tous secours C; tout le cours JK; tout son cours RRa; tous ses cours St. 1906 **Ne** Nen JK. **recours** secours E.

Au moins l'aime il, et son cuer la compaigne.
Dont n'est ce assez?
Doit il estre de li amer lassez?
Certes, nennil! Car on n'est pas amez,
Ne conjoïnz toudis, n'amis clamez:
Non, et sans doubte!
Raison, folz est amans qui vous escoute,
Ne qui ensuit vos dis, ne vostre route;
Et qui le fait, je dis qu'il ne voit goute.
Et par ma foy,
Nous ferons tant, Amours, ma dame, et moy,
Que son cuer yert si pris et en tel ploy,
Que nuit ne jour ne partira de soy.
Ne vos effors,
Ne doubtez pas, ne sera ja si fors
Que le fin cuer de cest amant soit fors
De la tres belle ou pou treuve confors.
Qu'Amour, ma dame,
Qui son cuer art, taint et bruit et enflame
Et moi qui sui encor atout ma flame,
En ceste amour le tenrons; car, par m'ame,
Il le couvient.
Et se des malx dolereux plus li vient
Qu'a la dame qui delez lui se tient,
Fort est assez; bien les porte et soustient."
Lors s'avisa
Li gentilz roys, et bonnement ris a
De Joinece qui ainsi devisa;
Mais onques mains pour ce ne l'en prisa,
Qu'elle faisoit
Tout son devoir de ce qu'elle disoit,
Et de son voeil plus chier denree avoit
Que .x. livres de son proffit n'avoit.
Si dist: "Joinece,
Belle dame, vous estez grant maistresse f. 93v
Qui cest amant tenez en grant destrece,
En povreté, en misere, en tristrece,
Vous et Amours.
Vez que li las a perdu tout secours,
Ne ses cuers n'a refuge ne recours,

fuge or recourse except in Death, who's rapidly approaching. You seek to cause him too much suffering and destroy him completely. Now, if you please, he's found a good and faithful counselor; you'd do well to let him be advised, for he's caught in such a tight bind that he knows no trick or device to escape."

"Indeed, sir, he'll do nothing of the sort; rather, he'll continue to love the beauty he loves so much. And should he die, everyone will call him 'Love's Martyr' and it will be to his honor to die for love."

When Youth had finished her discourse, the king spoke to them and said: "We are not gathered here to say whether he should love the lady or not, but to determine which of these two suffers more and for which one love's troubles are the bitterest, as it seems to me. Now you are completely agreed that more pain is concentrated in this lover than in this lady; nor do I dissent from this decision; rather, I concur with it and support it entirely, for this lover is farther from consolation than this lady, whom God consoles.

"So I shall render judgment as best I know how; for I am not accustomed to such things, and I well know that another would do it better. So I say the following: having rightly considered Reason's foregoing opinion, and the arguments of you who seek justice, and of

1907 **a** qua RRa. **a li vient** vient a li C. 1909 **trop** vous E. 1910–11 *om* RRa. 1910–13 *om* Ar. 1912 **Si** Vous St. 1913 **estroit** destroit C; tres fort St. 1914 **scet tour** scet tout E; se tient RRa. **në engien** ny engien JK; en engin RRa; na engin Ar. 1915 **ferai** ferons P; fera CArSt. 1916 **Ainz** Mais RRa. 1918 **y** en JK. 1919 **fera** sera CERArRaSt. 1920 **li** lui JKRRaSt. 1921 **ot** eust RRa. **parler** penser E. **assouvy** feni JK; furni Ar. 1923 **yci** cy E. 1925 **amer sa dame** sa dame amer E; la dame amer JK. 1927 **plus sent** sont plus C; plus sont JK. **crueux les malx** les maulx crueux St. 1928 **me** moy EJKArSt. 1929 **en** dun PAr; a C. **tout ensemble** tuit ensemble P; ce me semble EJKRa; et me semble St. 1930 **en** a RRa. **s'assemble** assamble JSt; se samble RRa. 1931 **Qu'en . . . ne** Que la dame na RRa. 1933 **Ainçoiz . . . tout** Ainçois du tout mi tiens EJK; Ainsi me tien du tout RRa. **et m'y accort** a mon accord RRa. 1934 **cilz** cest EJKRArRa. **de** du RRa. 1935 **soit** fait RRa. 1937 **ainsi com je** au mieus que je EJK. **sarai** seray Ar. 1938 **Car tel** Qua tel E; Car celle RArPc. **acoustumé** acoustumer St. 1939 **Et uns** Et vous JK; Mais ung RRa; Et nuls Ar. **vraiement bien le** bien vraiement je RRa. 1941 **Je** Si EJK. **ainsi consideré** ainssi et considere C. **a** ou Ra. 1942 **endroit** adroit C. 1943 **les raisons** la raison RRa. 1944 **Et** De RRa. 1945 **a** *om* RRa.

Fors a la mort qui a li vient le cours;
Car traveillier
Le voulez trop et du tout exillier.
Or a trouvé, s'il vous plaist, conseillier
Bon et loyal; lessiez le conseillier,
Si ferez bien,
Car il est pris en si estroit lïen
Qu'il ne scet tour d'eschaper, në engien."
"Certes, sire, de ce ne ferai rien;
Ainz amera
La tres belle pour qui tant d'amer a.
Et, s'il y muert, chascun le clamera
Martyr d'Amours, et honneur li fera,
S'il muert pour li."
Quant Joinece ot son parler assouvy,
Li roys parla a eulz et dit ainsi:
"Nous ne sommes pas assemblez yci
Pour deputer
S'il doit amer sa dame ou non amer,
Mais pour savoir li quelx a plus d'amer,
Et qui plus sent crueux les malx d'amer,
Si com me semble.
Or estes vous en acort, tout ensemble,
Que plus de mal en cest amant s'assemble
Qu'en la dame; ne pas ne me dessemble
De cest accort,
Ainçoiz m'y tieng du tout et m'y accort, f. 94
Que cilz amans est plus loing de confort
Que la dame ne soit, que Dieux confort.
Si en ferai
Le jugement ainsi com je sarai;
Car tel chose pas acoustumé n'ay,
Et uns autres vraiement, bien le sçay,
Mieux le feroit.

[J]e di ainsi: consideré a droit
L'entencion de Raison ci endroit,
Et les raisons de vous qui voulez droit,
Et Loyauté
Qui en a dit la pure verité,

Loyalty who spoke the pure truth, without artifice or deceit, of Love too who spoke persuasively, and of Youth, that this lover endures more sadness and that Love's troubles wound him more deeply than this very noble lady, and that he is farther from consolation, which he greatly needs, I therefore state and give my judgment, that he endures more suffering, tribulations, and distress than does she."

When the good king had rendered his decision as Reason had prescribed it, the knight in his presence rose and thanked him, while the lady became so deeply lost in her melancholy that she didn't say a word. Nonetheless, in the end she consented to respect the judgment handed down by the king, for he was so wise and true that he never treated anyone unreasonably.

Thereupon the king, smiling, took them by their hands and had them sit upon Norwegian rugs, so that there were just the three of them, apart from the others. He exhorted and begged each of them to be consoled, for if their hearts toiled long under such cares, both he and she might die. He hoped that this would never happen, but that each would find new strength, for the heart that immerses itself in so much sorrow and grief utterly cripples and destroys itself. One often sees it written that one must quickly forget what he clearly sees he cannot redress, and what he cannot reclaim through tears and lamentations. If they did this, he asserted, they would not sin against Loyalty;

1946 **Ne** Qui RRaSt; Quil Ar. **n'y chace** ny cacha Ar; richesse Pc. 1947 **D'amours** Amour St. **en a bien** bien en a RRa. 1949 **cilz** cel C; cest EJK; chieult Ar. **sueffre plus de** est plus pres de EJK. 1950 **d'amer** damours EJKRArPcRa. 1951 **ou** qui Ra. 1953 **de** le RRa. **dont . . . bien** dont il a bon EJK; de lamant dont il a RRa; dont il a grant St. 1954 **di** dit E; tiens St. **et doing** a bon St. RRa *replace this line with*: Et de tourment qui fort au cueur le point. 1955 *om* RRa. **qu'elle . . . soing** quel na et plus de soing P; quel na de besoing C; quelle na et grant soing JK; quelle nait de soing Ar; et plus quelle na soin St. 1957 **ot** eust RRa. **rendu** donne C. 1958 **faite** fone (*sic*) Pc. 1959 **illuec** se lieue JK; louyt RRa. 1960 **L'en** Le JK; Et len RRa. 1961 **s'oublia** loublia JK. 1963 **Mais** Et JK. **ottroia** lottroia J. 1966 **Car si** Car bien si St. **sages** sachiez Pc. 1967 **Qu'envers nulluy** Que vers nulz C; Que pour nului E; Que vers nully RRa. **feroit** fesoit JK. 1969 **a** *om* J. 1970 **assist** fist soir St. **sur les** sous les E; sur ung RArSt. **norois** noirs RRa. 1971 **Loing** Loingnet ArSt. **si** *om* C. **qu'il** que Ar. **n'y ot qu'eulz** ny eust a eulz Ra. 1973 **se** ce K. **conforte** deporte CRArPcRaSt. 1974 **se** ce K. **li cuers** leurs cuers EJK; cellui corps RRa. **longuement tel mal** tel mal longuement PC; longuement et mal RRa. 1975 **porroit . . . morte** porra estre mors elle morte P. 1978 **destruit** destraint CPc. 1979 **plour** point Ar. **et tel** et en tel PCRa. **se** *om* PRRa. 1981 **Voit** Ot EJKArSt. **c'on** com Ar. **tost** tout Ar. 1982 **Ce c'on** Ce quen C; Ce com KAr; Et on St. **c'on ne** com ne K; qu'en ne Pc. 1983 **par plaindre** par plaint C; pour plaindre Ar. **ne plorer** ne par plourer C. 1985 **ce dit pas** pas ce dist EJK; je di pas ArSt.

Ne n'y chace barat ne fausseté,
D'Amours aussi qui en a bien parlé,
Et de Joinece,
Que cilz amans sueffre plus de tristrece,
Et que li mals d'amer plus fort le blece
Que la dame, ou moult a de noblece,
Et que plus loing
Est de confort, dont il ont bien besoing;
Et pour ce di mon jugement et doing,
Qu'il a plus mal qu'elle n'a, plus de soing
Et de grevance."
[Q]uant li bons roys ot rendu sa sentence
Dont par Raison fu faite l'ordennance,
Li chevaliers illuec en sa presence
L'en mercia,
Et en pensant, la dame s'oublia
Si durement que nul mot dit n'y a.
Mais nonpourquant en la fin ottroia
Qu'elle tenoit
Le jugement que li roys fait avoit; f. 94v
Car si sages et si loyaux estoit
Qu'envers nulluy fors raison ne feroit.
Adonc li roys
En sousriant les a pris par les dois
Et les assist sur les tapis norois,
Loing des autres, si qu'il n'y ot qu'eulz .iii..
Si leur ennorte
Et deprie chascun qu'il se conforte;
Car se li cuers longuement tel mal porte,
Il en porroit mors estre, et elle morte;
Que ja n'aviegne,
Mais chascun d'eulz bon courage repreigne;
Car li cuers trop se destruit et mehaigne
Qui en tel plour et tel dolour se baigne.
Et recorder
Voit on souvent c'on doit tost oublïer
Ce c'on voit bien c'on ne puet amender,
Ne recouvrer par plaindre ne plorer.
Se ainsi le font
Vers Loyauté, ce dit, pas ne meffont;

but if they dissolved into such tears for love's sake, they would destroy their souls and their lives.

Afterwards the king called together his household: there came Sincerity, Honor, Courtesy, Beauty, Desire, cheerful Happiness, and Bravery, Valor, Love, Loyalty, Generosity, and Will, Thought, Wealth, and Youth, and then Reason who was mistress over all. He commanded each of them to strive to honor these two lovers, for Love forbade them Melancholy. Then he ordered that food be prepared, for it was already near day's end. They did his bidding without delay, like good and well-instructed people. Then they went to the lovers without further ado; and each of them did his best to do what he thought would suit and please them, for they were all filled with good will.

The lovers asked leave to go, but were roundly refused, for Courtesy, Sincerity, Honor and his beloved Generosity, the noble king who never forgot himself, and all the others sweetly begged them to remain.

It was near the supper hour. At this word horns within the castle sounded the call to wash, and the loud trumpets too. They arose and entered the hall two by two; next they politely washed their hands; then they sat down, and drank and ate fittingly, for there was an abundance

1986 **s'en ce** ce en ce C; sen tel JK; sans ce RRa. **se deffont** se meffont C; ce deffont K. 1987 **Omicides** Comme homicide RRa. **ames** amer RRa. **seront** feront E. 1990 **S'y vint** Sa viens RRa. **franchise . . . courtoisie** honneurs franchise courtoisie Ar. 1991 **Beauté** Loyaute et P; Loyaulte RRa. **desir leece** delis et leeche Ar. **l'envoisie** renvoisie C. 1993 **loyauté** souvenirs P; et beaulte RRa. 1994–95 *inverted in* JK. 1994 **Vouloir** Valour Ra. **avec** et C. 1995 **de tous fu** sur tous est P; du compter fut RRa. 1996 **Si** Et RRa. **commande** demande ERRa. 1997 **d'eulz a honnorer** a honneur faire RRa. 1998 **qu'amours** que amer C; moult JK. 1999 **aprez que la** apres que leur RRa; apres che que la Ar; decy que la St. 2000 **Soit** Fu soit St. 2003 **Com** Comme Ra. **endoctrinee** ordonnee RRa. 2006 **a fait** le fait ArPc; li fait St. 2007 **Ce qu'il pense** Ce quilz pensent E; Tout ce que pense RRa; Et che quil pensent ArSt. **qui leur aggree** quilz leur aggree E; qui leur aide RRa; quil leur agree Ar. 2008 **Qu'entalenté** Quatalente C. 2009 **En estoient** Estoient JK; En estoit RRa; Tout en estoyent Ar. **de** en RRa. 2011–79 *missing in* K. 2011 **a baudement** abandonnement C. 2014 **qui** que JAr. 2015 **leur** les CEJRRa. 2016 **De** Du RRa. 2017 **Et . . . heure** Il estoit prez de leure P; Et il estoit pres deure J. **heure de** leure du Ar. 2018 **ce** cest C; cel St. **on prist** ont pris RRa; prist Ar. **l'yaue** leans J. **a corner** a tourner RRa. 2019 *om* St. **a** de Pc. 2021 **.ii. et .ii.** deulz et .ii. C; doy a doy RRa; doi et doi Ar. **en . . . en** ensamble sen RRa; sus en la sale Ar. 2023 **Puiz** Et puiz PEJRRaSt (+1). **si burent** et burent EJRArRaSt. 2025 **ot** eust RRaAr. **foison** faison E.

Mais s'en ce plour pour amer se deffont,
Omicides de leurs ames seront
Et de leur vie.
Aprez li roys appella sa maisnie:
S'y vint Franchise, Honneur, et Courtoisie,
Beauté, Desir, Leece l'envoisie,
Et Hardiece,
Proece, Amours, Loyauté, et Larguece,
Vouloir, Penser, Richece, avec Joinece,
Et puiz Raison, qui de tous fu maistresse.
Si leur commande
Que chascun d'eulz a honnorer entende f. 95
Ces .ii. amans, et qu'Amours leur deffende
Merencolie; aprez, que la viande
Soit aprestee,
Car il estoit ja prez de la vespree.
Et il ont fait son voeil sanz demoree
Com bonne gent et bien endoctrinee.
Lors se sont trait
Vers les amans, sanz faire plus de plait;
Et chascun d'eulz a son pooir a fait
Ce qu'il pense qui leur aggree et plait,
Qu'entalenté
En estoient de bonne volenté.
Et li amant ont congié demandé;
Et on leur a baudement refusé,
Car Courtoisie,
Franchise, Honneur, et Larguece s'amie,
Li gentilz roys qui pas ne s'y oublie,
Et chascun d'eulz moult doucement leur prie
De demorer.
Et il estoit prez heure de souper.
Et a ce mot on prist l'yaue a corner
Par le chastel, et forment a tromper.
Si se leverent
Et .ii. et .ii. en la sale en alerent;
Aprez leurs mains courtoisement laverent;
Puiz s'assistrent, si burent et mengerent
Selon raison,
Car il y ot plenté et a foison

of whatever one might have or say was good. After eating, the noble king drew them by their robes and said to them: "You'll stay for several months, because I want to rid you at this time of those melancholy thoughts that are causing you anguish."

The knight began to excuse himself, and the lady likewise, who said she could tarry no longer. Finally the king detained them happily for a week, and upon their departure gave them generously horses, trappings, jewels, gold, and silver. At the end of the week they took leave of the king and departed, saying they'd never seen so good and noble a king, nor been treated with so much honor. Honor accompanied them, as did Courtesy, Youth, Love, cheerful Wealth, and many another whose name I cannot recall. These mounted their horses and kept the two company until each reached home, then returned to the king at Durbuy.

Here I'll end my account and rhyme no more, for I've enough rhymes to write elsewhere. But at the end of this little book I'll ensure that he who wants to learn truly my name and surname can clearly perceive it in the final line of the booklet, provided that he separates the first seven syllables and rearranges the letters in a different fashion, without omitting or forgetting any. In this way he who wishes can dis-

2026 **canqu'on . . . n'avoir** canque len porroit avoir P; quanquon pot dire et avoir C; quanqui pot dire navoir E; Quanques on peut dire navoir RRa; quanquez on poeut avoir Ar. 2027 **giron** gieron E. 2029 **Et . . . dist** Et dist RRa; Et lor dist Ar. 2031 **Les pensees** Les pensers RRa; Les vos pensees Ar. **moult vous font** vous font moult CRRa. **d'ennoys** destrois J. 2033 **l'en** le RRa. 2035 **pooit** se pot P; peust RRa. **ce** si RRa. **de** du Ar. 2036 **Et finalment** Finablement EJRRaSt. 2037 **.viii.** .vii. P. 2038 **larguement** de largent RRa; liement Ar. 2039 **harnoys joyaux** joyaulx assez RRa. 2040 **Si se** Et se CPc; Et sen RRa. 2041 **Au . . . .viii.** A .viii. P (−1); Au chief des .viii. E; Au bout de .viii. RRa; Au chief de che huit. Ar. **et** *om* Ra. **du roy** au roy PAr; *om* St. **congié prinsrent** congie si prirent RRa; le congie prinrent St. 2042 **Ou tant orent** Qui tant heurent RRa. **d'onneur qu'il** damour qui RRa; de grant honnour quil Ar. 2043 **Qu'onc** Quains EJSt; Que RPcRa. **ne si gentil** ne fu ne si gentil Ar. 2045 **aussi fist** et si fist C; et aussi (fist *om*) St. 2046 **richesse** leece P. **l'envoisie** li aisiee C; le aisie ArPcSt. 2047 **maint** pluisour Ar. 2048 **Car** Qua E. 2049 **tant** tout St. 2050 **leur hostel** leur chastel P; son hostel CERArRa. 2051 **au roy a Durbuy** daroy a dambury RRa; au roy de durbuy St. 2053 **ne plus ne** ne plus nen CE; et plus ne RRaSt; et plus nen Pc. 2054 **autre** dautre PE. **ay** lay Ra. 2055 **ce livret** cest livret C; ce livre RRaSt. 2057 **Vourra mon nom** Vaurra mon nom P; Mon nom vouldra RRa. **de voir** pour voir P; avoir Ar; savoir St. 2058 **le** *om* RRa. **percevoir** apparcevoir R. 2059 **Ou . . . ver** Au derrenier (ver *om*) P; Au derrenier ver ERRa. 2061–79 *missing in* P. 2061 *om* RRa. **premieres** premiers E. **d'ensemble** desamble E; je dessamble St. 2063 **nulle** ne nesune Ar.

De canqu'on peut dire n'avoir de bon.
Aprez mengier les prist par le giron
  Li gentilz roys,
Et si leur dist: "Vous n'en irez des mois, f. 95v
Car je vous voeil oster a ceste fois
Les pensees qui moult vous font d'ennoys."
  Le chevalier
Moult humblement l'en prist a mercïer,
Et aussi fist la dame qui targïer
Ne pooit plus, ce dit, de repairier.
  Et finalment
Li roys les tint .viii. jours moult lïement,
Et au partir leur donna larguement
Chevaux, harnoys, joyaux, or, et argent.
  Si se partirent
Au chief de .viii. jours et du roy congié prinsrent,
Ou tant orent trouvé d'onneur qu'il disrent
Qu'onc si bon roy ne si gentil ne virent.
  Mais compaignie
Leur fist Honneur; aussi fist Courtoisie,
Joinece, Amour, Richesse l'envoisie,
Et maint autre que nommer ne sçay mie.
  Car il monterent
Sur les chevaux et tant les convoierent
Que chascun d'eulz en leur hostel menerent,
Et puiz au roy a Durbuy retournerent.
  Ci fineray
Ma matere, ne plus ne rimeray;
Car autre part assez a rimer ay.
Mais en la fin de ce livret feray
  Que qui savoir
Vourra mon nom et mon surnom de voir,
Il le porra clerement percevoir
Ou derrein ver du livret et veoir,
  Mais qu'il dessemble
Les premieres .vii. sillabez d'ensemble
Et les lettres d'autre guise rassemble,
Si que nulle n'en oublie në emble.
  Ainssi pourra
Mon non savoir, qui savoir le vourra;

cover my name; but he'll not think more of me because of this. Despite all this I'll not be any less a faithful, happy, joy-filled lover, for had I nothing in this world more than the fact that I love my innocent and lovely lady against her inclination, yet do I have enough, for Love has honored me and richly rewarded my pain, since thus I've given my heart to my lady forever. And this consoles my heart in its tribulations that, when first I felt Love's sorrows, I hoped for humble relief for my sweet sorrow.

2066 **ja . . . ne** pour ce mieulx ja ne RRa. 2067 **Et . . . ja** Maiz nonpourquant E; Et non tant la R. 2068 **je** *om* RRa. 2069 **amis jolis** amans joyaux EJ; amans jolis Ar. 2071 **j'aim** jayme RRa. 2072 **Contre** Outre E; Et de J. 2073 **je** *om* Ar. **honnouré** hoonnoure (*sic*) Pc. 2074 **Et richement** Richement et RRa. 2075 **ainsi** ay si RArRa. 2076 **Ai** Mais Ar. **a** *om* E. 2077 **ce** se EJ; ont RRa; com Ar. 2078 **Que quant** Quant au E; Et quant Ar. **les maulz** le mal J. 2079 **A** Ou EJ. **gentil** gentilz J. **cuide** cuiday EJ.

Explicit Ci fenist le temps pascour C; Explicit EPc; Explicit le jugement J; Explicit le jugement damours etc. R; Explicit le Jugement damours Ra; Ce livre compila et fist maistre guillam de Machaut St; Explicit le jugement du roy de behaingne Kr.

Mais ja pour ce mieulz ne m'en prisera.
Et nonpourquant ja pour ce ne sera
  Que je ne soie
Loyaus amis, jolis, et plains de joie;
Car se rien plus en ce monde n'avoie
Fors ce que j'aim ma dame simple et coie
  Contre son gré,
Si ai je assez, qu'Amours m'a honnouré
Et richement mon mal guerredonné,
Quant a ma dame ainsi mon cuer donné
  Ai a tous jours.
Et ce mon cuer conforte en ses doulours
Que, quant premiers senti les maulz d'Amours,
A gentil mal cuidë humble secours.

Explicit

REMEDE DE FORTUNE

He who wishes to learn any skill must take heed of twelve things: first, he must choose something to which his heart most leads him and for which he has a natural inclination, because a person does not willingly finish what he seeks to do contrary to his will, since Nature stands against him. He should love his master and his profession above everything; and he must honor, obey, and serve them; and he must not feel he is enslaving himself, for if he loves them, they will love him; and if he hates them, they will hate him: he can gain nothing otherwise. He must receive instruction meekly; and he must be careful to follow it, for learning is difficult to retain and easily forgotten when it is not put into practice. He should be diligent, assiduous, and eager for knowledge, for thus can he attain wisdom. And he should seek it at an early age, before his heart turns to wickedness through too much experience; for the true state of innocence is like the white and polished tablet that is ready to receive the exact image of whatever one wishes to portray or paint upon it. And it is also like wax that can be written upon, and which retains the form and imprint exactly as one has imprinted it.

Title Missing CPe; Ci commence remede de fortune JK; Ci commence lescu bleu E. 4 **le tire** se tire EJKPe. 5 **Et** *om* E. **n. l'encline** n. plus lencline Pe. 6 **define** se fine J; ce fine K. 7 **Qu'en** Com JKPe. **gre** cuer JKPe. 10 **est m.** est bien m. Pe. 11 **et** *om* EKPe. 13 **s'il** cil K. 14 **s'il** si JK. 17 **Et** Mais EJKPe. **se** ce K. 19 **et** *om* JK. 20 **continuee** continue K. 21 **penser desir** desir penser J. **de** et C. 22 **si** il JK. 23 **l'entreprengne** lautre preingne JK. 24 **son courage** sencourage E. 25 **Mue** Que E. 26 **d'innocence** de jouvence JK. 28 **Blanche polie** Blanche et polie E; Blanche et poli Pe. 30 **c'on** com JK. **paindre** prindre K. **ou** et EPe. 35 **Ainssi** Ausi Pe.

(Miniature 1) [*No caption*]

Cilz qui veult aucun art aprendre f. 23a
A .xii. choses doit entendre:
La premiere est qu'il doit eslire
Celui ou ses cuers mieus le tire
Et ou sa nature l'encline;
Car la chose envis bien define
Qu'en veult encontre son gré faire,
Quant Nature li est contraire.
Aimme son maistre et son mestier
Sus tout; et ce li est mestier
Qu'il l'onneure, obeïsse et serve;
Et ne quide pas qu'il s'asserve,
Car s'il les aimme, il l'ameront,
Et s'il les het, il le harront:

Profiter ne puet autrement. f. 23b
Doctrine rechoive humblement;
Et bien se gart qu'il continue,
Car scïence envis retenue
Est et de legier oublïee,
Quant elle n'est continuee.
Soing, penser, desir de savoir
Ait, si pourra scïence avoir.
Et l'entreprengne en joene aage,
Ains qu'en malice son courage
Mue par trop grant cognoissance;
Car le droit estat d'innocence
Ressamble proprement la table
Blanche, polie, qui est able
A recevoir, sans nul contraire,
Ce c'on y veult paindre ou pourtraire;
Et est aussi comme la cire
Qui sueffre dedens li escrire,
Ou qui retient forme ou emprainte, f. 23va
Si com on l'a en li emprainte.

Ainssi est il certainement
De vray humain entendement

Truly it is the same with human understanding, which is ready to receive whatever one wishes and can apprehend whatever one sets it to: arms, love, other art or letter. For there is nothing so difficult that it cannot master it if it so chooses, provided it is willing to work and toil in accordance with what I have said above.

For this reason I have said that when I was in the state of innocence, when Youth governed me and kept me in idleness, my works were fleeting; my heart was changeable: whatever I saw was the same to me, except that my heart and all my thoughts were ever on my lady, who is proclaimed by all to be the most beautiful and best above all. Everyone rightly gives her this name. And she has so many of the gifts that Nature can grant her creatures that she is the sovereign flower above all human creatures.

Therefore my heart was inclined towards her, and Nature taught it this, I believe; because truly in accord with my youthful understanding I was ever eager to see her; for my ways and paths, my games, my thoughts, my recourses were ever in her person; and without seeing her I could not have perfect joy.

And when Love saw that I'd reached this point, she didn't hesitate,

37 **ables** able C (−1). 38 **c'on** com CJK. 39 **tout** *om* JK. **a** en E. 41 **chose** choses Pe. **puet** peuent E. 43 **faire** face JK. 46 JK *replace this line with* De jouvence quant je y estoie. 50 **varians** variaux JK. 52 **enclinoie** menclinoie JK. 63 **car** *om* Pe. 65–66 *reversed in* JK. 69 **n'avoir** mavoir E. 70 **parfaite** pour faire E. 73 **se** ce K.

Qui est ables a recevoir
Tout ce c'on veult et concevoir
Puet tout ce a quoy on le veult mettre:
Armes, amours, autre art, ou lettre.
Car chose ne puet si fort estre,
S'il veult, qu'il n'en deviengne mestre,
Mes qu'il veulle faire et labeure
A ce que j'ay dit cy desseure.

Pour ce l'ay dit que, quant j'estoie
De l'estat qu'innocence avoie,
Que Jonnesce me gouvernoit
Et en oyseuse me tenoit,
Mes oeuvres estoient volages;
Varians estoit mes courages:
Tout m'estoit un quanque veoie,
Fors tant que tousdis enclinoie
Mon cuer et toute ma pensee
Vers ma dame, qui est clamee
De tous sur toutes belle et bonne.
Chascun par droit ce non li donne.
Et de tous les biens que Nature
Puet ottroier a creature
Ha tant, qu'elle est fleur souveraine
Seur toute creature humaine.

Pour ce a lui mes cuers s'enclinoit,
Et Nature li aprenoit,
Ce m'est vis; car certainement
Selonc mon jonne entendement
La veoie moult volentiers;
Car mes voies et mes sentiers,
Mi gieu, mi penser, mi retour
Estoient en son noble atour
Tout adés; n'avoir ne pouoie,
Sans li veoir, parfaite joye.

Et quant Amours vit qu'en ce point f. 23vb
Estoie, elle n'atendi point,
Ains se mella par tel maniere

but rather intervened in such a way that then and always I must love, obey, serve, and honor her above everything God has made, with my whole heart and actions, and be entirely hers at every time and moment according to the law of the lover. For this was my first love and will be my last; therefore I shall die serving her and will never love another. Now may God grant that her love be mine, for in this world I want nothing more.

Thus Love, by her skill, which gently enflames many a noble heart, caused my lady's great beauty to carry away my heart when first I saw her. When I was kindled by her love, I was young and inexperienced, and I had much to learn if I wished to embark upon such a course. What am I saying? I had already embarked upon it, having asked advice and leave only of my heart and her eyes, which often laughingly bid me so sweetly to love her that I dared not and could not refuse their wish. My heart wanted me to be hers entirely, and I too wanted it, and therefore I heeded their advice. Thus, God help me, I was captured by Sweet Laughter and Sweet Looks. Yet truly, if I were so gifted as to be as wise as Solomon, and if all the world were completely mine, and I were

81 **ç'a** sa JKPe. 86 **Qu'en** En JK. 87 **fist** fu E. 91–150 *om* JK. 93 **mestier** besoing E. 96 **conseil ne congié** congie ne conseil E. 101 **ne p.** ne ne p. EPe. 107 **se** ce E. 109 **com** comme CEPe (+1).

Que puis ne fu, ne jamais n'iere,
Que sur tout quanque Dieus a fait
Ne l'aimme de cuer et de fait,
Obeïsse, serve, et honneure,
Et qu'en tous temps et en toute heure
Ne soie tous siens sans demi
A loy de tres loyal ami.
Car ç'a esté m'amour premiere,
Et si sera la derreniere;
Pour ce en li servant finerai,
Ne jamais autre n'amerai.
Or doint Dieus que s'amour soit moie,
Qu'en ce monde plus ne voudroie.

Ainssi fist Amours par son art
Qui maint franc cuer doucement art
Que, quant premiers ma dame vi,
Sa grant biauté mon cuer ravi.
Et quant de s'amour fui espris,
Jonnes estoie et desapris,
S'avoie bien mestier d'aprendre,
Quant tel fait vouloie entreprendre.
Que dis je? Ains l'avoie entrepris,
Qu'ains conseil ne congié n'en pris
Fors a mon cuer et a ses yeus,
Qui en riant m'ont en maint lieus
Prié que par amours l'amasse
Si doucement, que je n'osasse
Leur veul refuser, ne peüsse.
Et mes cuers vouloit que je fusse
Touz siens, et je aussi le vouloie,
Et pour ce a eulz me conseilloie.
Si qu'ainssi fui, se Dieus me gart,
Pris par Doulz Ris et Douz Regart.

Et certainement, se je eüsse
Tant de bien en moy que je fusse
Aussi sages com Salemons, f. 24a
Et fust miens quites tout li mons,
Et aussi preus comme Alixandres
Ou comme Hector, qui gaire mandres

as valiant as Alexander or as Hector (who was scarcely less brave than he) and if I had as much honor as Godfrey of Bouillon, and the beauty of Absalon, and Job's great patience, and the steadfastness and constancy of Judith and of Socrates, who always held to one position, because he would not change it for loss or for gain, no matter how great; and if I had in addition the humility of Esther and the faithfulness of Abraham, in truth I would still not be worthy to love a lady of such rank. But Love made me do it, who made me her liege man when first I saw her; so I am hers without reserve, come what may, and will be hers as long as I live, nor shall I ever love another.

(2) *How Love chastises the Lover*

And when Love had made me her captive and a loyal lover, she clearly perceived my youth, my innocence, my inexperience; and since I was still a child, she took me under her guidance. She showed me the right path: how I must love, serve, obey, honor, humbly believe and adore my lady, and fear her above all creatures as my love and my

115 **ot** eust E. 118 **et** *om* C. **constance** contestance C. 120 **estoit** estoient E. 121 **Car** Que C. 133 **com** comme Pe. 135 **m'ot** mont E. 136 **fuy** sui E. 138 **innocence** juvence E. 146 **Com** Comme EPe.

Ne fu de li quant a valour,
Et sc'eüsse autretant d'onnour
Comme ot Godefroy de Buyllon,
Et la biauté qu'ot Absalon,
Et de Job la grant pasciensce,
L'estableté et la constance
Et de Judich et de Socratés,
Qui en .i. point estoit adés,
Car pour gaaingne ne pour perte
Ne se mouvoit, tant fust aperte,

Et avec ce l'umilité
Que Hester ot, et la loyauté
De Abraham, a verité dire,
Ne peüsse je pas sousfire
Pour dame amer de tel affaire.
Mais Amours le me firent faire
Qui m'i donnerent liegement,
Quant je la vi premierement;
Si que siens sans riens retenir
Sui, quoy qu'il m'en doie avenir,
Et serai, tant com je vivray,
Ne jamais autre amour n'avray.

(Miniature 2) *Comment Amours chastie l'Amant*

Et quant Amours m'ot a ce mis f. 24b
Que pris fuy et loyaus amis,
Elle congnut bien ma jonnesce,
Mon innocence, ma simplesce;
Et pour ce qu'estoie en enfance,
Me prist elle en sa gouvernance.
Si me moustra la droite voie:
Comment ma dame amer devoie,
Servir, obeïr, honnourer,
Humblement croirre et aourer,
Et cremir sur toute autre rien
Com m'amour et mon dieu terrien;
Et que tousdis eüsse l'ueil

earthly god; how I must constantly be alert to do her will and her desire, while preserving her honor and her tranquility; how, if pain or suffering were to come to me from loving, or melancholy or sadness, I should welcome it submissively and not consider myself aggrieved; also she showed me how I must be careful to make this love last, and ever, near and far, have desire, thought, and care to acquire her love and her grace, never desiring or seeking any other; and how I must be loyal and secret. These are the points and articles that Love taught and instructed me in when she took me under her guidance; and I learned them so well that never afterwards did I violate a single one of them.

And also my very sweet lady, whom, by my soul, I desire and love in my heart, without any unworthy thought, more than ever Paris did Helen, was my mirror and exemplar for desiring and doing all that is good. And for the good I saw in her, I strove with all my might to do only what was right and to keep from doing wrong, so that no one could find fault with me, because her goodness gave me the heart and will to do so.

And her perfect humility assured that I behaved humbly and gently to all and was my shield, defense, and sentinel against Pride, who en-

149 **s'onnour** samour E. 151 **Me . . . doulour** Ne navoie nulle d. JK. 152 **Ou** *om* JK. **ou** ne JK. 153 **tout** *om* JK. **humblement r.** humblement ne r. JK. 154 **grevés** gueriz JK; greurs E. **m'en** me EPe. 162 **les poins** les les poins Pe. 164 **gouvernance** gouvernement J. 166 **ne** nen C. 170 **Plus que** Et plus que E. 174 **tout bien** touz biens JK. 176 **me** men EPe. 184 **maintenisse** tenisse C (−1).

A faire son bon et son veul,
En gardant s'onnour et sa pais;
Et que, se de l'amoureus fais
Me venoit painne ne doulour,
Ou merancolie, ou tristour,
Que tout humblement recueillisse,
Et qu'a grevés ne m'en tenisse;

Et aussi que bien me gardasse
Que ceste amour continuasse,
Et qu'adés, de prés et de loing,
Desir, penser eüsse et soing
De s'amour et sa grace aquerre,
Sans autre desirer ne querre;
Et que loyaus fusse et secrez.
Ce sont les poins et les degrez
Qu'Amours m'ensaigna et aprist,
Quant en gouvernance me prist;
Et je les ai si bien apris
Que puis en un seul ne mespris.

Et aussi ma tres douce dame,
Que je desir et aim, par m'ame,
De cuer, sans pensee vilaine,
Plus que Paris ne fist Helaine,
M'estoit mireoir et examplaire f. 24va
De tous biens desirer et faire.
Et pour le bien qu'en li veoie,
De tout bien faire me penoie
Et me gardoie de mesprendre,
Si qu'on ne me peüst reprendre,
A mon pouoir, car sa bonté
M'en donnoit cuer et volenté.

Et son humilité parfaite
M'estoit escus, desfense, et guaite
Qu'Orgueux ne me peüst seurprendre,
Qui maint mal nourrist et engendre,
Et qu'envers tous tres doucement
Me maintenisse et humblement.

genders and nourishes many evils. And truly I can say that she is the font and wellspring of humility; never was turtledove (he or she), lamb, pigeon or little dove, maiden or virgin more free of pride, or more filled than she with humility, joined with pity, in all instances and places. And it is properly so indeed, because it comes to her by birthright; and in this she does not forsake her inheritance.

Her confident manner, praised by man and woman alike, her fair demeanor and noble bearing that I hold to be without peer, taught me, as the master teaches the child, how to be. Nothing more than the memory of them improved my own comportment, manner, and bearing when I was far from her and remembered them. Therefore, when I saw her face to face and contemplated her demeanor, her comportment, her manner, which were more constant and harmonious than any I have ever seen, it was quite fitting that I retain from them some memorable lesson, since through memory alone Sweet Thought often amended my behavior.

And her gracious way of speaking, which was not capricious or foolish, unkind or malicious, nor haughty, but was moderate, well-

186 **et** a JK. 193 **endrois** adrois Pe. 200 **n'ont** not E. 202 **m'aprenoient** maprenoit C (−1); maprenoie E. 205 **Loing** Lors C. 212 **qu'en** que JK. 215 **douce** mainte E. 216 **maniere** mame Pe. 220 **affremee** affermee EPe; afervee J; afirvee K. 221 **saison** raison E.

Et vraiement bien dire puis
Que d'umblesce est fontaine et puis;
Qu'onques turtre ne turterelle,
Aigniaus, coulons, ne coulombelle,
Damoyselle, ne pucellete
Ne pot estre d'orgueil plus nette,
Ne plus plaine d'umilité,
Acompaignie de pité,
En tous cas et en tous endrois,
De li. Certes, et c'est bien drois,
Car il li vient de droite ligne;
Pour ce en ce cas pas ne forligne.

Et sa maniere asseüree,
De tous et de toutes loee,
Son biau port, son gentil maintien
Qui pareil n'ont, si com je tien,
Tout aussi com l'enfant le mestre
Aprent, m'aprenoient a estre.
Car, sans plus, de leur remembrance,
Maintieng, maniere, et contenance
Loing de li souvent me venoit
Meilleur, quant il m'en souvenoit.
Si que dont, quant je la veoie
Vis a vis et que remiroie
Son port, son maintien, sa maniere, f. 24vb
Qui plus est estable et entiere
Que nulle qu'onquez mes veïsse,
Bien estoit droiz qu'en retenisse
Aucun notable ensaignement,
Quant dou souvenir seulement
Maintez foys par Douce Pensee
Ma maniere estoit amendee.

Et sa gracieuse parole,
Qui n'estoit diverse ne fole,
Estrange ne mal ordenee,
Hautaine, mes bien affremee,
Cueillie a point et de saison,
Fondee sur toute raison,

chosen, and appropriate, based wholly on reason, so pleasant and sweet to hear, causing everyone to be cheerful, bridled my speech to keep me from saying anything that might be called slander. But I was given rein to speak what was good, for one should never say of another what he does not want to hear about himself. She forbade me to speak frivolously; she ordered me to speak measuredly, without boasting and bragging, without lying and flattery; because it's a very honorable thing to be truthful in speaking, and Truth seeks no angles and has no time for lies.

Her honor and great courtesy forbade me base actions and directed me to honor everyone and think little of myself; for he has honor who acts honorably, not he to whom honor is paid. And if the Gospel is not wrong, he who exalts himself is humbled, and he who humbles himself is exalted. This is why my lady's name is so exalted through all the world, for she abounds in humility, honor, and courtesy more than any lady alive; and even though everyone accords her the prize and crown of honor, she has so much honor that she believes herself to be the least of all. She knew nothing of foolish giving, nor of the pettiness of

226 **de ce** a tout ce JK. 227 **qu'on** com KEPe. 228 **laisse** lessier J; lessiez K; laissie E. **avoit pour** avoir pour C; le et JK. 235 **c'est** est J. 236 **son** *om* C (−1). 242 **que** *om* Pe. 245 **se** ce JK. 246 **qui s'essausse** que ce essauce J; que se essauce K. 247 **s'umilie essauciés** sessauce humiliez CJPe; lessauce humiliez K. 250 **habonde** sabonde E. 252 **que** quen JK. 253 **comment** doint E. 255 **Estre** Questre E.

Tant plaisant et douce a oïr,
Que chascun faisoit resjoïr,
Me metoit .i. frain en la bouche
Pour moy taire de ce qui touche
A tout ce qu'on claime mesdire.
Mais laisse avoit pour le bien dire,
Car nulz ne doit dire d'autrui
Ce qu'il ne veult oïr de lui.

Le trop parler me deffendoit;
Parler a point me commandoit,
Sans baudour et sans vanterie,
Sans mentir et sans flaterie;
Car c'est chose moult honourable
D'estre en son parler veritable,
Et Verité ne quiert nulz angles,
N'elle n'a que faire de jangles.
S'onneur et sa grant courtoysie
Me deffendoient villainnie
Et vouloient que je honourasse
Chascun, et que pou me prisasse;
Car cilz a l'onnour qui le fait,
Non pas cilz a qui on la fait.

Et se l'Evangille n'est fausse,
Humiliez est qui s'essausse,
Et qui s'umilie essauciés. f. 25a
Pour ce est li noms si essauchiez
De ma dame par tout le monde,
Qui en humilité habonde,
En honnour et en courtoysie,
Plus que dame qui soit en vie;
Et comment que chascuns li donne
Le pris d'onnour et la couronne,
Estre cuide, tant a d'onnour,
Entre les autres la menour.

Ne congnoissoit fole largesce,
Ne d'escharseté la simplesce,
Ne la destresce d'avarice,

cupidity, nor of the misery of avarice, which is a great vice in the human heart. Whenever she gave, she prudently reckoned her gifts and unfailingly knew what, when, how much, to whom, and why. She gave promptly and willingly, making her gift more valuable; for he who gives promptly, gives twice. In this she was a good instructor to me, by teaching me not to be a foolish giver, nor avaricious, nor stingy, which Generosity hates mercilessly, and above all to avoid the head and shaft of the arrow of avarice, which causes every other good to perish wherever it manages to strike. For no matter how honored a man may be, his reputation will be destroyed and he will lose wisdom, honor, spirit, praise, and worth if he has been grasping.

And her great sweetness never left my heart on any account, because it made its home and dwelling therein night and day. And just as sweet balm reduces and eases the pain of a wound, her great sweetness eased the suffering that Love and Desire caused me, who gave me many a painful blow for which I don't lament or complain, since I feel no pain or suffering, but receive them meekly, simply, and joyfully.

And her very sweet pleasant glance attracted my heart to it, by its

264 **et** ne JK. 270 **Que n.** Que je n. Pe. 272 **Que** Qui JK. **het** ait E. 273 **fer ne f.** ferme f. E; feit ne f. Pe. 274 **fust** sceust E; feust Pe. 275 **perir** porrir E. 276 **se** ce K. 277 **tant** si K. 278 **ne** nen JK. **devourez** demourez JK. 279 **s'il a pris** sil la pris CPe; si la pris J. 280 **ame . . . pris** laime et p. E. 282 **se** ce K. 283 **et** a E. 284 **Y** Il JK. 286 **trait** entrait E. 290 **Qui** Que E. **estour** assault EPe. 292 **ne dueil** ne pau dueil E. 293 **les** le EJK. 296 **Atraioit** Atroit E. **de** a EJK.

Qui est en cuer humain grant vice.
Mes tousdis, quant elle donnoit,
Ses dons sagement ordenoit
Et savoit certainement quoy,
Quant, comment, a qui, et pourquoy.
Tost le faisoit et volentiers,
S'en estoit ses dons plus entiers;
Car qui tost donne, .ii. foys donne.
De ce m'estoit mestresse bonne
Qui m'aprenoit a bonne escole
Que n'eüsse largesce fole,
Avarice, n'escharseté,
Que Largesce het sans pité,
Et sur tout qu'en moy fer ne fust
Du dart d'avarice ne fust,
Qui tout autre bien fait perir
Partout ou il se puet ferir.
Car ja hons n'iert tant honourez,
Que ses biens ne soit devourez
Et qu'il n'en perde, s'il a pris,
Sens, honnour, ame, los, et pris.

Et sa grant douçour a nul fuer
Ne se departoit de mon cuer,
Car sa demeure et son sejour
Y faisoit de nuit et de jour.
Et aussi com le doulz entrait f. 25b
La doulour d'une plaie trait
Et adoucist, sa grant douçour
Faisoit adoucir la doulour
Qu'Amours et Desirs me faisoient,
Qui maint grief estour me donnoient,
Des quielz je ne me plaing ne dueil,
Car je n'en ay painne ne dueil,
Ainçoys les recueil humblement,
Bonnement, et joyeusement.

Et son tres doulz plaisant regart
Atraioit mon cuer de sa part
Tout aussi, par son doulz attrait,

sweet attraction, just as a magnet attracts iron. And this kept my heart joyful, for when I perceived this sweet glance, nothing contrary to joy could find lodging in me. And her beauty, which surpasses all other, bound my heart in her service and her love and binds it more and more from day to day, and taught me, by its power, to know Sweet Hope and to desire Love's mercy, for which I thank her profoundly. For indeed I did not know Hope or Desire when her beauty put me on the path to meet them, in order to increase my love and my joy, for Love increases and prompts Desire, and Joy brings Hope.

And her beautiful, fair, and noble attire, which, as everyone says, is modest, elegant, stylish and lovely, taught me and still teaches me to dress elegantly, properly, and handsomely, with good taste; for he who dresses extravagantly, indeed, does not dress well; but the best thing to do is to attain the happy mean.

Thus her excellent goodness, her perfect humility, her constant manner, her noble demeanor, her modest comportment, her fair words, her high honor, her unerring courtesy, her open generosity, her

298 **Com** Comme Pe. 299 **ce** se CE. 300 **ce** son JK. 302 **qui fust** qui faist C; quil fust E; qui fu Pe. 303 **qui** que J. 307 **par** en E. 314 **m'amour** amour E. 315 **desir et e.** et desirs e. CE. 319 **faitis a.** fait a. E. 320 **encor acointe** encour a. C; encore a. E; encor macointe JK. 323 **pou** pour Pe. **qui se d.** qui trop se d. C (+1); sui se E; qui ce d. K. 326 **a tenir** a maintenir Pe. 333 **franche** franch K.

Com l'aymant le fer attrait.
Et ce tenoit mon cuer en joie,
Car quant ce doulz regart veoie,
En moy ne prenoit son repaire
Rien qui fust a joie contraire.
Et sa beauté, qui toutes passe,
Enlaçoit mon cuer et enlace
De plus en plus de jour en jour
En son service et en s'amour,
Et m'aprenoit, par sa poissance,
A congnoistre Douce Esperance
Et a desirer la merci
D'Amours, dont moult la remerci.
Car certes, je ne congnoissoie
Espoir ne Desir, quant en voie
Me mist sa beauté du congnoistre,
Pour m'amour et ma joie acroistre,
Qu'Amours croist Desir et enorte,
Et Esperance Joie apporte.

Et son noble atour bel et gent,
Qui est, au dit de toute gent,
Simple, faitis, appert, et cointe,
M'acointoit et encor acointe
Que me tenisse cointement,
Nettement, et joliëment,
Trop ne pou; car qui se desguise, f. 25va
Certes, ce n'est pas belle guise;
Mes qui puet au moien venir,
C'est le plus seür a tenir.

Ainssi son exellent bonté
Et sa parfaite humilité,
Sa maniere qui n'est volage,
Son gentil port, son maintien sage,
Son beau parler, sa haute honnour,
Sa courtoysie sans errour,
Sa franche liberalité,
Sa douçour plaine d'amisté,
Son doulz regart, sa beauté fine,

friendly sweetness, her sweet glance, her pure beauty, and her attire offered me a splendid example and much good, if I could imitate them well. And even though I could but little imitate the many perfections I saw in her, I would have done very badly had I not shown some improvement. But if I have profited, I'll not willingly brag about it, because praise grows dim in the mouth of him who praises himself. Nevertheless, without boasting and without lying I want to say, in her praise only, that if ever I am worth anything in my life, it will have come straight from her, to whom I yield my heart, body, and soul.

Thus the fair one, whose person expresses all good lessons, taught me this very noble lesson, which is so precious and fine. And for a long while I served her so lovingly with my heart that I paid no attention to anything other than her love to which I was inclined. But she knew nothing of any of this, nor of how she'd captured me, because nothing could compel me to reveal or tell her of the love in my heart; nor could I have revealed it to her if I'd wanted to or known how; instead, I bore this love secretly and hidden, making no complaint or outcry about it, for I was burning so with love for her. Nonetheless, when I felt the

336 **atour** estour Pe. 337 **Me . . . bien** Me moustroient et moult de b. JK; Me moustroient a maint b. E; Me moustroient et maint b. Pe. 343 **se** ce JK. 344 **diroie** disoie K. 345 **assourdist** absordist C; ensourdist JK. 352 JK *replace this line with*: En cuer en corps en ame en vail. 354 **Qui** Que Pe. 357 **la** lai Pe. 360 **je tendoie** jentendoie E. 364 **ne deïsse** ne li deisse JK. 369 **en** *om* E. 372 **espart** esgart E.

Et son atour belle doctrine
Me demoustroient et maint bien,
Se je les retenisse bien.
Et ja soit ce qu'en li veïsse
Tous biens, et pou en retenisse,
Ne puet estre que miulz n'en vaille,
Ou ce seroit mal fait sans faille.
Et se retenu les avoie,
Volentiers pas ne les diroie,
Pour ce que löenge assourdist
En bouche qui de li le dist.
Et nonpourquant tant en vueil dire
Sans vanterie et sans mesdire
A sa löenge seulement,
Que de li venra proprement,
S'en toute ma vie rien vail,
A qui cuer, corps, et ame bail.

Ainssi la tres noble doctrine
Qui tant est precieuse et fine
De la belle me doctrina,
Qui toute bonne doctrine a.
Et je la servi longuement
De cuer si amoureusement,
Qu'a nulle autre rien n'entendoie
Fors a s'amour ou je tendoie.
Mais de tout ce riens ne savoit, f. 25vb
Ne comment elle pris m'avoit;
Car pour riens ne li descouvrisse
L'amour de mon cuer, ne deïsse,
Ne descouvrir ne li peüsse,
Se je vousisse ne sceüsse;
Ains portoie couvertement
Ceste amour et celeement,
Sans faire en plainte ne clamour,
Tant estoie espris de s'amour.

Nonpourquant, quant de son regart
Sentoie le tres doulz espart,
Je perdoie toute vigour

sweet spark of her glance, I lost all strength under its force and power; it caused me to grow pale and flush, to shake, tremble, and shudder. Then one could well perceive that I loved her without deceit over five hundred thousand times more than myself, without pretense and with a lover's heart. So I spent my youth in Sweet Thought, in Memory, in Hope of attaining the grace of my sweet noble lady, whom I desire so much that I have no other desire.

Thus I felt many wounds, at one moment sweet, at another bitter, at one pleasant, at another disagreeable, at one sad, at another joyful. For the heart that feels Love's wound is not always in one mood, nor sure of joy or tribulation; rather, it is subject to the whims of the fortune of Love. But with head hung like a bear, I accepted her sweet biddings, whether for joy or for sorrow, meekly like a perfect lover, loyal in word and deed.

And since I was not always in one mood, I learned to compose chansons and lais, ballades, rondeaux, virelais, and songs, according to my feelings, about love and nothing else; because he who does not compose according to his feelings falsifies his work and his song. Nor could I show my lady, who is the charming inspiration for my song,

374 **sa . . . rigour** la force de sa vigour JK. 381 **S'usoie** Usoie JK. 382 **ma tres douce dame** ma dame tresdouce dame E. 388 **l'autre** les autres J. 393 **ou** ne JK. 397 **son . . . vouloir** sans tresdoulz valloir E. 400 **Et loyaus** Amoureus JK. 403 **Mis en** Mais a J; Mis a K. 410 **Les** Telz JK. 412 *om* JK.

Par sa force et par sa rigour,
Et me faisoit taindre et palir,
Fremir, trembler, et tressaillir.
Lors pouoit bien aperchevoir
Que l'amoie sans decevoir
Plus .v.c. mille foys que mi,
Sans faintise et de cuer d'ami.
S'usoie ensement ma jouvente
Pour ma tres douce dame gente
En Dous Penser, en Souvenir,
En Esperance d'avenir
A sa grace, que tant desir
Que je n'ai nul autre desir.

Si sentoie maintes pointures,
Une heure doucez, l'autre sures,
L'autre plaisant, l'autre enuieuse,
L'autre tristre, l'autre joieuse.
Car cuers qui sent d'Amours le point
N'est mie tousdis en .i. point,
N'asseür de joie ou de paine;
Ainçoys couvient qu'il se demainne
Selonc la fortune d'Amours.
Mais la teste encline comme ours
Recevoie son doulz vouloir,
Fust de joye, fust de douloir,
Humblement comme amis parfais f. 26a
Et loyaus par dis et par fais.

Et pour ce que n'estoie mie
Tousdis en un point, m'estudie
Mis en faire chansons et lays,
Baladez, rondeaus, virelays,
Et chans, selonc mon sentement,
Amoureus et non autrement;
Car qui de sentement ne fait,
Son oeuvre et son chant contrefait.
Ne moustrer aussi ne pouoie
Les maulz d'amours que je sentoie
A ma dame, qui en chantant
Me va si bel comme enchantant.

the pains of love I felt. All the songs I composed I made for her praise, thinking that, if my song should come before her, she could realize how much I love her and am subject to her. And my heart took great pleasure when my lady led me to sing a song in her praise and honor, for love of her. For singing is born of a cheerful heart, and tears come from sadness. And because Sweet Thought is enclosed within my heart, along with Memory and Good Hope and Loyalty, in whom I have placed all my trust, I composed this piece that is called a lai:

(3) *How the Lover composes a lai about his feelings*

I

He who has no other pleasure
in love
than Sweet Thought
and Memory
with Hope of satisfaction,
would be wrong
if he sought
the aid
of any other comfort; because to satisfy

413 **chans . . . ditoie** maux que d. J; maux que je d. K. 415 **s'il** cil JK. 416 **devant** devers JK. 419 **s'i** cy K. 421 **Qua** Que C. **s'onnour** samour CJK. 424 **vient** nest JK. 425 **douce pensee** deusse chanter JK. 426 **S'est** Cest CJK; Est E. **dedens . . . enfermee** mon cuer dedens enfermer JK. 427 **et** est JK. 430 **qu'on** com JK. 433 **penser** espoir J. 439 **Voloit** Voloir E.

Et tous les chans que je ditoie,
A sa löenge les faisoie

En pensant que, s'il avenist f. 26b
Que mes chans devant li venist,
Qu'elle pourroit savoir comment
Je l'aim et sui en son comment.
Et mes cuers moult s'i deduisoit
Quant ma dame a ce me duisoit
Qu'a sa löenge et a s'onnour
Me faisoit chanter pour s'amour.
Car chanters est nes de leesce
De cuer, et plours vient de tristrece.
Et sur ce que Douce Pensee
S'est dedens mon cuer enfermee.
Souvenirs et Bonne Esperance
Et Loyauté, ou ma fiance
Ai si toute qu'ailleurs ne l'ay,
Fis je ce dit qu'on claimme lay:

(Miniature 3) *Comment l'Amant fait un lay de son sentement*

[LAY]

I

Qui n'aroit autre deport
En amer
Fors Doulz Penser
Et Souvenir
Aveuc l'Espoir de joïr,
S'aroit il tort
Se le port
D'autre confort
Voloit rouver;
Quar pour .i. cuer saouler

and sustain a heart,
he who loves deeply
must not seek
further reward.

Yet there remain many consolations:
to remember,
or to imagine,
to see, to hear,
in sweet pleasure, his lady,
her noble mien,
the recollection
of the goodness that issues
from her speech
and from her sweet look,
whose glance
can preserve
and protect
a lover from death.

II

And should anyone want more—
I dare not conceive
such a foolish notion
that he who is not satisfied with such benefits
can love whole-heartedly;
for he who seeks more wants to cheat,
when Love has held him so dear
that with her arrow
she deigned propel the knowledge of these
through his eye into his heart.

For one cannot value
or esteem them too much,
since easily
they can lighten all burdens,
and by their great powers make
a wounded heart healthy and supple,
with no conflict,

448 **En** Et CEJK. 449 **vëoir oÿr** veoir et oyr JK. 450 **Son . . . port** Et son gent p. J; Et sont gent p. K. 451 **recort** recoit JK. 458 **Amant** Avant E. 463 **tiels** ces JK. 468 **d'eaus** de deux E; doulz JK. 469 **les** *om* Pe. **esprisier** espuisier JK. 473 **leur** *om* JK. 474 **et** de C. **legier** entier Pe.

Et soustenir,
Plus querir
Ne doit merir
Qui aime fort.

Encor y a maint ressort:
Remembrer,
Ymaginer,
En dous plaisir
Sa dame veoir, oÿr,
Son gentil port,
Le recort
Dou bien qui sort
De son parler
Et de son douls regarder,
Dont l'entrouvrir
Puet garir
Et garantir
Amant de mort.

II

Et qui vourroit plus souhaidier— f. 26va–vb
Je n'os cuidier
Si fol cuidier
Que cilz aime de cuer entier
Qui de tiels biens n'a souffissanche;
Quar qui plus quiert, il veult trichier,
S'Amours tant chier
L'a que fichier
Deigne par l'oel de son archier
En son cuer d'eaus la cognoissanche.

Car on ne les puet esprisier,
Ne trop prisier,
Quant de legier
Pueent de tous maulz alegier,
Et faire par leur grant poissanche
Un cuer navré sain et legier,
Sans nul dangier,

and they can exile
sadness and bring joy,
merely through remembrance of them.

III

And thereby Sweet Thought
is engendered
and enclosed within my heart,
for I constantly recall
the one I long for,
the source of my joy,
whereby the hope that comes to me
from her is doubled.

She will be honored,
served, praised,
feared, obeyed, and loved.
This must be so;
for according as it pleases her,
I'll have a happy fate
or a hopeless death;
it all depends on her.

IV

But when I see
her lovely body
smartly dressed
in beautiful, simple,
modest attire,
and when I hear
her speak calmly,
by my faith,
I so rejoice
that I have every happiness.

I must do so,
if I love and trust her;
for joy grows
within me,

480 **S'est** Cest JK. 483 **desiree** desire E. 487 **ert** est Pe. 488 **Servie loee** Servie et loee EJK. 489 **Crainte obeïe** Crainte et obeye Pe. 494 **a li** il li C. 497–498 *om* JK. 507 **en** de Pe. 508 **Joye en croy** A lottroy Pe.

Et eslongier
De mal, et de joie aprouchier,
Seulement de leur remembranche.

III

Et pour ce engendree
S'est Douche Pensee
En mon cuer et enfremee,
Qu'adez me souvient
De la desiree,
Dont ma joie est nee
Et l'esperance doublee
Qui de li me vient.

S'en ert honnouree,
Servie, loee,
Crainte, obeïe, et amee,
Faire le couvient;
Car si li aggree,
J'arai destinee
Bonne ou mort desesperee;
Dou tout a li tient.

IV

Mais quant je voy
Le tres bel arroy
Simple et quoy,
Sans desroy,
De son corps, le gay,
Et que je l'oy
Parler sans effroy,
Par ma foy
Si m'esjoy
Que toute joye ay.

Faire le doy,
Se je l'aim et croy;
Car en moy
Joye en croy,

since my true heart
lives in her,
and from her I derive such favor
that I've had no
bitter suffering
since I fell in love with her.

V

And if I experience any sorrow
from Desire, I don't complain,
for her sweet laughing eye
completely soothes
the sorrow born of Desire;
and it so pleases and delights me
that I enjoy bearing it,
more than I have before,

Because of her beauty without pride that
surpasses all others, to my mind,
and because of her Fair Welcome
which is ever smiling;
so that it nourishes my heart
with pleasure and so enriches me
that to live thus is all I need
and all I want;

VI

Except that, in no way does
my dear lady,
who is the treasurer and
door-keeper of my heart,
know that she is my first love
and my last.
And I love her more than myself or anything I have,
not with a vain and frivolous love,
but so wholly
that I'd rather be in my coffin

509 **Pour ce mon** Et de mon Pe. 510 **Remaint** Demeure JK. 512 **Que** Quainc Pe. 516 **m'en** me E. 524 **Qui . . . vueul** Que toute a mon v. JK. 525 **tres** doulz E. 528 **m'enrichist** enrechist Pe. 538–544 *inverted with* 545–551 *in* JK.

Pour ce mon cuer vray
Remaint en soy,
Dont tel bien rechoy
Que puis n'oy
Grief anoy
Que je l'enamay.

V

Et se par Desir recueil
Aucun grief, pas ne m'en dueill, f. 27a–b
Quar son tres dous riant oeil
Tout adouchist
Le grief qui de Desir ist;
Si me plaist et abelist
Tant que au porter me delit,
Plus que ne sueil,

Pour sa beauté sans orgueil
Qui toutes passe, a mon vueul,
Et pour son tres Bel Accueil
Qui tousdis rit;
Si qu'en plaisance norrist
Mon cuer et tant m'enrichist
Qu'einssi vivre me sousfist,
Ne plus ne vueul;

VI

Fors tant, qu'en aucune maniere
Ma dame chiere,
Qui de mon cuer la tresoriere
Est et portiere,
Sceüst qu'elle est m'amour premiere
Et derreniere.
Et plus l'aim que moy ne mon bien,
Non pas d'amours vaine et legiere,
Mais si entiere,
Que mieulz ameroie estre en biere

than be unfaithful to her
or have any deceitful thought in me.
Thus shall I always be,
though she knows nothing of this;

For I am not worthy to
request her love,
nor so much seek out her favor
as to ask her for it;
for my heart that lies caught in her snare
could pay very dearly
for such an entreaty.
Therefore I don't let it show,
so that I'll receive
no refusal to repel me
or drive me away from her;
for if her sweetness were denied me
Love would be my murderer,
this I well know.

VII

Thus there is no chart
that can guide me
to reveal my love to her
by any means;
for nothing would prevent
my dying
if I were
refused; and if I lived
my happiness
would be sorrow.

I'd be a fool
were I to ask for
anything more than to devote to her
my body, honor,
heart, and love;
I should not desire
any other joy,

541 **Qu'a** Que EJK. 542 **Fust n'en** Fust en EJK. 544 **Comment** Combien JK. 550 **Telle** Celle JK. 553 **je n'acquiere** je ni a. C (+1). 558 **sai je** scet on JK. 559–680 *om* JK. 562 **nul tour** nul retour E.

Qu'a parchonniere
Fust, n'en moy pensee doubliere.
Telz tousdis iere,
Comment qu'elle n'en sache rien;

Car ne sui tielz qu'a moy affiere
Que s'amour quiere,
Ne que de son vueul tant enquiere
Que li requiere;
Car moult pourroit comparer chiere
Telle prïere
Mes cuers qui gist en son lÿen.
Pour ce n'en fai semblant ne chiere,
Que je n'acquiere
Refus qui me deboute ou fiere
De li arriere;
Car se sa doucheurs m'estoit fiere,
Amours murtriere
Seroit de moy, ce sai je bien.

VII

Si n'est voie
Qui m'avoie
Comment descouvrir li doie
Par nul tour;
Quar sans retour
Je mourroie
Se j'avoie
Refus; et se je vivoie
Ma baudour
Seroit tristour.

Fouls seroie
Se rouvoie
Riens plus, fors qu'en li emploie
Corps, honneur,
Cuer, et amour;
Qu'autre joye
Ne devroie

when I can sufficiently contemplate
her sweetness
and her worth.

VIII

Now how will the good
and sweet one know
that seeing her
has caused a new love
to lodge in my heart, which renews me
and brings me
happy news,

and whose spark
makes my true heart
burn within my breast?
So I tremble and shake,
that man or woman,
lady or maiden,
cannot know it,
so I carry it concealed.

IX

Love to whom I pray,
who desired and permitted
me, when first I saw her,
to dedicate myself to her at once,
could easily tell her
that I burn for love of her
without complaint or cry,
and that I give myself to her,
as to the most noble choice
I could select,

And that I choose no other;
instead Love has granted
that I never reveal it,
wherefore I've suffered many sighs

596 **voult** vault EPe. 604 **Que peüsse** Que je puisse Pe. 605 **tri** cry E. 607 **Qu'onc ne** Quonques ne E.

Voloir, se assés remiroie
Sa douçour
Et sa valour.

VIII

Dont la bonne et belle, f. 27va–vb
Comment sara elle
Que de li veoir
En mon cuer s'ostelle
Une amour nouvelle,
Qui me renouvelle
Et me fait avoir
Joieuse nouvelle,

De quoy l'estancelle
Fait sous la mamelle
Mon fin cuer ardoir?
S'en frit et sautelle,
Que hons ne damoyselle,
Dame ne pucelle,
Ne le puet savoir,
Si le port et celle.

IX

Amours que j'en pri,
Qui voult et souffri
Qu'a li, sans detri
Quant premiers la vi, m'offri,
Li porra bien dire
Que pour s'amour fri
Sans plainte et sans cri,
Et qu'a li m'ottri,
Comme au plus tres noble tri
Que peüsse eslire,

Et qu'autre ne tri;
Ainçoys a l'ottri
Qu'onc ne descouvri,
Dont maint souspir ay murdri

that have found no physician.
But if Love opposes
my prayer,
I do not wail or cry out,
nor give vent to my woe in any other way,
nor think of getting angry.

X

For in this manner
I wish joyfully,
happily,
and gaily
to spend all my life
so sincerely
loving my lady faithfully,
that truly
if I am tormented,
I want no
relief, other than to endure humbly
my sweet malady.

Secretly
and sensibly,
patiently
and purely,
and very lovingly was
it nourished within my heart;
for well
and sweetly,
and very soon,
if Hope does not lie,
my suffering will be rewarded most generously
a hundred times over.

XI

For although Desire assails me
and battles ceaselessly against me,
and shoots me with his amorous dart,

609 **Qui puis n'orent** Que puis morent E. 610 **s'en** sous Pe. **mon** moy C. 612 **n'en** ne C. 614 **pense** peusse E. 632 **norrie** *om* Pe.

Qui puis n'orent mire.
Mais s'en mon depri
Met Amours estri,
Je n'en bray ne cri,
N'autrement ne m'en deffri,
Ne pense a defrire.

X

Car ensement
Vueil lïement,
Jolïement,
Et gaiement,
En ma dame amer loyaument
User toute ma vie
Si franchement,
Que vraiement
Se j'ai tourment,
Aliegement
N'en veul, fors souffrir humblement
Ma douce maladie.

Celeement
Et sagement,
Pacïenment,
Et nettement
Ert et tres amoureusement
Dedens mon cuer norrie;
Car bonnement
Et doucement,
Prochainement
S'Espoirs ne ment,
M'ert ma paine tres hautement
A .c. doubles merie.

XI

Car comment que Desirs m'assaille
Et me fache mainte bataille f. 28a–b
Et poingne de l'amoureus dart,

which frequently slices my heart
secretly with its shaft and point,
indeed he wastes his efforts,
for all is healed by her Sweet Glance,

That feeds my heart the food
of love, and so imprints her
perfect beauty within by its art
that there's nothing else for which I care,
and it offers me so many amorous gifts
that there is no joy that does not come
to me from her—may God keep her!

XII

And therefore without objection
I wish
to endure and hide
the burning desire
that seeks to lessen my joy
by subtle craft;
I bear it
without discomfort
and I want to bear it.
For though it makes my heart quake,
grow wan and pale,
and tremble,
I am fully prepared
to endure it.

It inspires me to honor,
serve, protect,
and obey
my lady, and so cherish her
that I rejoice
in its afflictions.
When it torments
and seeks to wound me,
I have only to think of her

644 **se** me E. 654 **Endurer** Veul celer E. 655 **Vueul et celer** Sanz faulx penser E. 669 **Servir celer** Celeement et tendrement E. 670 **Et** *om* E. 672 **Qu'en** Que E.

Qui souvent d'estoc et de taille
Celeement mon cuer detaille,
Certes bien en vain se travaille,
Quar tout garist son Dous Regart

Qui paist d'amoureuse vitaille
Mon cuer, et dedens li entaille
Sa beauté fine par tel art
Qu'autre n'est de quoy il me chaille,
Et des biens amoureus me baille,
Tant qu'il n'est joye qui me faille
Que n'aie de li, que Dieus gart.

XII

Et pour ce, sans nul descort,
Endurer
Vueul et celer
L'ardant desir
Qui vueut ma joye amenrir
Par soutil sort;
Si le port
Sans desconfort
Et vueul porter.
Quar s'il fait mon cuer trembler,
Taindre et palir,
Et fremir,
A bien sousfrir
Du tout m'acort.

Il me fait par son ennort
Honnourer,
Servir, celer,
Et obeïr
Ma dame, et li tant cherir
Qu'en son effort
Me deport.
Quant il me mort
Et veult grever,
Mais qu'a li vueulle penser

whom I love and desire
forever
without regret;
from that my comfort comes.

Thus my lady inspired me to compose this lai you've heard me recite, although she did not know at all that she had inspired me to write it. But I composed it to her praise in accord with the skill I possessed, and as near to my feelings as I well could. And then it happened by chance that this lai came into her presence (and I too was there, which afterwards caused me no little anxiety) and that she ordered me to read it.

(4) *How the Lady has the Lover read the lai he'd composed*

I dared not refuse her, but rather read it from beginning to end, with trembling heart and bowed head, fearing there might be some mistake, since I had composed it. And when I had read it all to her and she had carefully considered it, she asked me who had written it, because she didn't know. As soon as she'd asked me this, I couldn't have said a single word were I offered the whole Roman Empire; no one can imagine how I lost my composure and strength; for shame, love, beauty, fear, and the fact that I wanted to hide from her the amorous malady I

681 **fist** fait E. 683 **riens n'en s.** rien s. C (−1); riens en s. E. 684 **fait faire** faire faire E. 687 **si** ci K. 690 **Qu'en . . . cilz** Que sa p. ce E. 692 **puis assez** asses puis E. 694 i *of* li *added above line in* C. 695 **li lui** la lui C; le leu Pe. 696 **A** De JK. 697 **qu'il** que J; qui KPe. 700 **l'ot bien** bien leut JK. 705 **toute** tout Pe. 706 **penseroit** pensoit C (−1). 709 **li** le JK. 710 **sentoie** pensoie JK.

Qu'aim et desir
Sans partir,
Ne repentir;
La me confort.

Einssi me fist ma dame faire f. 28a
Ce lay qu'oÿ m'avez retraire,
Ja soit ce que rien n'en sceüst
Qu'elle fait faire le m'eüst.
Mais selonc le sens que j'avoie,
A sa loenge le faisoie, f. 28b
Et si pres de mon sentement
Com je pouoie bonnement;
Tant que par aventure avint
Qu'en sa presence cilz lays vint
Et venus y estoie aussi,
Dont j'oy puis assez de soussi,

(Miniature 4) *Comment la dame fait lire*
A l'Amant le lay qu'il a fait

Qu'elle me commanda au lire. f. 28va
Si ne li osay escondire,
Ains li lui tout de chief en chief,
A cuer tremblant, enclin le chief,
Doubtans qu'il n'i eüst mesfait,
Pour ce que je l'avoie fait.
Et quant je li eus tout leü
Et elle l'ot bien concheü,
Me demanda qui fait l'avoit,
Pour ce qu'elle ne le savoit.
Et si tost qu'elle dist le m'ot,
Je n'eüsse dit .i. seul mot
Pour toute l'empire de Romme;
Car nulz cuers ne penseroit comme
Je perdi maniere et vigour;
Car honte, amour, beauté, paour,
Et ce que celer li vouloie
L'amoureus mal que je sentoie,

felt so stripped me of my memory and five senses that I cannot believe any lover was ever in such straits, nor so incapable of reply. My heart, which was trembling in fear, was so knotted up that I could find no way to speak. And truly it seemed to me that if I'd said, "I wrote it," I'd have been totally confounded and, perhaps, in danger of a cruel, bitter, and harsh death, because I'd have revealed and shown her how much I love her. And had she treated me the least bit harshly, whether by her glance, her manner, her words, or otherwise, I know for a fact that I'd have died on the spot for fear of losing her favor: not because she was mine, but because I hoped she'd become mine; so for this reason I dared not reply to her question or answer her.

But I would have been even less true to myself had I lied to her, for a lover must not lie to his lady even were it to cost him his life and soul; instead he must always tell her the truth as nearly as he knows it. And indeed, my lady is so good and wise that she'd know by my expression as soon as I tried a ruse, no matter how well I colored it. It made my heart quake not to know which to tell her, the truth or a lie. And

715 **Car je** Ne je CE; Ne ja Pe. 717 **qui** que CE. 719 **Se j'eüsse** Que se jeusse JK. 722 **crueuse amere** amere crueuse JK. 723 **que** qua Pe. 725 **Et s'un** Et un E. 727 *om* JK. 733 **despondre** espondre JK. 734 *om* J. 738 **ne** ou EJKPe. 740 **qu'il** com JK; qui Pe. 743 **se** ce K. 745 **ce** si JK; se Pe. 748 **com** que CEPe. **se** ce CEJKPe.

Me tollirent si le memoire
Et les .v. sens, que ne puis croire
Qu'onquez amans fust en tel point,
Ne de parler si mal a point.
Car je n'i savoie moyen,
Tant estoit en estroit loyen
Mes cuers, qui de paour trambloit.
Et vrayement, il me sembloit, f. 28vb
Se j'eüsse dit: "Je le fis",
Que trop me fusse desconfis

Et mis, espoir, en aventure
De mort crueuse, amere, et dure,
Pour ce que li eüsse ouvert
Comment je l'aim, et descouvert.
Et s'un poy de durette chiere,
Ou de regart, ou de maniere,
Ou de parler, ou autrement,
M'eüst fait, je sçay vrayement
Qu'eüsse esté mors en la place
Pour paour de perdre sa grace:
Non pas pour ce qu'elle fust moie,
Mes en esperance en estoie;
Et pour ce n'osoie despondre
Sa demande, n'a li respondre.

Mais encor plus me deceüsse
Assez, se menti li eüsse,
Car mentir ne doit a sa dame
Amans pour mort de corps ne d'ame;
Ains li doit tousdis dire voir
Au plus pres qu'il le puet savoir.
Et certes, si bonne et si sage
Est ma dame, qu'a mon visage
Sceüst tantost se je bourdasse,
Ja si bien ne li coulourasse.
Et ce faisoit mon cuer defrire
Que ne savoie le quel dire,
De verité ou de mençonge.
Et pour ce aussi, com se fust songe,

therefore, as if in a dream, lost in the depths of melancholy, without answering and without further delay, I left the presence of my honored lady without taking leave, in such a state that I didn't know what to do or where I was.

Sighing as I departed, I began to weep so copiously that my heart, completely overcome, melted in tears and weeping. And for all the world I could not have restrained this torrent of tears from running freely down my cheeks. It was very fortunate that there was no one there except the two of us who might see or understand anything, for all the others were some distance away in an alcove where they were having a good time playing "The King Who Does Not Lie."

Thus I left my dear lady and went away miserable, sad, downcast, and sighing, melancholy, and eager to reach some hidden place where I could cease my weeping and regain my composure. I left hurriedly because I didn't want to be stopped by anyone, and because I didn't want anyone to notice my tears and sadness.

I went along thus for a while, ever lost in my thoughts, until I saw a

750 **De** *om* CJK (−1). 755 **Et** Car JK. 760 **Je** Ne JK. 763 **fui** fu EJKPe. 764 **fors que** J. **deus** deuls C. 766 **qui** que Pe. 768 **un** *om*. C (−1). 781 **par** pour JK. **on n'aparcheüst** on apperceust JK. 782 **ne** ou JK.

Ravis en parfonde pensee,
De devant ma dame honouree
Sans respondre et sans plus attendre
Me departi, sans congié prendre,

En tel point que je ne savoie
Qu'il me failloit, ne ou j'estoie.
Et au partir souspiranment
Pris a plourer si fondanment f. 29a
Qu'en plours et en lermes fondoit
Mes cuers qui tous s'en confondoit.
Et pour gaaingnier tout le monde,
Je n'eüsse retenu l'onde
De ce plour, que parmi le vis
Ne me coulast a son devis.
Mais de ce fui trop eüreus
Qu'ame n'i avoit, fors nous deus,
Qui s'en peüst aperchevoir,
Ne qui riens en peüst savoir.
Car tuit li autre assez loignet
Estoient mis en un coignet
Et s'esbatoient bonnement
A jouer au "Roy qui ne ment".

Einssi laissai ma dame chiere
Et m'en parti a simple chiere,
Tristes, pensis, et souspirans,
Merancolieus, desirans
De venir en aucun destour
Ou finer peüsse mon plour,
Tant qu'a moy fusse revenus.
Si m'en alai les saus menus,
Pour ce que s'aucun encontrasse
Que tant ne quant n'i arrestasse,
Et par quoy on n'aparcheüst
Qu'en moy plour ne tristresce eüst.

S'alai ainssi moult longuement,
Sans issir de mon pensement,
Tant que vi .i. trop bel jardin

very beautiful garden called the Park of Hesdin. Then I headed straight for it and didn't stop until I'd come there; but I couldn't enter because it was surrounded and enclosed by high walls, and the road was not open to one and all. Nonetheless I followed the paths and trails I saw before me until I reached a closed gate, which was beautifully and nobly situated in a remote spot, far from people. I raised the latch of a small wicket; and after I'd lifted it, I went in. But I saw no one within, which made me happier, because I wanted to be alone if possible. And when I'd succeeded in entering and found myself all alone, I bolted the lock on the wicket. I walked along among the plantings, which were more beautiful than any I'd ever seen, nor will I ever see any so beautiful, so fair, so agreeable, so pleasing, or so delightful. And I could never describe the marvels, the delights, the artifices, the automata, the watercourses, the entertainments, the wondrous things that were enclosed within. Nonetheless I can well say that one could not seek any diversion in the air, in water, or on land that he'd not find there immediately, always ready to answer his wish.

I wandered up hills and down until I came upon a valley in which I

786 **Qu'on** Com JK. 789 **g'y vins** y vins JK; je y ving E. **je** *om* JK. 791 **murs** meurs JK. 793 **ne** et JKPe. 794 **Nonpourquant** Et n. C (+1). **sivi les routes** en vy les rotes JK. 796 **Jusqu'a** Jusques a E. 797 **Qui** Que JK. 801 **levé l'eus** levai leu C. **entrai** entre Pe. 803 **fui car** fu que EJK. 804 **se** ce K. 805 **assevi** assouvy EPe; assui JK. 806 **et . . . vi** a tous ceulz que vy E. 809 **estoit si biaus** si biaux estoit JK. 815 **esbas** abas Pe. 817 **descrire** escrire JK. 820 **en l'iaue** en la mer JK. 821 **Qu'on** Com JK. 822 **A** De E. **sans . . . demeure** et sanz grant d. JK.

Qu'on claimme le Parc de Hedin.
Lors celle part m'acheminai,
Et de cheminer ne finai
Tant que g'y vins; mais je n'i pos
Entrer, car il estoit enclos
De haus murs et environnez,
Ne li chemins abandonnez
N'estoit pas a tous në a toutes.
Nonpourquant je sivi les routes f. 29b
Qu'a terre vi et les esclos
Jusqu'a un huis qui estoit clos,
Qui trop bel seoit et trop gent
En un destour et loing de gent.
S'i avoit .i. petit guichet,
De quoy je levai le clichet;
Et quant levé l'eus, j'entrai ens.
Mais je ne vi ame leans,
Dont plus liez fui, car je vouloie
Estre tous seulz, se je pouoie.

Et quant j'eus mon veul assevi
D'entrer ens, et tous seulz me vi,
Le guichet fremai au verreul.
Si m'en alai parmi le brueul
Qui estoit si biaus qu'onquez mais
Ne vi, ne ne verray jamais
Si bel, si gent, si aggreable,
Si plaisant, ne si delitable.
Et les merveilles, les deduis,
Les ars, les engins, les conduis,
Les esbas, les estranges choses
Qui estoient dedens encloses,
Ne saroie jamais descrire.
Et nonpourquant je puis bien dire
Que homme ne saroit deduit querre
En l'air, en l'iaue, n'en la terre,
Qu'on n'i trouvast prest a toute heure
A son vueul, sans faire demeure.

S'alai tant amont et aval
Que je m'embati en .i. val

saw a fountain that was perfectly clear and beautiful, surrounded by trees and grass; and around it had sprung up a little hedge of wild roses. But I saw no beaten or well-trod path or trail, only the thick, sharp-bladed grass. I surmised that few people came there, so I set off in that direction. I passed through the little hedge and came to the clear, limpid fountain, where I washed my face and eyes; afterwards I sat down, because the place I'd thus reached seemed very secluded.

Then I grew deeply despondent, blaming myself for having left my lady as I did. I felt that it would no doubt have been better if my heart had burst for love of her in her presence than for me to have behaved in the silly manner I've told about here, because it would have been for her, and she'd have known it. Nonetheless, I couldn't make amends, even if I were lord over all that God has made. Yet the offense wasn't so immense, because no one can act beyond his own powers; nor was this offense mine, for I didn't commit it; instead, it was committed by Love who, I now saw better than I had before, does not mete out discipline, rules, order, reason, or moderation to hearts in love. It was not

827 **D'arbres** Derbres K. 830 **n'i vi voie** ne vi voie E; ny avoit ne voie J; ni a voie K. 831 **froïe** froiee JK. 844 **se** ce K. 845 **et** *added above line in* C; *om* JK. 848 **j'ay** *om* C (−1). **j'ay cy devant** ci devant ay E. 849 **Ce** Et C. 850 **et elle** et quelle EJK. 852 **se** si J. 853 **quanque** quanquil K. 855 **outre** contre JK. 859 **ne** et J; *om* K. 860 *om* JK. 861 **m'en vois** le voy E; me vois JK.

Ou je vi une fontenelle
Qui estoit moult clere et moult bele,
D'arbres et d'erbe environnee;
Et si estoit environ nee
Une haiette d'esglentier.
Mais n'i vi voie ne sentier
Qui fust froïe ne batue, f. 29va
Fors l'erbette poignant et drue.
Si pensai que petit repaire
Avoit la; pour ce m'i vous traire.
Si me mis oultre la haiette
Sus la fontaine clere et nette,
Ou mon vis lavai et mes yeus;
Et puis je m'assis, car li lieus
Ou ainssi m'estoie arrivez
Me sembloit estre moult privez.

Lors pris a penser durement,
En moy blasmant quant tellement
De ma dame estoie partis.
Car se li cuers me fust partis
Pour s'amour et en sa presence,
Il me vausist mieus, sans doubtance,
Qu'avoir fait telle niceté
Com j'ay cy devant recité,
Ce m'estoit vis, puis que ce fust
Pour lui, et elle le sceüst.
Nonpourquant je ne le peüsse
Amender, se sirez deüsse
Estre de quanque Dieus a fait.
Si n'est pas si grant le mesfait,
Car outre pouoir ne puet nus;
Ne cilz mesfait n'est pas venus
De moy, car je ne le fis pas;
Ains le fist Amours qui compas,
Reigle, ordre, raison, ne mesure
Es cuers amoureus ne mesure,
Je m'en vois bien aparchevant
Mieus que n'avoie fait devant.
Car gaires n'a que je disoie

long ago that I said that a lover was always happy; now I see and feel just the opposite in my own case, and I cannot feel otherwise. But I had not learned all Love's ways when I began to love her; so I'll have to learn them and take the bit with my teeth if I want to live in Love's service. I see no surer way, because I sense and see clearly through my own experience, and not otherwise, that the heart of a lover who loves deeply is now joyful, now mournful, now laughing, now crying, now singing, now lamenting, now happy in its plaint, now trembling, now sweating, now hot, now cold, and no longer cares what assault Love may make upon it; now it is pleased, now it cannot be pleased, for the lover's heart is happy or sad depending on whether Love wishes to console it and on the mood of Fortune, who brings good fortune to one lover and bad to another, and to others according to her whim. What Fortune does she unfailingly and abruptly undoes, for in her there is no stability, love, pity, or permanence; instead it is ever her custom to cut down and humiliate and bring into subjection unto death those whom she builds up.

And while I was in this mood, I decided to compose about Fortune and my sorrows, my thoughts and my griefs, a piece called a com-

865 **Or sent et voy** Or en voy bien JK. 866 **ne je n'en** mes je ne JK. 870 **Et** Si JK. 876 **Or a joie or** Quil a joie ou JK. 877 **or plaint** et plaint E. 878 **se** ce K. **en son** or se J. 881 **qu'amours** damours E. 894 **Que ceulz** Que cilz E; Car ceulz JK. **tonde** couve JK. 897 **Et en ce p.** Entente p. JK. 900 **mes pensers** me pensers K. 901 **qu'on** com JPe. 902 **Ou il averoit** Ou il li averoit C (+1); Ou il avoit E; Ou il y aroit JK.

Qu'adez estoit amans en joie;
Or sent et voy tout le contraire
En moy, ne je n'en puis plus faire.
Mes pas n'avoie bien apris
Tous ses tours, quant l'amer empris;
Si faudra que je les aprengne f. 29vb
Et que le frain a mes dens prengne,
Se je vueul vivre en son servage.
Je n'i voi plus seür passage,
Car je sen et voy clerement
Par mon fait, et non autrement,
Que cuer d'amant qui aimme fort
Or a joie, or a desconfort,
Or rit, or pleure, or chante, or plaint,
Or se delite en son complaint,
Or tremble, or tresue, or a chaut,
Or a froit, et puis ne li chaut
D'assaut qu'Amours li puisse faire;
Or li plaist; or ne li puet plaire;
Car selonc ce qu'Amours le veult
Deduire, il s'esjoïst ou duet,
Et selonc l'estat de Fortune
Qui les amans souvent fortune,
L'un bien, l'un mal, l'autre a sa guise,
Selonc ce qu'elle se deguise.
Car sans faute, ce qu'elle fait
Moult soudainement le desfait,
Car en li n'a estableté,
Amour, pité, ne fermeté;
Einçoys est tousdis sa coustume
Que ceulz qu'elle fait tonde et plume
Et sousmette en subjection
Telle comme a destruction.
Et en ce penser ou j'estoie
Je m'avisai que je feroie
De Fortune et de mes doulours,
De mes pensers et de mes plours,
.I. dit qu'on appelle complainte,
Ou il averoit rime mainte,

plainte, in which there would be many rhymes and a sad subject. So I began in this manner:

COMPLAINTE

(5) *How the Lover writes a complainte about Fortune and her Wheel*

He laughs in the morning who weeps in the evening,
and he believes Love works
for his benefit while she is attacking him
and doing him wrong;
and he thinks Joy is hastening
to help him, while she lags behind.
Fortune does all this harm
as she turns her wheel,
and she doesn't wait for daybreak
to turn it; she doesn't stop,
but turns it, turns it some more, and turns it upside down,
until she brings to the top
him who was lying flat in the gutter;
him who was exalted she brings down low,
and makes the happiest man sad and gloomy
in no time at all.

For she's not fixed or stable,
just, loyal, or true;
when you think
she's charitable, she's stingy,
hard, fickle, frightening,
traitorous, biting, deceptive;
and when you think she's amiable,
then she's bitter.
For even though she appears a friend,
sweet as honey, true as a mother,
the viper's bite
which is incurable
is nothing compared to her,

903–904 *om* JK. 907 **court** queurt JK. 909 **que** qua JK. 913 **Qui** Et JK. 914 *om* JK. 916–918 *om* JK. 924 **avere** amere E. 929 **ce** *om* E. 932–933 *om* J. 932 **incurable** inoatable *or* incatable C.

Qui seroit de tristre matiere.
Si commenchay en tel maniere:

COMPLAINTE f. 30a–b

Tieus rit au main qui au soir pleure,
Et tieus cuide qu'Amours labeure
Pour son bien, qu'elle li court seure
Et mal l'atourne;
Et tieus cuide que Joie acqueure
Pour li aidier, qu'elle demeure.
Car Fortune tout ce deveure,
Quant elle tourne,
Qui n'atent mie qu'il ajourne
Pour tourner; qu'elle ne sejourne,
Ains tourne, retourne, et bestorne,
Tant qu'au desseure
Met celui qui gist mas en l'ourne;
Le seurmonté au bas retorne,
Et le plus joieus mat et morne
Fait en po d'eure.

(Miniature 5) *Comment l'Amant fait une complainte de Fortune et de sa roe*

Car elle n'est ferme n'estable, f. 30va
Juste, loyal, ne veritable:
Quant on la cuide charitable,
Elle est avere,
Dure, diverse, espouantable,
Traïstre, poignant, decevable; f. 30vb
Et quant on la cuide amiable,
Lors est amere.
Car ja soit ce qu'amie appere,
Douce com miel, vraie com mere,
La pointure d'une vipere
Qu'est incurable
En riens a li ne se compere,

because she'd betray her own father
and cast him from a place of honor
into unspeakable misery.

If Fortune loves, it's from afar;
she's never there when needed
and cares for no one,
good or bad.
And I testify she's so false
that she'd bear false witness
to entrap the best friend
she has in the world.
She flays more than she shears,
and she abounds in wickedness,
whereby she destroys her nursling;
she doesn't give a rotten apple
for what she knocks down,
and wants her works to be destroyed,
in this there's no one like her.
I call her:

"Stupid, squint-eyed, false, and miserly."
She's never satiated with doing evil.
She doesn't give a fig for anyone,
rather she treats them all
just as the moon behaves,
which is now full, bright, and shining,
yet in two weeks
has neither form nor brightness;
except that Fortune fixes no month, week,
day, or appointed hour,
instead her vengeance is sudden;
that's well known,
for when a person is at the peak of his
honor and of the riches of this world,
she brings him to naught with a turn of her wheel.
Such is Fortune.

Take, for example, two buckets in a well,
to which I can compare her well:

934 **elle traïroit** trayroit elle Pe. 940 **Soit vil** Soit vif E; Sele vit JK. 943 **coing** soing C. 944 **ou** en KPe. 948–1263 *om* K (*two leaves missing*). 948 **coing** soing C. 950 **ses** ces E. 954 **n'est geüne** ne fut jeune J. 955 **Tout . . . prise** Ne prise le monde J; Tout le monde ne prise E. 960 **N'a en quinsainne** Ne en quisaine E. 962 **prefix** profix J; presix E. 966 **D'onneur** Damour E. 969 **Pren** Tien E.

Car elle traïroit son pere f. 31a
Et mettroit d'onnour en misere
Desraisonnable.

Se Fortune aimme, c'est de loing;
Elle faut tousdis au besoing,
N'elle n'a de personne soing,
Soit vil ou monde.
Et pour si fausse la tesmoing,
Qu'elle porteroit faus tesmoing
Pour le mieudre amy mettre en coing
Qu'elle ait ou monde.
Plus escorche qu'elle ne tonde,
Et en mauvais malice habunde,
Parquoy sa norriçon confonde;
Un pourri coing
Ne prise chose qu'elle fonde,
Qui vuet que ses ouvrages fonde,
En ce n'a pareil ne seconde.
Ce nom li doing:

"Lorde, borgne, fausse, et enfrune."
De mal faire onques n'est geüne.
Tout le mont ne prise une prune,
Ains le demainne
A la semblance de la lune
Qui or est plainne, clere, et brune,
Et fourme ne clarté nesune
N'a en quinsainne;
Fors tant que n'a moys ne semainne,
Jour prefix, në heure certainne,
Ains est sa venjance soudainne;
Chose est commune,
Car quant la personne est plus plainne
D'onneur, de richesce mondainne,
De son tour a nïent le mainne.
Telle est Fortune.

Pren moy .ii. seaus en un puis,
Qu'assez bien comparer li puis:

one is full, the other empty;
and if one is drawn up,
the other goes down; in like manner I find
that Fortune by her actions
raises the one, lowers the other, and
doesn't worry at all if he is
king, duke, peer, or count:
she gives honor to one and shame to the other;
she demotes the one, promotes the other;
it's her pleasure;
she weakens and overthrows all pride.
But Boethius tells us
that we must pay no heed
to the pain she inflicts.

Fortune knows more ways
than a master of medicine,
of divinity, of logic,
or a beggar
to find a devious path;
she flatters, she stabs, she stings,
she makes a long nose at everyone,
smiling all the while.
She makes one a beggar, the other a noble;
she pushes one back and the other forward;
she laughs one minute and cries the next; she doesn't
know when she loves, so
her advances are most deceptive.
She never keeps her promises
and, to conclude, she's always
trying to knock you down.

(6) *How Nebuchadnezzar dreamt that he saw a figure named Statua*

Nebuchadnezzar relates
that in a dream he saw a statue,
large and tall, with a
hideous face,

971 **li autre** et l'autre EJ. 973 **ainssi** aussi J. 974 **ses** ces C. 977 **a duc a per** na duc na per J. 978 **et** *om* Pe. 980 **C'est ses d.** Et cest d. J. 983 **Qu'on** Com J. 984 **anuis** amis C. 985 **scet** soit J. **de** que J. 986 **ne** *om* E. 988 **Et** Ne J. 994 **arrier et l'autre** arriere lautre E. 997 **sont** son E. 998 **ait** est J. 1002 **Qu'il** Qui JPe.

Li uns est plains, li autre vuis;
Et se l'un monte, f. 31b
L'autre descent; tout ainssi truis
Que Fortune par ses conduis
Monte l'un, l'autre avale, et puis
Rien n'i aconte
A roy, a duc, a per, n'a conte:
L'un donne honnour, et l'autre honte;
L'un desgrade; l'autre seurmonte;
C'est ses deduis;
Tout orgueil amolie et donte.
Mais Boeces si nous raconte
Qu'on ne doit mie faire conte
De ses anuis.

Fortune scet plus de pratique
Que ne font maistre de fisique,
De divinité, de logique,
Et mendiant,
Pour trouver une voie oblique;
Elle oint, elle point, elle pique,
Elle fait a chascun la nique,
En sourriant.
L'un fait petit, l'autre fait grant;
L'un met arrier, et l'autre avant;
Or rit, or pleure, or ne scet quant
Elle aimme, si que
Si attrait sont trop decevant.
Riens ne tient qu'elle ait en couvant,
Et, pour conclure, en trebuchant
Tousdis s'aplique.

(Miniature 6) *Comment Nabugodonosor songa qu'il veoit une figure qui se claimme Statua*

Nabugodonosor figure f. 31va
Qu'il vit en songe une estature
Grande et haute, qui la figure
Horrible avoit,

its head of rich, fine gold,
its arms and chest of silverwork,
its belly and thighs were made
of bronze;
it was standing on legs of iron,
its feet were part iron and
part earthenware. And then he saw
that by chance
a stone, untouched by any hand, came down
and struck its feet,
and shattered it to dust
and refuse.

The statue he presents here
seems to me to be none other
than Fortune, who doesn't rest for
a day, or even an hour.
Her head, in which all wealth is enclosed,
is gold, if I dare say so,
or so it seems to the fools she flatters,
who live in
the greatest of all possible error;
for she has no power or strength
to give anything except pain and strife.
Remember this and gloss it properly,
for her joys are nothing but tears,
and her riches are like ice in an oven.
Therefore he who opposes her does
the very best thing.

For if you are very wealthy
you will never have true happiness,
only pain, misery, and sadness,
and you will be fearful
of losing your wealth, which will wound you deeply,
or you will acquire the hardness and asperity
of avarice, the mistress
of calamity.
And if you wallow in poverty

1013 **sans main venoit** en sa main tenoit J. 1015 **l'acraventoit** les c. J. 1023 **Ce** Se E. 1025 **qu'il** qui EJPe. 1026 **n'a** ait J. 1029 **joies** joaies J. 1031 **trop** *om* Pe. 1032 **s'i** ci Pe. 1034 **vraie** grande E. 1037 **trop** tout C. 1039 **est maistresse** est la m. C (+1).

Et la teste d'or riche et pure,
Les bras, le pis d'argenteüre,
Ventre, cuisses de sa faiture
D'arain portoit,
Jambes de fer sus qu'elle estoit,
Des piez l'une part fer estoit,
L'autre terre. Et encor veoit
Que d'aventure
Une pierre sans main venoit
Qui parmi les piez la feroit,
Si qu'en pourre l'acraventoit
Et en ordure.

L'estature que ci pourpose
Estre ne me semble autre chose
Que Fortune qui ne repose
Heure ne jour.
La teste a d'or, se dire l'ose,
Ou toute richesce est enclose,
Ce samble aus musars qu'elle alose,
Qui en errour f. 31vb
Vivent telle qu'il n'est greigneur;
Qu'elle n'a pouoir ne vigour
De donner, fors painne et labour.
Retien et glose;
Car ses joies ne sont que plour,
Et ses richesces glace en four.
Pour ce fait cilz trop le meillour
Qui s'i oppose.

Car se tu yes en grant richesce,
Jamais n'avras vraie leesce,
Fors paine, misere, et tristesce,
Et en doubtance
Seras dou perdre, qui trop blesce,
Ou l'ardeur aras et l'apresse
D'avarice qui est la maistresse
De pestilence.
Et se tu gis en mendiance,

you will lack patience,
and every morning will find you
on the verge of thievery.
Therefore, don't treasure such power
in which there is no peace, security,
or satisfaction—only grief and mischance,
tears and distress.

Her arms and chest are silver,
but it's only an illusion:
because they shine brightly
she startles and blinds
the eyes of many people
to whom she makes grand promises,
while secretly plotting treason
in her breast.
With one arm she places them upon her wheel
more lightly than an aloe;
with the other she strikes them such a blow
on the cheek
that she knocks them off into the mud,
and then she makes a face at them.
This is how Fortune endows
those she takes under her wing.

Her belly and thighs are bronze;
that's to show more clearly
to all those near her
that her transformations are
for the worse. Here you see it proven,
since first her head is gold,
afterwards comes silver, not tin.
Tell the truth: do I lie?
Now comes base and unfit bronze;
Certainly this is not a good transformation.
One's a fool to hold out his hand
to accept such gifts,
for by such transformations she takes vengeance
on those she flatters and cajoles,

1045 **pris . . . puissance** prise rien tel p. J. 1046 **pais seürté** pais ou s. Pe. 1047 **N'a** Nas J. 1049 **Les** Ses e. **le pis** les pis CJ; les piest e. 1051 **ce qu'il luisent** ce qui reluist C; ce qui luisent EPe; qui le vise J. 1055 **pis couvertement** pis est c. E. 1059 **joe** roe E. 1066 **c'est . . . plain** ce est pour moustrer a p. J. 1069 **si** ci J; *om* Pe. **le** de E. 1073 **d'arain . . . estrange** darin vil est e. C. 1075 **telz dons s'arrange** ces doulz servage J. 1077 **Car** *om* C (−1).

Tu n'aras mie pascïence,
Ains sera ta main en balance
D'estre larrenesse.
Si ne pris riens telle puissance
Ou pais, seürté, sousfisance
N'a, fors doulour et mescheance,
Plour et destresse.

Les bras et le pis ha d'argent,
Mes ce n'est que decevement:
Car ce qu'il luisent clerement
Les yeus esbloe
Et aveugle de mainte gent
Cui elle promet largement,
Et en son pis couvertement
Traïson noe.
D'un des bras les met sus sa roe
Plus legierement c'unne aloe;
De l'autre les fiert en la joe
Si fierement
Qu'elle les trebuche en la boe,
Et puis elle leur fait la moe. f. 32a
Ainssi Fortune tous ceulz doe
Qu'elle entreprent.

Ventre et cuisses porte d'arain,
Mes c'est pour moustrer plus a plain
A touz ceaus qui li sont prochain
Qu'elle se change
En pis. Si vois tu le certain,
Que d'or est son chief premerain,
Aprés d'argent, non pas d'estain.
Di le voir: ment je?
Or est d'arain vil et estrange;
Certes, ce n'est mie bon change.
Foulz est qui a telz dons s'arrange
Ne tent sa main,
Car par tel change elle se vange
De ceulz qu'elle flate et losange,

and takes away their honor and glory
from one day to the next.

She's set on legs of iron,
showing that he who has her
does not in any way fear
tempest, storm, wind,
actions, or words.
But it's a covering and deception,
for her feet are of mud,
slippery and soft.
And since she's not built
on rock foundation, but on worthless sand,
he who thinks enough of her
to heed any of her blandishments
truly shames and degrades himself;
for she constantly mocks her pupils,
babbles their misfortunes all about,
and denigrates them.

I don't consider someone very clever
who expects to build a tall structure
on a worthless foundation
without great loss;
for when he is in the midst of
construction the foundation fails,
which causes the whole edifice
to tumble and fall.
In like manner Fortune the uncivilized,
when she's built some structure
and one's on the top story,
causes a wind and a storm
of adversity to come sweeping through,
which rips up everything—
foundation, roof, and walls—
with a single blow.

Fortune has more than a thousand tricks
to grab and deceive her own;
but, wretch, she has nothing

1082 **moustrant** moustra J. 1083 **orage vent** orage ne vent E. 1085 **craint** crient EJPe. **s'est** cest CJ. 1086 **c'est** est E. 1087 **Car . . . terre** Car cilz les piez de t. J. 1089 *follows 1090–91 in* J. 1090 **fors** que C. 1093 **Qu'il retient** Qui r. E; Quil ne r. J. **riens** *om* J. 1097 **quaut** baut CPe. 1101 **saut** haut J. 1102 **deffaut** li faut E. 1107 **on** len J. **en** au C; ou EJPe. 1113 **Fortune** Sortune E.

Et leur oste honnour et loange
D'ui a demain.

Seur jambes de fer est asisse,
En moustrant que par nulle guise
Tempeste, orage, vent de bise,
Fait ne parole
Ne craint cilz ou elle s'est mise.
Mais c'est couverteure et faintise,
Car les piés ha de terre glise
Gliant et mole.
Et quant sur pierre ne seur mole
N'est fondee, fors seur frivole,
Cilz se honnist bien et afole
Qui tant la prise
Qu'il retient riens de son escole;
Qu'adez ses escoliers rigole
Et partout leur meschief flajole
Et les desprise.

Je ne tieng pas celui pour quaut
Qui veult faire .i. ouvrage haut
Seur fondement qui riens ne vaut,
Sans grant dommage; f. 32b
Car quant il est en plus grant saut
D'ouvrer, li fondemens deffaut,
Dont tresbuchier et cheoir faut
Tout le megnage.
Ainssi Fortune la sauvage,
Quant elle a fait aucun ouvrage
Et on est en plus haut estage,
Fait en tressaut
Venir un vent et un orage
D'aversité qui tout esrage,
Fondement, comble, et massonnage,
D'un seul assaut.

Fortune a plus de mil engiens
Pour penre et decevoir les siens;
Mais la dolante, elle n'a riens

she can give them.
She can promise plenty,
but you're a real fool if you believe
that there's anything which is yours.
While sitting she flees;
her right side is soft, the other sharp;
her right holds flowers, leaves, and fruit,
the other is empty, sterile, and void
of earthly goods.
The right shines brightly,
the other resembles darkest night,
and she's split between
gold and excrement.

Fortune is hateful love,
unhappy happiness,
she's avaricious generosity;
she's misery;
she's sad and suffering health;
she's niggardly wealth;
she's nobility, poor and shameful
and disloyal;
she's proud humility;
she's envious charity;
she's dangerous security,
not to be trusted;
she's power in poverty;
she's repose in adversity;
she's famine in a satisfied heart;
she's bitter joy.

She's unyielding suffering;
she's covetous plenty;
she's sad, troubled peace;
she's vanity;
she's restless patience;
she's lazy diligence;
she's careful forgetfulness
against friendship;
she's the tree of inhumanity,

1116 **donner puist** puist donner J. 1117 **Promettre** Promette C; Promectre J. 1119 **ait** aist C; est J. 1121 **droit . . . cuist** droit les est dont lautre c. CPe; droit lun est doulz lautre c. E; don doulz est et lautre c. J. 1126 **samble** ressamble J. 1133 **tristre** male J. 1135 **noblesse** richesse J. 1145 **rigoureuse** rigoieuse C. 1153 **de inhumanité** de humanite E.

Que donner puist.
Promettre assez puet de ses biens,
Mes tu es trop foulz se tu tiens
Qu'il en y ait nul qui soit tiens.
En seant fuist;
Son droit lés est doulz, l'autre cuist;
Le droit porte flour, fueille, et fruist,
L'autre est desert, brehaigne, et vuit
Des biens terriens.
Le droit moult clerement reluist,
L'autre samble a l'oscure nuist;
Et mi partie est par deduist
D'or et de fiens.

Fortune est amour haïneuse,
Bonneürté maleüreuse;
C'est largesse avaricïeuse;
C'est orphenté;
C'est santé tristre et doulereuse;
C'est richesce la souffraiteuse;
C'est noblesse povre et honteuse,
Sans loyauté;
C'est l'orguilleuse humilité;
C'est l'envïeuse charité; f. 32va
C'est perilleuse seürté;
Trop est douteuse;
C'est puissance en mandicité;
C'est repos en adversité;
C'est famine en cuer saoulé;
C'est joie ireuse.

C'est souffrance la rigoureuse;
C'est souffisance couvoiteuse;
C'est pais dolente et rioteuse;
C'est vanité;
C'est pacïence dongereuse;
C'est diligence peresseuse;
C'est oubliance la songneuse
Contre amisté;
C'est l'arbre de inhumanité,

rooted in falsity;
the trunk signifies that in her truth
she lies;
the flowers are of disloyalty
and the leaves of iniquity,
and the fruit is of harsh
and bitter poverty.

Her head is half bald;
with one eye she laughs, and with the other weeps;
one cheek has the color of life,
the other is like death;
if one of her hands is your friend,
the other will be your mortal enemy;
one foot is straight, the other lame;
she twists the straight.
Her faith is that she's faithful to no one;
Her strength is that she's strong in falling;
laughing, she brings misfortune,
tears, and woe;
in comforting she makes one sad;
she favors her own by mistreating them;
she takes pleasure in every sort of grief,
whatever one may say.

Fortune is above the courts;
she makes her own statutes and laws
over emperors, popes, and kings,
and these three
can present no opposition,
no matter how bold, proud, or firm they are,
because Fortune breaks and overthrows
all their resistance.
It's true enough that she strives
and struggles to elevate them,
and lends them honor and status
for I don't know how many months.
But everywhere she wanders

1154 **seur** sanz J. 1155 **L'estoc est qu'en** Lescot quen en J. 1156 **Est** Soit EJPe. 1164 **com** comme C (+1). 1165 **t'est** est E. 1166 **t'iert** test EJ. 1169 *om* J. 1170 *After this line J adds*: En desconfort se reconforte. 1171 **meschëance** mescheant J. 1172 **haschie** haitie J. 1174 **foulant** volant J. **entreporte** autres porte E. 1175 *J replaces this line with*: Et les assiest jouste la porte. 1178 **loys** drois J. 1179 **empereurs** emperiere J. 1181 **mettre de ces** mettre nulz de ces E. 1182 **fiers orgueilleus** fiers ou contes J; orguilleus fiers Pe. 1184 **abat** debat E. 1186 **combat** debat E. 1188 **quans** queus C; quen J.

Enraciné seur fausseté;
L'estoc est qu'en sa verité
Est mensongeuse;
Les flours sont de desloyauté,
Et les fueilles de iniquité,
Mais li fruis est de povreté
Dure et crueuse.

La teste a pelee a moitie;
D'un oeil rit, de l'autre lermie;
L'une joe a couleur de vie,
L'autre est com morte;
Se une de ses mains t'est amie,
L'autre t'iert mortel anemie;
Un piet a droit, l'autre clopie,
La droite torte.
Sa foy est qu'a nul foy ne porte;
Sa force est qu'en cheant est forte;
En riant mescheance aporte,
Pleur et haschie;
En confortant se desconforte;
En foulant les siens entreporte;
En tous maus faire se deporte,
Quoy que nulz die. f. 32vb

Fortune est par dessus les drois;
Ses estatus fait et ses loys
Sus empereurs, papes, et roys,
Que nulz debat
N'i pourroit mettre de ces .iii.,
Tant fust fiers, orgueilleus, ou roys,
Car Fortune tous leurs desroys
Freint et abat.
Bien est voirs qu'elle se debat
Pour eulz avancier, et combat,
Et leur preste honnour et estat
Ne sçay quans mois.
Mais partout ou elle s'embat,

she gets such pleasure from her tricks
that in victory she exclaims proudly:
"Checkmate!"

(7) *How the Lover laments over Fortune*

Fortune has treated me, I believe,
just as I've told you here;
for once I abounded in
every sort of joy,
but now with a single twist she's brought me so low
that my laughter has turned to bitter tears
and all the good I had
is left behind.
Because now I wouldn't dare
look in the face of
the beauty to whom my heart is devoted,
whom I could not love more.
And I desire so much to see her
that my sad heart goes mad;
so I don't know what I should do,
I'm so miserable.

Love! Love! You've done this to me,
you who made me commit the offense
that is destroying all my joy!
For I can well say
that your arrow so afflicted my heart
that I couldn't have spoken a word
were I offered the whole empire
unconditionally.
Why did you have me choose a lady
for whom my heart sighs so deeply
that it cannot tell joy from sorrow,
and why do you want to destroy me
completely for love of her?
When you make my sad heart burn
and melt in loving martyrdom,
is this well done?

1194 **que** qui J. 1198 **grief . . . mué** grief et plour tourne J. 1199 **li . . . est** mes biens sont E. 1205 **si** ce J. 1206 **dolens cuers** cuers dolens J. 1210 **mesfait** mal fait E. 1213 **estraignis** estranges C. **de ton trait** estoit de ton t. J. 1219 **ne** no J. 1220 **a fait** affait C; de fait J. 1221 *After this line J erroneously repeats line 1225.*

De ses gieus tellement s'esbat
Qu'en vainquant dit: "Eschech et mat!"
De fiere vois.

(Miniature 7) *Commant l'Amant se plaint de Fortune*

Einsi m'a fait, ce m'est avis,
Fortune que ci vous devis;
Car je souloie estre assevis
De toute joye,
Or m'a d'un seul tour si bas mis f. 33a
Qu'en grief plour est mué mon ris,
Et que tous li biens est remis
Qu'avoir souloie.
Car la belle ou mes cuers s'ottroie,
Que tant aim que plus ne porroie,
Maintenant veoir n'oseroie
En mi le vis.
Et si desir tant que la voie
Que mes dolens cuers s'en desvoie,
Pour ce ne sçay que faire doye,
Tant sui despris.

Amours, Amours, ce m'as tu fait,
Qui m'as fait faire le mesfait
Qui toute ma joye desfait!
Car bien puis dire
Que si estraignis de ton trait
Mon cuer, qu'on n'en eüst mot trait,
S'avoir deüsse sans retrait
Toute l'empire.
Pourquoy me feïs tu eslire
Dame pour qui mes cuers souspire
Tant qu'il ne congnoist joye d'ire,
Et tout a fait
Me vueus pour s'amour desconfire?
Quant mon dolent cuer fais defrire
Et fondre en amoureus martire,
Est ce bien fait?

Alas! what do you ask from me?
I love you with all my strength.
Now you hate me and have knocked me
from high to low,
and have so flogged me with your whip
in your prison where you've thrown me
that I yield myself to you
vanquished and overthrown.
You are very wrong to beat me
when I acknowledge defeat and you've captured me,
for one should not beat or strike
a prisoner under any circumstance
when he's been defeated;
rather, one should seek to heal him.
Alas! Now you beat me while I am bound,
captive and submissive!

I don't believe it does you honor
for me to serve you in such faith
that I humbly consent to die,
if you wish it,
for my lady whom I no longer see.
For I fear, which astounds me,
that her gentle heart is
angry at me.
Therefore I'm poorly served,
sad, disconsolate, unhappy,
since you've turned away all my happiness,
I don't know why.
My face is pale on this account
and my heart overflowing with tears
mingled with melancholy sighs,
all because of you.

Nonetheless I'm not surprised—
when her sweet eye's glance
and her shining face, white and rosy,
which radiates
more beauty than gold in the sun,
and her body with its unparalleled

1228 **De . . . bas** Que me subas J. 1229 **tes** ces C. **de . . . batu** de verges si fort batu J. 1231 **me rens** met cuer J. 1235 **Car** Son J. 1238 **respas** repas J. 1239 **me bas** me as J. 1243 **Que** Et J. **a mourir** a toy J. 1249 **atournés** arrivez J. 1251 **Quant** Quen J. **as** mas J. 1256 **par** pour E. 1257 **me merveil** mesmerveil E. 1262 **Et . . . gent** De son corps gent E; Et son gent corps JPe.

Helas! que me demandes tu?
Je t'aim de toute ma vertu.
Or me hez et m'as abatu
De haut en bas
Et de tes verges si batu
En ta chartre ou m'as embatu
Que je me rens dessous l'escu
Vaincus et mas.
Si fais trop mal, se tu me bas
Quant je me ren et que pris m'as,
Car prisonnier on ne doit pas, f. 33b
S'on l'a vaincu,
Batre ne ferir en nul cas,
Ains doit on vouloir son respas.
Helas! or me bas en tes las,
Pris et rendu!

Ce n'est pas ton honour, ce croy,
Quant je te serf en telle foy
Que humblement a mourir m'ottroy,
Se c'est tes grés,
Pour ma dame que plus ne voy.
Car doubte ay, dont je me marvoy,
Que ses gentilz cuers envers moy
Ne soit irés.
Dont je sui trop mal atournés,
Tristres, pensis, desconfortés,
Quant tous mes biens as destournés,
Ne sçay pourquoy.
S'en est mes vis descoulourés
Et mes cuers de plours saoulés,
De griés souspirs entremellés,
Et tout par toy.

Nonpourquant pas ne me merveil—
Quant le regart de son douls oeil
Et son cler vis blanc et vermeil
Qui resplendist
De biauté plus que or en solleil
Et son corps gent qui n'a pareil

sweetness, were graciously
turned toward me—
that my vision was troubled,
that my words dried up,
and my strength waned.
For it was through your wish
that Nature began to trouble me
and my senses grew weak,
which makes my heart tremble and shake;
this is why I lament.

(8) *How the Lover caught sight of his Lady*

Therefore her perfect beauty,
fresh and sweet as a summer flower,
and the stunning brightness
of her visage,
by which I found myself illuminated,
and the all-powerful beam of her eye
had soon overcome my five senses;
I could do nothing.
Alas! I've had so many troubles
that I don't know where to turn,
nor does my joy return to me,
or my happiness;
because since I love without transgression
you seek to destroy me completely,
unless the sweet gentle lady
is merciful.

The power is yours, you must admit,
because I am yours, for better or for worse.
But I beg you to remember
how I bear
in my heart the amorous sign
of the sorrow of love that cripples me,
and that there's nowhere that affords me
any comfort.
And if my lady has in mind

1265 **s'en esblouïst** ses esbloist E; sen esbahist JK. 1266 **Se . . . m'en** Et ma parole sen JK. 1268 **ton** trop E. 1269 **s'en esbahist** sanz estanchist E. 1270 **sens s'en esvanuist** cuers sen esmanuit E. 1273 **sa** fu E. 1277 **vi** sui J. 1279 **Mes** Maiz E. **tost** tout E. 1280 **N'en** Ne E. 1284 **gaieté** leesse JK. 1293–94 *inverted in JK*. 1294 **Du** De J. 1295 **Si qu'il** Et qui JK. 1297 **se** si E.

De douceur, de cointe appareil
Vers moy guenchist—
Se mes regars s'en esblouïst,
Se la parole m'en tarist,
Se ma vigour en amenrist.
Car par ton vueil
Nature en moy s'en esbahist
Et mes sens s'en esvanuist,
Dont li cuers me tramble et fremist;
De ce me dueil.

(Miniature 8) *Comment l'Amant entrevit sa dame*

Ainssi sa parfaite biauté, f. 33va
Fresche et douce com fleur d'esté,
Et la merveilleuse clarté
De son viaire
Dont je me vi enluminé,
Le ray de son oeil que plus n'é,
Mes .v. sens eurent tost maté;
Plus n'en pos faire.
Helas! s'en ay tant de contraire
Que je ne sçai quelle part traire,
N'en moy joye plus ne repaire,
Ne gaieté;
Car pour ce que j'aim sans mesfaire,
Tu me vueus de tous poins desfaire,
Se la tres douce debonnaire
N'en a pité.

En toy en est, bien t'en couviengne,
Car je sui tiens, comment qu'il prengne.
Mais je te pri qu'il te souviengne
Comment je port
En mon cuer l'amoureuse ensaingne
Du mal d'amours qui me mehaingne, f. 33vb
Si qu'il n'est lieu dont il me viengne
Aucun confort.
Et se ma dame est en acort

to harm me, I implore you
to show her that she's wrong,
and that she has me
so firmly in her power that if she is intent
on hurting me, she's destroyed me,
and that she is my life and death,
come what may.

I know of no other solution
unless I want to drive off love.
But that cannot be,
because, without lying,
if all those whom God has caused to be born
were just as learned as
Seneca in arts and letters,
they could not make me
abandon her even on threat of death,
because I love and desire her above all women.
She is the source of all my pleasures;
she is my right hand;
she is the one who can heal me
and make me happy again,
if only she deigned to nourish
my desire with her glance.

Alas! Woe! Now I dare not hope
that she would ever be so tender to me
as to deign to let her sweet glance
fall upon me;
for you caused me to do so badly
by parting from her without asking leave
and without saying anything at all
that early and late
this unhappy departure causes me to
lament and weep, and by its effect
reduces my hope from a hundred thousand
to less than a fourth;
I'll die of this, so help me God,
if she does not grant me through you

1304 **Quoy** Que JK. 1305 **mettre** meittre C; mectre J. 1312 **deguerpir** deguerpist E. 1313 **feroient** feroie E. 1315 **mi plaisir** mon plaisir C; mi desir JK. 1317 **qui** que Pe. 1319 **Se de son r.** Se son douls r. C. 1322 **Qu'envers** Que vers E. 1330 **Plaindre plourer** Plaindre et plourer J. 1331 **dou** de .i. JK. 1332 **Mon** Son JK. 1334 **par toy** de soy JK.

De moy grever, je te pri fort
Que tu li moustres qu'elle a tort;
Et qu'elle tiengne
Tant de moy que, s'elle s'amort
A moy grever, elle m'a mort;
Et qu'elle est ma vie et ma mort,
Quoy qu'il aviengne.

Je n'i sçay autre conseil mettre,
Se je ne veul l'amer demettre.
Mais c'est chose qui ne puet estre,
Car sans mentir,
Se tous ceuls que Dieus a fait naistre
Estoient tuit aussi grant maistre
Com Seneque d'art et de lettre,
Li deguerpir
Ne me feroient pour mourir,
Car sus toutes l'aim et desir.
C'est celle ou sont tuit mi plaisir;
C'est ma main destre;
C'est celle qui me peut guarir
Et faire en joye revenir,
Se de son regart mon desir
Daignoit repaistre.

Las! dolens! or ne m'ose attendre
Qu'envers moy fust jamés si tendre
Qu'elle sur moy daignast descendre
Son douls regart;
Car tu me faïs tant mesprendre,
De moy partir sans congié prendre
Et sans nulle autre raison rendre,
Que tempre et tart
Me fait ce doulereus depart
Plaindre, plourer, et par son art
Fait de cent mil a mains dou quart
Mon espoir mendre; f. 34a
Dont je mourrai, se Dieus me gart,
S'elle par toy ne me depart

some share of her sweetness
to protect me.

For my sad heart is so downcast,
because my true hope is
not there, that I feel no joy at all.
This torments me;
this causes me many a mortal wound;
this confounds me; this wounds me;
such that there's not a sorrow that other lovers feel
that I don't bear.
Because when I was young I gave my love,
heart, body, soul, life, and mind
to my very sweet lady, who is noble,
pleasing, and gay.
Alas! Now I languish in sorrowful expectation
and live with sad memories:
this is the reward, these the wages
that Love pays me.

Love, it's not right at all
to give me gifts of sadness
instead of a happy reward;
rather it's wrong,
since I've put myself
unconditionally under your power.
Now you who should have guided me
have destroyed me
and trampled me underfoot,
and you have caused the dice to turn on me,
and by you I've been exiled from joy
without cause
and parted from my lady.
But if you are thus harsh with me,
I cannot hope for consolation or healing
for my troubles.

And since Hope does not attach herself
to my heart, but rather detaches herself,
it's no wonder
if Foolish Hope joins itself to it,

1337 **tant** trop JK. 1339 **qu'il . . . que** quel joie que Pe. 1340 **Ce** Se E. 1341 **Ce** Se E. 1342 **Ce . . . se** Se me confort se E. 1346 **Cuer . . . vie** Cuer corps vie J; Cuer et corps vie K. 1349 **atente** entente JK. 1350 **Et . . . pensee** Car je vif en p. E. 1353 **ce** se Pe. 1357 **sans** sus J. 1362 **Car** Et JK. 1364 **occoyson** achoison EJK. 1366 **s'auques** se onques E. 1367 **n'espoir** naray JK. 1370 **A** En C. **desjoint** destaint E. 1371 **se** ce K.

De ses douceurs aucune part
Pour moy desfendre.

Car mes dolens cuers tant s'esmaie,
Pour ce que m'esperance vraie
N'est pas, qu'il n'est joye que j'aie.
Ce me tourmente;
Ce me fait mainte mortel plaie;
Ce me confont; ce me deplaie;
Si qu'il n'est mauls que je ne traie
Qu'autre amis sente.
Car m'amour donnay en jouvente,
Cuer, corps, ame, vie, et entente,
A ma tres douce dame gente,
Plaisant et gaie.
Las! or langui en grief atente
Et vif en pensee dolente:
C'est le guerredon, c'est la rente
Qu'Amours me paie.

Amours, ce n'est mie raison
De me donner tristresce en don
En lieu de joieus guerredon;
Ains est pechiés,
Quant je suis sans condicion
Tous mis en ta subjection.
Or me mes a destruction
Et entrepiés
Qui deüsses estre mes chiés,
Car par toy m'est li dés changiés,
Et par toy de joie essilliez
Sans occoyson
Sui, et de ma dame eslongiés.
Mais s'auques einssi dure m'iés,
Confort n'espoir de mes meschiés,
Ne guarison.

Et quant Esperance ne joint
A mon cuer, einçoys s'en desjoint, f. 34b
Se Fol Espoir a li se joint

because you behave so badly
that your wickedness has defeated me
and trapped me in a tight corner,
like it or not.
There, I receive nothing good;
there, my face is bathed in tears;
there, there is nothing to console me,
or give me any
comfort for the trouble that assails me;
there I feel unparalleled grief;
there Pity sleeps; there Desire keeps watch,
who goads me excessively.

There I'm worse off than in a fever;
there I feel grief besetting me;
there my heart shakes and sweats;
there I am sure
that my Hope is gone,
if the bitter grief persists
that so grips my heart
that I'll never again
be happy; and if I swear this,
God knows that I'm not lying.
Therefore I forswear all joy,
which must be
lost in me, for I love with a pure heart;
and all the trials that I bear
for my lady are always harsher;
this destroys me.

(9) *How the Lover laments to himself*

Alas! Woe! This is what blots out
in me the grace of Hope;
this is what drives me to death
and reminds me

1374 **et empoint** en tel point JK. 1376 **ne** non E. 1377 **La** Las JK. 1378 **La** Las EJK. *After this line J inserts line 1382, as well as in its proper place.* 1379 **La** Las JK. 1381 **qui me** que je E. 1382 **La** Las JK. 1383 **La** Las EJK. **la . . . veille** et desirs vueille E; las desirs veille JK. 1385 **La** Las JK. 1386 **La** Las JK. 1387 **La** Las JK. 1388 **La** Las JK. 1389 **esperdue** perdue JK. 1391 **tant . . . tenue** tient mon cuer en continue JK. 1393 **se j'en** si en JK. 1398 **adés** asses J. **plus dur** perdur JK. 1403 **ce qui a** ce qua Pe.

N'est pas merveille,
Puis que tu fais si mal a point
Que tu m'as maté et empoint
Par ton mesfait en l'angle point,
Vueille ou ne vueille.
La n'est il bien que je recueille;
La mon vis de lermes se meulle;
La n'est il riens qui me conseille,
Ne qui me doint
Confort dou mal qui me traveille;
La san je doulour nompareille;
La Pytié dort; la Desirs veille,
Qui trop me point.

La suis je pis qu'en continue;
La sens je douleur qui m'argue;
La tremble mes cuers et tressue;
La m'asseür
Que m'esperance est esperdue,
Et la grief doulour continue,
Qui tant s'est en mon cuer tenue
Que bon eür
N'arai jamais; et se j'en jur,
Dieus scet que je ne m'en parjur.
Pour ce toute joye forjur,
Qu'estre perdue
Doit en moy, quant j'aim de cuer pur;
Et tout adés me sont plus dur
Li mauls que pour ma dame endur:
Ce me partue.

(Miniature 9) *Comment l'Amant se complaint a lui meïsmes*

Las! dolens! C'est ce qui esface f. 34va
En moy d'esperance la grace;
C'est ce qui a la mort me chace
Et fait penser

that just as a hunting hound
pursues and chases its prey
and follows its track everywhere
in order to kill it,
so Desire to satisfy
my foolish eyes by gazing sufficiently
at the sweet visage
of the beautiful, good, and peerless lady,
strikes and pursues me unceasingly,
intent on driving me to death.
But I wish to endure meekly
whatever he does to me.

Yet he has not so much strength
to cause me grief
as I have good heart to accept it;
let it be made clear:
if on this account I have little hope
of seeing my sweet lady
and Love holds me in contempt,
what will Desire do to me?
Will he kill me? He cannot,
for my loyalty will save me.
What did I say? Rather it will
oppose me, perhaps;
because, since Love will torment me,
as well as Fortune who's shamed me,
my great loyalty will slay me,
just as I wish.

For my heart cannot feign
love for my lady, nor can it cease to love her;
rather, the love that abides in me
is greater each day,
and nothing can put it out;
for when she most causes me to grow pale,
grieve, moan, and complain,
then she most enslaves me.
I've heard many people say
that when a sick person complains,
his pain causes a little of his complaint

1405 **de chace** deschace E. 1406 **sa** la JK. 1409 **desirs** desseus E; dessus JK. 1410 **folz** sos C. 1411 **belle et bonne** bonne et belle J. 1412 **face** chiere JK. 1413 **berse** berte K. 1416 **qu'il me face** qui me fiere JK. 1427 **me sera** maydera J. 1429 **Car puisqu'amours** Quamours qui puis JK. 1430 **qui** que Pe. 1433 **se** ce K. 1436 **maint** vient C. 1437 **Ne . . . estaindre** Ne ce pourroit de rien e. JK. 1438 **Car** Que JK. **plus** *om* E. 1440 **m'enceint** mentaint E. 1442 **se** ce K.

Qu'ensement comme uns chiens de chace
Aprés sa beste fuit et chace
Et la sieut partout a la trace
Pour li tuer,
Einssi Desirs de saouler
Mes folz ieus d'assés remirer
De la belle et bonne sans per
La douce face
Me berse et chace sans cesser
Et me cuide a la mort mener.
Mes humblement vueil endurer
Quoy qu'il me face.

Mes il n'a pas si grant pouoir
De moy faire douleur avoir
Com j'ay bon cuer dou recevoir;
Or y parra:
Se pour ce que j'ay povre espoir
De ma douce dame veoir
Et qu'Amours m'a en nonchaloir,
Qu'il me fera? f. 34vb
M'occira il? Il ne pourra,
Car ma loyauté m'aidera.
Qu'ai je dit? Einçoys me sera
Contraire, espoir;
Car puisqu'Amours me grevera
Et Fortune qui honni m'a,
Ma grant loyauté m'occirra,
Si com j'espoir.

Car mes cueurs ne se pourroit feindre
D'amer ma dame ne refraindre;
Ainçoys est tousdis l'amour greindre
Qui en moy maint,
Ne riens ne la porroit estaindre;
Car quant elle me fait plus teindre,
Dementer, gemir, et complaindre,
Tant plus m'enceint.
J'ay oÿ recorder a maint
Que quant uns malades se plaint,
Que sa doulour fait de son plaint

to remain.
Alas! This is what darkens my heart;
this is what touches it most rudely;
this is what destroys my happiness,
without hope for joy,

that my desired lady
knows nothing of my troubles
(she whom my heart loves
above all creatures),
and nothing of the harsh fate
allotted me on her account,
nor of how love for her
is smoldering in the center
of my heart, which is entirely hers,
nor of how I weep and moan frequently
and tremble for her love,
which is flaming
within me, and which makes me cry out: "Ah, me!
Esteemed lady, will you then
slay your beloved by the hands of
his enemy?"

This is the work of Desire, who enflames my heart
and consumes it with such a pernicious flame
that in this world there's not any
man or woman who knows the
remedy for it, except my lady,
who burns it, singes it, enflames
and sears it with Love's flame,
unendingly.
Fortune is its cruel neighbor,
and Love assails and tortures it,
wherefore I think I'll die in short order
blameless.
But if my life ends thus,
I wish to render up my soul
with clasped hands and head bowed
to my lady whom I love with a pure heart.

1445 **et** *om* E. **taint** ataint E. 1446 *om* J. **ce** celle C (+1). 1452 **de mi** dami JK. 1455 **Ne** Et JK. 1456 **Est** Et JK. **tout** toute CE. 1465 **C'est de desir** Cest desirs E. 1469 **se ce** ce ce JK. 1473 **dure** droite JK. 1475 **mourir** mort JK. 1477 **s'ainssi** ainssi J.

Un pou remaindre.
Las! et c'est ce qui mon cuer taint;
C'est ce qui plus griefment l'ataint;
C'est ce qui tout mon bien estaint,
Sans joye ateindre,

Pour ce que riens de ma pensee
Ne scet ma dame desiree,
Seur toute creature amee
Dou cuer de mi,
Ne la tres dure destinee
Qui m'est pour lui amer donnee,
Ne comment s'amour embrasee
Est tout en mi
Mon cuer qui est siens sans demi,
Ne comment je pleure et gemi
Souvent pour s'amour et fremi,
Qui enflamee
Est en moy, dont je di: "Aymi!
Occirrés vous dont vostre ami f. 35a
Entre les mains son anemi,
Dame honnouree?"

C'est de Desir qui mon cuer flamme
Et point de si diverse flamme,
Qu'en monde n'a homme ne fame
Qui medecine
Y sceüst, se ce n'est ma dame,
Qui l'art, qui l'esprent, qui l'enflame
Et bruït d'amoureuse flame,
N'elle ne fine.
Fortune est sa dure voysine,
Et Amours l'assaut et le mine,
Dont mourir cuit en brief termine
Sans autre blanme.
Mais s'ainssi ma vie define,
A ma dame qu'aim d'amour fine,
Les mains jointes, la chiere encline,
Vueil rendre l'ame.

(10) *How Hope came to comfort the Lover*

And when I had sufficiently debated and struggled alone, and had made my lament and cry about bitter Fortune and Love, about the great griefs and tribulations that had been overwhelming me and had sought to bring me suffering through fasts and vigils, through sighs drowned in tears, I had wandered far from the way of sense, memory, energy, and every other power. For this reason I'd fallen into a trance, like someone who sees and senses his death fast upon him. I turned my head a little as I uttered the sad moan of a weak, defeated, and listless man, and opened one of my eyes just barely—for it was all I could do—because I wished to look about me. And I saw seated beside me the most beautiful lady I'd ever seen, by my soul, excepting only my own lady. She was as perfectly beautiful, noble, and well adorned as if God had formed her with his own hands; in manner she was seemly, good, noble, sweet, and refined. But as I looked at her face, I didn't think she was human or of this world, which astounded me greatly. For her

1486 *om* JK. 1487 **m'ourent** mavient JK. 1489 **noiez** baigniez CPe; baillies E. 1490 **fui . . . desvoiez** fui tous d. C (−1); sui je tous d. E; com touz desavoiez JK. 1492 **autre** *om* JK. 1498 **vains . . . langoureus** mas vains et l. E. 1507 **Belle gente** Belle et g. EJK. 1509 **s'estoit** cestoit JK. 1511 **fu** fust J. 1512 **je l'esgardai** la regarday JK. 1517 **faite** fait CE.

(Miniature 10) *Comment Esperance vint conforter l'Amant*

Et quant a par moy debatus
Me fu assés et combatus,
Et fait ma plainte et ma clamour
De Fortune amere et d'Amour, f. 35b
Des grans douleurs et des meschiez
Dont j'estoie et sui entechiez,
Qui m'ourent voulu traveillier
De jeüner et de veillier,
De souspirs en lermes noiez,
Aussi fui je tous desvoiez
De sens, de memoire, et de force,
Et de toute autre vigour. Pour ce
Estoie je cheüs en transe
Aussi com cilz qui voit et pense
Sa mort devant li toute preste.
Si tournay un petit ma teste
En jetant un plaint doulereus,
Com homs vains, mas, et langoureus,
Et entre ouvri l'un de mes yeus
Un petit, car je ne pos mieus,

Pour ce que vouloie veoir
Entour moy. Mes je vi seoir
Delez moy la plus belle dame
Qu'onques mes veïsse, par m'ame,
Fors ma dame tant seulement.
Car tant estoit parfaitement
Belle, gente, et bien acesmee,
Que se Dieus de ses mains fourmee
L'eüst; s'estoit elle d'asfaire
Bel, bon, gent, doulz, et debonnaire.
Mes il ne me fu mie avis,
Quant je l'esgardai vis a vis,
Que ce fust creature humaine
De li, ne qu'elle fust mondaine,
Dont j'avoie moult grant merveille;
Car sa face blanche et vermeille,
Par juste compas faite a point

white and rosy face, so perfectly proportioned that there was no fault in it, shone so brightly that its brightness lit up the shadows, the dark night of my unhappy adventure, and its ray pierced the cloud that had long loomed troubled, black, shadowy, and gloomy over my heart and my countenance; so that, although I was so distressed that I was afraid I'd die, I most willingly gazed upon her, because in seeing her I felt just a little consoled in my harsh afflictions.

For just as a good physician by applying a precious stone heals and mends an eye dulled by a cataract, from which he must skillfully remove a white film that impedes and refracts the light so as to restore its original brightness, in like manner her brightness and splendor restored light to my heart, memory, and vision, and brought me out of the shadows into the sun.

Moreover, from her sweetness there came a fragrance so precious and a scent so lovely that never was there a sweeter thing encompassed by heaven, sea, or earth, nor was there ever any fragrance or sweetness so pure, so perfect, that it was not bitter in comparison, as gall to balm; and the garden where I lay was filled with it, and I well sensed that the

1518 **ot** a JK. 1523 **perchoit** partoit E. 1524 **s'estoit** cestoit JK. 1525 **onuble** obscure JK. 1527 **que** *om* JK. **comment qu'a** comment a Pe. 1528 **Tel** Telle E. 1529 **la** le CPe. 1530 **ce qu'a** quen E; ce quaq JK; ce quen Pe. 1533 **drame** dame E. 1535 **de** en JK. 1538 **clarté tient** char retient E. 1539 **sa** la JK. 1540 **einssi** aussi JK. 1541 **De** Du JK. 1542 **me** *om* E. 1548 **en mer** nen mer E. **n'en terre** en terre JK. **enclose** close E. 1551 **n'eüst** nest E. 1552 **fiel** fil E.

Si que mesfaçon n'i ot point,
Si clerement resplandissoit
Que sa clarté esclarcissoit
Les tenebres, la nuit obscure
De ma doulereuse aventure, f. 35va
Et de son ray perchoit la nue
Qui longuement s'estoit tenue
Trouble, noire, onuble, et ombrage
Seur mon cuer et seur mon visage;
Si que, comment qu'a meschief fusse
Tel que de mort paour eüsse,
Moult volentiers la regardoie,
Pour ce qu'a veoir me sentoie
Un petitet reconfortez
De mes dures maleürtez.

Car tout aussi com d'une drame
Le bon maistre guarist et drame
L'ueil empechié de cataracte,
Dou quel il couvient qu'il abate
Par soubtil enging une toie
Qui la clarté tient et desvoie,
Et li rent sa clarté premiere,
Tout einssi me rendoit lumiere
De cuer, de memoire, et de l'ueil,
Et me mettoit d'umbre en solleil
Sa clarté et sa resplandour.
Et aussi venoit une oudour
De sa douçour tant precieuse
Et de saveur si gracïeuse
Qu'onques ne fu plus douce chose
En chiel, en mer, n'en terre enclose,
N'onques odeur ne fu si fine,
Ne douceur, tant fust enterine,
Qui n'eüst encontre li blasme,
Tel com le fiel contre le basme;
Si que li pourpris ou j'estoie
En estoit plains, et bien sentoie
Qu'oudour de li tant douce issoit

fragrance wafted so sweetly from her that it softened my grief, even though my nature was more overcome than I can say.

Then, like one accustomed to sighing, I uttered a lament and sigh from the depths of my heart, accompanied by weeping and washed in tears; and with great effort I turned toward her my flushed, pale, sad, sorrowful, and weeping face, full of suffering. But I said nothing to her because I was unable to speak; instead, I gazed fixedly at her. When she perceived my condition, she smiled most sweetly; then she approached me very courteously in order to determine my state, and took my right hand in her white, smooth one, to know more of my malady; she felt my pulse and vein, which was feeble, weak, and faint. But she never lifted her hand from the vein that comes from my heart, for the good and wise lady well perceived that the madness that so bitterly troubled me came from my heart and from nowhere else.

And after she had taken the time to observe my condition at leisure and knew the whole extent of my suffering, with nothing hidden, and that I was in such sorrow because of the troubles of love that I felt, like

1557 **Comment** Combien JK. 1561 J *repeats this line at the top of the following column.* 1562 **en** de Pe. 1564 **pale** mate E. 1565 **De maniere** La marrie E. 1569 **la** *om* E. **a estat** en estat JK. 1571 **sousrist** souffrist E. 1572 **se** et JK. 1575 **De** *om* JK. **sienne** siene C. **onnie** polie JK. 1577–1606 *om* JK. 1579 **m'ostoit** nostuet E. **a** en C. 1582 **du** de E. 1588 **toute** *om* Pe. 1590 **Des** De CPe. 1591 **Com . . . qui** Comme celle que Pe. 1592 **la** sa E.

Que ma doulour adoucissoit,
Comment que Nature esbahie
Fust en moy, plus que je ne die.

Lors, com hons qui souvent souspir
Jetay un plaint et un souspir f. 35vb
De parfont cuer, acompaigniez
De plours et en lermes baigniez;
Et tournai vers li a grant paine
Ma chiere tainte, pale, et plaine
De maniere desconfortee,
Tristre, dolente, et esplouree.
Mais nulle riens ne li disoie,
Pour ce que parler ne pouoie;
Ains la regardoie a estat.
Et quant elle vit mon estat,
Si en sousrist moult doucement;
Lors se traÿ courtoysement
Vers moy pour savoir de mon estre,
Et si me prist par la main destre
De la sienne, blanche et onnie,
Pour miulz savoir ma maladie;
Si senti mon pous et ma vaine
Qui estoit foieble, mate, et vaine.
Mes sa main n'ostoit a nul fuer
De la vaine qui vient du cuer,
Car bien pensoit, la bonne et sage,
Que du cuer me venoit la rage
Qui si griefment me demenoit,
Et que d'ailleurs ne me venoit.

Et quant elle ot a son plaisir
Veü mon estre, et a loisir,
Et qu'elle sot sans couverture
De mon mal toute l'encloueure,
Et qu'en telle doulour estoie
Des maulz d'amours que je sentoie,
Com celle qui la theorique
Toute savoit et la pratique

one who knew all the theory and practice needed to heal me, and who understood the fluids of the eyes of the heart, whose essence was love, and who knew more about comforting than Fortune did discomforting, and who wished to console me for the troubles that grieved my heart, for there is no food so savory as good comfort to a sick man; like a skillful, learned, clever, and consoling physician, with a beautiful, clear, and rich voice, sweeter than any pan-pipe, she said after having felt my pulse:

"Fair friend, how do you feel? And what is the source of this sorrow that causes you to grow pale in this manner? Indeed, I believe it grips your heart and comes from loving. You should not destroy yourself in this manner and give yourself up to martyrdom, for it's a great shame and a great mistake to pity yourself for loving her, since you are neither cruel nor false to the lady you love.

"I've often heard you say that you'd not want to choose any blessing or contentment other than to have forever Memory and Sweet Thought of her sweet countenance, so that these two might heal you of all troubles that came to you. Who prevents you from having them? You prevent yourself by being too distressed; because your lady grows

1593 **Qu'il** Qui Pe. 1596 **faite** forte E. 1603 **Com** Comme Pe. 1606 **douçaine** fontaine E. 1610 **destaint** estaint E; destraint JK. 1614 **a** au E. 1615 **c'est . . . honte** cest honte E. 1616 **n'es** niers JK. 1618 **Quant** Qui CE. 1622 **sa** ta E. 1625 **Et . . . te** Et cil dui qui te JK. 1628 **qui** que JK.

Qu'il failloit a ma medecine,
Et qui bien congnoissoit l'orine
Des yeus du cuer, qui fondanment
Estoit faite amoureusement,
Et qui plus savoit de confort
Que Fortune de desconfort, f. 36a
Et qui conforter me vouloit
Des mauls dont mes cuers se doloit,
Car il n'est viande si sade
Com bon confort a un malade;
Com fisicienne soubtive,
Sage, apperte, et confortative,
D'une belle vois, clere et saine,
Plus douce que nulle douçaine,
Me dist, quant elle m'ot sentu:
"Douls amis, comment te sens tu?
Et dont te vient ceste doulour
Qui ainssi destaint ta coulour?
Certes, je croy qu'elle te tiengne
Au cuer et que d'amer te viengne.
Si ne te dois pas desconfire
Ainssi, ne toy mettre a martire,
Car c'est grant honte et grant desfaus,
Puis que tu n'es mauvais ne faus
Envers ta dame que tu aimmes,
Quant pour li amer las te claimes.

Je t'ay pluseurs foys oÿ dire
Que tu ne vousisses eslire
Autre bien n'autre souffissance,
Fors que de sa douce semblance
Souvenirs et Douce Pensee
Fussent en toy sans dessevree,
Et que cil .ii. te garissoient
De tous les mauls qui te venoient.
A qui tient il que ne les aiez?
Il tient a toy qui trop t'esmaies;
Car ta dame, de jour en jour,
Croist en beauté, sans nul sejour,

unceasingly day by day in beauty, in sweetness, and in all the blessings one can imagine, of this I am sure.

"And since she is increasing and abounds more than any other woman in the world in all one can call good, you must not pity yourself if you love her well, nor be dismayed that she doesn't pay you a thousand times more than you deserve for loving and serving her. And besides, it's next to nothing for her to repay you, for the very least reward she is able to give you, of which she has endless and numberless ones, is worth, at true reckoning, five hundred times more than you could deserve were you to love and serve her, not all the days of your life, but as long as the kingdom of this world endures. And I can loyally swear to you that if she rewards you every day in a thousand lavish, expensive, and costly ways, she will be none the poorer for it; because goodness so abounds in her that the more she gives, the more she has, as long as Good Love consents. And since Love has directed you to hope for her good graces, you must not despair because of a small misstep, for to tell the truth there was no wickedness or deceit, only fear, modesty, and simplicity mingled with Love, when you were

1632 **Qu'on** Com JK. **penser** prisier K. 1635 **qu'on** com JK. **bien** bon JK. 1636 **pas** point E. 1638 **doie paiier** doie bien p. EPe. 1639 **mil** mile JK. 1644 **De . . . te** De quoy elle te E. 1645–46 *inverted in* JK. 1650 **autant com** tant comment J; tant comme K. 1657 **s'abandonne** s'abonde E. 1658 **plus . . . donne** plus a quant elle plus d. EJK; plux a quant plux d. Pe. 1659 **s'i** se E. 1660 **Et** En JK. 1661 **sa** *om* JK. 1662 **Tu . . . pas** Tu ne te dois JK; Pas ne te dois Pe. **desperer** desesperer EJKPe. 1664 **traïson** mesprison E. 1667 **s'i** se EJ; ce K.

En douçour et en tout le bien
Qu'on peut penser, ce sçai je bien.

Et quant elle croist et habonde
Plus que dame qui soit ou monde
En tout ce qu'on puet bien nommer,
Tu ne te dois pas las clamer f. 36b
Se tu l'aimes bien, n'esmaiier
Qu'elle ne te doie paiier
Plus mil foys que ne desers
En ce que tu l'aimes et sers.
Et aussi c'est chose petite
A li de rendre a toy merite,
Car tout le mendre guerredon
De qu'elle te puist faire don,
Dont elle a sans fin et sans nombre,
Vaut .v.c. foys, s'a droit le nombre,
Plus que deservir ne porroiez
Se tu l'amoiez et servoiez,
Non pas tous les jours de ta vie,
Mes autant com la monarchie
De ce monde porra durer.
Et loyaument te puis jurer
Que tous les jours en .m. manierez,
Riches, precieuses, et chieres,
Elle te guerredonnera,
Que ja plus povre n'en sera;
Car biens en li tant s'abandonne
Que plus en a, quant plus en donne,
Mais que Bonne Amour s'i consente.
Et quant Amours t'a mis en sente
De sa bonne grace esperer,
Tu ne te dois pas desperer
Pour un petit de mesprison,
Car mauvestié ne traïson
N'i ot, quant a la verité,
Fors paour, honte, et niceté,
Avec Amours qui s'i mesla,
Quant servis fus de ce més la

served that viand that caused the abscess on your heart and turned your sweetness bitter.

(11) *How Hope teaches and instructs the Lover*

"And also you must believe, in order to stop your worrying—not only believe, but know, if you wish to find joy and peace once more—that since she possesses perfectly all the qualities one can properly imagine, describe, or conceive, which increase constantly within her, and since she is enriched with virtues and free from all vices, she must of necessity have Sincerity and Pity, Humility and her friend Charity. And therefore you must not be so despondent, because Pity, who is above Justice, could never stand to see you surrendered to death because you love, that's for certain, nor could Sincerity, who is close to Charity and Humility. And if you say that Love wounds you, you would sound like one who will listen to no one, preferring to torment himself and to suffer when things are going well.

"And indeed, you wrong her in telling her that she is cruel to you; it's a sin of ingratitude as well as rude, bad manners. Didn't you say in your lai—you did, if I remember well—that Love, whom you were im-

1669 **l'apostume** la coustume E. 1671 **dois tu** tu dois E. 1674 **joye et pais** pais ou joie J; pais et joie K. **ravoir** avoir EJK. 1676 **qu'on** com JK. 1679 **des** de E. 1682 **Qu'en** Que J. 1687 **Qui** Que JK. **porroit** pourra E. 1688 **offrir** souffrir JK. 1692 **se** ce K. 1693 **vueus ressambler** me ressambles JK. **a** *om* Pe. 1694 **se** ce K. 1695 **se . . . coresce** ce tourment et c. K. 1696 **adresce** s'adresse JK. 1698 **De . . . li** De li a li Pe. 1699 **c'est** sest Pe. 1701 **N'as** Nays Pe. 1702 **as** ais Pe. **se** ce K.

Qui te mist ou cuer l'apostume
Dont ta douçour en amer tume.

(Miniature 11) *Comment Esperance ensaigne et aprent l'Amant*

Encor dois tu penser aussi f. 36va
Pour toy meitre hors de soussi—
Non mie penser, mes savoir,
Se tu vueus joye et pais ravoir—
Que puis qu'elle a parfaitement
Tous les biens qu'on puet bonement
Ymaginer, dire, ou penser,
Qui croissent en li sans cesser,
Et qu'elle est des vertus paree
Et de tous vices separee,
Qu'il couvient de neccessité
Qu'en li soit Franchise et Pitié,
Humblesce, et Charité s'amie.
Et pour ce tu ne te dois mie
Ainssi mettre a desconfiture,
Car Pitiez est dessus Droiture,
Qui jamés ne porroit sousfrir
Toy veoir a la mort offrir
Pour amer, c'est chose certaine,
Ne Franchise qui moult prochaine
Est de Charité et d'Umblesce.
Et se tu dis qu'Amours te blesce,
Tu vueus ressambler a celui
Qui ne se loe de nului, f. 36vb
Ains se tourmente et se coresce
Quant sa besoigne bien adresce.

Et certes, tu li fais injure
De dire a li qu'elle t'est dure,
Et c'est pechiez d'ingratitude
Et maniere mauvaise et rude.
N'as tu mie dit en ton lay—
Si as, se bien retenu l'ay—
Qu'Amours, que tu en supplioiez,

ploring, could easily tell the lady you love of your martyrdom, because you didn't know how to tell her yourself? And Love, who is sincere and honest, heard and carried out your request, for she told and revealed to your lady in such a judicious and sensitive way the love you have kept hidden so long, that there never was nor ever will be anyone who could tell her so well, so agreeably, so appropriately, or in such manner that you feel the sting of True Love because of her charming and unspotted beauty—and Love told her this without uttering a word. It's a good saying I've heard: let your actions speak for themselves. So I don't know why you complain of Love, because she has done as you asked and has accomplished even more than you hoped. But a dog that's made to swim isn't grateful to get across; he just barks. Fair sweet friend, you are behaving in like manner, and it isn't worth a straw, for there's nothing so wasted as goodness unrecognized.

"Do you think that an esteemed, intelligent, loyal, and prudent lady would care for someone who implores her love with polished, deceitful words and who, in begging her, colors his speech to play the sage, or who asks boldly and impertinently for her love? Indeed not! This can-

1714 **qui** que Pe. 1715 **bien si bel** bel si bon Pe. 1717 **sens** sanz EJK. 1720 **en** len Pe. 1724 **Qu'elle** Quella ac. JK. **a acompli** acomplisse E. a *of* accompli *added above line by scribe* C. 1727 **qu'on . . . paie** quon nage est bien du paie JK; *om* Pe. 1730 **Et** Car K. 1732 **Que** Com JK. 1734 **Sage loyal** Sage et l. C. 1737 **en priant** empraint J. 1739 **qui la** quil le E. 1741 **ce** se Pe. 1742 **laisse** laira JK. **gens** jus E.

A ta dame que tu amoiez
Porroit bien dire ton martire,
Car tu ne li savoiez dire?
Et elle, com franche et honneste,
A oÿ et fait ta requeste,
Car elle a dit et descouvert
L'amour que tu as tant couvert
A ta dame si sagement,
Et de si tres bon sentement,
Qu'onquez ne fu ne jamais n'iere
Personne qui en tel maniere,
Si bien, si bel, ne si a point,
Li peüst dire que du point
De fine amour sens la pointure
Pour sa biauté plaisant et pure—
Ja soit ce qu'elle li deïst
Sans ce que parole en feïst.
Mes belle chose oy tesmoignier:
Pou parler et bien besoignier.
Si ne sçai que tu li demandez;
Qu'elle a acompli tes demandez
Et fait plus que tu ne vouloies
De ce que tu li requeroies.
Mais chien qu'on nage, en liu de paie,
Quant il est passez, il abaie.
Biaus douls amis, ainssi fais tu,
Et tout ce ne vaut .i. festu,
Car il n'est chose si perdue
Que bonté qui n'est congneüe. f. 37a

Cuides tu que dame honnouree.
Sage, loyal, et avisee,
Prise celui qui s'amour rueve
Par mos polis, plains de contreuve,
Et qui en priant son langage
Farde pour miulz faire le sage,
Ou qui la requiert baudement
De s'amour, et hardiement?
Certes, nennil! Ce ne puet estre;
Ains laisse tielz gens a senestre

not be. Instead, she shunts aside such people and considers them as nothing. But they have no mortification, shame, or anger if they are refused, because they are so wicked and sly that they're not troubled by what ladies say when they reject them, but go elsewhere instead, to test other ladies and beg their mercy.

"But when a worthy lady sees a lover who is ill at ease, who practices no deceit, but instead has trembling limbs and heart, discolored and darkened by fear when he wants to beg her mercy; and when she sees him so beset that Love forcefully squeezes out the liquid that falls drop by drop from his eyes to his cheeks, and he is forced to cut short his words and interrupt them with sighs, drawn from the depths of his being, that render him mute and silent, and he has no choice but to remain speechless and turn away from her in shame; and when she soon perceives that Love colors his face with three or four colors due to the troubles of love he's suffering, and that the power of Love causes him to lose his mind, you can be sure that she immediately recognizes by his comportment that he loves without pretense and with a true lover's heart; that is the sum of it. Nor is there in this world any man so subtle or clever who could pretend to be a lover without giving away his hand; nor could anything make me believe he could suddenly and

1743 **n'i** *om* E. 1747 **qu'on** quil C; com K. 1748 **quant on** et com J; ce com K. 1749 **merci rouver** aiey trouver JK. 1755 **destaint** destraint JK. **nerci** nouri E. 1758 **espraint** estraint J. 1759 **des** ces K. 1761 **qu'il** qui JK. 1762 **Ses** Des JK. 1764 *om* J. 1765 **qu'il** qui JK. 1766 **de honte** delpute C. 1767 **en** quen JK. 1771 **Qu'il** Qui JK. 1772 **peris** espris JK. 1773 **Saches** Sachiez C. 1776 **si** *om* E. 1777 **appers** aspres JK. 1779 **eüst** est J. 1781 **Quë il** Quil E.

Com celle qui riens n'i aconte.
Mes il n'ont vergoigne, ne honte,
Ne courrous, s'il sont refusé;
Car si mauvais et si rusé
Sont qu'il ne doubtent ce qu'on dist
A eulz, quant on les escondist;
Ainçoys aillours merci rouver
Vont pour les dames esprouver.

Mais quant une dame de pris
Voit l'amant qui est entrepris,
Qui n'use pas de faus semblant,
Ains a menbres et cuer tremblant,
De paour destaint et nerci
Quant il li vueult rouver merci;
Et qu'elle le voit si estraint
Qu'Amours de li par force espraint
La liqueur qui des yeus degoute
Parmi sa face goute a goute,
Et qu'il li couvient recoper
Ses paroles et sincoper
Par souspirs puisiez en parfont,
Qui mut et taisant le parfont,
Et qu'il l'estuet par force taire
Et de honte ensus de li traire;
Et qu'elle voit en petit d'eure
Qu'Amours son visage couloure
De .iii. ou de .iiii. couleurs
Pour les amoureuses doulours f. 37b
Qu'il reçoit, dont ses esperis
Par force d'Amours est peris,
Saches que tantost a sa guise
Congnoist qu'il aime sans faintise
De vray cuer d'ami; c'est la somme.
N'ou monde n'a si soubtil homme,
Tant soit appers, qui sans mesfaire
Sceüst un amant contrefaire,
Qu'il n'i eüst trop a reprendre;
Ne riens ne me feroit entendre
Quë il peüst soudainement

appropriately take on the four colors of a true lover: white, black, red, or blue.

"But Love does it anytime she wishes. And therefore I want to instruct you, by showing you that you are wrong to complain of the trials of love, or of anything Love does to you; for she has blessed you more than you could earn in serving her five hundred thousand years. I wish to tell you how: Love has made you the loyal lover of the best and most beautiful woman alive. But she has also done you a very great courtesy of which you are totally unaware, because by her power she has given your lady sure knowledge through subtle and knowing ways of the love sparkling within you, decreeing that your heart is loyal and discreet, in the manner mentioned above, which is the most profitable way, and the one that should be most willingly received and held dear; for in this case, whatever anyone may say, a man cannot describe as effectively in words his malady as he can show how touched by Love his heart is by being unable to say what is the matter, or of what he's lamenting; and so it is with you. Now I say that you're behaving foolishly, since your situation is improving and since Love, who has more right to complain of you than you of her, has become your friend.

1792 **li** la JK. 1794 **t'a** te E. 1795 **et** a EJ. 1796 **Qui** Que Pe. 1798 **Laquelle tu** L. que tu E. 1803 **approvant** deprouvant JK. **decret** secret JK. 1804 **as** *om* E. 1806 **qui** que Pe. 1807 **Et** Ce Pe. 1809 **quoy que** que que J. 1813 **Au** A E. 1814 **a** la CK. **se** ce K. 1816 **qu'il** qui K. 1818 **t'amie devient** taime de ce vient J. 1820 **tu . . . doies** tu ne ten dois C (−1); ne te devroies JK.

Sa couleur müer proprement
En .iiii. manieres diverses,
Blanches, noires, rouges, ou perses.

Mais Amours le fait a son vueul;
Et pour ce chastoier te vueul,
En toy moustrant que tu fais mal
Qui te plains de l'amoureus mal,
Ne de chose qu'Amours te face;
Car elle t'a fait plus de grace
Que ne pourroiez desservir
En li .v.c. mil ans servir.
Et si te vueil dire comment:
Amours t'a fait loyal amant
A la millour et la plus belle
Qui vive; mais encor t'a elle
Fait une moult grant cortoisie
La quelle tu ne congnois mie,
Qu'elle li a par sa poissance
Donné certaine congnoissance
Par maniere sage et soubtive
De l'amour qui en toy s'avive,
En approvant par son decret
Que cuer as loyal et secret,
Par la maniere dessus ditte
Qui est celle qui plus proufite
Et qui doit estre receüe
Plus en gré et plus chier tenue; f. 37va
Car en ce cas, quoy que nulz die,
Homs ne diroit sa maladie
Jamais si proprement de bouche,
Com fait cil a qui elle touche
Au cuer, si que dire ne peut
Qu'il a, ne de quoy il se dueut;
Et ainssi t'est il avenu.
Or dis qu'il t'est mesavenu,
Quant ta besoingne bien te vient
Et qu'Amours t'amie devient,
Qui se deüst mieus de toy plaindre
Que tu ne t'en doies complaindre.

(12) *How Hope chastises the Lover*

"Furthermore, nothing you do more blots out joy in your heart and causes you such grief than living in such error as to take your lady for a fool. This is what is driving you mad and destroying you; because, it seems to me, you conceive and imagine in dreams or fantasies that she doesn't hearken to or recognize the love that swells up within your heart, and you believe she doesn't see it at all. But she does, never doubt it; because she is wise and perceptive enough to recognize a deceitful heart by its words and behavior; nor will it ever tell so subtle a story that she'll not see through it. But if she sees a heart given over to love with a true desire to live and die loyally, as you do and have done in heart, word, and action, she will easily recognize it, even though it is difficult for one who wants certain, true, and just knowledge to distinguish the loyal heart from the wicked and disloyal one—because this is a very subtle distinction. But your lady, who is considered the best and wisest of ladies, knows all your heart, since Love taught and instructed her through the true and loyal ensign that no false lover wears; for in a faithless heart Love dies, whereas she reigns happily and shines brightly

1822 **tant s'anulle** tant anulle E. 1828 **Ce . . . vis** Cest vis E. 1831 **n'i** ne JKPe. 1832 **si . . . doubte** de ce ne te doubte si fait C. 1833 **est** *om* K. 1834 **decevant** damant J. 1836 **soutive** soubtille E. 1837 **dira** diras EJK. **ne l'entende** nentende C (−1). 1838 **s'elle en voit** se elle voit E. **un** *om* Pe. 1842 **penser** pensee E. 1848 *om* J. 1852 **ton** *om* E. 1855 **ne** ny E. 1856 **elle** *om* EPe. 1857 **lïement** el rement JK. 1858 **et** *om* JK.

(Miniature 12) *Comment Esperance chastie l'Amant*

Aprés tu ne fais chose nulle
Dont joie en ton cuer tant s'anulle,
Ne dont tu aies tant d'irour,
Comme de vivre en telle errour
Que tu tiens ta dame pour fole.
Et ce te destruit et afole,
Car tu penses et ymaginez,
Ce m'est vis, songes ou devinez,
Qu'elle pas n'entende ou congnoisse f. 37vb
L'amour qui en ton cuer s'engroisse,
Et croiz qu'elle n'i voie goute.
Mais si fait, de ce ne te doubte;
Car elle est sage et parchevant
De congnoistre .i. cuer decevant
Au maintien et a la parole;
Ne ja si soutive parole
Ne dira qu'elle ne l'entende.
Et s'elle en voit .i. qui se rende
En amours de vrai sentement
Pour vivre et mourir loyaument,
Si com tu le fais et as fait,
De cuer, de penser, et de fait,
Legierement le congnoistra,
Comment que fort a congnoistre a
Cilz qui vueut avoir sans doutance
La juste et vraie congnoissance
Pour congnoistre le cuer loyal
Dou mauvais et du desloyal,
Car c'est chose moult reponnue.
Mais ta dame, qui est tenue
Pour la millour et la plus sage
Des dames, scet tout ton courage,
Qu'Amours li aprent et ensaigne
Par la vraie et loyal ensaigne
Que nulz faus amoureus ne porte;
Qu'en cuer desloyal elle est morte,
Et en cuer loyal lïement
Regne et resplendist clerement.

in a loyal heart. Do you know the ensign? Indeed not, because you are not that clever. Therefore I want to try to tell about it as I know it.

"It's a shield whose substance is suffering with meek countenance and whose field is of pure azure; but it is so unsullied and pure that there is no speck of any other color to spot or discolor it. In the center is a heart of gules, pierced through the middle by an arrow of sable; yet never was there such a tip as it has, which is of fire with five tongues of pure argent; and it is all the more beautiful and noble for being semé of tears. These are the exact, true, and complete arms of the faithful lover; but the shield-straps are made of Hope. If you do not understand this, I wish to describe and explain it to you.

(13) *How Hope explains Love's own arms to the Lover*

"It is recorded, and has often happened, that many have attained what they desired simply by suffering long and meekly; because suffering meekly weakens and wins many a hard heart, and the proverb that states: 'He who endures, conquers!' is good witness to this. Next I'll tell you the meaning of the colors on the shield, because you've not lived

1861 **mettre** meittre C. 1862 **con** comme Pe. 1867 **d'autre . . . tache** taint coleur ne t. JK. 1872 **qu'elle a** quella J. 1873 E *replaces with*: Aux labiaux qui sont dargent. 1875 **Ce qu'il est** Et quil est E; Mais quil soit JK. 1877 **Dou** De E. 1878 **d'Esperance** desesperance C. (+1). 1881 **An recorde** En recorde EK; En recorder J; On recorde Pe. 1884 **bien et** *repeated in* C. **souffrir bien** bien souffrir Pe. 1885 **Que** Qui E. **sousfrir a le fie** sueffre a la fie E. 1886 **amolie** humelie C.

La congnois tu? Certes, nennil;
Car tu n'es mie si subtil.
Pour ce me vueil mettre a l'essai
Dou dire, si con je le sçay.

C'est un escu dont la matere
Est de sousfrir a humble chiere,
Et le champ est de fin azur;
Mes il est si monde et si pur
Qu'il n'i a d'autre couleur tache, f. 38a
Qui le descouleure ne tache.
Un cuer de geules a en mi,
Feru d'une fleche par mi
De sable; mes onques ne fu
Tel fer qu'elle a, qui est de fu
A .v. labiaus de fin argent;
Et trop y affiert bel et gent
Ce qu'il est touz semez de lermes.
Ce sont les droites plaines armes
Dou fin amant sans disference;
Mais enarmés est d'Esperance.
Se tu ne scez que c'est a dire,
Moustrer le te vueil et descrire:

(Miniature 13) *Commant Esperance moustre les droites armes d'Amours a l'Amant*

An recorde, et ce est avenu
Souvent, que pluseurs sont venu
A leur entente seulement
Par souffrir bien et humblement;
Que humblement sousfrir a le fie
Maint dur cuer vaint et amolie,
Et li proverbe qui recorde:
'Qui sueffre, il vaint,' bien s'i acorde. f. 38b
Aprés des couleurs de l'escú,
Pour ce que n'as pas tant vescu
Que tu en saches l'ordenance,
Te diray la senefiance:

long enough to understand their arrangement: know for a fact that wherever one describes heraldry properly the blue color is called 'azure,' if it's properly named, the red 'gules,' the black 'sable,' and the white 'argent'; and without fabrication I tell you that the green is called 'sinople' and the yellow 'or.'

"Now I want to teach you how these colors must be understood in Love: know that blue signifies loyalty that hates duplicity; and red signifies the fire of love born from loyal and pure love; black means by its tint grief; white is joy; green, inconstancy; and yellow, falsity. So hold fast to the first four and forsake the last two; because if they were placed in the shield the arms would be ruined. The flaming tip of the arrow that constantly burns and dries up the heart, know well that it burns and sears so subtly that no spot, burn, trace, wound, or injury shows; and it smolders and glows like charcoal beneath the ashes. Yet though the heart can feel this fire, it is invisible, as is the one who lights it. This is Desire, who laps and sucks up from the heart the blood and matter that is purified in this fire. Nonetheless, it is a fact that a noble

1893 **vray** veoir E. **qu'en** que JKPe. 1894 *om* JK. *Blank line left in* J. **descript** escript E. **a droit** est droit E. 1898 **sans** cest JK. 1900 **sineple** surople E; si noble JK. 1901 **ces** des E. 1905 **Et** *om* E. 1907 **te moustre** demoustre JK; se moustre Pe. 1910 **c'est fausseté** faussete cest C; fait faussete E. 1911 **retien** je tieng E. 1913 **Car** Et E. 1915 **fer** fert Pe. 1919 **Qu'il n'i** Quil ne E; Qui ny JKPe. **arsure** mesure E. 1921 **se cueve** ce quouve E; se lienne JK. 1923 que *added above line in* C. 1926 **lappe** happe EJK. 1930 **Qu'en . . . doulour** Que ce fu ne d. E. 1931 **qu'est . . . nature** Qui est domme n. E.

Saches de vray qu'en tout endroit
Ou en descript armes a droit
La coulour de pers est clamee
Azur, s'elle est a droit nommee,
Le rouge geulez, le noir sable,
Et le blanc argent; mais sans fable
Je te di c'on appelle encor
Le vert sineple et le gaune or.
Or te vueul ces couleurs aprendre
Com en Amours les dois entendre:

Saches que le pers senefie
Loyauté qui het tricherie,
Et le rouge amoureuse ardure
Naissant d'amours loyal et pure;
Le noir te moustre en sa coulour
Segnefiance de doulour;
Blanc joie, vert nouvelleté;
Et le jaune, c'est fausseté.
Mes retien les .iiii. premieres
Et lesse les .ii. derrenieres;
Car s'en l'escu fussent poseez
Les armes en fussent fausseez.
Mes le fer ardant de la fleche
Qui le cuer tousdis art et seche,
Sachiez certainement qu'il art
Et bruïst par si subtil art
Qu'il n'i pert tache ne arsure,
Trace, plaie, ne bleceüre;
Et aussi se cueve et engendre
Com li charbons desous la cendre.
Mais comment que cilz fus sensibles
Soit au cuer, il est invisibles,
Et aussi est cilz qui l'alume.
C'est Desir qui lappe et qui hume f. 38va
Le sanc du cuer et la substance
Qui en tel feu fait sa penance.
Nonpourquant, c'est chose certaine
Qu'en ce feu n'a doulour ne paine
Uns cuers qu'est de bonne nature,

heart feels no hurt or pain in this fire; instead, it draws sweet nourishment and enjoys itself like a fish in water.

"Now I've instructed and sketched out for you—if you have understood and retained it—how your lady can know that you love her truly, for you bear the arms fully in your heart, on your face, and in your manner, except that the shield-straps are broken from the shield for no reason, because it seems to you that you lack Hope, through your own fault. But if you're willing to trust me, I'm here to repair them; I'll make them better than new, and better than any others you know or can find, provided you heed the lesson which I explain above: that is, you must not be so imperceptive that you believe your lady so foolish as not to have seen that Love has captured and received you into her sweet religion, to make your profession of faith, with no second thoughts or regrets; and that she does not see that you'll be true to death; and that she is not pleased that you are hers.

"Therefore I urge you to believe me, for I swear to you on my faith that if you will be governed by me I shall support, aid, and console you in all your needs, very loyally and willingly, and shall never leave you in health or sickness, for better or for worse, no more than a wife would leave her husband. Now take heart and cheer up, fair sweet

1941 **enarmes** armez CE (−1). 1944 **Ce** Se E. **par** pour E. 1945 **se** ce K. **me** le E. 1946 **renouer** ravoier C. 1950 **de toy** je tay C. 1953 **n'ait** nest JK. 1954 **t'a** test JK. 1956 **parfaire profession** parfaite p. E; p. parfection JK. 1957 **pensee** penser JKPe. **ne** *om* E. 1958 **jusqu'a** jusques a C (+1). 1959 **Et qu'il** Qui li JK. **que . . . soiez** que tout siens soies J. 1962 **S'estre** Cestre K. 1967 **lié** liee E. 1968 **femme** dame E.

Ains y prent douce norreture
Et s'i delite en tel maniere
Com li poissons en la riviere.

Or t'ay devisé et apris—
Se retenu l'as et compris—
Comment ta dame puet savoir
Que tu l'aimes sans decevoir,
Car les armes portez entieres
En cuer, en vis, et en manieres,
Fors tant que les enarmes toutez
Sont sans cause en l'escu desroutez,
Pour ce qu'Esperance te faut,
Ce te semble, par ton desfaut.
Mais se tu me vueus avouer,
Je sui ci pour les renouer;
Si les ferai meilleurs que neuves,
Ne qu'autres que sachez ne trueves,
Mes que tu tiengnes le pourpos
Que de toy ci dessus propos:
C'est qu'en toy n'aiez si grant vice
Que ta dame cuidez si nice
Qu'elle n'ait bien apparcheü
Qu'Amours t'a pris et receü
En sa douce religion
Pour parfaire profession,
Sans pensee avoir ne remort;
Que n'i soiez jusqu'a la mort;
Et qu'il li plest bien que siens soiez.
Pour ce te pri que tu me croiez,
Car je te jur sur ma croiance,
S'estre vueus en ma gouvernance,
Qu'a tous besoins te porteray,
Aiderai, et conforteray, f. 38vb
Tres loyaument et de bon vueul,
Ne jamais lessier ne te vueul,
Sain, malade, lié, ne mari,
Nes que la femme son mari.
Or pren cuer et te reconforte,
Biaulz doulz amis, car je t'aporte

friend, because I bring you the health you desire; and truly, I desire it also. But to distract you a little and bring your sorrows to joy, I want to sing you a new song, because new things are always pleasing."

(14) *How the Lover falls asleep listening to Hope sing*

Then at my side in a sweet, harmonious voice—clear and rich—she began her song with such a melody that soon I fell asleep; but not so deeply that I didn't accurately hear how her new song began beautifully and gaily:

CHANT ROYAL

Many who fall in love find joy,
pleasure, sweet sustenance, and a life of honor;
and there are many who find only hurt,
distress, sorrow, tears, sadness, and bitterness.
They say this, but I cannot
agree, for there is no pain
in the sufferings Love brings,
because whatever comes from her
is pleasing to a lover's heart;

for True Love in a lover's heart creates
very Sweet Hope and amiable Thought:
Hope attracts Joy and Good Luck;
Sweet Thought causes Pleasure to enter the heart;
so he who has good Hope,
Sweet Thought, Joy, and Pleasure
must not ask for more;
for I tell you, if he demands more,
Love will abandon him.

1972 **Et** Quar Pe. 1977 **voys clere** voie douce E; vois douce JK. 1978 **Douce** Clere EJK. 1988–93 *om* JK. *Space is provided in both MSS.* 1988 **Doulour ardour** Ardour doulour E. 1989 **Ce** Le E. 1998 **Si ne doit** Se ne doy E. 2000 **et** *om* JK. 2002 **guerpi** gueri E.

La santé dont tu as desir;
Et vrayement, je la desir.
Mes pour toy un petit deduire
Et pour tes mauls a joie duire,
Te vueil dire un chant nouvellet;
Car chose plaist qui nouvelle est."

(Miniature 14) *Commant l'Amant s'endort en ooiant chanter Esperance*

Lors d'une voys clere et serie,
Douce, sainne, en tel melodie
Commença son chant delez mi,
C'un petitet m'i endormi;
Mes ne fu pas si fermement
Que n'entendisse proprement
Qu'ainssi commença par revel
Joliëment son chant nouvel:

[CHANT ROIAL]

Joye, plaisance, et douce nourreture, f. 39a–b
Vie d'onneur prennent maint en amer;
Et plusseurs sont qui n'i ont fors pointure,
Doulour, ardour, plour, tristesse, et amer.
Ce dient; mais acorder
Ne me puis, qu'en la sousfrance
D'Amours ait nulle grevance,
Car tout ce qui vient de li
Plaist a cuer d'ami; f. 39a

Car vraye Amour en cuer d'amant figure
Tres dous Espoir et gracieus Penser:
Espoir atrait Joie et Bonne Adventure;
Dous Penser fait Plaisance en cuer entrer.
Si ne doit plus demander
Cilz qui a bonne Esperance,
Doulz Penser, Joye, et Plaisance;
Car qui plus requiert, je di
Qu'Amours l'a guerpi.

Therefore he who lives on such sweet nourishment
can easily and must live a life of honor,
for he has all blessings in abundance,
more than another heart would dare desire;
nor does he have the heart, desire, or longing
to implore any other reward,
because he has Sufficiency;
nor can I name here
any other reward to ask for.

But those who are sad, distressed,
weeping, moaning, and in constant sorrow,
and who say that Love treats them so harshly
that they cannot go on any longer without dying,
I cannot conceive
that they love without deceit
and that they are not overwhelmed
by Desire. They are in such a state
because they have deserved it;

for Love, who is of such a noble nature
that she well
knows who loves without duplicity,
knows well how to pay lovers their due:
she satiates the loyal with joy
and has them savor her
sweetnesses abundantly;
but the wicked are banished
by decree from her court
as traitors.

ENVOY

Love, I know beyond a doubt
that you have rewarded those who've served you
a hundred times over.

THE LOVER SPEAKS

And when she had finished her song, she nodded her head in my di-

2003 **Dont** Com E. 2005 **a a comble** an comble C (−1). 2006 **n'en** ne JK. 2010 **Ne** Et EJKPe. 2012 **tristresse en ardure** tristresse et en a. CE (+1). 2013 **En . . . plains** En plains en plours E; En plours plaintis JK. 2015 **ne peuent** ne peut E; ne le pueent JK. **plus durer** endurer JK. 2018 **Et** Ne JK. **trop ne s'avance** point savance JK. 2019 **ce** *om* Pe; ce se E. **sont** soit C. 2020 **Qu'il l'ont** Qui lont EK; Quil ont J. 2022 **scet** sot E. 2025 **d'eaus** des biens E. 2026 **Ses** Les E. **en** et E. 2028 **com traîtres** comme traitres CPe (+1); contraites E. 2029 **sa court** secours E. 2033–38 *om* E.

Dont cilz qui vit de si douce pasture
Vie d'onnour puet bien et doit mener,
Car de tous biens a a comble mesure,
Plus qu'autres cuers n'en saroit desirer;
Ne d'autre merci rouver f. 39b
N'a desir, cuer, ne beance,
Pour ce qu'il a Souffissance;
Ne je ne sçay nommer cy
Nulle autre merci.

Mais ceulz qui sont en tristresse, en ardure,
En plours, en plains, en doulour sans cesser,
Et qui dient qu'Amours leur est si dure
Qu'il ne peuent sans morir plus durer,
Je ne puis ymaginer
Qu'il aiment sans decevance
Et qu'en euls trop ne s'avance
Desirs. Pour ce sont ainssi,
Qu'il l'ont deservi;

Qu'Amours, qui est de si noble nature
Qu'elle scet bien qui aimme sans fausser, f. 39va
Scet bien paier as amans leur droiture:
C'est les loyaus de joye saouler
Et d'eaus faire savourer
Ses douçours en habondance;
Et les mauvais par sentence
Sont com traïtres failli
De sa court bani.

L'ENVOY

Amours, je sçay sans doubtance
Qu'a .c. doubles as meri
Ceuls qui t'ont servi.

L'AMANT PARLE

Et quant elle ot son chant finé,
Vers moy a son chief incliné

rection, laughing sweetly, like an innocent maiden; then she put her hand upon my head and asked me forthwith:

(15) *How Hope asks the Lover if she'd sung well*

"How do you like it? What do you say? Have I presented your case well? What do you think of my song? Are there any arguments or themes that please you or displease you, or make you feel better? What do you say? Won't you tell me if I sing well or poorly? Were I not to flatter myself, I'd say that my song was well sung. Since you don't want to answer, I'm not sure if you can, but I think you're just hesitating to speak because you don't want to. I beg you, fair sweet friend, not to be so remiss as to allow yourself to be destroyed in this fashion; for you must seize and hold to my earlier instructions, and not waste your time in idleness and badinage. Abandon all melancholy and everything that leads to it except loving, for unless one seizes his opportunity he will lose it. Only a real fool seeks his destruction and death because of a foolish opinion, since he can easily change it. And therefore I want

2035 **com** comme C (+1). 2036 **vierge et p.** vierge p. J. 2043 **ou** et E. 2047 **Se** Ce K. 2049 **c'est** ce Pe. 2050 **se** ce K. 2051 **te faignes** refraignes JK. 2052 **ou** et JK. 2053 **Or** Si EPe; Je JK. 2056 **te dois** doies Pe. 2058 **le . . . tenir** tenir le temps E. 2063 **en prent** emprent J. 2064 **s'est** cest JK. 2067 **qu'il** qui Pe.

En riant doucement, com celle
Que je tieng pour vierge et pucelle;
Si mist sa main dessus mon chief
Et me demanda derechief:

(Miniature 15) *Comment Esperance demande a l'Amant s'elle a bien chanté*

"Comment t'est? Que me diras tu? f. 39vb
Ay je ton chief bien debatu?
Que te samble de ma chançon?
Y a il noyse ne tençon
Qui te plaise ou qui te desplaise,
Ou dont tu soies plus aaise?
Que c'est? Ne me diras tu rien,
Se je sçay chanter mal ou bien?
Se ce n'estoit pour moy vanter,
Je diroie de mon chanter
Que c'est bien dit. Quant tu ne veus
Respondre, ne sçay se tu peus;
Mais je pense que tu te faignes
De parler, ou que tu ne daignes.

Or te pri, biaus tres dous amis,
Que tu ne soies si remis
Que tu te laisses ainssi perdre;
Car tu te dois prenre et aerdre
A ce que j'ay dit cy devant,
Non pas le temps tenir devant
En oyseuse et en trusferie.
Laisse toute merencolie
Et tout ce qui te puet mouvoir,
Fors l'amer; qu'on ne puet avoir
De bon temps fors ce qu'on en prent.
Et s'est trop fols qui entreprent
Pour une fole opinion
Sa mort et sa destruction,
Puis qu'il le peut bien amender.
Et pour ce te vueul commander,

to command, urge, enjoin, and request that you make peace in this war you're waging against yourself, for it's a foolish enterprise and a foolish idea. And I promise and swear to you that I'll reassure you about that of which you are in such great doubt. Now take comfort and don't be afraid, because you'll be healed if you wish; and if you don't, you'll be shamed. Take the kernel and leave the chaff: forget your sadness, because he who sees clearly yet chooses wrongly does right to repent. And I offer you all my help as your good and perfect friend. You must not idle away your time so much that you refuse my offer; for it is said: 'If you don't act when you can, you won't when you want to; it's time to strike when the iron's hot.' I don't want to lecture you any more, but I do want you to be assured that your concerns will be mine, because I should and do love you."

THE LOVER SPEAKS

Then she took a beautiful, fine, valuable, precious, and expensive ring from her finger and gently slipped it onto mine.

And I, who was still dozing—but not deeply, because I had heard what she'd sung and said: rhyme, music, and words—felt the cold metal of the ring; then I turned drowsily as best I could toward her and

2071 **toy** moy E. 2077 **se** ce K. 2082 **s'il** si E. **repent** reprent Pe. 2084 **parfaite** loyal Pe. 2085 **si tant m.** yci m. E. 2087 **Qu'on** Com JK. **qui** quil EK. 2090 **m'en** me JK. 2094 **prist** pris C. 2095 **Bel bon** Bel et bon E. **chier** *om* CE (−1). 2098 **car** que E. 2100 **En** Et E. 2102 **pou** plus CEPe.

Deprïer, enjoindre, et requerre,
Que pais faces de ceste guerre
Qu'empris has contre toy meesmes,
Car s'est fole emprise et fols esmes.
Et je te promet et te jur f. 40a
Que je te feray asseür
De ce dont yes en si grant doubte.
Or te conforte et ne te doubte,
Car se tu vueus, tu es garis,
Et se ce non, tu es honnis.
Pren le grain et laisse la paille;
De tristresse plus ne te chaille,
Car cilz qui bien voit et mau prent,
C'est a bon droit s'il s'en repent.
Et je te offre toute m'aïe,
Con ta bonne et parfaite amie.
Si ne dois pas si tant muser
Que tu la doies refuser;
Qu'on dit: 'Qui ne fait quant il peut,
Il ne fait mie quant il vueut;
Et le fer chaut, on le doit batre.'
A toy ne m'en quier plus debatre;
Mes je vueil bien que certains soies
Que tes besoignes seront moies,
Car je t'aim et faire le doy."

L'AMANT PARLE

Lors prist .i. anel en son doy,
Bel, bon, chier, precïeus, et riche,
Et doucement ou mien le fiche.

Et je qui encor soumilloie—
Non pas fort, car bien entendoie
Ce qu'elle avoit chanté et dit
En rime, en musique, et en dit—
Senti la froideur de l'anel;
Et lors d'esperit pou ysnel
Me tournay au mieus que je pos
Vers li et lessay le repos

awoke from the sleep that, as I've told you, had been brought on by her beautiful, clear, and rich voice, sweeter than the voice of any siren, who casts a spell over men by the sweetness of her singing. In turning I bathed my heart and my eyes and my breast all over with tears, heaving a sad moan like one who is in great sorrow and affliction. But just as the brightness of this lady had lit up the darkness of my heart, which Love had colored and blackened, and her sweetness had sweetly lessened my torment, in like manner her very comforting words when I heard her speak brought back to my heart speech, which I'm using even now, because I'd lost it entirely. Then I spoke, as best I could, and told her without delay:

"My lady, blessed was the hour you were conceived and born and came here, since the powers with which you are endowed have restored health, joy, and life in me. For I was in the presence of Death, and would truly have died, my lady, were it not for you, and had you not looked mercifully upon me with the eyes of your heart. But you have raised me to life, and I pray you devoutly as humbly as I can, my lady,

2106 nulle voix de EPe. 2111–12 *om* CEPe. 2112 **ma poitrine** maportant JK. 2114 **se** ce K. 2123 **la** sa JK. 2124 **cy** si K. 2125 **perdu** perdue CEJK (+1). 2127 **sans . . . demeure** si com je pouoie JK. 2130 **cy** si K. 2131 **Quant** Car JK. 2132 **M'ont** Moult JK. 2133 **presente** presentee E. 2135 **se** ce K. 2136 **se** *om* E; ce K. **esgardé** regarde JK. **m'eüssiés** mussies JK. 2139 **depri** prie CPe. 2140 **Et tant com** Tant com C (−1). 2141 **qu'il** qui E. **plaire** plaise K.

Ou sa belle voys clere et saine,
Plus douce que nulle seraine,
Qui les hommes scet enchanter
Par la douçour de son chanter,
M'avoit mis, si com dit vous ay.
Et en moy tournant arrousay f. 40b
De larmes mon cuer et mes yeus
Et ma poitrine en pluseurs lieus,
En getant un doulereus plaint
Com cil qui moult se dueut et plaint.
Mais tout aussi com la clarté
De ceste dame l'oscurté
De mon cuer avoit esclarcy,
Qu'Amours avoit taint et nercy,
Et que sa douçour doucement
Avoit adoucy mon tourment,

Tout ainssi le tres douls parler
De li, quant je l'oÿ parler,
Me remist ou cuer la parole
Dont cy presentement parole,
Car de tous poins perdu l'avoie.
Lors parlai, si com je pouoie,
Et li dis sans faire demeure:
"Dame, ce fu a la bonne heure
Que fustes nee et conceüe
Et que vous estes cy venue,
Quant li bien dont estes garnie
M'ont rendu santé, joie, et vie.
Car presente m'estoit la Mors,
Dont vraiment j'estoie mors,
Ma dame, se vous ne fussiés
Et se esgardé ne m'eüssiés
Des yeus de vo cuer en pitié.
Mes vous m'avez resuscité;
Si vous depri devotement,
Et tant com je puis humblement,
Ma dame, qu'il vous vueille plaire
Que je sache de vostre afaire
Vostre non et vostre venue,

that it may please you to tell me your name and where you came from, and how you came here; because, by my soul, I've never desired anything as much as knowing this, except my lady's love."

(16) *How Hope tells the Lover of her power*

"My friend, I'll be glad to tell you without making a long story of it, for whatever pleases you, pleases me. I am comfort for lovers who obey Love's commandments; I aid them; I advise them; I'm of their privy council; I defend them; I cheer them up; I help them; I comfort them in the face of Desire, who assails them with many an unpleasant assault; I am their castle and fortress; I am their servant and mistress; I am their lady and chambermaid; I carry their banner everywhere; I keep them happy and joyful; I set them on the path of honor; I give them heart and strength to act boldly; I bring them to great honor; I cause them to be in love; I make them speak, laugh, play, sing, and dance expertly; I keep them gay and cheerful; I comfort the afflicted; I nourish them; I suckle them; I am their mother, lover, and sentinel; I am their physician and protectress; I defend and keep them from all harm; they adore me; I honor them; they implore me and I remain beside them; I

2144 **cy** si K. 2150 **te . . . plait** me plait il te pl. C. 2153–54 *inverted in* E. 2155 **je** et K. 2159 **fortresse** forteresse C (+1). 2160 **sui** *inserted by scribe above line in* C. **servante** sergens E. 2162 **la** leur JK.

Et comment estes cy venue,
Ne par ou; qu'onques mais, par m'ame,
Se ce n'est l'amour de ma dame,
Nulle riens tant ne desiray."

(Miniature 16) *Comment Esperance dit a l'Amant quel pover elle a*

"Amis, et je le te diray f. 40va
Volentiers, sans faire lonc plait,
Car ce qui te plait, il me plait.
Je sui li confors des amans
Qui font les amoureus commans;
Je les aide; je les conseil;
Je sui de leur estroit conseil;
Je les deffen; je les deporte;
Je les secour; je les conforte
Contre Desir qui les assaut
Et fait maint doulereus assaut;
Je leur sui chastiaus et fortresse;
Je leur sui servante et maistresse;
Je leur suy dame et chamberiere;
Je porte partout la baniere;
Je les tiens jolis et en joie;
Je les met d'onneur en la voie;
Je leur doing cuer et hardement
D'entreprendre hardïement;
A haute honnour les fais venir;
Amoureus les fais devenir;
Je les fais sagement parler,
Rire, jouer, chanter, baler;
Je les tieng gais et envoisiés; f. 40vb
Je rapaise les despaisiez;
Je les nourri; je les alaite;
Je leur sui mere, amie, et gaite;
Je leur suy phisicienne et garde;
De tous mauls les deffen et garde;
Il m'aourent, je les honnoure;
Il me prïent, et je demeure;
Je sui leur resort, leur recours

am their resort, their recourse by custom and agreement; by calling for me in their thoughts, and nothing more, they find me ready in every need, because I heed their thoughts, if they're not too disordered. But they are of such weak stock that they can do nothing without me. And when they need me, I tell you as I would my friend, I don't need to run or go far or near to help them; and I'll tell you why at once, if you want to hear."

[THE LOVER]

"Yes, my lady, I beg you to tell me."

[THE LADY]

"Listen, then; I'll answer your request. I tell you and make clear in your sight that just as the sun lights up the world with its rays and with its pure and shimmering brightness, and the earth, which has been barren and waste in winter, covered with ice and snow, enlivens and bedecks itself at the approach of summer, germinating, sweetening, and greening in the great warmth it feels from the sun shining upon it, so that beautiful Nature clothes it in a new dress colored like a panther, bedecking itself to welcome the springtime—it is said that the panther is speckled and trimmed with every color—for there is no shoot so wild

2182 **penser** pensee E. 2183 **pensees** pensez JK. 2184 **desordonees** desortenees C; desmesurez JK. 2185 **tant** tous E. 2186 **il** eulz E. 2191 **si** ce K; se Pe. 2193 **et** *om* EJK. 2194 **donc je** dont et je Pe. **depri** detri JK. 2195 **Je . . . a** Je di et moustre bien a E. 2196 **com** comme C (+1). 2197 **De ses rais** De ses raies C (+1); Des rais JK. 2199 **qu'encontre** quant entre JK. 2202 **De noys** Des nefs E. 2204 **Germe** Terre JK. 2206 **seur li d.** dessus d. E. 2210 **se pere** sapere E. 2211 **A . . . est** A dire quelle est E; Et diriez quelle est JK. 2212 **et** est E.

Par coustume et par entrecours;
A tous besoings me truevent preste
Par penser, sans autre requeste,
Car je obeï a leur pensees
Se trop ne sont desordonees.
Mais tant sont de fieble marren
Que sans moy il ne peuent rien.
Et quant il ont mestier de mi,
Je te di comme a mon ami
Qu'aler ne me faut ne courir
Loing ne pres pour eulz secourir;
Et si te dirai sans atendre
Comment, se tu y vueus entendre."

[L'AMANT]

"Oïl, dame; et je vous em pri."

[ESPERANCE]

"Oy donc; je ferai ton depri:

Je te di, et le moustre a l'ueil,
Que tout aussi com le solleil
De ses rais le monde enlumine
Et de sa clarté pure et fine,
Et qu'encontre le temps d'esté
La terre, qui moult a esté
En yver brehaigne et deserte,
De noys et de glaces couverte,
Se resjoïst et se cointoie,
Germe, adoucist, et renverdoie
Pour la grant chaleur qu'elle sent
Du solleil qui seur li descent,
Si qu'adonc Nature la belle f. 41a
Li vest une robe nouvelle
De la coulour d'une pantere
Dont contre le printemps se pere,
—A dire est qu'elle est dyapree
De toutes coulours et paree—
Car racine n'est tant diverse

that in this springtime it doesn't set to producing, according to its nature, flowers, fruit, leaves, seeds, or greenery (unless it has stopped blossoming and has no greenery or seed), and therefore the earth is so pretty, so beautiful, so fair, so elegant, because it has taken off its damp and dirty winter coat; and nothing more than the attractiveness of springtime has made it so attractive—thus, I say, in like manner and just as the sun's light brings to the globe even to its farthest reaches, brightness, warmth, joy, and pleasure by its rays, whose power causes the happy earth to smile and become pretty and gay, so similarly my radiance that shines here now brightens the whole world, spreading everywhere and living forever in lovers who are in love, both here and across the seas, giving them brightness, warmth, joy, and pleasure in their love.

"But I who am their true mother bring them a brightness so bright, so becoming, so fitting, that the shoot grafted onto their heart buds with flowers, leaves, new fruit, and seeds, and makes them twenty times fairer than the earth in springtime. Thus, just as the sun bestows its light far and wide, without limit, so does my royal radiance shine

2215 **sa** la CPe. 2216 **fueilles . . . verdure** fueille et v. E; fueilles greine v. JK. 2217 **telle** celle JK. **sime** suive E. 2218 **qu'il** qui CJKPe. **chime** suive E; sime JK; cyme Pe. 2223 **Et . . . pour** Sanz plus et pour E. 2224 **est si** ainssi CEPe. 2226 **Que . . . com** Que tout ainsi com E; Que aussi comme JK. 2229 **joye pl.** joie et pl. E. 2230 **rais qui par** raies qui pour E. 2233 **li** le Pe. 2234 **cy** si EJK. 2236 **et . . . siecle** par tout le siecle E. 2237 **Es** Et E. 2238 **Tant . . . dela** Tant com deca mer com dela C (+1); Tant deca comme dela E; Tant com de sai mer com de la Pe. 2239 **clarté ch.** clarte et ch. CE (+1). 2240 **Joye pl.** Joie et pl. Pe. 2241 **droite** vraie JK. 2243 **si bien o.** et si o. E. 2244 **entee** entree JK. 2246 **fueille . . . germe** fueille fruit nouvel et g. C; fruit noel et g. E; fueille fruit noiel et g. Pe. 2247 **fais** fait JK. 2248 **en** a E; au JK. 2249 **com** que E. 2250 **loing et pres** prez et loing Pe. 2253 **se** ce K.

Qui a ce printemps ne se aërse
A geter, selonc sa nature,
Fleur, fruit, fueilles, graine, ou verdure,
(Se telle n'est que plus ne sime
Et qu'il n'i ait verdeur ne chime,)

Et pour ce est la terre si cointe,
Si belle, si gente, et si jointe,
Qu'elle a sa robe despoillie
De l'yver crotee et moillie;
Et sans plus pour l'acointement
Dou printemps est si cointement—
Einssi, di je, en semblant maniere
Que tout aussi com la lumiere
Du solleil donne par le monde,
Tant comme il tient a la reonde,
Clarté, chaleur, joye, plaisance
De ses rais qui par leur puissance
Font que la terre qui s'esgaie
En rit et devient cointe et gaye,
Qu'ensement de moy li resplent
Qui cy presentement resplent
Donne clarté par tout le siecle,
Par tout s'espant et par tout siecle
Es amans vivans en amer,
Tant deça mer com dela mer,
Et leur donne clarté, chalour,
Joye, plaisance en leur amour.
Mes je qui sui leur droite mere
Leur doing une clarté si clere,
Si a point, si bien ordenee,
Que la racine qui entee
Est dedens leur cuer d'amours germe f. 41b
Fleur, fueille, fruit, et nouvel germe,
Et les fais plus cointes vint temps
Que la terre n'est en printemps.
Si qu'einssi com le solleil donne
Sa clarté loing et pres, sans bonne,
Ainssi fait mon resplant royal
Partout en cuer d'ami loyal.
Et se Nature soubtille oeuvre

everywhere in the hearts of loyal lovers. And if Nature subtly works to reclothe and cover the earth, to remove its soiled winter dress, and attires it in a new dress, I can compare myself quite well to her, because I make a lover pretty and fair. Do you know how? You'll know it for certain; write down what I've said above. For if Nature causes a shoot to flower and a briar to bear roses, in like manner I make a heart flower in complete joy and cause sorrow to die out; for I cultivate it until no weed of sorrow remains. And with my sweetness that you sense, which is much sweeter than incense, I soothe, console, and anoint it, if it is deserving, whether near or far. And since I knew that you were disconsolate and joyless, and my role is to console lovers, I came here. I came in my true character, as your faithful and good friend, in such manner that you've neither seen nor perceived me, because I am invisible; yet when I want to be, I am visible. And since you want to know my name, you can learn it easily, because I don't wish to be hidden from you: I am called Hope."

(17) *How the Lover spoke to Hope*

When I saw that this was Hope, I took more comfort and hope in

2254 **reveste** revest E; rouesce JK; revesce Pe. 2255 **que** vi E; quen J. **crostee** croicie JK. 2256 **temps** tant JK. **ostee** ascie JK. 2258 **cy** je JK. 2262 **qu'ay devant** que jay devant E. 2263 **s'elle fait** celle fait C; se le fay E; elle fait J. 2264 **rose** robe JK. 2265 **aussi** ainssi JKPe. 2266 **fais** fas Pe. 2267 **l'esserbe** leesse erbe E; laserbe JK. 2271 **le c.** la c. C. 2272 **S'il le desert** Si le dessers EPe; Si le sert JK. **soit pres ou l.** ou pres ou l. E; soit prez ou soit l. JK; soit prez soit l. Pe. 2274 **nu** nue E. 2276 **cy** si EK. 2279 **tel** celle JK. 2288 **confort et espoir** au fort espoir JK.

Dont la terre reveste et cueuvre,
Pour ce que sa robe crostee
De l'yver temps li est ostee,
Et li donne robe a parer,
Trop bien me puis cy comperer
A li, car je fais un amant
Cointe, joli. Sces tu comment?
Tu le sauras sans contredit;
Recorde ce qu'ay devant dit.
Et s'elle fait d'une racine
Yssir flour, et rose d'espine,

Tout aussi fais je un cuer flourir
En toute joie, et fais mourir
En li douleur; car je l'esserbe,
Si que de mal n'i demeure herbe.
Et de ma douçour que tu scens,
Qui moult est plus douce qu'encens,
L'adouci, le conforte, et l'oing,
S'il le desert, soit pres ou loing.
Et pour ce que je te savoie
Desconforté et nu de joie
Et qu'a conforter sui tenue
Les amans, sui je cy venue.
Mes c'est en ma propre personne,
Com ta certaine amie et bonne,
Par tel maniere que veü
Ne m'avoies, n'aperceü,
Pour ce que je sui invisible;
Et quant je vueil, je sui visible.
Et de mon non que voeus savoir, f. 41va
De legier pues apercevoir,
Qu'a toy ne vueil estre celee:
Esperance sui appelee."

(Miniature 17) *Comment l'Amant parle a Espera[n]ce*

Quant je vi que c'iert Esperance,
Je pris confort et espoir en ce

this matter than I had before, so that I summoned up all my senses together and then forced myself to speak and said to her in more lively fashion:

"My dear and revered lady, worthy of praise and honor, perfect in every quality heart can imagine, eyes see, ears hear, hand draw, mouth say, keen understanding describe, taste savor, touch feel, desire or will or heart sense; loved-one of God, Nature, and every created thing; true exemplar, mirror of happiness, bright star that leads lost hearts to safe harbor; sorrow's antidote, health, happiness; healing and curative from death; flower, stem, and very root from which come joy and every sweetness wherever you're remembered. If every one of God's creatures who's lived or is yet to live were each not merely just as gifted, but a hundred thousand times more gifted in enumerating than Arithmetic and Pythagoras and Music, Michalus and Milesius and skillful Orpheus, and if they were all to burden themselves with enumerating your numberless blessings and sweetnesses, Lady, they would only be chasing their shadows, for they'd never succeed, any more than they could dry up the sea.

2291 **ensemble mis** ensamble et mis JK. 2293 **vive** vivre E; lie JK. 2294 **reverent** reverence E. 2302 **vouloir** valoir E. 2307 **desvoiés** avoyes E. 2310 **estoc** escot JK. 2312 **Ou vo remembrance** Onnor embrance JK; En vo r. E. 2313 **Se** Et C. **tuit** tint K. **que** qui J. 2317 **En** A E. **que** *om* E. 2321 **se** cé K. **vousissent em.** voissent tous em. Pe. 2322 **douçours** decours E. 2324 **S'abaieroient** Sabaroient C (−1); Si oublieroient J; Si oublieroit K. **ombre** nombre JK.

Plus que devant n'avoie fait,
Si que mes esperis a fait
Tous ensemble mis a force ay,
Et lors de parler m'esforçay
Et li dis de plus vive chiere:
"Ma dame reverent et chiere,
Digne de loenge et d'onneur,
Exellent en toute valour
Que cuers porroit ymaginer,
Yeus veoir, oreille escouter,
Main figurer, ne bouche dire,
Soultis entendemens descrire,
Goust savourer, ne tast sentir,
Desirs, vouloir, cuers assentir;
De Dieu amie et de Nature
Et de toute autre creature; f. 41vb

Examples vrais, mireour de joye,
Estoille clere qui ravoie
Les cuers desvoiés a droit port;
Contre doulour, santé, deport,
Retour de mort, et medecine;
Flour, estoc, et droite racine,
Dont joye et toute douçour vient
Ou vo remembrance seurvient.
Se tuit cilz que Dieus a fait estre
Et cilz qui sont encor a nestre
Estoient chascun plus soubtil,
Non pas une foys, mais cent mil,
En bien nombrer que Arismetique
Et Pytagoras et Musique,
Michalus et Millesius
Et que li soubtis Orpheüs,
Et se vousissent emcombrer
Des biens et des douçours nombrer,
Dame, dont vous avés sans nombre,
S'abaieroient il leur ombre;
Car jamais n'i asseveroient,
Ne que la mer espuiseroient.

"And since, noble lady, I have neither wit nor power to relate all your blessings and sweetnesses—as I should and would willingly do, but I would labor in vain, my lady—I very humbly offer you grace, thanks, and praise a hundred thousand times, and hail you; for I am at the port of salvation, I feel, when I look at you, and I place heart, body, and soul completely in your care; because there is nowhere I could better place them in order to employ my time happily. And I swear to you faithfully that I want to spend my life and my time in your sweet company; for I see clearly that he who loses you is lost himself. Therefore I never want to leave you. But I beg and request, my lady, that you not be displeased if I ask one more thing on account of my troubles."

HOPE

"Indeed not; ask with confidence!"

(18) *How the Lover thanks Hope*

THE LOVER

"Gladly, my lady. You have told me, as well you can, how I must behave if I wish to be restored to health; how Love has helped me; how

2329 **et** ou E. 2330 **com je le d.** com je les d. C; comme je d. E. 2331 **Et** Si JK. 2333 **tres . . . ren** a vous doucement ren E. 2334 **A . . . mercy l.** Tres humblement grace et l. E. 2340 **les** le CEPe. 2342 **si vous promet** ce vous prengne E. 2345 **bien** *om* E. 2350 **Se** Et E. 2356 **je** *om* Pe.

Et pour ce, dame de vaillance,
Qu'en moy n'a pas sens ou scïence
Pour vos biens et douçours retraire—
Si com je le deüsse faire
Et com volentiers le feroie,
Mais en vain me traveilleroie,
Ma dame—tres humblement ren ge
A vous grace, mercy, loenge
.c. mille foys, et vous salu;
Car je suy au port de salu,
Ce m'est vis, quant je vous regarde,
Si met du tout en vostre garde
Cuer, corps, ame; car il n'est lieus
Ou mettre les peüsse mieus
Pour mon temps user lïement.
Et si vous promet loyaument f. 42a
Qu'en vostre douce compaignie
Vueul mon temps user et ma vie,
Quar je voy bien tout en apert
Que cilz qui vous pert, il se pert.
Pour ce jamais partir n'en quier;
Mes je vous depri et requier,
Ma dame, qu'il ne vous desplaise
Se de ce qui moult me mesaise
Vous fais encor une demande."

ESPERANCE

"Nennil; seürement demande!"

(Miniature 18) *Commant l'Amant mercie Esperance*

L'AMANT

"Volentiers, dame. Dit m'avés,
Si com bien faire le savés,
Comment je me doy maintenir
Se je vueil a santé venir;
Comment Amours m'a secouru;

you have come promptly to aid and comfort me; the arms lovers must bear, and the meaning of their colors and design, for all of which I thanked you sincerely; how you've wed me with your delightful ring and sung your amorous song; how lovers who want to leave you can do nothing, for you are all their strength, their wall, their castle, their comfort; how your brightness shines far and near upon lovers; next, how your sweetness, sweeter than any other sweetness, alleviates their sorrows; and you have told me your provenance and your most noble and renowned name, and the nature of mercy, for which I thank you a hundred thousand times.

"But you have said nothing about Fortune, who makes the world's fortune, who is not and never was constant, but when she most reassures her own, they are the ones she most mercilessly punishes and strikes down from their high estate. I know well what to expect, because memory alone of her assaults, her attacks, her false laughter, her false tricks so frightens me that all my limbs tremble just at the thought of it. For this reason, my lady, I ask you to tell me how I can defend myself against Fortune, because her game is to break a heart, especially

2358 **Comment** Et comment C (+1). 2363 **sceü vous é** vous sceu ey K. 2367 **li amans** lamoureux JK. **puellent** puent C; peuent E; puevent J. 2368 **se** ce K. 2369 **Car** Que C. **tous leur** tour leur C. 2370 **murs** meurs CEJK. 2374 **leur maus** les maus C; amans E. 2377 **chose** *om* JK. 2379 **n'avés** ne maves C (+1). 2380 **Qui** Que JK. **ainssi le monde** le monde ainsi Pe. 2381 **n'onques ne fu** onques ne feust E; nonques ne fust J. 2383 **sont** *om* E. 2384 **de plus haut** plus de haut J. 2387 **assaus . . . estours** assaux et de ses tours E; assaus de ses atours JK. 2388 **de . . . tours** et de ses tours CPe. 2390 **En** Me E. **m'en** mi E. 2393 **Je me pourray** Me pourroie JK. 2395 **de** dun E.

Comment vous avés acouru
Pour moy aidier et conforter;
Les armes qu'amans doit porter,
De quel fust la senefiance
Des couleurs et de leur semblance,
Dont moult bon gré sceü vous é; f. 42b
Comment vous m'avés espousé
De vostre anelet savoureus
Et chanté vos chans amoureus;
Comment li amans riens ne puellent
Qui departir de vous se veulent,
Car vous estes tous leur effors,
Leurs murs, leur chastiaus, leur confors;
Comment vos clarté loing et pres
Esclarcist les amans; aprés
Comment vostre douçour, plus douce
Qu'autre douçour, leur maus adouce;
Vostre venue et vostre non
Qui est de moult noble renon,
Et quelle chose est de merci,
Donc .c. mille foys vous merci.

Mais riens n'avés dit de Fortune
Qui ainssi le monde fortune,
Qui n'est, n'onques ne fu seüre;
Mais quant les siens plus asseüre,
Ceuls sont qu'elle plus griefment bat
Et qu'en bas de plus haut abat.
Je m'en sçay bien a quoy tenir,
Car seulement dou souvenir
De ses assaus, de ses estours,
De ses faus ris, de ses faulz tours
Ay tel paour que tuit mi membre
En fremissent quant il m'en membre.
Pour ce, dame, je vous demant
Qu'a moy vueilliés dire comment
Je me pourray de li desfendre,
Car si gieu sont pour un cuer fendre,
Mais que il soit de loyal amant
Et fust plus dur que dyamant,

if it belongs to a loyal lover and is harder than a diamond; and to others, like me, she is so cruel and of such a perverse nature that she'd have killed me, had God not led you here to me to turn aside the blow she meant to deal me."

(19) *How Hope speaks to the Lover about Fortune*

"Fair sweet friend, what should I tell you about Fortune? I cannot tell you more about her than you said in the complainte you composed, except that in olden days the ancients customarily attributed two faces to her, one in front and the other behind. This proves clearly to you that Fortune is sweet and bitter: for she will be sweet to you when she observes you with the face she has in front, generously promising you sweetness, joy, and happiness, all cloaked in sadness; for thus you must understand it, although the world doesn't wish to take it so; yet this is the correct understanding, wherefore many who believed too firmly in her promises have been deceived, and trusted in her so far that in the end they were destroyed.

"And if you are observed by the other face, be careful, because For-

2397 **si** *om* EPe. 2400 **tost ci** *in* C *these words were inverted, then corrected by scribe.* 2401 **estordre** destordre JK. 2404 **t'en** te E. 2405 **dit as** as dit E. 2406 **que ditas** que tu as dit E; dictas JK. 2407 **usages** un sages E. 2409 **arrier** arriere EJ. 2410 **derrier** darriere EJ. 2411 **Ce te** Ceste E. 2415 **Du** Dun CE. **visage** mesage C. 2417 **bonneürté** et debonnairete E. 2421 **le** *om* JK. 2423 **maint** moult Pe. 2424 **couvent** commant E. 2425 **s'en** se E. 2426 **s'en . . . fin** souspendoient a laffin E. 2428 **lance sur f.** lance sous f. C; lente seur f. JK; lance senz f. Pe. 2429 **Se** Ce K. **combatre** embatre E.

Et se as autres est si diverse
Et de nature si perverse
Comme a moy, qu'elle eüst oci,
Se Dieus ne vous eüst tost ci
Amenee pour moy estordre f. 42va
Dou mors dont elle me vueut mordre."

(Miniature 19) *Comment Esperance parle a l'Amant de Fortune*

ESPERANCE PARLE

"Biaus douls amis, que te diroie
De Fortune? Ne t'en saroie
Plus dire que tu en dit as
En ta complainte que ditas,
Fors tant que jadis fu usages
Que li ancien .ii. visages
Li faisoient ça en arrier,
L'un devant et l'autre derrier.
Ce te demoustre chose clere,
Que Fortune est douce et amere:
Car adonc douce te sera
Quant elle te regardera
Du visage qu'elle a devant,
Et largement t'ara couvant,
Douçour, joie, bonneürté,
Afflublés de maleürté;
Car ainssi le doys tu entendre,
Ja soit ce que li mondes prandre
Ne le vueille mie ensement;
Mais c'est le droit entendement,
Dont maint ont esté deceü f. 42vb
Qui trop ont son couvent creü,
Et tant s'en faisoient afin
Qu'il s'en perdoient a la fin.

Et se regardez ies de l'autre,
Garde toy; car lance sur fautre
Se vient encontre toy combatre

tune is attacking you with lance at the ready, to drive you from every honor, without formal threat or defiance; you should place no more trust in her than in the club of a bully; and, if you wish my opinion, take no pleasure in any of the benefits she sends and gives you. So thus in her face you see both sweet and bitter fortune, for the ancients who depicted her gave her such form. And because I've sought you out and you've asked me with humble heart how you should defend yourself when Fortune assails you with the eye of her rearward face which strikes without warning, so that no man can protect himself from it, I want to ask you which in your opinion is the better of these two goods: the good you cannot lose, or the good you could easily lose?"

THE LOVER SPEAKS

"My lady, the answer is easy."

HOPE ANSWERS HIM

"Say it, then."

THE LOVER

"Indeed, dear lady, the good that one doesn't lose is better."

HOPE SPEAKS

"Therefore, that which one loses is worse."

2432 **dois** doies E. 2433 **d'un** de EPe. 2434 **Et selonc** Selon ce E. 2435 **et** ou C. 2436 **De** Se Pe. 2437 **sa** la JK. 2439 *om* JK. **telle** celle Pe. 2440 *after this line* J *adds*: A ce samblant la cognoissoient 2443 **desfense** deffaulte E. 2445 **sa** la JK. 2446 **ainçoys** avant E. 2447 **qu'il** qui Pe. 2448 **Le** Ni E. 2450 **ces** ses CK. 2453 **Dame la response** Response dame JK. 2454 **Di la donc** Di donques E; **Di la** JK. **certes dame** certes ma dame CJK (+1).

Pour toy de toute honnour abatre,
Sans menace et sans deffier;
Si que tu ne t'i dois fier,
Ne qu'en baston d'un champion;
Et, selonc mon oppinion,
Des biens qu'elle donne et envoie,
De l'un pren ne de l'autre joye.
Si qu'ainssi vois par sa figure
La douce fortune et la seure,
Car telle fourme li donnoient
Li ancien qui la figuroient.
Et pour ce que je t'ay acquis,
Et que de humble cuer m'as enquis
Quelle desfense il te faudra
Avoir quant elle t'assaudra
De l'ueil de sa derraienne face,
Qui fiert ainçoys qu'elle menace,
Si qu'il n'est homs qui amender
Le puist, je te vueil demander,
A ton avis, le quel tu tiens
Estre meilleur de ces .ii. biens,
Ou le bien que tu ne porroies
Perdre, ou celui que bien perdroies?"

L'AMANT PARLE

"Dame, la response est ligiere."

ESPERANCE LI RESPONT

"Di la donc."

L'AMANT

"Certes, dame chiere,
Le bien qu'on ne pert est millour."

ESPERANCE PARLE

"Dont est cilz qu'on pert le piour."

THE LOVER REPLIES

"My lady, that is true; I agree."

HOPE SPEAKS

"So now we're in agreement; I want to show you clearly that you've made the right choice: do you think that if prosperity is in Fortune, felicity and true happiness are there likewise? Don't trouble yourself to answer, because these things can never be found together. And here is how I reach this conclusion: sovereign happiness and unfailing felicity are sovereign goods of Nature, who is governed by uncorrupted Reason; and such goods cannot be lost; therefore, Fortune's goods cannot be compared to them or preferred over them. For one sees, and it's well known, that he who has the most, loses the most. Therefore I show you clearly there is nothing certain in Fortune, neither felicity nor happiness. And if you want to protect yourself from her, I'll tell you what you can do to achieve happiness. Is there anything more precious to you than yourself?"

THE LOVER

"My lady, no!"

HOPE SPEAKS

"Then hold Fortune's power in contempt and be your own master.

2458 **en** a EPe. 2459 **Si te** Je te E. 2463 **Aveuc** Avecques JK. 2466 **ce** *om* EPe. **me muet** meuet C (−1). 2470 **use** usent JK. 2473 **s'i** ci K. **cil** sil C. 2477 **Qu'en** Que JK. 2478 **ne** en CEPe. 2480 **dirai que faire** diroie que ne JK. 2482 **n'as** na K. 2483 **Comme** Com E.

L'AMANT RESPONT

"Dame, c'est voirs; je m'i acort." f. 43a

ESPERANCE PARLE

"Or sommes nous donc en acort;
Si te vueil moustrer clerement
Que tu as fait bon jugement:
Cuides tu, se prosperité
Est en li, que felicité
Aveuc la beneürté vraye
Y soient? De ce ne t'esmaie,
Car c'est chose qui ne se puet
Joindre. Et vesci ce qui me muet:
La beneürté souveraine
Et la felicité certaine
Sont souverain bien de Nature,
Qui use de Raison la pure;
Et tels biens, on ne les puet perdre;
Pour ce comparer ne aërdre
Ne s'i puent cil de Fortune.
Car on voit, et chose est commune,
Que qui plus en a, plus en pert.
Si que je te moustre en appert
Qu'en Fortune n'a riens seür,
Felicité ne boneür.
Et se de li garder te voeus,
Je te dirai que faire pues,
Et pour estre boneüreus.
Dont n'as tu riens si precïeus
Comme toy?"

L'AMANT

"Ma dame, nennil!"

ESPERANCE PARLE

"Or tien donc son pouoir si vil
Qu'aies de toy la seigneurie.

See that Reason rules you and that you are patient and have the virtue of sufficiency, for happiness truly comes from enduring patiently; and I believe there's no man who, when he becomes impatient, wouldn't trade his position for something unknown; and this makes him be unhappy and live in perilous plight. Also you should not fear or esteem in your heart Fortune's power or her mutability, but rather hate, flee, and despise them, and not wish for her goods for yourself. And if you remember my warning, you will never lack for the blessings Fortune cannot take from you.

"And although you've lamented bitterly in your complainte and contend that Fortune has been hard, bitter, inconstant, and uncertain toward you, and that you've often called her a false and proven traitor and your enemy in every situation, I wish to be her advocate and prove to you by reason that she never betrayed you, nor was she ever your enemy, but rather was your good friend, in so far as she knows what love is and can be compassionate in her bitterness. And so as better to show your mistake, I want to ask you this: does he who fulfills his duty do wrong?"

2486 **Gardes** Garde JKPe. 2491 **N'il n'est** Ni nest E; Nil est Pe. **a** en E. 2493 **Qui** Quil Pe. 2495 **le** les JK. 2499 **douter ne prisier** amer ne penser JK. 2501 **ses . . . desire** telz biens ne dire JK. 2505 **te** ten E. 2506 **que** *om* E. 2510 **fausse traïtre** fausse tristre C (−1); faulte tristrece E. 2517 **scet** veult E; soit JPe. 2518 **Et** *om* E. 2521 **Fait . . . qui** Meffait cilz qui JK.

Gardes que Raisons te maistrie
Et qu'aies en toy pacïence
Et la vertu de souffissance,
Car beneürtés vraiement
Vient de souffrir pacïenment;
N'il n'est homme, a mon enscïent,
Que quant il est impascïent,
Qui ne vousist avoir fait change f. 43b
De son estat a un estrange;
Et ce le fait maleüreus
Et vivre en estat perilleus.
Aussi ne dois tu la puissance
De Fortune ne sa muance
En ton cuer douter ne prisier,
Mais haïr, fuïr, desprisier,
Ne ses biens ne desire en toy.
Et se tu retiens mon chastoy,
Tu aras le bien sans faillir
Qu'elle ne te porroit tollir.

Et comment que moult fort te plaignes
En ta complainte, et que tu teingnes
Que Fortune t'a esté dure,
Amere, diverse, et obscure,
Et que maintes foys appellee
L'as fausse, traïtre prouvee,
Et ton anemie en tous cas,
Je vueul estre ses advocas
Et te vueil prouver par raison
Qu'onques ne te fist traïson,
N'onques ne te fu anemie;
Ainçoys t'a esté bonne amie,
Selonc ce qu'elle scet amer
Et estre douce en son amer.
Et pour mieus prouver ton contraire,
Te vueil ceste demande faire:
Fait cils mal qui fait son devoir?"

"Indeed not, my lady."

[HOPE]

"You speak the truth. But yet as you are my witness, I speak in accord with reason and testify that, although Fortune has taken away the joy you felt, which has caused you much sorrow, she did not betray you or do you wrong; for she is only doing what she must, as I'll point out to you. If she were constant and behaved reasonably, so that she was just and true to everyone, she would not be Fortune. But because she is not stable, but is fickle, changing, and capricious in fact, word, and reputation, she is called Fortune. Although her instability in changing is her true stability, this is her station, this is her nature, this is her normal behavior, this is her right. Therefore, since she behaves as she must, I say that you were wrong to slander and curse her, and to defame her works; for if you fell into tribulation because of her sudden, singular, fickle, and ruthless shifting, which made your heart stagger, indeed, my friend, you are not the only one, for she does the same without rhyme or reason to those who live in pagan lands; and her

2523 **ton** te E; *om* Pe. 2525 **osté** este E. 2528 **ne fist** na fait JK. 2529 **elle fait** elle a fait JK. 2530 **Et . . . doit** Et en ce te moustray je au d. E; Et ce te moustrai je au d. JKPe. 2533 **tous** *om* Pe. 2536 **se** ce K. 2538 **Est elle** Et elle est C. 2539 **mobilité** nobilite E. 2540 **soit estableté** est abilite E. 2541 **ses** ces C. 2542 **ses** ces C. **meurs** murs K. 2546 **ses** ces J. 2548 **sa** la JK. 2550 **Qui** Que E. 2553 **en paienime** en paiennie C; en sa doctrine E. 2554 **ne rime** nermie C.

(Miniature 20) *Comment l'Amant parle a Esperance*

"Nennil, ma dame." f. 43va

[ESPERANCE]

"Tu dis voir.
Mais encor avant ton tesmoing
Je di par raison et tesmoing
Que, se Fortune t'a osté
De la joie ou tu as esté,
Dont tu as receü maint mal,
Que traïson ne fist, ne mal;
Car elle fait ce qu'elle doit,
Et ce te moustrerai au doit:
S'elle estoit tousdis en un point
Et de raison usoit a point,
Si qu'envers tous fust juste et une,
Elle ne seroit pas Fortune.
Mais pour ce qu'elle ne sejourne,
Ains se change, mue, et bestourne
En fait, en dit, en renommee,
Est elle Fortune nommee.
Comment que sa mobilité
En mouvant soit estableté,
C'est ses estas, c'est sa nature,
Ce sont ses meurs, c'est sa droiture.
Dont, puis qu'elle fait son deü,
Je di que tu as tort eü
De li laidengier ne blasmer,
Ne de ses oeuvres disfamer;
Car se tu ies cheüs en peine
Par sa mutation soudaine,
Estrange, diverse, et sauvage,
Qui fist chanceler ton corage,

Certes, amis, tu n'ies pas seuls;
Car autant en fait elle a ceuls
Qui demeurent en paienime,
Sans resgarder raison ne rime;

wheel was not built for you alone, nor will it be dismantled for you, because it makes its power known to monk and layman alike. And since you knew it well, tell me why you climbed upon it? If your face has gone pale because of it, it's more your fault than hers. When you began to love, you set out to sea amongst perilous, welling, cresting, and breaking waves that roll quickly along, one over the other, making the ocean rage and swell, so that the whole sea is turbulent; and so you became a slave to Fortune, who is so clever that no one can join her court unless he immediately enslaves his freedom, once he strives to serve her.

"If to the winds you unfurl your sail, made of broadcloth by a master's hand, you are well aware that your ship will go wherever the wind blows it, because without question your ship's freedom has been committed to the wind. Thus it is, since you've so enslaved yourself to Fortune that you serve her and have entered her servitude, that you must sail and row as she sails and rows, and that you must conform in every shape and manner to her behavior, since you are of her house-

2555 **Ne** Et JK. **seul ne fu pas f.** seule ne fu f. C; seul ne fu f. EPe. 2563 **empreïs** en pris CPe (−1). 2566 **c. et plates** c. plates EPe. 2568 **dessous** dessus EPe. 2569 **se** *om* C (−1). 2570 **Si** Et E. **toute** *repeated* J. 2573 **devient** remaint E. 2574 **Qu'il** Qui C. 2575 **Qu'il** Qui Pe. 2576 **fera tant qu'il** sera temps qui E; face tant qui JK. 2578 *om* CPe. **et** *om* E. 2581 **sans plus** semplus E. 2582 **nef** neif C. **sera mise** se ravise C. 2583 **tant t'assers** tant assers E. 2587 **nagier et a rime** nage a la rive E; nagier et a rive JK. 2588 **nage et rime** nage et rive EK; na et rive J. 2589 **qu'a . . . tu** qua ce tu C (−1); quasses faiz tu E; a sez fes tu Pe. 2591 *om* JK.

Ne pour toy seul ne fu pas faite,
Ne pour toy ne sera deffaite
Sa roe qui se fait congnoistre f. 43vb
Entre les mondains et en cloistre.
Et quant tu bien la congnoissoies,
Di moy pourquoy tu i montoies?
Se tu en as le vis pali,
C'est plus par toy que n'est par li.
Car quant tu enpreïs l'amer,
Tu te meïs enmi la mer
Entre les perilleuses ondes
Cornues et plates et rondes,
Qui se transportent en pou d'eure,
L'une au dessous, l'autre au desseure,
Dont la mer s'engroisse et se trouble,
Si que toute l'iaue en est trouble;
Et si te meïs en servage
De Fortune, qui tant est sage
Que nulz ne devient de sa court,
Qu'il ne couveingne brief et court
Qu'il face sa franchise serve,
Puis qu'il fera tant qu'il la serve.

Se tu estens au vent ton voile,
Fait de main de maistre et de toile,
Tu scés bien que ta nef ira
La ou li vens la conduira,
Pour ce, sans plus, que la franchise
De ta nef au vent sera mise.
Einssi est, puis que tant t'assers
A Fortune que tu la sers
Et ies mis en sa servitude,
Il couvient par force que tu te
Mettes a nagier et a rime,
Selonc ce qu'elle nage et rime,
Et qu'a ses meurs tu te conformes
En tous cas et en toutes formes,
Puis que tu yes de ses maignies.
Prouvé le t'ay, se tu le nies.

hold. I've proven it to you, even if you deny it. Now hasten to answer me, because I still want to defend her against your earlier assertion that you found her bitter; and this has moved me to ask: Has she brought you more trouble or more good?"

[THE LOVER]

"More trouble, my lady; of this I'm certain."

[HOPE]

"Indeed, you don't know what you're saying. I think you're naive and that your heart feels the opposite, not in one instance, but a hundred."

[THE LOVER]

"It does, my lady?"

[HOPE]

"Yes, and I'll prove it to you."

[THE LOVER]

"I beg you to do so, because I find nothing in myself to boast of, except the great joy and good that I derive from your presence."

[HOPE]

"It comes from lack of knowledge; for if you were well-informed,

2597 **m'a** mas JK. 2598 **dou quel tu as** tu que tu as E; dont duquel as JK. 2600 **de** du E. **ce** se C. 2602 **Il** Y Pe. 2606 **car** que JK. 2607 **Riens** Biens K. **m'en** me EJK. 2612 **En** Et E.

Mes or me respon sans muser,
Car encor la vueil escuser
De ce que devant as prouvé
Que tu l'as amere trouvé; f. 44a
Et ce a demander m'a meü:
Di, dou quel tu as plus eü
De li, ou de mal ou de bien?"

[L'AMANT]

"Dame, de mal. Ce sçay je bien."

[ESPERANCE]

"Certes, tu ne sces que tu dis.
Il m'est vis que tu arrudis,
Que tes cuers le contraire en sent,
Non pas en un cas, mais en cent."

[L'AMANT]

"Fait, dame?"

[ESPERANCE]

"Oïl, je le te preuve."

[L'AMANT]

"Je vous en pri; car je ne trueve
Riens en moy dont loer m'en doie,
Fors dou bien et de la grant joie
Qui me vient de vostre presence."

[ESPERANCE]

"C'est par desfaut de congnoissance;
Car se tu fusses bien apris
En ton cuer eüsses compris

you would have understood in your heart that when you came forth from your mother's womb Fortune was not bitter toward you, but amiable, sweet, courteous, and loving; so you are not compelled to condemn her. For you were naked, and she immediately took you and nursed you devotedly with her milk—that is, with her riches, her honors, her splendours—and was your nurse and mistress, the glad dispenser of your glory, and surrounded you with all possessions within reason, possessions that are under her jurisdiction. And you complain? Is it right? What more do you want her to do for you? Has she not blessed you sufficiently when she—if you understand me well—gave you gifts that were not yours? For they are not yours, but rightfully belong to her. And since none of this is yours, you are a fool to consider yourself ill paid if she wishes to take back from one day to the next what is hers.

"You are very much like someone who has borrowed from another, and when it comes time to repay, becomes angry if he's asked to do so. This is no more and no less than what you're doing. But since you are in the hands of Fortune of whom I speak, I beg you to remember from my teaching that there where she is are her blessings; and if she leaves, they go as well; and whoever she helps, is helped, and whoever she

2614 **te** *added above line in* C. **fu** feust E. 2615 **fu** fust E. 2617 **pas . . . tenus** au blasmer tenus C (−1); au blasmer la tenus EPe. 2618 **biens** *om* Pe. **nus** nulz E. 2619 **elle** celle E. 2623 **te** se E. 2624 *line added in* C *at bottom of column, with pointing finger to indicate its proper position.* 2625 **t'avironna** ten environna E. 2626 **ou** en E. 2628 **a droit** au droit JK. 2631 **se . . . gloses** si bien les gloses E; si bien ses choses JK. 2632 JK *replace this line with*: Moustrees par tieute et par gloses. 2633 **mie** pas Pe. 2634 **et** *om* CEPe (−1). 2635 **riens n'i a qui** ny a riens qui E. 2636 **te** ten E. 2637 **S'elle** Elle C. 2638 **a** et Pe. 2640 **de** *om* E. 2641 E *replaces this line with* : Quant il est tenus de le rendre. 2642 *om* K. J *replaces this line with*: Un autre vient qui le li emble 2643 **Ainssi** Ains E. 2644 **tu** *om* CPe (−1). 2648 **Et . . . il** Elle sempart et il JK. 2649 **cui** qui E. 2650 **Qui** Cui C.

Qu'a l'issir dou ventre ta mere
Elle ne te fu pas amere,
Ainçoys te fu moult amiable,
Douce, courtoise, et charitable;
Si n'ies pas au blasmer tenus.
Car de tous biens estoies nus,
Et elle te prist erraument
Et t'alaita diliganment
De son lait—c'est de ses richesses,
De ses honneurs, de ses noblesses—
Et te fu nourrice et maistresse,
Favorable admenisteresse
De la gloire, t'avironna
De tous les biens ou raison a,
C'est des biens qui sont de son droit.
Et tu t'en plains? Fais tu a droit?
Que vueus tu qu'elle plus te face?
Ne t'a elle fait assés grace f. 44b
Quant elle t'a—se bien le gloses—
Fait user des estranges choses?
Car elles ne sont mie tiennes,
Ainçoys sont de son droit et siennes.
Et quant riens n'i a qui soit tiens,
Fouls yes s'a mal paiés te tiens,
S'elle vueult ravoir en sa main
Ce qui sien est, d'ui a demain.

Tu sembles trop bien a celuy
Qui a emprunté de l'autruy,
Et quant il est temps qu'il le rende,
Il a courous s'on luy demande.
Ainssi fais tu, ne plus, ne mains.
Mais pour ce que tu yes es mains
De Fortune dont je parole,
Je te pri, retien de m'escole
Que la ou elle est, si bien sont;
Et s'elle s'en part, il s'en vont,
Et cui elle aide, il est aidiés,
Qui elle laist, il est laissiés,

abandons is abandoned, I believe; because everyone today lives within her circle. But it seems, if I'm not mistaken, that you want to control her and compel her to remain stable, or else you'll complain. Yet indeed, you have much to complain about if you wish to change her nature, which has always been and ever remains the same, and will never be different until the world ends.

"You behold the sea calm and peaceful at one moment, then you see it frightening and stormy, because the wind is howling so strongly that the breakers are rising and falling more swiftly than any horse, nor could the whole world stop them.

"So Fortune changes, and no force and no sweet talk can ever restrain her when once she decides to move. She carries off wealth, honors, and all possessions as properly her own, and no one shares them unless she grants it by her grace; so you should not complain. But to reach the truth about the trouble you say she's caused you, I say she's done you no wrong, but rather has favored you greatly."

[THE LOVER]

"How, my lady? Tell me!"

2651 **m'est avis car** mest vis car C (−1); mest avis que JK. 2656 **doie** doies J. 2657 E *reads*: Quautrement tu complaindre as. 2662 **li siecles** le monde E. 2663 **paisible** plaisible C. 2664 **et** est E. 2665 **et** est E. 2670 **l'arester** arrester JKPe. 2677 **part** pert E. 2678 **repart** repert E. 2682 **que . . . meffait** quelle ne ta riens m. Pe.

Ce m'est avis; car par son cerne
Au jour d'ui chascuns se gouverne.
Mais il semble, a bien discerner,
Que tu la vueilles gouverner
Et que tu la vueilles contraindre,
Si qu'estable doie remaindre,
Ou autrement tu t'en pleindras.
Mes certes, assés a pleindre has
S'oster la vueuls de sa nature,
Qui tous jours a duré et dure,
Ne jamais autre ne sera
Tant que li siecles fenira.

Tu voys la mer quoye et paisible
Aucune foys, et puis orrible
La voys et plaine de torment,
Pour ce que le vent si forment
Y fiert, que ce sont mons et vaus,
Plus tost courans que nulz chevaus, f. 44va
Ne tous li mondes contrester
Ne porroit pas pour l'arester.

Tout ainssi Fortune se mue,
Ne jamais ne seroit tenue
Par force, ne par biau parler,
Si tost qu'elle s'en vueut aler.
Mais richesce et honnour emporte
Et tous biens qui sont de tel sorte
Com siens propres, ou nuls ne part,
Se sa grace ne l'en repart;
Si ne t'en deüsses pas plaindre.
Mais pour la verité ateindre
Dou mal que dis qu'elle t'a fait,
Je di que riens ne t'a meffait,
Ainçoys a fait assés pour toy."

[L'AMANT]

"Dame, comment? Dictes le moy."

"Gladly! She left your senses unharmed, and what you love and desire most is the life of which you are master. So if afterwards she has twisted her double face, which is two-sided in word and deed, less than a quarter turn in your direction and has cast a sidelong glance, must you lament, complain, weep, and suffer?

"If you were wise, you would take heart and hope for improvement through her mutability. Is it not said that the wild man rejoices when he sees it rain, and sings? What moves him to it? His merrymaking expresses his hope that after the storm will come good weather. Nor can you know what joy is unless you've suffered. And I also teach and show you that good Fortune is properly the sign of bad to come. You should have remembered when you had risen so high that you could fall down at any time. But Love, who blinds many a heart, blinded your eyes and heart so that you never thought of leading any other kind of life that she might give you, except the present one. But in all you plan you must be aware of how things come out; and if they come out

2686 **Ton scens** Tous ceulz E. 2688 *om* JK. 2689 **s'elle** ce elle C. 2692 **fait de travers** fay dentravers E. 2693 **T'en** Tant JK. **dementer** demander J. 2700 **Qui li** quil li C. 2701 **quil** qui CK. 2704 **c'est joye** cest de joie E. 2706 **proprement f.** f. proprement Pe. 2712 **te fist** se fist CPe. 2716 **du** *om* C (−1). 2719 **en meschiet** mal en chiet CEPe.

(Miniature 21) *Comment Esperance parle a l'Amant*

"Volentiers! Elle t'a laissié
Ton scens qu'elle n'a point blecié,
Et ce qu'aimmes plus et desires,
C'est la vie dont tu ies sires.
Aprés s'elle a sa face double, f. 44vb
Qui en fait et en dit se double,
Tourné vers toy a mains dou quart
Et fait de travers un regart,
T'en faut il ainssi dementer,
Plaindre, plourer, et tourmenter?

Tu deüsses en sa muance
Penre cuer et bonne esperance
De mieus avoir, se fusses sages.
Ne dit on que li homs sauvages
S'esjoïst quant il voit plouvoir,
Et chante? Qui li fait mouvoir?
L'espoir qu'il prent en son revel
Qu'aprés le lait il fera bel.
Ne tu n'as pouoir de savoir
Que c'est joye sans mal avoir.
Et aussi je t'apreng et moustre
Que proprement Fortune est moustre
De maleürté a venir.
Si te deüst bien souvenir,
Quant en si haus degrés estoies,
Qu'en aucun temps descenderoies.
Mais Amour qui maint cuer aveugle
D'eus et de cuer te fist aveugle,

Si que tu ne pensoies mie
A mener jamais autre vie,
Qu'elle ne te faisoit present,
Fors seulement du temps present.
Mais en tout ce que tu proposes
Dois regarder la fin des choses;
Et s'aucune foys en meschiet,
Pour une, .c. foys bien en chiet,

wrong one time, they go right a hundred, because every rule has its exception. I've offered you this proverb so that henceforth you'll be careful to keep your eye on how things come out. And had you been well aware of this, you'd never have complained so about Fortune or Good Love, for everything they did was for your advancement, and all for you. Therefore I want to and must ask forgiveness on their behalf, since they've given you by their sweetness a hundred joys for every sorrow. Yet you maintain the contrary, which you must not do.

"I urge you not to let this happen again, and always to remember from now on not to give a fig for the gifts of Fortune. Don't worry if they come and go; and if they don't stay with you, that shouldn't faze you one way or the other, because they are flightier than a bird. The more one has of Fortune's gifts, the more one needs: thus kings are more wanting than commoners in gold, silver, and precious gems, through lack of sufficiency, because a burning brand of cupidity is twisting and striking within their hearts, that burns and enflames their very entrails; and as long as they are burning so, all their hopes fail. I don't say that Nature is easily satisfied; but if the world were filled from the sky to the earth with whatever goods a heart could seek,

2722 C *reads*: Pour ce prouver le te baille (−1). 2723 **d'or en avant** dores en avant E. 2729 **ont fait c'est** a fait et JK. E *reads*: Car quanquelle a fait cest pour toy. 2730 **les** le E; la JK. 2731 **Que** Quelle JK. **t'ont** ton E; *om* JK. **leur** sa JK. 2732 **joies** joie CPe. 2733 **tu** qui E. 2734 **Ce que pas** Que tu pas E. *First* e *of* deusses *added above the line in* C. 2735 **Si** Se Pe. 2736 **et souviengne** et te s. C (+1). 2742 **Car** Que C; Ne E. **que oyselés** dun oysel JK. **sont** *om* E. 2745 **menue** menus C. 2746 **nue** nus C. 2748 **se . . . lance** sa bonte lance E. 2749 **raim** raan J. 2750 **si** *om* EJ. 2751 **Qu'il** Qui CEJK. 2752 **sont** font E. **esplois failles** espoirs failles C; explois frailles E. 2757 **jusqu'a la t.** jusques a la t. CE (+1); jusques a t. Pe. 2759 **Dire . . . d'avoir** Dire ymaginer savoir C (−1); Dire ymaginer davoir EPe.

Car il n'est regle qui ne faille.
Pour ce ce proverbe te baille,
Que d'or en avant bien te gardes
Que la fin des choses regardes. f. 45a
Et se bien prins garde y eüsses,
Ja de Fortune ne te fusses
Ainssi plains, ne de Bonne Amour,
Car ç'a esté pour ton millour
Quanqu'elle ont fait, c'est tout pour toy.
Pour ce escuser les vueil et doy,
Que donné t'ont par leur douçour
Cent joies pour une doulour.
Et tu maintiens tout le contraire,
Ce que pas ne deüsses faire.

Si te pri que plus ne t'aviengne,
Et qu'il te ramembre et souviengne
Que tu ne prises une prune
Desormais les biens de Fortune.
Ne te chaille s'il vont et viennent;
Et së avec toy ne se tiennent,
N'en dois estre liés ne dolens,
Car plus que oyselés sont volens.
Cilz qui plus en a, plus li faut:
Dont ont li roy plus grant desfaut
Que n'ont la povre gent menue,
D'or, d'argent, et de joiaus nue,
Et par deffaut de souffissance,
Car en leur cuer se voute et lance
Un ardant raim de couvoitise,
Qui si les embrase et atise
Qu'il les art jusques es entrailles;
Et si sont tous leurs esplois failles,
Tant comme il sont en telle ardure.
Je ne di mie que Nature
De pou de chose n'ait assés;
Mais se li mondes entassés
Estoit dou ciel jusqu'a la terre
De quanque cuers porroit requerre,
Dire, et ymaginer d'avoir,

imagine, or ask for, there could never be enough there to satisfy a covetous heart, if the truth be told, not even if five hundred thousand worlds were filled five hundred thousand times—as I believe. Do you know why not? In my humble opinion, I think nothing can satisfy avarice; wherefore it is manifest that he who covets everything, loses everything, because one loses soul and body, joy and honor. This is my opinion.

"Moreover, I beg you from the bottom of my heart never to forget the two precious virtues that I named for you above: one is beautiful Sufficiency; the other is Patience, her handmaiden. If you possess them, you needn't concern yourself with two-faced Fortune, because these virtues are so powerful, so worthy, and so precious that they can ignore Fortune's dominion and fickleness and safely set man on the road to Happiness. Happiness, it seems to me, is what brings us these six virtues—Glory, Delight, Esteem, Power, Honor, and Sufficiency. It's the sovereign and perfect good that comes from the First Master, who is beginning and end, three united in one, one in three, and one single good, in whom nothing is lacking.

2760 **N'en y** Nen il Pe. 2761 **droit** bien E. 2762 **couvoiteus** amoureux JK. 2763 **certes** pas a E. 2765 **le** les CPe. 2770 **Que** *om* JK. **tout c. tout** plus c. plus E. **tout pert** tretout pert JK. 2772 **Joye honnour** Joie et h. J. **et** *om* E. 2773 **prie trop de** prie je de E; pri trop de JK. 2781 **si** ci K. 2785 **mettent l'omme** lome mectent JK. 2786 **En c.** Et en c. E. 2787 **ce** se K. 2788 **qui** que Pe. 2792 **dou maistre** de nostre Pe. 2794 **conjointement** commencement JK. 2795 **Uns** Ou E.

N'en y pourroit il tant avoir f. 45b
Qu'il peüst jamais, a droit dire,
A un cuer couvoiteus souffire;

Non certes .v.c. mille mondes
Qui par .v.c. milles foys combles
Fussent, si com je le devis!
Sces tu pour quoy? Il m'est avis
Que, selonc mon jugement nice,
Riens ne souffist a avarice,
De quoy on voit tout en apert
Que qui tout couvoite, tout pert;
Car on en pert l'ame et le corps,
Joye, honnour. Et c'est mes acors.

Encor te prïe trop de cuer
Que tu n'oublies a nul fuer
Les .ii. precïeuses vertus
Que je t'ay nommé cy dessus:
L'une est Souffissance la belle,
L'autre est Pacïence, s'ancelle.
Se tu les as, tu n'as regart
De Fortune au double regart,
Car elles sont si vertueuses,
Si dignes, et si precïeuses,
Que riens ne prisent le dangier
De Fortune, ne son changier,
Ains mettent l'omme a seürté
En chemin de Bonneürté.
Bonneürtés est, ce me semble,
Ce qui donne ces .vi. ensemble:
Gloire, Delit, et Reverence,
Puissance, Honnour, et Souffissance.
C'est bien parfait et souverain
Qui vient dou Maistre Premerain,
Qui est fin et commencement,
Trebles en un conjointement,
Uns en .iii. et un tout seul bien,
Ou il ne failli onques rien.
Je ne vueil mie que tu penses

"I don't want you to think I'm forbidding you to love; instead, I'm wanting and sincerely urging you to love loyally, for in proper reckoning true lovers are not counted among the goods of Fortune, but among the goods of virtue. Therefore I instruct you to have a true heart as long as you live, for then will you have joy and glory. And never despise Loyalty, even if you gain nothing by it here below, for it can never be lost, but will be rewarded a hundred times over. If it's not repaid here, truly it will be in the seat of glory.

"I've told you what to do and what you'll discover to be true; if you do it, good will come to you from it; and if you don't, things will go badly. I shall leave you and go away. But on leaving I assure you that if you need me you'll find that you always have my undivided friendship. It's not good for you to delay any longer before going to your lady. But take good care not to become disheartened; for she'll never be so haughty toward you that she'll scold or hurt you, unless it be with her very sweet, laughing, attractive, and artful eyes. But I attest that they are such that their blows are not mortal, because their wound is sweet and their sting pleasant.

"And if you are so taken with seeing your worthy lady that you

2801 **vray** vras J. **en compte** sans conte CEPe. 2802 **biens f.** biens de f. E. 2805 **Aies** Aras E. 2806 **grant . . . gloire** tres grant joie JK. 2808 **ça jus** heu nen JK. 2812 **Si** Se EPe. **en . . . gloire** en haut de g. C (−1); en siecle de g. JK; ou ciel de g. Pe. 2816 **Et se** Et ce C; Ce se E. 2817–18 *reversed in* J. 2822 **bon** bien C. 2823 **te traies** te retraies E. 2828 **Rians** Biaux C. 2833 **tu . . . pris** estoies si fort pris JK.

Que d'amer te face desfances; f. 45va
Ains vueil et te pri chierement
Que tu aimmes tres loyaument;
Qu'ami vray ne sont pas en compte
Des biens Fortune, qui bien conte,
Mes entre les biens de vertu.
Et pour ce t'enseingne que tu
Aies cuer vray, tant com vivras,
Car grant joie et gloire en aras.
Et loyauté ja ne despite,
Se ça jus n'en as la merite,
Qu'elle ne puet estre perdue
Qu'a .c. doubles ne soit rendue.
Se cy ne l'est, c'est chose voire,
Si l'iert elle en siege de gloire.

Je t'ay dit ce que tu feras
Et qu'en verité trouveras;
Se tu le fais, bien t'en venra;
Et se non, il t'en mescherra.
Je te lairay, si m'en yray;
Mais au partir tant te diray
Que, se tu as mestier de my,
Amie entiere sans demi
Me trouveras a toutes heures.
Si n'est pas bon que plus demeures,
Que vers ta dame ne te traies;
Mais garde bien que ne t'esmaies,
Car ja ne te sera si fiere
Qu'elle te laidenge ne fiere,
Se ce n'est de ses tres douz yeus
Rians, atraians, et soutieus.
Mes je les tesmoigne pour tieus
Que leurs coups ne sont pas mortels,
Car douce en est la bleceüre
Et aggreable la pointure.

Et se tu estoies si pris
De veoir ta dame de pris
Que ne peüsses endurer

cannot endure her sweet eyes, nor stand against them, and are so overwhelmed by true love, shame, and fear that you grow pale and lose your composure, always remember me, however it may be; for their attack will never be so powerful that they'll not be wholly overwhelmed, as long as you don't forget me, because I never forget my friends. But if you do forget me, you may be absolutely sure and certain that you'll be defeated within the hour.

"I'm leaving; I commend you to God. But first I'll sing you a baladelle in my limpid voice, with new words and music, which you'll carry off with you, singing it to cheer up your heart as you go along, if it's troubled by any concern.

(22) *How Hope offers the Lover a song and sings it for him*

[BALADELLE]

To be in love is a sweet
and happy life,
if one knows how to live it,
because the malady's so pleasing,
when it's sustained
by amorous desire,
that it emboldens the lover
to seek
how it spreads.
It's a sweet trouble to bear,

2836 **n'encontre** ne contre EJK. 2837 **qu'entrepris** quentepris J. 2838 **cremour** paour JK. 2843 **desconfies** desconfites EJ. 2844 **Du tout** Nen doubt JK. 2845 *om* JK. **mes** mais C. 2845–46 *reversed in* E. 2847 **et tous fis** et fis E. 2849 **te** ten E. 2852 **ditté** dit EPe. 2855 **se** si C. 2860 **maladie** melodie JK. 2861 **Quant** Que JK. 2862 **amoureus** lamoureux E. 2863 **Que** Quer JK. 2865 **mouteplie** multipi J.

Ses doulz yeus n'encontre eulz durer, f. 45vb
Et qu'entrepris de fine amour
Fusses, de honte et de cremour,
Si que coulour et contenance
Perdisses, aies remembrance
De moy tousdis, comment qu'il aille;
Car ja n'iert si fort leur bataille
Qu'elles ne soient desconfies
Du tout, mais que tu ne m'oublies,
Qu'adonc mes amis pas n'oubli.
Et se tu me mes en oubli,
Soies tous seürs et tous fis
Qu'en l'eure seras desconfis.

A Dieu te commant; je m'en voys.
Mais ainçoys de ma clere voys
Te diray une balladelle,
De chant et de ditté nouvelle,
Laquelle tu emporteras
Et en alant la chanteras,
Afin que tes cuers s'i deduise
S'il a pensee qui li nuise.

(Miniature 22) *Comment Esperance baille a l'Amant une chançon et la chante devant li*

[BALLADELLE]

En amer a douce vie f. 46a–b
Et jolie,
Qui bien la scet maintenir,
Car tant plaist la maladie
Quant norrie
Est en amoureus desir,
Que l'amant fait esbaudir
Et querir
Comment elle mouteplie.
C'est doulz mauls a soustenir,

which brings joy to
a lover's and a lady's heart;

Because Love by its lordship
abases
the loving heart to suffer,
and rules it by its
noble mastery,
so that in everything it feels
it finds
the joyful taste
of pleasure, I have no doubt.
Thus she fulfills
without fulfillment
a lover's and a lady's heart.

So Love must be cherished
and served,
since she can help
everyone who requests and invokes
her aid
without diminishing her treasure.
She can protect and save
from death
a heart that begs for health;
she fills with sufficiency
and liberates
a lover's and a lady's heart."

(23) *How Hope leaves the Lover*

When she had finished her ballade, which was very pleasant and agreeable to my ears and in my heart, since I'd never before heard such sweet harmony, I was overjoyed. But if the sweet music pleased me,

2868 **d'ami et d'amie** dami et dami J. 2877 **prengne** prendre E. 2878 **merir** mourir C. 2884 **qui . . . prïe** quil r. ou p. E; qui le r. et p. JKPe. 2889 **qui . . . mendie** de qui de sante m. K. 2891 *om* JK. 2892 **Fait** Puet JK. 2896 *om* JK. 2898 **durement m'en esjoÿ** doucement me resjoy E. 2899 **m'en** me EPe. 2900 **Tel** Telle JK. **dit me f.** dit f. JK.

Qu'esjoïr
Fait cuer d'ami et d'amie;

Qu'Amours par sa signourie f. 46va
Humelie
L'amoureus cuer a souffrir,
Et par sa noble maistrie
Le mestrie,
Si qu'il ne puet riens sentir,
Que tout au goust de joïr
Par plaisir
Ne prengne, je n'en doubt mie.
Ainssi saouls de merir,
Sans merir,
Fait cuer d'ami et d'amie.

Si doit bien estre cherie
Et servie,
Quant elle puet assevir
Chascun qui li rueve ou prïe
De s'aïe,
Sans son tresor amenrir.
De la mort puet garantir
Et garir
Cuer qui de santé mendie;
De souffissance enrichir
Et franchir
Fait cuer d'ami et d'amie."

(Miniature 23) *Comment Esperance se depart de l'Amant*

Quant elle ot finé sa ballade, f. 46vb
Qui moult me fu plaisant et sade
Dedens le cuer et a l'oÿe,
Pour ce qu'onques mais armonie
Si tres douce n'avoie oÿ,
Moult durement m'en esjoÿ.
Mais se li douls chans m'en plaisoit,
Tel joie le dit me faisoit

the words brought me more joy than anyone could conceive. So I made a great effort to learn it, and memorized it so quickly that before she'd left the place or had even finished singing it, I knew both the words and the music.

And so I'd not forget it, I had to imprint it upon my memory; but as I fixed its image in my heart and imprinted it with such ardor, that every disposition of my five God-given senses was so intent upon it that I had no heart or desire to think of anything else (except that I constantly remembered her who was the source of my good), the lady vanished. In all my life I'd never seen anything disappear so quickly; for I lost sight of her so suddenly that I didn't know what had become of her.

Then more than ten or twenty times I looked behind the hedgerow, but I saw there only grass, trees, leaves, flowers, and greenery; for there was no one there but myself alone. When I saw that Hope had told me all she wanted and had suddenly and secretly flown away, I fell into very deep thought and began to go over all she had taught me point by point, for I felt I'd yet have great need of it.

2901 **ne** *om* J. 2902 **moult** *om* C (−1). 2903 **soz** souls C. 2906 **soz** soulz C. 2909 **com** comme E. **je l'ymaginoie** je ymaginoie CE (−1). 2913 **.v. sens** .v.c. JK. 2917 **Fors** Fort Pe. 2920 **en** a J. 2922 **si la veüe** sitost la veue E. 2925 **Regarday** Regarda Pe. **haiette** chambrette JK. 2928 **il** y K. 2935 **a** *om* E. 2938 **grant** *added by scribe at end of line.*

Que ne savoie au quel entendre.
Si mis moult grant paine a l'aprendre,
Et la soz en si poy d'espasse
Qu'ains qu'elle partist de la place,
Ne que toute l'eüst pardit,
Je la soz par chant et par dit.

Et pour ce que ne l'oubliasse,
Failloit il que la recordasse;
Mais si com je l'ymaginoie
En mon cuer et la recordoie
De si tres bonne affection,
Que toute l'inclinacion
Des .v. sens que Dieus m'a donné
Y estoient si ordené
Que n'avoie cuer ne penser
Que lors peüsse aillours penser,
(Fors tant qu'adés me souvenoit
De celle dont mes biens venoit,)
La dame fu esvanuïe.
Mais onques en jour de ma vie
Ne vi chose si tost perdue;
Car j'en perdi si la veüe
Que je ne sos qu'elle devint.

Lors plus de .x. foys ou de .xx.
Regarday entour la haiette,
Mes je n'i vi riens fors herbette,
Arbres, fueille, fleur, et verdure;
Car il n'i avoit creature
Fors moy seulet. Et quant je vi f. 47a
Qu'Esperance avoit assevi
Tout ce que dire me vouloit,
Et qu'ainssi elle s'envoloit
Soudainement a recelee,
Je chaÿ en moult grant pensee
Et par ordre a recorder pris
Tout ce qu'elle m'avoit apris
De point en point, car bien pensoie
Qu'encor grant mestier en aroie.

And to fix the memory of everything about her and her story, just as I've written it out above, it was inscribed in my heart by true and certain understanding a hundred times more accurately and exactly than any clerk could write it out by hand on parchment or wax tablet. And since I wanted to go to her whom Reason instructs, it was necessary that I follow Hope's teachings and recall them constantly, so that, if it happened that Love became haughty toward me, and Beauty disdained me, and Sweet Glance were so harsh as to refuse to see me, I could be strong and valiant enough against their mighty power to withstand their assaults by enduring them all patiently. For it shows great strength and courage to vanquish one's adversary by enduring patiently with a noble heart.

When I had noted it all word for word, leaving nothing out, having imprinted in my heart the sweet imprint of her teachings, I felt myself much more confident, stronger, calmer, maturer. Then I stood up and went toward the small wicket through which I had entered. I saw

2950 **j'ensiuisse** nenfrenisse JK. 2952 **Par** Pour JK. 2959 **vassaus** versaus JK. 2961 **Par** Pour EJK. 2963 **Est** Et E. 2964 **Par** Pour E. 2968 **emprainte** empraindre E. 2969 **m'en** me C. 2974 **bien** *om* E.

Et par maniere de memoire
Tout le fait de li et l'ystoire,
Si com je l'ay devant escript,
Estoit en mon cuer en escript
Par vray certain entendement
Mieus .c. foys et plus proprement
Que clers ne le porroit escripre
De main en parchemin ne en cire.

Et c'estoit chose neccessaire,
Puis que je me voloie traire
Vers celle que Raisons doctrine,
Que j'ensiuisse sa doctrine
Et que souvent m'en souvenist,
Par quoy, se li cas avenist
Qu'Amours fust vers moy dangereuse
Et Biauté fine desdaigneuse,
Honte dame, Paour maistresse,
Et Douls Regars en telle aspresse
Fust qu'il ne me daignast veoir,
Qu'encontre leur puissant pooir
Fusse vigueureus et vassaus
Pour recevoir tous leurs assaus,
Par tout souffrir en pacïence.
Car grant vertus et grant vaillance
Est de vaincre son adversaire
Par souffrir de cuer debonnaire.

Quant j'eus tout recordé par ordre,
Si qu'il n'i avoit que remordre,
Et en mon cuer la douce emprainte f. 47b
De ses ensaingnemens emprainte,
Je m'en senti trop plus seür,
Plus fort, plus rassis, plus meür.
Lors en mon estant me dreçay
Et vers le guichet m'adreçay
Par ou j'estoie la venus.
Mais je m'aperchu bien que nus
N'estoit alez par ceste voie,

clearly that no one had come that way since I'd entered, for the sharp-bladed grass had not been disturbed and the bright, sparkling dew was still on the thick grass.

And in more than thirty thousand places the birds, wide-throated, were trying to out-sing one another, as if it were a contest, making the whole orchard ring; and it's no lie that prior to Hope's visiting me in my need, my senses had been so distorted that I'd not noticed the birds or their clamor, or how merry they all were. But this should not be held against me, because there are two things that falsify the senses and cause them to react irrationally: these are great joy and great sadness. And I had been so much in the grip of great sadness that my mind had played me false and I could think of nothing but the intense sorrow I felt. But now their sweet singing so delighted me that before sunset I felt restored in heart, body, and health, as much for the sweet memory I had of Good Hope as for the thought that soon I'd see my lady. And since I was on my way back to see her very noble self again, I composed at once the words and music I shall now sing:

2977 **Qu'en** Qui E. **depassee** repassee JK. 2980 *initial* a *of* abatue *added above line by the scribe.* 2981 **qui** que EPe. 2982 **.xxx.** .xxv. JK. 2983 **aussi** ainsi EJ. **par** pour E. 2984 **baees** bees C (−1). 2985 **Si** Et JK. 2993 **ce . . . tourner** ce a mal me devoit t. C; ce mal ne me doit t. E; a mal ne me doit t. JK; ce a mal me doit t. Pe. 2994 **font** me font C (+1). 2995 **et** ou E. 2996 **Ce sont g.** Cest g. C (−1); Ce g. Pe. 2999 **Si** Et JK. **n'entendoie** ne tendoie C. 3001 **leur** li JK. 3012 **Ce ci que** Cesti que E.

Depuis que venus y estoie:
Qu'en riens n'i estoit depassee
L'erbe poignant, et la rousee
Clere et luisant sur l'erbe drue
N'estoit pas encore abatue.

Et cil oysillon qui mieus mieus
En plus de .xxx.m. lieus
Tout aussi com par estrivees
Chantoient, les geulez baees,
Si qu'il faisoient retentir
Tout le vergier; et sans mentir,
Ains qu'Esperance visité
M'eüst en ma neccessité,
Mes sens estoit si pervertis
Qu'encor ne m'estoie avertis
Des oyssillons, ne de leur noise,
Ne comment chascuns se degoise.
Mes ce a mal ne me doit tourner,
Car .ii. choses font bestourner
Le sens et müer en folour:
Ce sont grant joye et grant doulour.
Et grant doulour tel m'atournoit
Que mon memoire bestournoit

Si qu'a nulle riens n'entendoie,
Fors au grief mal que je sentoie.
Si m'abeli tant leur douls chans,
Qu'ainçoys qu'il fust soleil couchans
Je me senti a volenté
De cuer, de corps, et de santé,
Tant pour la douce remembrance f. 47va
Que j'avoie en Bonne Esperance,
Comme de ce que je pensoie
Que briefment ma dame verroie.
Et pour ce qu'estoie au retour
De veoir son tres noble atour,
Tantost fis en dit et en chant
Ce ci que presentement chant:

[BALLADE]

Lady, from whom all my joy comes,
I cannot love or cherish you too much,
or praise you enough, or serve, fear,
honor, and obey you as is fitting;
for the pleasing hope,
sweet lady, that I have of seeing you
brings me a hundred times more joy and good
than I could deserve in a hundred thousand years.

This sweet Hope keeps me alive
and nourishes me with amorous desire,
and places within me everything that is needed
to comfort and bring joy to my heart;
nor does it abandon me morning or evening,
but rather induces me to receive sweetly
more of the sweet goods that Love sends her own
than I could deserve in a hundred thousand years.

And since Hope who is fixed in my heart
causes such joy within me
when I'm far from you, my lady, if I were
to see your beauty that I desire so much,
no one could imagine, comprehend, or conceive
my joy, I believe,
for I would have more
than I could deserve in a hundred thousand years.

Thus I composed and sang my song as I walked toward the wicket along the lush green path; but I didn't find it open, for it was closed just as I'd left it; so I unlatched it. When it was open, I passed through and relocked it carefully with the padlock. This done, I continued on my

3013 **qui** cui Pe. 3020 **porroie** porroiee C (+1). 3023 **qui** quil JKPe. 3027 **des** de E. **envoie** octroie EJK. 3029–end *missing in K.* 3031 **vous** moy E. **s'il** si E. 3032 **moult** tant J. 3034 **concevoir** recevoir E. 3039 **Par** Pour E. **fu** *om* J. 3043 **passay** passe C (−1).

(Miniature 24) *Comment l'Amant fait une balade*

[BALADE]

Dame, de qui toute ma joie vient, f. 47va–vb
Je ne vous puis trop amer, ne cherir,
N'assés loer, si com il apartient
Servir, doubter, honnourer, n'obeïr;
Car le gracïeus Espoir,
Douce dame, que j'ay de vous veoir,
Me fait .c. foys plus de bien et de joye
Qu'en cent mil ans desservir ne porroie.

Cilz douls Espoirs en vie me soustient f. 47va
Et me norrist en amoureus desir,
Et dedens moy met tout ce qui couvient
Pour conforter mon cuer et resjoïr; f. 47vb
N'il ne s'en part main ne soir,
Ainçoys me fait doucement recevoir
Plus des douls biens qu'Amours as siens envoie f. 48a
Qu'en .c. mil ans deservir ne porroie.

Et quant Espoir qui en mon cuer se tient
Fait dedens moy si grant joie venir
Lointains de vous, ma dame, s'il avient
Que vo beauté voie que moult desir,
Ma joye, si com j'espoir,
Ymaginer, penser, ne concevoir
Ne porroit nuls, car trop plus en aroie
Qu'en cent mil ans deservir ne porroie.

Ainssi fis mon chant et finay
Et au guichet m'acheminay
Par le chemin qui fu tout vert;
Mais ne le trouvay pas ouvert,
Car ainssi com je le fremai,
Estoit; adonc le deffremai.
Quant ouvers fu, je passay oultre
Et le refremai bien au ploutre.
Ce fait, je me mis a la voie.

way. I was very happy that no one knew anything of my adventure. So I went along singing and so happy in my song that before long I saw the place where my lady dwelled.

When I saw it, I stopped and as I stood there I thought a little about what I'd do and how I'd proceed; for my heart was trembling so greatly within my body that it seemed to me it was about to split in two or break. I didn't know what to do, because I was so frightened at seeing it and so dumbstruck that truly I'd have turned back had I not had Hope with me.

But Hope, who is ever attentive to help her friends in need, and who doesn't sleep or doze but stays alert to comfort them, was not sleeping at this moment; she said to me:

"Fair friend, I've not wasted my steps coming here. Say, who has alarmed you? What do you need? Why are you upset? You must tell me: what is the source of these foolish thoughts that needlessly torment you?"

(25) *How Hope holds the Lover by the hand and takes him to see his Lady's manor*

"On my word of honor, my lady, I don't know, except that I'm

3046 **trop** *om* Pe. 3050 **chant tant** chantant EPe. 3055 **petitet** petit bien J. 3059 **deüst partir** partir deust JPe. 3062 **estahis** esbahis EPe. 3064 **S'esperance avec moy** Savec moy esperance J. 3074 **Il** Y C.

Mes trop durement liez estoie
De ce que nulle creature
Ne savoit riens de m'aventure.
Si m'en aloie tout chantant
Et deduisant en mon chant tant
Que je vi en assez pou d'eure
Le lieu ou ma dame demeure.

Quant je le vi, je m'arrestay
Et pensé en mon arrest ay
Un petitet que je feroie,
Ne comment je me cheviroie;
Car li cuers ou corps me trembloit
Si tres forment qu'il me sambloit
Qu'en .ii. deüst partir ou fendre.
Si ne savoie conseil prendre,
Car j'estoie tous esbahis f. 48b
Dou veoir, et si estahis,
Que vraiement retournez fusse
S'Esperance avec moy n'eüsse.

Mais Esperance qui a soing
D'aidier ses amis au besoing,
Et qui ne dort pas ne sommeille
Pour euls conforter, ainçoys veille,
A celle heure ne dormi pas,
Ains me dist: "Biaus amis, mi pas
Ne sont pas cy endroit perdu.
Di: qui t'a einssi esperdu?
Que te faut? Ne que te demandes?
Il couvient que raison m'en randes:
Dont viennent ces pensees vaines,
Que sans cause ainssi te demaines?"

(Miniature 25) *Comment Esperance tient l'Amant par la main et le mainne veoir le manoir sa dame*

"Je ne sçay, dame, par ma foy,
Fors que je suy en grant effroy,

terribly afraid and dread has stopped me in my tracks, because I've seen the manor where my heart and my lady live. So I beg God to lead me there in joy, for if I have no better guide than Fear, I don't see how I'll get there."

[HOPE]

"What? Do you think that I'd fail you and break the promise I swore to you?"

[THE LOVER]

"Never, my lady."

[HOPE]

"Indeed you do, in my opinion, when you behave this way. Tell me what causes you to be so frightened and apprehensive. Are you afraid of your shadow? That's what I think is bothering you."

[THE LOVER]

"My lady, with all due respect, I'm not afraid of my shadow. But some strange heat that turned to cold surprised me and gripped my heart so suddenly that there's no way I could relate how I feel or how it stings me, for I'm hot and cold together and am sweating and shaking at the same time, and I've lost all strength, and was struck speechless in

3079 **m'estuet** me fait E. 3081 **et** ou E. 3082 **pri** prie C (+1). 3088 **je** *om* E. **couvent** couvenant E. 3093 **doubtance** paour Pe. 3098 **s'est** est E; cest J. **en** de E. 3103 **Chaut et froit** froit et chaut J.

Et en doubte m'estuet manoir,
Pour ce qu'ay veü le manoir
Ou mes cuers et ma dame maint.
Si pri Dieu qu'a joye m'i maint,
Car se je n'ai millour conduit
Que de Paour qui me conduit,
Je ne voy pas comment je y aille." f. 48va

[ESPERANCE]

"Comment? Crois tu que je te faille
Et que je fausse le couvent
Que je t'ai eü en couvent?"

[L'AMANT]

"Dame, nennil."

[ESPERANCE]

"Certes, si fais,
Ce m'est avis, quant ainssi fais.
Di moy dont te vient la poour
Que tu as, ne celle freour.
As tu doubtance de ton umbre?
Je croy que c'est ce qui t'encombre."

[L'AMANT]

"Dame, sauf vostre reverence,
De mon umbre n'ay pas doutance.
Mes je ne sçai quelle chalour
Qui s'est couvertie en froidour
M'a souspris et me tient au cuer
Si soudainement qu'a nul fuer
Ne porroie dire en quel point
Sui, ne comment elle me point;
Car j'ay chaut et froit si ensemble
Que tout a un cop sue et tremble,
Et s'ay toute vigour perdue,

the middle of my song like a dumb beast; wherefore my laughter, my joy, and my song are ended and I must remain silent, I don't know why, unless it's because I've seen the house that is more beautiful than any other spot except for earthly paradise. It's the place where my sweet love lives, and my heart too: I can find no other reason. And therefore I want to beg you, my lady, to advise me, else I'm lost and ruined, for in this world I don't desire anything as much as seeing my lady whenever I want; but I see no way or access without you, which is why my complexion has changed."

[HOPE]

"And how should I advise you? I would be exerting myself for nothing, because my words are wasted on you. A caged bird isn't as obtuse as you are! I've sworn to you, and swear again, that whenever you want me I'll be ready in every need, fair friend; and when you don't believe me, you only increase your troubles. Your present experience is proof of this, because to alleviate the grief that greatly distressed and now oppresses you, as soon as I knew of it I was here to help you

3107 **enmi** en me J. 3111 **Se** Et E. **pour** par J. 3116 **mes . . . demour** mon cuer tout aussi d. J. 3122 **vëoir** voir E. 3123 **ne** ny E. 3128 E *replaces this line with*: Un oisellon en un boscage 3134 *om in* J, *but space left.* **tes** telz Pe. 3136 **Car** Que J. **ta** la J; en Pe. 3137 **Qui** Que J. **a neü** as veu E; anue J. 3138 **sceü** seue J. E *replaces line with*: Aussi com je t'ay tost sceu. 3140 **Que ne** Que tu ne C (+1). **souhaidier** soushaidier C.

Et aussi comme beste mue
Sui esbahis enmi ces chans;
Dont mes ris, ma joye, et mes chans
Sont si feny, ne sçai pourquoy,
Qu'il me couvient taire tout quoy,
Se ce n'est pour ceste raison
Que j'ai veüe la maison
Qui trop plus belle est de tout estre,
Que ne soit paradis terrestre.

C'est li lieus ou ma douce amour
Et mes cuers aussi font demour:
Autre raison n'i sçay trouver.
Et pour ce vous vueil je rouver, f. 48vb
Dame, que vous me conseilliez,
Ou perdus sui et essilliez,
Qu'ou monde riens tant ne desir
Com veoir ma dame a loisir;
Mais je n'i voy tour ne attainte
Sans vous, dont ma coulour est tainte."

[ESPERANCE]

"Et comment te conseilleroie?
Pour neant me travailleroie,
Car je pers en toy mon langage.
Uns oyselez en une cage
N'a pas l'entendement si dur
Com tu as! Juré t'ai, et jur,
Qu'a tous besoings me trouveras
Preste quant mestier en avras,

Biaus amis, et tu ne m'en crois,
Dont tes maulz durement acrois.
Tu le vois par experïence,
Car pour alegier ta grevance,
Qui moult te grieve et a neü,
Aussi tost com je l'ai sceü,
Tu m'as plus tost pour toy aidier
Que ne peüsses souhaidier.

quicker than you could have hoped for. I had instructed and enjoined you to unite your heart to mine, so that, near and far, come what may, you will always be mindful of me.

"Now I see clearly that you don't remember, and this is why you must suffer so, for if you had remembered, this would never have happened to you. Take heart and go confidently to your lady, for truly I'll be a good sentinel, shield, defense, and fortress for you; and the promise I gave you, I'll keep, and will come to you without your having to beg me, as one who'll be your guide in happiness and woe. Therefore you should be full of confidence since thus I reassure you in every respect. And the heat that has turned to cold is the burning that was long hidden in your heart. Now it has been revealed and has spread through your body, which is shaking and sweating at the same time.

"And because you are nearing the fire of Love that stings you with its brands, you are losing your bearing and countenance, sense, joy, strength, and power. And remember what I taught you: 'He who's nearest the fire burns the most.' I'll not tell you more right now. Farewell; I shall leave, yet without leaving you; for I must divide myself into more than a hundred thousand shares, to be shared among

3142 **a** en E. 3143 **te** *om* Pe. 3146 **Et . . . ainssi** Einsi estre pour ce Pe. 3151 **Gaite** Grace E. **fortresse** forteresse C (+1). 3154 **priere** prier J. 3155 **seray** sera J. 3158 **partout ainssi** ainssi partout J. 3160 **c'est** en J. 3161 **s'est** cest CJ. 3162 **est** sest Pe. 3163 **corps** cuer E. 3164 **tremble et tressue** trop tramble et sue J. 3170 **s'art** art EJ. 3173 **toy me** moy te J. 3174 **je me parte** m'en departe E. 3177 **departiras** te partiras J.

Je t'avoie dit et enjoint
Que ton cuer fust a moy si joint
Qu'adés de moy te souvenist
Loing et pres, quoy qu'il avenist.
Or voy bien qu'il ne t'en souvient,
Et pour ce estre ainssi te couvient;
Car s'il t'en fust bien souvenu,
Ja ce ne te fust avenu.
Pren cuer et va seürement
Vers ta dame, que vraiement
Gaite, escus, deffense, et fortresse
Te seray bonne, et la promesse
Que je t'ai promis, te tendrai,
Et sans prïere a toy vendray,
Com celle qui seray tes chiez f. 49a
En tes biens et en tes meschiez.
Si dois estre moult asseür
Quant partout ainssi t'asseür.
Et la chaleur qui en froidure
Est couvertie, c'est l'ardure
Qui s'est moult longuement couverte
En ton cuer; or est descouverte
Et parmi ton corps espandue,
Dont a un cop tremble et tressue.

Et pour ce que le feu approuches
D'Amours qui te point de ses broches,
Pers tu maniere et contenance,
Sens, joye, vigour, et poyssance.
Et aussi retien de mon art:
'Qui plus est pres du feu, plus s'art.'
Orendroit plus ne t'en dirai.
A Dieu; je m'en departirai,
Sans ce que de toy me departe;
Car il couvient que je me parte
En plus de .c. mille parties
Qui aus amans sont departies.
Et quant de cy departiras,
Droitement celle part iras

lovers. And when you leave here, go straight to where you'll see your gentle lady, and you'll be on the right path."

(26) *How the Lover kneels in the pathway to his Lady's manor*

Then she left. I remained and in my heart I sweetly savored what she'd told me; and it was so very flavorful that I was completely reassured about the perturbations which had welled up so strongly in my heart that I could find no comfort. And since I was no longer afraid of anything, I knelt on both knees in the middle of the narrow pathway, with hands joined and my face turned directly toward the precious and worthy place that was a sign and manifestation to me of the hope that I would find my lady.

And because it was not proper that I go a single step forward without commending myself to the protection of Love and my guardian Hope, with devout heart and bowed head I began this prayer, first of all thanking them humbly for their blessings:

[PRAYER]

Love, I praise and thank you
a hundred thousand times and express my gratitude,
because my heart that you had darkened,
troubled, discolored and dimmed,
and tempered through suffering for your sake,

3184 **tres . . . savoit** tresbon goust me sambloit E; bon goust me savouroit J. 3194 **apparance** esperance J. 3196 **ja** la J. 3198 *om* J. 3203 **humblement** doucement J. 3205 **te** vous E. 3207 **avoies nerci** avies n. C (−1); avoies nouri E. 3208 **destaint** destraint J. 3209 **adurci** adverti C; adouci JPe.

Ou tu verras ta dame gente,
Et tu es en la droite sente."

(Miniature 26) *Comment l'Amant s'agenoille en la sente devant le manoir sa dame*

Lors s'en parti; je demouray f. 49b
Et moult doucement savouray
En mon cuer ce que dit m'avoit;
Et si tres bon goust me savoit
Que je fu tous asseürés
Des mouvemens qui figurés
Estoient en mon cuer si fort
Qu'en moy ne savoye confort.
Et quant riens plus ne resongnai,
A .ii. genoulz m'agenoillai
Enmi la sentellette estroite,
Les mains jointes, la face droite
Vers le lieu precïeus et digne
Qui m'estoit apparance et signe
A l'esperance que j'avoie
Que ja ma dame trouveroie.

Et pour ce qu'il n'afferoit pas
Qu'avant alasse .i. tout seul pas,
Que ne me meïsse en la garde
D'Amour et d'Espoir qui me garde,
De cuer devot, a humble chiere,
Encommenchai ceste prïere,
En eulz merciant humblement
De leurs biens tout premierement:

[PRIERE]

Amours, je te lo et graci
.c. mille foys et remerci,
Quant mon cuer qu'avoies nerci,
Troublé, destaint, et obscurci,
Et en ton martire adurci,

you have now deigned to love so much
through your power
that you've softened it with your sweetness
and brightened it with your light
and so sweetened its bitterness
that you make me desire mercy
with Hope.

Love, I want to adore
and fear you as my second god,
praise, serve, obey, and honor you
with all my strength
in heart, in body, and in thought;
for in my youth
you made me love loyally
and desire your blessings
and afterwards to desire
and savor them so sweetly
that in true faith I want to do
you homage.

Love, I knew nothing,
not even how to distinguish evil from good,
when to my true heart, which I hold
to be yours without limitation,
you gave by your subtle craft
the understanding
to love and be your captive,
and presented it directly,
along with my body and all I have,
to my lady; this I know well,
because I gave her everything
on account of her worth.

And if I foolishly lamented,
complaining and wailing within myself
about you and the sorrows of love
that filled me to overflowing,
I beg you with hands joined
that you not hold it

3211 **As** Mas EPe. **vueus** vois J. 3214 **son** sanz EPe. 3215 **Quant** Que J. **fais** fait E. 3219 **toutes** tous E. 3223 **faïs** fais tres J. 3225 *om* J. **les me** le me E; le mez Pe. 3233 **donnas** donnans C. 3238 **ce sçay je** que je say E. 3240 **Par** Pour J. 3242 **En** Et E. **dementez** demanter J. 3245 **te depri** te pri C (−1). 3246 **ce** *om* J.

Par ta puissance
As amé et vueus amer si
Que de ta douçour adouci,
Et de ta clarté esclarci
L'as et fait douls son amer cy
Quant desirer me fais mercy f. 49va
En Esperance.

Amours, je te vueil aourer
Com mon dieu second, et doubter,
De toutes mes vertus loer,
Servir, obeïr, honnourer
De cuer, de corps, et de penser;
Car en m'enfance
Me faïs loyaument amer,
Et les biens de toy desirer;
Aprés les me fais esperer
Et si doucement savourer
Qu'en vraye foy te vueil porter
Obedïence.

Amours, je ne savoie rien,
Né differer le mal du bien,
Quant a mon vray cuer, que je tien
Sans riens retenir pour tout tien,
Donnas par ton soubtil engien
La congnoissance
D'amer et d'estre en ton lien,
Et le presentas sans moien
Avec le corps et tout le mien
A ma dame, ce sçay je bien;
Car tout li ottroiay com sien
Par sa vaillance.

Et se folement me sui plains,
En moy dementez et complains
De toy et des amoureus plains
Dont j'estoie chargiez et plains,
Je te depri a jointes mains
Que ce a grevance

against me, and that it not affect
you one way or the other, for I remain yours.
So you must be more understanding in this case,
since you can see clearly and be certain
that you are my sovereign ruler
and the one in whom I believe.

And unless I shirk my duty I must also
praise and thank Hope, to whom I give
dominion over my heart and myself;
for if I am worth anything and if I strive to do well,
it is undoubtedly because
of her; for I was in mortal agony
between the hammer and the wedge,
so that I wouldn't give a garlic
for my life; but, my lady, you were
my subsistence, my friend and rampart,
my tower and bulwark.

Sweet Hope, she's the haven
of my joy and happiness;
she's my wealth, my resort;
it's she in whom I rejoice;
for from the pains of love I bear
I derive such pleasure,
because when they do their best
to harm me, I am most comforted;
and by her noble comfort alone
I am saved from the death
that, without her, would have slain
me without warning.

She has given more love to me,
more courtesy, more sweetness,
more honor, profit, tenderness
than to any other; for night and day
she holds fast against Desire,
who stings and pierces
my heart with the flame of love.

3247 **tourt** court E. 3248 **tiens** tieng E. 3249 **m'en** *om* E. 3250 **si** ce J; se Pe. **vois** veux E. **es** est Pe. 3253 **Aussi** Ainssi J. 3257 **Ne s'a** Ne a E. 3258 **C'iert** Car J. 3259 **car** qui J. 3260 **Fui** Sui J. **coing** coug C. 3266 **de** *om* J. 3269 **es** aus J. **d'amours** damer J. 3270 **plaisance** puissance J. 3271 **Car** Et CEPe. **plus** tout J. 3273 **Et** Car E. 3277 **Elle m'a** Celle me E. 3278 **c. de douçour** c. et de d. E.

Ne me tourt, et que plus ne mains
Ne t'en soit, car tiens sui remains.
Si m'en dois estre plus humains;
Et si vois bien et es certains
Que tu es mes chiés souverains
Et ma creance.

Aussi doy je, se trop ne fail, f. 49vb
Loer Esperance, a qui bail
De moy et de mon çuer le bail,
Et mercïer; car se rien vail
Ne s'a bien faire me travail,
C'iert sans doubtance
Par li; car en mortel travail
Fui entre le coing et le mail,
Si que je ne donnasse un ail
De ma vie; mes soustenail
Me fu, dame, amie et murail,
Tour et deffence.

Douce Esperance, c'est le port
De ma joie et de mon deport;
C'est ma richesse, mon raport;
C'est celle en qui je me deport;
Car es maulz d'Amours que je port
Ay tel plaisance,
Car quant il font plus leur effort
De moy grever, plus me confort,
Et tout par son noble confort
Sui je respité de la mort
Qui m'eüst, s'elle ne fust, mort
Sans deffiance.

Elle m'a fait trop plus d'amour,
De courtoisie, de douçour,
D'onnour, de proufit, de tenrour,
Qu'a nul autre; car nuit et jour
Contre Desir soustient l'estour
Qui point et lance
Mon cuer d'une amoureuse ardour.

She heals my sorrow;
she keeps me strong;
she's my refuge; she's my tower;
she's my every resource;
she's my faith.

She it was who acknowledged me
every time she saw me
devoid and deprived of joy.
Then she gently nourished me
with all the blessings she could,
and brought me relief.
She it was who lessened
my sorrows and increased my joy;
she provided me sweet comfort
without recompense or tribute,
when with the eyes of her heart she perceived
my suffering.

And since from you I derive such good
that I abound in every joy,
much more than ever before,
I beg you with humble heart and amorous
desire, as one who loves and desires
your aquaintance,
to lead me to the threshold
where I shall behold my lady's
Sweet Welcome; and should I suffer there,
if you do not keep your heart and eye
upon me, I'll die of grief
in her presence.

And if my lady—may God watch over her—
deigns to let fall her glance
upon me, even half or a quarter,
please see that I have sense or skill
to distinguish whether
the sparkle in her eye
comes from love or from elsewhere;
for if her sweet eye sends forth through Love
the amorous arrow in my direction,

3284 **ce** *om* C (−1). 3289 **C'est celle** Car cest celle E. 3290 **sceü** veu E. 3292 **La** Las J. 3295 *om* J. 3296 **acreü** escreu J. 3298 **salaire avoir** avoir salaire J. 3305 *om* J. 3307 **jusqu'au** jusques au E. 3308 **le douls a.** .i. bel a. J. 3316 **qu'aie** quaiez J. 3320 **repart** regart J.

C'est ce qui garist ma doulour;
C'est ce qui me tient en vigour;
C'est mon refuge; c'est ma tour;
C'est celle ou sont tuit mi retour;
C'est ma fiance.

C'est celle qui m'a congneü
Par tout ou elle m'a sceü
Nu de joye et despourveü. f. 50a
La doucement m'a repeü
De tous les biens qu'elle a peü,
Et d'aligance.
C'est celle qui a descreü
Mon mal et ma joie acreü;
De doulz confort m'a pourveü,
Sans salaire avoir ne treü,
Et des yeus de son cuer veü
En ma souffrance.

Et quant par vous tel bien recueil
Que de toute joye en l'escueil
Sui, plus assez que je ne sueil,
D'umble cuer et d'amoureus vueil
Vous pri, com cilz qui aimme et vueil
Vostre acointance,
Que vous me menez jusqu'au sueil
Ou je verray le Douls Accueil
De ma dame; et se lors me dueil,
Se vous n'avés le cuer et l'ueil
Vers moy, je serai mors de dueil
En sa presence.

Et se ma dame, que Dieus gart,
Deingne descendre son regart
Sur moy, a moytié ou au quart,
Je vous pri qu'aie sens ou art
Pour congnoistre de son espart
La difference,
S'il vient d'amours ou d'autre part;
Car se son doulz oeil me repart
Par amours de l'amoureus dart,

I'll never have eyes for anyone else.
If not, despair cannot come
soon enough.

You know also that I love, serve, and fear her
humbly, and that I desire her loyally
more than any other, or even myself,
and that I'm so sworn to her
that it is without separation
and without change.
So you must sweetly and lovingly
move her heart
to give me consolation
and to make her feel
as I feel, or else
my hope will be disappointed.

Now let it be as you like,
for without you I cannot attain
the joy I desire so much;
but I wish so to obey you
that I would die for my lady
patiently,
if that's your will; and if you wish
to reward me, without diminishing my lady's
honor, deign to enrich me by letting me
see and hear her to my heart's content.
Then I'll have peace, mercy, my desire,
and sufficiency.

And when I'd finished my prayer, I didn't remain kneeling there long, but stood up. Love, Desire, and Sweet Hope were admonishing me so insistently to see my dear lady that I took to the pathway and set

3322 **De riens** Dautre J. 3326 **crain** et E. 3327 **qu'autre** quautrui C. 3332 **Son** Mon C. 3336 **c'iert** cest J. 3343 **c'est** sest Pe. 3345 **voulez . . . m'enrichir** voulez vueilliez moy enrichir CPe (+1); vueilles et moy enrichir E. 3346 **li** la E. 3347 **merci pais** pais mercy J. 3350 **moult** trop J. 3352 **m'aloient** malerent E; maloie J. **amonnestant** esbanoiant J.

De riens n'aray jamais regart.
Se non, en moy sera trop tart
Desesperance.

Vous savés aussi que humblement
L'aim, serf, crain, desir loyaument
Plus qu'autre, ne moy proprement,
Et que siens sui si liegement
Que c'est sans nul departement f. 50b
Et sans muance.
Si devez mouvoir doucement
Son cuer et amoureusement
Pour moy donner aliegement,
Et li faire avoir sentement
Tel com je l'ai, ou autrement
C'iert decevance.

Or en soit a vostre plaisir,
Car sans vous ne puis avenir
A la joie que tant desir;
Mais je vous vueil tant obeïr
Que pour ma dame vueil mourir
En pacïence,
Se c'est vos grés; et se merir,
Sans l'onnour ma dame amenrir,
Me voulez, vueilliez m'enrichir
D'assés li veoir et oïr;
S'arai merci, pais, mon desir,
Et souffissance.

Et quant j'eus finé mon depri,
La ne fis pas moult lonc detri,
Ains me levai en mon estant.
Si m'aloient amonnestant
Amours, Desirs, et Douls Espoir
De ma chiere dame veoir,
Tant que tantost m'acheminai
Par la sente et mon chemin ai
Pris en bon espoir vers la tour

off, full of hope, along the way to the tower where my lady in her noble attire dwells. But I'd not gone even the distance of a bowshot when I saw near the tower a park with meadows and little fountains, in which there were ladies, knights, and maidens, and a great company of other people, dancing gaily amidst great joy and festivity. There were no instruments or minstrels, only delightful, bright, and courtly songs. I was happy when I saw the company, and even more so when I heard them.

Then I immediately headed in that direction. Love, who did not leave me, and Hope, my dear friend, stayed close beside me and guided me. And I, who couldn't refrain from going toward them, hurried past a hedgerow and was soon among them, where God so blessed me that I saw my lady. All my body, my heart, limbs, and blood were shaking when I saw her. I was shaking so much that, if God had given me the joy of encountering her, I'd have been afraid of falling.

But I remembered Hope; then truly, if I wanted to be victorious, I needed to have recourse to the account that Hope recited to me, and not neglect any of her sweet commandments and good teachings. I re-

3360 **vi** ot J. 3361 **ot** *om* E. 3366 **N'il . . . instrument** Ny ny avoit nul i. E; Nil navoient la J. 3367 **menestrelz** manetrez J. 3369 **je** ce E. **moult** je C. 3372 **ne part** depart J. 3374 **s'esloignierent** mesloingnierent E. 3377 **m'enhastai** me hastay J. 3378 **haiette hastai** haie passay J; haiete que hantai Pe. 3379 **tantost fu** fui tantost E. 3380 **Ou** Et J. 3382 **corps ne cuer ne** cuer ne corps ne E; cuer ne corps ni J; corps cuer ne Pe. 3383 **ne** me E. 3384 **car** que EJ. 3388 **adonc** avant E. 3390 **Que je recourusse** Que recourusse E; Que je recourisse J. 3391 J *replaces this line with*: Que javoie escript en mon cuer. 3392 **puer** pueur C; peur J.

Ou maint ma dame au gent atour.
Mais n'alay pas le trait d'un arc
Que pres de la tour vi un parc
Ou praiaus ot et fontenelles,
Dames, chevaliers, et pucelles,
Et d'autres gens grant compaignie
Moult joieuse et moult envoisie,
Qui dansoient jolïement;
N'il n'avoient nul instrument, f. 50va
Ne menestrelz, fors chançonnettes
Deduisans, courtoyses, et nettes.
Quant je les vi, moult m'esjoÿ,
Et plus quant je les entreoÿ.

Lors alai tantost celle part.
Mais Amours qui de moy ne part,
N'Esperance, ma chiere amie,
De moy ne s'esloignierent mie,
Ains me tenoient par le frain.
Et je, qui pas ne me refrain
D'aler vers euls, si m'enhastai
Qu'outre une haiette hastai,
Et puis tantost fu en la place,
Ou Dieus me fist si belle grace
Que je vi que c'estoit ma dame.
Mais je n'os corps, ne cuer, në ame,
Ne sanc, qui ne fremist en mi
Quant je la vi; car si fremi
Que, se Dieus de li me doint joye,
Grant paour de cheoir avoie.

Mais d'Esperance me souvint;
Et vrayement, adonc couvint,
Se je vouloie avoir victoire,
Que je recourusse au memoire
Qu'Esperance m'ot dit de cuer,
Et que ne jectasse en puer
Nulz de ses doulz commandemens,
Ne de ses bons ensaignemens.
Si recordai si ma leçon

viewed my lesson so carefully that my heart felt more confident by the time a girl who was singing had finished her song, for Sweet Hope was assuring it of some happiness.

Thinking only of my lady, I moved closer to where they were dancing. And the polite and well-bred one who is ruled and governed by Reason, who is so knowing and capable and worthy that no good is lacking in her, so favored me by her goodness that she turned her sweet eyes toward me. And this was done so very sweetly that it seemed to me, so help me God, that she loved me with a true love. When she had gone half the circle and was nearer to me, laughing graciously she called to me most courteously, saying:

"What are you doing there, fair sir? Dance with us!"

I fell at once to my knees and greeted her meekly. But as I spoke to her I changed colors several times, which made my face grow rosy and pale. And truly, it seemed to me that upon my face she could easily recognize my love, my desire, my passion, and all that these imply: how I was hers forever and how I was deeply in love with her. She returned my greeting, and rather swiftly, so that no one would notice that I was in this state out of love for her. She offered me her little fin-

3396 **qu'en** com J. **la c.** une c. J. 3397 *om* J. **pucellette** pucelle E. 3398 **plus seürs** a plus seur J. 3400 **Me** Le J. 3403 **et** est E. 3405 **scet tant puet** scet tant plus E; puet tant scet J. 3407 **m'enrichist** menrichi J. 3408 **guenchist** guejchi J. 3409 **ce** se Pe. 3410 **Qu'il** Qui Pe. **sembla** semble E. 3411 **fine** fole E. 3418 **tantost** atant E. 3423 **il** y C. 3426 **l'encloueure** lencloure EPe; lenclouture J.

Qu'ains qu'en eüst dit la chançon
Que une pucellette chantoit,
Mes cuers plus seürs se sentoit;
Car douce Esperance asseür
Me faisoit d'aucun bon eür.

Si me traï pres de la dansse
Com cilz qui a sa dame pense.
Mais la bonne et bien enseignie
Que Raisons gouverne et mestrie, f. 50vb
Qui tant scet, tant puet, et tant vaut
Que riens de bien en li ne faut,
De sa bonté tant m'enrichist
Que ses douls yeus vers moy guenchist.
Mes ce fu si tres doucement
Qu'il me sembla, se Dieus m'ament,
Qu'elle m'amast de fine amour.
Et quant elle ot fait demi tour,
Que plus de moy fu approuchie,
En riant de sa cortoysie
Moult courtoysement m'apella,
En disant: "Que faites vous la,
Beau sire? Danssiés avec nous!"
Et tantost me mis a genouls
Et humblement la saluay.
Mes couleur pluseurs foys muay,
Ainssi com je parloie a li,
Dont j'eus le vis taint et pali.

Et vrayement, il me fu vis
Qu'elle congnut bien a mon vis
L'amour, le desir, et l'ardure
De moy, et toute l'encloueure:
Comment siens a tous jours estoie
Et comment par amours l'amoie.
Si me rendi courtoysement
Mon salut et assés briefment,
Pour ce qu'on ne s'apercheüst
Que pour s'amour ainssi me fust.
Et me tendi son petit doy;

ger; and I, desirous and dutiful to her wish, was not remiss in taking it, and so I began to dance. But I had not danced long before she told me sweetly that I must make ready to sing, for it had come to my turn. I replied without hesitation:

"My lady, I want to do your bidding, but I know very little about singing. Yet since it pleases you I have no choice." Then without delay I began this virelai, which is called a chanson baladee; this is what it should be named.

(27) *How the Lover sings before his Lady*

[CHANSON BALADEE]

[Refrain:]

My lady, to you without reservation
I give my heart, thought, desire,
body, and love,
as to the very best
who can be seen,
or who can live or die
in this time.

I must not be held
a fool if I adore you,
for it's no lie
that you are more precious than goodness
and your sweet fragrance surpasses
every flower one might smell.
Your beauty makes every other

3434 *om* J; *space left for line.* 3435 **fu** fut J. 3436 **mis** pris E. 3437 **dansié n'ous pas** dansay non pas E. 3439 **Qu'il** Qui JPe. 3441 **venus estoie** venu estoit J. 3447 **qu'il** qui J. 3448 **ce** un J. 3449 **Que on** Com J. 3450 **clamee** nommee J. 3451–70 *om* J. 3463 **Que on puet** Con puist E.

Et je, qui faire vueil et doy
Son vouloir, ne fu pas remis
Du prendre, et a dansier me mis.

Mes dansié n'ous pas longuement
Quant elle me dist doucement
Qu'il couvenoit que je chantasse
Et que de chanter m'avissasse,
Car venus estoie a mon tour.
Je li respondi sans demour: f. 51a

"Ma dame, vo commandement
Vueil faire; mais petitement
Me sçai de chanter entremettre.
Mes c'est chose qu'il couvient estre,
Puis qu'il vous plaist." Lors sans delay
Encommenchay ce virelay f. 51b
Que on claimme chançon balladee;
Ainssi doit elle estre clamee.

(Miniature 27) *Commant l'Amant chante emprés sa dame*

[CHANSON BALLADEE]

Dame, a vous sans retollir f. 51a–b
Doins cuer, pensee, desir,
Corps, et amour,
Comme a toute la millour
Qu'on puist choysir,
Ne qui vivre ne morir
Puist a ce jour.

Si ne me doit a folour
Tourner, se je vous aour, f. 51va–vb
Car sans mentir,
Bonté passez en valour,
Toute fleur en douce oudour
Que on puet sentir.
Vostre beauté fait tarir

wither and fade away,
and your sweetness
surpasses all; I see your complexion
the color of roses,
and your glance can heal
every sorrow. [Repeat refrain]

Therefore, my lady, I gird myself
with all my strength
to serve you,
and I devote, without base artifice,
my heart, my life, and my honor
to pleasing you.
And if Pity grant
that you deign to hear
my appeal,
I wish no other recompense
for my troubles,
for no greater joy
could come to me. [Repeat refrain]

My lady, my every resource,
I must often lament and mourn
when far from you;
and, near you, I grow pale
since you don't know the passion
I have to suffer
for you whom I love and desire so much
that I can no longer hide it.
And if you show no
tenderness, I must end my days
in great sadness.
Nonetheless I remain yours
till death. [Repeat refrain]

After my song a lady, who had been dancing there and who seemed to me very charming, gracious and pretty, began at once to sing: "Dear

3468 **doy tenir** doi cremir Pe. 3471 **Pour . . . je** Douce dame je E. 3474 **met sans nul vilain t.** aussi met sanz nul t. E. 3475 **m'onnour** mamour J. 3476 **En** Et E. 3480 **ne** nen E. 3482 **Qu'il ne** Qui ne E. 3485–87 *om* E. 3491 **le** *om* J. 3499 **me** *om* E. **sembla** sembloit EJ.

Toute autre et anïentir,
Et vo douçour
Passe tout; rose en coulour
Vous doy tenir,
Et vos regars puet garir
Toute doulour. // Dame, a vous, etcetera. . .

Pour ce, dame, je m'atour f. 51va
De trestoute ma vigour
A vous servir,
Et met, sans nul vilain tour,
Mon cuer, ma vie et m'onnour
En vo plaisir.
Et se Pitiés consentir
Vueut que me daigniez oïr
En ma clamour,
Je ne quier de mon labour
Autre merir,
Qu'il ne me porroit venir
Joye greigneur. // Dame, a vous, etc.

Dame, ou sont tuit mi retour,
Souvent m'estuet en destour
Plaindre et gemir,
Et, present vous, descoulour
Quant vous ne savez l'ardour
Qu'ai a sousfrir
Pour vous qu'aim tant et desir,
Que plus ne le puis couvrir.
Et se tenrour
N'en avez, en grant tristour
M'estuet fenir.
Nonpourquant dusqu'a mourir f. 51vb
Vostre demour. // Dame, a vous, etc.

Aprés ma chançon commença
Une dame qui la dança,
Qui moult me sembla envoisie,
Car elle estoit cointe et jolie,
Si prist a chanter sans demeure:

God, when will the time and hour come that I may see the one I love?" And she finished her song with this refrain. When she'd finished it, my lady said: "That's nicely sung, but now it's time for us to return." Then they all set off after her in the direction of the manor, for there was neither lord nor lady there who'd contradict anything my lady might say. So they all stopped dancing and went happily along, some alone, some in pairs, some by threes and fours, all relaxing and enjoying themselves. My lady kept me at her side and spoke to me, just as she often did, inquiring all about my situation; she was very desirous to know where I'd come from and why I'd avoided her presence; and also what it was that had caused me to quit her company recently; for I'd parted very abruptly without taking leave, and never before, she said, had she seen me find cause to depart in that manner, and she wondered why I had not wanted to respond to her question or answer her, and insisted that I tell her the whole truth, where I'd been, without lying or dissimulation, and what had occasioned this behavior.

When she had made this reasonable and forthright request—for a

3503 **si** cy J. 3510 **N'il** Il E. 3514 **alerent** aloient J. 3516 **esbatre** abatre Pe. 3518 **d'encoste** de coste EJ. 3520 **elle** *om* Pe. 3531 **voulz despondre** vous respondre CPe.

"Dieus, quant venra li temps et l'eure
Que je voie ce que j'aim si?"
Et sa chançon fina ainsi.
Quant finé l'ot, ma dame dist:
"C'est bien et jolïement dit,
Mais il est temps de nous retraire."
Et lors se mirent au repaire
Vers le manoir tuit aprés lui,
N'il n'ot en la place celui
Ne celle qui contredeïst
Chose que ma dame deïst.
Si laissierent tuit le danser
Et s'en alerent sans tencer,
Ci un, ci .ii., ci .iii., ci .iiii.,
Pour eulz solacier et esbatre.
Et ma dame m'araisonna
Et d'encoste li me mena, f. 52a
En demandant de mon affaire,
Ainssi comme elle souloit faire;
Et m'enquist moult dont je venoie,
Et comment tant tenu m'estoie
Que je ne l'avoie veü,
Et aussi que j'avoie eü
Quant je parti derrainement
De li; car moult soudainement
M'en parti, sans penre congié,
Në onques mais si eslongié,
Ce dist, ne me vit de raison
Com la; et pour quelle occoison
Ce fu que ne li voulz despondre
Sa demande, n'a li respondre,
Et que toute la verité
Li deïsse, ou j'avoie esté,
Sans mentir et sans couverture,
Et dont venoit ceste aventure.

Quant elle m'ot fait sa requeste,
Qui fu raisonnable et honneste—
Car dame a loy de demander
Seur amant et de commander—

lady has the right to question and command a lover—I, who often sigh from my heart, sighed deeply, for I saw clearly that I had no choice but to reply. Then I quickly had recourse to my goddess Hope, who inspired heart and lips to say what touched me most deeply. So with great trepidation I replied quite ingenuously:

(28) *How the Lover speaks to his Lady*

"My lady, I cannot refuse your command, and since it pleases you I'll give you an honest answer and will never lie, so that I'll hide no truth from you, neither for gain nor loss; yet I'd gladly excuse myself from doing this, if it pleased you and I so dared. So I beg you, my lady, in God's name, if ever I should say anything that bothers you, that you make allowance for my deficiency; and I pray you to forgive me, for I would never willingly say anything that would displease you. Of this I want God to be my witness.

"My lady, right from the start I want to tell you the origin, the nature, the basis, and the root that determine the truth of what you ask, since you command me to do so. I was young and small, silly, childish

3542 **un . . . parfont** un plaint et un J. 3544 *om* J. 3545 **recouri** recouvri CEPe. 3549 **que** com J. 3555 **verité n'iert** niert verite Pe. 3558 **S'il** Si Pe. **dame** *om* C (−1). 3563 **pri** *om* C (−1). **escusés** escuser J. 3566 **vueil dieu** dieu vueil Pe. 3568 **le commencement** lencommencement Pe. 3569–70 *reversed in* E.

Je, qui souvent de cuer souspir,
Jetai un moult parfont souspir,
Car bien vi qu'il me couvenoit
Respondre, et il appartenoit.
Lors recouri je sans paresse
A Esperance ma deesse,
Qui me mist en cuer et en bouche
De dire ce qui plus me touche.
Si que moult paoureusement
Respondi assés simplement:

"Ma dame, refuser ne puis
Vostre commandement, et puis
Qu'il vous plaist, je vous en dirai
Le voir, ne ja n'en mentiray,
Qu'a vous verité n'iert couverte
De moy, pour gaaigne ne pour perte; f. 52b
Mais volentiers m'en deportasse,
S'il vous pleüst, dame, et je ossasse.
Si vous pri, ma dame, pour Dieu
Que, se je di en aucun lieu
Chose qui vous puist annuier,
Vueilliés mon deffaut supplier,
Et vous pri que escusés en soie;
Car voulentiers pas ne diroie
Chose qui vous deüst desplaire.
De ce vueil Dieu a tesmoing traire.

Ma dame, tout premierement
Vous diray le commencement,
L'estat, le fons, et la racine
Qui la verité determine
De ce que vous me demandés,
Puis que vous le me commandés.

(Miniature 28) *Commant l'Amant parle a sa dame*

J'estoie joines et petis,
Nices, enfes, et enfantis,

and infantile, void of sense and quite naive, of very weak understanding, accustomed to idleness, when first I saw you, my lady, and even now I am more that way than I'd like to be. So I set my imagination and inclination and all my pleasure on you, my lady, because without doubt you were my model and guide in all I should do; nor did I believe I could live without seeing you, and I so devoted my whole mind and heart and youth to you that your glance, your words, and your deeds were my true paradise.

"So I decided that I would compose, according to my feelings towards you and in praise of you, a lai, complainte, or original song; for I did not dare or know how to tell you otherwise how I felt, and it seemed to me better to tell in my new song what was oppressing and wringing my heart than to try by some other method. So I composed a lai about the feelings I had at the beginning, and it was brought to you, which caused me such distress that I was certain that nothing could keep Death from seizing me. For, my lady, you summoned me and commanded me to read it; and I read it to you from beginning to

3575 **d'ignossance** dignorance E; de jovence J. 3583 **mis** mit J. 3589 **si** ci J. 3601 **Ce** Et E. **destraint** estaint C; estraint E. 3608 **la** *om* C (−1); mis J. 3610 **lui** le E. 3612 **et . . . point** et le mis a p. J.

Nus de sens et plains d'ignossance,
D'assez petite congnoissance,
D'estre en oyseuse coustumiers,
Dame, quant je vous vi premiers,
Ja soit ainssi qu'encor en soie
Mieus garnis que je ne voudroie. f. 52va
Si que l'imaginacion
De moy et l'inclinacion
Si mis et toute ma plaisance
En vous, dame; que, sans doubtance,
Vous m'estiés examplaire et voie
De tout ce que faire devoie;
Në il ne m'estoit mie avis
Que sans vous veoir fusse vis,
Et en vous si toute m'entente,
Mon cuer metoie, et ma jouvente,
Que vostre oeil, vos fais, et vos dis
Estoient mon droit paradis.

Si m'avisay que je feroie
Selonc ce que je sentiroie
Pour vous et a vostre loenge
Lay, complainte, ou chançon estrange;
Qu'a vous n'osasse ne sceüsse
Dire autrement ce que je eüsse,
Et me sembloit chose plus belle
De dire en ma chançon nouvelle
Ce qui mon cuer destraint et serre,
Que par autre guise requerre.
Si fis un lay dou sentement
Que j'avoye au commencement,
Et fu devant vous aportés,
Dont puis fu si desconfortés
Que je cuiday bien que la Mort
M'eüst sans remede la mort.
Car, ma dame, vous m'appellastes
Et lui lire me commandastes.
Si le vous leu de point en point,
Rudettement et mal a point,

end, artlessly and inelegantly, like one whose great dread could not be mistaken.

"And since no one yet knew who had composed the lai, my lady, you asked me who had done it and requested that I tell you truthfully. And I, who would never do anything that might displease you, seeking only to please you, and who did not wish to lie to you—therefore, my lady, I dared not say I had done it, because I had done it and did not want to reveal to you the love I'd kept hidden so long, and that I could no longer conceal from you, since I would have to reveal it; so my heart was confused as to whether to answer or remain silent, because I didn't know which to do. For this reason, I took the middle road and left your presence, so sorrowful and upset that my heart nearly burst when my body left in this manner.

"And indeed, for all the money one could have or hope for, I couldn't have answered you, because I felt so troubled in mind, in strength, and in words. Thus I had to go off lamenting, weeping, and sighing, and seeking and hoping for death, until I came by chance to an enclosed place of exceptional beauty. I went to a secluded corner of it

3614 **qu'il** qui J. 3618 **Qui** Quil E. 3620 **qui** que E. **feïsse** deisse J. 3621 **qui** que E. 3622 *om* J. **peüst** pleust E. 3623 **qui** que J. 3625 **que ce** ce que EJ. 3627 **vous** *om* J. 3629 **couvrir** celer J. 3630 **descouvrir** descombrer J. 3631 **Estoit** Estueut C; Sestoit J. 3632 **respondre** rendre E. 3634 *follows* 3636 *in* Pe. 3635 **me parti** departir C. **de present** present de E. 3638 **corps** cuers E. **s'en** se EJ. 3640 **Qu'on** Com J. 3643 **force de p.** force et de p. J. 3644 **couvint aler** couvint il aler C (+1).

Comme cilz qui en grant frisson
Fu qu'il n'i eüst mesprisson.

Et pour ce que nulz ne savoit
Encor qui ce lay fait avoit,
Ma dame, vous me demandastes
Qui l'avoit fait, et me priastes f. 52vb
Que sans mentir le vous deïsse.
Et je, qui jamais ne feïsse
Riens qui desplaire vous deüst,
Fors ce qui plaire vous peüst,
Et qui mentir ne vous vouloie—
Et aussi, dame, je n'osoie
Dire que ce fust de mon fait,
Pour ce que je l'avoie fait
Et que je vous eüsse ouvert
L'amour que tant vous ay couvert,
Que plus ne la vous puis couvrir,
Ainçoys la m'esteut descouvrir—
Estoit mes cuers en fait contraire
Ou de respondre ou de moy taire,
Car le quel faire ne savoie.
Pour ce pris la moienne voie
Et me parti de present vous
En tel dueil et en tel courrous,
Qu'a pou que mes cuers ne partoit
Quant mes corps ainssi s'en partoit.

Et certes, pour trestout l'avoir
Qu'on porroit desirer n'avoir
Ne vous eüsse respondu,
Tant me senti je confondu
De sens, de force, de parler.
Et pour ce m'en couvint aler
Plaignant, plourant, et souspirant,
La mort querant et desirant,
Tant que je vins par aventure
En une trop belle closture.
Si m'en alay en .i. destour,
Et la fis je de ma tristour

and there I composed a complainte about my sad state and about Fortune, who had extinguished my joy. And truly I was dying, with no regret at losing life; but Sweet Hope quickly appeared, who helped me in my need and was a thousand times more beautiful than any creature fashioned by Nature; because, in short, she seemed a heavenly being and I'd never seen anything so beautiful or radiant. And there she swore love, loyalty, companionship, fidelity, help, comfort, and aid to me, if I would follow her and flee despair. There she sweetly comforted me; there she healed me; there she brought me peace, joy, honor, and wealth, and banished sorrow and sadness. She taught me to recognize, without ever forgetting or confusing, the meaning of the shield of true lovers, and the powers of the colors; and how Fortune's constancy is her mutability; she taught me not to fear Fortune and showed me with manifest argument how she is bitter when she seems sweet.

"Afterwards, my lady, her guidance led me to you; because, by my soul, I'd not be here had Hope not accompanied me. Therefore I implore you with devout heart, dear lady—since she has desired and still desires you to have my whole heart, my whole body, and my whole life—that you do nothing contrary to what she's promised me. Be-

3653 *om* J; *blank line left.* 3656 **me** ma C. 3660 **Qu'elle** Quel J. 3661 **Qu'onques** Nonques J. 3663 **loyauté c.** loyaute et c. C (+1). 3666 **desesperance** desperance C (−1). 3668 **la m'aporta** et conforta J. 3669 **santé richesse** et richesse C (−1); sante leesse E. 3670 **et** de J. 3671 J *replaces this line with*: Les armes qui sont en lescu. 3674 **ne** sans E. 3675 **comment** comme E; forment J. 3676 **mouvant** nommant E. 3677 **M'osta** Moste E. 3679 **si duit** seduit E. 3680 **Qu'elle** Elle J. **jusqu'a vous conduit** jusques a vous duit E. 3681 **Car** Et E. 3683 **suppli** depri J. 3688 *om* J.

Et de Fortune une complainte,
Par qui ma joie estoit estainte.
Et vraiement, j'estoie mors
Sans avoir de vie remors;
Mais Douce Esperance acouri
Qui au besoing me secouri f. 53a
Et vint en trop plus belle fourme
Mil foys que Nature ne fourme.
Car, a briés mos, elle fu telle
Qu'elle sambla esperituelle,
Qu'onques mais riens si bel ne vy,
Ne si cler. Et la me plevy
Amour, loyauté, compaignie,
Foy, secours, confort, et aïe,
Se je la vouloie ensievir
Et desesperance fuïr.
La doucement me conforta;
La me gari; la m'aporta
Pais, joye, honnour, santé, richesse,
Et m'osta doulour et tristresse.
La demoustrance de l'escu
Des vrais amans, et la vertu
Des couleurs m'aprist a congnoistre,
Sans oublïer ne descongnoistre,
Et comment Fortune ha constance
En li mouvant; ceste doubtance
M'osta et dist par raison clere
Comment en douçour est amere.

Aprés, dame, elle m'a si duit
Qu'elle m'a jusqu'a vous conduit,
Car, par m'ame, jamais n'i fusse
Venus, s'aveuc moy ne l'eüsse.
Si vous suppli de cuer devost,
Chiere dame—puis qu'elle vost
Et vueut encor que sans partie
Aiés mon cuer, mon corps, ma vie
Que vous ne la vueilliés desdire
De ce qu'elle m'a volu dire.
Car, dame, se vous l'avoués,

cause, my lady, if you agree, I'll be right where I hope to be; and if not, I must leave my heart behind and die a very bitter martyrdom because of you, for there is no way, my lady, that I could beg you for joy or favor; because a lady's refusal destroys a lover's body and soul, dear lady, and were I to be refused, indeed I know I'd die. I'd rather Hope be refused than me; but if she's accepted, I'll have everything my heart desires; it should more than satisfy me.

"And if it please you, my dear lady, to consider the last little song I sang, of which I composed both words and music, you can easily tell whether I'm lying or speaking the truth. I beg you to recall it and take pity on me, for I am so truly yours and will always be, that I'll never love another."

When I had finished my reply, my lady, who heals and restores my troubles, my sorrows, my afflictions and all my misfortunes with her sweet glance, answered me: "So help me God, this is a splendid story, however improbable. I'm surprised because I've never before heard anything like this. But is it true you composed the lai you recited to me?"

3691 **se** ce C. **faurra** convenra Pe. 3695 **depri** depru C. 3697 **perit** perist CJPe. 3698 **corps** cuer J. **esperit** esperist C. 3700 **sçay** croy J. 3702 **s'elle** celle J. 3703 **J'aray** Je tay C. 3705 **s'il** si EJ. 3709–10 *om* CPe. 3711 **pri** *om* Pe. 3712 **vous** *om* Pe. 3713 **si** li E. 3715 **j'os parfiné** jos fine C (−1); jeus parfaite E. 3726 **Est ce v.** Esse v. E.

La serai ou je sui voués;
Et se non, il faurra partir
Mon cuer et mourir com martir
Pour vous tres doulereusement,
Qu'a moy n'appartient nullement, f. 53b
Dame, que je face depri
A vous de joie ne d'ottri;
Car refus de dame perit
En amant corps et esperit,
Chiere dame, et se je l'avoie,
Certes, bien sçay que je morroie.
S'aim mieus qu'elle soit refusee
Que moy, et s'elle est avouee,
J'aray quanque mes cuers desire;
Si me devra plus que souffire.

Et s'il vous plaist, ma dame chiere,
A regarder la dairreniere
Chançonnette que je chantay,
Que fait en dit et en chant ay,
Vous pourrez de legier savoir
Se je ment ou se je di voir.
Si vous pri qu'il vous en souviengne
Et que pytié de moy vous preigne,
Car si vostres sui et seray
Que jamais autre n'ameray."

Quant j'os parfiné ma response,
Ma dame, qui rest et qui ponse
Mes mauls, mes annuis, mes durtés
Et toutes mes maleürtés
Seulement de son doulz regart,
Me respondi: "Se Dieus me gart,
Ceste aventure est gracïeuse,
Comment qu'elle soit merveilleuse,
Qu'onques mais n'oÿ la pareille
Et pour ce en ai je grant merveille.

Mais de ce lay que vous me dites,
Est ce voirs que vous le feïstes?"

[THE LOVER]

"Yes indeed, my lady."

[THE LADY]

"No one helped you?"

[THE LOVER]

"No one, my lady, except you alone who inspired my song, rhyme, and joyful subject."

(29) *How the Lady speaks to the Lover*

THE LADY SPEAKS

"And for whom did you compose it?"

THE LOVER REPLIES

"For you, my lady, to whom I'm totally devoted."

THE LADY

"You are?"

THE LOVER

"Yes."

THE LADY

"That's hard to believe."

THE LOVER

"By my soul, it's as true as the Lord's Prayer that I wrote it and that

3728 **dame** certes E. 3729 **seule** dame E. 3735 **Aussi** Ainssi JPe.

[L'AMANT]

"Certainement, ma dame, oïl."

[LA DAME]

"Vous aida nuls?"

[L'AMANT]

"Dame, nennil,
Fors vous seule en qui je prenoie
Chant, rime, et matiere de joye." f. 53va

(Miniature 29) *Comment la dame parle a l'Amant*

LA DAME PARLE

"Et pour qui le feïstes vous?"

L'AMANT RESPONT

"Pour vous, dame, a qui je sui tous."

LA DAME

"Estes?"

L'AMANT

"Oïl."

LA DAME

"C'est fort a croirre."

L'AMANT

"Par m'ame, c'est parole voire,
Aussi comme est la patenostre,

I am yours, my lady, and may your honor be preserved, which I love, want, desire, seek, and save, as much as I want to save my eternal soul."

THE LADY

"And did you see Hope in the shape and form you've described to me here?"

THE LOVER SPEAKS

"Yes, my lady. And had I pondered and thought a hundred years about her, I couldn't tell you the hundredth part of her goodness, her great beauty, or the perfect loyalty she swore to me. For this reason she made me come here and promised me a happy life, and that you would be gracious to me. And you must carefully reflect before you deny her request. I don't care to lie: if I beg and request anything of you, it's through her and in her name, which is so nobly renowned that there's not a land or kingdom in the world where she cannot be found, where she does not reign, and where everyone who is capable of joy through her is not happy.

"Nonetheless, my lady, you are so wise and noble of heart that you can see proven by my plaint that he who laments has much to request.

3738 **vueil desir** desir vueil C. 3740 **qu'ay a** que jay a E. 3743 **ci le m'avés** vous mavez ci J. 3744 **Et** *om* C (−1). 3746 t *of* tans *added above line in* C. 3748 **la** sa E. 3750 **venir** tenir J. 3751 *before this line* J *adds*: Et ma promis vie jolie. 3753 **devés moult** devez bien E; moult devez Pe. 3756 **ou** ne E. 3757 **son** mon J. 3762 **Qui** Que C. **puet** veult J. 3764 **et** *om* CPe.

Que le fis et que je suis vostre,
Ma dame, et vostre honnour soit sauve
Que j'aim, vueil, desir, quier, et sauve,
Com celle que je vueil sauver
Tant com m'ame qu'ay a sauver."

LA DAME

"Et veïstes vous Esperance
En la fourme et en la semblance
Que ci le m'avés devisé?"

L'AMANT PARLE

"Ma dame, oÿl. Et se visé
Y avoie et pensé .c. ans,
Ne diroie je de .c. tans f. 53vb
Sa bonté, ne sa grant beauté,
Ne la parfaite loyauté
Qu'elle m'a promis a tenir.
Et pour ce m'a fait cy venir
Et m'a promis vie joyeuse,
Et qu'a moy seriés gracïeuse.
Si vous devés moult aviser
Que sa requeste refuser
Ne voeilliés. Et mentir n'en quier:
Se riens vous depri ou requier,
C'est de par lui et en son non
Qui est de si noble renon
Qu'au monde n'a païs ne regne
Qu'elle n'i soit, qu'elle n'i regne,
Et que chascuns ne se resjoie,
Qui de li puet avoir la joie.

Nonpourquant vous estes si sage,
Dame, et de si noble courage,
Que veoir poués a mon pleint
Qu'assés rueve qui se complaint.
Mes riens demander ne vous ose
Amour, mercy, në autre chose

But I dare not ask anything of you—love, pity, or anything else—for it is not my place to do so, and it is commonly said that asking comes from ill breeding, while giving is born of courtliness."

[THE LADY]

"You speak the truth; that's what they say. And also he who is refused should feel shame, if he has any sense, be he noble, commoner, valet, or page. He who doesn't reflect before asking must be reckoned a fool. Likewise, one often gets into trouble by speaking when he should keep silent, for they say that talking too much is harmful. And truly I believe that he who covets more than he ought will be ruined by his covetousness. And to ask out of covetousness is contrary to honesty; nor should one climb so high that he's ashamed of coming back down, but rather he should choose the mean, for I've often heard it said that he who climbs higher than he ought falls from higher than he'd like. Therefore it is good to speak openly, wisely, avisedly, and to the point, sweetly, not boorishly, and to ask for what is due, because a proper request will elicit a proper response.

"And, fair sir, I believe that Good Hope, who is worthy and powerful, has advised you wisely, in the manner of one who is intelligent,

3772 **donner . . . courtoysie** Et louenge de c. J. 3773 **ce que on** que on C (−1); ce com J. 3774 **que on** com J. 3776 **vallés** varlet E. 3778 **Qui** Quil E. 3780 **De** Et E. 3781 **cuist** nuit E. 3783 **qu'il** qui E. 3785 **couvoitise** courtoisie J. 3786 **contre** de J. 3788 **Qu'on** Com J. 3789 **moyen** moyem C. 3792 **haut** bas C. 3795 **Doucement** Justement E. **sans** par J. **ruste** rude E; juste J.

Qu'a moy n'appartient nullement,
Et on dist que communement
Demander vient de villonnie,
Et donner nest de courtoysie."

[LA DAME]

"Vous dites voir; c'est ce que on dist.
Et aussi cil que on escondist
Doit estre honteus, s'il est sages,
Soit grans, petis, vallés, ou pages.
Il couvient que pour fol se rende
Qui ne s'avise ains qu'il demande;
Et aussi vient souvent contraire
De parler quant on se doit taire,
Car on dist que trop parler cuist.
Et vrayement, si com je cuit.
Qui plus couvoite qu'il ne doit, f. 54a
Sa couvoitise le deçoit.
Et demander de couvoitise
Est engenrés contre franchise;
N'on ne doit pas si haut monter
Qu'on ait honte dou desvaler,
Ains doit on le moyen eslire;
Car meintes foys ai oÿ dire:
Qui plus haut monte qu'il ne doit,
De plus haut chiet qu'il ne voudroit.
Pour ce fait bon parler a point
Par scens, par avis, et par point,
Doucement, sans maniere ruste,
Et demander ce qui est juste,
Car encontre bon demandeur
Appartient bon escondisseur.

Et, biau sire, Bonne Esperance
Qui moult a valour et puissance,
Comme sage et bien doctrinee,
Loyal, juste, et bien avisee,
Vous ha conseillié sagement,
Ce m'est avis. Et vraiement,

learned, loyal, just, and perspicacious. And truly she is so worthy, so wise, so powerful, so helpful, so exemplary, so necessary to everyone, so courteous, well-bred, good, gentle, bountiful, lovable, loyal, noble, forthright, trustworthy, generous with joy and comfort, liberal in consolation, disposed to reason and doing good, and she is so undefiled, pure, and spotless in deeds and morals that her actions show their goodness wherever she performs them. She is so good and true in nature that it is my feeling one should never oppose anything she says or does.

"So I would be unworthy if I were to fail her or deny her anything. Therefore with all my heart I yield to her pleasure and her will, for I want whatever she wants; nor will my heart resist what she's said and promised of me, but rather will gladly submit, without condition or delay. So therefore, fair sweet loyal friend, I avow, ratify, and will hold to all she has promised you, and will never oppose her. For this reason I beg you henceforth to be charming, gay, happy, loyal and discreet, without bragging, for you have a loyal sweetheart.

"And indeed, my friend, I was sure that you loved me even though

3806 **tant puet valoir** et valoir J. 3807 **pour** a J. 3808 **courtoise** courtaise C. **et** *om* E. 3810 **honneste c.** honneste et c. E. 3815 **et** *om* Pe. **meurs** mains J. **que** quen Pe. 3816 **Bonne** *om* E. 3818 **qu'a** quen E. 3820 **penser** faire J. 3823 **la** li C. 3824 **s'ottroie** otrie J. 3828 **Qu'elle . . . et** De ce quelle a E. 3829 **iert** est EJ. 3833 **ratefi** certefi C; je de sy E. 3835 **que desormais** que desoremais E; des ore mais J.

Tant vaut, tant scet, tant a pouoir,
Tant puet aidier, tant puet valoir,
Tant est pour chascun neccessaire,
Tant est courtoise et debonnaire,
Bonne, gentil, franche, amiable,
Loyal, noble, honneste, creable,
Large de joie et de confort,
Abandonnee en reconfort,
A bien faire et raison encline,
Tant par est nette, pure, et fine
En fais et en meurs, que son oeuvre
Bonne appert partout ou elle oeuvre.
Tant est bonne en condicion
Et vraie, qu'a m'entencion
On ne devroit riens escondire
Qu'elle vousist penser ne dire.

Si ne seroie pas vaillant f. 54b
Se je li estoie faillant,
Ne s'en riens la desavouoie.
Pour ce dou tous mes cuers s'ottroie
A son plaisir et a son vueil,
Car tout ce qu'elle vueut je vueil;
N'a ce mon cuer n'iert anemi
Qu'elle a dit et promis de mi,
Ains iert bonnement avouee,
Sans penre terme ne journee.
Si que, biaus douls loyaus amis,
Tout ce qu'elle vous a promis
Aveu, ratefi, et tenray,
Si que ja contre ne venray.
Pour ce vous pri que desormais
Soiés cointes, jolis, et gais,
Loyaus, secrés sans vanterie,
Car vous avés loial amie.

Et certes, amis, bien pensoie
Que la vostre amour estoit moie,
Comment que riens n'en deïssiez
Et que semblant n'en feïssiez.

you said nothing and gave no sign of it. But since Hope has become involved, I shouldn't rebel against her wish, but instead grant you faithfully the gift of my love; for she has told me that you love me and want to be called my beloved."

(30) *How the Lover thanks his Lady*

Then I immediately fell to my knees to thank her. But she as quickly bent down to stop me, preferring that I rise and talk with her as we walked along. So I stood upright and thanked her, as was proper, not as well as I should, but as best I knew how.

And when I had thanked her a hundred thousand times and expressed my gratitude for the honor she'd done me in having thus soothed my heart—although I was entirely hers, and want to remain hers as I have said above—once again I renewed my promises and gave her my heart, body, fidelity, and lover's loyalty for evermore and inseparable, until death parts me from her. And my heart was enflamed with joy as she received and accepted them.

And so that no one might perceive or learn anything of our love,

3844 **ne** nen Pe. 3849–90 *om* J. 3854 **a li parlasse** a lui me parlasse E. 3856 **la** len E. 3857 **je** *om* E. 3862 **Quant** Quen E. 3863 **Comment** Comme E. 3865 **Ainssi** Aussi E. 3871 **les** *om* C (−1). **prist** print Pe. 3872 **esprist** esprint Pe. 3873 **n'aperceüst** aperceust C. 3874 **ou** et E.

Mes quant Esperance s'en melle,
Je ne doy pas estre rebelle
A son vouloir, ains vous otroy
Loyaument de m'amour l'otroy,
Qu'elle m'a dit que vous m'amés
Et vueut qu'amis soiés clamés."

(Miniature 30) *Comment l'Amant mercie sa dame*

Adonc me mis sans detrïer f. 54va
A genouls pour li mercïer.
Mais elle tantost s'abaissa
Vers moy et pas ne m'i laissa,
Ainçoys vost que je me dressase
Et qu'en alant a li parlasse.
Si que je me levay tous drois
Et la merciay, ce fu drois,
Non pas ainssi com je devoie,
Mais si com faire le savoie.

Et quant je l'os remercïé
.c. mille foys et gracïé
De l'amour qu'elle me faisoit
Quant mon cuer ainssi appaisoit—
Comment que, sans riens retenir,
Siens fusse, et siens me vueil tenir,
Ainssi com si dessus dit l'ay—
Encores li renouvelay
Et li donnai le cuer de mi,
Corps, foy, et loyauté d'ami
A tousjours mais, sans decevrer,
Tant que mors m'en fera sevrer.
Et elle les reçut et prist,
Dont mon cuer de grant joie esprist.

Et pour ce que on n'aperceüst
Riens de nos amours, ou sceüst,
Une damoyselle appella,

she summoned a damsel, who quickly harkened to her call. She spoke to her of other things; and then I fell back among other ladies and damsels who asked me news of myself and sang me several songs which debated love and its adventures. Indeed my replies were very far from what I was thinking, for I constantly made white black for them, until we came to the manorhouse that was not far distant. We all followed after my lady, who went there before us. This was proper, for Reason wished it.

When we got there, it was to my liking. We climbed the stairs to a very beautiful chapel, painted in gold by a master's hand, and with the very finest colors I'd ever seen. There they prepared for mass, which was devoutly said and heard. And there I made my prayers and acts of humility to God, asking that He deign to preserve my lady in honor, in both body and soul, and to give me the happiness, wisdom, grace, and strength to protect her tranquility and honor, and the power to serve her according to my wishes, and to have her accept as reasonable my pleasant little attentions. This was the aim of my prayer.

When mass was over, I heard a chamberlain sounding a trumpet

3877 **Si** De E. 3878 **je me** si men E. 3881 **me** *om* Pe. 3884 **je** *om* C Pe (−1). 3891 **ce** si C. 3894 **D'or et** Dori J. **maistre** mente C. 3897 **messe** maisse C. 3898 **Devotement** Doucement E. 3899 **je** *om* C (−1). 3901 **sauver** garder E. 3903 **vigour** honour CEPe. 3907 **com** coup E. 3909 **Ce** Ee (*sic*) C.

Qui tost oÿ son appel a.
Si li parla d'autre matiere;
Et lors je me traï arriere
Devers dames et damoyselles
Qui enquierent de mes nouvelles
Et me firent pluseurs partures
D'amours et de ses aventures.
Certes, et je leur respondoie f. 54vb
Moult loing de ce que je sentoie,
Car tousdis leur fis dou blanc noir,
Tant que nous fumes au manoir
De quoy nous estions assés pres.
Si y venimes tuit aprés
Ma dame qui devant aloit.
Drois fu, car Raisons le voloit.

Quant la fumes, ce fu mes grés.
Si montames par les degrés
En une chapelle moult cointe,
D'or et de main de maistre pointe
Et des plus tres fines coulors
Qu'onques mais veïsse que lors.
Si fu la messe appareilliee,
Devotement ditte, et oÿe.
Et la fis je mes oroisons
A Dieu, et mes afflictions,
Qu'il me vousist sauver ma dame
En honnour, en corps, et en ame,
Et qu'eür, scens, grace, et vigour
De garder sa pais et s'onnour
Me donnast, et de li servir
Pouoir, si com je le desir,
Et qu'elle eüst com raisonnable
Mon petit service aggreable.

Ce fu la fin de ma prïere.
Quant la messe fu dite entiere,
J'oÿ sonner une trompeste
Dont uns chambrelans haut trompete.

loudly. You should have seen all the servants! Each hurried to his station, one toward the pantry, another to the wine cellar, the others to the kitchen, according to what each prepared. Messengers and stable boys set up benches, trestles, and tables. It was quite a sight to see them hurrying to and fro, bringing rushes, spreading rugs, shouting, hollering, and sweeping—it was bedlam to hear them call to one another in French, Breton, German, Italian, English, Occitan and Norman, and in many other unusual languages. It was a marvel to see elsewhere the carvers arranging, polishing, decorating, and straightening things, readying the water, and slicing bread for their masters, preparing the plates, calling for tablecloths, removing cheeseskins with their own hands, one sitting down, the other scurrying along, yet another scrubbing off dirt, others washing and cleaning their hands, one more and the other less, before going to sit down. They were making quite a racket, with everyone shouting and exclaiming: "Hurry up! Mass is ended and they've sounded the trumpets for dinner long since!" When the entire mass had been sung, each person went to his own room to remove his tight-fitting vest and put on a looser coat.

3914 **court** acourt E. 3915 **L'un** Li uns J. 3916 **bouteillerie** peueliere J. 3917 **vont** veint E. 3920 **dressent** dressont E. 3924 **a** et E. **raisonner** araisonner J. 3925 **et** *om* C (−1). 3926 **oc** *om* E. 3928 **C'estoit** Estoit J. 3931 **Vallés** Varles E. 3932 **pain** bien J. 3933 **tailloirs** taillours C. 3937 **leur** ses E. 3940 **C'estoit** Estoit CJ. 3944 **l'iaue** leure J. **grant . . . cornee** pieca corne C (−1); pieca cornee E; grant piesa tournee J; piece a cornee Pe. 3947 **corset** surcot E.

Qui adonc veïst gent de court!
Chascuns a son office court:
L'un devers la paneterie,
Et l'autre en la bouteillerie,
Li autre vont en la cuisine
Selonc ce que chascuns cuisine.
Messagiers et garçons d'estables
Dressent fourmes, trestiaus, et tables.
Qui les veïst troter et courre, f. 55a
Herbe aporter, tapis escourre,
Braire, crïer, et ramonner
Et l'un a l'autre raisonner,
Françoys, breton, et alemant,
Lombart, angloys, oc, et normant,
Et meint autre divers langage,
C'estoit a oïr droite rage.
Qui d'autre part veïst pignier,
Polir, cointoyer, alignier
Vallés trenchans et eaulz parer
Et pour leur mestre pain parer,
Faire tailloirs, demander napes,
Et de leur mains oster les rapes,
L'un seoir jus, l'autre troter,
Et l'autre ses crotes froter, f. 55b
Laver et netoier leur mains,
A l'un plus et a l'autre mains,
Ainçoys qu'on alast asseoir,
C'estoit merveilles a veoir.
Car il menoient moult grant noise,
Ainssi com chascun crie et noise:
"Faites tost; la messe est chantee,
Et l'iaue est grant pieça cornee."
Quant en ot chanté tout a trait,
Chascuns ala a son retrait,
Qui dust son corset desvetir
Pour le sercot ouvert vestir.

(31) *How the Lover attended his Lady's dinner*

Next everyone came into the main hall, which was in no way vulgar or mean, where all, I believe, were paid due honor and served with wine and food as their bodies and appetites required. And there as I ate I observed the demeanor, bearing, conduct, and deportment of her in whom is found all my happiness.

And after the meal you should have seen the musicians arrive, all combed and comfortably attired. They played various harmonies, for there all in a circle I saw vielle, rebec, guitar, lute, Moorish guitar, small psaltery, cittern, and the psaltery, harp, tabor, trumpets, nakers, portative organs, more than ten pairs of horns, bagpipes, flutes, musettes, douçaines, cymbals, bells, timbrels, the Bohemian flute and the large German cornett, willow flutes, a fife, pipe, Alsatian reed pipe, small trumpet, buisines, a psaltery, a monochord (which has a single string), and a straw pipe all together. And it certainly seemed to me that such a melodious sound had never been perceived or heard; because I heard and perceived each one of them, according to the pitch of his instrument—vielle, guitar, cittern, harp, trumpet, horn, flute, pipe,

3950 **ne fu** nestoit J. 3957 **le m.** de m. J. 3961 **puré** pur EPe. 3964 **rubelle g.** rebebe et g. E. 3965 **Leü** La EPe; Leust J. **micanon** micanum C; et le micantun E; michanon J; le mi cantun Pe. 3966 **et le psalterion** et psalterion CE (−1); et le certherion J. 3968 **dis** .ii. EPe. 3969 **flajos ch.** flajos et ch. C (+1). 3970 **simbales cl.** cimbales et cl. E. 3971 **fleüste br.** fluste br. C (−1); flahute de br. E. 3973 *This line added at end of column by scribe of C, with little hand pointing to where it should be inserted.* **de . . . pipe** dessus et sculepique E; de sans fistule pite J. 3975–76 *reversed in* E. 3975 **eles** et les E; et le J. 3978 **il** y C. 3981 **d'eaus** danse E. 3983 **guiterne** guinter J.

(Miniature 31) *Comment l'Amant fu au disner sa dame*

Aprés vint chascuns en la sale f. 55va
Qui ne fu villainne ne sale,
Ou chascuns fu, ce m'est avis,
A point honnourés et servis
Ainssi de vin et de viande
Com corps et apetis demande.
Et la pris je ma soustenance
En regardant la contenance,
L'estat, le maintieng, et le port
De celle ou sont tuit mi deport.
Mais qui veïst aprés mangier
Venir menestreuls sans dangier,
Pigniés et mis en puré corps,
La firent meins divers acors;
Car je vi la tout en un cerne
Violle, rubelle, guiterne,
Leü, morache, micanon,
Cytolle, et le psalterion,
Harpe, tabour, trompes, nacaires,
Orgues, cornes, plus de dis paires,
Cornemuses, flajos, chevretes,
Douceinnes, simbales, clocettes,
Tymbre, la flëuste brehaingne,
Et le grant cornet d'Alemaingne,
Flajos de Scens, fistule, pipe,
Muse d'Aussay, trompe petite,
Buissines, eles, monocorde
Ou il n'a c'une seule corde,
Et muse de blef tout ensemble.
Et certainement, il me samble
Qu'onques mais telle melodie
Ne fu veüe në oÿe,
Car chascuns d'eaus, selonc l'acort
De son instrument, sans decort,
Viole, guiterne, cytolle,
Harpe, trompe, corne, flajole,
Pipe, souffle, muse, naquaire,

bladder pipe, bagpipe, naker, tabor, and whatever could be played with finger, pick, or bow—performing in perfect harmony there in the little park.

After they had performed an estampie, the ladies and their company went off by twos and threes, holding hands, to a very beautiful room; and there all the men and women alike who wanted to relax, dance, sing, or play at backgammon, chess, or parsons found all they needed at hand and ready for games, singing, and music. And there were musicians more skilled and knowledgeable in both the new and old styles, and who could sing better than Music, who writes the songs, or Orpheus, who sang so well that he charmed all the inhabitants of Hades by the sweetness of his song.

After we had been a long while together, a knight quickly called for the wine and spices. This was evidently his function, because immediately and without delay the squires hastened there. It was past midday and approaching three o'clock when we'd had the spices and drunk the wine. It was time to depart, so everyone asked leave in the accustomed manner. I waited for the last to depart, attentive to nothing except my

3988 **parchet** porchet Pe. 3991 **S'en** Si E. 3993 **Jusqu'en** Jusques en C (+1); Jusqua E. 3994 **la n'ot il** la ny ot il E; ni ot il J. 3996 **chanter** jouer E. 3997 **de** ou J. 4008 **sceûst** sot C (−1). 4009 **rusé** chante J. 4014 **Y** Il J. 4016 **ce vermeillet** vermeillet C (−1); vin vermeillet Pe; vermeillet vin E. 4017 **la** et J. 4018 **ce** *om* Pe. 4020 **la** sa J. 4021 **tous des** tous les E; touzdis li J; dez Pe. 4022 **cilz** *om* Pe.

Taboure, et quanquë on puet faire
De dois, de penne, et de l'archet f. 55vb
Ouÿ je et vi en ce parchet.
Quant fait eurent une estampie,
Les dames et leur compaignie
S'en alerent, ci .ii., ci .iii.,
En elles tenant par les dois,
Jusqu'en une chambre moult belle;
Et la n'ot il celuy ne celle
Qui se vousist esbanoier,
Dancier, chanter, ou festoier
De tables, d'eschés, de parsons,
Par gieus, par notes, ou par sons,
Qui la ne trouvast sans arrest
A son vueil l'esbatement prest.
Et s'i ot des musicïens
Milleurs assez et plus scïens
En la vieus et nouvelle forge
Que Musique qui les chans forge,
Ne Orpheüs, qui si bien chanta
Que tous ceaus d'enfer enchanta
Par la douçour de son chanter,
Devant eaulz ne sceüst chanter.

Quant en ot rusé longuement,
Uns chevaliers isnelement
Hucha le vin et les espices;
Bien croy que ce fu ses offices,
Car en l'eure, sans delaier,
Y courirent li escuier.
Quant en ot espices eü
Et de ce vermeillet beü,
Midi passa; la nonne vint.
Pour ce prendre congié couvint;
Si le prist chascuns et chascune
Selonc la maniere commune.
Mais j'atendi tous des desrains,
Com cilz qui ne pensoie a riens,
Fors a ma douce dame gente

sweet noble lady whom I saw before me. And when I perceived that it was time to go to her, I didn't hesitate, but went at once to commend myself to her and ask her leave. In a whisper and very innocently I said to her: "I commend to you my heart and my being, as one who cannot live without loving you truly, for your love keeps me alive and happy."

She, like the worthy, courteous, good, and wise woman she was, answered me in a low voice: "My dear friend, since Love has brought us to join our two hearts together completely and inseparably, and wishes to make two into one, in God's name, let us make them equal; for they will be lost and shamed if they are not kept alike and united in both good times and bad, always equal, with no thought of mastery, supremacy, or lordship. For there are always quarrels and disputes between mastery and love. And above all we must each keep honor and peace with the other. And for my own peace of mind, I want to know where this ring came from, for I've never before noticed you wearing a ring."

4024 **la presente** en ma presente J. 4025 **qu'il** qui EJPe. 4032 **et** *om* E. 4036 **vie . . . joie** joie et en vie Pe. 4037 **com** comme Pe. 4040 **vous** nous Pe. 4044 **paire** parte E. 4046 **Se** Et E. 4047 **qu'en** que J. 4048 **et en tous** en tous C (−1); entre tous E; en trestouz Pe. 4049 **pensee** penser E. 4050 **et** ou J. 4051 **rumour** rancour E. 4052 **Entre . . . et** Quadez s. est J. 4053 **seurtout** seurtant J. **regarde** se garde E. 4054 **Qu'onnour** Qu'amour E.

Que je veoie la presente.
Et quant je vi qu'il fu a point f. 56a
D'aler vers lui, n'atendi point,
Ainçoys m'alai recommander
A li et congié demander.
Si li dis d'une voys bassete
Et de maniere assez simplette:
"Moy et mon cuer vous recommant,
Ma dame, et a Dieu vous commant,
Com cilz qui vivre ne porroie,
Se par amours ne vous amoie,
Car l'amour de vous me soustient
En vie et en joie me tient."

Elle, com vaillant et cortoise,
Bonne et sage, sans faire noise,
Me respondi:

[LA DAME]

"Mes chiers amis,
Puis qu'Amours a ce vous a mis
Que nos .ii. cuers ensemble joindre
Vueut sans partir et sans desjoindre,
Et que faire vueut .i. de .ii.,
Pour Dieu, ne faisons paire d'eus;
Car il sont perdu et honni,
Se si pareil et si onni
Ne sont qu'en bien et mal commun
Soient, et en tous cas comme un,
Sans pensee avoir de mestrie,
De hausaige, et de seigneurie,
Qu'adés ha tençon et rumour
Entre seignourie et amour.
Et seurtout que chascuns regarde
Qu'onnour et pais a l'autre garde.
Et pour ma pais je vueil savoir
Dont cilz aneiés vint, qu'avoir
Ne vous vi onques mais anel."

[THE LOVER]

I said: "My lady, I'm pleased for you to know, and you shall know it; and, if you want, you shall have it. Hope gave it to me, when she so yielded to me that she promised me her faith and love, and put it from her finger onto mine."

[THE LADY]

"Did she?"

[THE LOVER]

"Yes, truly, my lady."

[THE LADY]

"I would like a loving exchange of your ring for mine, and may they represent our agreement."

[THE LOVER]

Overjoyed by this, I answered her in ecstasy: "Dear lady, may God bless you for this!"

Then she began to smile sweetly and took from her smooth, white, round, soft, unwrinkled hand an exceptionally beautiful diamond which she placed on my finger as a sign that I was to be her blissful beloved, and she took Hope's ring, just as it is.

(32) *How the Lady and the Lover exchange rings*

4059 **si** se Pe. 4060 **voulez** voulois C. 4062 **s'abandonna** sumelia J. 4066 **vueil qu'am.** vueil am. E. 4073 **polie** jolie E. 4074 **Poteleuse** Petelleuse E. **onnie** jolie J. 4075 **En . . . d'eüreus** Et en signe de vray E. 4078 **D'esperance** Esperance E.

[L'AMANT]

Je dis: "Ma dame, ce m'est bel
Que le sachiez; si le sarés,
Et se vous voulez, vous l'arés.
Esperance le me donna f. 56b
Quant a moy tant s'abandonna
Que foy et amour me promist,
Et de son doit ou mien le mist."

[LA DAME]

"Fist?"

[L'AMANT]

"Ma dame, oïl, vrayement."

[LA DAME]

"Et je vueil qu'amiablement
De vostre anel au mien changons,
Et que ce soient nos changons."

[L'AMANT]

Et je, qui de ce grant joie eus,
Li respondi com moult joieus:
"Chiere dame, Dieus le vous mire!"
Lors prist doucement a sousrire
Et de sa blanche main polie,
Poteleuse, nette, et onnie,
En signe d'eüreus amant
Me mist .i. trop biau dyamant
En moy doy, et prist l'anelet
D'Esperance, tel com il est.

(Miniature 32) *Comment la dame et l'Amant changent d'aniaus*

But even as she was holding my finger, Sweet Hope suddenly appeared between the two of us to complete this alliance, which made us very happy and joyful to have her to advise us, because, should one say or do anything against the other, she could set it right and judge, according to the transgression, before Love and Loyalty, who have the sovereignty and are judges of lovers; because Hope judges each rightly and can testify that my lady gave her love to me with a loyal heart, and I to her. Therefore each of us with perfect heart agreed to this by word and deed.

Thereupon I left my lady, but she accorded me a glance so true and of such sweet meaning that she kept my heart as hostage. I was so happy and overjoyed by it that everything made me happy, since Hope had kept her promise to me so well; and for the joy I felt I composed this rondelet as I went along:

(33) *How the Lover departs singing*

[RONDELET]

My lady, my heart stays with you,
although I myself must leave you.
With true love I bear within,

4079 **ainssi** aussi J. 4081 **douce** bonne J. 4085 **deïst** vousist J. 4086 **ou** ne J. 4089 **Avant** Avec EJ. 4090 **ont** sont J. 4094 **que** *om* E. 4095 **je li** je a lui E. 4103 **joyans** joyaux E. 4104 *om* J, *blank line left.* **joians** joyaux E. 4105 **assevi** assouvy E; ensevi J. 4108 **fis en** fis je en E. 4109–16 Pe *gives the following rondelet*: Tant doucement me sens emprisonnes / Quonquez amant not si douce prison / Jamas nen quier estre desprisonnes / Tant doucement etc. / Quar tous biens mest en ceste prisonnes / Que dame puet donner sens mesprison / Tant doucement etc. 4111 **Par** De J.

Mais tout ainssi qu'elle tenoit f. 56va
Mon doit, soudainement venoit
Entre nous .ii. Douce Esperance
Pour parfaire ceste aliance,
Dont moult liés et moult joieus fumes
Quant a nostre conseil l'eümes,
Pour ce que, se li uns deïst
Riens contre l'autre ou meffeïst,
Qu'elle le peüst corrigier
Et selonc son mesfait jugier
Avant Amour et Loyauté,
Qui ont la souverainneté
Et qui sont des amoureus juge;
Pour ce que chascuns a droit juge,
Et qu'elle peüst tesmoignage
Porter, que de loyal corage
Me donna s'amour et je li,
Si que de nous n'i ot celuy f. 56vb
Qui adonc par dit et par fait
Ne l'acordast de cuer parfait.

Atant de ma dame parti;
Mais d'un regart me reparti
Si vray et d'un si doulz langage,
Qu'elle retint mon cuer en gage.
Dont si liés fu et si joyans
Que de tous les biens fu joians,
Quant Esperance ot assevi
Si bien ce qu'elle m'ot plevi;
Et pour la joye que j'avoie
Ce rondelet fis en ma voie:

(Miniature 33) *Comment l'Amant s'en va chantant*

[RONDELET]

Dame, mon cuer en vous remaint, f. 57a–b
Comment que de vous me departe.
Par fine amour qui en moy maint, f. 57a

my lady, my heart stays with you.
Now I pray God that your heart will love me,
without being shared with any other.
My lady, my heart stays with you,
although I myself must leave you.

When I'd finished this rondelet, I took a little path that led me to an open field, where everyone was finding great pleasure in arms, love, merriment, jousting, and tourneying, and in every other pleasant pastime. I joined the company and imitated according to my small skill what I saw the others were doing, although I couldn't do it properly; but I needed to learn, for he who doesn't learn in his youth regrets it in his old age, if he could have learned: for learning is a most noble endeavor. My heart took pleasure in this, because my lady inspired me to it. I remaïned there a long while in joy and relaxation, until it was time to return to her in whom is my every desire. I returned at once toward her noble and elegant, pretty and fair self; but I arrived at such a time that I believed, as God is my witness, that my heart would break. For I saw her sweet eyes turn from me and cast their brightness elsewhere; I didn't know whether she did this deliberately, but I was certainly about

4112 C: Dame mon cuer etc. 4113 **que li vostres** que vostre cuer E. 4114 **qu'en** qua E. **amour** autre J. 4115–16 C: Dame mon cuer etc. 4117 **ce** cest E; mon J. 4122 **et** *om* C (−1). 4125 **fis a mon** feis mon J. 4126 **je pos** je y pos E. 4128 **Et** Si JPe. **qu'il** qui E. 4129 **ne le f.** je le f. E; ne f. J. 4130 **il** *om* J. 4132 **repent** reprent E. 4133 **qui** quil CE. 4135 **s'i** se J. 4136 **Que** Car J. 4137 **longuettement** longuement E; moult longuement J. 4143 **bel s'i** bel et si C (+1). **telle** celle J. 4145–46 *A small patch in the parchment of* C *obliterates the last words of these lines*: dëust partir; departir. 4148 **leur** le E. **espart** regart J. 4149 **so** say J. 4150 **je** jen J.

Dame, mon cuer en vous remaint.
Or pri Dieu que li vostres m'aint,
Sans ce qu'en nulle autre amour parte.
Dame, mon cuer en vous remaint,
Comment que de vous me departe.

Quant j'eus finé ce rondelet,
Je me mis en un sentelet
Qui me mena en une marche
Ou toute joie maint et marche,
D'armes, d'amours, de festoier,
De jouster, et de tornoier, f. 57b
Et de toute autre bonne vie.
Si me mis en la compaignie
Et fis a mon petit pouoir
Selonc ce que je pos veoir
Que li autre se demenoient,
Et vos faire ce qu'il faisoient,
Comment qu'a droit ne le feïsse;
Mais il failloit que j'aprenisse,
Car qui n'aprent en sa jonnesse,
Il s'en repent en sa viellesse,
S'il est tel qui le sache entendre: f. 57va
Car trop noble chose est d'aprendre.
Pour ce mes cuers s'i deduisoit,
Que ma dame a ce me duisoit.
La demouray longuettement
En joye et en esbatement,
Tant qu'il fu temps de reparier
Vers celle ou sont mi desirier.
Si me mis briefment au retour
Vers son gent et faitis atour
Cointe et bel; s'i vins a telle heure
Que je cuidai, se Dieus m'onneure,
Que li cuers me deüst partir;
Car je vi de moy departir
Ses tres doulz yeus, et autre part
Traire et lancier leur doulz espart;
Et ne so se ce fu a certes,
Mais je fu pres de morir, certes;

to die, for I thought that the appearance and demeanor, the affection, look, and expression that a lover deserves from his lady had changed, and I imagined she did this because someone else pleased her more.

I again became dispirited and fell into such sad, heavy, and bitter dejection that no joy or soothing chrism remained in my heart because of the fear that gripped it. Then I became very melancholy, like one who ponders and is tormented, who weighs possibilities, reflects, and muses whether this were a ruse or true, or whether her heart was trying to wound me in this manner in order to test me. But she did it so very circumspectly and so subtly that I could never distinguish the true from the false.

(34) *How the Lover speaks to his Lady*

So I decided what I would do, and thought I would tell her: "My dear lady, you know how you have captured my heart and myself, how I love you forever, how you can destroy and slay me, if you wish, by taking your sweet look from me. My lady, if you are of a mind to receive the homage of another or to keep me disconsolate by venturing to be untrue to me, or by banishing me, who am in your sweet power, then as God is my witness, my lady, you care so little for me that you

4155 **le** li C. 4156 **qui** que Pe. 4159 **pesme** presme E. 4162 **doulour** doubte J. 4166 **ruse** muse J. 4167 **se** *om* E. 4169 **aviseement** amiablement J. 4171 **le** *om* J. **voir** veoir EJ. 4174 **diroie** disoie J. 4181 **vous** lors E. 4187 **fiez** fier J. 4188 **que vous m'occiés** que ne mocies E; car vous mocier J.

Car de semblant et de maniere,
De cuer, de regart, et de chiere
Qu'amis doit recevoir d'amie,
Me fu vis qu'elle estoit changie,
Et pensai qu'elle le faisoit
Pour autre qui mieus li plaisoit.

Lors renouvella ma pesance,
Et cheï en une doubtance
Si grief, si pesant, et si pesme,
Que de joie ne que de cresme
Dedens mon cuer ne demouroit
Pour la doulour qui l'acoroit.
Lors fu en grant merencolie
Comme cilz qui pense et colie,
Contrepense, estudie, et muse,
S'a certes estoit, ou par ruse,
Ou se ses cuers ainssi plaier
Me vouloit pour moy essaier.
Mes si tres aviseement
Le faisoit et si soutivement,
Que je ne pos onques le voir f. 57vb
De la mensonge concevoir.

Si m'avisai que je feroie,
Et pensai que je li diroie:
"Ma chiere dame, vous savez
Comment moy et mon cuer avez,
Comment je vous aim sans retraire,
Comment vous me poués deffaire
Et mettre a mort, se vous voulés,
Se vos doulz regart me tolés.
Dame, et se vous avez courage
D'autre recevoir en hommage,
Ou de moy tenir en penser,
Qu'envers moy daignissiez fausser,
Ou de moy de vous estrangier
Qui sui en vostre dous dangier,
Pour Dieu, dame, tant vous fiez
De moy, las! que vous m'occïés,

kill me by saying openly that you no longer care for me; for it is much better that I die for you at a single blow than languish forever." In this way I told her without hesitation all my thoughts and feeling. She listened attentively to me and replied at once: "Fair sweet friend, don't be worried by anything I say and do; I do it for the best and in order to conceal our love better, because a lover who does not know how to feign cannot attain great joy, if he does not have the strength to hide well what he doesn't want to reveal; for society is so inconstant, so slanderous, and so perverse and full of such false deceit that today people say and imagine things that were never before conceived. My friend, for this reason I've decided to treat everyone the same, with no special marks of favor, except, at the proper time, for you alone. Your heart will never find anything in me to cause it to fear that my love is not entirely yours, in honor and loyalty, without a trace of disloyalty."

Thus my lady reassured me and swore this most insistently. Although I later had to bear many fears, many harsh assaults and many

4192 **a** *om* J. 4200 **vostre** nostre J. 4201 **scet** soit J. 4202 **a** *om* E. 4203 **N'il** Quil E. 4207 **Et . . . fausse** Et si plains de f. Pe. 4212 **sans** ceulz J. 4214 **Ne** Que E. 4215 **doubte** honte J. 4219–56 *om* J. 4219 **Ma** La C. 4223–24 *reversed in* E.

En moy disant sans couverture
Que vous n'avés mes de moy cure;
Car il me vaut trop mieus morir
Pour vous a un cop que languir."

Si que tout ainssi, sans attente,
Li dis tout mon cuer et m'entente.
Si m'escouta diliganment
Et me respondi erranment:
"Biaus douls amis, soiés en pes
De tout ce que je dis et fais,
Car je le fais pour le milleur
Et pour mieus celer vostre amour;
Car qui en amour ne scet faindre,
Il ne puet a grant joye ataindre,
N'il n'a pouoir de bien celer
Ce qu'il ne vorroit reveler;
Car li mondes est si divers,
Si mesdisans, et si pervers
Et plains de si fausse contrueve,
Qu'au jour d'ui on dit et contrueve
Ce qui onques ne fu pensé. f. 58a
Amis, et pour ce ay je pensé
De faire un semblant general
A tous, sans riens d'espicial,
Fors a vous seul, quant point sera.
Ne ja vos cuers ne trouvera
En moy, dont doiés avoir doubte
Que m'amour ne soit vostre toute,
En honnour et en loyauté,
Sans nul raim de desloyauté."

(Miniature 34) *Comment l'Amant parle a sa dame*

Ma dame ainssi m'asseüra
Et de ce moult fort me jura.
Comment que puis mainte paour,
Maint dur assaut, et maint estour,
Mainte dolour, mainte morsure,

attacks, many sorrows, many biting torments and many sudden pangs, many sorrowful sighs, much anguish, and much deep melancholy, nonetheless I was determined in every respect to believe firmly that she was speaking the truth. For he who distrusts his lady quarrels and fights with himself, and cannot rightfully be happy because he cannot rejoice in joy.

And besides, pure Loyalty, Goodness, Reason, Wisdom and Righteousness, Sincerity, Honor and Gentility, Shame, Truth and Nobility, in company with all the good virtues that adorn her fair person and accompany, guard, nourish, and instruct her constantly, would never deign permit her to be false in any way. Moreover, he who loves blamelessly must believe his lady in every instance, as he himself wishes to be believed. So therefore I believed her and felt that in friendship she told me the unadulterated truth, that I was in her good graces. Now may God grant that I never do anything that might cause me to lose her, that I may find her my beloved and lady, as I am her lover, devoted and given to her, inseparable in death and in life: for he who loves well is slow to forget.

At the end of this treatise that I've compiled and composed, I want to place my first and last names, without omitting a syllable or letter; and he who wishes to know them

4225 **grief** dur E. 4227 **M'en ait** Maint ai Pe. 4229 **a fermement** afferment C. 4236 **et** ou CPe. 4237 **et** *om* E. 4240 **gens** *om* E. 4241 **l'acompaignent** le compaignent E. 4244 **Qu'en . . . laissassent** Que rien lui l. E. 4247 **c'on** com C. 4249 **m'iert** mest EPe. **qu'en** en Pe. 4251 **bonne** pure E. 4253 **quoy** quo Pe. 4254 **truisse** tenisse E. 4258 i *of* aimme *added above the line in* C. 4262 **sillabe oublier** silabe doubler E; oblier sillabe Pe.

Et mainte soudaine pointure,
Maint grief souspir, mainte haschie,
Et mainte grant merencolie
M'en ait couvenu soustenir;
Nonpourquant je me vos tenir
De tous poins a fermement croirre
Qu'elle disoit parole voire.
Car cilz qui encontre lui pense f. 58b
A par li se riote et tence,
N'a droit ne se puet resjoïr,
Qu'il ne puet de joie joïr.

Et d'autre part, Loyauté pure,
Bonté, Raisons, Scens, et Droiture,
Franchise, Honnour, et Gentillesce,
Honte, Verité, et Noblesce,
Avec toutes bonnes vertus
Dont ses gens corps est revestus,
Qui a toute heure l'acompaignent,
Gardent, norrissent, et ensaignent,
Ne se daignassent assentir
Qu'en riens la laissassent mentir.
Et aussi qui aimme sans blasme
En tous cas doit croire sa dame,
Ainssi comme il vueut c'on le croie.
Si que pour ce je la creoie,
Et qu'il m'iert vis qu'en amistié
Me disoit pure verité,
Que j'estoie en sa bonne grace.
Or doint Dieus que jamais ne face
Chose de quoy perdre la puisse,
Et qu'amie et dame la truisse,
Ainssi com je li sui amis,
Qui a li sui donnés et mis,
Sans partir en, n'a mort, n'a vie:
Car qui bien aimme, a tart oublie.
Mais en la fin de ce traitié
Que j'ay compilé et traitié
Vueil mon non et mon seurnon mettre,
Sans sillabe oublïer ne lettre;
Et cilz qui savoir le vourra

can easily discover them; for the fourth line from the end is the beginning, middle, and end of my name, which is there in its entirety, not lacking a quarter or third. But not a single letter of this fourth line need be changed or omitted, for if one were to change anything he would never find my name, for there would be too many or too few letters.

And because I am in the hands of faithful Love whom I so love, I pay him homage and say thus:

"Good Love, I pay you homage with hands, mouth, and heart, as your dutiful, true, loyal, discreet, and constant liege, and I place my heart, body, soul, strength, desire, thought, happiness, and honor completely in you along with my life, as one who wishes to live and die in your service, forever. And it is certainly proper that I do so, since you give me such hope that I constantly hope for better, and that my dear sweet lady will see with good heart and happy countenance this dit that I have rhymed, even though I rhyme rather poorly. And this Hope within me, that my dear lady loves me, so sweetly cheers my heart that its sorrow is changed to great joy and comfort, when you tell me that my dit will be welcomed by her. Now may God grant that she accept it gladly, and that I never err in serving her."

4266 **et** ne E. 4270 **lettre n'oster** lettre noter C; mettre noster J. 4280 **Fins** Suis E. 4282 **plaisance h.** plaisance et h. Pe. 4284 **vueut** vueil Pe. 4287 **espoir** pouair J. 4288 *om* J. 4290 **a** en EJ. 4292 **nicement** sotement J. 4293 *repeated in* E *at top of next folio*. 4294 **Qu'encor** Quencore E; Quant tout J. 4296 **santé** se ten C; secre EPe. 4299 **qu'en** que Pe. 4300 **qu'en** que J.

Explicit Amen. Ci fenist remede de fortune C; Explicit E; Explicit Remede de fortune J; Amen Pe.

De legier savoir le porra;
Car le quart ver, si com je fin,
Commencement, moyen, et fin
Est de mon non, qui tous entiers
Y est, sans faillir quart ne tiers.
Mais il ne couvient adjouster f. 58va
En ce quart ver lettre, n'oster,
Car qui riens y adjousteroit,
Mon non jamais n'i trouveroit,
Qu'il n'i eüst ou plus ou mains.
Et pour ce que je suy es mains
De loyal Amour que j'aim si,
Li fais hommage et di ainssi:
"Bonne Amour, je te fais hommage
De mains, de bouche, de courage,
Con tes liges sers redevables,
Fins, loyaus, secrés, et estables,

Et met cuer, corps, ame, et vigour,
Desir, penser, plaisance, honnour
Du tout en toy avec mon vivre,
Com cilz qui voeut morir et vivre
En ton service, sans retraire.
Et certes, je le doy bien faire,
Quant tu me donnes tel espoir
Qu'adés mieus recevoir espoir,
Et que ma douce dame chiere
De bon cuer et a lie chiere
Verra ce dit qu'ay mis a rime,
Comment qu'assez nicement rime.
Et cil espoir qui en moy maint
Qu'encor ma chiere dame m'aint,
Mon cuer si doucement resjoie
Qu'en grant santé et en grant joie
Li change mal, u tu me dis
Que pris en gré sera mes dis.
Or doint Dieus qu'en bon gré le prengne,
Et qu'en li servant ne mesprengne."

Amen
Ci fenist Remede de Fortune.

APPENDICES

APPENDIX I: MUSICAL WORKS IN *REMEDE DE FORTUNE*

INTRODUCTION

From a musical point of view, Guillaume de Machaut is today regarded as the most important composer active in the fourteenth century. In terms of the number of works extant, he is one of the most prolific as well, since his compositions total nearly 150 works. We owe the survival of this rich mine of music to a singular circumstance: almost alone among medieval composers, Machaut took great interest in the preservation of his oeuvre in manuscript. The great majority of his compositions are thus known to us not from the so-called repertory manuscripts containing the music of many composers, but from seven manuscript collections devoted entirely to his works, manuscripts which include most of his music as well as his poetry.

Though he composed a justly famous Mass and some twenty-three motets, the emphasis in Machaut's music is overwhelmingly on the secular song, which seems to have been the main focus of his composition throughout his musical career. His skill as a poet no doubt directed his musical interest particularly towards the genres of lai, virelai, rondeau, and ballade, with an increasing emphasis on the latter two types. All four genres (including two kinds of ballade) are found among the seven musical works in *Remede de Fortune*, as are the complainte and the chant royal, two singular genres to which Machaut never returned musically.

Remede de Fortune, as has been discussed in the Introduction, is a relatively early work, dating from the 1340s. The function of the musical numbers in the poem is twofold: both to instruct and to entertain. The entertainment aspect is self-evident; the narrative calls for songs, and Machaut supplies them. The didactic aspect stems from two factors. First, the poet/composer includes all the types of lyric vernacular song found in fourteenth-century France, in narrative contexts that illuminate their social function and milieu. Second, as several scholars have pointed out, the seven pieces proceed from the most complex poetic form, the lai, to the simplest, the rondeau. This is true despite the fact that it is the two ballades and the rondeau that are set in melismatic polyphony, which adds a purely musical sort of complexity.

The first published transcription of all seven musical works in *Remede de Fortune* was done by Friedrich Ludwig and included as an appendix to Ernest Hoepffner's 1911 edition of the poem.[1] Ludwig later published a complete edition of Machaut's musical works, using the manuscript Vg as his primary source.[2] By the time Leo Schrade brought out a second complete edition of the music in 1956 as part of the series *Polyphonic Music of the Fourteenth Century*,[3] the manuscript Vg was unavailable to him for comparison, and he based his transcriptions on manuscript A, a slightly later and more complete source.

Recently François Avril's more precise dating of several of the principal Machaut manuscripts has established that manuscript C, long acknowledged to contain the earliest state of the repertory, is the earliest manuscript as well, produced in the early 1350s rather than the fifteenth century.[4] In terms of the *Remede de Fortune*, both Vg and A (from the 1370s) represent a later tradition than C, which serves as the principal source for this edition. These differences can be seen in various small rhythmic and melodic variants which read one way in the early tradition and a slightly different way in the later manuscripts.[5]

Besides manuscript C, the other representatives of the earliest musical tradition of the *Remede* are manuscripts E, K, and Pe. Though Pe (from the early fifteenth century) is the latest of the four sources, its musical readings are the closest to those of C. The most singular divergence from the early tradition in Pe is the choice of a different (and undoubtedly later) rondeau for the final musical number in the poem, a choice found in no other source of the *Remede*. Manuscript K (dated 1371), whose copy of the *Remede* is incomplete, contains music only for the two ballades, though it was evidently intended to have more. The text scribe of K left what he considered to be the necessary amount of space for the musical numbers at their proper places in the poem, but in most cases the music was never entered. In K's copy of the baladelle (no. 4), the musical scribe was sufficiently uncertain of his material and its layout that he omitted the top voice of the composition, even though space was allowed for it by the text scribe.

The misleadingly neat appearance of manuscript E (ca. 1390) belies the fact that it is the one most likely to differ from the other three sources, both through outright error and through a certain amount of "contamination" from the later tradition. The most striking musical variant in the *Remede* among C, E, K, and Pe is indicative of such contamination in E. The ballade *Dame, de qui toute* (no. 5) has only two parts in C, K, and Pe, but four in E and all manuscripts of the later tradition, suggesting that Machaut eventually came to find a fuller polyphonic texture more satisfying.

The *Remede de Fortune* rightfully occupies a valuable position in Machaut's musical oeuvre not only because of its excellent examples of his lyric art but also because of its picture of the function of music in the courtly society of fourteenth-century France. As a skilled and talented participant in that society, Machaut offers us a perspective of unique value.[6]

Notes to Appendix I

1. *Oeuvres de Guillaume de Machaut*, ed. Ernest Hoepffner, Société des Anciens Textes Français, vol. 2 (Paris: Firmin-Didot, 1911).
2. *Guillaume de Machaut, Musikalische Werke*, vols. 1–3 edited by Friedrich Ludwig; vol. 4 edited by Heinrich Besseler (1926–1943; reprint, Leipzig: Breitkopf und Härtel, 1954).
3. *Polyphonic Music of the Fourteenth Century*, ed. Leo Schrade, vols. 2 and 3, *The Works of Guillaume de Machaut* (Monaco: Editions de L'Oiseau-Lyre, 1956).
4. François Avril, "Les Manuscrits enluminés de Guillaume de Machaut," in *Guillaume de Machaut*, Colloque–Table Ronde organisé par l'Université de Reims, Actes et Colloques, no. 23 (Paris: Klincksieck, 1982), 117–34.
5. Such variants may be seen by comparing the transcriptions published here with those published by Ludwig and Schrade, since their editions follow later sources.
6. Two handy sources of additional information about Machaut the musician and his compositions are Richard Hoppin's *Medieval Music* (New York: Norton, 1978), pp. 396–432, and Gilbert Reaney's article on Machaut in *The New Grove Dictionary of Music and Musicians*, ed. Stanley Sadie, 20 vols. (London: Macmillan, 1980), 11: 428–36.

fol. 26-28
LAI
ll. 431-680
1a. Qui n'a- roit au- tre de- port En a- mer
b. En- cor y a maint res- sort: Re- mem- brer,
Fors Doulz Pen- ser Et Sou- ve- nir A- veuc
Y- ma- gi- ner, En dous plai- sir Sa da-
l'Es- poir de jo- ïr, S'a- roit il tort
me ve- oir, o- ÿr, Son gen- til port,
Se le port D'au- tre con- fort Vo- loit rou- ver,
Le re- cort Dou bien qui sort De son par- ler
Quar pour un cuer sa- ou- ler Et sous- te-
Et de son douls re- gar- der, Dont l'en- trou-
nir, Plus que- rir Ne doit me- rir Qui ai- me fort.
vrir Puet ga- rir Et ga- ran- tir A- mant de mort.
2a. Et qui vour- roit plus sou- hai- dier
Quar qui plus quiert, il veult tri- chier,
2b. Car on ne les puet es- pri- sier,
Un cuer na- vré sain et le- gier,
Je n'os cui- dier Si fol cui- dier Que cilz ai-
S'a- mours tant chier L'a que fi- chier Dei- gne par
Ne trop pri- sier, Quant de le- gier Pus- ent de
Sans nul dan- gier, Et es- lon- gier De mal, et
me de cuer en- tier Qui de tiels biens n'a
l'oel de son ar- chier En son cuer d'eaus la
tous maulz a- le- gier, Et fai- re par leur
de joie a- prou- chier, Seu- le- ment de leur

souf- fis- san- che;
co- gnois- san- che.
grant pois- san- che
re- mem- bran- che.
3a. Et pour ce en- gen- dre- e S'est Dou-
De la de- si- re- e. Dont ma
3b. S'en ert hon- nou- re- e. Ser- vi-
Car si li a- gre- e, J'a- rai
che Pen- se- e En mon cuer et
joie est ne- e Et l'es- pe- ran-
e, lo- e- e. Crainte, o- be- ïe,
des- ti- ne- e Bonne, ou mort des-
en- fre- me- e. Qu'a- dez me sou- vient
ce dou- ble- e Qui de li me vient.
et a- me- e. Fai- re le cou- vient;
es- pe- re- e; Dou tout a li tient.
4a. Mais quant je voy Le tres bel ar- roy Simple et quoy,
Et que je l'oy Par- ler sans ef- froy, Par ma foy
4b. Fai- re le doy, Se je l'aim et croy; Car en moy
Re- maint en soy, Dont tel bien re- choy Que puis n'oy
Sans des- roy, De son corps, le gay,
Si m'es- joy Que tou- te joye ay.
Joye en croy, Pour ce mon cuer vray
Grief a- noy Que je l'en- a- may.

5a. Et se par De- sir re- cueil
Le grief qui de De- sir ist;
5b. Pour sa beau- té sans or- gueil
Si qu'en plai- san- ce nor- rist
Au- cun grief, pas ne m'en dueill, Quar son tres dous
Si me plaist et a- be- list Tant qu'au por-ter
Qui tou- tes passe, a mon vueul, Et pour son tres
Mon cuer et tant m'en- ri- chist Qu'eins-si vi- vre
ri- ant oeil Tout a- dou- chist
me de- lit, Plus que ne sueil,
Bel Ac- cueil Qui tous- dis rit;
me sous- fist, Ne plus ne vueul;
6a. Fors tant, qu'en au- cu- ne ma- nie- re Ma da- me chie- re,
Non pas d'a- mours vaine et le- gie- re, Mais si en- tie- re,
6b. Car ne sui tiels qu'a moy af- fie- re Que s'a- mour quie- re,
Pour ce n'en fai sem- blant ne chie- re, Que je n'ac- quie- re
Qui de mon cuer la tre- so- rie- re Est et por- tie- re,
Que mieulx a- me- roie estre en bie- re Qu'a par- chon- nie- re
Ne que de son vueul tant en- quie- re Que li re- quie- re;
Re- fus qui me de- boute ou fie- re De li ar- rie- re;
Sce- üst qu'elle est m'a- mour pre- mie- re Et der- re- nie- re.
Fust, n'en moy pen- se- e dou- blie- re, Tels tous- dis ie- re
Car moult pour- roit com- pa- rer chie- re Tel- le pri- e- re
Car se sa dou- cheurs m'es- toit fie- re, A- mours mur- trie- re

Et plus l'aim que moy ne mon bien,
Com- ment qu'el- le non sa-che rien;
Mes cuers qui gist en son ly- en.
Se- roit de moy, ce sai je bien.
7a. Si n'est voi-e Qui m'a- voi-e Com- ment des- cou-
Je mour- roi-e Se j'a- voi-e Re- fus, Et se
7b. Fouls se- roi-e Se rou- voi-e Riens plus, fors qu'en
Qu'au- tre joy-e Ne de- vroi-e Vo- loir, se as-sés
vrir li doi-e Par nul tour, Quar sans re- tour
je vi- voi-e Ma bau- dour Se-
li em- ploi-e Corps, hon- neur, Cuer, et a- mour,
re- mi- roi-e Sa dou- çour Et
roit tris- tour.
Sa va- lour.
f27v
8a. Dont la bonne et bel-le, Com-ment sa-ra
Une a-mour nou- vel- le, Qui me re-nou-
8b. De quoy l'es-tan- cel- le Fait sous la ma-
Que hons ne da- moy- sel- le Da-me ne pu-
el- le Que de li ve- oir En mon cuer s'os-tel-le
vel- le Et me fait a- voir Joi-eu-se nou- vel-le,
mel- le Mon fin cuer ar-doir? S'en frit et sau-tel-le,
cel- le, Ne le puet sa-voir, Si le port et cel-le.
9a. A- mours que j'en pri, Qui voult et souf- fri Qu'a
Que pour s'a-mour fri Sans plainte et sans cri, Et
9b. Et qu'au-tre ne tri; Ain-çoys a l'ot- tri Qu'onc
Mais s'en mon de- pri Met A- mours es- tri, Je

li, sans de- tri Quant pre-miers la vi, m'of- fri,
qu'a li m'ot- tri, Comme au plus tres no- ble tri
ne des-cou- vri, Dont maint sous-pir ay mur- dri
n'en bray ne cri, N'au-tre-ment ne m'en def- fri,
Li por- ra bien di- re
Que pe- üsse es- li- re,
Qui puis n'o- rent mi- re.
Ne pense a de- fri- re.
10a. Car en- se- ment Vueil li- e- ment, Jo- li- e- ment, Et
Si fran- che-ment, Que vrai- e- ment Se j'ai tour- ment, A-
10b. Ce- le- e- ment Et sa- ge- ment, Pa- ci- en- ment, Et
Car bon- ne- ment Et dou- ce- ment, Pro-chai- ne- ment, S'Es-
gai- e- ment, En ma dame a- mer loy- au- ment U-
lie- ge- ment N'en vuel, fors souf- frir hum- ble- ment Ma
net- te- ment Ert et tres a- mou- reu- se- ment De-
poirs ne ment, M'ert ma pai- ne tres hau- te- ment A
ser tou- te ma vi- e
dou- ce ma- la- di- e.
dens mon cuer nor- ri- e;
cent dou- bles me- ri- e.
11a. Car com- ment que De- sirs m'as- sail- le Et me fa-
Qui sou- vent d'es- toc et de tail- le Ce- le- e-
11b. Qui paist d'a- mou- reu- se vi- tail- le Mon cuer, et
Qu'au- tre n'est de quoy il me chail- le, Et des biens

f28
che main- te ba- tail-le Et poin-gne de l'a-mou-reus
ment mon cuer de- tail-le,
de-dens li en- tail-le Sa beau-té fi- ne par tel
a-mou- reus me bail-le
dart,
Cer-tes bien en vain si tra-vail-le, Quar tout ga-rist son
art
Tant qu'il n'est joy-e qui me fail-le Que n'ai-e de li,
12a. Et pour ce, sans nul des- cort,
Dous Re- gart 12b. Il me fait par son en- nort
que Dieus gart.
En-du-rer Vueul et ce-ler L'ar- dant de- sir
Hon-nou-rer, Ser-vir, ce-ler, Et o- be- ïr
Qui vueut ma joye a-men- rir Par sou-til sort;
Ma dame, et li tant che- rir Qu'en son ef- fort
Si le port Sans des-con-fort Et vueul por- ter. Quar s'il
Me de-port. Quant il me mort Et veult gre- ver, Mais qu'a

fait mon cuer trem- bler, Taindre et pa- lir, Et fre-mir,
li vueul- le pen- ser Qu'aim et de- sir Sans par-tir,
A bien sous-frir Du tout m'a- cort.
Ne re-pen- tir; La me con- fort.

fol. 30
COMPLAINTE
ll. 905-1480
1. Tieus rit au main qui au soir pleu- re,
Et tieus cui- de que Joie ac- queu- re
Et tieus cui- de qu'A- mours la- beu- re
Pour li ai- dier, qu'el- le de- meu- re.
Pour son bien, qu'el- le li court seu- re Et mal l'a-
Car For- tu- ne tout de- veu- re,
tour- ne; Quant el- le tour- ne.
Qui n'a- tent mi- e qu'il a- jour- ne
Met ce- lui qui gist mas en l'our- ne;
Pour tour- ners, qu'el- le ne se- jour- ne,
Le seur- mon- té au bas re- tor- ne.
Ains tour- ne, re- tour- ne, et bes- tor- ne, Tant qu'au des-
Et le plus joi- eus mat et mor- ne
seu- re Fait en po d'eu- re.
(36 strophes)

fol. 39
CHANT ROYAL
ll. 1985–2032
I. Joy-e, plai- sance, et dou- ce nour-re- tu- re,
Et plus-seurs sont qui n'i ont fors poin- tu- re,
Vi- e d'on- neur pren-nent maint en a- mer;
Dou- lour, ar- dour, plour, tris- tesse, et a- mer.
Ce di-ent; mais a-cor- der
Ne me puis, qu'en la sous-fran- ce
D'A- mours ait nul-le gre-van- ce,
Car tout ce qui vient de li Plaist a cuer d'a- mi.
[Envoy] A- mours, je sçay sans doub-tan- ce
Qu'a cent dou-bles as me- ri Ceuls qui t'ont ser- vi.
(5 strophes and envoy)

fol. 46
BALADELLE
ll. 2857–2892
[Triplum]
[Cantus]
Tenor
[Contra-tenor]
En a- mer a dou- ce vi- e
Car tant plaist la ma- la- di- e,
Et jo- li- e, Qui bien la sent main- - - te- - - - - - nir,
Quant nor- ri- e Est en a- mou- - - - reus de- - - - - - - sir,
Que c'est

20
l'a- - - ment fait es-bau- - dir Et que-rir
doulx mauls a sous-te- - nir, Qu'es-jo-ir
25
Com- - - ment el-le mou-te- - - pli- -
Fait cuer d'a-mi et d'a- - mi- -
1
30
2
e.
e.

2.

Qu'Amours par sa signourie
Humelie
L'amoureus cuer a souffrir,

Et par sa noble maistrie
Le mestrie,
Si qu'il ne puet riens sentir,

Que tout au goust de joïr
Par plaisir
Ne prengne, je n'en doubt mie.

Ainssi saouls de merir,
Sans merir,
Fait cuer d'ami et d'amie.

3.

Si doit bien estre cherie
Et servie,
Quant elle puet assevir

Chascun qui li rueve ou prie
De s'aïe,
Sans son tresor amenrir.

De la mort puet garantir
Et garir
Cuer qui de santé mendie;

De souffissance enrichir
Et franchir
Fait cuer d'ami et d'amie.

fol. 47v-48
BALLADE
ll. 3013-3036
[Cantus]
Tenor
Da- me,
N'as- sés
de qui toute ma joy-e vient,
lo- er, si com il a-par- tient,
Je ne
Ser- vir,
Vous doub- puis
ter,
trop a-mer, ne che- rir,
hon-nou-rer,
n'o- be- ir;
Car le gra-ci- eus Es- poir, Dou-ce da- me, que

2\.

Cilz douls Espoirs en vie me soustient
Et me norrist en amoureus desir,
Et dedens moy met tout ce qui couvient
Pour conforter mon cuer et resjoïr;
N'il ne s'en part main ne soir,
Ainçoys me fait doucement recevoir
Plus des douls biens qu'Amours as siens envoie
Qu'en cent mil ans deservir ne porroie.

3\.

Et quant Espoir qui en mon cuer se tient
Fait dedens moy si grant joie venir,
Lointains de vous, ma dame, s'il avient
Que vo beauté voie que moult desir,
Ma joye, si com j'espoir,
Ymaginer, penser, ne concevoir
Ne porroit nuls, car trop plus en aroie,
Qu'en cent mil ans deservir ne porroie.

fol. 51-51v CHANSON BALLADEE ll.3451-3496

1, 5. Dame, a vous sans re-tol-lir Doins cuer, pen-se-e, de-sir, Corps,
4. Vos-tre beau-té fait ta-rir Toute autre et a-ni-en-tir, Et

et a-mour, Comme a tou-te la mil-lour Qu'on puist choy-sir, Ne qui vi-vre
vo dou-çour Pas-se tout; rose en cou-lour Vous doy te-nir, Et vos re-gars

ne ma-rir Puist a ce jour. 2. Si ne me doit a fo-lour Tour-ner, se je
puet ga-rir Tou-te dou-lour. 3. Bon-té pas-sez en va-lour, Tou-te fleur en

vous a-our, Car sans men-tir,
douce ou-dour Que on puist sen-tir.

2.

2. Pour ce, dame, je m'atour
De trestoute ma vigour
A vous servir,
3. Et met, sans nul vilain tour,
Mon cuer, ma vie et m'onnour
En vo plaisir.
4. Et se Pitiés consentir
Vueut que me daigniez oïr
En ma clamour,
Je ne quier de mon labour
Autre merir,
Qu'il ne me porroit venir
Joye greigneur.
5. Dame, a vous, etc.

3.

2. Dame, ou sont tuit mi retour,
Souvent m'estuet en destour
Plaindre et gemir,
3. Et, present vous, descoulour,
Quant vous ne savez l'ardour
Qu'ai a sousfrir
4. Pour vous qu'aim tant et desir,
Que plus ne le puis couvrir.
Et se tenrour
N'en avez, en grant tristour
M'estuet fenir.
Nonpourquant dusqu'a mourir
Vostre demour.
5. Dame, a vous, etc.

fol. 57
RONDELET
ll. 4109 - 4116
[Triplum]
[Cantus]
1.4.7. Da-
3. Par
5. Or
Tenor
ms, mon
fine a-
pri Dieu
cuer
mour
que
En
qui
li
Vous
En
vas-

20
re-
moy
tres
25
maint,
maint,
m'aint,
2. 3Com-
6.Sans
30
ment
ce
que de
qu'en nulle

35
Vous
me de-
par-
autre
a-mour
par-
40
te.
te.

NOTES TO THE TRANSCRIPTIONS

The primary source for the musical transcriptions is manuscript C; manuscripts E, K, and Pe have been drawn upon when the reading of C appears to be in error. Accidentals written on the staff are according to those in C; mention is made only when the other manuscripts differ from C or when clarification is needed. The editorial suggestions placed above the staff include most of the accidentals that appear in the other three sources, as the notes below indicate. Natural signs in the manuscripts are written as either sharps or flats: b sharp for b natural, c flat for c natural, etc., but have been converted to modern usage in the transcriptions. In C, the only voice part to be labeled is the tenor; K labels none of the parts, while E and Pe label everything but the cantus.

Abbreviations in the notes for each piece include L for long, B for breve, SB for semibreve, M for minim, li for ligature, and m. for measure. Mention of pitches is in lowercase letters, is not octave-specific, and is usually without accidentals. The designation aSB gSB fB indicates three single notes, while agSBfB indicates a three-note ligature. A clear-cut error in a given source is labeled as such, particularly when the note values do not add up correctly, but alternative pitch readings are sometimes listed merely as variants.

In performance, these works are meant for soloists, with the cantus being the only vocal part. When there is more than one instrumental voice, instruments of contrasting timbres should be used so that each part will be a distinctive line in the polyphony.

1. Lai **Qui n'aroit autre deport** *a1*

SOURCES

C, f. 26; E, f. 23; Pe, f. 4.

OBSERVATIONS

Typical of its genre, the lai has twelve stanzas, each divided musically into repeated halves. Stanzas two through eleven, in fact, divide each half stanza in half, so that the same music is heard four times instead of two. Stanza twelve repeats the music of stanza one but transposes it up a fifth. Except for a plica in m. 164, the music moves entirely at the retrospective level of longs, breves, and semibreves, making no use of minims. This requires a transcription level in which the long rather than the breve equals the measure. The lai has the widest pitch range of any piece in the *Remede*; it is one note short of covering two octaves.

ACCIDENTALS

1–52	C, E, and Pe have a b♭ signature in stanzas one and two.
13	Pe lacks f♯.
17	Pe writes in b♭ again.
20	C has c♯ and c♭ (for natural); E, Pe have c♯ only.
34, 36	E, Pe have f♯.
38	E writes in b♭ again.
43	E, Pe lack f♯.
46	Pe has f♯ here and not in 47; E has neither.
57	E has b♭ (beginning of a line).
84	Pe has f♯.
87	E lacks c♯.
94	E lacks b♮.
97	E, Pe have b♮.
99–100	Pe writes f♯ here rather than in 101.
101, 109	E lacks f♯.
110	E, Pe lack b♮.
111	Pe has c♯.
125	E, Pe lack f♯.
127	Pe has c♯.
145	Pe has g♯.
146	E has b♭.
148	E, Pe lack f♯.
149	E has b♭.
152	E lacks f♯.
155	E has b♭ but lacks f♯; Pe has a♯ after 1st li (error for f♯?).
156	E has f♯.
161	E lacks c♯.
166	E has f♯.
170	E, Pe lack c♯.
174	Pe lacks f♯; E lacks f♯ in line 10b.
178	E has f♯.
203	E lacks c♯.
210	E, Pe lack c♯ but write it in 211.
217	Pe has g♯ (error for f♯?).
221	E has f♯ sign between the f and gB.

VARIANTS

3	In Pe the last li is afSB instead of gfSB.
16	In Pe the imperfect L rest is missing (error).
19	In Pe the first dB has a descending plica.
37	In E the gL is written as gB with imperfect L rest.
44	In E the fL has no plica.

45 In line 2b in E, the 3 SB are separate instead of 1 + 2 li.

46 On the second beat in E, gfSB is written as gfB (error); this is followed by gB instead of the gSB eSB in C.

47 In E both notes are written a third too high (error).

49–50 In line 2b in E, the last two notes of 49 and the note in 50 are written as 3 li.

51 C intends 49 to be repeated unchanged for the second ending, writing out only the gL in 52, but E and Pe both make the distinction written out in brackets as 51.

51–52 In E the last three notes are written as 3 li.

55 In Pe the second li is feSB instead of fdSB.

56 In Pe the cB has a descending plica.

58 In Pe the aL has a descending plica.

59 In line 3a in E, the four notes are 2 + 2 li instead of 4 li.

62 In E both notes are written a third too high (error).

64 In E note values are reversed to read dL eB.

66 In line 3b in E, the first note is dB instead of cB.

67 E has eB with imperfect L rest instead of eL.

68 C omits the cL of the second ending (error).

74 In E and Pe, the gL is written as gB with imperfect L rest.

79 In E line 3a has eB with imperfect L rest.

87 In C, because of a clef change before cL, the sharp is written between cL and cB rather than before cL.

91 In Pe the dB has a descending plica.

94 In E the first beat is aB instead of baSB.

99 In Pe the aB has a descending plica.

102 Line 6a in E has a perfect gL followed by gB and an imperfect L rest, taking two mm. instead of one (error).

105 In E the last li is edSB instead of fdSB; in Pe the eB has a descending plica.

113 In Pe the cB has a descending plica.

115 In Pe the gL has a descending plica.

116 In Pe the gL has an ascending plica.

118 In line 6a in E, the last li is caSB instead of baSB; in line 6b it is agSB.

124 In C the breve rest is missing (error); in Pe the second dB has a descending plica.

133 This m. is missing in C, which has only the dL of 134.

136 In Pe the second dB has a descending plica.

143 In Pe the second d is an imperfect L, not a B.

146 In E the aL is perfect, with no SB rest; the bSB begins 147.

147 In E the first beat is bSB aSB instead of aB.

151 In Pe the second dB has an ascending plica.

152 In E after the first aB comes agSB gfSB instead of gB fB.

153 In line 9a in E, the first beat is efSB instead of feSB.

160 In Pe the bL has a descending plica.

161 In C the c♯ is written as a L instead of a B (error) and is followed by what appears to be a breve rest (error); it is at the end of a line, however, and may have been intended as a custos for the dB beginning the next line. If so, it may be the source for the erroneous breve rest in later copies. In E and Pe, the cB is clearly followed by a breve rest (error). On the third beat dB, Pe has a descending plica; E has deSB.

162 In Pe the second 2 li is fdSB instead of edSB.

164 Instead of the plicated aB, E has agSB.

165 In E, the last note is aB instead of bB.

169 In Pe the eL has a descending plica.

171 In E the first note is bB with B rest; in Pe the bL and aB both have a descending plica.

172 In Pe the dL has a descending plica.

173 In E the first two beats are efSBeB.

176 In E the last note of the 3 li is written as a L (error); in Pe this m. is not copied again for the second ending.

188 In Pe the cL has a descending plica.

190 In C after the first ending comes a dL with finis punctorum, as though it were the second ending (error). In Pe the eL has a descending plica.

191 In E the first note is gB instead of eB.

195 In Pe the cL has a descending plica.

201 E and Pe have dL with B rest instead of dB with imperfect L rest.

204 In Pe the eB has a descending plica.

205 In Pe the second 2 li is fdSB instead of edSB.

211 C has an erroneous dot separating the cL and dB.

217–18 In Pe the second 2 li and eB are a step higher, written agSB fB.

219 In Pe the dL has a descending plica.

223 In E the first note gB is written twice, once as the last note on f. 24r and again as the first note on 24v. In Pe the gB has a descending plica.

224 In Pe the cB is written as cL with imperfect L rest (error).

2. *Complainte* Tieus rit au main *a1*

SOURCES

C, f. 30; E, f. 25; Pe, f. 8.

OBSERVATIONS

This work, like the lai, requires an older-style level of transcription in which the breve equals a quarter note rather than a half note. The overall form of the music is the same as that of the baladelle, *a a b b*. Besides its thirty-five repetitions, the musical stanza of the complainte manifests a certain rhythmic repetitiveness through its frequent use of four patterns. Each line of the poetic stanza begins with a measure composed of three breves; this pattern occupies ten out of forty measures. And each line except those in mm. 11–14 and 31–34 ends with a two-measure pattern of a perfect long followed by a breve and an imperfect long rest; this pattern occupies sixteen of the remaining thirty measures. Another frequent pattern is a measure of long plus breve (mm. 12, 14, 22, 27, and 34), and the rhythmic pattern of m. 3 reappears in mm. 13, 28, and 33. These four most frequent rhythmic figures are united at the end of the *a* and *b* sections in a pitch repetition that forms a five-measure musical rhyme. The repetitiveness of the musical material mirrors the reiteration of theme in the poetry.

ACCIDENTALS

1 In C, the b♭ signature disappears at m. 31 (beginning of a line); in E, it is not repeated at the beginning of the second line, m. 12. Pe has a b♭ signature throughout.

15 Since this m. matches 35, the f should be sharped.

18 E, Pe lack f♯.

21 In E the *b* section begins with a b♭ signature.

28 In E the ♭ sign is written in the higher octave with the note b.

33 Though C has no flat here, this m. duplicates 13, which does flat the b; both E and Pe write in a b♭ in 33.

35 E, Pe lack f♯.

38 Since this m. matches 18, the f should be sharped.

VARIANTS

In Pe, several longs and breves have descending plicas.

2–3 In E, instead of 2 li + 1, the bcSB dB are a 3 li that reads 3 B (error).

8 E conflates two different readings, the one found in C and Pe and the version fB edSB cbSB from other manuscripts, to produce a reading with an erroneous extra breve: fB fB edSB cbSB.

13 In E, the cbSB is written as cbB (error).

14 In E, an erroneous dot appears between aL and gB.

28 In E, the last two notes are written gfSB instead of agSB.

35 In E, the first note is aB instead of gB (error).

3. *Chant royal* Joye, plaisance *a1*

SOURCES

C, f. 39; E, f. 28v; Pe, f. 17.

OBSERVATIONS

Like the lai and the complainte, the chant royal requires a retrospective level of transcription for fourteenth-century works, one in which the long rather than the breve equals the measure. A particularly old-fashioned feature is the absence of any minims; the note values are confined to longs, breves, and semibreves. Though the musical stanza form of the chant royal resembles that of the fourteenth-century ballade, *a a b*, this work is actually closer to many thirteenth-century trouvère songs, since it has five stanzas plus an envoy. It also lacks the textual refrain line characteristic of the three-stanza ballade.

ACCIDENTALS

1	E has a b♭ signature for the whole piece but also adds a b♭ at 21.
10	C and Pe write in the b♭.
17	Pe has a b♭ signature throughout the *b* section (17–34).
21	In C, the b♭ is the second note of a line and functions as a signature for the rest of the line (through 25).
26	In C, a line begins here with a b♭ sign, which covers the remaining b's in the section (in 28 and 29).

VARIANTS

4	The bL has a descending plica in Pe.
7	E has an extra cL (error), because the musical scribe did not coordinate his work carefully with the already-copied text.
16	E has no rest or finis punctorum (error); in Pe the rest is a perfect L.
17	In E and Pe, the dB has no plica.
18–19	In Pe the reading is dB cbB, cL, followed by a perfect L (instead of a B) rest.
19	In E the rest after cL appears to be an imperfect L (error) instead of a B rest.
23	In Pe the gL has a descending plica; in E the rest after gL appears to be an imperfect L (error) instead of a B rest.
28	In E and Pe the dB has no plica.
31	In Pe the aL has a descending plica; in E the B rest is missing after aL (error).

4. *Baladelle* En amer a douce vie *a4*

SOURCES

C, f. 46 (triplum, cantus, tenor, contratenor); E, f. 31 (triplum, cantus, tenor, contratenor); K, f. 59v (cantus, tenor, contratenor); Pe, f. 23v (triplum, cantus, tenor, contratenor).

OBSERVATIONS

En amer is a form of ballade that repeats both the *a* and *b* sections, each of which has a first and a second ending. Measures 22–32 of the second *b* constitute the refrain, and the musical stanza form is thus *a a b b (R)*. Despite the four parts found in three of the four manuscript sources under consideration, the baladelle is a three-part work, for according to Gilbert Reaney the textless triplum and contratenor are alternatives and only one should be performed with the cantus and tenor. Since *En amer* is Machaut's only work composed before 1349 with this disposition of parts, it would appear to be his first song (as opposed to motet) to use a contratenor. The contratenor is well matched to the tenor part in both rhythmic activity and counterpoint, but the busy triplum, as the highest part, tends to distract attention from the texted cantus voice. It is not impossible to perform the baladelle as a four-part work, but it sounds better without the triplum. Though its omission may well have been a scribal error, by not including the triplum manuscript K adopts the more forward-looking texture of cantus, tenor, and contratenor, the standard arrangement of chanson parts in the second half of the fourteenth century.

ACCIDENTALS

Triplum

13 — E, Pe lack f♯.

15 (for 16) — E puts the sharp sign at the beginning of the *b* section in 15 (end of a line) and does not repeat it in 16, even though that begins a new line with the f intended to be sharped; E's exemplar probably began a new line with 15.

20 — E, Pe have f♯.

22 — Pe has f♯.

31 — E has f♯.

Cantus

1 — Section *a* has a b♭ signature in C, E, K, and Pe.

15 — Pe lacks e♭.

17 — Pe lacks b♭ here, but has one starting at m. 13, which begins the line.

24 — E, K, and Pe lack e♭.

27 — E lacks e♭.

29 — E has e♭, which begins the last line as if a signature.

31 E and K do not write in e♭ again in this m.

Tenor

9 Pe lacks f♯.

22 K has e♭.

26 E, K lack b♭.

29 K, Pe have e♭.

Contratenor

4 Pe lacks b♮.

7 K, Pe lack f♯.

13 E, Pe lack f♯.

20 K lacks f♯.

24 Pe lacks b♭.

26 K has b♭ (beginning of last line).

VARIANTS

Triplum

1–16 In Pe, the entire *a* section and first 2 mm. of *b* are written a third too low.

8 After the second M rest, E has 3 aM (instead of 2 gM) before dSB (error).

15 In E, the first gM is written as aM.

24 In E, the first aM is written as gM; the final d is SB instead of M (error).

29 E's reading is aSB imperfected by gM; fSB imperfected by gM; and 3 M, gfg.

Cantus

1 In Pe, the cB has a descending plica.

2 In K, the aM is written as aSB (error).

3 In K, the SB rest is written as a B rest (error).

9–18 In C, coordination between music and text is poor.

10 In E, the M rest is a SB rest (error).

11 In K, the first note is cSB instead of cM (error).

13 E has 2 M rests (error); K begins with M rest, followed by cM dM.

16 In K, the first note is dSB instead of dM (error).

22 In K, the last note is bSB instead of bM (error).

22–24 In C, coordination between music and text is poor.

26 In E, all notes are M's, with dM inserted before the final e c.

27 In E, the first note, bSB, is imperfected by an added dM.

28 In C, the e♭ SB is written as eM (error).

31 In Pe, the last 2 notes are cM bSB instead of cSB bM.

Tenor

3 In C, the SB rest is missing (error).

12	In E, the dL is missing (error).
28–29	In K, the bcSB dSB are written as 3 li (instead of 2 + 1) with the last note dB (error).
31–32	K has a variant reading of cSB dBcL (1 + 2 li).
Contratenor	
4	In K, the third note is dSB instead of dB (error).
4–5	In K, the d and c are single notes rather than 2 li.
13	In C, E, and Pe, m. 10 is copied again for the second ending, but only in this part.
13–14	In E and Pe, the three notes are written as 3 li instead of 1 + 2 li.
17	In E, the first note cSB is missing (error).
18	In K, the first two SB's are single notes rather than 2 li.
20–21	In K, the f (♯) B is imperfected by gSB (followed by a dot); the cB in 21 is perfect.
22	In E, the first 2 SB are written as 2 li.
26	In E, the first 2 SB are written separately, not as 2 li.
27	In Pe, the aB comes before the SB rest instead of vice versa.
29–30	In E and K, the three notes are written as 3 li instead of 1 + 2 li.

5. Ballade Dame, de qui toute ma joye vient *a2*

SOURCES

C, f. 47v (cantus, tenor); E, f. 32 (triplum, cantus, tenor, contratenor); K, f. 60v (cantus, tenor); Pe, f. 25v (cantus, tenor).

OBSERVATIONS

The two-voice version of this work in C, K, and Pe represents an early stage of *Dame, de qui toute.* In all other musical sources, including manuscript E, a textless triplum and contratenor have been added. As in the baladelle, however, these two added parts are meant to be alternatives; one or the other should be selected to form a three-part texture. (For a transcription that includes the two additional parts, see the editions of Schrade and Ludwig.) The form of the three-stanza ballade is *a a b (R)*, with the refrain occupying mm. 40–49. A three-measure musical rhyme unites the end of section *a* (mm. 23–25) with that of section *b*.

ACCIDENTALS

Cantus

1	K and Pe have a b♭ signature throughout.
1–25	E has a b♭ signature throughout the *a* section.
14	In C, the b♭ signature drops out here (the beginning of line two in the manuscript), perhaps prompted by the f♯ in 16.

18 In C, the b♭ reappears.

26 In E, the *b* section begins without a b♭ signature.

31 In E, the b♭ reappears (beginning a line).

34 E, K, and Pe lack e♭.

35 Pe has a c♭ sign (for ♮) following the first c.

46 E, Pe lack e♭.

48 E has b♭.

Tenor

1 C and K have a b♭ signature throughout; E has an f-clef with e♭ signature throughout.

3 E has a b♭ which, since it precedes the first b, may be intended as a signature for the whole line (the entire *a* section); Pe has a b♭ here also.

7 K adds an e♭ signature just before the gSB (beginning of a line) that lasts to the end of the piece.

15 Pe has b♭.

22 C, Pe add a b♭ in the lower octave.

32 C and K add another b♭ despite the b♭ signature already present; Pe has b♭; and E has a b♭ also, which may apply to the b in 43 as well.

34 Pe adds an f♯.

44 E adds another e♭ (as in C and Pe) despite the e♭ signature already present.

VARIANTS

The triplum and contratenor in E are omitted from consideration.

Cantus

7 C has dM instead of dSB (error); in Pe the first eSB is written as eB (error).

9 In Pe the dB has a descending plica.

10 After the rest, E, K, and Pe have gM fM eSB instead of gM fSB eM; in K the eSB is followed by a SB rest (error).

10–19 In K, the coordination of text and music is quite different in line two of the text and in its repetition (through 25); at the end of 12 this results in a second gSB (error).

14–15 In E, the last note of 14 (dM) and the first note of 15 (cM) are written a third too low (error).

15 In K, the first note is cSB instead of cM (error).

20 In C and E, the aSB beginning 18 is repeated unnecessarily to begin 20 (the second ending); the syllable *hon-* appears only once. K and Pe do not repeat 18 to form 20; the text for 20 is underlaid at 18.

21–25 In K the second ending has no text underlaid, because *n'obeir* appears under *ne cherir* of the first ending (error).

22 In K, the first three notes are bSB cM dM instead of bM cM dSB.

26 In Pe, the fB has a descending plica.

28 In C and Pe, the bSB is written as bM (error); E follows C's reading of 28 (dM cSB bM aM gM) but dots the aSB in 29 to avoid dropping a M beat.

33 In E, K, and Pe, the dB is followed by a breve rest (error).

48 In E, the second b (SB) is written as bM (error).

Tenor

5–6 In E, the fL is written as fB (error).

15–17 Instead of 4 li, K has 3 li + 1; the aB in 16 is written as aL (error).

20 In K, m. 18 is not written out again for the second ending.

26–27 In E, K, and Pe, the bB and dB are written as 2 li.

29–31 In K, the notes edSB cbB are written as 4 li.

33 In C, E, K, and Pe, the gB is followed by a breve rest not matched in the cantus (error).

41–42 In C, the 3 li ends with fL instead of fB (error); it is correctly written in K.

41–43 E, Pe have a 4 li, fgSBfbB.

6. Chanson balladee Dame, a vous sans retollir *a1*

SOURCES

C, f. 51; E, f. 33v; Pe, f. 29.

OBSERVATIONS

This virelai, which moves entirely in semibreves and minims, exhibits the composer's delight in the kind of syncopations found in mm. 3–6 on the one hand and in mm. 9–10 and 14–15 on the other hand. The snappy rhythms and 6/8 meter—both typical of Machaut's works in this genre—enhance the dance-like character of the music, which has the overall form *A b b a A b b a A b b a A.*

ACCIDENTALS

1 C has a b♭ signature for both the *A* and *b* sections, but on the written-out repeat of *a* (line 4), the flat drops out in mm. 9–11 (the last line of music). In E, the entire repeat of *a* (line 4) lacks the flat. In Pe, a b♭ signature begins every line of the score except that comprising mm. 10–11, which contains no b.

9 In Pe, a natural sign follows the cM on *qui* in line 1; at the same place in line 4, a sharp sign precedes the cM on *vos.*

Though each is squarely on the c line, they probably mean that the bM is natural rather than flatted.

VARIANTS

1 In E, the second note in line 1 is bM instead of aM (error); in line 4 it is correct. In line 4, a clef change from c3 to c4 should precede the word *beauté* (*beauté* in manuscript E); thus the remainder of the line (through m. 4) is a third too high (error).

3 In E, line 1 has the first note aM instead of gM (error).

4 In E, line 1 has an extra aSB before the last note on *corps* (error), the result of poor coordination of music and text by the musical scribe.

5 In C, line 1 omits the M rest; line 4 has a SB rest (both errors).

7 In E, line 4 has an extra gM on the second syllable of *coulour* (error), the result of poor coordination of music and text by the musical scribe.

8 In C, line 4 has gSB instead of gM for the second note (error). In Pe, line 1 has the first note fSB instead of fM (error).

9 In C, line 4 has an extra bM after the fSB, so that the last cM is not altered.

16 In C, the first note is dM instead of dSB (error).

7. *Rondelet* Dame, mon cuer *a3*

SOURCES

C, f. 57 (triplum, cantus, tenor); E. f. 35v (triplum, cantus, tenor). Pe includes a different rondeau, *Tant doucement* (no. 9), in place of *Dame, mon cuer* in the *Remede*.

OBSERVATIONS

This work is apparently Machaut's earliest musical composition in rondeau form, since there are no other rondeaux in the first section of manuscript C. Thus unlike that of the virelai, this genre was polyphonic from the first in his oeuvre. Most of Machaut's three-part works have as the third part a textless contratenor rather than a textless triplum; use of the latter in this rondeau may be taken as an early characteristic. Another early trait is the absence of musical rhyme between the *a* and *b* sections. But a notable feature of this rondeau is the use of the same clef (c3) and range for cantus and tenor (found elsewhere only in Rondeau 1, *Doulz viaire gracieus*). This no doubt prompted the passages of voice crossing, voice exchange (mm. 29–30), motivic repetition (tenor mm. 4, 8, 26, 39; cantus mm. 5, 9, 25–26, 27, 40), and outright imitation (mm. 5–7, 10–12, 15–19, and 34–38, tenor leading). When compared with the skillful duet of these two parts, the triplum often seems a poor fit. Of all the types of songs included in the *Remede*, the rondelet has the least amount of text (eight lines) and the greatest amount of melismatic writing and musical repetition. As part of the overall form of *A B a A a b A B*, the 23-measure *a* section is heard five times.

ACCIDENTALS

Triplum

28	E has c♯.
35	E has an intended f♯ (actually a♯ because of a clef error).

Cantus

1	E has a b♭ signature throughout. In C the first and second lines of the score have a b♭ signature that carries through the first half of m. 33; the flat is reiterated in 16.
10	E lacks f♯.
17	E adds c♯.
32	E lacks f♯.
35	In C, the last note is the only b not flatted.
37	E lacks c♯.

Tenor

1	Both C and E have a b♭ signature throughout.
7	E has an f♯.
24	C has a flat sign (for f♮) not present in E.

VARIANTS

Triplum

1	In E, the first note is fB instead of dB (error).
14	In E, the eSB is written as eM (error).
16	In E, the second note is dM instead of fM.
17	In E, the m. begins with two M rests, and the fSB is without a dot.
25	In E, the notes are 4 M instead of M SB M SB (error).
30	In E, the last note is aM instead of bM.
31	In E, the first two note values are SB M rather than vice versa.
31–35	In E, the pitches are written a third too high (error).
35	In E, the note values are 3 M instead of M M SB (error).
38	In E, the first four pitches are agagM rather than vice versa.

Cantus

1–23	In E, music and text are poorly coordinated in section *a*.
4	In E, the SB rest looks more like a M rest (error).
14	In E, the third note is eM instead of fM.
16	In E, the rest is a SB instead of a M (error).
18	In C, the syllable *re-* appears both at the beginning of this measure (error) and again in 19.
22	In E, the last two notes are SB M rather than M SB.
25	In E, the third note, cM, is followed by a dot (error).
26	In E, the rest is a SB instead of a M (error).

Tenor

4	In C, the first note is cSB instead of cM (error).
11–15	In E, this passage is omitted due to a skip by the copyist from m. 10 to the same figure in m. 15 (error).
16	In E, the first note is gSB instead of aSB (error).
22	In E, the SB rest is written as 2 M rests.
23	In E, the gB is written as gSB (error).
29	In E, gfSB is omitted (error).

APPENDIX II: MINIATURES IN *REMEDE DE FORTUNE* (MANUSCRIPT C)

INTRODUCTION

The series of thirty-four miniatures which illustrate *Remede de Fortune* in manuscript Bibliothèque Nationale fonds français 1586 (manuscript C) complements superbly Machaut's poetic text and musical notation, making the fusion of verse, music, and art in the manuscript a nearly unmatched aesthetic success. The paintings themselves are masterpieces, and they supply invaluable interpretive and stylistic commentary on Machaut's text. In their subject matter the illuminations well represent the narrative, and the combination of convention and realism in the pictorial style provides an appropriate counterpart to the poetic style.

Until François Avril's recent art-historical studies of the Machaut manuscripts,[1] manuscript C was thought to be a fifteenth-century copy of an early stage of Machaut's collected works. In showing that the manuscript was no copy, but rather probably executed between 1350 and 1356 under the poet's supervision, Avril has demonstrated that its illustrations constitute one of the most distinguished programs of manuscript illumination in fourteenth-century France. He finds that it was painted by three artists, with the painter of *Remede de Fortune* "visiblement le chef du file."[2] Avril further associates this artist's work with major manuscripts done for Jean le Bon, notably with a celebrated "Bible moralisé."[3] An assumption that manuscript C was likewise done for King Jean agrees well with our identification of the lady of the poem with Bonne of Luxembourg, Jean's wife who died in 1349 (see above, pp. 33–36). The codex would then form something of a memorial to Bonne. The order in which the works are presented, different from the standard order of the other collections, suggests this,[4] with *Remede* being preceded only by *Jugement*, which celebrates Bonne's father. Even more compelling evidence is provided by the facts that *Remede* has by far the most elaborate program of illustration of any work in the codex,[5] that it is the only poem with which the chief painter concerns himself, and that the miniatures constitute his most important identified work. Avril identifies the anonymous artist as the "Master of the *Remede de Fortune*."

In characterizing the style of the artist Avril points particularly to his emphasis, quite novel for the time, on direct observation of nature and people; in this regard he notes particularly the representation of spatial depth, the individualization of the characters, and the outfitting of them in close-fitting garments which had come into vogue in the 1340s. The conjunction of these characteristics is especially apparent in the six larger miniatures of the series (miniatures 1, 3, 5, 27, 31, and 33). Three of these are particularly interesting for their presentation of court life: the picture of the carole or round dance (miniature 27) in which the participants take turns singing virelais *a capella*; the representation of the banquet with the bustling serving-people and blaring trumpets (miniature 31); and the jousting ground with the grandstand from which the ladies can observe (miniature 33). The other three large miniatures are particularly important as images of poetic creativity, a major theme in the work. In the first (miniature 1), which keynotes the poem, Amant with his serving-man observes pensively from one side, while his lady standing before her castle instructs three damsels, no doubt about love: the lady and Amour are the poet's theme. The second (miniature 3) depicts Amant writing a lai on a long scroll. The other (miniature 5) is a double miniature occupying three-fourths of the page. In the upper part Amant sits in the walled Park of Hesdin composing the complainte, while in the lower part is found the prime image of the complainte, Lady Fortune, blindfolded and turning her cleverly engineered wheel. (See frontispiece.)

The other twenty-eight miniatures are single-column, averaging about a third of a column in length. Twenty-one of them have two figures, with sixteen of those (miniatures 10–23, and 25–26) presenting Amant and Esperance together in various poses—she comforting, instructing, and singing to him; he complaining and questioning. The miniaturist perceptively sees this as the central relationship of the work. Only two of the pictures show Amant and the lady alone together (miniatures 29 and 34); another (miniature 2) shows him with the God of Love; and in another (miniature 7) he is pointing to Lady Fortune. The other illumination that has two figures (miniature 6) depicts Nebuchadnezzar dreaming of the statue with the feet of clay. Two small miniatures show Amant alone (miniatures 9 and 24); and five show him and the lady with others: with the king and some people (miniature 4), with a girl holding the lady's train (miniature 8), with two other couples going to the château (miniature 28), with three ladies looking on while Amant kneels (miniature 30), and with Esperance who presides over their exchange of rings (miniature 32).

As would be expected, a consideration of the miniatures for *Remede* in all the manuscripts confirms the early/late division between them. E and Pe, the two early-text manuscripts besides C, have two and one illuminations respectively; the second one in E and the only one in Pe are placed immediately after the complainte, where the tenth miniature of C is also found. Manuscript E here depicts Amant and Esperance in a walled garden, while C and Pe—very similar—show Esperance holding Amant's hand. None of the other manuscripts have an illumination at this point, though several of the late-text manuscripts are amply illustrated. Manuscripts A and Pm both have twelve miniatures, found at identical points in the poem; the artist of Pm follows A very closely in subject matter, though he modernizes the style to suit fifteenth-century tastes.[6] Despite the large number of miniatures in C, which are generally placed at natural breaks in the poem, only four miniatures of A and Pm occur at the same points as those in C, and there is no significant concord between A, Pm, and C in the representations. Among the other manuscripts of the poem, J has five illuminations, with K retaining three that almost duplicate those of J. In contrast to the text of the poem, in which the variants of J and K are not allied consistently with either the early or the late text, the placement of the miniatures and their contents in J and K are very similar to A. The three miniatures in Vg evidently were produced independent of the other manuscripts; the congruencies with others are not notable.

Notes

1. François Avril, *Manuscript Painting at the Court of France: The Fourteenth Century* (New York: Braziller, 1978); "Les Manuscrits enluminés de Guillaume de Machaut," in *Guillaume de Machaut*, Colloque–Table Ronde Organisé par l'Université de Reims, Actes et Colloques, no. 23 (Paris: Klincksieck, 1982), pp. 117–33.

2. "Les Manuscrits enluminés," p. 119.

3. See "Un Chef d'oeuvre de l'enluminure sous le règne de Jean le Bon: La Bible moralisée, manuscrit français de la Bibliothèque nationale," *Monuments et Mémoires de la Fondation Jean Piot* 58 (1972): 112–14.

4. In the other collections, either the *Louange des dames* or the *Dit dou vergier* is placed first, and both judgment poems as well precede *Remede*.

5. For a table of the miniatures of manuscript C, see Lawrence M. Earp, "Scribal Practice, Manuscript Production, and the Transmission of Music in Late Medieval France" (Ph.D. diss., Princeton University, 1983), pp. 382–89.

6. "Les Manuscrits enluminés," pp. 129–30.

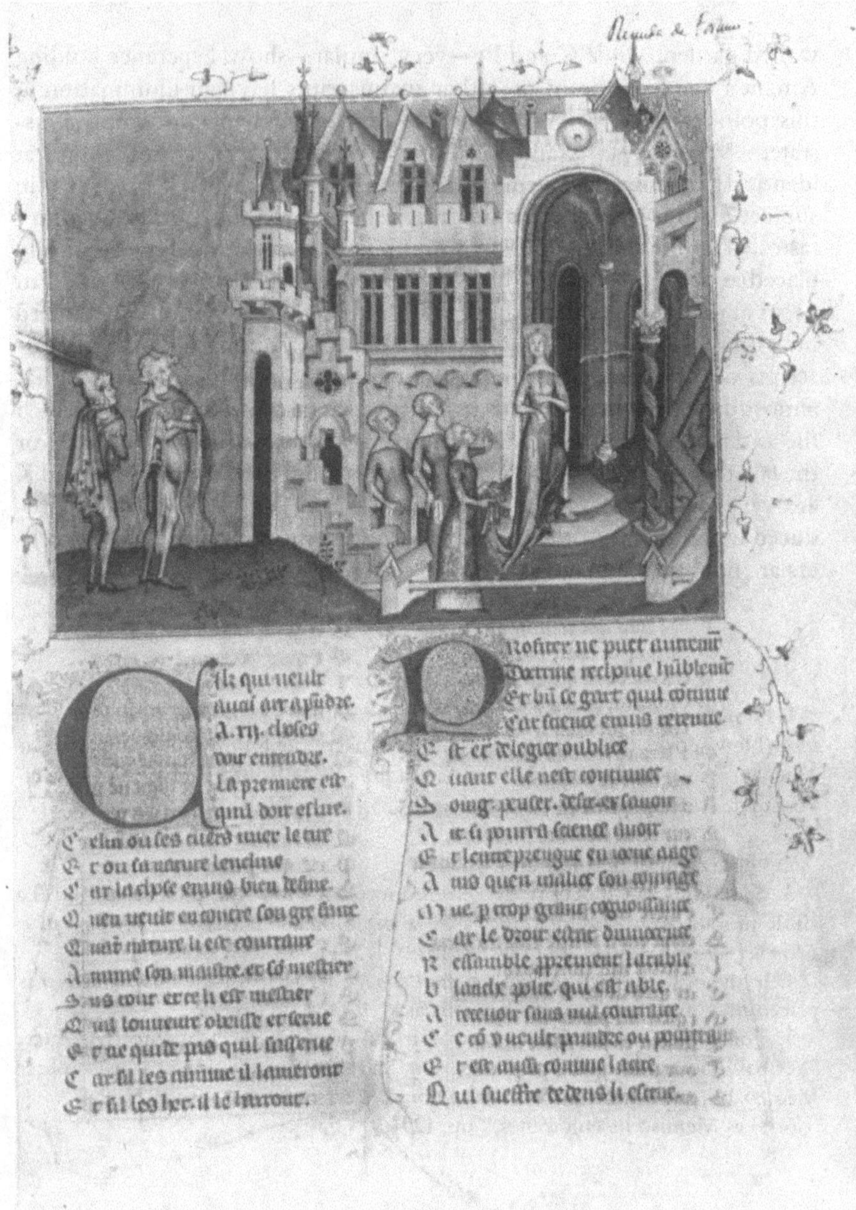

Miniature 1. The Lover approaches the Lady's castle and observes her. Fol. 23a–b.

Miniature 2. How Love chastises the Lover. Fol. 24a (line 134).

Miniature 3. How the Lover composes a lai about his feelings. Fol. 26a–b (line 414).

Miniature 4. How the Lady has the Lover read the lai he'd composed. Fol. 28va (line 692).

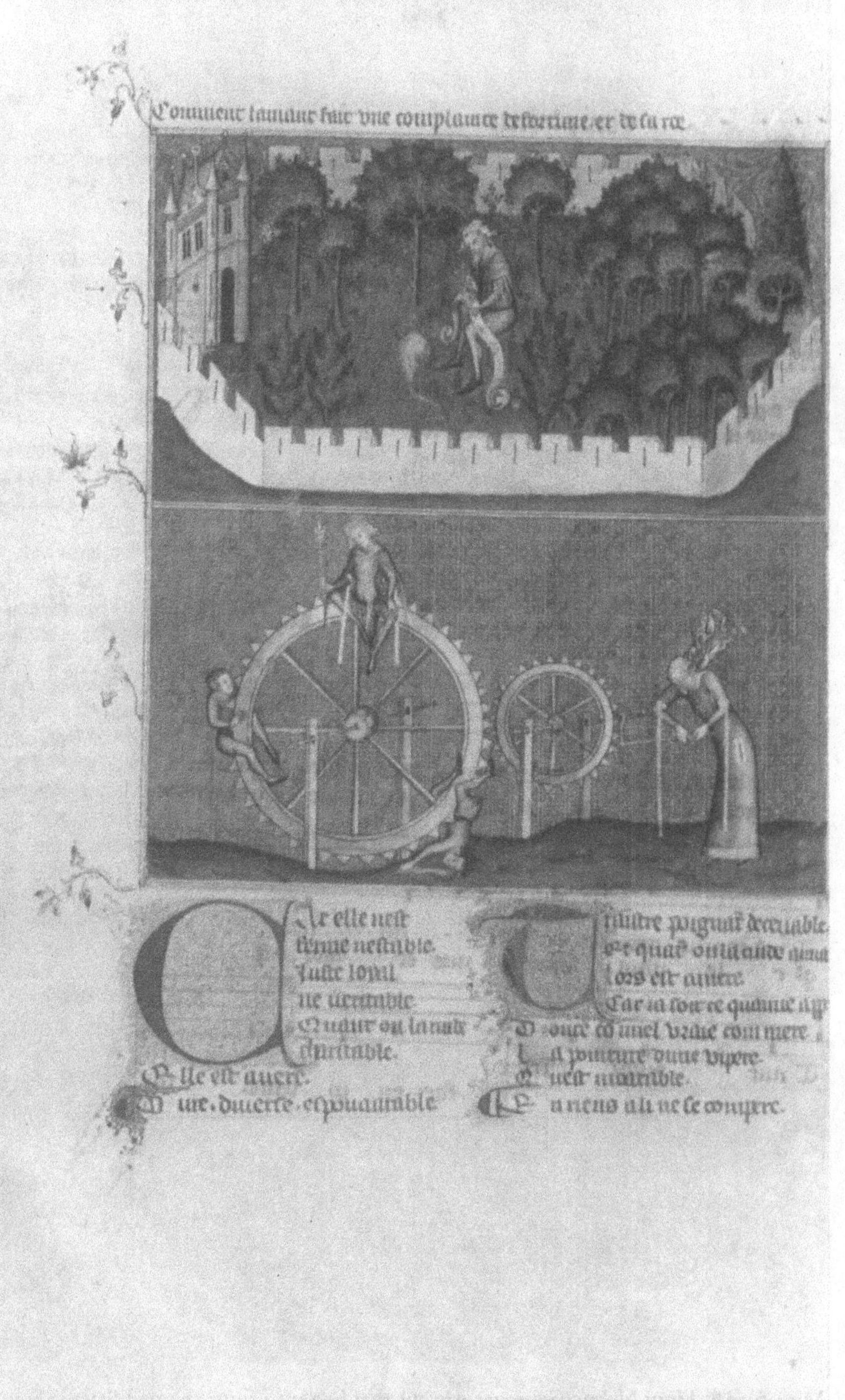

Miniature 5. How the Lover writes a complainte about Fortune and her Wheel. Fol. 30va–vb (line 920).

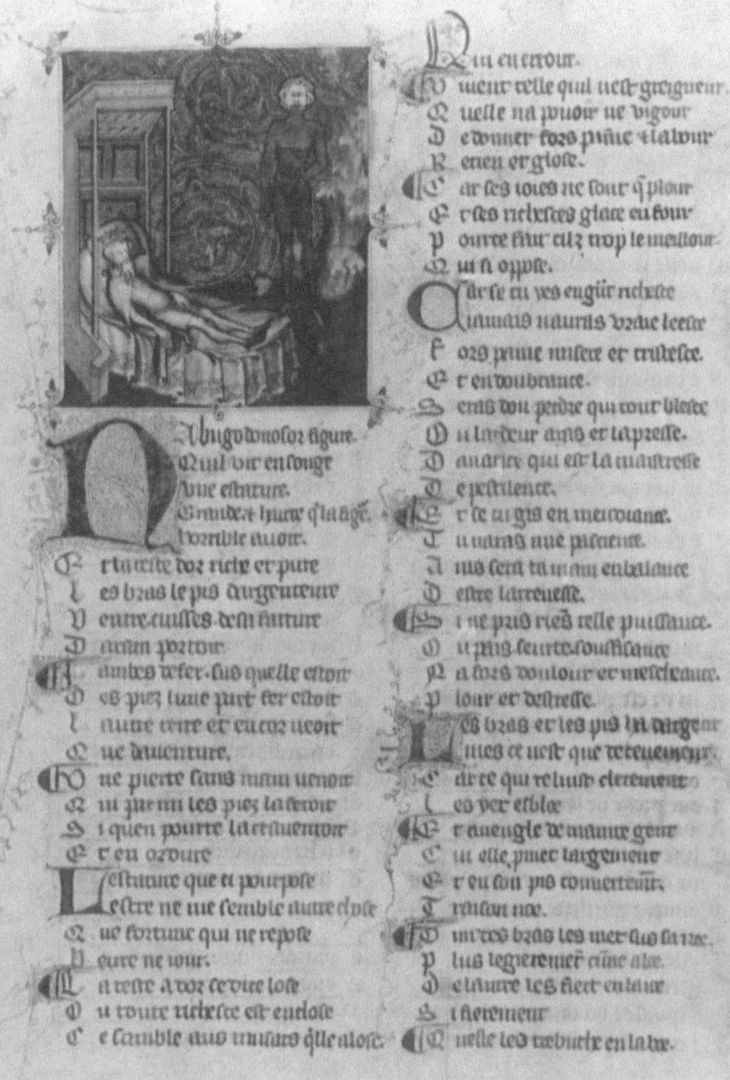

Miniature 6. How Nebuchadnezzar dreamt that he saw a figure named Statua. Fol. 31va (line 1000).

Miniature 7. How the Lover laments over Fortune. Fol. 32vb (line 1192).

Miniature 8. How the Lover caught sight of his Lady. Fol. 33va (line 1272).

Miniature 9. How the Lover laments to himself. Fol. 34va (line 1400).

Miniature 10. How Hope came to comfort the Lover. Fol. 35a (line 1480).

Miniature 11. How Hope teaches and instructs the Lover. Fol. 36va (line 1670).

Miniature 12. How Hope chastises the Lover. Fol. 37va (line 1820).

Miniature 13. How Hope explains Love's own arms to the Lover. Fol. 38a (line 1880).

Miniature 14. How the Lover falls asleep listening to Hope sing. Fol. 38vb (line 1976).

Miniature 15. How Hope asks the Lover if she'd sung well. Fol. 39va (line 2038).

Miniature 16. How Hope tells the Lover of her power. Fol. 40va (line 2147).

Miniature 17. How the Lover speaks to Hope. Fol. 41va (line 2286).

Miniature 18. How the Lover thanks Hope. Fol. 42a (line 2352).

ʌiniature 19. How Hope speaks to the Lover bout Fortune. Fol. 42va (line 2402).

Miniature 20. How the Lover speaks to Hope. Fol. 43b (line 2521).

Miniature 21. How Hope speaks to the Lover. Fol. 44va (line 2684).

Miniature 22. How Hope offers the Lover a song and sings it for him. Fol. 45vb (line 2856).

Miniature 23. How Hope leaves the Lover. Fol. 46va (line 2892).

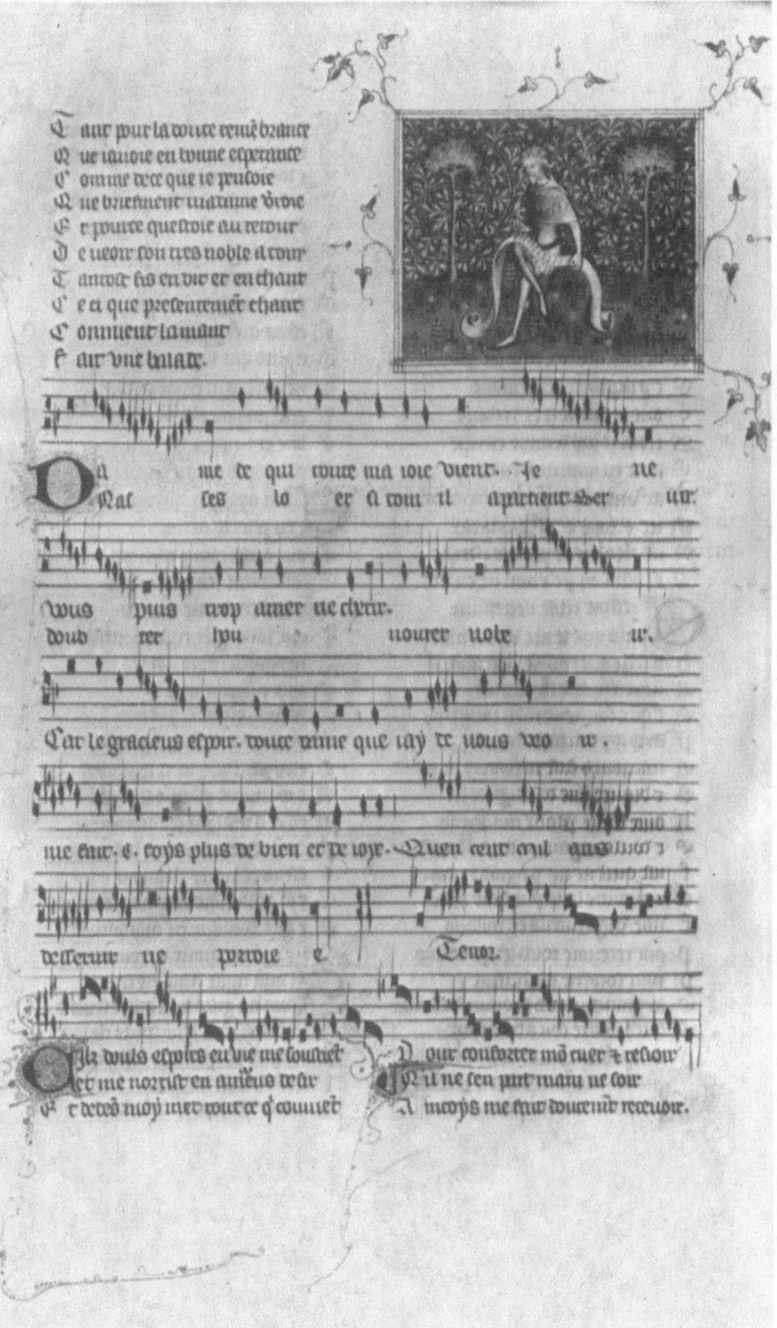

Miniature 24. How the Lover composes a ballade. Fol. 47vb (line 3012).

Miniature 25. How Hope holds the Lover by the hand and takes him to see his Lady's manor. Fol. 48b (line 3076).

Miniature 26. How the Lover kneels in the pathway to his Lady's manor. Fol. 49a (line 3180).

Miniature 27. How the Lover sings before his Lady. Fol. 51a–b (line 3450).

Miniature 28. How the Lover speaks to his Lady. Fol. 52b (line 3572).

Miniature 29. How the Lady speaks to the Lover. Fol. 53va (line 3730).

Miniature 30. How the Lover thanks his Lady. Fol. 54b (line 3848).

Miniature 31. How the Lover attended his Lady's dinner. Fol. 55a–b (line 3948).

Miniature 32. How the Lady and the Lover exchange rings. Fol. 56b (line 4078).

Miniature 33. How the Lover departs singing. Fol. 56va–vb (line 4108).

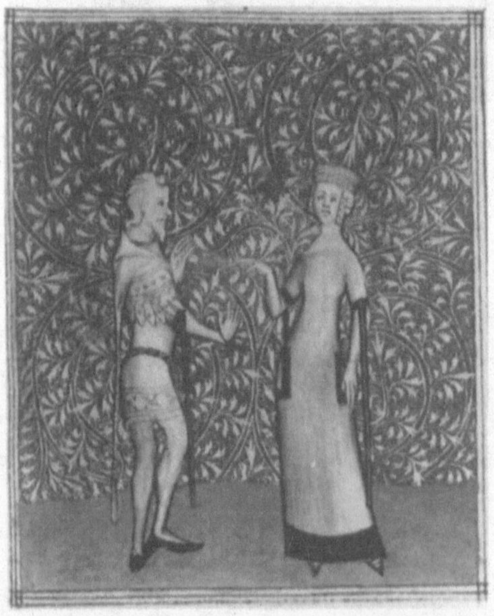

Miniature 34. How the Lover speaks to his Lady. Fol. 58a (line 4218).

NOTES

NOTES TO THE TEXTS

These notes to the texts of Machaut's poems deal with three matters: they specify the relationships between Machaut's and Chaucer's works, both by quoting parallel lines from Chaucer's poetry and by explaining how the various readings of the Machaut manuscripts agree with, or differ from, the readings Chaucer evidently knew; they identify and quote Machaut's sources; and they explicate textual questions. Chaucer's works are quoted herein from *The Works of Geoffrey Chaucer*, ed. F. N. Robinson, 2d ed. (Boston: Houghton, 1957).

The following abbreviated references are to works that are frequently cited in the notes:

Chaucer's works:

AA	*Anelida and Arcite*
BD	*Book of the Duchess*
CA	*Complaint d'Amour*
CM	*Complaint of Mars*
CT	*Canterbury Tales*
For	*Fortune*
HF	*House of Fame*
LGW	*Legend of Good Women*
PF	*Parliament of Fowls*
TC	*Troilus and Criseyde*

Other texts:

Boet	Boethius. *The Consolation of Philosophy*. Edited by H. F. Stewart and E. K. Rand. Cambridge: Harvard University Press, 1962.
Chichmaref	Guillaume de Machaut. *Poésies lyriques*. Edited by V.-F. Chichmaref. 2 vols. Paris: Champion, 1909.
Foulet	Foulet, Lucien. *Petite syntaxe de l'ancien français*. 3d ed. Paris: Champion, 1930.
Hassell	Hassell, James W., Jr. *Middle French Proverbs, Sentences, and Proverbial Phrases*. Toronto: Pontifical Institute of Medieval Studies, 1982.
Hoepffner	*Les Oeuvres de Guillaume de Machaut*. Edited by Ernest Hoepffner. Société des Anciens Textes Français. 3 vols. Paris: Firmin-Didot, 1908–21.
Ménard	Ménard, Philippe. *Syntaxe de l'ancien français*. Vol. 1 of *Manuel français du moyen âge*. Edited by Yves Lefèvre. Rev. ed. Bordeaux: Société Bordelaise de Diffusion des Travaux de Lettres et Sciences Humaines, 1973.

Morawski	Morawski, Joseph. *Proverbes français antérieurs au xve siècle*. Paris: Champion, 1925.
Palmer	Guillaume de Machaut. *The Judgment of the King of Bohemia*. Edited and Translated by R. Barton Palmer. Garland Library of Medieval Literature, ser. A, vol. 9. New York: Garland, 1984.
RR	Guillaume de Lorris and Jean de Meun. *Le Roman de la Rose*. Edited by Félix Lecoy. Classiques Français du Moyen Age. 3 vols. Paris: Champion, 1966–70.
Whiting	Whiting, Bartlett J., and Helen W. Whiting. *Proverbs, Sentences, and Proverbial Phrases from English Writings Mainly Before 1500*. Cambridge: Harvard University Press, 1968.

NOTES FOR *LE JUGEMENT DU ROY DE BEHAIGNE*

1–12 With this *reverdie* opening, cf. *RR* 45 ff. Especially cf. *Jugement* 1 with *RR* 49, "el tens ou toute rien s'esgaie"; and *Jugement* 2 with *RR* 64, "et de maintes colors divers."

5 Since the daughter of Jean l'Aveugle, king of Luxembourg, was named Bonne, it may be significant that Machaut frequently personifies Love as Bonne Amour and consistently treats it as feminine. See introduction to *Remede*. In Chaucer's *BD* Love is masculine.

13 *BD* 341 And *ful attempre* for sothe hyt *was*

14 *BD* 340, 342

Blew, bryght, clere was the ayr . . .
For *nother to cold* nor hoot yt nas.

17 *BD* 340 *Blew*, bryght, *clere* was the ayr.

Chaucer's manuscript reading:
m'esbleuissoit mesbloissoit ABD*E*FMVg; mebluissoit *JK*.
In the pattern of borrowing "Blew" may have been suggested by the unusual spelling of the third person preterit of "esbloir" in the early-tradition manuscripts.

19 *BD* 336 And throgh the glas the *sonne shon*

26–27 *BD* 397 And *I hym folwed* and *hyt forth wente*

As the bird leads the narrator here, so the dog in *BD* acts as guide to Chaucer's narrator.

30 *BD* 400 With *floures fele*, faire under fete

43–44 *BD* 398–99

Doun by a floury grene *wente*
Ful thikke of gras, ful softe and swete.

50 *BD* 452 A wonder wel-farynge knyght

59 *BD* 533–34

. . . and fond hym so *tretable*
Ryght wonder skylful and resonable

60–62 *BD* 503–4

And *grette hym*, but *he spak noght*,
But *argued* with his owne *thoght*

70 *BD* 520–21

I herde the not, to seyn the soth
Ne I sawgh the not, *syr, trewely*.

71 *BD* 509–10

So, throgh hys sorwe and hevy *thoght*,
Made hym that he herde me noght.

73–74 *BD* 525 *Foryive me, yif I have mystake*.

74 *BD* 519 He sayde, "*I prey the*, be not wroth."

75–76 *BD* 529 Loo! how *godly spak thys knyght*

77 *BD* 526–27

"Yis, th'*amendes* is lyght to make,"

Quod he, "for *ther lyeth noon therto*."

78 *BD* 528 *Ther ys nothyng myssayd nor do*.

79–80 Cf. *BD* 555 And telleth me of your sorwes smerte.

79, 86 *BD* 538 Have more knowynge of *hys thought*.

88 *BD* 547 Me thynketh *in* gret *sorowe I yow see*.

89 *BD* 553 For, *by my trouthe*, to make yow hool

90 *BD* 548–49

But certes, sire, *yif* that yee
Wolde ought *discure me youre woo*

91 *BD* 554 *I wol do al my power hool*.

92 *BD* 551 *Amende hyt*, yif I kan or may.

93 *BD* 560 "Graunt *mercy*, goode frend," quod he

94–96 *BD* 563 *No man may my sorwe glade*

97 *BD* 564 *That maketh my hewe to falle and fade*.

105 This line is hypermetrical in all manuscripts, as well as in Hoepffner's and Palmer's editions.

123–24 *BD* 749–50

"*Blythely*," quod he, "com sytte adoun!
I telle the . . . "

125 *BD* 37, 759

That I have suffred this *eight* yeer
"*Syr*," quod he, "sith first I kouthe . . ."

126 *BD* 764–65

Dredeles, I *have* ever yit
Be tributarye and yiven *rente*

127 *BD* 766 *To Love*, hooly with good entente

128–29 *BD* 759–60

"Syr," quod he, "*sith first I kouthe*
Have any maner wyt *fro youthe*
Chaucer's manuscript reading:
sa cognoissance congnoissance *J*.
The omission of the possessive "sa" changes the sense from "first knew her" to "first had understanding," making *J* closer to Chaucer's sense. But cf. 261 below.

130–33 *BD* 767–70

And *throgh plesaunce* become his thral
With good wille, *body, hert, and al*
Al this I *putte in his servage*
As to my lord, and dide *homage*.

147 In spite of Palmer's note and variants, the later manuscripts (except M and B) have *amoureux discrez*.

149–50 *BD* 1036 Was hooly *al my love leyd*

151–59 *BD* 1038–40

My suffisaunce, my lust, my lyf,
Myn hap, myn hele, and al my blesse,
My worldes welfare, and my goddesse

159 The terminology here is biblical and Marian. See James I. Wimsatt, "The

Apotheosis of Blanche in *Book of the Duchess,*" *Journal of English and Germanic Philology* 66 (1967): 41–42. Machaut does not develop an analogy of the lady with the Virgin, however, as Chaucer does with Fair White in *BD*.

166 *BD* 1289 *Our hertes wern so evene a payre*

167 *BD* 1290–91

That never nas that oon contrayre
To that other, for no woo.

169–72 *BD* 1292–94

For sothe, ylyche they *suffred* thoo
Oo blysse, and eke oo sorwe bothe;
Ylyche they were bothe glad and wrothe.

173 *BD* 1295 Al was us oon, *withoute were*

Chaucer's manuscript reading:

.ii. deulx *CJK*.

The word "deulx" can mean "sorrow/anxiety" as well as "two." If Chaucer's "withoute were" means "without anxiety," rather than "without doubt" as it is usually glossed, then "deulz" was probably the reading of Chaucer's manuscripts.

177–87 Cf. *RR* 4263–4310.

184–85 *BD* 609–10

To *derke* ys turned al my lyght,
My wyt ys foly, *my day ys nyght*

186, 191 *BD* 608 *In drede* ys al my *sykernesse*

194 *BD* 476 That *joye gete I never non*

Chaucer's manuscript reading:

n'attendra nateindra ABCFM*Ar*PmVg; ne tendra *St*.

Although the reading "n'ateindra" of *C, Ar,* and the later manuscripts is more suggestive of Chaucer's "gete" than "n'attendra" of early-tradition manuscripts, it provides a less accurate rhyme and is probably due to scribal intervention.

Allas, *deth,* what ayleth the,
That thou noldest have *taken me*

197–99 The word play on *mort, mordrir, mordre* (death, murder, bite), involving *rime équivoque* (homophonic rhyme), produces an effect particularly prized in Middle French poetry.

199–200 *BD* 483 Whan thou *toke my lady swete*

201 *BD* 478 *Which I have loved* with al my myght

Chaucer's manuscript Reading:

de fin cuer loyaument *JK*; de cuer fin *RRa*.

"De fin cuer" seems closer to Chaucer's "with al my myght" than *J* and *K* "loyaument."

204 *BD* 475 I have of *sorwe so great* won

Chaucer's manuscript reading:

grief grant *EJKRRa*.

"Grant" is closer than "grief" to Chaucer's "great."

213 *BD* 507 Hym thoughte hys *sorwes* were so *smerte*

215 *BD* 488–89

Hys sorwful hert gan faste faynte,
And his spirites wexen dede.

TC III 1088–89

And every spirit his *vigour* in knette,
So they astoned or oppressed were.

These passages in Chaucer also have a source in *Remede* 1490–92.

217 *BD* 510 Made hym that he *herde* me *noght*.

220 *BD* 488

Hys sorwful hert gan faste *faynte*

TC III 1092

And down he fel al sodeynly *a-swowne*.

221–23 *TC* III 1114–15

Therwith his pous and paumes of his hondes
They gan to frote, and wete his temples tweyne.

227–28 *TC* III 1119–20

And at the laste, he gan his *breth to drawe*,
And of his swough sone after that adawe

232–33 *BD* 714–15

"A, goode sir," quod I, "say not soo!
Have som pitee on your nature"

234 *BD* 725 And ye for sorwe mordred yourselve . . .

246 The reading of all early-tradition manuscripts except *St* is hypermetrical; Palmer's variant, *N'est pas meru*, is a misreading of Hoepffner's variant, where *meru.* is an abbreviated form of *merveille*. There is no reason to posit an intervention by Machaut.

253–56 *BD* 749–52

"Blythely, quod he;"com sytte adoun!
I telle the upon *a condicioun*
That thou shalt hooly, with al thy wyt,
Doo thyn entent to herkene hit."

254 *BD* 555–56

And telleth me of your *sorwes* smerte;
Paraunter hyt may ese *youre herte*.

261 *BD* 759–60

"Syr," quod he, "*sith* first I *kouthe*
Have any maner *wyt* fro youthe"

Cf. note to 128–29 above.

262 *BD* 761–62

Or kyndely understondyng
To *comprehende*, in any thyng

263 *BD* 763–64

What love was, in myn owne wyt,
Dredeles, I have *ever yit*

Chaucer's manuscript reading:

Qu'estoit amer Que cest amer ABDFMPmVg; Que cest amour *C*; Que cest damer *EPcSt*; Que ciert damer *JKKr*; Quest vraye amour *RRa*. Past tense of "estre" in *P, J, K*, and *Kr* matches Chaucer's "was."

265 *BD* 775 And this was *longe*, and many a yer

266 *BD* 776 *Or that myn herte was set* owher

268 *BD* 766 *To Love*, hooly with good entente

269 *BD* 771 And ful *devoutly* I prayed hym to . . .

Chaucer's manuscript reading:

devote devottement *E*; parfaite *St*.

Adverb "devottement" perhaps represents Chaucer's reading.

270–71 *BD* 772, 774

He shulde besette myn herte

And *worship* to my lady dere.

272–73 *BD* 773 That hyt plesaunce to hym were

281–82 *BD* 805, 807–8

Hit happed that I cam on a day

Trewly, the *fayrest companye*

Of ladyes that ever man with ye

284 *BD* 811 That broght me there? Nay, but *Fortune*

285 *BD* 812 *That ys to lyen ful comune*

Cf. also *TC* IV 5 traitour comune.

286 *BD* 817–18

Among these ladyes *thus* echon,

Soth to seyen *y sawgh oon*

Chaucer's manuscript reading:

une lune ABDFM*Pc*Vg.

Chaucer's borrowing here is manifest. Reading of earlier manuscripts without the definite article matches *BD*.

287 *BD* 821, 824

That *as the* someres *sonne* bryght . . .

The *moone*, or the sterres seven

288 *BD* 822 Ys fairer, *clerer*, and *hath more lyght*

Chaucer's manuscript reading:

Vaint de Veint la ABDVg; Veint sa Pm; Passe de *Kr*; Veu que de *RRa*.

Reading "Veint de" of earlier manuscripts conveys Chaucer's comparatives, "clearer," "more." "Veint la" signifies "overcomes."

289–90 *BD* 826–27

Surmounted hem alle of beaute,

Of maner, and of comlynesse.

Chaucer's manuscript reading:

les autres toutes les autres D.

The word "toutes" in D matches Chaucer's "alle," but at a cost of two superfluous syllables.

292–96 Cf. *BD* 895–903 (Ineffability of White's beauty.)

292 The comparison introduced by *tant estoit* in the preceding line and continued by the conditional *porroit* in 293 requires the conjunction *que*, rather than the *car* of C, Ar, St and the later manuscripts.

297 *BD* 848 *I sawgh hyr daunce so comlily*

298 *BD* 849 Carole and *synge so swetely*

299 *BD* 850 *Laughe and pleye so womanly*

300 *BD* 853 That, certes, I trowe *that evermor*
301 *BD* 854 *Nas seuyn so blysful a tresor*
Chaucer's manuscript reading:
plus si *EKrPmSt.*
The word "si" matches Chaucer's "so."

302–95 Machaut follows the model of medieval rhetorical treatises, enumerating traditional features of ideal beauty in a head-to-foot portrait. For comparable descriptions, cf. the twelfth-century treatises in Edmond Faral, ed., *Les arts poétiques du xiie et du xiiie siècles* (Paris: Champion, 1930), especially the *Poetria Nova* of Geoffrey de Vinsauf, lines 562–99.

302 *BD* 855, 858
For every *heer* on hir hed . . .
Me thoghte most *lyk gold* hyt was.

The preference for golden hair is standard. Cf. *Poetria Nova* 564, Crinibus irrutilet color auri.

303 *BD* 857 *Ne nouther yelowe, ne broun hyt nas.*

304–11 *Poetria Nova* 564–66 emphasizes the same contrast of black and white:
. . . lilia vernent
In specula frontis; vaccinea nigra coaequet
Forma supercilii.

312 *BD* 859 *And whiche eyen* my lady hadde!

314–15 *BD* 866–67, 883
Hir eyen semed anoon she wolde
Have mercy.
But many oon *with hire lok* she herte
Chaucer's manuscript reading:
rigeur acueil D; regart *JK*; vigueur *RRaSt*; doulceur Pm.
In the context of borrowing, "regart" of *JK* is more likely to be Chaucer's reading.

316–18 *BD* 860–61
Debonaire, goode, glade, and sadde,
Symple, of good mochel, noght to wyde.

The "greye" eyes of Chaucer's Prioress, *CT* A 152, probably match the "vair" of the eyes here. In *Poetria Nova* 570 the lady's eyes shine with "luce smaragdina"; i.e., with bright green.

321 *BD* 872 Had made hem opene by mesure
Chaucer's manuscript reading:
clingnetans clinans tant D; Clinet et *JK*; clingniet *ArKr.*
Derivatives of "cliner" ("to lower") in D, *J*, and *K* perhaps express the sense of Chaucer's description better than the participles from "clignier" ("to blink") of the other manuscripts.

322 *BD* 861 Symple, of good mochel, *noght to wyde.*

323 *BD* 864–65
Hyt *drew and took up, everydel,*
Al that on hir gan beholde.

326 *BD* 883 But many oon with hire lok she herte

329 *BD* 866–67

Hir eyen *semed* anoon she wolde
Have mercy; fooles wenden soo.

330 *BD* 874 Hyr lokynge *was not foly sprad*

The weight of the early manuscript evidence here suggests the reading *N'estoient mie*, but this is hypermetrical. It is possible that Machaut composed a hypermetrical line here (as he may have at 105), but it seems preferable to take the evidence of *J, K,* and *Kr* and accept *N'estoient pas* as Machaut's reading. The later manuscripts have *N'estoit mie*, taking *leur regars* in line 328 as singular rather than plural.

331–35 Cf. *BD* 883–87 (The effect of Fair White's glance.)

331 Cf. *TC* I 325 Right with hire look thorugh-shoten and thorugh-darted.

337–38 Cf. General Prologue *CT* A 150 Hir nose tretys

340–42 The lady's mouth in *Poetria Nova* 573–75 is comparably small, red, and tumescent:

Splendeat os forma spatii brevis et quasi cycli
Dimidii; tamquam praegnantia labra tumore
surgant, sed modico rutilent. . . .

341 Cf. General Prologue *CT* A 153
Hir mouth *ful smal* and therto *softe and reed.*

342 Cf. Miller's Tale *CT* A 3261
Hir mouth was sweete as bragot or the meeth.

346 Cf. Miller's Tale *CT* A 3735 Ful savourly. . . .

Poetria Nova 577–78 similarly specifies the sweetness of the lady's breath:

. . . thuris et oris
Sit pariter conditus odor.

357–58 *BD* 904–5
But thus moche dar I sayn, that she
Was whit, *rody, fressh, and lyvely hewed.*

Cf. *Jugement* 710.

359 The change from the early to the later tradition here is one of the few that the poet might have made, in this case to achieve accuracy, for one could plausibly argue that the rose on the branch would be fresher before (*eins que*) it was picked than after, or "when" (*quant*).

361 *BD* 942, 947
Hyt was *white, smothe*, streght, and pure flat
Of good gretnesse, and noght to gret.

362–63 *BD* 939–41, 43, 45
But swich a fairnesse of *a nekke*
Had that swete that *boon nor brekke*
Nas ther non sene that myssat. 943
Withouten hole; or canel-boon 945
Hyr throte . . .

362 The reading of *P, J, K,* and *Ar* (*gorgete*) can be defended if *ne os* is read as one syllable rather than as *në os*. Lack of elision in all manuscripts, the frequent non-elision of the negative in this poem, the possible confusion with the pronoun *nos*, and the significant number of manuscripts with *gorge*, all argue in favor of the reading we have adopted.

364–66 *Poetria Nova* 586–90 is also expansive in describing the arms, hands, and fingers:

. . .placeantque lacerti,
Tam forma gracili quam longa deliciosi.
Confluat in tenues digitos substantia mollis
Et macra, forma teres et lactea, linea longa
Et directa: decor manuum se jactet in illis.

365–66 *BD* 952–54

Ryght faire shuldres and body *long*
She had, and armes, every lyth
Fattyssh, flesshy, not gret therwith.

Chaucer's manuscript reading:
Qui estoient Quelle avoit *JK*.
The pattern of borrowing testifies strongly to Machaut's influence. "Qu'elle avoit" ("that she had") is closer to Chaucer's line 953.

367 *BD* 955 Ryght *white handes*, and nayles rede

369–70 *BD* 956 *Rounde brestes* . . .

Poetria Nova 591–92 is less specific but more suggestive than Machaut in describing the lady's breasts:

Pectus imago nivis, quasi quasdam collaterales
Gemmas virgineas producat utrimque papillas.

373 *BD* 952 . . . and *body* long

374–75 *BD* 954 *Fattyssh, flesshy, not gret therwith*

376–77 *BD* 956–57

. . . and of good brede
Hyr hippes were, a streight flat bak.

380–87 Concerning the hidden beauties of the lady, *Poetria Nova* 593–94 similarly preserves adamant silence:

Taceo de partibus infra :
Aptius hic loquitur animus quam lingua.

382 *BD* 959 That al hir lymmes nere pure *sewynge*

382–83 *TC* I 282–83

But *al hire lymmes* so wel answerynge
Weren to wommanhod . . .

Chaucer's manuscript reading:
tout estoit estoit tant *JKSt*.
The phrase "tant respondant" of *J* and *K* matches Chaucer's "so wel answerynge." Chaucer echoes the next sixty lines of *Jugement* throughout his picture of Criseyde in *TC* I.

390 *BD* 950 She was both fair and *bryght*.

391 Cf. Canticle of Canticles 4:7 "Thou art all fair, O my love, and there is not a spot in thee." With a line such as this Machaut may have helped to suggest Chaucer's references to Canticles in *BD*, esp. lines 310, 905, 946, and 397–433 *passim*. Cf. also *CT* E 2146, "No spot of thee ne knew I al my lyf."

393 The reading of the later manuscripts, *tendrette de*, is less satisfactory than the comparison presented in the early ones, since *de* is used only to introduce expressions of disparity (cf. Ménard, 256).

394 Cf. *TC* I 289–91, where Criseyde's "chere" is said to be "somdel deignous."

398–99 *BD* 908–9

For certes, *Nature had swich lest*
To make that fair, that trewly she . . .

402–3 *BD* 910–11

Was hir chef *patron of beaute*
And chef *ensample* of al hir werk.

TC I 297–8

That *in his hertes* botme gan *to stiken*
Of hir his *fixe* and depe *impressioun.*

412 Cf. *TC* I 366 In which he saugh al holly hire *figure.*

418 Plaisance is Machaut's equivalent of Deduit, the proprietor of the garden in *RR*; cf. 430 below.

421–22 For the conventional comparison see Hassell, G10, O3; Whiting, O17.

421 *BD* 368, 1056, 1060

Syr, th'emperour *Octovyen*
Thogh I had had al the beaute
. . . al the *richesse*

422 *BD* 1072 Or *ben as wis* as Mynerva

434–36 The process presented figuratively here abbreviates that in *RR* involving the God of Love's arrows and his capture of the lover.

437–39 *TC* I 289–91

Gan for to *like* hire mevynge and hire *chere*
Which somdel *deignous* was, for she *let falle*
Hire loke . . .
Chaucer's manuscript reading:
ses cilz ABCDFM*ArPc*Pm*St*Vg; son *E.*
The phrase "ses regars" of *E, J, K,* and *P* is like Chaucer's "Hire loke." The pattern of borrowing in *TC* strongly favors influence of *Jugement* here.

440–41 *TC* I 301 Unnethes *wiste* he how to loke or wynke.

442 *BD* 1218 For *wit, maner, and al* was goon.

442–44 *TC* I 306–7

That sodeynly hym thoughte he felte dyen,
Right with hire look, the spirit in his herte.

451–52 *TC* I 361, 363

And *thought* ay on hir so, withouten lette
Right of hire look, and gan it newe avise.

453–56 Cf. *BD* 1186–91 (Knight's fear of confessing his love.)

457–59 *RR* is the original for Bel Acueil, Dous Regart, and Dous Espoirs (Esperance).

461–62 *BD* 1196–98

Ne formed never in creature
So moche beaute, trewely,
And bounte, *wythoute mercy.*

TC I 898–99

. . . sith thy lady vertuous is al,
So foloweth it that there is som pitee . . .

466 *BD* 1191–92
Allas! what shal I thanne do?
In this *debat* I was so wo

468–70 *BD* 1212–14
Softe and *quakynge* for pure *drede*
And *shame*, and styntynge in my tale
For *ferde*, and myn hewe al pale . . .

471 *BD* 1211 With sorweful *herte*, and *woundes* dede

473 *BD* 1218 *For wit, maner, and al was goon.*
Chaucer's manuscript reading:
maniere mesure *PC*.
Chaucer's "maner" helps confirm that the proper reading is "maniere" despite the usual authority of *P* and *C*.

474 Cf. *TC* III 79 . . . wax neither quyk ne ded

480 Dous Penser is another personification originating in *RR*.

499 *BD* 1214–15
For *ferde*, and myn hewe al pale,
Ful ofte I *wex bothe pale and red.*

504 *BD* 1224 With hool herte I gan hir *beseche*

505 *BD* 1219 I seyde '*mercy*!" and no more.

505–6 Cf. Franklin's Tale *CT* F 978
Have mercy, swete, or ye wol do me *deye*.

509 *BD* 1236 *And whan I had my tale y-doo.*

oy, os, eus, etc., are all variant spellings of the first person singular preterit of *avoir*, which is here used with the past participle *dit*. This should be translated as a past tense, "told," and not as "dared tell" (Palmer): *oser* would be constructed with an infinitive, not a past participle. So also in line 554.

521 Cf. General Prologue *CT* A 119 . . . ful simple and coy.

541–48 Cf. *BD* 1239–44 (White's abrupt rejection of Knight).

580–81 *BD* 917–18
Yn al *hir face* a wikked sygne;
For hit was sad, symple, and benygne.

582 *BD* 910–11
Was hir chef patron of beaute
And chef ensample of al hir werk.

596–97 *BD* 1261–63
. . . *and she wel understod*
That I ne wilned thyng but god,
And worship, and to kepe hir name
Chaucer's manuscript reading:
je tendoie a ne tendoye qua *St*
St reading here matches Chaucer's phraseology very closely.

598 *BD* 1264 *Over alle thyng*, and drede hir shame

610 Cf. *BD* 1271 Savynge hir worshippe, by al weyes.

622 *BD* 1277–78

As helpe me God, I was as blyve
Reysed, as fro deth to lyve

Cf. *TC* III 1243

And from his deth is brought in sykernesse

623 *BD* 1280 The gladdest, and the moste at reste.

635 *BD* 1216 Bowynge to hir, I *heng the hed*.

641 *BD* 1270 *The noble yifte of hir mercy*. Cf. *Jugement* 670.

656 *BD* 1227–28

Ever to be stedfast and trewe,
And love hir alwey fresshly newe.

658 *BD* 1230 *And al hir worship for to save*

659–60 *BD* 1234–35

And never to false yow, but I mete,
I nyl . . .

663 *BD* 1040 My *worldes* welfare, and *my goddesse*

Cf. *LGW* F Prologue 95 As to myn erthly god to yow I calle

665–67 *TC* III 1294–95

. . . so that I *thorugh myn ignoraunce,*
Ne do no thing that *yow be displesaunce.*

Chaucer's manuscript reading:

negligence ignorance *JKAr.*

"Ignorance" of *J*, *K*, and *Ar* evidently accounts for Chaucer's word. Similarity of rhymes and the pattern of borrowing in *TC* and *BD* argue for specific influence of *Jugement* here.

670 See 641n.

671–74 Cf. *TC* III 1493–1518; IV 671–74 (Criseyde's pledge to Troilus).

675–77 *BD* 1296–97

And thus we lyved ful many a yere
So wel, I kan nat telle how.

684–85 Cf. *TC* IV 2–3

. . . ythonked be Fortune
That semeth trewest whan she wol bygyle

686–88 Cf. *RR* 5814–16, where Raison advises Amant,

Le dieu leras qui ci t'a mis,
et ne priseras une prune
toute la roe de Fortune.

686 Cf. *TC* III 1271 And *me bistowed in so heigh a place*

688–90 Cf. *RR* 8009–11, where Ami says that his friends:

. . . me firent tretuit la moe
quant il me virent souz la roe
de Fortune envers abatu.

688 *TC* IV 7 Than laugheth she, and *maketh hym the mowe.*

689 *TC* IV 8–9

From Troilus *she gan her brighte face*
Awey to writhe, and tok of hym non heede.

690–91 *TC* 6, 11

And whan a wight is from hire whiel ythrowe
And *on hire whiel she sette up* Diomede.

Cf. *RR* 3961–62:

et celui qui est sor la roe
reverse a un tour en la boue.

Cf. also *RR* 4865–66.

710 The adjectives repeat *Jugement* 358; see note above.

722 Cf. *BD* 488 Hys sorwful hert gan faste faynte

Chaucer's manuscript reading:

partir palir *CJKRRa*.

If there is a relationship between *Jugement* and *BD* here, it would be through variant "palir."

723–24 *CM* 191–92

To whom shal I pleyne of my distresse?
Who may me helpe?

Chaucer's manuscript reading:

prendre plaindre *JKKr*; complaindre *RRa*.

"Plaindre" may well have been the reading of Chaucer's manuscript. The verbal parallel here extends to a parallel of situation. *Jugement* 849–50 (see note below) shows a similar "plaindre/prendre" variant.

725–40 Cf *Boet* I Prose i, 29–31: Hi semper eius mores sunt ista natura. Servavit circa te propriam potius in ipsa sui mutabilitate constantiam

733 The early-tradition reading, *fait monter*, accords better with the Knight's conception of himself as a victim of Fortune than *voit monter*, the reading of the later manuscripts. It also is consonant with Boethius' presentation.

740 *BD* 631 To lyen, for *that ys hyr nature*.

747 *CM* 193 *Shal I compleyne unto my lady fre?*

Chaucer's manuscript reading:

Puiz Veuil *JK*. **ma** *om JK*.

"Vueil" seems closer to "Shal I" than "puis," but at the same time *J* and *K* lack the possessive "ma" which Chaucer translates.

808–9 *CA* 57–58

Yit is al this no lak to hir, pardee,
But *God or Nature* sore wolde I blame.

811 *CM* 268 *That putte such a beaute in her face*

826 Cf. *BD* 608 In drede ys al my *sykernesse*.

830 Despite Palmer's objection, Hoepffner's reading (*ne m'onnour*, based on F but supported by M, B, Vg, *P, E, J, K*, and *R*) is not metrically incorrect and must be maintained.

834–36 Cf. *BD* 1049, 1052–53

. . . she was the beste
. . . alle that hir seyen
Seyde and sworen hyt was so.

842 For the proverb, see Hassell, O69; Whiting, G295. Most of the proverbs in *Jugement* are found after line 1000.

848–50 *CM* 191 *To whom shal I than pleyne of my distresse*?
Chaucer's manuscript reading:
me prenray men prenray *CEArSt*; men plaindray *JK*.
"Men plaindray" translates Chaucer's meaning exactly. See similar variant in 723–24.

852–53 Cf. note to 808–9.

854–55 *CM* 267–68
But he that wroghte her, also mot I the,
That put *such a beaute* in her face

861–62 Cf. *BD* 1129–30
How ye sawe hir first, and where.
But wolde ye *tel* me *the manere* . . .

861–63 Cf. General Prologue *CT* A 715–16
Now have I toold you soothly, in a clause,
Th'estaat, th'array, the nombre, and eek the cause

906 The reading preferred by Hoepffner and Palmer, *Aucune joie face en vous, qui remestre*, although supported by P and the late-tradition manuscripts, should be rejected as hypermetrical.

943 The rhythm of the sentence, with a major pause after *Esperance*, suggests that one read *D'Esperancë*, rather than *Dë Esperance*. Also, there are no instances of the non-elision of the preposition *de* in our text, but several of elision at the fourth syllable (1050, 1182, 1695, etc.).

980–83 The omission of these lines in manuscripts of the later tradition destroys the syntax and logic of the passage and must be due, as we have argued in the introduction, to scribal error rather than to a deliberate omission on the part of the poet. Hoepffner rightly included them in his edition of the poem.

1000–1001 For this popular proverb, see Hassell, N35; Whiting, U8.

1002–3 Also proverbial; see Hassell, L101; Whiting, W450.

1011–15 The pronouns here are ambiguous. *P* reads *li* (1011), *le* (1013), and *il* (1015), suggesting the masculine *Souvenir* as antecedent. Most early manuscripts, including *C*, have *li, la, il*, indicating some confusion as to the intended antecedent. *J* and *K* have *li, la, el*, which would indicate either *Pensee* or *la dame* as the antecedent. We have gone with the weight of the early tradition, seeing *Pensee* as the antecedent for 1011–14, and a conflation of both *Pensee* and *Souvenir* as the referent for *il* in 1015 (whence the masculine form). *Le* for feminine *la* is attested in *P*.

1039 Cf. *BD* 616 Allas, how myghte I fare werre?

1071 A very common proverbial phrase. See Hassell, F75; Whiting, A216, L147. Cf. *TC* III 1200, and *LGW* 2648.

1072 *BD* 645 . . . for hyt ys nothyng *stable*

1074 *BD* 646 *Now by the fire, now at table*.
Chaucer's manuscript reading:
ore au feu ore a (*JKRRa*) au feu et a la *PAr*; or au feu a la ABDFMPm*Pc*Vg; ore au feu ore aū *E*; or a feu ore a *St*.
The reading of *J, K, R*, and *Ra* matches Chaucer's line exactly; the others deviate in various details.

The image here suggests the conventional presentation of the month of January in medieval picture calendars, in which the dining table and the fireside are the foci of activity.

1078 *BD* 648 *She ys pley of enchauntement*

1097–99 Cf. *TC* II 925–30 (In her dream an eagle takes Criseyde's heart.)

1105–7 The instinctive fidelity of plants and animals to their natures is the theme of *Boet* III meter 2. Cf. Chaucer's Squire's Tale *CT* F 604–20.

1105–6 For the proverb, see Hassell, L92.

1114 The spelling *nulz* of *J* and *K* and the later manuscripts must be rejected as an obvious error in inflection. There are numerous examples of the use of oblique forms for nominatives in this text, not only scribal but attested at the rhyme (e.g., 1640, 2032), but this case of nominative for oblique is unique and erroneous.

1143 *BD* 1115–17

> "Repentaunce! nay, fy!" quod he,
> "Shulde y now *repente me*
> *To love?*"
>
> 1145 *Chaucer's manuscript reading*:
> **repentoie** departoie ABCDFM*ArPc*Pm*St*Vg.
> Repetition of "repent"/"repentaunce" in *BD* 1114–16 may have been suggested by similar repetition in most early-tradition manuscripts (cf. l. 1143, "repentir").

1155 The conjuction *car* of *P* or *et* of *E*, *J*, and *K* is preferable to the relative *qua* (*qu'a*) of *C*, *R*, and *Ar* and the later manuscripts. One could easily see *qua* as a spelling variant of *car* indicating an attenuated pronunciation of final *r*. On the use of *que* for *car*, see Foulet, 428 and Ménard, 232.

1204–13 There are relatively few small domestic dogs in medieval fiction. Tristan's Petitcreiu is one, but he is a fairy dog, quite unreal, whereas Machaut's dog here, as Chaucer's after him, acts in a naturalistic manner.

1204 Cf. *BD* 389 A whelp, that fauned me as I stood

1212 Cf. *BD* 395 I wolde have *kaught hyt*

1224–25 *BD* 529, 533–34

> Loo! how goodly spak thys knyght
> . . . so tretable,
> Ryght wonder skylful and resonable

1226 *BD* 454 Of good mochel, and ryght yong therto

1233 The spelling *attrait* is found only in *C* and the later manuscripts. The adverbial phrase of the early-tradition manuscripts makes much better sense and should be maintained.

1234–51 A number of details of the lady's portrait here are like the portrait of White in *BD* 895–1005, but Chaucer's chief source is the description in lines 302–95.

1237 A proverbial comparison. See Hassell, F25; Whiting, F27. Chaucer's Prioress, *CT* A 152, has "eyen greye as glas"; and Absalon in the Miller's Tale, CT A 3317, has "eyen greye as goos."

1273 *BD* 398–99

> . . . a floury grene wente
> Ful thikke of gras, ful softe and swete.

1292–1343 This passage is Machaut's tribute to his longtime employer and patron, Jean l'Aveugle of Luxembourg, King of Bohemia.

1296–7 *BD* 1059–65 similarly mentions Alexander and Hector, but Chaucer's source probably is *Remede* 111–12. Alexander's riches and generosity were both proverbial; see Hassell, A75 and A77. Likewise, Hector was brave, strong, and valiant; Hassell, H20, H21, H22; Whiting, H317, H318.

1326–27 For Ovid as the expert in the ways of Amour, cf. *RR* 10492. Chaucer calls Ovid "Venus' clerk," *HF* 1487.

1337 It is appropriate that an adventurous king like Jean should have a battle cry. Most such slogans (like Charlemagne's legendary *Montjoie*) were place names. Lembourc perhaps refers to Limburg, the historic territory of the Low Countries to which the House of Luxembourg had claims, though it was controlled by Brabant after 1288. That was the year in which Henry III of Luxembourg, Jean l'Aveugle's grandfather, lost Limburg and his life at the battle of Worringen. Henry IV seems to have settled the issue of Limburg amicably in 1292 by marrying the daughter of the Duke of Brabant.

1338–41 Henry IV of Luxembourg, Jean l'Aveugle's father, was crowned Holy Roman Emperor, as Henry VII, at Rome on June 29, 1312. Contrary to Machaut here, Henry's wife Margaret, though she had been crowned with her husband at Milan, died before the party arrived in Rome. See William M. Bowsky, *Henry VII in Italy* (Lincoln: University of Nebraska Press, 1960). Jean l'Aveugle's son also became Holy Roman Emperor as Charles IV (1355–78).

1350 Since the knight is responding (*respondi*) to the narrator here, the *vous* of the earlier versions seems more logical than *nous* in P and the later manuscripts.

1364–66 Machaut obviously was proud of his close personal ties to the king.

1379–1422 The description evokes Luxembourg city, with its wide river and steep bank, famous up to World War II as the "Gibraltar of the North," whose fortifications Jean l'Aveugle's father had commenced. But the castle referred to probably was at or near the modern village of Durbuy, now in the Belgian province of Luxembourg, about 30 kilometers north of Bastogne, which also had fortifications on an impressive river site up until the eighteenth century.

1412–22 With Machaut's description of the fountain here, cf. *RR*, the description of the pool of Narcissus, 1430–32, 1528–34; and the description of the river, 103 ff., esp. 110–12:

> clere estoit l'eve et ausi froide
> come puis ou come fontaine,
> si estoit poi maindre de Saine.

1415 "Cold as ice": proverbial in the fourteenth century, as now. See Hassell, G36; Whiting, I1.

1423 Cf. *BD* 43 Our first mater is good to kepe

1448ff. From the time Honneur and Courtoisie greet the new arrivals until they are sent away with handsome gifts, all in the Castle of Durbuy is done *comme il faut*. The whole poem is a mirror of courtly behavior, this last part especially.

1466–67 Cf. the "paved parlour" which Pandarus enters in *TC* II 80–82.

1474–75 *TC* II 83–84

Herden a mayden reden hem the geste
Of the siege of Thebes, while hem leste.

By pointedly declaring his inability to name the clerk who is reading, Machaut may be humorously pointing to a literary associate in Jean's entourage, or perhaps he is suggesting an alter ego of himself.

1497 *Le prisa* ("praised/esteemed him") of the earlier manuscripts is more in keeping with Courtoisie's character than the later *l'esprisa* ("judged him").

1513 Cf. *BD* 301–2

And songen, everych in hys wyse,
The moste solempne servise . . .

RR 659–62 is probably a source for both Chaucer and Machaut.

1525–26 Cf. *BD* 502–3. But 60–62 above are main source. See note.

1540–41 Cf. *BD* 537–38. But 86 is main source.

1577 The earlier *a li* brings out more forcefully the pathos in the Lover's situation, referring directly back to *nouvel ami* (1574), than does the less precise *ailleurs* of the later manuscripts.

1581 *Nos* of the early versions would refer back to the whole discourse, in which the Lover set forth both cases, rather than merely to his own situation (*mes*).

1595–96 Here the knight talks about his story as a written presentation, as in 1782 below. Cf. the pilgrim Chaucer's words in *CT* B 2154 After the which this murye tale I write.

1609 *Leurs* in the later versions seems preferable here, in keeping with *nos* in 1581.

1617 *Si en* counts for a single syllable.

1642 Cf. *BD* 1049–50

Yow thoghte that she was the beste,
And to beholde the alderfayreste

1643 *C* and *R*'s *soy*, and in a more distant way *P*'s *aussi*, support *Ar* and the later manuscripts' *foi*. Even *E*'s *li* and *J*, *K*, and *St*'s *lui* could be attributed to a scribal misreading of *foi*, given the similarities in the vertical risers of *f*, *s*, and *l*.

1668–69 Proverbial comparison. See Hassell, C209; Whiting, W102.

1676–78 Cf. *TC* IV 423–24, 427

Or elles selde seynge of a wight,
Don olde affecciouns alle over-go.
Absence of hire shal dryve hire out of herte.

1687 See preceding note.

1699 Not worth a "pomme (pourrie)" is a common expression. For many occurences, see Hassell, P232; Whiting, A166.

1709–18 Raison's analysis of love as "carnal affection" motivated by delight accords with the presentation in *RR*, where the garden of love is the property of Deduit and its delights are all physical in nature. Raison in *RR* nonetheless tends to be more prescriptive in moral matters than Raison here with her generally practical advice.

1709–11 Cf. *TC* IV 418–20

Swich fir, by proces, shal of kynde colde;

For syn it is but casuel plesaunce,
Som cas shal putte it out of remembraunce

1750–51 This expression of the notion that the lover ought to respond in accord with the lady's treatment of him certainly has the ring of a proverb. The sentiment is related to that of lines 1822–23 below. Both image and sentiment are like line 1839.

1753 Cf. *BD* 843–45

. . . myn owne thoght
Seyde hit were beter serve hir for noght
Than with another to be wel.

1782 Cf. note to 1595–96 above.

1788–1811 The assumptions in Amour's response to Raison are similar to those of Troilus' response to Pandarus, *TC* IV 435–518.

1796–99 Cf. *TC* I 818–19

And thynk it is a guerdon, hire to serve,
A thousand fold moore than he kan deserve.

Primary source is *Remede* 1636–48.

1803–4 *TC* I 813, 816

What? *sholde he therfore fallen in dispayr*
Nay, nay . . .

1805–7 Cf. *TC* I 810, 812

What! many a man hath love ful deere ybought . . .
That never yet his lady mouth he kiste.

1817 The reading of *E, J,* and *K* and the later manuscripts appears preferable, but that of *P* and *C* and the early versions need not be rejected out of hand. *Que* could be added to give an exclamatory sense of disbelief to the question.

1822–23 Cf. Wife of Bath's Prologue *CT* D 484, 487

I made hym of the same wode a croce
That in his owene grece I made hym frye

For the common French proverb, "Rendez luy de tel pain souppes," see Hassell P7; Morawski, 869; and cf. 1750–51 note above.

1826–27 For the proverb, see Hassell, B199; Whiting B604.

1831 *P, R, Pc, Ra,* and *St*'s *fausse* seems to fit the context better than the other manuscripts' *haute*.

1839 Cf. 1750–51 and note above.

1848–51 With the presentation of Jeunesse here and following, cf. *RR* 1257–76 and 4409–4514.

1850 One could read *n'acomptë a don n'a* or *n'acompte a don në a,* as we have. Since the vast majority of the cases of non-elision of feminine *e* in *Jugement* are with the negative *ne,* the latter is to be preferred.

1861 *Topasse* here provides another example to support the thesis that Chaucer's name for Sir Thopas is meant to suggest effeminacy. See R. M. Smith, *Modern Language Notes* 51 (1950): 314–15.

1861–84 These lines are omitted in both *P* and *C* and the later manuscripts. As we have shown in the introduction, this is more likely due to scribal error than to a deliberate omission on the part of Machaut in revising his poem. Our text for these lines is based on Pc.

1885 This line is short by one syllable in both Hoepffner's and Palmer's editions. The meter requires the repetition of *et*, sanctioned by most early manuscripts.

1918–20 Cf. *TC* IV 623 And *if thow deye a martyr*, go to hevene! Cf. also IV 327–29.

1986–88 Cf. *BD* 723–25

Though ye had lost the ferses twelve
And ye for sorwe mordred yourselve,
Ye sholde be dampned in this cas . . .

Cf. *TC* I 823–24

That for to slen hymself myght he nat wynne,
But bothe don unmanhod and a synne

1995 Raison has an authority in the Castle of Durbuy which she does not enjoy in the garden of *RR*.

Chaucer's manuscript reading:
deffont meffont ABCFMPmVg.
The more drastic "deffont" of the earlier manuscripts accords better with the idea of suicide expressed in Chaucer's passage.

1997 The future form *seront* is to be preferred to the present tense after a hypothetical clause in the present.

2012–43 The king's entertainment of the knight and lady here has a number of points in common with King Sarpedoun's hospitality to Pandarus and Troilus, and their leave-taking,in *TC* V 435–48, 477–504.

2055ff. The ingenious solution of Ernest Hoepffner, "Anagramme und Rätselgedichte bei Guillaume de Machaut," *Zeitschrift für romanische Philologie* 30 (1906): 405, to the anagram contained in the last line remains the best. We translate: "The normal spelling *Guillaume de Machaut* cannot be derived from this line; two letters, *a* and *u*, are missing; two others, *i* and *n*, are left over. Since *Machaut* cannot be altered, we must seek to account for them in *Guillaume*. The form *Guillemin* readily suggests itself. That this form of the name was common at that time is proven among other ways by its presence in the *Combat des Trente*." The same solution works the anagram at the end of *Remede*.

NOTES FOR *REMEDE DE FORTUNE*

1–25 The twelve commandments of the apprentice or neophyte sound traditional, but we have not located a source. This opening passage is quite appropriate for *Remede*, which is strongly didactic throughout.

3–8 Cf. "Nature passe nourriture." Hassell, N6; Whiting, N25.

4 The direct object pronoun of *C* offers a better parallel to line 5 than does the reflexive of the other manuscripts.

23 *BD* 793 For-why *I tok hyt of so yong age*

Chaucer's manuscript reading:

"Lautre preigne" of *J* and *K* not Chaucer's reading.

24–25 *BD* 794–96

That *malyce* hadde my *corage*
Nat that tyme turned to nothyng
Thorgh to mochel knowlechyng.

Chaucer's manuscript reading:

qu'en que Pm.

Of all manuscripts Pm alone lacks the preposition "en" (24), reading "ains que malice," as Chaucer's manuscript probably did. Manuscript *E*'s "Sencourage" (24) and "Que" (25) are not Chaucer's.

26 Cf. *BD* 797 For that tyme Yowthe, my maistresse

26–30 *BD* 779–83

Paraunter I was therto most *able*,
As a *whit* wal or a *table*,
For hit ys redy to cacche and take
Al that men wil theryn make,
Whethir so *men wil portreye or peynte.*

Chaucer's manuscript reading:

ou et AB*E*FM*Pe*PmVg.

"Ou" rather than "et" evidently represents Chaucer's model for "portreye *or* peynte."

31–34 Cf. (Merchant's Tale) *CT* E 1429–30, 2117

But certeynly, a yong thyng may men gye,
Right as men may warm wex with handes plye.
In warm wex hath *emprented* the clyket

37–40 *BD* 786–88

I was *able* to have lerned tho,
And to have kend as wel or better,
Paraunter, *other art or letre*.

45–48 *BD* 797–99

For that tyme *Yowthe*, my maistresse,
Governed me in ydelnesse;
For hyt was in my firste youthe . . .

49–51 *BD* 801–4

For al *my werkes were flyttynge*
That tyme, and al my thoght *varynge*;

Al were to me ylyche good
That I knew thoo; but thus hit stood.

Chaucer's manuscript reading:
varians variaux *JK*.
The *J* and *K* reading evidently is further from Chaucer's than "Varians" of the others, though the orthographic difference is slight.

54–56 *BD* 948–51

And *good faire White* she *het*
That was my *lady name right.*
She was bothe fair and bryght;
She had not hir name wrong.

Chaucer's punning reference to Blanche of Lancaster matches Machaut's here to Bonne of Luxembourg; see lines 268–69, 3815–20, and 4277 below, and introduction to *Remede*.

54–56 *BD* 1049–53

Yow thoghte that she was the *beste*
And to beholde the *alderfayreste*,
Whoso had loked hir with your eyen.
With myn? nay, *alle* that hir seyen
Seyde and sworen hyt was soo.

55–60 Physician's Tale *CT* C 7–12

Fair was this mayde in excellent beautee
Aboven every wight that man may see.
For *Nature* hath with *sovereyn* diligence
Yformed hire in so greet excellence,
As though she wolde seyn, "Lo! I *Nature*,
Thus kan I forme and peynte a *creature* . . ."

57 Nature here seems more specifically the manifestation of God's creative force in the world, as in *RR* 15863 ff. and Alain de Lille's works, than in *Remede* 8 and 62. The alternation of more specific and more general significances for Nature seems typical of Chaucer's and Machaut's frequent references to her in their poetry.

61 Cf. *BD* 1092 Whan my herte wolde yerne

64 *BD* 1095 *After my yonge childly wit*

65 *BD* 1101 For *wonder feyn I wolde hir se.*

89 *BD* 1089 *Whan I first my lady say?*

92–95 *BD* 1090–93

I was ryght *yong*, soth to say,
And ful gret nede I hadde to lerne;
Whan my herte *wolde* yerne
To love, hyt was a gret *empryse.*

96–98 *BD* 839–42

So sodenly, *that I ne tok*
No maner counseyl but at hir lok
And at myn herte; for-why *hir eyen*
So *gladly*, I trow, myn herte seyen . . .

107–27 Machaut enumerates here nine nonpareils, five from the Bible, four from classical tradition. In the comparable passage in *BD* 1056–72, Chaucer names only six classical figures, duplicating only Machaut's Alexander and Hector (both from the traditional list of Nine Worthies).

109 *BD* 1072 Or ben *as wis as* Mynerva

110–11 *BD* 1059–61

And therto had the *worthynesse*
Of *Alysaunder*, and al the rychesse
That ever was in Babyloyne . . .

112–113 *BD* 1064–65

And therto also *hardy* be
As was *Ector*, so have I joye

116 *BD* 1056–57

Thogh I had had al *the beaute*
That ever *had* Alcipyades

118–122 Cf. *BD* 717–19

Remembre yow of Socrates,
For he ne counted nat thre strees
Of noght that Fortune koude doo.

The passages in *Remede* and *BD* both go back to *RR* 5814–20.

121 Although *que* for *car* is a common feature of many Old French texts, it is not usual in *C* and has therefore been rejected.

123–24 *BD* 986–87

Had as moche *debonairte*
As ever *had Hester* in the Bible

Cf. also *LGW* F 250 *Hester*, ley thow thy *mekenesse* al adoun; and Merchant's Tale, *CT* E 1744–45.

130 Cf. *BD* 1129; cf. also 89 above.

131 Cf. *BD* 1146 On hir was al my love leyd.

132–33 *BD* 1226–28

And swor, and hertely gan hir hete
Ever to be stedfast and trewe,
And love hir alwey fresshly newe

134 *BD* 1229

And *never other lady have*

Chaucer's manuscript reading:

autre amour navray autre nameray ABFMPmVg.

Chaucer's wording matches closely the reading of *C*, *E*, and *Pe* for this line.

137–40 *BD* 1285–86

In al my *yowthe*, in al chaunce,
She tok me in hir governaunce.

Cf. also *BD* 1090–91, 1095.

143–44 *BD* 1098 To do hir *worship* and the *servise* . . .

146 *BD* 1040 My *worldes* welfare, and my *goddesse*

147–49 *BD* 1262–63

That I ne *wilned* thyng but *god*,
And *worship*, and *to kepe* hir name

Cf. *TC* III 165–66

And myn honour with wit and bisynesse
Ay kepe.

164 Cf. 140 above, which is the likely source for *BD* 1286.

167–356 The lover now describes the lady's character and bearing, which inspired and instructed him much as the God of Love's lecture instructed the lover in *RR*. There are correspondences in *Remede* to the god's caution against villainy (*RR* 2074 a–j; *Remede* 239–40) and against pride (*RR* 2113–28; *Remede* 179–96, 245–52), and his counsel to proper dress (*RR* 2129–52; *Remede* 317–26). But the more practical Ovidian detail and tone of *RR* (e.g., in 2132–2212) are foreign to Machaut's poetry.

171 *BD* 911–12

And chef *ensample* of al hir werk,
And *moustre*.

Cf. *Jugement* 402–3, 582, and notes. Despite its orthography, *mireoir* counts for but two syllables in the versification.

197 *BD* 833 She had so stedfast countenaunce

TC I 182 With ful *assured lokyng* and *manere*.

198 Cf. *BD* 1052–53

Alle that hir seyen
Seyde and sworen hyt was soo.

Cf. also *TC* I 173 Hire goodly lokyng gladed al the prees.

TC I 176 . . . as folke seyde everichone.

199 *BD* 834 So *noble port* and *meyntenaunce*.

200 Cf. *TC* I 174 Nas nevere yet seyn thyng to ben preysed derre

209 Cf. 199 above, which is the probable source of *BD* 834.

217 *BD* 919 And which a goodly, softe speche . . .

219–22 *BD* 921–22

So frendly, and so wel *ygrounded*,
Up al resoun so wel yfounded

Chaucer's manuscript reading:

affremee affermee *EPe*; afervee *J*; afirvee *K*; afrenee ABFMPmVg.

Chaucer's manuscript clearly seems to have read "affermee"/"affremee" ("grounded") of *C, E,* and *Pe,* rather than "affrenee"/"enfrenee" ("bridled") of the others. "Affermee" is the *lectio durior*; "affrenee" assimilates the image of bridling one's speech found in 225 below.

226–27 Cf. *BD* 930–31

That ther was never yet throgh hir tonge
Man ne woman gretly harmed.

229–30 "Nota" in margin of A, B, F, M, Pm, and Vg; the proverb here is the Golden Rule, found in Matt. 7:12 and Luke 6:31; but Machaut's negative wording is more closely matched by Tob. 4:16. See Hassell, F4; Whiting, D274.

232–37 Cf. *BD* 927 Ne trewer tonged, ne skorned lasse

238 *BD* 937 Ne chyde she koude never a del.

243–44 "Nota" in margin of F, Pm, and Vg. For proverb, see Hassell, H60.

245–47 Matt. 23:12; Luke 14:11. "He who humbles himself shall be exalted, and he who exalts himself shall be humbled." As the variants show, only the inept *E* scribe got the biblical allusion straight. Machaut's own wording may have been confused.

249–50 Cf. *BD* 1052–53, quoted above 198n.

252 *Que* of *C, E,* and *Pe* completes the comparison of his lady with other ladies better than *qu'en* of *J* and *K* and the later manuscripts, which grammatically compares *dame* to the adjectives in the preceding two lines rather than to *dame* of 249.

257, 270 Fole Largesse is a conception of *RR* (7867, 7924, etc.); there it is an attribute of the lover who is trying to spend his way to success.

267 "Nota" in margin A, F, and Vg. For the proverb, see Hassell, D119; Whiting, G76. Cf. *LGW* F 451–52.

268–69 This is another possible punning reference to Bonne of Luxembourg. Cf. 54–55 above and note.

274–75 The presentation of avarice as the slayer of all good reformulates the conception of it as the root of all evil enunciated by Chaucer's Pardoner, *CT* C 334. Cf. Hassell, A215, C294; Whiting, C491.

289 The personification Desire figures importantly in Machaut's and Chaucer's poems; interestingly, the personification does not appear in *RR*.

297–98 Cf. the image of the magnet in *RR* 1157–60.

299–302 *BD* 1102–5

So mochel hyt amended me
That, whan I saugh hir first a-morwe,
I was warished of al my sorwe
Of al day after, til hyt were eve.

308 This is the first mention of Esperance, who assumes a body and great importance later in the poem. The figure originates in the God of Love's promise in *RR* 2601–28 that Hope will comfort the lover in his sufferings.

316 "Nota" in margin of Vg; nevertheless, a rather plain sentiment.

318 Cf. 249–50n above.

330 Cf. 199, 209 and notes above.

359–61 *BD* 1146–47

On hir was al my love leyd;
And yet she nyste hyt never a del

363–64 *BD* 1149–50

For be ryght siker, I *durste noght,*
For all this world, telle hir my thoght

371–78 Cf. Troilus' first interview with Criseyde, *TC* III 78–98. Both Chaucer's and Machaut's lovers endure physical sufferings comparable to those produced in *RR* by the God of Love's arrows, 1694–1704, 1766–68, etc.

375 *BD* 1215 Ful ofte *I wex bothe pale and red.*

396 *BD* 1216 Bowynge to hir, I heng the hed.
Chaucer eliminates the inelegant comparison of the lover's bowed head to a bear's.

402–3 *BD* 1156–57

Trewly *I dide my besynesse*
To make songes, as I best koude

Chaucer's manuscript reading:

403 "a faire" in *J* and *K*, rather than "en faire" of all others, perhaps represents Chaucer's reading, though the case is not strong.

Cf. *BD* 471 He sayd a *lay*, a maner *song*

403–4 Cf. Franklin's Tale *CT* F 947–48
Of swich matere made he manye *layes,*
Songes, compleintes, *roundels, virelayes*

405 *BD* 1171–72
Algates *songes* thus I made
Of my felynge, myn herte to glade.

Cf. Franklin's Tale *CT* F 944–45.

407–8 "Nota" in margin of B and Vg.

414 In our translation, the rubric for miniature no. 3 has been moved from after this line to after line 430 so as not to interrupt the flow of the narrative.

423–24 Cf. 405n above.

430 *BD* 471, 1171
He sayd a lay, a maner song
Algates songes thus I made

431–652 The lai was reputed to be the most difficult of the generally demanding Middle French *formes fixes.* It has twelve sections, each section divided into matching halves. The metrical structures and the rhymes of the sections differ except for the first and last, which are supposed to be identical. See Hoepffner, II: xxxvii–xxxviii. The accompanying music, which is monodic, is different for each of the eleven differing stanza forms.

433, 434, 435, 454 Dous Penser, Souvenir, Espoir, and Dous Regard, whose consoling powers the lover celebrates in this lai, are the comforters that the God of Love promises in *RR* 2601–2734.

436–39 Cf. *TC* I 969 Stond faste, for to good port hastow rowed. Cf. also *TC* I 526. The familiar image is also found in 2306–7, 2336 below.

497 Cf. *CT* A 119 . . . ful symple and coy. These adjectives were commonly joined in personal descriptions.

508–10 The substantial difference in the text of the early-tradition manuscripts from the late at this point is discussed in the introduction to the manuscripts.

662–664 Cf. *BD* 1211–15. See also 371–78n above.

685–702 This is perhaps the most noteworthy of several passages in *Remede* which provide valuable testimony to the anonymous circulation of fourteenth-century court poetry and to its presentation. Though the lai is supplied with music in the manuscripts, the lover does not sing it here.

693–98 Cf. *BD* 1212–17. *Jugement* 466–76 is primary source.

703–7 Cf. *TC* III 78–81
This Troilus, that herde his lady preye
Of lordshipe hym, wax neither quyke ne ded,
Ne myghte o word for shame to it *seye,*
Although men sholde smyten of his hed.

705 Cf. *BD* 310 That certes, for the toun of Tewnes . . .
Machaut's source perhaps is *RR* 1074 Plus que trestoz li ors de Rome.

708 Cf. *BD* 1218 For wit, maner, and al was gone. *Jugement* 473 is primary source.

733–34 *BD* 1250 *I durste no more say therto*
Chaucer's manuscript reading:

d'espondre respondre ABFMPmVg.

Readings of *C, E, J, K,* and *Pe* are to be preferred, since *rime eqúivoque* (identical rhyme) demanded that either the part of speech or the meaning vary, as they do not if "respondre" is used here. "Espondre" ("to explain") better represents Chaucer's meaning in *BD* 1250.

737–38 The readiness of the lover to sacrifice his soul in the cause of love has a counterpart in the narrator's sentiment expressed in *TC* III 1319–20, though Machaut seems to be reaching for a rhyme here.

748 The early-text tradition is unsatisfactory in all manuscripts. Neither *C, E,* and *Pe*'s *que ce fust songe* ("for this was a dream") nor *J* and *K*'s *com ce fust songe* ("as if this were a dream") is satisfactory in light of the context.

751–52 Cf. *BD* 1250–51

I durste no more say therto
For pure fere, but stal away.

757 *TC* I 543 Till neigh that he *in* salte *teres dreynte.*

760–61 "Wave of tears" perhaps is drawn from *Boet* I Prose ii, 17, "oculosque meos fletibus undantes," which Chaucer translates in *Boece* as "wawes of my wepynge."

770 For the game "Roy qui ne ment," see Ernest Hoepffner, "Frage- und Antwortspiele in der französischen Literatur des 14. Jahrhunderts," *Zeitschrift für romanische Philologie* 33 (1909): 695–710.

786 The Parc de Hesdin is the famous park of the castle at Hesdin in northwest France. See Introduction, *Remede*, "Occasion, Contents, Sources, and Influence."

787–801 With the high-walled garden that the lover enters by way of a "petit guichet," cf. *RR* 495–516.

808–27 Amant's describing the garden as he walks along until his arrival at a "fontenelle" certainly derives from the comparable passage in *RR* 1283–1425, in which the lover leaves the carole and eventually arrives at the "fontaine" of Narcissus.

830–32 Cf. *BD* 398–401

Doun by a floury grene wente
Ful thikke of gras, ful softe and swete.
With floures fele, faire under fete,
And litel used, hyt semed thus.

836–37 Cf. *RR* 118–19

De l'eve clere reluisant
Mon vis refreschi et lave.

858–60 Cf. *Boet* III xi, 47

Quis legem det amantibus?
Maior lex amor est sibi.

Cf. Knight's Tale, *CT* A 1164.

870 Cf. *RR* 3051 Pren durement au denz le frain.

In *RR* Reason is telling the lover to take the bridle between his teeth in order to resist Love.

877–80 Cf. *RR* 2263–66

Lors te vendront soupirs et plaintes,

Friçons et autres dolors maintes;
Em plusors sens seras destroiz
Une heure chaut, autre eure froiz . . .

883–96 The characterization of Fortune here is the first of a number of such passages in *Remede*. The main source is *Boet* II, and *RR*. The situation and statement at this point is generally comparable to *RR* 3950–57, where Amour and Fortune are also closely associated.

891 *BD* 645 . . . *for hit is nothyng stable*

905–1480 This complainte is the longest of the intercalated lyrics of *Remede*. As Hoepffner says, there is no doubt that Machaut here is presenting the complainte as one of the standard lyric genres, but it never gained general acceptance as a *forme fixe*. See Hoepffner, II, xxxvii–xl, for a thorough analysis of the form. There are thirty-six stanzas of sixteen lines each; the monodic melody could be repeated for each stanza, but a full performance would be very lengthy and repetitive.

905–1000 The various characteristics of Fortune enumerated here, and the images associated with her (the wheel, the two buckets, etc.) are of course conventional (See Howard Patch, *The Goddess Fortune in Medieval Literature* [Cambridge: Harvard University Press, 1927], *passim*), much of their tradition being derived from *Boet*, the central source of *Remede*. Boethius is cited by name in line 982.

For 905 cf. *BD* 599–600

My song ys turned to pleynynge,
And al my laughtre to wepynge

Machaut's line is proverbial; see Hassell, R55; Whiting, M688.

912–14 *TC* I 848–50

For if *hire whiel stynte any thyng to torne*,
Than cessed she Fortune anon to be.
Now, sith hire whiel by no way may *sojourne*

916–18 *TC* IV 10–11

But caste hym clene out of his lady grace,
And on hire whiel she sette up Diomede.

Cf. also *Jugement* 690–91.

918 *BD* 635 *That ys broght up, she set al doun*.

920 In our translation, the rubric for the miniature (no. 5) has been moved from mid-stanza to the beginning of the *complainte*.

926 Cf. *BD* 620, 813

The trayteresse fals and ful of gyle
The false trayteresse pervers!

Machaut's Motet VIII, 17, is the main source for these lines of Chaucer. Cf. also 2510 below.

In manuscript *C* this line begins with a large decorative initial placed beneath the miniature to balance the initial of line 921. It does not mark a natural division, so we have not included our customary space before this line in the edition.

930 Proverbial comparisons; see Hassell, M151, M127.

945 Cf. proverb, "Qui une foiz escorche deus foiz ne tont," Morawski, no. 2179.

955 The wording here is from *RR*, 5815 Tout le monde (Fortune) ne prise une prune.

982–84 Cf. *BD* 718–19

For he ne counted nat thre strees
Of noght that Fortune koude doo.

The primary source for Machaut and Chaucer is *RR*, 5814–20.

988–90 Cf. *BD* 636–41; Merchant's Tale *CT* E 2059.

1000–1112 Nebuchadnezzar's dream of the statue with the feet of clay is told in Dan. 2:31–35. The allegorization of the statue as Fortune is perhaps original with Machaut. Daniel assigns it an historical significance. As Hoepffner points out (II, xxxii–xxxiii) Nebuchadnezzar was often included among the victims of Fortune, which probably accounts for the association here.

1052–53 *BD* 647 For *many oon* hath she thus *yblent.*

1052–56 Cf. *TC* IV 5 That she hem hent and blent, traitour comune!

1054 *BD* 621 That *al behoteth*, and nothyng halt

1057 Cf. *TC* IV 11 And *on hire whiel she sette up* Diomede

1059–60 Cf. Wife's Prologue *CT* D 792 I with my fest so *took hym on the cheke*

1061–62 *TC* IV 6–7

And whan a wight is from hire whiel *ythrowe,*
Than laugheth *she, and maketh hym the mowe.*

1078 Cf. *BD* 637, 639.

1113–14 *BD* 673–74

For *Fortune* kan so many a *wyle,*
Ther be but fewe kan hir *begile*

1122–28 The contrasting doors of Fortune's domicile evidently represent an elaboration of *RR* 6049–91, the description of Fortune's house. See Patch, *Goddess Fortune*, pp. 136–43.

1129–53 Cf. anaphora and oxymoron in these lines with *BD* 598–615. Machaut's source seems to be *RR* 4263–4315, Reason's description of Amour, which begins, "Amors, ce est pez haïneuse."

1133 Cf. *BD* 607 Myn hele ys turned in seknesse

1138 *BD* 642 She ys *th'envyouse charite*

1153–60 Machaut's tree-image seems mostly original. For other trees of Fortune, see Patch, pp. 138–40.

1153–57 Cf. *BD* 630–31

Hir moste worshippe and hir *flour* ys
To lyen, for that ys hyr nature.

1156 The subjunctive of all manuscripts except *C* is not warranted by the syntax or sense.

1161–92 This is another series of attributes conventionally attached to Fortune. See Patch, *Goddess Fortune,* pp. 42–57.

1162 *BD* 633–34

She ys fals; and ever *laughynge*
With oon eye, and that other wepynge.

1167 *BD* 622 She goth *upryght* and yet she *halt*

1169 *BD* 632 *withoute feyth*, lawe, or mesure

Chaucer's manuscript reading:

Only *C, E,* and *Pe* have this line which, like Chaucer's, speaks of the faithlessness of Fortune. The wording here perhaps brought to the poet's mind Machaut's Motet VI, which he uses in the following passage of *BD*. Manuscripts A, B, D, *J*, M, Pm, and Vg replace 1169 with "En desconforte se reconforte" after 1170. See discussion in the introduction to the manuscripts.

1177 Cf. *BD* 632; but the main source for *BD* here is Motet VI.

1191 Cf. *BD* 659–60

Therwith Fortune seyde 'Chek her!'
And 'Mat!' in myd poynt of the chekker

Source for both Machaut and Chaucer is probably *RR* 6622.

1198 *BD* 599–600

My song ys *turned* to pleynynge,
And al *my laughtre to wepynge*
Chaucer's manuscript reading:
mué tourne *J*.

"Tourne" and the conjunction "et" ally *J* with Chaucer's lines here, but "est" in all other manuscripts is closer to his "is" plus past participle.

1209–1368 After attacking Fortune, the lover reproaches Amour. The association of Love with Fortune is conventional, but may be directly inspired by the lover's complaint in *RR*. See 883–96n above.

1216 See 705 and note above.

1229–43 Machaut develops the conventional imagery of Love's warfare and punishments in an original manner here.

1246–48 *BD* 1190 I am *adred she wol be wroth*.

1265–67 Cf. *BD* 1217–19

I durste nat ones loke hir on,
For wit, maner, and al was goon.
I seyde 'mercy!' and no more.

Jugement 467–76 is probably a more important source for this passage.

1270 Cf. *TC* I 274 And sodeynly he wax therwith astoned

1271 *BD* 1211–12

With sorweful herte, and woundes dede,
Softe and quakynge for pure drede

Cf. *TC* I 278–79

Therwith his herte gan to sprede and rise,
And softe sighed . . .

1278–80 Cf. *TC* I 305–7

Withinne the subtile stremes of hir eyen;
That sodeynly hym thoughte he felte dyen,
Right with hire look, the spirit in his herte.

Cf. also *TC* III 129, 306–7.

1289–90 Cf. *TC* I 422–23

. . . O lord, now youres is
My spirit, which that oughte youres be.

1304 Cf. *TC* I 427 But as hire man I wol ay lyve and sterve.

1311 In *CT* Chaucer cites Seneca for his wisdom several times. Jean de Meun tells the story of his death, *RR* 6155–6230.

1319–20 *TC* I 538

And *with* som *frendly lok gladeth me*, swete

TC III 129–30

That with the stremes of youre eyen cleere
Ye wolde somtyme frendly on me see

Chaucer's manuscript reading:

1319 reading of *C* which omits "de" and supplies "douls" seems both nearer to, and farther from, Chaucer's original.

1323–24 Cf. *TC* III 129–30, quoted in preceding note.

1351–52 Cf. *BD* 764–66

Dredeles, I have ever yit
Be tributarye and yiven *rente*
To *Love* . . .

1362 Cf. Knight's Tale *CT* A 1238

Wel hath Fortune yturned thee the dys.

1374–75 Cf. *BD* 659–60 (See 1191n above).

1403–16 This simile in which the lover becomes the game pursued by the hunting dog evokes the hunt-of-love allegories. See James I. Wimsatt, *Chaucer and the French Love Poets* (Chapel Hill: University of North Carolina Press, 1968), pp. 39–45.

1425–26 "Nota" in margin of Vg. That his loyalty will save the lover has various proverbial equivalents, one of them the biblical "Truth overcomes all things" (Esdras 3:12). See Whiting T509, T511, T513.

1441–44 For the proverbial idea that a complaining sick person is mending, cf. Hassell, M60, M62.

1445–59 Cf. *TC* I 544–46

Al was for noght, she herde nat his pleynte;
And whan that he bythoght on that folie,
A thousand fold his wo gan multiplie.

1460–74 The fire of love imagery here inspires the comparable passage in *TC* I 435–49.

1461–64 Cf. *TC* I 533–36

But now help, God, and ye, swete, for whom
I pleyne, ikaught, ye, never wight so faste!
O mercy, dere herte, and help me from
The deth . . .

1465–66 *TC* I 440 And *brende hym so in sondry* wise ay newe

1470–72 *TC* I 436, 490

The fyr of love . . .
That *the hote fir of love hym brende*

Cf. also *TC* I 445 his hote fir; 448 And ay the ner he was, the more he brende.

1481–82 *BD* 504–5

But *argued* with his owne thoght
And *in his wyt disputed* faste

TC IV 1083–84

And *whil he was* in al this hevinesse,
Disputyng with hymself in this matere

As in *Remede* the lover's debate with himself is followed by the appearance of

Esperance, so in the comparable passages in *RR*, *BD*, and *TC*, comforters (Reason, the dreamer, Pandarus) appear to the bewildered lovers. The situation stems ultimately from *Boet* I Meter i, Prose i, where Philosophy descends to Boethius.

1483 Cf. *BD* 487 *Whan* he *had mad* thus *his complaynte*

1488 Cf. *TC* I 484–85

And fro this forth tho refte hym love his slep,
And made his mete his foo . . .

1489 Cf. *TC* I 543 Til neigh that he in salte *teres dreynte*

Chaucer's manuscript reading:

noiez baigniez *CPe*; baillies *E*.

J and *K* and later manuscripts match Chaucer's "dreynte" better than *CPe* ("bathed"), or *E*.

1490–93 *TC* III 1088–92

And *every spirit* his *vigour* in knette,
So they astoned or oppressed were.
The *felyng* of his sorwe, or of his fere,
Or of aught eles, *fled was out of towne*;
And *down he fel* al sodeynly *aswowne*.

Chaucer's manuscript reading:

"Toute" without "autre" in *J* and *K* 1492 makes them closer to *TC* III 1088, but the line is left a syllable short, and "aught elles" of III 1090 is left without a counterpart.

1491–93 *BD* 488–89

His sorwful hert gan faste *faynte*,
And his *spirites wexen dede*.

1499–1500 Cf. *BD* 184–85, where the God of Sleep casts up "oon eye." Chaucer's primary source, however, is Machaut's *Fonteinne amoureuse*, 632.

1502–5 As suggested in the note to 1481–82 above, the advent of Esperance here is modelled both on the coming of Reason to the lover in *RR* 2955–81, 4191–98, and on Lady Philosophy's appearance to Boethius in *Boet* I, Prose i. The *Consolation* provides the primary source for the interview of the lover with Esperance. Much of their conversation involves word-for-word translation.

1516–43 The imagery which depicts the lover as blind and sick, and Esperance as a bringer of light and a healing physician, is derived from *Boet*, esp. I Meter i–Prose iii.

1519–26 *Boet* I Meter iii,1–2.

Tunc me discussa liquerunt nocte tenebrae
Luminibusque prior rediit uigor.

1533–43 Cf. *Boet* I Prose ii,17–18, and I Meter iii.

1544–58 The sweet savor of Esperance evidently is an original conception of Machaut.

1567–77 *Boet* I Prose ii 9–11 Cumque me non modo tacitum sed elinguem prorsus mutumque vidisset, admouit pectori meo leniter manum . . .

1572–73 Cf. *BD* 450,502

Anoon-ryght I wente ner.
I went and stood ryght at his fet

1577–84 Cf. *BD* 490–92

The blood was fled for pure drede
Doun to hys herte, to make hym warm—
For wel hyt feled the herte had harm

1627 C's *aiez* is a graphy for second singular *aies* (for the confusion of *s/z*, see especially Pope, S807).

1629–30 *BD* 906 And *every day* hir *beaute* newed.

1636 cf. *TC* I 813 What? sholde he therfore fallen in dispayr

1639–40 *TC* I 817–19

To *serve and love* his deere hertes queene,
And thynk it is a guerdon, hire to *serve,*
A thousand fold moore than he kan deserve.

1643–48 *TC* I 817–19 (quoted above).

1662–63 *TC* I 813–14

What? *sholde he* therfore *fallen in dispayr,*
Or be recreant for his owne tene?

1671–82 *TC* I 897–900

And also thynk, and therwith glade the,
That sith thy lady vertuous is al
So foloweth it that there is som pitee
Amonges al thise other in general.

1681–82 Franchise and Pitié are also personified attributes of the lady in *RR*, but Humblesse and Charité are not found there; cf. 1690–91 below.

1684 *TC* I 901 *And forthi* see that thou, in special . . .

1686 *TC* III 1282 Here may men seen that *mercy passeth right.* Cf. also III 1267 But if thi grace passed oure desert; Knight's Tale *CT* A 3089 For gentil *mercy oghte passen right*; and *LGW* F 161–62 Yet Pite . . . made *mercy passen right.* This statement involving familiar Christian doctrine is recorded often in English after Chaucer. See Whiting, M508. Not listed in Hassell's or Morawski's collections.

1721–22 "Nota" in margin of F, K, M, and Vg. See Hassell, P48. Cf. *TC* I 807–8

But love a woman that she woot it nought
And she wol quyte it that thow shalt nat fele.

1727–28 "Nota" in margin of F, K, and Vg. This version of "The dog that bites the hand that feeds him" is also found in *RR* 14868. See Hassell, C153; and 2639–42 below.

1733–84 The contrast between the glib deceiver and the true lover who has extreme difficulty in declaring his love is like the contrast between Troilus in *TC* III and Diomede in V.

1737–38 Cf. Squire's Tale *CT* F 510–11

That no wight koude han wend he koude feyne,
So depe in greyn he dyed his coloures.

1751–75 Cf. *TC* III 82–98 (Troilus changes color, trembles, and lies mute before Criseyde in their first interview, while she looks on approvingly.)

1790–92 Cf. *TC* I 818–19, quoted above, note to 1639–40.

1794–96 Cf. *TC* I 879–89 (Pandarus expatiates on how well "Love hath byset" Troilus).

1836 For "soutive parole," manuscripts A, B, F, M, Pm, and Vg substitute "soutile parabole," which is probably preferable in the light of the rules for *rime équivoque* (see note to 733 above).

1863–78 This description of the ensign of the true lover is a feature of *Remede*. In manuscript *E* the incipit identifies the whole poem as "L'escu bleu," and miniatures in A, *C*, *J*, *K*, and *Pm* depict the shield as presented in this passage.

1865–69 Cf. *TC* III 1370–71

> But wel I woot, a broche, gold and asure,
> In which a ruby set was lik an herte.

The azure ground and the heart of gules give the shield an interesting resemblance to the brooch.

1887–88 Cf. *TC* IV 1584 Men seyn, "*the suffrant overcomith*," parde. "Nota" in margin of A and *K*. The proverb was common in French and English. See Hassell, S108; Whiting, T213. Cf. 2485–90 and note below.

1901–10 The meanings for lovers of the various colors are referred to and drawn on several times by Machaut and Chaucer. See James I. Wimsatt, "Guillaume de Machaut and Chaucer's Love Lyrics," *Medium Aevum* 47 (1978): 70. "True blue," of course, was and remains proverbial; see Hassell, P135; Whiting, B384. So was "fickle green," at least after Machaut and Chaucer. See Hassell, V75; Whiting, G452.

1931 *qu'est* = *qui est*

1933–34 A proverbial comparison. See Hassell, P226.

1950 Esperance's references here and elsewhere to what she said "above" suggests reading rather than oral presentation. Cf. *Jugement* 1595–96, 1782; William Calin, *A Poet at the Fountain* (Lexington: University of Kentucky Press, 1974), p. 48. Cf. Chaucer's similar "confusion" of speaking and writing in *CT* B 2154.

1961–68 With Esperance's vow of faithfulness, cf. that of Lady Philosophy, *Boet* I, prose iii.

1976 Proverbial: "De nouveau tout est beau." See Hassell, N36; Whiting, T143.

1985–2023 The chanson royal is the third of the intercalated lyrics set to music in *Remede*. The five stanzas on the same rhymes with envoy are standard, though the line lengths here are exceptional. See Hoepffner, II: xli–xliv. Like Lady Philosophy, Esperance sings comforting songs to her protegé.

1993–2020 The notion that the lover should be satisfied with Hope and Sweet Looks takes up a theme of the lover's earlier lai. See 432–58 above and notes.

2010 *Ne* of *C* provides a better parallel with 2007 and the negative context than does *Et* of the other manuscripts.

2035–36 The lines embody the proverbial comparison, "Doux comme une pucelle." See Hassell, P294; Whiting, F434. Chaucer applies the related "meek as a maid" to two male figures, *CT* A 69 and 320.

2039–49 Cf. *HF* 853–87. The insistent questioning and self-approval of Esperance here provide a precedent for the eagle's comic interview with Geffrey. There is humor, of course, in the light suggestion of feminine vanity which Machaut conveys here in the presentation of Esperance.

2053 We have retained the dynamic adverb *Or* of *C* (supported by adverbial *Si* in *E* and *Pe*) rather than the flat *Je* of *J*, *K*, and the later manuscripts.

2064–66 "Nota" in margin of *K*. For related proverbial statements, see Hassell, F148; Whiting F434.

2079 Cf. Nun's Priest's Tale *CT* B 4633 Taketh the fruyt and lat the chaf be stille. Machaut uses versions of this proverb seven times. See Hassell, G46; Whiting, C428, F693, S 824; Bernard F. Huppé and D. W. Robertson, Jr., *Fruyt and Chaf* (Princeton: Princeton University Press, 1963), pp. 3–29.

2081–82 "Nota" in margin of Pm. For this common proverb, see Hassell, B93; Whiting, F431, T152.

2087–88 "Nota" in margin B, F, *P*, and M. This and 2089 again represent very familiar proverbs. See Hassell, F13; Whiting, W275.

2089 Cf. *TC* II 1276 Felte iren hot, and he bigan to smyte. "Nota" in margin B, F, and Pm. See Hassell, F51; Whiting, I60. Chaucer uses the image also in Tale of Melibee *CT* B 2226.

2090–93 "Nota" in margin of B and *K*. Esperance continually presents herself as the proverbial "friend in need." See also 2819–21 and 3065–66 below; Hassell, A100; and Whiting, F634.

2094–96 Cf. *BD* 1273 And therwith she yaf me a ring. Later in *Remede*, 4075–76, the lover gives this ring to his lady.

2106–8 Proverbial comparison; see Hassell, S100.

2133–38 Cf. *BD* 1277–78

. . . I was as blyve
Reysed, as fro deth to lyve

This passage and several nearby (2128–29, 2181–82, 2186) evoke biblical statements..

2173–77 With Esperance as nurse and physician, cf. presentation of Philosophy, *Boet* I prose iii, 1–6.

2181–82 Cf. Matt. 6:8 Your father knows what you need before you ask him.

2191–94 *BD* 752–55

"Doo thyn entent to herkene hit."
"Yis, syr." "Swere thy trouthe therto."
"Gladly." "Do thanne holde hereto!"
"I shal ryght blythely . . .

2199–2222 Cf. *BD* 410–15; *LGW* F 125–29. Primary source for *Remede* here and both passages of Chaucer is *RR* 53–66.

2205–8 *LGW* F 128–29

Now hath th'atempre sonne all that releved
That naked was, and *clad him new agayn*.

2209 In the context of the borrowing here, the phonetic similarity of "panter" in *LGW* F 131 and "panthere" in this line may be significant.

2253–57 Cf. note to 2199–2222 above.

2277 The reading of later manuscripts, "a ta propre p.," adopted by Hoepffner, is much inferior. It is appropriate that a personification like Esperance should emphasize to the Amant her true nature.

2281–82 The ability of Esperance to make herself visible when she wishes is comparable to the power of angels who on occasion appear to men but otherwise are invisible.

2283–86 Cf. *LGW* F 510–19, when Alceste's name is revealed.

2294–2351 Much of this address to Esperance uses the language of a prayer of praise to the Blessed Virgin.

2296–97 Cf. *TC* II 835–36

> . . . al that bereth lif
> Ymagynen ne kouthe how to be bet.

2305 Cf. *TC* II 842 Of trouthe grownd, mirour of goodlihed

2306–7, 2336 Cf. note to 436–39 above.

2310–11 Cf. *TC* II 844–45

> Of vertu roote, of lust fynder and hed,
> Thorugh which is alle sorwe fro me ded

2317–26 Cf. *BD* 435–42. *RR* 12760–70 is the primary source for both Machaut and Chaucer in these lines, but while Jean de Meun and Chaucer name Algus (Argus) as the exemplary counter, Machaut enumerates a series of six experts, none of whom is Algus.

2324 "To bark at one's shadow" is surely proverbial, but not recorded in Hassell, Morawski, or Whiting.

2326 Cf. Morawski 1307, "Moult a affaire qui la mer a a boire." See Whiting, S140; cf. *RR* 5052, Il bee a boivre toute Seine. Cf. Whiting, S110, S112.

2336 Cf. *TC* I 969 . . . for to good port hastow rowed.

2364–65 One may compare *AA* 131 Hir herte was to him *wedded* with a ring. In both cases the marriage is figurative.

2370 Cf. *BD* 1003–5

> That Trouthe hymself, over al and al
> Had chose hys maner principal
> In hir, that was his restyng place

2379–84 Cf. Hassell, F127; Whiting, F523, F546. As noted before, much of the description of Fortune in *Remede* is proverbial. We have not endeavored to document it all.

2407–48 While the two faces of Fortune became common in her medieval iconography, it is not clear to which "ancients" Machaut refers here. Boethius briefly imputes to her two faces, *Boet* II prose i, 33, "ambiguos vultus."

2448 Esperance's manner of catechizing the lover is indebted to the question-and-answer exchanges of Philosophy and Boethius, and no doubt derives ultimately from the dialogues of Plato.

2461–63 *TC* III 813–14, 817

> . . . worldly *selynesse*,
> Which clerkes callen fals *felicite* . . .
> Condicioun of veyn *prosperitee*.

The similarity of wording is reinforced by a similarity in situation. Both Esperance and Criseyde are moralizing, somewhat speciously, about Fortune.

2467–73 *Boet* II prose iv, 79–84. Si beatitudo est summum naturae bonum ratione degentis nec est summum bonum quod eripi ullo modo potest, quoniam praecellit id quod nequeat auferri, manifestum est quoniam ad beatitudinem percipiendam fortunae instabilitas adspirare non possit.

2475 Listed as proverb by Hassell, P209. Cf. 2770 below.

2485–90 *TC* IV 1583–88

> And forthi sle with *resoun* al this hete!
> Men seyn, "the *suffrant* overcomith," parde;
> Ek "whoso wol han *lief,* he lief moot lete."
> Thus maketh *vertu* of necessite
> By *pacience,* and thynk that *lord* is he
> Of Fortune . . .

Chaucer's use of the proverb, "The suffraunt overcomith," may have been prompted by his reading "vient de souffrir" of 2490 as "veint de souffrir" ("conquers by suffering"), though no extant manuscript has the latter reading. See 1887 and note above. Cf. also Franklin's Tale *CT* F 773–75.

2489–94 *Boet* II prose iv, 63–66. Beata sors omnis est aequanimitate tolerantis. Quis est ille tam felix qui cum dederit impatientiae manus, statum suum mutare non optet?

2497–2504 The advice not to prize the goods of Fortune in one's heart, and to gain the never-failing good that cannot be taken away, echoes words of the Sermon of the Mount, Matt. 3:19–21; Luke 12:33–34.

2510 Cf. note to 926 above.

2512 Cf. *Boet* II prose ii, 1–2. Vellem autem pauca tecum fortunae ipsius verbis agitare.

2531–40 *TC* I 848–51

> For if hire whiel stynte anythyng to torne
> *Than cessed she Fortune anon to be.*
> *Now sith* hire whiel by no way may *sojourne,*
> What wostow if *hire mutabilite* . . .

Cf. *Boet* II prose i, 59–62. Tu vero uoluentis rotae impetum retinere conaris? At . . . si manere incipit, fors esse desistit.

2539–42 *Boet* II prose i, 29–31. Hi semper eius mores sunt ista natura. Seruauit circa te propriam potius in ipsa sui mutabilitate constantiam.

2541 *BD* 631 To lyen, for *that ys hir nature.*

2552–58 Cf. *Boet* II prose ii, 45–47. Tamen ne animo contabescas et intra commune omnibus regnum locatus proprio uiuere iure desideres.

2577–80 *Boet* II prose ii, 55–56. Si ventis vela committeres, non quo voluntas peteret sed quo flatus impellerent promoveres.

2583–91 Cf. *Boet* II prose i, 58–59. Fortunae te regendum dedisti; dominae moribus oportet obtemperes.

2613–27 *Boet* II prose ii, 9–13. Cum te matris utero natura produxit, nudum rebus omnibus inopemque suscepi, meis opibus foui et . . . fauore prona indulgentius educaui, omnium quae mei iuris sunt affluentia et splendore circumdedi.

2628 *Boet* II prose ii, 16. Quid igitur ingemiscis?

2630–38 *Boet* II prose ii, 13–16. Nunc mihi retrahere manum libet. Habes gratiam velut usus alienis, non habes ius querelae tam prorsus tua perdideris.

2639–42 The quarrelsome debtor resembles the proverbial dog that bites the hand that feeds him. See 1727–28 and note above.

2649–50 Cf. John 20.23. Whose sins you shall forgive, they are forgiven them, and whose sins you shall retain, they are retained. Here as elsewhere in *Remede* the application of Christian terminology to Fortune is probably for ironic effect.

2660–62 In this case the phraseology of the Gloria Patri ("Lesser Doxology") is applied to Fortune: ". . . sicut erat in principio et nunc et semper et in saecula saeculorum."

2663–65 *Boet* II prose ii, 25–27. Ius est mari nunc strato aequore blandiri, nunc procellis ac fluctibus inhorrescere.

2675–77 *Boet* II prose ii, 17–18. Opes honores ceteraque talium mei sunt iuris . . . me abeunte discedunt.

2685–88 *Boet* II prose iv, 27–28. Cum igitur praecipua sit mortalibus vitae cura retinendae.

2692 Cf. *BD* 623 That baggeth foule and loketh faire.

2705–7 *Boet* II prose i, 44–45. Quid est aliud fugax quam futurae quoddam calamitatis indicium.

2706 Cf. *Fortune* 10 To knowen frend fro fo in thy mirour.

2709 Cf. *TC* III 1271 And me bistowed *in so heigh a place*

2717–18 *Boet* II prose i, 45–47. Neque enim quod ante oculos situm est, suffecerit intueri; rerum exitus prudentia metitur.

The proverb, "Look on the end," which Machaut enunciates again in 2722–24, is recorded in Hassell, F88; Whiting, E84.

2721 Also proverbial. See Hassell, R16.

2722–24 See note to 2717–18 above.

2735–40 Cf. *Jugement* 982–84n.

2742 Related to the conventional "fly like a bird." See Hassell, O46; Whiting, B311. Cf. also Hassell, O44; Whiting, F567, F569.

2743 "Nota" in margin of B. See Hassell, P208; Whiting, M675.

2744–49 "Nota" in margin A, B, F, and *K*. The passage is a version of "Tel convoite qui a assez," Morawski, no. 2334. Cf. Hassell, A214; Whiting, C115.

2754–55 *Boet* II prose v, 44. Paucis enim minimisque natura contenta est.

2770 "Nota" in margin A, B, F, and *K*. See Morawski, nos. 2164–65; Whiting, A91. Cf. 2475 above.

2787–90 *Boet* III prose ii, 46–48. Habes igitur ante oculos propositam fere formam felicitatis humanae—opes, honores, potentiam, gloriam, uoluptates.

Also III prose ix, 81–83. Nam nisi fallor ea vera est et perfecta felicitas quae sufficientem, potentem, reuerendum, celebrem laetumque perficiat.

2791–96 *Boet* III prose x, 37–38. Veram igitur beatitudinem in summo deo sitam esse necesse est. Christian trinitarian concepts supplement here the phraseology of the *Consolation*.

2793 Apoc. 1:8 I am Alpha and Omega, the beginning and the end.

2801 Cf. *Boet* II prose viii 21–26; and *RR* 4894–4944.

2819–21 Cf. note to 2819–21 above.

2857–92 This "baladelle" (2751) is a special variety of the ballade. It has the usual three stanzas on the same rhymes with a one-line refrain, but each stanza consists of four rather than three parts. See Hoepffner, II: xliv–xlvi.

2902–16 This passage provides an interesting witness to the medieval talent of learning by heart.

2961–64 This is a variant of the proverb found in 1887–88 above. See note; also note to 2485–90.

2993 No early-text manuscript has a totally satisfactory reading. *J* and *K* omit the antecedent *ce*, attested in all other manuscripts; *E* omits the verb; and *C* and *Pe* omit the requisite negative. The reconstruction is based on a comparison of all manuscripts, including the later ones.

2994–96 "Nota" in margin B. Proverb not recorded.

3013–36 This ballade has one of the more common eight-line stanzas, a favorite of Machaut's. The general form is standard. See Hoepffner, II: xlvii.

3065–66 Cf. 2092–93 and 2819–21 above.

3069–94, 3125–30 With the tenor of Esperance's reproaches here, cf. Lady Philosophy's words to Boethius, *Boet* I prose ii 7–9; prose iv, 1–6; II prose i, 61.

3093–94 Cf. *TC* III 737 Artow agast so that she wol the bite? For Machaut's proverbial image, see Hassell, F72; Whiting, S177.

3106 For the proverbial comparison, see Hassell, B54; Whiting, B125.

3113–14 Cf. *RR* 633–34; and Merchant's Tale *CT* E 1332 His paradys terrestre and his disport.

3128–30 For the proverbial comparison, see Hassell, O52; Whiting, B307.

3168 Cf. *TC* I 448–49

And ay the ner he was, the more he brende.
For ay the ner the fir, the hotter is.

Cf. *RR* 3168. For proverb, see Hassell O59; Whiting, F193.

3190–92 Cf. *TC* II 1201 And held his hondes up, and sat on knowe

3201–2 Cf. *LGW* F 2268–69

And this was, day by day, al hire *preyere*,
With al *humblesse* of wifhod, word and *cheere*

Cf. also Clerk's Tale *CT* E 141

His meeke *preyere* and pitous *cheere*

3205–3348 This "prayer" is not one of the *formes fixes*, and it is the only intercalated piece of *Remede* which Machaut does not set to music. It has twelve stanzas of twelve lines each. See Hoepffner, II: liii.

3225 Though only A and Pm omit this line, Hoepffner deletes it from his edition, evidently because of the authority he accords to A. It is needed for the stanza form, and seems quite adequate.

3241–48 One might compare here *TC* I 932–38, Troilus' prayerful apology to love for his former irreverence.

3260 For the expression, see Hassell, C244.

3261–62 Also proverbial; see Hassell, A53, *RR* 12889.

3267 Instead of "raport," late-tradition manuscripts have "ressort." The former maintains the string of five rhymes on "port," yields good sense, and is the *lectio difficilior*. It is clearly preferable.

3379 Cf. *BD* 805–6

Hit happed that I cam on a day
Into a *place ther that I say* . . .

3381 Cf. *BD* 832 Hit was my swete, ryght as hirselve

3382 The spelling "jame" of later manuscripts, instead of "ame," was perhaps introduced by a scribe to avoid the elision with "ne." But Machaut is not averse to hiatus in this position, and "ame" yields much better sense.

3395 *TC* III 50 *Recordyng his lesson in this manere*

3419–20 *TC* II 1257–58

With that *he gan hire humbly to saluwe,*
With dredful chere, and *oft his hewes muwe.*

3420–22 *BD* 1215

Ful ofte I wex bothe *pale and red.*

TC III 94–95

Goodly abaist and *now* his *hewes rede,*
Now pale . . .

3424–26 *TC* III 85 Criseyde al this aspied wel ynough

3451–96 This virelai, which Machaut insists is properly called a "chanson baladée," consists of three thirteen-line stanzas and a seven-line refrain that commences the piece and is repeated after each stanza. In our line numeration the refrain is counted only one time. Virelais were commonly sung at dances without instrumental accompaniment, as here. See lines 3365–66 above and Nigel Wilkins, "A Pattern of Patronage: Machaut, Froissart and the Houses of Luxembourg and Bohemia in the Fourteenth Century," *French Studies* 37 (1983): 267–68. For further discussion, see Hoepffner, II: xlvii–li.

3502–3 Hoepffner, II: vii, takes this refrain to be part of a rondeau. See his further discussion, pp. liii–liv.

3533–36 Cf. *BD* 746–48

Good sir, telle me al hooly
In what wyse, how, why, and wherfore
That ye have thus youre blysse lore.

3537–38 Cf. *TC* 148–49

Lo, here an hard *requeste,*
And *resonable* a lady for to werne!

3556 Although elsewhere *aa* always counts for two syllables (e.g., lines 23, 121, 759, 2044), here the *aa* in *gaaigne* must count for only a single syllable if the line is not to be hypermetrical.

3572 In the translation, the rubric for miniature 28 has been moved from mid-speech to the beginning.

3578 Cf. *BD* 1129 How ye *sawe hir first,* and where

3692 Cf. *TC* 623 And if thow *deye a martyr,* go to hevene!

3723–24 These lines are missing in A and Pm, and Hoepffner omits them from his edition, no doubt in accord with the authority he assigns to A. From this point our line numbers run two higher than Hoepffner's.

3735 For the proverbial comparison, see Hassell, P76; Whiting, P48.

3765–66 See Hassell, D21.

3771–72 Both the narrator (3770) and the lady (3773) assert proverbial status for these lines. In manuscripts A, B, F, J, M, Pm, and Vg, line 3772 reads "Et loenge de courtoisie." The earlier reading involves better grammatical parallel and sharper lexical contrast ("demander"/"donner"), and therefore seems more characteristically proverbial. Hassell shows as proverb, but lists only two quotes from Machaut. Not in Whiting.

3774–76 This is the first of twelve maxims which the lady presents in rapid-fire order in lines 3774–98 in response to the lover; nine of them have versions recorded in Hassell and/or Whiting. This one is not recorded.

3777–78 This is a version of "Look before you leap." See Whiting, L435; S576.

3779–80 See Hassell, C286; cf. Whiting, L67.

3781 See Hassell, P51, G53; Whiting, T 37.

3783–84 See Hassell, C289.

3785–86 Proverb not recorded.

3787–88, 3791–92 Two related proverbs. See Hassell, M176; Whiting, C296; M724.

3789 Cf. "Mesure en toutes choses," Hassell, M1; Whiting, 464.

3793–95 See Whiting, W586, W595.

3796 Proverb not recorded.

3797–98 "Nota" in margin Vg; see Hassell, D24.

3815–20 For Machaut's continuing play on the name Bonne see note to 54–56.

3819–20 That the lady should be obliged to do what Hope has suggested to the lover is allegorically suspect. In *Remede* Esperance usually acts, and is responded to, more strictly in accord with her abstract character. Subtle characterization of the lady may be involved.

3861 Rather than "l'amour," the later manuscripts have "lonneur," which seems to accord better with the verb "faisoit."

3867–70 The language here evokes the marriage service, as does the subsequent exchange of rings; see 4039–44 below. Cf. also 4075–78 below. But there seems no question of an actual marriage having taken place.

3885 See Hassell, B105, N24; Whiting, B330.

3892–4300 The ensuing description of the service in the chapel, the dinner, and the games indoors and outdoors provide valuable circumstantial description of the activities in a fourteenth-century court.

3903 The word "honour" instead of "vigour" in *C, E,* and *Pe* is clearly wrong, no doubt picked up from "s'onnour" in the next line.

3944 Again, no early-text reading is perfectly satisfactory, but their combined witness, plus that of the later manuscripts, favors the reading adopted.

3959–88 This scene of musical entertainment, with its enumeration of instruments, bears comparison with the comparable scene in Chaucer's *HF* 1201–59. Many of the instruments have not been identified with absolute certainty. (See Hoepffner, II: ix, note 1.)

3961 *En pure corps* is a variant of the common expression, *en pur le corps*. See Tobler-Lommatzsch, *pur*.

3965 In this and the following lines we have given all the significant spelling variants of the different musical instruments mentioned, since this could be of interest to students of medieval music. *C*'s *micamon* is most likely the result of the scribe's inadvertant addition of an extra minim (as at 3695, 3789, 3933, etc.).

3989 The *estampie* was originally a song characterized by its pairs of musical phrases. The sung estampie was replaced in the fourteenth century by the instrumental estampie, which Machaut clearly presents here, following as it does his list of musical instruments and not being accorded any lyrics such as he provides for all other fixed form poems to which he alludes in *Remede*. On the estampie, see Jacques Handschin, "Ueber Estampie und Sequenz," in *Zeitschrift für Musikwissenschaft* 12 (1929–30): 1–20 and 13 (1930–31): 113–32; and Patricia W. Cummins, "La musique et la poésie dans l'estampie," *Romania* 103 (1982): 259–77.

3995 Cf. *BD* 51 Then play either at chess or tables.

3997 If parsons is a game, it is mentioned only here. Hoepffner suggests it could be a variant of *partures* (line 3881), a type of debate on the subject of love (*Oeuvres*, II: ix, note).

4001–8 *BD* 1160–70 is roughly comparable to this discussion in *Remede* of the quality of a musical performance, implicating ancient and legendary practitioners: Tubal and Pythagoras in Chaucer, Orpheus and Musique in Machaut.

4003 The "nouvelle forge" is the contemporary Ars Nova.

4039–44 The wording here again suggests that the lovers have a quasi-marital relationship. See note to 3867–70 above, and note to 4079–84 below.

4049–54 Franklin's Tale *CT* F 745–47

Of his free wyl he swoor hire as a knyght
That nevere in al his lyf he, day ne nyght,
Ne sholde upon hym take no maistrie

CT F 764–66

Love wol nat been constreyned by maistrye.
Whan maistrie comth, the God of Love anon
Beteth his wynges, and farewel, he is gon!

CT F 794–95

Thanne was he bothe in *lordship* and servage.
Servage? nay, but in *lordship above*

Of the several precedents that have been adduced for Chaucer's discussion of lordship in marriage in the Franklin's Tale, this passage in *Remede* seems to offer the fullest parallel. For the proverb of 4049–50, see Hassell, A126; Whiting, L544.

4075–78 Cf. the exchange of rings in *TC* III 1368, and White's gift of a ring to the Black Knight in *BD* 1273. For other parallels to the marriage service, see note to 3867–70 above and the note which follows.

4075 In our translation, we have moved the rubric for miniature 32 to its logical position before the exchange of rings.

4079–84 Esperance's role as "priest" in this "marriage" can be compared to Pandarus' role in *TC* III.

4085–88 Cf. *TC* III 136–38

And I to han, right as yow list, comfort,
Under yowre yerde, *egal to myn offence*,
As deth, if that I breke youre defence.

4089 The later-text tradition reads "Avec" rather than "Avant." The latter is much more consistent with the legal metaphor of 4083–93, and is to be preferred.

4109–16 This is the simplest form of the Middle French rondeau (*AB aA ab*

AB), and the form which Machaut favored. See Hoepffner, II, liii, and Poirion, pp. 318–26.

4130–34 The theme of learning with which Machaut opens the poem is carried through to the end. When the narrator speaks here of learning while he is still in his youth, there is a strong suggestion that the persona of the Amant should be distinguished from the poet's proper person. Machaut doubtless was well past thirty-five when he composed the work.

4199–4200 Cf. *TC* V 1606 It semeth nat ye take *it for the beste.*
TC V 1610 For that I tarie is al for wikked speche.
One may suspect that the lady's explanation here in *Remede* is deceptive, just as Criseyde's is in *TC* V 1604–10.

4218 In our translation, the rubric for miniature 34 has been moved to its logical position before the Lover's speech.

4258 Proverbial. See Hassell, A63; Whiting, L56. It is the first line of Machaut's *Lay de Plour* (Chichmaref, II: 459). It also occurs in some manuscripts of Chaucer's *PF* at the head of the rondeau (beginning line 679).

4277 For the probable reference to Bonne here, see note to 54–56 above.

4291 Cf. *BD* 1331 Fonde to *put* this sweven *in ryme*

4292 Cf. Man of Law's Prologue *CT* B 47–48
That Chaucer, thogh he kan but *lewedly*
On metres and on rymyng *craftily* . . .

4297 This line is an anagram on the author's name; see 4263–66. For an explication, see the note to *Jugement*, line 2055.

www.ingramcontent.com/pod-product-compliance
Lightning Source LLC
Chambersburg PA
CBHW012003120726
47902CB00016B/2118
* 9 7 8 0 8 2 0 3 5 3 5 3 1 *